D0111883

Ukraine

the Bradt Travel Guide

Andrew Evans

edition
2

www.bradtguides.com

Bradt Travel Guides Ltd, UK
The Globe Pequot Press Inc, USA

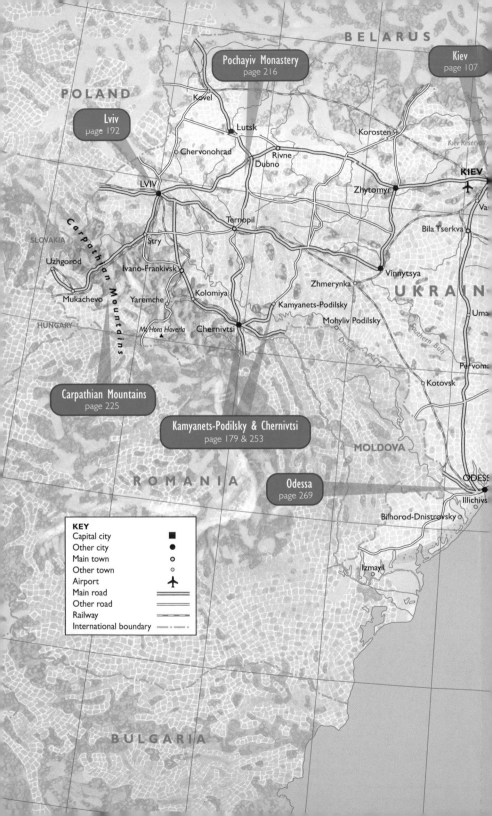

Kharkiv
page 395

Dnepr River
page 359

Crimea
page 299

RUSSIA

Chernihiv

Glukhiy

Sumy

KHARKIV

Kupyansk

Cherkassy

Poltava

Izyum

Severodonetsk

Kremenchuk

Slovyansk

Luhansk

Oleksandriya

DNEPROPETROVSK

Pavlohrad

Gorlovka

Alchevsk

Kirovohrad

Krasnoarmiysk

Makeyevaka

Kryvy Rih

Zaporizhzhya

DONETSK

Nikopol

Volnovakha

Mykolayiv

Melitopol

Berdyansk

Mariupol

Taganrogskiy Zaliv

Kherson

Nova Kakhovka

Sea of Azov

Dzhankoi

Crimea

Kerch

Yevpatoria

Kalamita Bay

Simferopol

Feodosiya

Kerchens'ka Protoka

Sevastopol

Alushta

Yalta

BLACK SEA

N

Bradt

0 — 50km

0 — 50 miles

Ukraine
Don't
miss...

Churches
St Andrei's Church, Kiev
(MW) page 144

Countryside
Sunflowers, Sloboda
(AE) page 38

above   New high-rise apartment buildings, Kiev's Obolon District on the Dnepr River (RD)

below   Façade of the History Museum, Ploscha Rynok, Lviv (PK) page 207

above   **Ploscha Rynok, Lviv** (AG) page 192

right   **Secessionist architecture, Lviv** (PK) page 205

below   **Broken-down trolley bus, Kharkiv** (AE) page 395

top	Table Mountain, Crimean Mountains (RD)
above left	Carpathian deer, Yaremche (AE) page 227
above right	Carpathian woodlands (AE)
below	Demerdzhi, Crimea (DZ) page 349

above Hiking in the Gorgany range, Carpathian Mountains (RD) page 250

below left Ski slopes in the Chornohora range, Carpathian Mountains (RD) page 239

below right Tysa River, running between the Chornohora and Svidovets ranges, Transcarpathia (RD) page 245

<table>
<tbody>
<tr><td>top</td><td>Fishermen on the ferry docks, Sevastopol (AE) page 319</td></tr>
<tr><td>above left</td><td>Maize and kalina berries, Galicia (AE)</td></tr>
<tr><td>above right</td><td>Salted fish for sale, Khmelnytsky, Podillya (AE)</td></tr>
<tr><td>left</td><td>Babushka with herbs, Dikanka, Sloboda (AE) page 418</td></tr>
</tbody>
</table>

above **Carpathian foothills, Yaremche** (AG)

right **17th-century wooden church, Museum of Folk Architecture and Life, Lviv** (PK) page 208

above left   **Kievo-Pechersky Lavra, Kiev** (AE) page 147

top right   **Mosaic, Alexander Nevsky Cathedral, Yalta, Crimea** (AE) page 338

above right   **Gravestone, Lychakivsky Cemetery, Lviv** (PK) page 210

below   **Mother of God Icon, Kievo-Pechersky Lavra, Kiev** (PK) page 147

top **Sudak Fortress, Crimea**
(HS) page 353

centre **Armenian Cathedral, Lviv** (PK) page 206

right **Detail from a house on Krakivska Street, Lviv** (PK)

above **'Walrus' swimming in December, Vorskla River, Poltava** (AE) page 414

left **Crimean coast near Balaclava** (DZ) page 328

below **Yalta** (DZ) page 321

above **Beach near Sudak, Black Sea** (HS)

below **Waves crashing, Black Sea** (AE) page 269

next page **Swallow's Nest Castle, Yalta, Crimea** (HW/SC) page 341

Author

Andrew Evans first arrived in Ukraine in 1994, where he lived and worked for two years as an LDS missionary. His love for such a rapidly changing country kept him returning wearing many different hats – as a NATO analyst, student, political consultant, and finally as the author of *Ukraine: The Bradt Travel Guide*. He received a postgraduate degree in Russian and East European Studies from Oxford University and went on to work in international development. Andrew now works as a freelance writer and offers regular travel lectures at the Smithsonian Institution. Among his publications are *Kiev: The Bradt City Guide* and the forthcoming *Iceland: The Bradt Travel Guide*. Andrew lives in Washington, DC, and can be reached through his website: www.walkedandwalked.com.

PUBLISHER'S FOREWORD   *Hilary Bradt*

The first Bradt travel guide was written in 1974 by George and Hilary Bradt on a river barge floating down a tributary of the Amazon. In the 1980s and '90s the focus shifted away from hiking to broader-based guides covering new destinations – usually the first to be published about these places. In the 21st century Bradt continues to publish such ground-breaking guides, as well as others to established holiday destinations, incorporating in-depth information on culture and natural history with the nuts and bolts of where to stay and what to see.

Bradt authors support responsible travel, and provide advice not only on minimum impact but also on how to give something back through local charities. In this way a true synergy is achieved between the traveller and local communities.

*   *   *

In the first edition of this guide I wrote: 'The essence of a good guide is when the author has "painted the picture" – especially in a country that is little known to travellers – and has injected his personal enthusiasm into the text ... But such enthusiasm needs to be balanced with accurate practical information. Andrew Evans has achieved this and more.' I learned just how much more when the readers' letters started coming in, all saying that this Ukraine guide is the best on the market. Here's an example: 'Kudos to the author for an insightful guide that provided a wealth of historical and cultural background that really enhanced my experience.' And the new edition is even better!

Second edition January 2007 First published 2004

Bradt Travel Guides Ltd
23 High Street, Chalfont St Peter, Bucks SL9 9QE, England; www.bradtguides.com
Published in the USA by The Globe Pequot Press Inc, 246 Goose Lane,
PO Box 480, Guilford, Connecticut 06437-0480

Text copyright © 2007 Andrew Evans
Maps copyright © 2007 Bradt Travel Guides Ltd
Photographs and illustrations copyright © 2007 Individual photographers and artists

British Library Cataloguing in Publication Data
A catalogue record for this book is available from the British Library
ISBN-10: 1 84162 181 1   ISBN-13: 978 1 84162 181 4

Photographs *Text* Rick DeLong (RD), Andrew Evans (AE), Alan Grant (AG), Piotr Krakwiec (PK), Mark Wadlow/Russia & Eastern Images (MW), Helga Wilcox/Sylvia Cordaiy Photo Library (HW/SC), Dmitry Zamorin (DZ)
Front cover St Mikhayil's Monastery, Kiev (allOver photography/Alamy)
Title page Mosaic, Alexander Nevsky Cathedral, Yalta (AE), Sunflowers, Sloboda (AE), Kiev's Obolon District (RD)
Back cover House on Krakivska Street, Lviv (PK), Kara Dag Reserve, Crimea (DZ)

Illustrations Carole Vincer
Maps David Priestley, Steve Munns

Typeset from the author's disc by Wakewing
Printed and bound in Italy by Legoprint SpA, Trento

Acknowledgements

My heart is full of thanks to friends, family and strangers who all reached out to make this book even better. I have been overwhelmed by the love and sincere interest that everyone has shown me, and grateful for all the new people I have met along the way. A good guidebook takes many minds and hands; thank you all – *Duzhe dyakuyu vsem vam!*

I would like to acknowledge and thank the guest contributors in this edition, Dr Mark Von Hagen and Christy Quirk.

In England: thank you to the entire team at Bradt Travel Guides, to Hilary Bradt for her enthusiasm and to Tricia Hayne and Adrian Phillips for editing and managing the project, to Sally Brock for the extra-complicated typesetting, to both Debbies for their continuous help, to Caroline Mardall for marketing the book, to Janet for managing correspondence, and Anna Moores for editing and doing more than I probably know. Thanks, also, to Regent Travel for another great opportunity to explore Ukraine.

Thank you to Sandy Petrasek and the Globe Pequot Press in America.

In Washington, DC: my gratitude goes to His Excellency Ambassador Oleh Shamshur, to cultural attaché Natalia Holub and to the Embassy of Ukraine. A very special thank you to the Global Fairness Initiative – to Steven Bennett, Lindsay Parker, Sally Painter and Karen Tramontano for their ongoing support and interest in my work and their work in Ukraine. To Inci Bowman and the International Committee for Crimea (ICC) for editorial input and John Kun of the US–Ukraine Foundation. And thank you to Faye Browning and Mary McLoughlin and the Smithsonian Institution for their interest in what I have to say about Ukraine.

My sincere gratitude to Aerosvit Airlines for providing flights to and from Ukraine. A very special thank you to Marijka Helbig, a passionate woman and noble travel companion with so many wonderful friends. *Dyakuyu* Marijka!

Hundreds of people went out of their way to make me feel welcome in Ukraine. I want to thank all those who helped me conduct the research for this edition – in Kiev: to Olymp Travel and the Institute of Tourism for hosting me, to Yevhen Savchuk, Natalia Ostapenko and Alex Metelsky, and to Vladislava Osmak for her goodwill and research; in Lviv: to the Mayor of Lviv, to Ivanka and the wonderful folks at the Ukrainian Catholic University for their kindness and hospitality, and to Vasyly Popovich and Natalka of Lviv-Intrutrans; in Vinnytsya: to Sandra Jacobs for fact-checking and suggestions and Rabbi Israel Meir Gabay and the Hasidic community in Medzhybizh for their time and kindness; in Odessa: to Zhanna Belousova (Eugenia Travel) for information and ongoing support, and Amelia Botovkina for such a wonderful tour, and the insider's insights of Jonathon Oakes; in Kamyanets-Podilsky: to Aleksander Niedzelsky for his impromptu tour of the old city, *dziekuje!*; in Donetsk: to Sergei Borzenkov, Yulia Melnikova and Alexander Vasilchenko; in Yalta: to Sergei Sorokhin for his suggestions and checking maps,

Maksim Ponomarenko and Palmira Palace for their hospitality, Lilia and the stalwart women of Intourist, and to Lutfi Osmanov in Bakhchisarai; to Bulgarian Alex who gave me a lift back from Romania; in Uzhgorod: to Andrea Kacsivaja for an engrossing tour, good conversation and a wealth of information; to the kind man who drove me across the Hungarian border and to the two *sigaretchiki* who snuck me back into Ukraine; to Kelly Rooney in Drohobych and Andrij Juzjuk of Kolomiya; to Natalia Hotsul and the good people of Eco-Play in Yaremche. In Zhytomyr, to Gillian Gloyer for her insights and suggestions and Daniel Reynolds for fact-checking. And to all those whose names I didn't catch, thank you for directions, ideas, and for answering my questions!

Thank you to all those fellow travellers who sent me updates and suggestions: Brady Caneer, Janet Chadwick, Sonia Damko, Vyacheslav Gromlyuk, Richard Hand, Peter Henderson, Peter and Janet Iley, Johann Knigge, Peter Marbais, Jason Pratt, Basil Ridha, Phil Wilcox and Tim Wilson.

Also to my good friends in Kiev, Andrei, Natasha and Ilyusha Tugai, and a big thank you to Anatoly and Nadezhda Shiyan for their goodness and kind hospitality. My deepest gratitude and appreciation to their wonderful son Max, a true and trusted friend.

To my good friends who encouraged me throughout: to Debdeb, Brett, Heidi Stalla and Kirsti Samuels. To my wonderful parents and family for backing me along the way; and to Grandpa Bob for always listening and for reading my books.

And to Brian, for making it all possible, for patience and believing, and for being simply fabulous.

FEEDBACK REQUEST

Just like Ukraine, a good guidebook is alive and constantly evolving. It is impossible for one person to capture the breadth of experience available in any country, especially one as huge and varied as Ukraine. When I'm on the road, I always love discovering new things, but I am especially grateful when others are willing to swap stories and share their ups and downs from their own trips. Your impressions, adventures, advice and insight are all very welcome. I am always so grateful for those people who take the time to write and who help me keep the book fresh and accurate. I do read all your letters and do my best to respond to each in person – many thanks to all of you who wrote in for this second edition!

I also want to know how the guide has proven helpful or where you may have found it lacking. I especially appreciate hearing your experiences, recommendations, and receiving any information on hotels, restaurants, transportation, and most importantly those truly wonderful spots you may have discovered. Remember that your contributions will help make the path a little lighter and more interesting for your fellow travellers to Ukraine. Please send all correspondence to: Andrew Evans, c/o Bradt Travel Guides, 23 High Street, Chalfont St. Peter, Bucks SL9 9QE, England; e info@bradtguides.com.

Kindest regards,
Andrew Evans

Contents

Introduction

A week after the revolution had officially ended, I stood and watched a humble policeman ticket and tow a black BMW parked on a sidewalk in the centre of Kiev, despite the furious protests of the car's well-dressed chauffeur. I was genuinely fascinated by the scene before me – after nearly 15 years of travelling to and through Ukraine, I had just witnessed someone receiving their first parking ticket, saw my first Ukrainian tow truck and met a policeman who remained totally unswayed by powerful threats.

Indeed, the past few years have been a time of many firsts for Ukraine: the first real elections, the first fruits of democracy, and the first disappointments that come with rule of law (eg: parking tickets). In actuality, the Orange Revolution may have had a more immediate effect on the rest of us than it has on Ukraine. At a time when the state of the world left many of us feeling apathetic, depressed or helpless, the people of Ukraine stood up against injustice and oppression in a most spectacular way, reminding us of a simple but important lesson: *razom nas bohato* – together we are many. History will surely reference their courageous example.

In spite of media attention and the common catchphrase, there is no 'new' Ukraine. Ukraine has always just been Ukraine – a timeless land of human struggle and simple beauty. The only real difference now is that Ukraine is free to be all of Ukraine, which is why there has never been a better time to travel there. Today, most of us don't need visas; you can take a direct flight to Kiev from almost any English-speaking country in the world, and you get to participate in a country that is rediscovering itself. Surely, this is an exciting time and the burst of creative energy almost demands a rephrasing of the national anthem: Ukraine is alive and kicking.

This is why I love travelling in Ukraine, for every time I return, I feel like I have arrived in some terra incognita that is ripe for exploration. The open field, the endless city, the borderless climes of Ukraine's great middle – it's all a recipe for sheer wanderlust, an emotion that many Ukrainians are feeling for the first time and what made researching the second edition of this book so much fun. Everyone I met on the road had something new and fascinating to show me. Hopefully, their mutual efforts will show through on these pages. I also got to delve back into all

NOTE ON PRICES

Ukraine's vigorous economy accounts for a slow but steady increase in the standard of living for many Ukrainians, as well as a not-so-steady increase in prices. As the country struggles to establish stability in the global marketplace, prices continue to fluctuate. In this book, most prices are listed in US dollars to account for real value; however, the current wave of economic growth has resulted in prices that may or may not correspond with listed references.

those things that have kept me coming back to Ukraine again and again. I still love the calculated trains and the people you meet on them, the uncluttered city squares and silver widths of the Dnepr, the round haystacks and rustic windmills in the countryside, the rocks and wildflowers in Crimea, the feeling of never wanting to leave Odessa, and a realisation that Transcarpathia may just be the most picturesque corner of planet earth. May you find Ukraine as inspiring a country as the millions who live there. *Schaslivoyi Dorohy*!

PLACE NAMES AND LANGUAGE

Ukraine is a land inhabited by many people who speak many different languages. For that reason, many cities are called several different names, and there are streets in Ukraine that are still commonly known by four or five different names. With admiration and respect to Ukrainian sovereignty, I completely welcome the present movement to standardise Ukrainian place names and language. For that reason, I have, for the most part, employed place names transliterated from the Ukrainian spelling (eg: Kharkiv, Kirovohrad), with the exception of those areas where the majority of a population in a particular location may use an alternate spelling to the Ukrainian. In a few chosen cases I have opted to use the more commonly known English names for certain Ukrainian cities as opposed to their official Ukrainian transliteration, hence Kiev instead of Kyiv, and Odessa instead of Odesa. This editorial preference is intended solely as a means of assistance to English-speaking travellers and does not in any way intend to promote a particular cultural preference or political ideal.

The transliteration of Russian and Ukrainian languages follows generally accepted English equivalents, with certain noted exceptions. In an attempt to provide readers with a more user-friendly guide, I have relied on the basic phonetic of Latin script in those cases where official or scholastic transliterations appear complex or jumbled. For the sake of simplicity, I have also omitted all soft and hard signs from transliterations.

FCO TRAVEL ADVICE
know before you go
fco.gov.uk/travel

Bradt Travel Guides is a partner to the 'know before you go' campaign, masterminded by the UK Foreign and Commonwealth Office to promote the importance of finding out about a destination before you travel. By combining the up-to-date advice of the FCO with the in-depth knowledge of Bradt authors, you'll ensure that your trip will be as trouble-free as possible.

www.fco.gov.uk/travel

Part One

GENERAL INFORMATION

Location Eastern Europe, 49°N and 32°E. Borders Russia, Belarus, Poland, Slovakia, Hungary, Romania and Moldova. Black Sea forms an extended coastline in the south.

Size 603,700km²

Geography Steppe and flat plateaux, divided by Dnepr River, with the primary mountain ranges along the western borders and the Crimean Peninsula in the south.

Climate Continental, with cold winters and warm, breezy summers. Average temperature in January −6°C, in July 24°C. Southern coast of Crimea is Mediterranean in climate and vegetation.

Status Republic

Population 48 million (estimate)

Life expectancy Women 75.3 years; men 64.4 years

Capital Kiev

Other major cities Kharkiv, Donetsk, Dnepropetrovsk, Lviv, Odessa

Administrative divisions 24 oblasts, one autonomous republic (Crimea)

People Ethnic Ukrainian 78%, Russian 17%. Remaining 5% includes Poles, Belarusians, Hungarians, Romanians, Jews, Crimean Tatars, Armenians, Greeks and Roma.

Languages Ukrainian and Russian. Also Tatar and some Romanian, Hungarian and Polish

Currency Ukrainian Hrivnia (UAH)

Exchange rates US$1 = 5.25UAH; £1 = 10UAH; €1 = 6.7UAH (November 2006)

National airport/airline Kiev Boryspil (KBP)/Aerosvit (Ukrainian Airlines)

International dialling code +380

Time GMT + 2 hours (7 hours ahead of New York City)

Electrical voltage AC is 200 volts, and the frequency is 50 hertz

Flag Two equally sized horizontal stripes of light blue and yellow gold

National anthem *Sche Ne Vmerla Ukrayina* (Ukraine has not yet perished)

National flower Sunflower

Public holidays 1 January (New Year's Day), 7 January (Ukrainian Christmas), 14 January (Old New Year's Day), 8 March (Women's Day), 1 May (May Day – workers' solidarity and the pagan rites of spring), 9 May (Victory Day – a jubilant tribute to the end of World War II), 24 August (Ukrainian Independence Day), 7 November (Anniversary of the Great October Revolution)

I

The Country

GEOGRAPHY

Ukraine is situated in eastern Europe at 49°N and 32°E, and shares borders with Russia, Belarus, Poland, Slovakia, Hungary, Romania and Moldova. The Black Sea forms an arched coastline in the south, interrupted by the Crimean Peninusla, which juts out as the country's southernmost point. The Sea of Azov is off the southeastern coast. The greatest distance inside Ukraine (from east to west) is about 1,350km (850 miles), and the country's widest point (north to south) is 850km (530 miles), from Crimea to Belarus. The country covers an area of 603,700km² (232,000 square miles); in comparative terms, that's slightly larger than France but slightly smaller than Texas. Ukraine is also the second-largest country in Europe, if you want to count Russia as Europe. Ukrainians don't, stating with pride that Ukraine is the largest democracy in Europe. Ukrainians also claim that their country lies at the very centre of Europe, pointing to the tiny Carpathian village of Dilove where Austrian geographers set up a stone marker in 1887. Indeed, Ukraine's assertion as Europe's geographical centre holds merit, but ironically only when Russia *is* counted as Europe.

Ukraine is mostly made up of vast steppe and flat plateaux and is world renowned for its rich black soil or *chornozom*. The Dnepr River runs south down the middle, dividing the country into traditional territories of right and left banks. Other major rivers include the Dnistr, Southern Buh, Pripyat along with the Danube delta south of Odessa. Roughly half of the Carpathian mountain chain lies inside western Ukraine, running diagonally southeast. The country's highest peak is Mount Hoverla at 2,061m (6,762ft). Along the southeast coast of the Crimean Peninsula lie the Crimean Mountains, the highest being Roman Kosh at 1,543m (5,061ft). A few low rolling hills define Ukraine's far east, and wide forests mark the northern borders, but

GEOGRAPHICAL IMPRESSIONS OF UKRAINE

As far as their country, the tract of land whereof I have been speaking is all a smooth plain, and the soil deep. [It] has no marvels except its rivers, which are larger and more numerous than those of any other land. These, and the vastness of the great plain, are worthy of note.

Herodotus, *Histories, Book 4*

How intoxicating, how magnificent is a summer day in Little Russia! [sic]
Nikolai Gogol, *Evenings on a Farm Near Dikanka*

It is a beautiful spot.

Mark Twain, *The Innocents Abroad*

A strategic position at the crossroads between Europe and Asia.

CIA Factbook

other than these, Ukraine boasts almost no natural boundaries, a fact that explains a turbid past and the controversial political borders today. The country's very beginnings and continual existence can be attributed to its position as a free-moving crossroads of land, river and sea routes between Europe, Asia and the Middle East.

CLIMATE

Ukraine has a temperate continental climate, which means cold white winters and beautiful warm summers. Spring and autumn seem somewhat short and mild, but can also be rather sunny. The further inland you go, the more extreme the weather, so that northeastern Ukraine suffers from the coldest temperatures in the country, while the south becomes very hot in summertime. The Carpathian Mountains also tend to experience more rainfall (750mm; 30 inches/year) and cooler summers than the rest of the country. On a whole, Ukraine's average January temperature is –6°C, and the average July temperature is 24°C. For reference, that's a lot warmer than Russia, but a bit colder than Italy.

The most notable exception to Ukraine's wintry caricature is the southern coast of Crimea, which is decidedly dry and Mediterranean year-round, both in climate and vegetation. Either way, most foreign visitors are surprised by the climate they encounter: Ukraine is either far warmer or far colder than they had expected.

POPULATION

The total population of Ukraine is estimated to be around 47 million, although a proper census has not been taken for more than a decade. Ethnic Ukrainians constitute the majority (78%) along with a significant Russian presence (17%). The remaining 5% include Poles, Belarusians, Hungarians, Romanians, Jews, Crimean Tatars, Armenians, Greeks and Roma. Ethnic distribution varies, but most Russians live in the eastern half of the country and in Crimea. Crimean Tatars obviously live in Crimea and Jews once made up at least a third of the population in Lviv, Odessa and Kiev. The people you meet will answer that they are one ethnicity or another, but keep in mind that Ukraine is one of the most ethnically diverse countries in Europe, and has been from the beginning.

Despite Ukraine's agricultural heritage and close ties to the countryside, over 70% of Ukrainians are city dwellers. Life expectancy is 75.3 years for women, but just 64.4 years for men, a worrisome statistic although still slightly higher than the world average. Following Ukraine's independence in 1991, its population fell quite drastically, due first to some emigration to Russia. The hardships of the early to mid-1990s also took a toll, showing a significant increase in Ukraine's death rate, a decrease in the birth rate, followed by huge waves of emigration of youth seeking better opportunities abroad. Since the year 2000, that trend has started to reverse itself, with life expectancy having stabilised and the standard of living improving to the point that Ukrainian labourers working abroad have begun to return. In addition to the country's sizeable labour force, which has attracted the attention of international investors, Ukrainians also enjoy one of the highest literacy rates in the world – close to 99.8% – thanks to strong standards of universal education.

ADMINISTRATION

Ukraine is divided into 24 oblasts and one autonomous republic, Crimea. Each oblast has a regional capital, and Kiev is the national capital. Kharkiv, Donetsk, Dnepropetrovsk, Lviv and Odessa are the largest cities.

GOVERNMENT

Ukraine regained independence in 1991 and now functions as a constitutional democracy, led by a president and ruled by a 450-seat parliament, the Verkhovna Rada. Members of the Rada serve five-year terms and their seats are allocated on a proportional basis to those parties that gain 3% or more of the national electoral vote. The exact balance of power between the president and Rada is still a point of conflict in these early years of democracy, while political corruption has been a plague to every administration back to Prince Vladimir.

Leonid Kravchuk won the first elections of an independent Ukraine in 1991 but his presidency was troubled by incredible inflation and so much public unrest that the next elections were brought forward, and Leonid Kuchma was voted in as the new president in 1994, then re-elected in 1999 for a second five-year term. The Kuchma presidency saw some small improvements in the field of domestic economics, due largely to the oligarch businessmen that he empowered during his regime, who came to be known as the Kuchma clan. Kuchma is remembered as a stubborn autocrat who lacked vision and relied on mafioso tactics to run the country, stashing hundreds of millions of dollars outside the country and ridding himself of any dissenting voice. One such reformer was the then prime minister Viktor Yuschenko, who was sacked following some much-needed economic reforms, including stabilisation of the currency. Kuchma's presidency continued with a slew of corruption scandals propped up by a shady legal process. Increased repression and a lack of freedom of speech led to major demonstrations in Kiev throughout the latter half of 2002, and to widespread discontent among Ukrainian voters.

Nearing the end of his term, Kuchma sought a successor with whom he could carry out a classic post-Soviet handover of power, while securing protection for himself and his family. He picked Viktor Yanukovych, who emerged from the Donbas clan of southeastern Ukraine and was well funded by industry interests. Meanwhile, Victor Yuschenko had forged a viable coalition with the charismatic Yulia Timoshenko, later founding the opposition party of Nasha Ukrayina – Our Ukraine. Throughout 2003, Our Ukraine was able to drum up majority support countrywide, despite major government action against their campaign. After the Kuchma regime tried to steal the presidential election in late 2004, Our Ukraine led an urgent call to the streets. The outpouring of public fervour and the sheer determination of the ensuing protest went down in history as the famed Orange Revolution.

Ukraine's Supreme Court has always acted as the more independent branch of Ukraine's government: with mounting international pressure and the streets still filled with protestors two weeks after the election, the Supreme Court ruled to annul the elections and reset the run-off between candidates Yuschenko and Yanukovych. Under the watchful eye of international monitors and the Ukrainian people, Viktor Yuschenko won the final round of elections and was officially inaugurated as President of Ukraine on 23 January 2005.

The Orange Revolution marked a turn towards confidence for the Ukrainian people. They had become heroes to the rest of the world, and the euphoria of the revolution raised high hopes that all the problems of the past would simply disappear under a true democracy. Clearly, some immediate changes were noted, and yet as democracy flourishes in Ukraine, so do some of its challenges. Alas, many lost heart when Yushchenko decided to sack his government in September 2005 due to charges of corruption and the resignations of key members of Yushchenko's cabinet. The sacking included the dismissal of then prime minister Yulia Timoshenko, who resented Yushchenko's decision and vowed a comeback in the March 2006 elections.

The voters' circus that ensued was shocking to the rest of the world, but fitted well with other periods of Ukraine's history, when a rainbow of factions rushed the political field. Optimists would say that it represented the healthy signs of a vigorous democracy, others noted how the pro-Russian Regions Party won the majority of votes, expressing a strong opposition to Yuschenko. After months of confusing deliberations and indecision between the various political blocs, President Yuschenko entered into a reluctant political pact with his former enemy Viktor Yanukovych, naming him prime minister and handing over several cabinet seats to his party. Together, these strange bedfellows faced a number of concerns, including the gas crisis, Ukraine's membership in NATO, relations with Russia, economic reform, corruption, and everything that plagues Ukraine. Finding a middle ground among Ukraine's divergent domestic and foreign policy goals has been a real challenge, worsened by a general lack of compromise among political leaders.

Ukrainians still look back on the Orange Revolution as a vital catalyst for social and governmental change, which has led to an improvement in the right to freedom of speech, the public accountability of elected officers, and institutional reform within the government. Ukrainian politics is far more invigorating than any of the national sports shown on Ukrainian television, and there will always be a new story to follow. Ukrainians tend to be both highly pensive and politically vocal, so that if you don't read about it before your trip, you will hear about it on your trip.

INTERNATIONAL RELATIONS

Ukraine occupies a difficult position in the world as the country is wedged between giant Russia, the recently expanded European Union, the turbulent Middle East and the Caucasus. Following independence from the Soviet Union, Ukraine sought distance from Russia through attempted EU and NATO membership, but the process was delayed by obvious complications and lack of preparedness.

Recent relations between Ukraine and Russia are fraught with much antagonism and bickering. Russia disapproves of Ukraine's push towards the West and leverages their shared history, cultures and economies to keep Ukraine subservient. After putting to rest early disputes about energy payments and control over the Black Sea fleet, Ukraine panicked in 2003 when Russia began construction of a long dam across the Kerch Strait with the aim of joining it to Tuzla, a minute Ukrainian island in the Sea of Azov. Such symbolic aggression continued prior to the Orange Revolution, when the Kremlin's sinister interference into Ukraine's electoral politics did not improve relations between the two countries. On New Year's Day 2006, Russia shut off gas supplies to Ukraine (not for the first time) and suddenly demanded market rates for future fuel resources. This time the international community intervened, especially the EU, which faced an energy crisis of its own if the gas dispute remained unresolved. A new deal was reached, forcing Ukraine to pay double what it had been paying and spawning a political crisis in the Rada. Thus Russia meddles with Ukrainian politics while Ukrainians argue amongst themselves about the extent of their partnership with their largest neighbour. A troubled friendship continues. Protecting Ukraine's sovereignty from Russia will always be a prime national security interest.

Today, Ukraine's primary foreign policy goals involve full integration with Western democracies and the global market economy, starting with full membership in the WTO, EU and NATO. Such ambitious goals have met with obstacles as domestic politics repeatedly hampers the efforts of progressive leaders. A continued lack of reform meant that Ukraine was passed up for WTO membership in 2005. In this same light, the Ukrainians have approached European integration far more realistically, working closely with the permanent EU–Ukraine Dialogue, which oversees all forms of joint EU co-operation and tracks Ukraine's progress towards adopting European standards and moving closer to EU membership.

Ukrainian opinions on NATO vary widely, particularly among the older generation who remember NATO as the enemy. With the type of strong military force it inherited from the Soviet Union, and the geo-strategic position it holds in the region today, Ukraine continues to be a leading priority for the international alliance. In 1994, Ukraine signed an agreement with the United States to get rid of its nuclear arsenal in return for US$1 billion in aid. In 1997, the NATO–Ukraine charter was signed as a treaty of co-operation in conflict prevention. Relations turned sour when it was discovered that President Kuchma had allowed the illegal sale of a nuclear radar system to Saddam Hussein's Iraq. Ukraine still holds a sizeable arsenal of small arms and military technology which, given the country's economic situation, make Ukraine a preferred destination for illegal arms dealers worldwide. When a munitions dump exploded in southern Ukraine in 2004, the country feared that its ageing arsenal had also become problematic for Ukrainians themselves. Since Yushchenko has become president, Ukraine has signed the Intensified Dialogue with NATO, with future membership contingent upon Ukraine's fulfilment of necessary military and political reforms.

Ukraine is a member of the United Nations and served on the United Nations Security Council from 2000–01. Ukraine is also a member of GUAM (Georgia, Ukraine, Azerbaijan, Moldova), an international organisation founded as an alternative to the defunct CIS (Commonwealth of Independent States), but which is now in danger of becoming defunct itself. In addition to close ties with Georgia, Ukraine benefits from particularly strong relations with Poland, Great Britain and the United States. Ukraine was one of the very first European countries to criminalise human trafficking and Ukrainian troops joined the 'coalition of the willing' in Iraq until late 2005.

ECONOMY

Ukrainians are survivors at heart, having already experienced every economic tragedy known to humankind in the last 100 years of their history, if not the last ten. They recognise the ups and downs of the global marketplace, but at the end of the day, they rely solely on themselves. The current bustle in Ukraine's economy is thrilling enough for many to be taking full advantage of new opportunities, but that sense of confidence is built upon the firmer foundation of self-reliance: at any moment, Ukrainians know they can pack up their bucket and shovel, retire to their little *dacha* (cottage) in the countryside, dig for potatoes, collect mushrooms in the forest, and make it through another winter.

Travellers to present-day Ukraine can experience the heart-rending sights of poverty alongside the glittery lifestyles of the rich, as well as the majority of everyday people going to and from work. It's not unlike a visit to Manhattan or London or Hong Kong, except that the phenomenon is a recent one for Ukraine.

RECENT HISTORY Within the context of the much larger Soviet Union, Ukraine's was a highly co-dependent economy. The Ukrainian SSR produced raw industrial material and grain in exchange for the consumer goods and energy of the other socialist republics, especially Russia. After independence, the country was left to its own devices in the global marketplace, hoping that a swift liberalisation would effect only a temporary inconvenience. Unlike Poland, where a year of 'shock therapy' was followed by steady economic growth, Ukrainians often claim they got the shock without the therapy.

The early 1990s were harsh years for Ukraine. A lack of institutional reform meant the command government continued to command with little regard for the 'invisible hand' of the free market. Because so many people had worked for the Soviet military industry or for factories producing uncompetitive goods, output collapsed and unemployment soared. Those who continued to work would sometimes go eight months (or more) without getting paid. In order to deal with these debts, the government simply printed more money, so that between 1993 and 1994 inflation reached over 10,000%. Of all the former Soviet republics at the time, Ukraine was the poorest, and for a while even Russian roubles were coveted currency.

Shuffling through pages of horrific statistics, international organisations bewailed Ukraine's impending doom, and yet people somehow survived year after year. Suddenly the experts began referring to Ukraine's ability to 'muddle through' and to the pervasive shadow economy that encompassed elusive forms of black-market activity and the more innocent system of *blat* – a long-standing custom of exchanging favours for goods or services. At one point it was estimated that over half of Ukraine's money was kept outside the banking system.

Blatant corruption was the major culprit for Ukraine's continual economic setbacks. In the mid-1990s, foreign investors shunned Ukraine for its Byzantine bureaucracy and prevalent criminal activity. Paying bribes was common practice, no matter what size the transaction. The 'privatisation' of Ukraine's economy constituted a few men divvying up Ukraine's natural resources and creating massive industrial monopolies. Seeking an edge, the oligarch owners of big business moved into the political arena and found government to be a more lucrative enterprise. The emergence of Ukraine's élite class of billionaires was proof of a consolidation of the country's industrial wealth with political power, from which a series of mafia-like clans battled for control of Ukraine's economy and trade. The most recent example was the 2004 sale of Ukraine's massive steelworks Kryvorizhstal, which despite competitive bids from abroad, was sold at a much lower price to a pair of billionaires, one of whom happened to be the then president Kuchma's son-in-law. Back in 2005, Transparency International awarded Ukraine 113th place on its Corruption Perceptions Index (out of 158 countries), not exactly a vote of confidence. Things have not greatly improved since.

Despite everything that appeared wrong with Ukraine, the country's economy appears to have stabilised and real economic growth was achieved from the year 2000 onwards. Ukrainians continue to hope, but keep planting their summer gardens just in case.

PROMISING DEVELOPMENTS Ukraine represents one of the largest markets in Europe, a fact that keeps investors coming back despite getting seriously burned during the country's upheavals of the past decade. The Orange Revolution raised hopes that the Ukrainian economy was going to boom overnight, provoking a short-lived 'orange rush' among impatient Ukrainians and foreigners who thought the obstacles of the past had suddenly been lifted. More cautious investors waited for real change in economic policy, which was slowed to a halt by Ukraine's very conflicted parliament. To some extent, the delay in policy change continues, so that instead of a boom, Ukraine continues to experience a slow and steady growth.

In general, there is hope that all the necessary changes will eventually occur. Ukrainians feel a lot more confidence in their own country and the market.

GDP (purchasing power parity) US$320 billion. Ukraine ranks 32nd out of 232 countries, between Belgium and Colombia.
Per capita GDP US$6,800. Ukraine ranks 114 out of 232, between Belize and Bosnia.
Human Development Index (HDI – the United Nations' composite score measuring a nation's economic and human welfare) Ranks 78th out of 177 countries, between Saudi Arabia and Peru.
Growth rate 4.4%
Unemployment 10% (unofficial)
Population living below the poverty line 29%
Number of millionaires in Ukraine (US$1 million) 1,800

Statistics taken from the CIA World Factbook and the United Nations' Human Development Index 2005

President Yushchenko's past life as an economist and former director of Ukraine's National Bank has proven helpful to a certain extent, although the drawn-out gas crisis of 2006 exposed the tangles surrounding Ukraine's economic sovereignty and development. One of the most positive changes in recent years has been that of tax law reform, which has sparked a nationwide movement of entrepreneurs. For nearly a decade, small businesses were subject to random tax collections that favoured the corrupt and bankrupted start-ups. New laws require business owners to pay a base fee every month only, after which they keep all profits. It seems simple, but the change has been revolutionary for Ukraine and now you will see all types of private enterprises flourishing.

Ukraine's new-found freedom of the press has done much to combat corruption, and as the Ukrainian economy becomes better integrated with Europe, corruption of the sort that was once prevalent throughout Ukraine is now becoming more of a disadvantage in business. An adoption of western European standards and improved codes of conduct has also been the creed of a new generation of self-made businessmen that view plenty of ripe opportunities in their own country. Self-help business manuals are bestsellers and having an MBA is all the rage. Young people who had emigrated to USA, Britain, Portugal or Italy have also begun to return with hard currency in hand, ready to start businesses or invest. Yet the external show of prosperity in cities like Kiev or Odessa should not fool anyone into thinking that life is not a day-to-day struggle for many. Most of the adults you will meet have probably seen their life savings disappear and have gone hungry (or seen their children go hungry), but pulling through tough times is nothing new.

STANDARD OF LIVING It's fair to say that Ukrainians today live far better than they have during any other time in their history. In 1998, the country's GDP per capita was a lowly US$750, while by 2006 it had risen to US$6,800. More importantly, this figure seems to have translated into the day-to-day for the average Ukrainians, allowing them more financial independence and opportunity. Some Ukrainians will still bemoan their very small salaries versus the price of goods in today's world, but for many, this is the aftershock of capitalism still talking. Those who suffer most are elderly recipients of government pensions or labourers receiving official minimum wage, which at US$50 a month does remarkably little, even in Ukraine. In 2007, a decent, liveable salary in Kiev would be around US$500 to US$1000 a month, whereas in the rest of the country, most people are earning around US$300 a month and can still afford their own accommodation, food, clothing, transport, and save enough surplus to pay for annual holidays. This emerging middle class tends to be urban and connected to business of some sort, while Ukraine's rural areas continue to suffer from a lack of cash but also tend to be more self-sufficient. Unemployment hovers around 10%.

Today an estimated 29% of Ukrainians live beneath the poverty line, a fact that is evident when travelling in certain regions of the country, typically in the most rural areas and among the elderly. Many people still live without very basic amenities, such as running water or gas heating. A common site outside larger towns is the rows upon rows of vast unfinished brick shells of magnificent dream homes, cobbled together with odd building materials. These new Ukrainian subdivisions are long-term works in progress, where people get some cash and build until it runs out, then go and get some more. It's not a sin to be poor in Ukraine, but it is a sin to look poor. Hence, the young woman that passes you on the street may in fact be wearing a real Gucci dress, but she rides only the trolley and eats a lunch of tomatoes that she's planted and picked with her own hands. The younger generation seem to have a better hold on the new economy and better jobs – many in their twenties–thirties are supporting their parents. Since 2002, Ukraine has bumped its way up 25 places on the UN's Human Development Index (HDI), but Ukrainians are tired of being content with less and will tell you so.

TRADE AND EXPORTS A drive through the Ukrainian countryside provides a vivid show of Ukraine's leading agricultural exports today: fields of grain (mainly wheat), sunflower seeds and sugar beets. Vegetables, beef and milk are also major exports. Returning Ukraine's agriculture to Soviet capacity (back when it produced more than a fourth of the USSR's output) has been a challenge due to unchanged land laws that leave unclear notions about land ownership and usage. These are in the process of changing now, and there are plenty of stories of EU farmers who lease fertile farmland in Ukraine and then sell their goods to the EU. There is a very good chance that what was once the breadbasket for Russia will soon become the breadbasket of Europe.

The industrial strengths of the Dnepr region and the Donbas are also visible testaments to the sheer industrial might that Ukraine still exhibits. Electric power, coal and metallurgy make up the country's leading industrial exports, followed by sugar refining, a Ukrainian enterprise for the past 150 years.

Ukraine sends the majority of its exports to Russia, about 12% to the EU and 5% to the United States.

CURRENCY Early travellers to Ukraine were often amazed at the mathematical abilities of Ukrainians, who could immediately calculate a given price in Russian roubles, American dollars and German marks. The hrivna (abbreviation UAH) was officially introduced in September 1996 as the new currency, and in the last few years has remained a very stable currency, pegged to the US dollar. Inflation is nowhere near what it was in the 1990s, but it continues to fluctuate.

CONSERVATION AND NATURAL HISTORY

By tradition, Ukrainians live closely with the earth and esteem nature and wildlife as a vital part of their environment and culture; however, the push towards an effective preservation of Ukraine's natural spaces and wildlife is a contemporary struggle. A recent legacy of environmental degradation is the direct result of Soviet governance, but these days poverty entices continued misuse of the few remaining natural areas. International development schemes have tended to focus on Ukraine's economic woes and democratisation rather than the environmental concerns of the country, but you'll find most Ukrainians are very concerned about protecting that which was lost in the past.

In Ukraine, the percentage of cultivated land is higher than any other country in Europe and only 4% of the country is preserved in a series of very young, underdeveloped national parks.

A 'national park' in Ukraine rarely carries the attitude of protection that we often expect. Once land is designated, quotas are established to demarcate what percentage of the park should be 'protected', what may be used for agricultural purposes or for industrial development, and where people may live. Travellers will find that some parks are filled with villages, roads and even factories. Then there are certain 'preserves' that exist beneath the veil of Soviet secrecy, where nobody is allowed in. Presently, Ukraine has 17 nature reserves, 12 national nature parks and four biosphere reserves (established by international bodies). The parks are concentrated in three areas: the Carpathians, the Crimea and Black Sea area, and the eastern steppe along the Russian border. The Ukrainian government has taken big steps towards fully protecting these areas in the last five years, but a few people can destroy it for everyone.

Serious water pollution and deforestation are the most serious threats to Ukraine's landscape. Rivers, wetlands and the coastline are still recovering from decades of Soviet industrial waste. An estimated 15% of Ukraine is still forested, and most of this territory lies in the north of the country (Polissya and Volhynia) and in the Carpathians. Oak and silver beech are prominent species in the north, and mixed deciduous and evergreen constitute the mountain forests. These are rare ecosystems and important wildlife habitats; however, visits to these protected 'virgin forests' often reveal areas where lumber poachers have entered and cut down thousands of trees.

Ukraine's flora and fauna were once a rare blend of European woodland species and the grasses and creatures of the Asian steppe. Today the scattered forests and grasslands still support small populations of deer, elk, wild boar, fox and hare. In the mountains of the Carpathians and Crimea there are still bears, wolves, lynx and wild mountain sheep (moufflon). A very few European bison also remain in Ukraine, and parks like Askania Nova have preserved animal populations that once thrived on the Ukrainian steppe, such as the Saiga antelope and Przewalski's horse. The Red Book of Ukraine is a reference publication that keeps track of Ukraine's endangered species (both plant and animal); however, it is used more frequently as a field guide, which reveals the state of Ukrainian wildlife. Most national parks and natural history museums will have an illustrated copy; it is only printed in Ukrainian but always lists Latin names. With the dire state of animal life, travellers are strongly discouraged from participating in 'hunting tours' offered by many local tour operators. Remember that it is a lack of regulation rather than an abundance of wildlife that caters to foreign hunters.

Ecotourism has already helped to influence positive conservation measures in the most immediate areas of concern, and your visit to any natural area only encourages increased protection. Ukraine's bird species are a plentiful and unique resource in this respect, and bird lovers will be pleased and surprised by the species they can see here. For serious birders, the Black Sea wetlands and the Dnistr and Dnepr river deltas are a must-see, as these are an important migration stop, and the nesting grounds for literally hundreds of species. Other unique areas to see birdlife are in the Carpathian Mountains and the parks of Volhynia and Polissya.

2

History

A visit to Ukraine is pointless without some knowledge of all that has transpired in this land – few countries boast a landscape so closely tied to their history. I should tell you to sit back and relax – it is a long story, and it's not over. The fact that you are reading a guidebook on Ukraine is a historical feat in itself.

Very little history is written in English about Ukraine as a land and people. Theirs tends to be treated as a peripheral history – historically it has been a peripheral land. Reading the histories of Russia, of Poland, Lithuania, the Jews, Turkey, Greece and Austria will give you a few slight glimpses into what happened in Ukraine. Only since independence has the country been treated as a whole in the context of its current borders.

Most aspects of Ukrainian history seem to breed controversy and so any attempted summary of the country's tumultuous past should be treated with sensitivity. The uncertainty of what these events mean today makes the past a minefield. Does history show Ukraine as a land of inherently independent, civilised people, or are they really just the descendants of barbarians and serfs? The intertwining of Russian and Ukrainian history makes the task more difficult. Even the way words are spelt and pronounced can express a particular political view and distort the truth.

Neither the greatest written tragedies nor the most adventurous Hollywood films could compete with Ukraine's history. There are no good guys or bad guys, only heroes and victims. The awe that visitors feel will be inspired by the story of the land as much as by the land itself.

ANCIENT HISTORY

Soviet propagandists liked to focus on the USSR's prehistoric beginnings in order to show a continued line of development from crouched-over bipeds clutching spears to the glory of space age socialist industry and organised communist society. The humble beginnings of man were elevated to such dizzying heights because they lived in this particular homeland that held an individual destiny. To a certain extent these Soviet propagandists were right. Beneath the melting glaciers of the Ice Age lay very rich soil that allowed Neolithic people to cultivate grain and raise livestock. Much earlier prehistoric sites have been found along the shores of the Black Sea, the Dnepr River and the Dniestr, showing that Palaeolithic man was also resident in Ukraine. These inhabitants ventured further from the riverbank as the land ice cleared, and permanent settlements were known from 5000BC onwards. One of the first groups of people given a name is the Trypillians. They lived in what is now southwest Ukraine and later expanded eastwards. Since the first millennium BC numerous 'civilisations' have been identified all over the region through archaeological digs that show distinct agricultural societies living in the Ukrainian steppe, mixed with the effects of nomadic tribes from the east.

The Scythians provided a colourful ancestry for Ukrainians today. A nomadic civilisation of Iranian origin, they lived in thick felt tents and wandered the southern Russian plains and central Asian steppe in wagons pulled by horses. Around 750BC, those passing into the western steppe of modern-day Ukraine settled and began cultivating grain and raising animals, most likely assimilating with the local population. Almost all of what we know about the Scythians was recorded by the ancient Greek historian Herodotus, who described a peculiar race of wandering warriors descended from Heracles (Hercules) with a penchant for bloodthirsty ritual. Scalps were taken in conquest and used as personal napkins by each warrior, and the skulls of enemies were padded with gold and leather and used as drinking chalices. They wore elaborate tattoos, developed an ornate art-form of animal symbols, practised human sacrifice, and took steam baths infused with marijuana. The Scythians left their mark on the landscape in the form of extensive burial mounds, known as *kurhany*, which can be seen in south-central Ukraine and Crimea today. A closer reading of Herodotus's *Histories* reveals some gentler references to later Ukrainian culture, including the Scythians' reverence for the linden tree, the use of wheat straw in religious rituals, and the ingenuity used in finding food in the forests and rivers. In their language, the Scythians called themselves *Skolotoi*, and a few Ukrainian folk songs refer to the *Sokoli* as inhabitants of their country. Yet throughout modern Ukrainian history the legacy of the Scythians has been either highlighted by militaristic regimes, or else downplayed by those who wish to disassociate Ukraine from an uncivilised Asian context.

Weakened by attacks from Persia and Macedonia, the Scythians were finally overshadowed by the Sarmatians who dominated the region from 250BC. The Sarmatians were Iranian in origin but supposedly more Slavic in appearance. They had blond hair and wore padded trousers and leather boots. Most noted were their women, who were skilled in horseback riding and warfare, so that some historians claim them to be the inspiration for the famed Amazon warriors feared by the Greeks. Their 'reign' lasted until AD250 when their infighting prevented them from defending themselves.

From the 6th and 7th centuries BC, the Greek Empire had also been expanding. Trading outposts were established around the Black Sea coast where the raw materials of nomadic tribes were exchanged for the luxuries of civilisation. Crimean ports like Chernoseus and Theodosia soon became the bustling crossroads of a declining Greece, with the dawn of Rus. Other semi-nomadic tribes crossed into Ukraine for certain periods, attracted by raw materials and river trade routes. The Ostrogoths came from Sweden and would either protect or attack the local trading posts, depending on their mood. In AD600, the Khazars of the Caucasus established their own empire touching the eastern half of the region. Their presence brought some discipline to the area and protection of the trade routes, allowing for two centuries of relative peace and prosperity. It was during this time that the first Hellenic Jews arrived in Ukraine. Many believe this marks the entrance of the Jews into eastern Europe.

KIEV AND THE EASTERN SLAVS From whence come the Slavs? Controversy surrounds the debate, fuelled by changing notions of national image today. By the 6th century AD, a definitive cultural and linguistic group was living in eastern Europe and it is accepted that this was an indigenous population mixed with the various nomadic overlords. From this emerged three groups of tribes. The south Slavs moved into the Balkans, the western Slavs moved into modern-day Poland

and central Europe, and the eastern Slavs moved into what is now Ukraine, Belarus and Russia.

Nature was the predominant force in the life of the eastern Slavic tribes. Their beliefs and everyday tasks centred on their relationship with the natural world. In the woods of northern Ukraine lived the Derevlianians (from the Slavic *derevo*, 'tree'). On the rolling plain of central Ukraine lived the Polianians (from the Slavic *pol'*, for 'field' or 'plain'). These people were known for being skilled in agriculture and cattle-raising. They produced grain in the fields and caught fish in rivers and streams. In the forest they hunted game and collected honey and wax from beehives. Every natural element had its own spiritual manifestations. Perun was the popular god of thunder and lightning. Svaroh was the sky, and he had two sons: Dazhboh, the sun, and Svarozhych, fire. Before war, sacrifices and prayers were offered to Volos, god of animals. Lesser spirits inhabited the forests, marshes, fields and bodies of water.

In a land that was relatively flat, the eastern Slavs used the available hilltops to build protective fortresses. These fort cities were called *horodyshcha*, from which comes the modern Ukrainian word for city: *horod*. Legend tells us that Kiev started as just such a town in AD560, and that its founding was a family affair. Kii, Shchek and Koriv were three brothers of the Polianian tribe. Their sister, Lybed, is often shown standing at the helm of a Viking longboat with her three brothers rowing her gently onwards. She pointed out the spot that felt right, and each sibling settled a separate hillside. A city emerged in between which they named after their eldest brother Kii. Three hills in Kiev still bear their names today.

THE VARANGIANS While the eastern Slavs were beginning to secure their land with strongholds, another civilisation was busy tearing down fortresses in other parts of the world. The Vikings had ravaged most of western Europe by the 9th century AD and were now ruling over several scattered kingdoms, diversifying their traditional pillaging with some trading. They were especially keen to access the more extravagant goods of the Byzantine Empire and sought an alternate route to Constantinople. Cutting through the lands of the eastern Slavs seemed to be the best solution, and several of the local tribes were already paying tributes to the Varangians (the Slavic term for the Norse tribes). At first the Varangians made a route from the Baltic, down the Volga, and into the Caspian Sea, but this area of the Khazar Kaganate was under more frequent attack and the route eventually proved unstable. The established route from the Varangians to the Greeks went from the Baltic Sea over to Lake Ladoga, to Novgorod, down the Lovat River, down the Dnepr, and across the Black Sea to Constantinople. Kiev swiftly became an important trading centre because of its midway point on the route to Byzantium, as well as its axis point on the east–west caravan routes that connected Europe to the Silk Road. The journey from Kiev to Constantinople took six weeks and was the most dangerous part of the voyage. Raids were common, especially during the passing of rapids on the Dnepr, some of which had to be portaged. Usually, two or three sailors would strip naked and ride the boat through the white water, while the remaining crew would hold a line to the boat from both banks and keep watch for attack.

Controversy surrounds the exact relationship between the Varangians and the Slavs. Based on the chronicles that have been kept, there was no general law applicable to the tribes collectively, which led to frequent warfare amongst the eastern Slavs. In an attempt at peace, the Slavs sought an overlord and went to the Varangians with the ever-famous line: 'Our land is great and rich, but there is no order in it. Come rule over us.' Politicians and academics do not like the idea of importing Germanic tribes to establish law and discipline, but this is the history that the average Ukrainian likes to remember.

Rus civilisation officially began with the reign of the Varangian princes over the regions' trading posts in the latter half of the 9th century. Kiev was 'discovered' by Askold and Dir, two close associates of Rurik, Lord of Novgorod. They ruled the city and took tribute from the local Polianians. In AD860, they raided Constantinople and came back with enough booty to make Novgorod jealous. When Oleh (Helgi), a fellow Varangian prince, heard the news, he relocated to Kiev, killed Askold and Dir and became the first prince over all of Rus. He made Kiev his capital, and spent the majority of his reign bringing the other eastern Slavic tribes under his rule. The empire of Kievan Rus was expanded, eventually extending from the Black Sea in the south to the Gulf of Finland in the north. Oleh also had his turn with Constantinople, dramatically nailing his shield to the city gates before his massive looting. A treaty was finally signed with Byzantium, exempting Kievan Rus from paying tributes or duties, which encouraged trade between the two societies. Byzantium traded their gold, silk, exotic fruit and spices for the furs, wax, honey and slaves of Kievan Rus. These raw materials were taken as tribute from the various Slavic tribes, and slaves were taken in war with outsiders and from recalcitrant tribes.

Ihor (Ingvar) succeeded Oleh and lived out a highly unglamorous reign. He spent most of it trying to get unruly tribes to pay their taxes. The Pechenegs, a Turkic people of the Volga region, disrupted trade and stability with their frequent raids between 915 and 920. Ihor launched one failed strike on Constantinople leading to the loss of favoured-trading status with the Byzantine Empire. He was finally killed by the Derevlianians, who were annoyed by the irregularity of his tribute collections. His wife Olha (Helga) stepped into his place and sought vengeance for her husband's death in a series of bloody massacres meted out to the Derevlianians. Legend holds that she held a funeral feast for her dead husband, letting the Derevlianians drink themselves into a coma before having her retinue chop them to pieces. She then instated a new system for collecting tribute throughout the empire, localising the process and making it more practical and regular. Rather than attack Constantinople, she went on a diplomatic mission to the Byzantine capital seeking to reinstate favourable terms of trade. Here she converted to Christianity, was baptised and given the Christian name of Helena. The emperor Constantine was her godfather.

Helena's son, Svyatoslav (Sveinald), took after his father when it came to diplomacy, but fortunately found more success as a warrior. He came to power in 962 and soon after brought the Vitchian tribe into the empire. When the Khazar Kaganate asked for his protection against the Pechenegs, he attacked the eastern empire instead, razing their capital to the ground. He conquered the Volga Bulgars and then took over the Bulgarian kingdom with the help of the Byzantine emperor. He eventually lost Bulgaria to Byzantium and was killed by a Pecheneg ambush on his boat near some of the Dnepr rapids. In Scythian fashion, the Pecheneg khan made a drinking cup from his skull.

While Svyatoslav had spent most of his life outside Kievan Rus, his sons had been ruling the empire in his place. In 972, his eldest son Yaropolk became the grand prince in Kiev, Oleh ruled over the Derevlianians, and Volodymyr/Vladimir reigned in Novgorod. A feud between the two elder brothers led to blows and Yaropolk murdered Oleh. Fearing the same fate, Volodymyr went into hiding in Scandinavia. He returned to Novgorod with a Viking army and launched an attack on Kiev. He took the city easily and had Yaropolk executed as a murderer.

Volodymyr's reign was characterised by his will to civilise Kievan Rus and make it a secure and stable empire. He wrote out the first code of law which he called the Russkaya Pravda, and was probably the first ruler ever to grant paganism the status of a state religion. He also established a system for the transfer of power based on a collection of joint principalities under Kiev. During his reign, Rus reached its greatest territorial expanse, but Volodymyr did not dedicate himself to expanding his borders or launching raids in other lands. Instead, he established an order that would carry Slavic civilisation through the centuries.

As the story goes, the Byzantine emperor was indebted to Volodymyr for his swift response to quell a rebellion in the Byzantine Empire. As a reward, the emperor offered him his daughter, the imperial princess, with just one catch: the marriage would take place as soon as Volodymyr converted to Christianity, which he duly did. He might have done it for the girl, but he had probably been thinking about a new religion for a while. He was keen to strengthen his own empire and to integrate Kievan Rus with other surrounding empires, and Volodymyr had noticed how the organised religions of the Jews, Christians and Muslims had furthered their own empires and served as an effective diplomacy. According to legend, Islam was rejected because of the Koran's restriction on drink, and Judaism was rejected for all of its restrictions. Christianity already had a small presence in Kievan Rus, and during Justinian's reign in Constantinople, much of the Crimea was Christian.

In AD988, Volodymyr returned to Kiev with his new bride and a new state religion. All the people of Kiev were marched into the Dnepr, and the river's waters were blessed by Byzantine priests while Volodymyr watched from the bank. In this way all of Kievan Rus was baptised and the Slavic nation made Christian. The statues of Perun and other pagan gods were torn down and beaten with sticks. Churches were built in Kiev and throughout all of Rus. Volodymyr dedicated one tenth of the state revenue to the Church and its clergy. Despite his 800 concubines and known executions of Christians prior to his conversion, Volodymyr was canonised after his death. He is remembered as a wise ruler who brought enlightenment and security to Kievan Rus. Today, his statue stands on the left bank of the Dnepr behind St Mikhayil's Monastery of the Golden Domes, holding a tall cross in his hands.

Volodymyr's plan of an organised succession to power was quickly forgotten in a bloody and drawn-out sibling rivalry. His two sons, Boris and Hlib, accepted death from their elder brother Svyatopolk rather than break their Christian vow of peace, and were made saints. The fighting weakened the capital and made it vulnerable to repeated nomadic raids. Yaroslav of Novgorod rushed to Kiev and succeeded in fending off the Pecheneg invasion in 1024. In remembrance and gratitude to God, he built St Sophia's Cathedral. Now the established grand prince of Kievan Rus, Yaroslav 'the Wise' continued the more dignified traditions of his father Prince Volodymyr. His reign is marked by cultural growth, legal development and rapprochement with Byzantium. Through a series of seven strategic marriages – of his children and himself – he became a relative of the rulers of Sweden, Hungary, Norway, France, Poland, Byzantium and Germany. This was European integration at its best.

These same methods of 'international relations' were copied by Yaroslav's grandson Volodymyr Monomakh, who married the last Saxon princess of England. He was popularly known as a defender of the poor: the crowds in Kiev rioted for him to take the throne even though it was not his to take. His reign (1113–25) marks that of the last great ruler of Kievan Rus before separate principalities broke away and became self-governing. Kiev was still the largest city in the region but local principalities became more independent and competitive, destabilising the city through constant battles and changes of power. In 1169 Monomakh's grandson ransacked Kiev and left the city reeling.

THE GOLDEN HORDE

Nomadic invasion was no news for the citizens of Kiev so they paid little attention when the Mongols first attacked on the Kalka River in 1223. Instead of moving on to Kiev however, the Mongols retreated and returned from the north years later. At the onset of the winter of 1240, the grandson of Genghis Khan – Batu Khan – came and decimated Kiev, bringing the last of Rus into the Mongols' military confederation, the Golden Horde. The Mongols never colonised the region fully and respected the local culture and religion, even exempting the Church from tribute. They put locals in places of power and had them do the dirty work of extracting each city's payment. It was a despotic realm and discipline was cruel. Unlike the Russians, the Mongols stayed in Ukrainian land for less than a century.

LITHUANIA AND POLAND

If Rus had become the Asiatic East, then Lithuania was its Wild West. For centuries, the pagan tribes of the Baltic forests had been a divided society of mutual raiding. This changed when the warrior Mindaugas brought together a combined tribal force in order to fend off the armed proselytising of the Teutonic knights. They held them back in Prussia, and the Grand Duchy of Lithuania expanded eastward. By the latter half of the 14th century, the Golden Horde had begun to lose power in the region and from 1344 the Lithuanians already ruled the far western principalities of Galicia and Volhynia. Algirdas, grandson to Mindaugas, defeated the Mongols at the Battle of Blue Waters on the Dnepr in 1362 and took Kiev with the charge that 'all Rus simply must belong to the Lithuanians'. The Lithuanians returned some of the order from the days of Kievan Rus and were a welcome change from the Mongols. The local nobility was incorporated into a ruling class and the land became a collection of ordered principalities. Many Lithuanians adopted Orthodoxy and learned to speak the local language that was now being called Ruthenian.

Polish expansion began in Galicia when the Polish-born leader Boleslaw was murdered on suspicions that he was still too Catholic. Having previously signed a treaty of spoils with the King of Hungary, the Poles moved into these western principalities with the ideological support of a Roman Church that opposed Orthodoxy. The following century marked a severe cultural shift for Galicia. Catholicism was introduced, Latin became the official language, and Czech, Polish and Hungarian nobles were given land grants.

The Grand Principality of Lithuania was by far the largest in the area, yet they faced threats from all their neighbouring nations: the Teutons were crowding the Baltic coast in the north, Muscovy looked nostalgically towards the lands of Rus, and Mongol raids were still a force to reckon with in the far east. Fearing they would lose the Ruthenian lands to the Russians, or worse, the Tatars, they sought a union with Poland that would enable combined forces of defence. The joining of the two countries was solemnised in the form of a marriage between Grand Prince of Lithuania Jogailo and the Hungarian Queen of Poland Jadwiga (the Polish king, Casimir the Great, left no male heir). The prince converted to Catholicism and in less than two years, Jadwiga had annexed Galicia to Poland. The rest of the Lithuanian principality was not so easily absorbed.

Jogailo stayed in his seat as king, but his cousin Vytautas began to rule Lithuania as a separate state. This lessened the Polish influence on the country, but it did not last long. Laws were passed that gave Lithuanian boyars the same rights as the Polish nobles, if they were Catholic. As the ruling élite of Poland and Lithuania became closer, the Ruthenians became more disenfranchised. In 1430 Prince Svidrigaillo led a campaign to sever ties with Poland completely, but the Poles responded with their own puppet candidate who proved more popular with the

Lithuanian élite. Sigismund of Starodub became the effective ruler of Lithuania and the Poles began to control more Ruthenian territory.

Lithuania was forced to co-operate with the Poles, as the threat of Muscovy and the Tatars increased. In 1522, the traditional principality of Chernihiv was lost to Moscow, a city that was now on a mission to gather Orthodox lands. Tatar invasions continued and then a fully fledged war began with Muscovy. Lithuania was financially drained and sought help from Poland. In 1569, a meeting was held at Liublin to decide the terms of the agreement. Realising that the Poles sought only to annex their lands to Poland, the Lithuanian and Ruthenian delegates walked out. The meeting continued nonetheless and the union was sealed; when the delegates returned, they had to settle. The Polish *Rzeczpospolita* was formed which would have an elected king, a parliament, common currency and a joint foreign policy. The land of the Ruthenians became attached to the Polish crown and the Ruthenian élite were quickly assimilated into a joint ruling culture. These nobles now spoke Polish, worshipped as Catholics, and enjoyed the favoured status of the Polish royalty. The lower-class Ruthenians were pushed to the fringes of their own society. Complicated laws based on religious discrimination and language kept Ruthenians out of the cities and out of positions of power. 'Ruthenian' came to mean peasant, and the Ruthenian language became the tongue of the countryside. These divisions were favourable to the Poles, who were tapping into the growing wealth of western Europe by trading food, in particular grain. Lands were combined into larger estates, and Ruthenian peasants were now forced to offer free labour to the nobles in exchange for the use of their own plots. Inside the Polish Commonwealth, cultural and economic disparity grew with the exploitation of the Ruthenians by the nobility.

THE COSSACKS

By the 16th century, western Europe had had a long tradition of feudalism, but the Polish landowners had only just introduced the system, enjoying the cashflow from the grain trade. Uninspired by their new lot in life, many peasants simply fled to the central Dnepr basin, the lands stretching across the plains north of the Black Sea. Here was a no man's land of sorts, a shifting frontier, unregulated by any foreign nobility. Other peasants were sent to cultivate the area, sanctioned by the Polish nobles themselves. Hoping to increase grain production, the Polish Commonwealth offered massive tracts of land rent free for up to 20 years in the unsettled steppe of the east.

This system brought two benefits to the commonwealth. Firstly, more grain could be produced and bought at low prices and then sold to western Europe. Secondly, an effective buffer zone was in place, protecting the kingdom from outside invasion. This borderland kept separate the civilised worlds of Poland, Lithuania and Muscovy from the barbaric Muslims of the Crimean Khanate and Ottoman Empire. This land was 'on the edge' of civilisation, or in the local language, 'U-krayi-na.'

A series of fortresses had been built to create a safety line for the Polish Commonwealth, stretching from Kiev out towards the western lands of Volhynia and Galicia. The land outside this line was called the *dike polye*, or 'wild field'. Constant raids from the south made the *dike polye* a precarious place to settle. The Tatars of Crimea had been left behind in the ebbing tide of the Golden Horde and continued to launch attacks to the north. By the 1500s they controlled most of the Black Sea coast and its Greek and Genoese trading posts. Crimean Tatars and Ottoman Turks came at least yearly on slave-collecting sprees, robbing the settlers, wrecking farms and severely depopulating the frontier.

Without the protection of overlords, the locals began to take matters into their own hands. A new brand of fighter emerged, dedicated to protecting his crops, family and land from continuous invasion. They became talented horseriders and disciplined warriors, earning their place as the genuine heroes of Ukrainian folklore. They gave the country its national costume and many of its folk songs and dances. It is impossible to compare the Cossacks to warriors like knights, the samurai or the cowboys of the Wild West. It was a unique time in a very wild frontier. Trained and prepared, they still spent most of their time on the farm, gathering only when it was necessary to fend off invaders or else attack enemy cities. It was these enemies that christened them 'Cossack', the Turkic word for 'freeman'. They were outsiders, excluded from any of the surrounding civilisations, and who in turn had established their own loose-fitting system of rule of law and sword.

THE ZAPORIZHIAN COSSACKS The popularity of the Cossacks spread across eastern Europe and young men who tired of the plough and the master's whip dreamt of running away and joining one of the bands of rebels. The Zaporizhian Sich became the unofficial headquarters of the Cossacks, based in a fortress town built on an island in the middle of the lower Dnepr. Here the Zaporizhian Cossacks emerged as a vaguely democratic military regime. Any Christian male of any nationality and social class was free to join, or leave. Every member had equal rights and all voices were heard in the open-air *Rada* that became the forum for decision-making. Women and children were forbidden from entering the Sich. Leaders were elected to be the *hetmans* or leaders, but had no power during peacetime. Only during a campaign could they enforce strict discipline.

The attacks on the Turks began as basic counter-offensives but soon turned into lucrative shopping trips to supplement their own wealth. Over one 20-year period, the Cossacks raided all the Turkish ports along the Black Sea and set the city of Constantinople on fire twice. The oversupply of booty saw the price of slaves tumble. The neighbouring nations were grateful for this 'Christian force' against the infidel Turks, and would offer them commissions to protect against raids. Yet the Cossacks were really only loyal to themselves, and soon they were making their first forays into Polish Galicia. For the first half of the 17th century, organised Cossack raids in Poland were the norm. King Stefan tried to stop the invasions by offering hefty stipends to some Cossacks if they would join his army against Muscovy, as well as fight the 'rebel' Cossacks. This divided the Cossacks and made the Zaporizhian Sich more determined against Poland.

Of all the Cossack warriors, the most revered is Bohdan Khmelnytsky. Born of Ruthenian nobility, he had served in the Polish army and had spent two years as a prisoner of the Turks. He later moved to the 'wild field' and spent most of his life quietly farming in what is now central Ukraine. He was a Cossack in that he helped keep the peace of the countryside from time to time. In 1646, however, a Polish neighbour beat to death his young son and then kidnapped his betrothed. As a Ruthenian outsider, his story had little pull in the Polish courts. He turned to the Zaporizhian Sich and incited enough enthusiasm for a campaign against Poland. He then made an alliance with the Tatar Khan who gave him 4,000 cavalry to help in his attack.

Khmelnytsky's army smashed the Polish force that same year at Zhovti Vody ('Yellow waters'). He continued his march towards Warsaw with a mission to destroy the Commonwealth of Poland. Cossacks allied to the Polish king soon deserted and joined with the Sich, while the Ruthenian peasants used the state of anarchy to revolt against the nobility, government officials and Jewish financiers. It was a murderous campaign all around. Catholic churches were burned and the priests brutally tortured. Massive pogroms were carried out on Jewish towns, many of them led by Khmelnytsky himself. Within a few months, the Cossack *hetman* had driven out the Poles, and for three years he controlled the territory between Lviv and Poltava.

By this time, the Tatar support had gone home and the *hetman* found that his jurisdiction was no longer secure. He began to consider a new overlord that would offer protection from the Poles while giving a chance for autonomy. Khmelnytsky turned to the Orthodox tsar of Muscovy as the less evil option. In 1654 the *hetman* met the tsar's emissaries in a church in Pereyaslav, a town below Kiev on the Dnepr. After swearing loyalty to the tsar, the Cossack stormed out when the delegation explained the tsar's power was absolute and that they would never make a reciprocal oath to his subjects. Hours later he wearily returned and agreed to the deal. Muscovite officials were sent into all the towns, and the tsar became the 'autocrat of all Great and Little Russia'.

RUIN The next 30 years were less than glorious for Ukraine and are often referred to as the 'Ruin'. Russian, Polish, Cossack and Tatar armies marched back and forth fighting for control of their own piece of Ukraine. Khmelnytsky's successors were unpopular and the countryside fell into disunity. In the west, the *haidamaky*, a band of runaway serfs and peasants, lived in the woods and raided the nobles' estates. The Cossacks' ranks became bureaucratic and ineffective. Only in 1686 did Poland and Russia sign an accord of 'Eternal Peace' which split the land right down the centre. Kiev and all lands east of the Dnepr fell into the hands of Muscovy, while Poland ruled the west.

The Russian leaders had little interest in autonomy within their empire. Peter I and Catherine II were both determined to centralise their empire, and used the English subjugation of Ireland as their model. The countryside was strictly ruled and all economic activity regulated by Russia. Trade was restricted to Russia at fixed prices. Some Cossacks were employed by the tsar as a useful protective force, but he did not appreciate their loyalties to other Cossack bands. The Zaporizhians were soon dubbed enemies of the tsar and a warrant went out for their execution. The Sich fortress on Khortytsya islands was destroyed by the Russian army in 1775.

LITTLE RUSSIA AND THE RUSSIAN EMPIRE

The Russian Empire was now the largest in the world, and Catherine II was intent on settling the southern portions of Little Russia. In her own words, she had 'recovered that which was torn away'. She presented tracts of land to Russian nobles and her German compatriots to win co-operation and pay for favours. Special labour concessions enticed local and foreign peasants to come and work on these new estates. The colony of New Russia welcomed a million people to the area in less than 50 years. Orthodox Serbs persecuted under the Catholic Hapsburgs were given former Cossack lands and renamed it New Serbia. The Crimean Peninsula was won from the Turks and quickly colonised by Russians, Greeks, Armenians and Jews. All of Little Russia became a land of grain production to feed the Russian Empire and to provide it with the raw materials to trade with Europe.

Malorossiya (Little Russia) was divided into nine provinces, each ruled by a tsar-appointed governor. It was a harsh regime, in which the tsar had unlimited power over all his subjects, and a cruel police force to impose it. The military boasted a strong presence and mandatory conscription for 25 years of service increased their size. Press-gangs collected the masses of unwilling young men.

Dr Mark Von Hagen

The national anthem of Ukraine starts with the words 'Ukraine has not yet perished, nor its glory nor its liberty ...' This is a very different kind of patriotism from the Germans' 'Deutschland über alles' or the American 'Star-Spangled Banner'. The hymn reminds Ukrainians of how precarious has been their statehood in history. Although today's independent Ukraine dates from only 1991, there have been former states that have ruled over the peoples and lands of this region and which could claim some important measure of sovereignty. But those states, whether medieval Kievan Rus or the Cossack *hetmanate* of the early modern period were destroyed by hostile neighbouring or invading powers, from the Mongol Hordes of Genghis Khan to Catholic Poland and Orthodox Muscovy.

The discontinuous history of the Ukrainian state and, with it, a Ukrainian nation, has been a consequence of Ukraine's location on the borderlands between powerful rival civilisations. The Slavic founders of Kievan Rus were pagans who had much in common with the nomads who wandered the southern Eurasian steppes. Kievan Rus also had early contacts with the world of Norse tradesmen and fighters who were eager to trade with Byzantium and the Black Sea ports. The Mongol sack of Kiev and the surrounding lands in the 13th century left a political vacuum that was filled to the east by a rising Muscovite autocracy and to the west by an expanding Polish and Lithuanian Commonwealth, both of which fought over the lands and peoples of the Ukrainian borderlands.

The Cossack *hetmanate* of the 17th and 18th centuries is now viewed as Ukraine's 'golden age' and enjoyed a loosely republican rule that distinguished it from royal Poland and tsarist Muscovy. The Cossacks themselves were a classic borderland phenomenon – they emerged to guard the borders of Russia/Muscovy and Poland from the Turkish states to the south, but were composed of peasants and other vulnerable social groups who were fleeing Polish and Russian enserfment. This included not only Slavic peasants (today's Russians, Ukrainians and Poles), but also Turkic peoples such as Tatars and Bashkirs.

When Poland was removed from the map of Europe at the end of the 18th century, the lands of Ukraine were also divided between Russia and Austria. Over the course of the 18th century Russian emperors abolished all vestiges of Cossack autonomy and resettled their lands with serfs and foreign subjects, largely from central Europe and the Balkans. The former Cossack élites assimilated into the Russian imperial service, especially the military and clergy.

Ukrainian political thought in the Russian Empire sought inspiration in the Cossack period for its project of a federalist and democratic Russia, in which Ukraine would have equality and justice restored to it. Austrian Ukraine, the lands of Galicia and Bukovyna, kept alive the language, faiths (Greek Catholic and Orthodox) and institutions of Ukrainians in a constitutional monarchy until the outbreak of World War I.

With the partitions of Poland also came a very large Jewish population that was also divided between Russia and Austria. Despite different degrees of disenfranchisement and discrimination, including pogroms in the Russian Empire, Jewish culture and institutions

Life was a dim prospect for the millions of serfs who were owned, purchased and sold by their landowners.

Tsar Alexander I had a slightly more liberal regime, but was prone to indecisiveness. Discontent grew and talk of reform was the banter in St Petersburg salons. Hidden societies flourished. Following Alexander's death in 1825, the infamous Decembrist Revolt erupted in a failed attempt to oust the incoming tsar. Nikolai I responded with the standard trappings of later Soviet regimes: a secret flourished in both Ukraines, producing literary figures like Sholom Aleichem and political leaders such as Zev/Volodymyr Jabotinsky, a founder of the modern state of Israel. Ukrainian Jews participated in all the major currents of modern Jewish life, from the traditionalist Hasidim to the Enlightenment-inspired reforms of the Haskalah to secular Jewish movements, including the socialist Bund and Zionism. Odessa and Kiev both emerged as important centres of Jewish life in the Russian Empire.

World War I brought horrible destruction to the borderlands of Ukraine, as well as Poland (which, incidentally, sings a national anthem that begins, 'Poland has not yet perished, as long as we are alive'). The imperial breakdown and rivalry also enabled the rise of several modern, if short-lived Ukrainian governments, including the Ukrainian Central Rada and National Republic (1917–18), the Hetmanate (1918), the Directory (1919) and a West Ukrainian Republic (1918–19). The war and civil war that followed in its wake ended, however, in yet another partition of Ukrainian lands, this time between a reborn Polish republic and the new USSR, largely recreating the former Russian–Austrian divide. In both the Soviet and Polish states, Ukrainian culture and politics had measures of renaissance during the 1920s. Increasing state repression on both sides of the border, including the devastating manmade famine in Soviet Ukraine in 1932–33, gave rise to militant Ukrainian nationalist movements that challenged the inter-war order.

World War II made Ukraine once again a bloody battleground between the Soviet Union and Hitler's Germany. Ukraine's Jews were murdered as part of the Europe-wide Holocaust that swept up Roma and other minorities. Ethnic Ukrainians and Russians were conscripted into forced labour in the Third Reich or in occupied Ukraine. The Soviet army's liberation of Ukraine in 1944 reunited the two parts again with the redrawing of Poland's borders after the war. Ukrainian partisan forces continued to fight the Soviet occupiers, as they had the Germans, but were crushed by the early 1950s, their leaders sent to Stalin's camps across Siberia.

Ukrainian culture and language enjoyed a moderate revival under Nikita Khrushchev's rule, but his successor, Leonid Brezhnev, resumed the Russification policies of Stalin and provoked a Ukrainian movement of dissent that helped fuel the opposition under Mikhail Gorbachev in the late 1980s. Ukrainian communist politicians joined forces with the democratic national opposition to create an independent state after 1991.

Today Ukraine's borderlands location continues to resonate in the struggle for its soul between Russia and the European Union, a struggle that has splintered the political élite and large parts of the citizenry. Inside the European Union, Poland, a traditional rival and overlord, has emerged as Ukraine's best friend. But Russian cultural ties, a large ethnic Russian minority (especially in the eastern and southern regions of Ukraine), and Ukraine's reliance on Russian oil and gas supplies mean that Ukrainian–Russian relations will also continue to present both threats and opportunities.

Professor Mark Von Hagen is chair of the history department at Columbia University, New York, as well as Boris Bakhmeteff Professor of Russian and East European Studies and a former president of the International Association for Ukrainian Studies.

police force, paid informers and strict censorship over printed material. He introduced brash cultural reforms aimed at making everyone more Russian. The local élite was quickly acculturated into the greater 'Russian tribe' and the class divide widened along cultural lines.

THE CHANGING EMPIRE The Crimean War (1854–56) highlighted the inefficiencies of the Russian Empire. Hundreds of thousands of peasants rushed to Kiev to join the fighting in the hope they would now be considered freemen. In battle, the Russian army came intimately close to Western foreigners and was made to witness its own backwardness. The empire could not compete with the leadership and industry of the Western nations, as seen in their ultimate defeat at Sevastopol.

Serfdom was the issue at hand, and Tsar Alexander took the throne in 1855 with the statement that it was better to 'abolish serfdom from above than to wait until the serfs abolish it from below'. Ukrainian peasants in the mid 19th century lived a life not dissimilar to the peasant farmers of feudal England. Their lives and their work were owned by their masters and living conditions were appalling. Life expectancy was never above 40 and alcoholism was rampant. Change was inevitable, but the delay was prolonged by the unresolved issues of land ownership. Russian nobles tended to understand the need to give some land away to the peasants, whereas the gentry in Ukraine were very reluctant to lose control of such a lucrative asset.

Serfdom was abolished in 1861 but the change did not ease the peasants' life. They were still not free to leave their village without specially issued passports. Land was distributed for their use, but they had to buy it from the government, which forced peasants into a tremendous debt that could last a lifetime. In addition, 20% of their payment was to be paid in labour obligations to the landowner. Serfdom remained de facto. The land they did receive as their own tended to be less fertile and much smaller in size than their former plots. The common land of forests and pastures went to the nobility and left the freed peasants with no access to wood or fodder.

New reforms eased the tension but did not resolve the ultimate issues of class and exploitation. Trials began to be held openly and military service decreased to six years. Education improved and local governments called *Zemstvo* were set up as committees to decide on tax spending for the region. But a head tax was issued which hit the peasants hardest, and most goods like sugar and tea were heavily taxed. Class differences were more noticeable between the peasants. The wealthiest group had somehow made their farms profitable and were known as *Kulaks*, while the middle (*Seredniaky*) and the poorest peasants (*Biadnaky*) worked for them, or hired themselves out to the gentry landowners. The nobility itself was in decline since few knew how to run an estate without free labour, but Ukraine remained the granary of Europe. At the turn of the century, Ukraine was producing 90% of the Russian Empire's wheat exports, while annually the Ukrainian peasant consumed one-third the amount of bread of a peasant in western Europe. Emigration became an increasingly attractive option, and Ukrainian national dress was a recognisable sight on the boats to Canada and America.

Industrialisation came late to Ukraine. Not until a railroad was built did a major industrial push begin in the 1890s. In the valley of the Don River, or Donbas, a furious coal extraction was carried out and mines soon covered the whole region. Such industry was often the work of foreign investors who sought to make a profit from cheap raw materials in a country that lagged severely behind western Europe. The Welshman, John Hughes, came to the Donbas to impart his knowledge of Welsh coal mining and gave his last name to the regional capital: Yuzovka. Iron became the purpose of Krivy Rih and Russia used the raw materials from both places to provide the steel needed to build a new industrial society. Workers were imported from Russia, the urban population grew, and the proletariat was born.

REVOLUTIONARY UNREST The ideas of Marxism spread quickly among the intelligentsia after the philosopher's books made headway in the 1870s. Within 20 years, the Russian Group of Social Democrats had been founded in Kiev, while other groups sprung up in Ukraine's industrial cities. These early Marxists were usually Russians and Jews – an honest reflection of the urban population that was interested in a predominantly Russian labour force. Agrarian socialism was its greatest contender for the revolutionary limelight. Earlier movements focused on the plight of the peasants, and used the peasant commune as a common symbol of Ukraine's inherent socialism. Sincere attempts were made to rally the peasants' support for a leftist political struggle against the tsar. The *khlopomany* movement (*narodnyky* in Russian, or 'People for the People') involved campaigns of students and intellectuals who would dress up like peasants and proselytise the revolution in the rural areas. The peasants rejected them as impostors.

Revolutionary enthusiasm was everywhere, but its ideas and representatives were split into odd-paired camps of ideologies and disparate brands of socialism. In 1881, the Narodnaya Volya ('People's Will' group), believing that only violent means would bring about needed change, assassinated Tsar Alexander II. In 1901, the populist Socialist Revolutionary Party was founded in Ukraine and also advocated political murder. Kiev was soon targeted for the new tsar's anti-revolutionary activity. The peasant uprising in Poltava of 1902 sent a strong nationalist message to Moscow and an individual brand of revolution was bred in the south. The Revolutionary Ukrainian Party was founded and became the vanguard for the Ukrainian nationalist political movement. Many of the leftist parties joined forces in the Union of Liberation of 1904, but those who were looking towards liberating Ukraine found the Marxist pull for centralisation discouraging. The parties did find common ground in their push for an end to autocracy and a parliament elected by universal suffrage. Tsar Nikolas II grew alarmed by this new coalition and sponsored a collection of violent ultra-rightist groups to put down the revolutionaries. Known as the Black Hundreds, they indiscriminately beat and killed anyone that was not tsarist, Orthodox or Russian. Blamed for the rise of revolutionary activity, the Jews suffered the bloodiest of pogroms in Ukraine, particularly in Odessa.

THE REVOLUTION IN UKRAINE

The Bloody Sunday massacre of 1905 occurred thousands of miles away in Petrograd (St Petersburg), but it set the revolution alight in Ukraine. A peaceful protest of factory workers ended when hundreds were gunned down by the tsar's troops. All the latent anger of revolutionary talk and party politicking turned to massive protests. In Ukraine, the proletariat led strikes that shut down the major cities. The peasants became more brazen and launched an expropriation of the Ukrainian countryside. Individually, they began to openly steal the gentry's crops, wood, tools and livestock. Collectively, the peasants would meet in front of the church and head towards a chosen estate with crude weapons in hand. The landowner would be forced to sign his estate away to the village council and the adult males would then redistribute the newly acquired property amongst the villagers. The rising fury led to the tsar reluctantly issuing his 1905 October Manifesto, which granted the vote to all Russian men and called for the establishment of an elected State Duma, to be led by the reformer Stolypin.

The new parliament found its powers were severely limited by the autocrat. Strikes and protests continued across the empire, and maintaining the peace became a violent task. Stolypin sought a soft revolution and supported a vision of conservative loyalists gradually implementing social change. The Duma was dissolved repeatedly and Stolypin's reforms were too little too late. He was shot during an intermission at the Kiev Opera House, while in the midst of conversation with Tsar Nikolas II.

Within days of the news of the February Revolution of 1917 reaching Kiev, the nationalist movement had mobilised. The Rada was established in March, modelled after the Cossacks' self-governing assembly. It assumed the most representative body, and soon the Ukrainian Socialist Revolutionary Party joined, as well as the Peasant Congress. By May they had issued a list of requests to the provisional government who were now attempting to hold the empire together. The Rada demanded recognition of Ukraine's autonomy, separate Ukrainian army units, and Ukrainians to take up the civil posts in Ukraine. The provisional government ignored the document, embroiled in its own confusing struggle for authority. The Rada then published its First Universal Declaration that called for a *Sejm* – Ukraine's own national assembly with a sovereign general secretariat. When it was granted to them, Ukraine's ethnic Russians were outraged. Kiev's provisional government eventually collapsed, unable to deal with the conflicting aspirations of Ukrainians and Russians.

WORLD WAR I AND UKRAINIAN INDEPENDENCE The internal mayhem of the revolution was made worse by the external war on the empire's borders. On the eastern front of World War I, Russia once again witnessed its own backwardness against the powers of the West in the most tragic manner. The faltering government stranded the army, millions were killed, and industry came to a standstill. Ukrainians found themselves fighting each other as soldiers in the ranks of the Austro-Hungarian and Russian imperial armies and by 1917, Ukraine was being suffocated. The Bolsheviks had come to power in Russia and were now fighting for a universal 'dictatorship of the proletariat'. In Ukraine, this proletariat lived mostly in the industrial eastern regions of the country. Like Lenin, they viewed nationalism and the independence movement as bourgeois and old-fashioned. The Bolsheviks had originally joined the Rada, but broke away after many disagreements and relocated to Kharkiv. Here they declared the creation of a Soviet Ukrainian Republic.

The Rada backdated its Fourth Universal Declaration to 22 January 1918, in which they declared Ukraine's independence. It was a frantic move in the shadow of an imminent Bolshevik takeover and the Rada looked for outside help. Not trusting Lenin to represent Ukraine's best interests, the Rada sent its own delegation to the talks at Brest-Litovsk. German occupation of the country, in exchange for food, seemed the best option. Even as the agreement was made, the Bolsheviks invaded Kiev. Miniature militias stood up against the army, albeit symbolically. One defiant group of 300 youths was surrounded and shot in Kiev. Yet within three weeks, the German/Austrian advance arrived and forced the Bolsheviks back to Kharkiv. However, the Germans found the country disorderly and were displeased with the inefficiency of the promised food deliveries. The authority of the Rada was uncertain and they could not satisfy their protectors' demands. Out of pure frustration, the German army disbanded the Rada at the end of April 1918.

A conservative government was put in its place that mimicked the monarchic Cossack *hetmanate*. The leader, Skoropadsky, was generally disliked, but was a welcome presence for the terrified nobles fleeing Russia. For a brief time, Kiev became a safe haven of hedonist escapism for the dispossessed gentry. Ukraine became the new theatre where the central powers fought for a Bolshevik downfall. However, when the armistice was signed, the Germans quickly retreated from Ukraine, leaving the vast territory at the mercy of its subterranean tension.

CIVIL WAR

The inconsistencies and contradictions of the Russian Revolution were gruesomely played out on Ukrainian soil over the span of three years of civil war. The Bolsheviks' Red Army invaded Ukraine from the north hoping to expand the revolution and secure its power over the former empire. The gentry and monarchists of Russia's imperial age backed the White Army. Keen to stop the ideological threat of communism and to quickly re-establish the old regime, the allies of the Entente – namely Britain and France – also gave military support to the White Army. The two armies competed in cruelty, which earned them a loss of support from both the peasantry and the proletariat. Food and horses were requisitioned by the passing forces, and the local men were forcibly conscripted. Both invading armies engaged in free-for-all violence: women were raped, homes looted, and towns destroyed. In the cities, factory workers were shot if they failed to meet the impossibly high industry quotas set to supply the ruling army.

The Ukrainian nationalists gathered in the west in the hope of rebuffing the foreign influence on their land and starting an independent state. A new nationalist government, the Directory, was founded in December 1918, but lasted only three months. A former leader of the Rada, Petlyura now led the largest nationalist band. Another independent Ukrainian state was proclaimed in Lviv after the fall of the Hapsburg monarchy, but was soon rejected by the Poles. The Galician rebels joined with Petlyura to fight in the civil war, but were betrayed when Petlyura made an agreement with the Poles to give up claims for Galicia in exchange for their assistance against the Bolsheviks. But after a quick defeat in Kiev, the Poles retreated.

The millions of peasants felt little allegiance beyond their village and carried out indiscriminate attacks on the nationalists, imperialists, Bolsheviks and Jews. These 'Green' peasant bands and 'Black' armies contributed to the pandemonium and sapped the energy of the greater armies. The most prominent of these fighters was Nestor Makhno. He was a home-grown Ukrainian hero with an intellectual bent for anarchy. Like many in his day, he had spent time in prison but also published academic essays on his political views. His competent army gained the respect of the local peasants who often collaborated in his terrorist forays.

The year of 1919 was one of bloodshed and chaos in Ukraine. Six separate armies ravaged the country, each with confused notions about its ultimate aim. Kiev changed hands five times in one year. The historian, Orest Subtleny, explained it best when he said: 'Ukraine was a land easy to conquer but almost impossible to rule.' Control of Ukraine's raw materials was a desired advantage for the greater war effort throughout the former empire. The Donbas was targeted, and the Red Army tried to implement some pre-emptive collectivisation on the peasantry. Neither the Red nor the White army could feed or clothe its soldiers. Desertion was the norm and in 1919 one million soldiers fled from the Red Army. Villages suspected of hiding deserters were decimated and soldiers fleeing combat were shot by their generals. Soldiers' uprisings were commonplace on both sides, and officers were cruelly tortured before being killed.

The Bolsheviks launched a successful invasion at the end of 1919 and took all of Ukraine in the following year. The Ukrainian Soviet Republic was reinstated. The Whites departed from Crimea, and the Ukrainian nationalist government retreated to Poland. Makhno went into hiding in Romania. The Bolsheviks had won the war, but at a tremendous price: 1.5 million of Ukraine's civilian population died in the scramble for power. The Jewish population suffered especially. Nationalists and anarchists carried out vicious pogroms that killed over 50,000 Jews. The Whites viewed the Jews as the chosen people of the Bolsheviks and killed over 100,000 of them. The Red Army simply killed Jews as bourgeois anti-revolutionaries, in spite of the Jewish leaders within the Bolshevik Party.

Bolshevik severity was justified as 'war communism' and meant Ukrainians were expected to release all belongings and food to the Red Army. Everything was nationalised, and grain was requisitioned from the peasantry. Out of protest, many peasants stopped planting. An accompanying drought led to a devastating famine, where hundreds of thousands died in Ukraine.

After moving Ukraine's capital to the eastern city of Kharkiv, the Ukrainian SSR joined the Soviet Union in a 1922 referendum of Bolsheviks in Ukraine. Lenin said Russia and Ukraine would be joined in a 'Union of Equals'. The new socialist republic included most of the territory of present-day Ukraine, with the exception of Galicia and Volhynia and certain borderlands. Kharkiv remained the republic's capital until 1934.

Lenin was sensitive to national sentiments and realised that, when presented in the colours of the local Ukrainian culture, the Bolshevik pill was more readily swallowed. A policy of *korenizatsiya* (making roots) was established to bring non-Russians into the Communist Party and earn co-operation from all Ukrainians. Ukrainian culture and language were preached like a new religion. Russian party officials had to study Ukrainian and speak it to their Ukrainian counterparts. Education turned Ukrainian and the plague of illiteracy disappeared. More people learned to read than ever in the history of the country, but the only Ukrainian books at hand somehow always featured the Communist Party and pictures of smiling Red Army soldiers.

Ukraine did not convert easily to communism. The years of war, the deadly famine and the present economic woes did not seem the shining end to the revolution they envisioned. The Bolsheviks were still very unpopular throughout the whole Soviet Union and peasant uprising continued in Ukraine. The Kronstadt Mutiny against the Red Army in St Petersburg alarmed the Bolshevik leaders and moves were taken to ease the tension between rulers and ruled. Before he died in 1924, Lenin introduced the New Economic Policy (NEP) which was aimed largely at appeasing the peasantry, albeit temporarily. Taxes were lowered, and peasants were permitted to sell grain at market prices. Collectivisation was halted and foreign investment encouraged. It was capitalism actually, and it gave immediate results. With new incentives, agricultural production increased, and industry flourished. The cities witnessed a new class of trade and businessmen that wore imported suits and sold foreign luxury goods.

THE TRAGEDY OF STALINISM Stalin had wangled the seat of party general secretary through sheer treachery and was now eager to push forth his concept of a centralised industrial union. Most of all, he hated the wealthy NEP men and the Kulak peasants who had prospered during the mid-1920s. In 1928 Stalin introduced his 'revolution from above' with a five-year plan. This was a series of gargantuan industrial goals for the cities and a major collectivisation of the countryside which was repeated in a second five-year plan. Sceptics of such massive change in so short a time were answered with Stalin's famous quote: 'You can't make an omelette without breaking eggs.'

Ukraine already had a large industrial base and hundreds of new factories were added. Ukrainians poured into the cities and dramatically changed the ethnic make-up of the workforce. Zaporozhia became a city of steel mills and Kharkiv started building tractors. The Dnepr hydro-electric plant made it all run. Living conditions were terrible and discipline severe. Everyone was pushed to the limits. On a summer day in 1935 a young coal miner in eastern Ukraine named Aleksei Stakhanov cut 102 tons of coal in just six hours. This was over ten times his mine's personal production goal. Stalin made him a national hero overnight, and a new cult of Stakhanovism had every worker sweating his way towards superhuman industrial achievements. Underneath the show of rapid industrialisation was the reality of waste, inefficiency and poor quality.

Soviet figures for industrial growth were based on parallel growth of the food supply. The state believed it would buy grain cheaply from the peasants, feed the cities and sell the surplus abroad for profit. When they offered to buy the grain at a minute fraction of market price, the peasants refused to sell. Hoarding grain drove up the market price even higher. Stalin called for the liquidation of the Kulaks as a class. Any peasant who owned something was suspect. During 1929–30, hundreds of thousands of Ukrainian peasants were packed onto freight trains, shipped to the frozen tundra of Siberia and ordered to settle the land. Most died of cold and starvation.

Collectivisation itself was a disaster. The remaining peasants revolted while the secret police and army used brutal force to take farms and move people. Resisters were shot on sight or else arrested and sent to Siberia. Out of protest, the peasants often killed their animals rather than let the government have them. Ukraine lost 50% of its livestock this way. The new collective farms were highly unsuccessful and directed by unskilled Russian party activists. Grain production fell drastically.

THE FAMINE Stalin called for even higher grain quotas and sent in military generals to supervise the seizure. Hired gangs went from farm to farm, tearing up floorboards and torturing peasants in search of hidden grain. Drought in 1931 killed the remainder of the failing crops. After two years of grain requisitioning, most of Ukraine's food supply had been confiscated and the countryside was left to starve. Peasants ate rats, bark, leaves, dirt, and one another. Skeletal bodies were a common sight in city streets and whole villages died together. The famine of 1932–33 was the ultimate tragedy for the Ukrainian nation. Figures vary widely, but it is generally believed that 3 to 6 million Ukrainians starved to death. The tragedy went unnoticed in the West and in much of the Soviet Union.

THE GREAT TERROR The 1930s also brought an end to *korenizatsiya* and any remaining idea of a union of equals. Stalin had no tolerance for opposition and targeted the intelligentsia. A new regime of terror rid the country of non-compliance. Scientists, church leaders, writers, editors, historians and musicians disappeared. The traditional Ukrainian *kobzari* (bards) were invited to a conference and shot on sight. Purges cleansed the party of infidels who were charged with all manner of '-isms' and lack of vigilance. The accused were shot or sent to the gulag prison camps of Siberia. In 1934, the Ukrainian Communist Party lost over 100,000 members in one year. New purges in 1937–38 eliminated the entire leadership of the Ukrainian Soviet government and the Ukrainian Communist Party. Soon, even the most random accusations would end in disappearances and executions. The Stalinist terror introduced a paranoia that kept people circumspect for the remainder of the Soviet Union's existence.

WORLD WAR II The Soviet army 'liberated' Galicia and Volhynia after Poland fell to the Germans in 1939. The policies of the Soviet regime were not well received in these western provinces and about half a million people were deported to Siberia. The Nazi attack on the USSR in June 1941 took Stalin by surprise. Resistance in Ukraine was futile. In western Ukraine, fascism sounded better than Stalinism. The German soldiers were perceived as liberators and given a hero's welcome in some towns.

Kiev was captured in September 1941 and soon after the whole country was occupied by Nazi forces. Knowing the advantage of raw materials in Ukraine, Stalin called for a scorched-earth policy in the Red Army's retreat. All political prisoners were shot, electricity plants destroyed, factories blown up and mines flooded.

The three-year Nazi occupation of Ukraine was brutal and exploitative. The collective farms of Ukraine were now feeding the Third Reich, and the Germans had a particular interest in such a fertile land. A common anecdote tells of train-loads of rich Ukrainian topsoil being shipped to Germany. Two million Ukrainians were also exported to Germany as forced labour. These *Ostarbeiter* (Eastern Workers) lived as slaves during the war, but were met with suspicion or imprisoned upon returning for their 'collaboration' in capitalist Germany.

There were approximately one and a half million Jews in Ukraine prior to the war. Days after the Nazi invasion, the calculated killing of Jews commenced. The majority of Ukraine's Jews were not sent to concentration camps, but rather were collected, shot and buried in mass graves. The 'final solution' was the annihilation of Ukraine's thousand-year-old Jewish community. Controversy surrounds the level of Ukrainian collaboration in the Holocaust and with the Nazis in general. Anti-Semitism has a long history in Ukraine, and many of the massacres of Jews were in fact carried out by the Ukrainians. As in the civil war, there was someone fighting for everything – Jews, Poles, Germans and Russians were all targets. Sizeable partisan armies fought against both Germans and the Soviet Army in attempts to liberate Ukraine.

By 1943 the Soviet Army had returned to Ukraine. Kharkiv was lost and re-conquered twice in a series of notorious tank battles on the Eastern Front. Within six months, only the environs of Galicia remained in German hands. At the Yalta Conference of 1945, Galicia and Volhynia were allocated to the USSR from Poland. One million Poles moved to the new Poland, while half a million Ukrainians relocated to the Ukrainian SSR. The borderlands of Transcarpathia and Bukovyna were also incorporated. By the war's end, it was estimated that one out of every six citizens of the Ukrainian SSR had been killed.

KHRUSHCHEV United in anger towards the German fascists, Stalin was able to direct the people's emotions towards rebuilding a wrecked country. Hundreds of war memorials still stand as symbols of overcoming one form of oppression in Ukraine. The mood was one of frenzy and inevitability. What had been destroyed had to be rebuilt quickly. Millions of Russians moved south to Ukraine, mostly to work in the factories. Cities exploded with growth.

Stalin died in 1953 and Nikita Khrushchev took his place at the helm of the Communist Party. Khrushchev was Russian by birth, but had climbed the political ladder in Ukraine, playing an instrumental role in the Kiev purges and overseeing the economic reconstruction in that republic. He had a folksy appreciation of the land, wore embroidered Ukrainian shirts and liked to hear Ukrainian songs on his visits. Khrushchev also liked to wax lyrical about the Slavic brotherhood of Ukraine and Russia. The year 1954 marked the 300th anniversary of the Pereyaslav Agreement between Khmelnytsky and the tsar. Big celebrations were planned and the Communist Party issued '13 theses' that spelled out the everlasting union of the Ukrainians and the Russians. As a commemoration gift, Khrushchev annexed Crimea to Ukraine. Most Russians say that he was drunk at the time. In fact, the Crimea proved to be a loaded present.

Khrushchev gained in popularity when he denounced Stalin and introduced the 'thaw' – a period of relaxed censorship and general freedom. The standard of living improved, and many families were given their own flats after decades of living in communal housing. The cookie-cutter concrete slab apartment buildings seen from Lviv to Vladivostok are Khrushchev's doing. In Russian, they were nicknamed '*khrushchoby*' – the general secretary's name crossed with the word for slum. They may be ugly, but the Soviet Union successfully housed its entire population in a very short time. Khrushchev moved between relaxing his grip and tightening the reins on Soviet society. The intelligentsia were periodically targeted, as were the churches.

The last decade of Soviet rule in Ukraine was one of decline and stagnation. The weaknesses of the centralised government only made the autonomy of Ukraine and the other republics more evident. Brezhnev was old and ill during his time as general secretary and both Chernenko and Andropov died soon after coming to power. These leaders were the old political élite who still glorified Stalin and ignored the telltale signs of internal degradation.

PERESTROIKA

The young reformer, Mikhail Gorbachev, then claimed the highest seat in the Communist Party in 1985. He held a firm belief in the superiority of socialism, but also had a distinct resolve to transform the clumsiness and rigidity of the Soviet Union. *Glasnost* (openness) allowed more freedom of expression than previously seen in the USSR. The reforms of *perestroika* (reconstruction) liberalised the economy and decentralised the political structure like never before.

On 26 April 1986, the Chernobyl nuclear plant exploded 100km north of Kiev. The initial disaster was exacerbated by the reluctance of the government to confess to the accident. Only after nearly a week did knowledge of the event reach the very people that were in the greatest danger. Hundreds died from the first heavy doses of radiation, but the real tragedy lay in the countless people living with chronic ailments and the thousands of deformed children born in the following months. While the power plant was a Soviet plant, it was located in Ukraine and the Ukrainians found that they would suffer most for it. The Soviet government proved ineffectual in remedying the situation, and Chernobyl has continued to be a festering sore with which the Ukrainians must still cope. Decades later, the political controversy around Chernobyl still prevents any comprehensive assessment of the true long-term effects on people's health, but the local ecology has made some recovery. More important is what Chernobyl has come to represent: a national tragedy for the people of Ukraine before they had their own nation.

Nationalist sentiment grew more vocal as people tested their boldness under the freedom of glasnost. In the summer of 1988, thousands gathered on several occasions in Lviv and Kiev with a variety of protests, but mostly for autonomy. This was probably the last time the KGB arrested anyone for being pro-Ukrainian.

All over the Soviet Union, people from every republic were speaking their minds and their message was freedom, but not necessarily independence. Gorbachev had never intended things to go this far and he tried frantically to keep some order to the union. In September 1989, the Ukrainian nationalist party, Rukh, was founded in opposition to the Communist Party in Ukraine. Gorbachev fired Ukraine's leading communist, Shcherbytsky, realising that repression of Ukrainian self-determination would only hurt his position with the other republics. In 1990, democratic elections were permitted for the first time at the republican level. The Supreme Soviet, or Verkhovna Rada in Ukrainian, would be open to non-communist parties.

In 1990, students from Lviv and Kiev camped out on the newly christened Maidan Nazelezhnosti (Place of Independence) and began a hunger strike calling for swift and major changes, including a stop to military service outside Ukraine and nationalisation of Communist Party property. Joined by politicians from Rukh, the demonstration was successful and the changes were announced in the Rada.

Meanwhile in Moscow, communist hardliners were conspiring against the liberal reforms. In August of 1991, Gorbachev was vacationing with his family in Foros, Crimea, when he was put under house arrest and a state of emergency declared for the whole Soviet Union. The ringleaders of the coup sought to put the Communist Party back on track and prove Gorbachev a traitor. The Ukrainian communists could either comply and fall under a supposed new dictatorship, or support the 'democrats' in the party and split the Soviet Union. The chairman of the Rada, Leonid Kravchuk, finally denounced the coup right before it failed. The collapse of the central government in Moscow left Ukrainian communists to rush for a decision on total independence and keep some aspect of authority in their own territory. The voting was almost unanimous, and on 24 August 1991, Ukraine was declared independent. Gorbachev made a final effort to keep some sort of union alive, but, in a hunting lodge outside Minsk, Yeltsin made a secret agreement with Kravchuk and Belarusian chairman Shushkevich that put the ineffectual CIS into place. The Soviet Union ceased to exist.

EARLY INDEPENDENCE

Kravchuk was elected president at the end of 1991 and it seemed that the same communist administration was in place as before, only under a different name. Privatisation of the country's wealth was a monument to shady deals, and a stark few turned astronomically wealthy overnight. Organised crime unashamedly ran business enterprises but seemed to be the only kind of organisation in the country. Mafia shootings were no longer shocking and corruption was the norm at all levels of government.

The following years were painful. Inflation rocketed to over ten thousand per cent. Cut-out paper coupons were printed as a temporary currency and made invalid before they'd come into wide use. People continued to go to work but received no salaries. The shops were either empty or closed, and food and clothing could be bought only on the streets. Winters were the hardest, with heat and electricity rationed. Russia threatened to shut off the gas supply to Ukraine when the country could not pay its bills.

Kuchma was elected in July 1994 as a progressive alternative to the Communist Party (see page 28). He was reported to dedicate hours to learning Ukrainian during his campaign in order to appeal to the hard-core nationalists of the west, but his support came mostly from his home town, the very industrial and Russian-speaking city of Dnepropetrovsk.

For a very short while, there were some fears Ukraine would split down the middle. Ukrainians in the west were speaking Ukrainian and feeling European. In the east, Russian speakers longed nostalgically for the convenience of the Soviet Union. The propaganda of Ukrainian culture began to dominate. Street names were changed and children nationwide started reciting the national poet Shevchenko at school. The new constitution appeared in newspapers everywhere in 1996 declaring Ukrainian as the only official state language – but most people couldn't read it.

Kuchma was re-elected in 1999, but his presidency was soon tangled in scandal when it was suspected he was linked to the brutal killing of Ukrainian journalist, Georgy Gongadze. The crime has yet to be solved. Other numerous scandals were then linked to the presidency and it was revealed the president was also connected to a private weapons deal with Saddam Hussein's Iraq, in breach of international sanctions. In October 2002, the Communist Party led days of protest in Kiev against Kuchma's corruption and abuse of power. NATO 'uninvited' the Ukrainian president to its Prague summit that year, but Kuchma attended anyway, inspiring a last-minute switch from English to French seating cards so that the United Kingdom and United States would not be seated next to Ukraine. Kuchma's reign became decisively less democratic. Ukrainian society continued to stagnate under severe corruption, and it looked as if the situation would continue even after Kuchma's second term was coming to a close.

THE ORANGE REVOLUTION

By the beginning of 2004, Ukraine faced a transfer of presidential power and lines had been drawn. The likely successor seemed to be Viktor Yanukovych, head of the 'Donetsk clan' and close ally to Kuchma. Employing a Kremlin-style campaign with plans for widespread election fraud, the Yanukovych team expected to walk into the presidency. Their staked opposition in the fall election was Viktor Yuschenko, an economist and Kuchma's former prime minister, and leader of the 'Our Ukraine' opposition bloc in the Rada. Composed of free-market, pro-democracy, Western-leaning members, the 'Our Ukraine' bloc won large support throughout the country and began posing a substantial threat to the Kuchma–Yanukovych camp. The pre-election dynamic was incredibly tense, and was only worsened after Viktor Yuschenko was poisoned in an attempted assassination just two months before the vote. International pressures mounted in favour of a free and fair election in Ukraine, and thousands of election observers were brought in.

Following a close but inconclusive first round of votes (a largely fraudulent ballot in and of itself), the second vote took place on 21 November 2004. Despite severe fraud, a strong condemnation of the vote from observers, and exit polls that clearly showed Yuschenko to be the victor, Yanukovych was quickly declared the winner and congratulated by Russian president Vladimir Putin. By 22 November hordes of 'Our Ukraine' supporters had gathered on the Maidan Nezalezhnosti (Independence Square) to protest the vote. Brandishing orange clothes and banners – the colour of the opposition bloc – the crowds soon turned into a mass demonstration that filled the centre of Kiev. In spite of roadblocks aimed at quelling the tide, supporters poured into the capital from all over the country. Over the next few days, up to one million people gathered in Kiev and succeeded in shutting down the city. Constructing park bench barricades and erecting a gigantic tent city, they closed off most of Khreschatyk and filled the square. As political tensions mounted, the protestors surrounded parliament, the presidential palace and the Supreme Court. Due to the corrupt elections, parliament finally passed a no-confidence vote in the Kuchma–Yanukovych government, but the government refused to step down. It was Ukraine's Supreme Court that finally intervened and declared the November election results invalid and set a date for a new election. All the while, the protestors kept vigil in freezing temperatures outside, not only in Kiev, but throughout all of Ukraine and in many other parts of the world. Their rallying cry was *razom nas bohato,* meaning 'together we are many' and they represented a broad mix of Ukraine's 48 million citizens. Together, they continued to hold the square up until the repeat second run-off vote took place on 26 December 2004 in which Viktor Yuschenko won the majority. The last protestors left and the tent city was removed only a few days before Viktor Yuschenko was sworn in as President of Ukraine on 23 January 2005.

The Orange Revolution represented a watershed moment for Ukraine, delivering a huge boost of confidence and self-determination to the Ukrainian people. In a country where oppression, corruption, fraud and violence had become the norm, a true show of people power had fought for change and succeeded – against all odds. Despite continuous analytical dissection of the revolution and its aftermath, 'orange fever' is responsible for a new sense of national consciousness and goodwill that has resulted in real improvements, be they economic, political, diplomatic or cultural. A new standard was set, and the people of Ukraine have begun to see their own future far more positively than they did five years ago.

MAKING HISTORY TODAY After the exhilaration of peaceful revolution and the celebration that followed, Ukraine began to experience the full brunt of responsibility that comes with independence, something they had been buffered from during the Kuchma regime. Reforms were slow and President Yuschenko found his powers limited in rooting out long-term corruption. Out of frustration, he sacked his entire government in September 2005. The ensuing 2006 parliamentary elections played out as a hectic circus in which dozens of parties competed against one another, each with its own colour and slogan (at least it looked like democracy). At the heart of the political debate was the price of gas – following an announcement that they would no longer provide Ukraine with subsidised energy, Russia shut off Ukraine's gas supplies on New Year's Day 2006. It was returned shortly thereafter, and many believed this was a political move to reinforce Kiev's dependency on Moscow in spite of the Orange Revolution. Yet the very forces that came together and stood against the Kremlin's influence were embroiled in months of bickering and blame that left the parliament paralysed. For a time, party coalitions shifted daily. Somehow, they came back to work in the end, but not without significant tension about the direction of long-awaited reforms. Coping with Russia and setting the right balance in that relationship will continue to be a vital issue in Ukraine's domestic and international politics.

Overall, independent Ukraine has made big changes in a very short time. The economic situation has stabilised, democracy is steadily finding its way and Ukrainians seem more hopeful about the future. But ten years is too short a time for generalisations and today the story of Ukraine still continues as it has for centuries. On one level, everything has begun to match the 'developed' world, but scratch the surface and the timelessness of earlier struggles is revealed. This turbulent past has cultivated a superhuman patience in Ukrainians so that the nation's deep resolve seems tied only to those things of proven regularity: the seasons, their families and the ability to survive. Ukrainians today are far more aware of their role in the country's history and take much more pride when looking back at the very difficult past.

What's more, this is the first time in their history that Ukrainians have been allowed to know all of their history, so that a current sense of jubilant national rediscovery inspires both those who live here and the travellers that arrive from abroad. It is difficult to go anywhere in Ukraine and not feel overcome by all that has transpired in this place.

3

The Ukrainians

PEOPLE

Anyone who has been to Ukraine knows that getting to know people is far more important than visiting any prescribed sights. Long after you've forgotten the name of some church in Kiev, you will recall individuals and their stories, even if your conversations were carried on by made-up sign language. The title 'Ukrainians' is meant to include everyone and anyone who lives in Ukraine – a truly diverse gathering of 48 million people. Ethnic Ukrainians make up the majority, but even that majority is made up of various shades of 'Ukrainian-ness'. The classic caricature of the Zaporizhian Cossack is still perceived as the ultimate Ukrainian personage, but travellers will find Ukrainians to be lots of things: a Poltava cabbage farmer, a Kiev professor, a Crimean Tatar, an Odessa Jew, a Galician student or a Russian coal miner.

Only a few, very broad, generalisations are worthy of describing Ukraine's people. First off, Ukrainians live closely to the earth. Every season has meaning, as does the blossoming of each plant. Urban Ukrainians will leave the city during the summer to live in their small cottages (*dachas*) and to work their individual plots. Historically, Ukrainians survived the winter by eating food they had produced themselves. Despite all the technological advances and pervasive e-culture of modern Ukrainian society, the people will always have a strong tie to the countryside and an appreciation of the simpler side of life.

As with most societies, families play a key role in Ukrainian life and loyalty is an integral value. Members of an extended family depend on one another; it's a strong support network that goes far beyond the limitations of the West's independence and individualism. Grandparents may raise children, young people look after the elderly and food and cash are shared all around.

Ukrainians like to have a good time by eating and drinking, singing songs, and telling stories and jokes. They like to talk a lot and most have a natural intellectual bent manifest in their conversational musings. By custom, Ukrainians are very hospitable and will gladly open their home to a stranger they have just met. Guests are always offered some sort of refreshment – at least tea, if not a meal, and Ukrainians always throw a good party.

LANGUAGE

Ukrainian is the official language of Ukraine, except in Donbas where Russian is officially recognised and in Crimea, where both Russian and Tatar are recognised (and spoken). The Russian language is still used throughout much of the country, but Ukrainian is coming into wider use with the growth of national consciousness. In the Carpathians, there are also areas where dialects of Romanian, Hungarian and Polish are spoken.

Ukrainian is an Indo-European language of the eastern Slavic family of languages. The original root language is now referred to as Old Church Slavonic,

Ukraine is NOT Russia. Just like Canada is not the USA, and Scotland is not England, Ukraine is too often defined by the shadow of its hefty neighbour. The last 15 years represent Ukraine's longest recognised independence in history, attributed by many to keeping Russia at bay in the post-Soviet era. In Ukraine, attitudes towards Russia range from friendly association to deep animosity, although most families embody the microcosm of a bi-national relationship: one parent might be Russian, the other Ukrainian, and relatives can be found on both sides of the border. In general, the two countries are neither too distantly related for total cultural separation, nor different enough to get along.

For now, Ukraine's recognised independence from Russia is the most important factor in the relationship and many Ukrainians now embrace everything that sets Ukraine apart from Russia. People will be quick to tell you that Russian civilisation was actually founded in Kiev, that Ukrainian is the older and more sophisticated Slavic language, and that famous Russian writers, or great Soviet leaders, were born and bred in Ukraine. Ukrainians like to consider their homeland to be inhabited by the more spirited and unconventional of the Slavs.

The current government-sanctioned cultural renaissance promotes all things Ukrainian, while Russian culture is considered somewhat politically incorrect. At school, children make cut-out paper sunflowers and learn Ukrainian folk dances. All official government business is conducted in the Ukrainian language and most place names have been changed, if only by one letter. This separate national consciousness has energised society somewhat, but has also led to feelings of self-alienation for those whose culture is more closely linked to Russia. The slang term Russians use for a Ukrainian is *Khokhol*, from the Tatar words for blue and yellow. In return, the Ukrainians will refer (rudely) to Russians as *Kotsap*, meaning 'little goat', but having the same effect as 'jackass' in English. Since the upset of the Orange Revolution, a more comfortable cultural balance has emerged, but travellers should be sensitive to the past struggle of Ukrainian cultural survival as they witness the present show(s) of nationalism. Keep in mind that, whatever Ukraine may be, it is not Russia, but it is the intertwining of the two histories and cultures that makes Ukraine such a fascinating place to explore.

as it is still used in the Orthodox liturgy. Discernible versions of Russian, Ukrainian and Belarusian had emerged from Slavonic by the mid 12th century. Two Byzantine missionaries, St Cyril and St Methodius, travelled to Ukraine in the late 9th century and established a written language for the land, hence the Cyrillic alphabet, which combines Greek and Latin letters to fit Slavic sounds.

After centuries of linguistic repression, it has become very important for Ukrainians to speak Ukrainian in a show of independence, individual identity and solidarity. This is the first time in the country's history that free linguistic expression has been permitted and society is taking full advantage. Thus everything is written in Ukrainian and in most of western Ukraine people will speak only Ukrainian. At the same time, Russian is a very important language in Ukraine, and visitors often wonder how similar/different the two languages actually are. The closest comparison to the relationship between Russian and Ukrainian might be Spanish and Portuguese. Ukrainians tend to have no difficulty understanding Russians, while ethnic Russians have more difficulty with Ukrainian. Ukrainian sounds much softer and is much more poetic in some respects, while Russian has benefited from centuries of high culture and literature, during which time Ukrainian was severely repressed and spoken mainly by the rural peasant population.

Newcasters and travellers are always trying to draw some kind of linguistic map for Ukraine that shows clear-cut boundaries and vivid trends. While it is fairly easy to generalise (Odessa, Donetsk, Dnepropetrovsk, Simferopol, and Kharkiv are all Russian-speaking cities; Kiev, Lviv, the Carpathians and Poltava are all Ukrainian), Ukraine's true linguistic landscape is as rich as its physical terrain and absolutely no rules apply fully. Throughout all of Ukraine you can hear a variety of interesting dialects and versions of both Ukrainian and Russian, and most people speak a fairly common mixture of the two, called *surzhyk*. Indeed, as choice of spoken language becomes de-politicised, Ukraine is developing into a multilingual European society, where Ukrainian is preferred and more generally used, but everyone can still speak Russian, if not some other language. A common sight nowadays (even on television) is one person speaking in Ukrainian, and another responding back in Russian, with both parties understanding one another and continuing the conversation in the two different languages.

Travellers should try to be sensitive to whatever the locals are speaking, although if you speak neither it's hard to tell. Contrary to exaggerated claims, nobody will shoot you for addressing them in the 'wrong' language. Still, the more effort you make to learn some Ukrainian (and Russian), the more likely you are to earn the respect of whoever it is you are speaking to. (And see *Appendix 1*, page 421.)

CULTURE

Ukrainian culture is evident everywhere you travel in the country, but most of what tourists will want to see is present only during country festivals, holidays or in more traditional areas. Allowing for exceptions, older Ukrainian traditions and customs are followed with more gusto in western Ukraine (Podillya, Galicia, Volhynia and the Carpathians), central Ukraine (Poltava and Cherkasy region) and throughout most rural areas.

SYMBOLS Ukraine's official coat of arms is a gold **trident** (*tryzub*) on a blue field, probably linked to the Greek god of the sea, Poseidon. Prince Rurik of Kievan Rus was said to have used the same symbol and old coins and bricks from the period of

THE UKRAINIAN CALENDAR

Names for the months in Ukrainian bear no relation to the Roman calendar, although Russian has adapted the Latin names. The Ukrainian year follows nature's tempo as a simple but poetic nod to earth's changes.

English	Ukrainian	Root and meaning
January	Sichen	*cut*; a cutting wind
February	Lyuti	*fierce*; cold and biting
March	Berezen	*birch*; the birch forests begin to bud
April	Kviten	*flowers* blossom
May	Traven	the *grass* grows
June	Cherven	*worms* crawl from the earth
July	Lypen	the *lime tree* blossoms; flowers are collected for tea
August	Serpen	*sickle*; the harvest begins
September	Veresen	the *heather* blossoms
October	Zhovten	*yellow*; wheat fields and forest leaves turn yellow
November	Lystopad	literally, *falling leaves*
December	Hruden	*balls* of snow fall

Prince Vladimir are also decorated with the trident. In the small bursts of independence in 1918 and in the Carpathians during 1939, the trident was re-adopted to show separatism from ruling powers. During the late Soviet period, nationalist demonstrators would flash 'trident' hand symbols with their three middle fingers held apart. The national emblem was made official in 1992. You will see it everywhere and on everything.

Plants, animals and trees are also important symbols for Ukrainians. The **sunflower** has always been used to represent Ukraine, and if you visit in summer you will see why. The *lipa* (lime tree or linden) is considered the most important and symbolic of Ukrainian trees, and Ukrainians use the flowers and leaves for all kinds of herbal remedies. The same goes for the **birch** tree, with its very strong pagan symbolism and healing powers. The **sickle** of the Soviet flag actually comes from Ukraine where it has always been an important symbol of the country's traditional agricultural lifestyle. Ukraine's own **flag** does look a lot like the Ukrainian landscape: a light blue sky over a golden field of wheat or sunflowers. The origins however date back to the Hapsburg monarchy in 1848 when the Supreme Ruthenian Council adopted the flag of a golden lion on a blue background. The lion eventually disappeared but the colours stayed. Cossack flags were generally red and white, and various nationalist peasant and anarchist bands have used banners of red, green and black.

NATIONAL DRESS The Ukrainian national costume typically is worn only for festivals and ceremonies (like weddings) but is the most prominent display of culture for most people. Traditionally, women wear a white embroidered tunic over which a scarlet woven *platya* (skirt) is wrapped and secured with a colourful belt. The ensemble is completed with leather boots, a flowered head-wreath with long coloured ribbons, and several red clay, beaded necklaces. Men wear baggy Cossack-style trousers tucked into low boots, a long silk sash belt, and the traditional *rubakha,* an open cotton shirt with intricate embroidery around the neck. A recent fad has Ukrainian businessmen substituting the sober shirt and tie of the West with the more colourful *rubakha.*

ARTS Classic romantic painting did not feature as strongly in Ukraine as it did among the European élite of Paris and St Petersburg, but there are a few important exceptions. Repin and Aivozovsky are the most renowned Ukrainian painters, and you'll find most art museums have at least one of their pieces, along with well-intentioned collections of other Ukrainian-themed paintings. The Odessa impressionists represent an important movement in art history, having made their mark a good 50 years after the French Impressionists. Soviet Ukrainian propaganda is only now being widely considered an art form, with its colourful posters and sober messages. A few permanent exhibits of Soviet artwork exist in Kiev and some souvenir shops sell prints.

The most traditional form of Ukrainian painting is *petrikivka*, bright, multi-coloured brushstrokes, typically depicting a repetitive floral motif, and usually painted on black lacquered platters or, in some areas, around the doorways and windows of homes. Colour is important and the designs symmetrical and full. Decorating the exterior of one's home is a wonderful Ukrainian tradition followed predominantly in the more rural areas of the country. Stamped metal patterns, coloured tiles, wooden stars and other shapes, shingles, shutters and glass are all used to express individuality on otherwise humble rural cottages. The results are always charming and people who appreciate rural art should make an effort to get out to a smaller village and witness some of these more traditional designs before everyone starts using aluminum siding.

Although religious in theme, **icon painting** is very much the ultimate Ukrainian form of rendering human images. Figures or faces of Christ, Mary, the apostles and saints are painted on wood and sometimes decorated with gold. Important Orthodox icon-painting schools existed in Kiev and Chernihiv, which set the standard for most Slavic icon imagery today. In homes, icons are placed in the corner of a room, usually opposite the door, and a small sheaf of wheat is placed underneath to ensure peace and prosperity for that home. Traditionally, this sheaf was cut from the last sheaf of good grain and tied with a ribbon during *Obzhynky*, the Harvest Festival.

HANDICRAFTS Ukraine's greatest artistic expression comes alive in the everyday experience of work and survival. For example, the large tile stoves of traditional Ukrainian homes were always the warmest part of the house. In winter, a family would spend most of the day (and night) on top of the warmed tiles. For a few centuries, painted stove tiles were revered as a high art from.

Eggs hold all kinds of symbolic meanings for Ukrainians, and eggs are often used in fortune-telling or folk cures. The quintessential Ukrainian craft is the decoration of *pysanky*, or Easter eggs. After blowing out the yolk and white from a small hole in the shell, melted wax and different coloured dyes are used in a batik-like process to produce a layered pattern of intricate designs. Traditional patterns are usually geometric or show basic representations of flowers or animals. Like all Ukrainian art, *pysanky* vary from region to region, and the craft has been kept alive largely by the diaspora (incidentally, if a woman gives a man a *pysanky* that leaves the top undecorated, he will go bald). **Rushniki** are the most basic art form in Ukraine but the most widespread in tradition. Calling them 'hand towels' doesn't do them justice, although technically that's what they are. The long white linen cloths are embroidered with bands at either end in simple geometric patterns. Traditional designs and colours differ by region, village and family. Mothers are supposed to embroider *rushniki* for their sons before they leave home, and a young bride will be sure to embroider enough for her trousseau. In Ukrainian homes, different cloths are used for special occasions: holiday meals, for holding newborn children or for a christening, for weddings, for welcoming guests with bread and salt, and for shrouds at funerals. In many Ukrainian churches, *rushniki* are draped over the icons and altars. Rather than cover the whole piece of material, Ukrainian embroidery on clothes decorates only the edges of simple white cloth with colourful geometric designs cross-stitched around the wrists, hems and neckline. Designs vary, but besides triangular and diagonal shapes, crosses, flowers and leaves are traditional. In the Carpathians, animal shapes hold special meaning.

Ukrainian **woodcarving** is either intentionally crude and rough, or else incredibly refined and inlaid with beads or tiny shells. Small, shaped boxes and lids are customary, along with bowls, plates, spoons, combs and pipes. Some are painted with red, gold and black *petrikivka* (see *Arts*, above), others are left natural or stained. Traditional **pottery** also embodies the true spirit of Ukrainian craft, combining the very rustic with the very refined and painstakingly beautiful. Black, ash-coloured pottery from the west of the country is an ancient art form with lovely results. Needless to say, even if you are dead set against knick-knacks, crafts and souvenirs, you're quite likely to leave Ukraine with something.

LITERATURE Ukrainians hold writers in such high esteem that they'll call you a journalist until you're dead (then they'll call you a writer). Needless to say, literature is taken very seriously and Ukraine's history is rich with individuals who have had to fight for the right to write in their own language. Taras Shevchenko is Ukraine's national hero and eternal poet laureate who wrote *Kobzar*, esteemed as the greatest written work in the Ukrainian language. His statues and portraits are ubiquitous and, as a rule, children memorise his poetry at school. Shevchenko was also an artist and many other things, and his personage continues to influence every aspect of Ukrainian culture, including its language. Nikolai Gogol, author of *Dead Souls* and *An Inspector Calls*, is probably better known in the West. His short stories take place in Ukraine's countryside and describe well the superstitious world of Ukrainians. Lesya Ukrayinka, whose pen name means 'Ukrainian forest', started the writer's circle called the 'Pleiades' and wrote lyrical poetry in Ukrainian while there was a ban on the language. Most cities have streets named after her, if not a memorial. Writers like Kotlyarevsky and Kotsyubinsky also wrote during a time of linguistic repression and their homes now stand as national shrines. Ukraine's literary canon also includes Russian writers like Pushkin and Chekhov who wrote and lived in Ukraine for part of their lives. Few people know that the English/Polish writer Joseph Conrad was also born in Ukraine, and Balzac spent a good deal of time in the country. For some suggestions on what to read before your trip, see *Appendix 2*, page 429.

Ukraine enjoys a 98% literacy rate and people enjoy reading. Writing and reciting poetry is also a national hobby. Owning books is a status symbol and most individuals harbour vast libraries of Ukrainian, Russian and international literature in the smallest of apartments. Soviet culture also permitted the reading of approved Western writers, namely Ernest Hemingway, John Steinbeck, Jack London and Sir Arthur Conan Doyle, so you will hear them mentioned often.

FOLK DANCING At weddings, holidays, festivals or indeed on any day, dancing is a very important part of celebrating. Folk dances are normally conducted by large groups of paired couples, but different dances have evolved from specific regional terrains. The wide open spaces of the Ukrainian steppe influenced the unique style of folk dancing that involves running, leaping and people forming extensive circles. Dances from the mountainous Carpathians are performed in small circles and involve more fancy footwork and jumping up and down. Ukraine's national dance is the *hopak*, a very energetic ensemble where women spin and encircle the men, who perform a number of difficult acrobatic stunts in the front, including the well-known squat kicks and split jumps of the Cossacks. Traditional Cossack dances excluded women and the *hopak* was originally a stage for physical competition between warriors. Now, nearly every folk dance performance will include at least part of the *hopak* in a charged mood of dancing, clapping and very fast music. Larger folk dance troupes tend to be based in Kiev, western Ukraine and around Poltava, where so many Ukrainian dances originated.

As a visitor you are more likely to witness the kind of dancing that takes place between courses at a banquet or in a nightclub. Despite modern influences and Ukrainian pop music, the trained eye can still see through all the free-form movement to the eager feet of what must be a genetic disposition to folk dancing.

MUSIC Ukrainians sing when they are very happy and when they are very sad. It seems as though the centuries of upheaval favoured the preservation of songs over any other kind of material culture, and if there is anything that brings Ukrainians together, it is their music. Today, most Ukrainians sing at large gatherings: birthday parties, weddings and holidays. Once they've started, they can sing for hours, and everyone in the room (of all ages) will know all the lyrics and the accompanying harmony.

The traditional Ukrainian instrument is the large tear-shaped *bandura*, normally with 60 strings. Strummed like a harp and tuned like a guitar, the *bandura*'s music has an enchanting sound. Once played by the Cossacks, today buskers play them in the streets and subway stations. Traditionally, blind children were taught to play and sing historical and religious songs in order that they might have an occupation. Named *kobzari* for the lute-like *kobzar* they played, these bards walked from village to village playing on request in exchange for food and alms. Many of the songs you hear date back to the era of the *kobzari*, with a series of short stanzas that tell a staggered story, sometimes through dialogue. It is not uncommon for a set tune to have over a dozen verses, with repeated choruses in between. The music is always in a minor key, which adds a melancholy tone.

Ukrainian folk songs are normally about love, vodka, or love and vodka. Some are ironic and humorous, but most are wistful or solemn. 'Kozak Viyizhdzhaye' is the conversation between a weeping girl and her Cossack, who is about to ride off into the unprotected 'wild field' of Ukraine. She begs to go with him, and in each verse he asks her what she will eat, where she will sleep, what she will do in far-off Ukraine? In 'Oi Verbo, Verbo!' a young maiden sings to a weeping willow tree, telling of her betrothal to the town drunkard and her plans to run away on a horse. Today, most people sing with a classic Russian guitar, accordion or without any accompaniment. Soviet folk songs also add to the national repertoire, and almost every adult male can sing you a song about being homesick and lonely out on the front.

If you want to buy some good folk music, check the stalls on the Maidan Nezalezhnosti in Kiev. Most of these sellers are from western Ukraine and are showing their patriotism by acquainting tourists with Ukrainian culture. Mariya Burmaka is one of the greatest Ukrainian folk singers, and her earlier cassettes add a fitting soundtrack to the landscape. Nina Matviyenko is known best for her haunting voice and pre-Christian folk songs, and most music dealers will have her recordings, as well as those of folk singer Mariya Mykolaychyk.

Traditional religious music is integral to Ukrainian culture and there are few sounds more heavenly than an Orthodox choir singing. Do everything you can to visit an Orthodox church during a musical service. The singers normally stand in a small balcony in the back of the church by the entrance and respond to the chanting priest throughout the service. Most churches and monasteries will have recordings of Orthodox chants and singing for sale.

Ukraine's national anthem is entitled 'She Ne Vmerla Ukrayina' ('Ukraine has not yet perished') and is meant to reinforce the country's perseverance through suffering. The anthem is played morning and night on the national radio station in the same fashion as the old Soviet anthem. There's also a popular jazz version that seems odd but is played regularly.

Ukrainian pop music is going full force in its artistic licence, sometimes mixing folk elements into modern beats. Best known for this style is Ruslana, the winner of the 2004 Eurovision song contest, who brought a strong Carpathian element to her musical performance. Ruslana continues to be hugely popular, but there are several very talented Ukrainian pop singers of the same genre (I also recommend Iryna Bilyk). Jazz is also a long-loved phenomenon among Ukrainians, and it's also surprising how easy it is to come upon a bona fide blues club in Kiev or any other city. Punk too is not dead in Ukraine, with some great Ukrainian contributions, including the hilarious band Borsch (as in the soup). Most nightclubs play rave or techno music, and the Russian/Ukrainian techno music that you hear in taxis, marketplaces and on long bus rides has a giveaway polka bass line that will stay in your head long after you've left the country.

BELIEFS AND RELIGION

ORTHODOXY For most Ukrainians, Orthodoxy and nationality are one and the same. Ukrainian Orthodoxy asserts that theirs is the original Church of ancient

Ukraine's human landscape features an abundance of old ladies who seem to be everywhere and are always very busy sweeping streets, carrying Atlas-sized bundles, or selling things. Why so many? In World War II, the Soviet Union lost over 20 million citizens, the majority of whom were male soldiers. Their sisters, widows and mothers survived, and now make up most of the elderly population. No other demographic group in Ukraine has endured as much as these women. After the devastation of the war, they spent their twenties and thirties rebuilding the country, and the rest of their working years keeping the USSR going. They retired just in time for Ukrainian independence and then watched their entire pension repeatedly devalue. Today, most female pensioners receive around US$30 a month and are left with no other choice but to go back to work. Enterprising grannies in their seventies and eighties have had to find ways to supplement their income, usually through very hard work. Many will sell roasted sunflower seeds, flowers, herbs and anything else out on the street. Others undertake hard-labour jobs that pay little but at least pay, and it is not uncommon to see old women carrying pick axes, shovels or large buckets to a construction site or through the market. *Bábushka* ('grandmother') is the respectful term used to address all elderly women (*babulya* or *babusya* in Ukrainian, or simply *baba*). *Babushki* play a vital role in Ukrainian culture and society, since most young mothers are expected to work, and traditionally, young married couples live with the bride's parents. In consequence, nearly all Ukrainian children are raised by their grandmothers. Ukrainians think fondly of their grandmothers, and will constantly quote them as a source of wisdom. Grandmothers are responsible for telling grandchildren stories, teaching them folk songs, religion and how to dance. Perhaps in detriment to their own image, grandmothers warn recalcitrant grandchildren of *baba yaga*, an evil grandmother witch who eats children and lives in a house with chicken legs deep in the Ukrainian forest (it helps to keep children in their beds).

Grannies also feel compelled to feed others: their families and their guests. Nothing compares to the privilege of eating a meal prepared by a real live *babushka*. For visitors to Ukraine, grannies also present a rare access to living history. Most have lived under the Stalinist regime, some have fought as partisans, and others have built tanks in factories or conducted scientific research in Siberia. They all know how to survive. Buying their sunflower seeds or flowers is a nice way to keep the grandmothers in business and if you ever want to give a gift, just think of what your own grandmother would like.

Kievan Rus, brought to them by the Apostle Andrew, and that the union of Slavic culture and Christianity was destined to occur in Ukraine. By nature, Ukrainian Orthodoxy is also highly mystical and meditative, and Ukrainians employ the outer rituals of prayer and fast plus iconography as methods to engage in a deeper spiritual process. The religion's philosophy is based largely on the writings of the early Christians and Gnostics of the wider Middle East, as well as a millennium of Slavic monastic work.

Orthodox **saints** (*svyaty*) are the holiest of religious symbols and most churches will hold at least one body of a saint, a physical remnant or an icon. Different saints perform different functions; for instance, Nikolai the Miracle Worker is popular in times of need or emergency. People will visit his icon in the church, pray to it and post a candle near it. Posting candles is both a sign of faith and an offering, and every church will sell different sizes of long beeswax candles for different degrees of prayer.

Icons are central to Orthodox worship and are much more than a picture of a favourite saint. Painted on wood or covered with gold and silver-plating, blessed icons carry holy powers of protection, healing and fortune. Believers visit and pray to icons in churches and monasteries and most taxi or bus drivers will keep an icon on their rear-view mirror to protect their vehicle. In homes, icons are placed in the top of the farthest corner opposite the door of a room to bless and protect the family's space.

Traditional Orthodox church buildings are built in the shape of a Greek cross. Those from the Byzantine era were made of stone with the typical rounded domes of the period. Traditional churches from the 15th to the 17th century are usually built from wooden beams criss-crossed in log-cabin style and fitted only with joints and pegs (no nails). Younger cathedrals are larger and made of stone, brick and mosaic, with the onion-shaped domes normally associated with Orthodoxy. On the inside, most churches have a highly decorated **iconostasis**, covered with images of the saints and closing off the back apse of the church. Only priests are allowed behind this sacred wall.

A normal Orthodox Sunday mass lasts about two and a half hours. Prayers are chanted and a small choir sings out chilling responses while aromatic **ladan** (incense) smoke fills the church. You'll notice there are no chairs inside, because it is considered a sin to pray or worship sitting down. Instead, believers will stand or periodically prostrate themselves on the ground. All-night vigils and extra-long church services are not unusual, and the faithful will continue to stand for up to seven hours. Shorter services during morning and evening weekdays are easier times to visit. Taking part in an Orthodox church service is an amazing experience and travellers should make it a priority during their stay in Ukraine. The problem is that most churches do not appreciate having tourists running around untethered. Visit churches only with a spirit of reverence: men should remove their hats and women are supposed to cover their heads. Even if the church's interior is beautiful, taking photographs indoors (especially during a service) is very offensive. You can avoid conspicuousness by buying a candle and lighting it in front of your favourite icon as you are walking around the church.

The Soviet era was a time of severe religious repression, but now Orthodoxy has become the most important sign of patriotism and independence. Society now divides itself among *verushy* and *neverushy* (believers and non-believers) and nearly every town will have at least one new church under construction. So much of the religious architecture that tourists see today was only renovated in the last five years, but historically Ukraine has always been considered the more spiritual country (compared with Russian Orthodoxy). In the USSR, Ukraine had more churches than all the other republics put together and a majority of Orthodox clergymen were Ukrainian. Two of the most holy sites in Slavic Orthodoxy are located in Ukraine: Kiev's Pechersky Lavra (Caves Monastery) and the Pochayiv Monastery near Ternopil. Today, in terms of numbers of physical churches, Ukrainian Orthodoxy is the largest Orthodox Church in the world; however, three separate Ukrainian churches consider themselves the Ukrainian Orthodox Church, and the government recognises four, as below.

Ukrainian Orthodox Church (Moscow Patriarchate)
Throughout the Russian Empire and the Soviet Union, the Church and Christianity fell under the jurisdiction of Moscow. After independence, the Ukrainian Orthodox Church that still recognised Moscow's ecclesiastical authority was named as such, and it is still the largest Church in the country. Followers exist all over Ukraine, but its presence is largest in Russian-speaking areas of the east and Crimea, though it still owns churches all over. In order to appeal to some Ukrainians, a few parishes are

Ukrainian-speaking, but traditionally, all services are read in Old Church Slavonic. The Caves Monastery in Kiev (see page 147) is the headquarters of this Church in Ukraine.

Ukrainian Orthodox Church (Kiev Patriarchate) In an attempt to break away from Russian influence after independence, the Ukrainian Metropolitan or ecclesiastical leader (with the government's help) formed an independent Orthodox Church in 1992 with the intention of offering a centrist version of Ukrainian culture that coincided with the political movement towards Ukrainian unity. The Moscow Patriarch excommunicated the Kiev Patriarch for his rebellion and both churches still bicker about property and territory. St Mikhayil's Monastery of the Golden Domes and St Vladimir's Cathedral in Kiev are the Church's most prominent sights.

Greek Catholics (Uniate) During the centuries of Polish rule in western Ukraine, the Orthodox believers made a symbolic compromise in order to appease the government and preserve their culture. The Ruthenians agreed to pay allegiance to the pope in Rome, but they would keep their Ukrainian Orthodox doctrine and service. The Church was made illegal in 1946 but was officially reinstated when Gorbachev met with the pope in 1989. Greek Catholic beliefs are a mixture of old Byzantium and Galician folk culture. Concentrated in western Ukraine and the Carpathians, Greek Catholics tend to promote a strong nationalist culture. St George's Cathedral in Lviv is their ecclesiastical centre. To identify a Greek Catholic church, look for any tapestry or picture of the pope and the absence of the traditional Orthodox iconostasis (the wall of icons separating the nave and sanctuary). In western Ukraine, Roman Catholics are called 'Polish Catholics'.

Ukrainian Autocephalous Orthodox Church During the window of Ukrainian independence at the time of the Russian civil war, nationally conscious Ukrainian believers sought autocephaly (self-rule) from the Russian Church, believing they should be able to worship in their own language. The Church was formed in 1919, but later fell victim to Stalin's early repression of nationalities, and was declared illegal in 1930. The Autocephalous Church survived in exile, mainly through the Ukrainian diaspora in North America, although the Church was said to meet frequently in Ukraine in the forest. The state gave official recognition to the Church in 1993. Like the Greek Catholic Church, the Autocephalous Church is concentrated in western Ukraine and is the most nationalist of Ukraine's churches. UAO churches are most easily recognised for their exquisite embroidered *rushniki*, used as simple but powerful decorations (although some Greek Catholic churches also have *rushniki*).

OTHER BELIEFS Many scholars believe that **Judaism** came to Europe from the Middle East via Ukraine. In the 19th century there were over three million Jews in Ukraine; today there remain about 250,000. Synagogues can be found in the cities of west and east Ukraine, many of which have just recently been returned to the local Jewish communities. Much of what is referenced as 'Jewish culture' in the West is in fact Ukrainian, whereas much of what Ukrainians refer to as their own culture is often heavily influenced by long-standing Jewish traditions.

Baptists constitute Ukraine's traditional form of evangelical Christianity, brought by missionaries over a hundred years ago from Germany. The Crimean Tatars are Sunni Muslims by faith so that **Islam** holds a visible presence in Crimea. As much of southwestern Ukraine was the frontier of prolonged war with the

- Never shake hands through a doorway. Doing so is a sign of insincerity, misfortune and ill will to the other person.
- Never cross paths with or move ahead of a funeral procession (even buses will wait until they pass). Doing so means you are searching for death.
- Whistling indoors means all your money will fly out the window.
- When you see a baby, do not faun over the child, look the baby directly in the eye, or tell the parent how cute and precious the baby is. It is bad luck – the child may get sick and you may inadvertently pass on the evil eye.
- Never give an even number of flowers – it symbolises death.
- To avoid jinxing yourself when tempting fate, spit over your left shoulder three times.
- Sit down before leaving on a long journey (preferably on your luggage). Rushing off brings bad luck on the road.
- If you sit at the corner of a table, you'll be single forever.
- Sitting between two people with the same first name brings good luck.
- If you a drop a knife, an unexpected male visitor is soon to arrive (a fork – female).

Turks, many of the castles and even some former churches in the region were once mosques. Since independence, Ukraine has seen a flood of missionary activity and a significant rise in religious pluralism. Slavic **paganism** has come back into open practice in recent years among small non-conformist groups, but with all due respect, most Ukrainian spirituality is already deeply rooted in early paganism.

THE SUPERNATURAL Despite a national pride in all things scientific and factual, a world of superstitions rules the lives of many Ukrainians. Be prepared to pick up a few of your own during your travels.

Orthodoxy and the trappings of organised religion have done little to hide the Ukrainian cultural connection between the natural and supernatural spheres, and between the pagan and Christian. According to Ukrainian tradition, all forms of nature have a spiritual personality: there are spirits in the fields and in the trees and evil water nymphs in the rivers called *rusalky*. The spiritual world can either help or harm, but most people just notice the harm.

The *nechysta sila* ('unclean power') is the cause of all wickedness, evil and human woes, and can be avoided only through spiritual *zaschyta* ('protection') that stems from a combination of Christian and pagan customs. During Christmas, for example, an axe is placed outside the door to ward off evil spirits. The headache of supernatural ailments is the evil eye, which can affect you in a number of ways: depression, fatigue, toothache, quarrelling with your spouse, bad luck or spoiled food. Wicked people can pass on the evil eye just by looking at you, as can nice people who simply look at you in the wrong way (with jealousy or condescension). The best protection against the evil eye is to wear small mirrors under your clothing (front and back) that reflects 'the eye' back to the sender.

Ekstrasensa is the Ukrainian/Russian version of spiritual foresight or ESP. The gifted (usually older women and *babushki*) can look into the future and work things for or against someone's favour through black or white magic. Rituals are based on physical manifestations of metaphysical ideas and usually involve Orthodox icons, Bibles and crosses. The use of herbal medicine is also normally combined with some sort of supernatural healing or with the help of 'bio-energy'.

The Ukrainians BELIEFS AND RELIGION

3

Most traditional Ukrainian holidays fit into a meticulous Orthodox calendar which changes from year to year. **Easter** is the most important of these holidays, and in Ukrainian Orthodoxy, believers will fast for the Lenten period by abstaining from meat and dairy products. All-night church services (standing!) and ritual parades around the church at midnight mark the beginning of the *Velyky Dehn* ('Great Day') and the festivities begin. Tall, yeasty sweet cakes called *paskhy* are baked at home and then brought into the priest for blessing, along with other food and decorated Easter eggs. The traditional greeting is *Yisus Voskres!* ('Christ is Risen!'), to which you are expected to reply *Va Istynno Voskres!* ('Truly, He is Risen!').

Ukrainian **Christmas** is a colourful and mystical holiday, celebrated quite differently from most Christian Christmases. On Christmas Eve, single youths will travel from house to house singing *kolyadki,* cheerful Ukrainian carols to wish a good evening and good health to neighbours and friends. Singers will stand beneath the main window of the house, brandishing large sacks, and will continue singing loudly until the window is opened and the homeowner drops Christmas treats into the bags. The practice goes on well into the night. In the home, a meal of 12 dishes is often served to symbolise the 12 apostles. A single candle is set inside a special braided bread loaf called *kolach* and the family eats *kutya*, a semi-sweet mixture of cooked wheat, honey and poppy seeds eaten only on Christmas Eve.

New Year became the most important holiday of the year during the Soviet era, where emphasis on 1 January detracted from any national or religious recognition of Orthodox Christmas on 7 January. Christmas trees (*yolka* in Russian, *yalynka* in Ukrainian) are put up for New Year and children receive gifts from *Dyed Moroz* (Father Frost) who wears dark blue robes and is accompanied by his helper, the princess *Snigorichka* (Little Snowflake). The evening is marked by a gigantic meal that is meant to last all night long, with heavy drinking, singing and dancing (in that order).

The most important summer holiday takes place on midsummer's eve from 6 July until the morning of 7 July. **Ivana Kupala** began as a pagan festival in honour of the deity of the summer, *Kupalo*, but the holiday's connotation was shifted towards Christianity's John the Baptist, hence *Ivana* (St John's) *Kupala* (Bathing) and the festival's common translation St John's Eve. Ritual cleansing through fire and water is the main objectives of the evening. In the early evening, medicinal herbs are gathered and couples search in the woods for a special fern that is meant to promise them happiness. Unmarried women are supposed to weave a head-wreath of leaves and flowers (*vynok*), place a candle in its centre, and set it into a flowing river. If the wreath floats, she will be married within the next year; if it sinks she will not (*vynok* symbolise love and protection, hence the Ukrainian word for marriage, *vynchaniya*). During the night of Ivana Kupala, participants immerse themselves completely in a lake or stream, and then, later, a roaring bonfire is lit and men and women hold hands and leap over the flames. The fire is meant to heal all ailments, and the couple who keep their clasp held through the flames will stay together. Ukrainians celebrate Ivana Kupala more than any other pre-Christian holiday.

The Soviet holidays of 1 May (Labour Day) and 9 May (Victory Day) are still widely celebrated with big military parades and fireworks. The October Revolution is remembered on 7 November but most businesses stay open. International Women's Day is celebrated on 8 March much like Mother's Day in the West. Flowers and cards are presented to women of all ages, and men are supposed to cook for their wives/mothers/girlfriends/sisters.

BIRTHS, DEATHS AND WEDDINGS The oak is one of many holy trees in Ukraine, and in the olden days, when a boy was born, a small oak branch was thrown into the water where he was bathed for the first time, so that he would grow up to be strong and solid, like an oak tree. When a girl was born, a clump of red *kalina* berries would be thrown into the water so that she would grow up to be beautiful. Nowadays, the most important event is a baby's baptism performed by an Orthodox priest. Until a baby is baptised, the child is highly susceptible to the evil eye and is more likely to fall ill. Infant baptisms are by immersion and a cross of silver or gold is placed around the child's neck to be worn for life.

When someone dies, the body will be set in an open coffin so neighbours, friends and family can pay their respects. Funeral processions make long slow parades that follow the deceased (usually on the back of a truck) towards the cemetery. It is bad luck to cross paths with a funeral procession and you will see traffic redirect itself for miles or completely stop. After the burial, families and friends will return at nine days, 40 days and a year after the person's death, as the spirit of the departed is said to be near the grave during this time. Flowers, candles and food are brought to the graveside and a meal is eaten on site. A small glass of vodka will be placed on the gravestone, from which the spirit will take 'sips' until the glass is empty.

In western Ukraine, a bride-to-be will travel from house to house with her friends all in national dress, inviting people to the wedding, singing folk songs and requesting blessings and good wishes from everyone in the village. Traditional Ukrainian weddings take place in October or November, after the harvest is over. Marriages in churches have come back into practice only during the last decade. During the Soviet period, weddings took place in front of a bust or painting of Lenin in special 'marriage palaces'. After the ceremony, couples would lay a bouquet of flowers near a war memorial or Lenin's statue. These days, the tradition continues, but the flowers are brought to Shevchenko's statue instead. After a vodka toast at a wedding dinner, guests will frequently shout *Gorko!* ('It's sour!'); the bride and groom must kiss one another to sweeten the other's lips. Shouts of *Gorko!* followed by kissing continue throughout the day, even without the vodka toasts. Wedding parties last for days, even after the bride and groom have left on their honeymoon.

FACE TO FACE WITH UKRAINIAN CULTURE

MANNERS AND MANNERISMS Ukrainians are incredibly hospitable and generally understand that foreigners are not always privy to their cultural idiosyncrasies. These are a lot more fun to figure out on your own, but here are a few tips:

- Greet people and introduce yourself as you would anywhere else. If you are a man, do not shake a woman's hand unless it is offered to you. Ukrainians love business cards and will pull them out at any opportunity. Bring some if you have them. When entering someone's home, take off your shoes near the entrance. Normally you will be offered slippers to wear. If you have been invited as a guest, bringing a small gift or flowers is customary.
- Turning down a drink is considered a very rude gesture and for some carries the same weight as refusing to shake hands. If you are a non-drinker or just want to hold back, a determined *nyet* will hardly do the trick. Stating religious or health reasons is met with more understanding and causes less offence. No matter how hardcore one's habits, don't ever expect to keep up with a Ukrainian drink for drink. I have yet to meet a non-Ukrainian who can.

- At birthday parties, weddings, anniversaries, holidays, and generally most gatherings, Ukrainians will make poetic toasts to one another and particularly those who are to be honoured. As a foreign guest, toasts will be made to you, and you are expected to toast in return. A mere 'thank you' or 'cheers' just won't do. Be vociferous and flowery, ending with very specific wishes of good will (eg: 'that our most wise and beautiful host discovers secret happiness and fortune throughout the next year').
- Before you eat, say '*Smachnoho!*' (like '*bon appétit*') to the others at the table. As a guest, you will be fed and fed and fed. If you completely empty your plate or bowl, it will be refilled. If you leave too much on your plate, your host will say you don't like his/her cooking and they will be offended. Either way, you can't win.
- The Soviet era created a society that was anything but service-oriented. Dealing with certain concierges, waiters, hotel clerks or ticket sellers can be a taxing experience, especially if you are used to a culture of Western customer service. Being ignored or shouted at can get frustrating. Sometimes it takes making a small fuss to get the attention of the person on the other side of the glass. Being polite but unwavering and persistent is the best policy.
- Standing in a queue (line) also gets you very little respect in Ukraine. As one very well-travelled Greek commentator wrote: 'When it comes to queuing, the Ukrainians are the very worst, even worse than the Greeks!' You may find that after waiting 20 minutes, someone will simply cut in front of you. Be assertive and try to come across as confident and even pushy. Always be prepared with your request – if you get to a window and are still fumbling for money or a ticket, then in their mind, they have the right to push you aside and take your place, and they will. When a bus, tram or subway appears, queues disappear and everyone pushes and shoves to get in. If you try to be your version of polite, you may never get on. Learn to throw your body into it and say *izvinitye* ('excuse me' in Russian) or *probachteh* (in Ukrainian).

POVERTY The people of Ukraine suffered tremendously during the economic crash and social ills of the early post-*perestroika* years. In less than ten years, Ukraine's population declined by more than eight million through massive emigration, a swift rise in the death rate and a dramatic drop in the birth rate. Begging is looked down upon culturally, but people still do it, although much less than in most countries. On the other hand, a small percentage of Ukrainian society has become extremely wealthy, especially the *byznesmeny* who got rich quick from privatisation 'deals'. These 'New Russians' are the subject of countless jokes that mock their lack of taste and value. Fortunately, a real middle class has emerged in Ukraine but overall, people are still quite poor and spend most of their time acquiring the basic needs of life. Coming to terms with dire poverty is something travellers must do all over the world, but in Ukraine the real shock stems from witnessing poverty among such an educated and technologically advanced people. Know that your presence in the country is already a sign of progress. Spend your money wisely, but make sure you spend it. Encouraging small private enterprise through patronage is one of the best ways to 'give something back' during your trip in Ukraine.

GIFTS There is no need to lug an extra suitcase of provisions to hand out to Ukraine's poverty-stricken. You can buy all the basics in the country and a lot more. Gift-giving in Ukraine is sentimental and highly symbolic, so don't feel compelled to make an overtly significant contribution. Plus, a lot of Ukrainians believe all foreigners are millionaires, so any irregular display of your financial

There are millions and millions of Ukrainians who do not live in Ukraine, following a number of mass emigrations throughout Ukraine's bumpy history. The largest and most well-known Ukrainian community is in Canada, concentrated in the western province of Alberta, as well as Toronto. Several other Ukrainian communities also thrive in the United States in cities like Philadelphia, Chicago, Newark, Baltimore, Cleveland, and, most recently, Brighton Beach, New York. Argentina and Australia also welcomed Ukrainian émigrés during the past century. All throughout Ukraine's very difficult past, the strength of the diaspora community has been instrumental in keeping Ukrainian culture and language alive and well. This same population continues to participate wholly in the country's present cultural and economic rebirth, in Ukraine and back in their countries of residence. From Britain to Buenos Aires to Pennsylvania, you can find a number of Ukrainian Orthodox churches, *banya* (baths), folk dance troupes, Ukrainian markets and schools.

A newer phenomenon has seen a wave of immigrants leaving Ukraine for a shorter time in order to work (legally or illegally) and save up a nice amount of hard cash with which to 'get started' back in Ukraine. Besides the United States, Poland, and the Czech Republic, Italy and Portugal seem to be primary destinations for working Ukrainians. For a while, there was a real concern that Ukraine was losing its very best people to better-paying manual jobs in the EU. That may still be the case, but a good number of this new wave of émigrés are returning with new skills, new languages, and new fortunes. For the most part, the cultural interplay has been a good thing for Ukraine.

prowess may bring you uncomfortable demands for sizeable loans or secret explanations of far-fetched business proposals. Token gifts showing appreciation are fine. If you are invited over for dinner, bring a box of chocolates, a cake, flowers (odd number) or a bottle of something. Creative and personal gifts will please even more: English books, nifty kitchen gadgets, and any luxury items that hold some merit when from another country (handbags, perfume, sports team paraphernalia, T-shirts, music and tourist knick-knacks).

3

50

4

Preparations

WHEN TO VISIT

Despite common misconceptions that Ukraine borders on Siberia and is normally freezing, summer is not the only time to visit. Really, Ukraine has four distinct seasons, and each provides different scenery. Travelling from June to September does promise warmth, sunshine, long days, green fields, leaves on the trees and lots of fresh fruit in the markets. Tourist facilities will also be in full swing and the more colourful cultural festivals take place towards the end of the summer season. Keep in mind that Ukraine gets hotter than you'd expect and air conditioning is still a rare luxury. Spring and autumn are generally warm and mild, and the October harvest is the most picturesque moment for Ukraine's countryside. Snow covers the ground from late November until April and the prettiest snowfall occurs in late December. January and February are the coldest months and you must plan your time to correspond with just seven hours of daylight. Travelling in the dead of winter requires a lot more patience but the season is a fact of life in Ukraine, so why not?

You should also consider holidays and festivals you may want to observe during your visit. Orthodox Easter (the weekend following Catholic Easter) is the biggest religious holiday of the year with lots of public display and ritual. May celebrations (1 May and 9 May) involve massive parades that still demonstrate the military fervour of Soviet holidays. For the most Ukrainian of Ukrainian events, Ivana Kupala falls at the end of the first week of July and is celebrated more passionately in western Ukraine. August visitors to eastern Ukraine will witness the sunflower fields in full bloom. The Christmas/New Year holiday is the very worst time to get around since the whole country shuts down for nearly two weeks, everything is booked up, and everyone is inebriated. If you are in the country then, stay in one place and join the party. Crimea sees its biggest tourist rush during July and August. If you want to avoid crowds on the peninsula but still want to catch the heat, go in June or September. The best time to hike the Carpathians is in late spring or autumn when there is little rain and the animals are most active.

HIGHLIGHTS AND ITINERARIES

HIGHLIGHTS Ukraine is such an expansive country with much to see. When time is limited, it does make sense to pinpoint your interests. Ideally, a thorough visit takes in some of the key cities, but does not miss an opportunity to experience Ukraine's countryside and its natural wonders.

- Kiev, the grandiose capital, the heart of Ukraine's cultural rebirth, and home to the sacred gold-domed Caves Monastery (see page 147).
- Lviv, Ukraine's most elegant city and a true architectural wonder (see page 192).

- Odessa, a lively seaside port renowned for its palaces and poetry (see page 269).
- Crimea, Ukraine's bustling Riviera with the famous resort town of **Yalta** (page 331) and the alabaster bastions of **Sevastopol** (page 319), home to the Black Sea Fleet and a stronghold of Russian imperialist nostalgia.
- The Carpathian Mountains, the most pristine natural area of the country, populated with the mixed cultures of Galicia, Bukovina and Transcarpathia.
- The Dnepr River, the country's primary waterway and legendary lifeline – namely Khortytsya Island (page 375).
- Kharkiv, Ukraine's second city and industrial giant, featuring early Soviet style (page 395).
- Other notable architectural treasures: the citadel and Magdeburg-era city of Kamyanets-Podilsky (page 179), Kievan Rus Chernihiv (page 159), Hapsburg Chernivtsi (page 253) and the 13th-century Pochayiv Monastery (page 216).
- Also, not to be overlooked are some of Ukraine's more detached towns and villages, namely the old Jewish *shtetl* of Medzhybizh (page 187), Crimean Tatar Bakhchisarai (page 313) and historic Peryaslav-Khmelnytsky (page 158).

SUGGESTED ITINERARIES Even the most intensive travel itineraries will leave vast expanses of Ukraine undiscovered. What's more, every region and city offers its own unique experience. Relegating the country to a list of tourist sites seems misguided, and every Ukrainian knows that you could spend your whole two weeks in Odessa or Lviv and feel quite content. For those who want a bit more guidance, I've listed a couple of different ideas on places and routes that could fit into an allotted time. Just know that there are no real limits to what you can see and do. Ukraine is quite an easy country to get around and anything is possible.

One week
City highlights Kiev–Lviv–Odessa–Kiev

Crimea Simferopol–Bakhchisarai–Sevastopol–Yalta–Simferopol

Carpathians Lviv–Ivano-Frankivsk–Kolomiya–Chernivtsi–Kosiv–Yaremche–Lviv

The East Kiev–Poltava–Kharkiv–Dnepropetrovsk–Kiev

Two weeks
City highlights Kiev–Lviv–Kamyanets-Podilsky–Odessa–Sevastopol–Yalta–Zaporizhzhya–Kharkiv–Kiev

Mountains and sea
Week 1 Lviv–Yaremche–Vorokhta (Mt Hoverla)–Odessa
Week 2 Sevastopol–Alupka–Yalta–Demerdzhi–Feodosiya

East and West (by car or bus from western Europe)
Week 1 Polish border–Lviv–Pochayiv–Rivne–Kiev–Poltava–Kharkiv–Luhansk
Week 2 Donetsk–Zaporizhzhya–Uman–Vinnytsya–Kamyanets-Podilsky–Ivano-Frankivsk–Uzhgorod–Slovakian border

Three weeks An ultimate, comprehensive tour to leave you totally exhausted:
3 nights Kiev (possible day trips to Chernihiv or Chernobyl)
1 night Kharkiv via Poltava
1 night Donetsk via Svyatogorsk
1 night Zaporizhzhya (Khortytsya Island)

2 nights Sevastopol via Bakhchisarai
2 nights Yalta via Balaclava
3 nights Odessa via Simferopol
1 night Kamyanets–Podilsky via Uman
1 night Chernivtsi
1 night Verkhovyna via Kolomiya and Kosiv
1 night Ivano–Frankivsk via Yaremche
3 nights Lviv (day trip to Pochayiv)
1 night Uzhgorod

PUBLIC HOLIDAYS

Modern Ukrainian holidays are a blend of traditional religious holidays, old and new Ukrainian national festivals, and Soviet anniversaries. Most businesses are closed on the following:

1 January	New Year's Day
7 January	Ukrainian Orthodox Christmas
14 January	Old New Year's Day (By the pre-revolutionary calendar. Why end the party?)
8 March	Women's Day
Spring	Orthodox Easter (2 weeks after Catholic Easter)
1 May	May Day (celebrating workers' solidarity and the pagan rites of spring)
9 May	Victory Day (A jubilant tribute to the end of World War II)
28 June	Constitution Day
24 August	Ukrainian Independence Day
7 November	Anniversary of the Great October Revolution

In addition, there is at least one Orthodox holiday for each day of the year, including name days. This fact does not correspond well with the belief that it is a sin to work on any Orthodox holiday.

TOUR OPERATORS

UK

Biosphere Expeditions Sprat's Water, Near Carlton Colville, The Broads National Park, Suffolk NR33 8BP; ☎ 0870 446 0801; e info@biosphere-expeditions.org; www.biosphere-expeditions.org. A non-profit-making organisation that arranges hands-on wildlife conservation projects. Expeditions involve collecting data on wolves and migratory birds on the Black Sea coast just north of the Crimea.
Interchange Interchange House, 27 Stafford Rd, Croydon, Surrey CR0 4NG; ☎ 020 8681 3612; f 020 8760 0031; e interchange@interchange.uk.com; www.interchange.uk.com. Offering tailor-made travel and accommodation throughout the country.
Intourist 7 Wellington Terrace, Notting Hill, London W2 4LW; ☎ 0870 112 1232; e info@intourist.co.uk; www.intourist.co.uk. Also offices in Manchester and Glasgow.

Regent Holidays 15 John St, Bristol BS1 2HR; ☎ 0870 499 0911; f 0117 925 4866; e regent@regent-holidays.co.uk; www.regent-holidays.co.uk. Offer individual, tailor-made itineraries for both holidays and city breaks to Ukraine. There is also the option to extend your trip to include Belarus, Moldova, Poland and Russia.
Russia House Chapel Court, Borough High St, London SE1 1HH; ☎ 020 7403 9922; f 020 7403 9933; e russiahouse@btinternet.com; www.therussiahouse.co.uk
Ukraine Travel Falcon House, Victoria St, Chadderton OL9 0HB; ☎ 0161 652 5050; f 0161 633 0825; e info@ukraine.co.uk; www.ukraine.co.uk. Custom-made trips for Ukraine, specialist travel and visa support.

4

US

Scope Travel 1605 Springfield Av, Maplewood, NJ 07040; ☎ 973 378 8998 or 1 877 357 0436; f 973 821 4855; e scope@scopetravel.com; www.scopetravel.com. Long serving the Ukrainian diaspora and all those who love Ukraine.
MIR Corporation 85c Washington St, Suite 210, Seattle, WA 98104; ☎ 206 624 7289; f 206 624 7360; e info@mircorp.com; www.mircorp.com.

CANADA

Astro Travel 2204 Bloor St West, Toronto, Ontario M6S 1N4; ☎/f 905 804 8826; e ukrainetour@ukrainetour.com; www.ukrainetour.com. Open since Ukrainian independence, specialising in professional, private and student travel, and tours and visas.

Exotic tours to exotic climes.
Eastern European Excursions 1874 Augusta Dr, Jamison, PA 18929; ☎ 215 343 6616; e info@eeevacation.com; www.eeevacation.com
Peter the Great Cruises 2606 E 15th St, Brooklyn, NY 11235; ☎ 718 934 4100; f 718 934 9419; cruiseruss@aol.com; www.cruiseruss.com. Dnepr River and Black Sea cruises.

RJ's Tours 11708 135A St, Edmonton, Alberta T5M 1L5; ☎ 780 415 5633; f 780 415 5639; e rjstours@tourukraine.com; www.tourukraine.com. Cruises and large, escorted, group tours.

IN UKRAINE Regional chapters give additional particulars about local tour agencies. Note that many travel agencies in Ukraine now specialise in helping Ukrainians plan their vacations to Egypt and Turkey. Instead, be sure to search for operators specialising in *priyom* ('incoming') tourism. The following are the largest and most secure of Ukraine's larger tour operators with a reputation for professionalism:

Albion Kiev, Chervonoarmiyska 26; ☎ 044 526 9296; e info@albion.com.ua; www.albion.com.ua. Bus tours to Crimea combined with Lviv and Kiev.
Eugenia Travel Odessa, Rishelyevskaya 23; ☎/f 0482 220 331; e janna@eugen.intes.odessa.ua; www.eugeniatravel.com. Black Sea cruises, Odessa and Crimea, as well as the rest of the country.
Hamalia Peremohy 22; ☎ 044 236 9550; f 044 236 9577; e incoming@hamalia.com.ua; www.hamalia.com.ua
Krymtour Simferopol, Schmidta 9; ☎ 0652 250 350; e info@krymtur.com; www.krymtur.com. Specialists for Crimea.
Lviv-Inturtrans Lviv 2/4 Kuznevycha, ☎ 0322 971 168; f 0322 926 114; e intur@mail.lviv.ua; www.lviv-inturtrans.com. International bus travel to Ukraine and lots of custom-made countrywide tours.
Mandrivnyk Kiev, Poshtova Ploscha 3; ☎ 044 490 6632; e info@mandrivnyk.com.ua; www.mandrivnyk.com.ua. Cruises and basic city visits.
Meest-Tour Lviv, Shevchenka 34; ☎ 0322 970 852; e office@meest-tour.com.ua; www.meest-tour.com. Trekking in the Carpathians and Crimea; adventure tourism.
New Logic Kiev Mikhayilivska 6A; ☎ 044 206 3322; e info@newlogic.ua; www.newlogic.com.ua. Best for young independent travellers.

Olymp Travel 24 Shovkovychna St, Kiev, 01024 Ukraine; ☎ 044 253 7108; f 044 253 8329; e welcome@olymp-travel.kiev.ua; www.olymp-travel.kiev.ua. A nationwide company offering comprehensive 'theme' tours. One of the most established, multilingual and professional travel companies in Ukraine.
SAM Kiev, Ivana Franka 40B; ☎/f 044 238 6959; e raskin@samcomp.kiev.ua; www.sam.com. The largest travel company in the country.
Sputnik Kiev Pushkinskaya 9; No 21; ☎ 044 531 9130; f 044 270 7358; e admin@traveltoukraine.info; www.sputnik.kiev.ua. Longer excursions and diverse tours combined with Russia trips.
Student Travel International Prorizna 18/1, No 6; ☎/f 044 490 5960; e sti@sti.com.ua; www.sti.com.ua
Terra Incognita Mala Zhytomyrska 16/3; No 4; ☎ 044 561 4022; f 044 279 5923; e info@terraincognita.info; www.terraincognita.info
Ukraine Rus Travel ☎ 044 483 2374; f 044 213 2374; e agency@ukr-rus.kiev.ua; www.ukraine-rus.kiev.ua. Innovative tours for every kind of traveller.
Ukrzovnishintour Kiev, Khmelnytskovo 26; ☎ 044 279 8464; e uit@uit.kiev.ua; www.uit.com.ua. Travel for business and leisure.

RED TAPE

Ukraine has turned bureaucracy into an art form that never fails to amaze Ukrainians and foreigners alike. Suspicion, indifference and micro-management are holdovers from the Soviet age and still linger about in the public sphere. The good thing is that attitudes are slowly changing – many Ukrainians now poke fun at authoritarian bureaucrats and being easy-going is becoming 'cool'. Be patient, and don't act like you're a consumer. A show of respect and saying please and thank you can do wonders when dealing with the hard-nosed officials you may encounter.

All Ukrainians are issued identification passports at the age of 16 and this is the document police want to see when they ask for *bumahy* (papers). Your passport is your 'papers' so never go anywhere without it on your person, as you will be asked to show it. Obviously, you should keep a photocopy of your passport's front page and Ukrainian visa separate from your passport, as well as any other valuable forms or information: if it's lost or stolen, it makes getting a new passport much easier. Foreigners and tourists are now a common sight in the capital and larger cities, so you should rarely have any run-ins with troublesome law enforcement. This was not always the case – in the not so distant past, lone foreigners appeared suspect to various authority figures, especially police. Only police have the authority to see your passport and they are under international obligation to return it immediately – if you don't trust them, don't hand it over. Random passport checks in the street are almost unheard of today – treating foreigners kindly has become de rigueur among Ukraine's police force, thank goodness. In fact, Ukraine is becoming more and more like a rich Western nation in that you are much more likely to be harassed by a private security guard than a policeman. If you find that you do get called into a police station or they want to search your bags, nonchalant co-operation is the best policy, but don't be afraid to put up a reasonable fuss (for instance, there is no need for anyone to open your camera). These days, people would rather chat with a foreign traveller than arrest them, so a frank and friendly demeanour will help any situation.

VISAS Hallelujah! Most of us **do not** need visas to visit Ukraine anymore. In fact, any citizen of the United States, Canada and the EU is allowed free entrance into Ukraine for travel of fewer than 90 days. Other countries that do not require a visa include: Andorra, Iceland, Liechtenstein, Monaco, Norway, Japan, San Marino, Switzerland, Turkey, the Vatican, and most of the former Soviet Union (with the exception of Turkmenistan and Tajikistan). Regardless of your nationality, you also do not need a visa if you are a passenger on a Black Sea cruise and stopping for a day or so in ports like Yalta and Sevastopol. The same applies for cities like Odessa and Simferopol, where special visas can be issued on site. As Ukraine's bureaucracy is in constant flux, however, it is always wise to double check the current visa regulations with the local embassy or consulate in your country.

If you are planning a longer stay or come from a country with less than optimal bilateral relations with Ukraine, then apply for a visa at the closest embassy or consulate. The process is much like getting a visa to anywhere – few applications are ever rejected, but the process can be lengthy, tedious and expensive. You must submit the visa application form with a passport still valid for six months *after your return* from Ukraine, two passport-size photographs and the initial fee, payable by money order only: £60 (US$100) for the normal ten-day processing; double that for 'speedy' three-day processing. Visas are based on 'purpose of visit' – Tourist, Business, Private or Transit – and each requires different forms and/or additional fees. There are also separate visas required for participants with religious or humanitarian missions. Be sure to apply for your visa well in advance. Some embassies will do a 'rush' order, but seeing as they are embassies, this is not likely. Mail-in applications often show a quicker turnaround.

Tourist visas would seem the most obvious choice, but they require an additional letter of invitation from a Ukrainian or foreign tourist agency, or a confirmation of booking from a hotel in Ukraine. If they are licensed, they can issue an invitation letter (for which you will be charged). Usual procedure has the Ukrainian party faxing the official invite to your country's embassy and presenting you with a confirmation number to be matched with your visa application. Organised tours often take care of all this for you.

A convenient sidestep to the tourist rigmarole is the **private visa**. Designed for foreigners visiting friends or family in Ukraine, you simply state the name and address of the person you are going to visit and where you might travel. If you don't know anybody in Ukraine, make some friends beforehand. Citizens of the EU, Canada, USA, Japan, Switzerland, Slovakia and Turkey *do not* require an invitation letter when applying for a private or business visa, cutting out the biggest headache of the application process. A private visa is also the best option for independent travellers, since you are not committed to a specific itinerary, and the process is the easiest when applying on your own.

Business visas do require an extra invitation from a legal entity in Ukraine and are far more restrictive.

Visas are generally issued for three months, and for six months if you are from a favoured nation (see above). It used to be that foreigners were required to register at the OVIR (Ministry of Interior's Office of Visas and Registration) within three days of entering any city, but this is only an issue if you are planning on staying in one area for longer than six months. If you seek to extend your visa, you must apply well in advance at the local OVIR office.

Passing overland between Russia and Europe requires the quicker and cheaper **transit visa**, which usually give you four days in the country. Applications require proof (another visa or a one-way ticket) that you will be moving on. If you are planning on leaving and re-entering, make sure to apply for a double- or multiple-entry visa, which adds significant cost but offers a safety measure for chronic wanderers. Visas are issued in person at the embassy or by mail and consist of an embossed full-page sticker in your passport. You'll find that your visa becomes a constant reference point during your travels as all hotel registrations and ticket outlets must take down your visa number (someone out there is tracking your movements!), and many need to see the page in order to know how to spell your name in Cyrillic.

IMMIGRATION AND CUSTOMS Compared with Heathrow or JFK, Kiev Boryspil feels like a breeze. Getting your passport stamped and your luggage through customs is no longer the nightmare that it used to be. Now that Ukraine is welcoming travellers with open arms, there are so many people pouring in that immigration officials are just trying to get you through their line so they can take their lunch break. In my experience, air and seaports are far quicker than land borders, which are either total cakewalks or half-day ordeals, depending on where you cross, what kind of vehicle you are in, and how much stuff you are taking in. Employ your very best traveller's wisdom: present yourself in the simplest manner and declare a specific goal or itinerary, even if you do plan on taking to the open road. At any given border entry point, you will be issued an 'Information Card' which is simply a slip of paper that you fill out in duplicate. The ripped copy of the slip is placed inside your passport. Don't lose it! This is your proof of legal entry and when you leave Ukrainian territory, you will be asked to show it.

Customs is much like that of the United Kingdom or the USA. Upon entering the country you will be issued a customs declaration form that you will need to fill in with details. The declaration is mainly to assess how much cash you are bringing into the country. Taking in a thousand bucks is no problem, US$5,000 may get you a raised eyebrow, and carrying in more than US$10,000 in cash is illegal (see *Money*, page 74). Everyone has their own way of dealing with border guards and there is no single word of advice applicable to the Ukrainian *tamozhniki* although, in general, it helps to be honest and open, but not too honest and open. For the most part, they are pretty friendly and far nicer than their counterparts in neighbouring countries. After losing a valuable amount to souvenir hunters, the Ukrainian government now prohibits the export of any national art treasures without special permission. These include antique icons, rugs and dishes, some Soviet medals, and coins. Most Ukrainian dealers are aware of the law and sell only goods that can be exported, and there tends to be one official at customs who knows what is legal and what's not.

Ⓔ EMBASSIES AND CONSULATES

Australia Level 12, St George Centre, 60 Marcus Clarke St, Canberra ACT 2601; ➘ +2 6230 5789; f +2 6230 7298; e ukremb@bigpond.com; www.ukremb.info

Austria Naaffgasse 23, 1180 Vienna, ➘ +43 1 479 7172; f +43 1 479 7147

Belarus Starovilenska 51, 220002 Minsk; ➘ +375 17 283 1990; f +375 283 19980; e emb_by@mfa.gov.ua

Belgium 30 Av Albert Lancaster, 1180 Brussels; ➘ +322 379 21 00; f +322 379 2179; www.ukraine.be

Canada Consular Section, 331 Metcalfe St, Ottawa, Ontario K2P 1S3; ➘ +613 230 8015; f +613 230 2655; www.ukremb.ca; Consulate General of Toronto, 2120 Bloor St West, Toronto, Ontario M6S 1M8; ➘ +416 763 3114; f +416 763 2323; www.ukrconsulate.com

Czech Republic De Gaulla 29, Prague 6; ➘ +42 02 33 342000; f +42 02 33 344 366

France 21 Av de Saxe, 75007, Paris; ➘ +33 1 43 06 07 37; f +33 1 43 06 02 94

Germany Albrechtstrasse 26, 10117 Berlin; ➘ +49 30 288 87 116; f +49 30 288 87 163; www.botschaft-ukraine.de

Hungary Stefania 77, Budapest H-1143; ➘ +36 1 422 41 20; f +36 1 220 98 73

Ireland 16 Elgin Rd, Ballsbridge, Dublin 4; ➘ +353 (1) 668 5189; f +353 (1) 668 8601; e emb_ie@mfa.gov.ua

Israel 50 Yirmiyahu, 62594 Tel Aviv; ➘ +97 23 602 1952; f +97 23 604 2512; www.ukraine-embassy.co.il

Japan 3-15-6 Nishi Azabu, Minato-ku, Tokyo 106-0046; ➘ +813 5474 9770; f +813 5474 9772; www.ukremb-japan.gov.ua

Moldova Sfatul Taril 55, 277004 Chisinau; ➘ +3732 582 151; f +3732 585 108

Poland Aleja Szucha 7, 00580 Warsaw; ➘ +48 22 625 0127; f +48 22 629 8103; www.ukraine-poland.com

Romania Calea Dorobantilor 16, Sector 1 Bucharest; ➘ +40 1211 6986; f +40 1211 6949

Russia Leontievsky 18, Moscow, 103009; ➘ +095 229 1079; f +095 924 8469

Slovakia Radvanska 35, 811 Bratislava 01; ➘ +42 12 5920 28 11; f +42 12 5441 26 51;

Switzerland Rue de L'Orangerie 14, CH 1202 Geneva; ➘ +41 22 740 3270; f +41 22 734 3801; e mission.ukraine@ties.itu.ch; www.ukremb.ch

Turkey Sancak Mahalessi 206 Solak N 17, Yildiz Cankaya, Ankara 06550; ➘ +90 312 441 5499; f +90 312 440 6815

UK Consular Department, 78 Kensington Park Rd, London W11 2PL; ➘ +44 20 7243 8923; f +44 20 7727 3567; Consulate in Edinburgh, 8 Windsor St, Edinburgh EH7 5JR; ➘ +44 131 556 0023, f +44 131 557 3460; www.ukremb.org.uk

USA 3350 M St NW, Washington DC 20007; ➘ +1 202 333 0606; f +1 202 333 0817; www.ukraineinfo.us; Consulate General of Ukraine in New York, 240 East 49th St, New York, NY 10017; ➘ +1 212 371 5690; www.ukrconsul.org; Consulate General of Ukraine in Chicago, 10 East Huron St, Chicago, IL 60611; ➘ +1 312 642 4388; f +1 312 642 4385; www.ukrchicago.com

GETTING THERE AND AWAY

✈ **BY AIR** Nowadays, there are so many different options for flying into Ukraine, travellers really can take their pick of whatever works for their budget and itinerary.

Several major European carriers fly to Kiev and other Ukrainian cities at least once a week, if not every day. **Aerosvit** (*www.aerosvit.com*) is Ukraine's largest international airline and offers the best connections between international flights and domestic destinations, with good deals for business-class travellers. **Ukraine International Airlines** (*www.ukraine-international.com*) flies to most European capitals and code shares with several western European airlines.

From Europe British Airways flies five days a week direct from London Heathrow to Kiev Borispol. Austrian Airlines (*www.aua.com*) has been flying to Ukraine the longest of any European carrier, and now offers regular services to Kiev, Kharkiv, Odessa and Dnepropetrovsk (all via Vienna; about two hours). They often code share with Ukraine International Airways, as does Air France (*www.airfrance.com*) from Paris de Gaulle, Lufthansa (*www.lufthansa.com*) from Frankfurt and Munich, and KLM (*www.klm.com*) from Amsterdam Schipol. Prices vary, but expect to pay around £250 (US$400) for any round-trip ticket from London to Kiev (three hours). Students with a valid ISIC card can usually find something slightly cheaper, while less expensive tickets are normally on offer via Eastern European carriers. Czech Airlines (*www.czechairlines.com*) flies every day to Kiev Zhulyany with an attractive optional stopover in Prague, and Lithuanian Airlines (*www.lal.lt*) offers similar deals via Vilnius. Besides their normal flights to Kiev, LOT Polish Airlines (*www.lot.com*) also flies to Lviv, and Malev Hungarian Airlines (*www.malev.hu*) flies to Odessa via Budapest. Another alternative is flying with Turkish Airlines (*www.turkishairlines.com*), with connections every other day from Istanbul to Kiev (two hours), Simferopol and Odessa.

With all the new budget airlines infiltrating eastern Europe, it has become quite cheap to fly quite close to Ukraine, a more popular option for backpackers. Ryanair (*www.ryanair.com*) flies every day from London Stansted to Rzeszów, Poland, from which it is only two hours by bus to Lviv, with prices for under £80 each way. easyJet (*www.easyjet.com*) also flies daily to Warsaw, Krakow and Budapest for under £120 return, all of which offer inexpensive rail and bus links to Kiev.

From North America Delta Airlines (*www.delta.com*) now flies five times a week to Kiev Boryspil from JFK. Prices range from US$600 to US$1,200 in the off season, to US$1,800 in summer. The only other direct flights from North America to Ukraine are on **Aerosvit** (*www.aerosvit.com*), which offers regular flights from Toronto and New York's JFK to Kiev. Prices range from £350 to £400 (US$500 to US$600). Otherwise, Austrian Airlines, British Airways, KLM and Lufthansa offer the most competitive and comfortable transatlantic connections to Ukraine via their respective hubs. Travellers tend to leave Canada or the US in the evening and arrive in Ukraine the following afternoon.

Other routes Various Ukrainian airlines and charter flights service all the recent hotspots for Ukrainian travellers: Bangkok, Malta, Egypt and Cyprus. **Aerosvit** flies to Beijing, Bangkok, Delhi and Dubai. Singapore Airlines advertises itself as the best connection from Ukraine to Australia, New Zealand or southeast Asia on the Star Alliance via Frankfurt. From Russia, **Transaero** and **Aeroflot** fly to all major Ukrainian cities, but this is not a convenient way to travel from western Europe since it requires a screwy airport change in Moscow and a long layover.

OVERLAND Ukraine is much closer than people realise, so that travelling across Europe to get there sounds more daunting that it actually is. From an American perspective, the trip from Paris to Kiev is the same as driving from New York to Denver. The route across Germany and Poland is the quickest, but many would argue that crossing the Czech Republic and Slovakia or Hungary makes for a much more beautiful drive. Either way, going overland can be a romantic endeavour and fairly cheap.

🚌 **By bus** Numerous bus companies travel from western Europe directly to Ukraine, most of which are Ukrainian companies offering direct services from Germany, Belgium, France and the UK to Kiev and Lviv (with **Lviv Inturtrans**; e *info@lviv-inturtrans.com.ua; www.lviv-inturtrans.com.ua*). Eurolines (*www.eurolines.com*) shares tickets on its one Antwerp–Kiev bus that can be joined from London, although this costs more than going to a Polish destination and then continuing on Ukrainian transport. The bus journey to Kiev from London takes two days and two nights, so you must consider whether the money you're saving is worth sitting upright for 48 hours and being forced to watch the latest Hollywood blockbusters dubbed into Polish. From the UK, the very cheapest way to get to Ukraine is on a two-day Eurolines bus from London Victoria to Rzeszów, Poland, usually costing £80 return (US$120). From Rzeszów there are frequent buses that cross the border to Lviv (three hours). Other options are quicker buses that travel to Warsaw or Krakow, and then continue on to Lviv or Kiev on an overnight train. These days though it really is becoming cheaper to fly there, or at least part of the way.

🚗 **By car** Everyone should drive across Europe at least once in their lifetime, and the trip from England to Kiev by car does not risk becoming too clichéd an adventure. For many, all is well until they get inside the country. If you have the luxury of bringing an old car that you don't mind losing, then do. There's also the option of driving to Ukraine, then switching to planes and trains to get around inside the country. The most direct route is from Brussels: follow the E-40 east and just keep driving across Germany via Cologne and Leipzig to the Polish border at Görlitz; in Poland drive via Wrocław, Krakow and Przemyśl to the border at Shehini. The E-40 continues in Ukraine through Rivne and on to Kiev, then through Kharkiv and Luhansk. Stay on the road and you'll end up in Kazakhstan. Slovakia and Hungary are also 'easy' border posts that are accustomed to lots of European traffic. The following chapter advises on driving inside Ukraine (see page 84).

🚆 **By rail** Ukrainian trains still travel from all of the former 'Eastern bloc' capitals, and this can be a fun way to make your entrance into the country. Direct overnight trains from Berlin, Belgrade, Budapest, Bucharest, Warsaw, Krakow, Bratislava, Prague and Sofia all go to Kiev, often via Uzhgorod or Lviv. With central European travel pretty standardised these days, budget-conscious travellers can save cash by combining a cheap flight or bus to Berlin or Prague followed by an overnight train. The fast train from Berlin Zoo Station to Warsaw Central takes only five hours and costs around US$35, and from Warsaw there are daily trains to Lviv (11 hours) or Kiev (20 hours). There's also the daily direct train from Berlin to Kiev (24 hours) which effectively instils a historical mood and is becoming the preferred path for the backpacking crowd.

There are so many trains between Russia and Ukraine it's not worth listing them all, but this is the most convenient way of getting into Ukraine from the north. The dozen or so Moscow trains usually pass through Kharkiv (12 hours) and Kiev (14 hours) on their way to Crimea and the Black Sea coast. A dozen more trains travel in from Russia's east and the Caucasus. Some might consider beginning or finishing their Trans-Siberian excursion in Ukraine, as there are regular trains between Vladivostok, Kharkiv and Kiev. There are also plenty of trains from the Baltic states; however, most travel through Belarus which requires a tricky transit visa and a lot of bureaucracy, and it's worth doing only if you intend to spend some time visiting Belarus. Otherwise, go through Russia or Poland. Remember that a US$5 surcharge is added when buying international rail tickets in Ukraine. For specific details on getting from London to Kiev by rail, check out this website: www.seat61.com/Ukraine.htm.

Crossing borders The Ukrainian border is no exception to general stereotypes about border guards, but things have improved so much over the past decade that the former peculiarities are hardly worth mentioning. As long as you have your visa sorted out beforehand, no border should pose any problems. If a situation does arise at the border, meekness is always the best policy.

If you are on a train, border checks are usually made in the middle of the night, which can be slightly annoying. The train will make its last stop in one country (say, Russia) and all the Russian immigration officers will come through and stamp your exit visa, followed by the customs officials who also look like soldiers. After the all-clear, you'll drift back to sleep while the train rattles on for 20 minutes or so, then a whole new set of immigration officers, this time Ukrainian, will come on, followed by their customs officials. Normally, the train conductor is expected to alert the guards when they have a foreigner among the passengers (ie: those with EU or US passports), which is why they seem to come straight to your compartment. The whole process can take from 15 minutes to an hour, with a lot of door slamming and hall conversation and flipping and re-flipping through your passport.

Crossing on a bus used to make for unpleasant experiences since most passengers were smuggling consumer goods to sell in Ukraine. Now, though, black-market activity is back to a minimum and buses are no longer targeted by unscrupulous, underpaid customs officials. Buses and cars may face very long queues at the border, with the heaviest traffic in the summer. Most border posts are open 24 hours now, but on the smaller roads the gates will close at midnight and open the following morning. If you are driving into Ukraine, make sure you have your vehicle registration, proof of auto insurance and a lot of patience.

Russia and the Caucasus Ukraine shares a love–hate relationship with Russia that seems to intensify at the border, where things are either remarkably easy or else inexplicably complicated. The two countries seem an obvious travel combination, but keep in mind that it is more difficult to get a Russian visa than a Ukrainian one and in my experience I've found there is less hassle in travelling from Russia into Ukraine than the reverse. The most clear-cut route is on the train from Moscow to Kharkiv via Kursk and Belgorod, but there are just as many Russian trains travelling to Kiev via Bryansk. Still, most Ukrainian trains follow the old Soviet plan, meaning they lead to Russia. Southern routes cross eastern Ukraine and head to the north Caucasus (Krasnodar) and the Russian Black Sea resorts (Sochi, Adler). It is no longer possible to take any direct trains to Georgia and Armenia since all the railroad tracks in Abkhazia have been blown up, although there is a train to Baku via all of the most dangerous places in Russia (eg: Dagestan). Most other routes are closed due to the war in Chechnya, so the alternative is taking a ship from Crimea to Turkey and then travelling overland to the Caucasus.

Belarus Belarus holds the proud title of Europe's last dictatorship, which is tragic, because it's such a beautiful place. Many argue that at least the dictator is a benevolent one who ensures that the streets are kept clean and the masses amused. The good thing is that travelling to Belarus feels just like going back in time, a spitting image of what it was like to travel in Ukraine, say, 15 years ago. Frequent trains travel from Minsk to Kiev via the Chernihiv–Gomel border post. A general animosity towards foreigners and the current state of fear mean it is not an easy experience, but nor is it terribly difficult, as long as your papers are in order. Receiving any kind of Belarusian visa can be daunting, and if you get so far as to be allowed into the country, be prepared to deal with being followed and watched. Anyone you interact with may also be interrogated once you've left. If you are simply passing through (trains to the Baltic states pass through Belarus), you must have a transit visa, a document that forbids more than one overnight stay in the country. Hopefully, things in Belarus will improve to facilitate travel.

Romania Odessa and Chernivtsi are the main transit point to and from Romania. The north of Romania is quite rural, which means that the Chernivtsi entry is never too busy. There are plenty of buses and *marshrutka* (minibuses) between Suceava and Chernivtsi, as well as regular overnight trains to and from Bucharest; more details on page 259. Now that Romania is in the EU, this border feels more accessible and user-friendly.

Moldova Anyone who complains about travelling in Ukraine has never been to Moldova. Travellers have often faced difficulty in crossing into Moldova from either the north (Chernivtsi) or the east (Odessa). Add the complexities of the trans-Dnistrian conflict, and it'll give you a headache that'll make you wish you'd stayed in Ukraine. Also, trains to and from Chisinau (Kishinev) have a reputation for theft. For more information, see page 274.

Poland Entering Ukraine from the west is the easiest and most obvious choice when travelling from Europe. Since Polish transport is frequent and reliable, it is easy to get right up to the border and then take any number of buses across. The two basic routes are Przemyśl–Lviv or Lublin–Lutsk. There are also more Ukrainian trains to and from Poland than any other country (besides Russia) so your options are varied. All trains must stop at the Polish–Ukrainian border, where the wheels are changed to fit a different gauge while the cars are suspended (with you still inside them). In summer, the Shehini border post gets busy, but an increase in checkpoints keeps traffic flowing to a degree. Coming through later at night will also mean less of a wait.

Hungary and Slovakia Uzhogorod is the main entry point from both countries, with frequent trains and buses from Budapest and Bratislava. From Slovakia, you can simply hike into Uzhgorod from Sobrance or take any number of buses, while the Hungarian border post and international train junction is at Chop, 20 minutes south of Uzhgorod. Both posts are known to be fairly relaxed as they deal with a lot of cargo traffic from Europe; however the queues at the Chop border can be horrendous. Coming into Ukraine is far easier than exiting.

BY SEA Passenger ships sail regularly to Ukraine (Sevastopol and Odessa) from Turkey (Istanbul and Samsun) and Israel (Haifa) – an unconventional Eurasian link that is only now being discovered. Black Sea cruises seem to be slowly regaining their former popularity, although for the present none originate in Ukraine, and they tend to spend no more than one day each in ports like Odessa, Sevastopol and Yalta. If you want to permanently disembark you will have to make prior arrangements with the cruise company. There is also the ferry from Russia to Kerch, although this is not so much a sea passage as it is an overland route from Russia's north Caucasus region. Private yachts docking on Ukraine's Black Sea coast are still considered a novelty, so be prepared for a lot of bureaucracy, especially in Sevastopol. For more information on travel by sea, check the regional chapters for Crimea and the Black Sea.

Despite US State Department warnings, Ukraine is not the dreaded Third World country it is often made out to be. Every country has its bugs to which travellers will always be more susceptible.

IMMUNISATIONS Although there are no specific vaccinations required for the Ukraine, it is recommended that visitors should be up to date with **tetanus**, **diphtheria** and **polio** (every ten years), **typhoid** and **hepatitis A**. A single dose of hepatitis A vaccine (eg: Havrix Monodose, Avaxim) lasts for one year. It can be boosted after this time to provide cover for up to 25 years. The vaccine is best taken at least two weeks before travel but can be taken even the day before, as the incubation period of hepatitis A is approximately two weeks. The vaccine has replaced immunoglobulin, which should no longer be used.

The newer typhoid vaccines (including the injectable Typhim Vi and the oral capsules, Vivotif) are about 85% effective and last for three years. It is worth taking, unless time is short and your trip is of one week or less. Vivotif capsules are currently available only in the US, but soon in the UK.

For trips of four weeks or more you should also consider **hepatitis B** and **rabies vaccinations**. Hepatitis B is especially relevant if you are working in a hospital or with children, and rabies jabs are recommended if you are either handling animals or are likely to be more than 24 hours from medical facilities. Ideally three doses of each are needed and should be taken at least three weeks before travel. However, if time is short then two doses, or even one of each, are better than nothing at all. For hepatitis B, only Engerix B is currently licensed for the rapid course.

Tuberculosis (TB) had reached epidemic proportions in Ukraine in the last decade but is now in decline; it is, however, known to be a highly persistent strain of the disease. The BCG vaccination for tuberculosis is routinely given in the UK between the ages of 11 and 13, whereas in the USA only high-risk individuals are vaccinated as a matter of course. If you have not been vaccinated, and are over 35, it is probably not worth having, as there is some doubt as to its efficacy. But don't worry, tuberculosis needs prolonged close contact with an infected individual and is still treatable. Symptoms of active TB include a permanent, crackling or dry persistent cough, fever (most often at night), fatigue and weight loss. Avoid long contact with anyone who coughs all the time, and if you think you may have been infected, or you've just spent a long time in Ukraine, get a TB test as a precaution. Treatment includes a long-term daily medication ritual, so the sooner you begin the better.

Tick-borne encephalitis is common in the Ukrainian forest. Travellers at risk include anyone visiting the Ukrainian countryside from April to August, but you should only consider being vaccinated if you are going into the country for more than three weeks or if you intend to spend most of your time in the woods. In the UK, the vaccine is available only on a named-patient basis, so it has to be pre-ordered. A new, faster schedule allows the three doses needed to be given over a four-week period. Whether or not you are vaccinated, you should always take general precautions against ticks: wear loose, long-sleeved shirts, long trousers that cover your limbs and are tucked into your socks or boots, and a hat. You should also use a tick repellent with DEET. At the end of the day, check for ticks on your body and hair. This is easier to do with another person as the ticks are small and hard to see. It is especially important to check the heads of children, who are more likely to get ticks from overhead branches. Hikers in the Carpathians tend to be prone to tick bites, since mountain paths can fade into scrubby woods where you

Dr Jane Wilson-Howarth

Asian ticks are not the prolific disease transmitters they are in the Americas, but they may spread Lyme disease, tick-bite fever and a few rarities. Tick-bite fever is a non-serious, flu-like illness, but still worth avoiding. If you get the tick off whole and promptly, the chances of disease transmission are reduced to a minimum, Manoeuvre your finger and thumb so that you can pinch the tick's mouthparts, as close to your skin as possible, and slowly and steadily pull away at right angles to your skin. This often hurts. Jerking or twisting will increase the chances of damaging the tick, which in turn increases the chances of disease transmission, as well as leaving the mouthparts behind. Once the tick is off, dowse the little wound with alcohol (local spirit, whisky or similar are excellent) or iodine. An area of spreading redness around the bite site, or rash or fever coming on a few days or more after the bite, should stimulate a trip to a doctor.

must push through low pine branches. For more information on what to do if you are bitten by a tick, see the box above.

TRAVEL CLINICS AND HEALTH INFORMATION A full list of current travel clinic websites worldwide is available from the International Society of Travel Medicine on www.istm.org. For other journey preparation information, consult www.tripprep.com. Information about various medications may be found on www.emedicine.com.

UK

Berkeley Travel Clinic 32 Berkeley St, London WIJ 8EL (near Green Park tube station); ☎ 020 7629 6233
Cambridge Travel Clinic 48a Mill Rd, Cambridge CBI 2AS; ☎ 01223 367362; e enquiries@ cambridgetravelclinic.co.uk; www.cambridgetravelclinic.co.uk. *Open Tue–Fri 12.00–19.00, Sat 10.00–16.00.*
Edinburgh Travel Clinic Regional Infectious Diseases Unit, Ward 41 OPD, Western General Hospital, Crewe Rd South, Edinburgh EH4 2UX; ☎ 0131 537 2822; www.link.med.ed.ac.uk/ridu. Travel helpline (0906 589 0380) open weekdays 09.00–12.00. Provides inoculations and anti-malarial prophylaxis and advises on travel-related health risks.
Fleet Street Travel Clinic 29 Fleet St, London EC4Y IAA; ☎ 020 7353 5678; www.fleetstreetclinic.com. Vaccinations, travel products and latest advice.
Hospital for Tropical Diseases Travel Clinic Mortimer Market Building, Capper St (off Tottenham Ct Rd), London WCIE 6AU; ☎ 020 7388 9600; www.thehtd.org. Offers consultations and advice, and is able to provide all necessary drugs and vaccines for travellers. Runs a healthline (0906 133 7733) for country-specific information and health hazards. Also stocks nets, water purification equipment and personal protection measures.
Interhealth Worldwide Partnership House, 157

Waterloo Rd, London SEI 8US; ☎ 020 7902 9000; www.interhealth.org.uk. Competitively priced, one-stop travel health service. All profits go to their affiliated company, InterHealth, which provides health care for overseas workers on Christian projects.
MASTA (Medical Advisory Service for Travellers Abroad) MASTA Ltd, Moorfield Rd, Yeadon LS19 7BN; ☎ 0870 606 2782; www.masta-travel-health.com. Provides travel health advice, anti-malarials and vaccinations. There are over 25 MASTA pre-travel clinics in Britain; call or check online for the nearest. Clinics also sell mosquito nets, medical kits, insect protection and travel hygiene products.
NHS travel website www.fitfortravel.scot.nhs.uk. Provides country-by-country advice on immunisation and malaria, plus details of recent developments, and a list of relevant health organisations.
Nomad Travel Store/Clinic 3–4 Wellington Terrace, Turnpike Lane, London N8 0PX; ☎ 020 8889 7014; travel-health line (office hours only) 0906 863 3414; e sales@nomadtravel.co.uk; www.nomadtravel.co.uk. Also at 40 Bernard St, London WCIN ILJ; ☎ 020 7833 4114; 52 Grosvenor Gdns, London SWIW 0AG; ☎ 020 7823 5823; and 43 Queens Rd, Bristol BS8 IQH; ☎ 0117 922 6567. For health advice, equipment such as mosquito nets and other anti-bug

devices, and an excellent range of adventure travel gear.

Trailfinders Travel Clinic 194 Kensington High St, London W8 7RG; ⟍ 020 7938 3999; www.trailfinders.com/clinic.htm

Irish Republic

Tropical Medical Bureau Grafton Street Medical Centre, Grafton Buildings, 34 Grafton St, Dublin 2; ⟍ 1 671 9200; www.tmb.ie. A useful website specific

USA

Centers for Disease Control 1600 Clifton Rd, Atlanta, GA 30333; ⟍ 800 311 3435; travellers' health hotline 888 232 3299; www.cdc.gov/travel. The central source of travel information in the USA. The invaluable *Health Information for International Travel*, published annually, is available from the Division of Quarantine at this address.

Connaught Laboratories PO Box 187, Swiftwater, PA 18370; ⟍ 800 822 2463. They will send a free list of specialist tropical-medicine physicians in your state.

Canada

IAMAT Suite 1, 1287 St Clair Av W, Toronto, Ontario M6E 1B8; ⟍ 416 652 0137; www.iamat.org

Australia, New Zealand, Singapore

TMVC ⟍ 1300 65 88 44; www.tmvc.com.au. 31 clinics in Australia, New Zealand and Singapore, including:
Auckland Canterbury Arcade, 170 Queen St, Auckland; ⟍ 9 373 3531
Brisbane 6th floor, 247 Adelaide St, Brisbane, QLD 4000; ⟍ 7 3221 9066

South Africa and Namibia

SAA-Netcare Travel Clinics P Bag X34, Benmore 2010; www.travelclinic.co.za. Clinics throughout South Africa.
TMVC 113 D F Malan Drive, Roosevelt Park,

Switzerland

IAMAT 57 Chemin des Voirets, 1212 Grand Lancy, Geneva; www.iamat.org

Travelpharm The Travelpharm website, www.travelpharm.com, offers up-to-date guidance on travel-related health and has a range of medications available through their online mini-pharmacy.

to tropical destinations. Also check website for other bureaux locations throughout Ireland.

IAMAT (International Association for Medical Assistance to Travelers) 1623 Military Rd, 279, Niagara Falls, NY 14304-1745; ⟍ 716 754 4883; e info@iamat.org; www.iamat.org. A non-profit organisation that provides lists of English-speaking doctors abroad.

International Medicine Center 920 Frostwood Drive, Suite 670, Houston, TX 77024; ⟍ 713 550 2000; www.traveldoc.com

TMVC Suite 314, 1030 W Georgia St, Vancouver BC V6E 2Y3; ⟍ 1 888 288 8682; www.tmvc.com

Melbourne 393 Little Bourke St, 2nd floor, Melbourne, VIC 3000; ⟍ 3 9602 5788
Sydney Dymocks Bldg, 7th floor, 428 George St, Sydney, NSW 2000; ⟍ 2 9221 7133
IAMAT PO Box 5049, Christchurch 5, New Zealand; www.iamat.org

Johannesburg; ⟍ 011 888 7488; www.tmvc.com.au. Consult website for details of other clinics in South Africa and Namibia.

FIRST-AID KIT A basic first-aid kit could sensibly include the following:
- antiseptic wipes
- plasters/Band-Aids, and blister plasters if you're hiking (compeed plasters or similar are particularly good for blisters)
- wound dressings such as Melolin, and tape
- sterilised syringes and needles
- insect repellent; antihistamine cream
- antiseptic cream
- oral rehydration sachets

IN UKRAINE 'Don't drink the water' fully applies to Ukraine and is the best advice to follow for a healthy trip. Never mind the lead pipes, dodgy sewage systems and a menagerie of gastrointestinal ailments; the water just tastes bad and will make you sick. Drink bottled or boiled water only; tea and hot drinks served in restaurants are safe. Avoid eating undercooked meat and freshwater fish, as they are known to carry worms.

Accept that you will get diarrhoea at some point and then you won't be so unhappy when you do, although good hygiene such as scrubbing your hands regularly with soap may help prevent infection. New food and new bacteria are the usual cause of diarrhoea in Ukraine and the condition should last only 24 hours. Even if you are taking anti-diarrhoea tablets like Imodium, be sure to drink lots of clear fluids to avoid dehydration. Rehydration sachets can be purchased in most pharmacies, but you can make the solution yourself with a teaspoon of salt, eight teaspoons of sugar and a litre of safe water. Bacillary dysentery usually fails to settle after 24 hours, and the diarrhoea may contain blood and/or slime or you may have a fever. This may be difficult to distinguish from amoebic dysentery. The latter is a much more serious ailment passed by contaminated food or water and human contact. Besides severe and bloody diarrhoea, there may be constant vomiting, stomach pains and a high fever. Another unpleasant, though rare, illness in Ukraine is giardiasis, caused by the protozoan *Giardia lamblia*. This gut infection includes greasy, bulky and often pale stools, stomach cramps and characteristic 'eggy' burps. It requires prompt treatment otherwise chronic infection may occur. Replenish all your lost fluids by drinking about four litres of rehydration fluid a day. Doctors in Ukraine will also prescribe antibiotic treatments, but if you think you will not be near medical facilities then carry your own supply. Ciprofloxacin – better known as Cipro (one 500mg tablet repeated 10–12 hours later) – will usually work for bacillary dysentery; however, you should still seek medical advice as sometimes it needs to be treated for longer. Suspected amoebic dysentery or giardiasis should be treated with 2g of tinidazole (Fasigyn) taken as four 500mg tablets in one go, repeated seven days later if symptoms persist. If your tummy feels fine, but your stools appear dark red, don't panic – you are probably eating a lot more beetroots (in the form of *borsch*) than you are accustomed to.

CHERNOBYL Chernobyl does not pose a serious health threat for travellers in Ukraine unless you plan on camping next to the reactor for an extended period of time. The general advice cautions against eating local food known to contain radiation, namely mushrooms and berries gathered from the Polissyan woods. Also, avoid freshwater fish from rivers and lakes in the vicinity.

ANIMALS All over Ukraine's larger cities, stray dogs move about in large packs and scavenge for food. Even if you think the puppies are cute, and others seem to be feeding them scraps of food, remember that these are wild animals that have been known to attack individuals. They also carry disease, rabies being the most obvious risk. Whether or not you are vaccinated, you are at risk of contracting rabies from being bitten, scratched or licked over open wounds. Wash the area immediately with soap and water and apply an antiseptic (or alcohol if you don't possess any antiseptic), then go as soon as you can for medical help. Having a pre-exposure rabies vaccine (see above) will reduce the number of post-treatment doses required. If you have had at least two doses of the vaccine then you will not need rabies immunoglobulin (RIG). The latter is very expensive and often unavailable, so it may pay to be vaccinated before departure. Rabies, if contracted and left untreated, is always fatal and is a horrific way to die.

In cheaper hotels, bedbugs can be a nuisance; known for the rows of small red bites you'll find in the morning, bedbugs do not spread disease and there's not much you can do about them, but calamine lotion or a proprietary antihistamine cream such as Anthisan can reduce the itching.

AIDS There is a serious AIDS crisis in Ukraine, spreading mainly through intravenous drug use and prostitution. Over 1% of the population is HIV positive, the highest rate in eastern Europe. Be wise. It is sensible to buy condoms before you leave to guarantee their quality, although most kiosks and shops sell good-quality ones in Ukraine.

UKRAINIAN HEALTH CARE Socialised medicine once supported a culture of efficient, long-term treatment, but with the current economic situation and severe supply shortages, the quality of care has dropped significantly. Ukrainian doctors are for the most part highly skilled, but paid miserably low salaries. Most continue to work with the incentive of receiving underhand gifts of cash in kind for medical services rendered. In my experience, travellers are welcome at public hospitals and will often be given priority. Be prepared to pay for any service, but don't be surprised if they refuse your money; there is prestige in treating a foreigner. However, there is a reciprocal health care agreement with the UK, so most medical treatment is free. This may also apply to dental treatment, but you will have to pay for prescribed medicine. Several private clinics have emerged in the larger cities where the staff speak English and the quality of care is comparable to that in the West.

When Ukrainians go to a public hospital, they are often expected to bring their own supplies along, including gauze, syringes and even anaesthetic. This has a lot to do with the lack of support that many hospitals still suffer. Travelling with a small first-aid kit is always a good idea (see page 64), and it is also wise to take a few packaged syringes and needles in case you need an injection. These days though, Ukrainian pharmacies are well stocked with high-quality medicine and medical supplies. Pharmacists also work as over-the-counter doctors. Simply pointing at or explaining an ailment in gestures will usually get you the right medicine or ointment.

Ukrainian folk medicine is a fascinating topic and you won't leave the country without being offered some sort of home remedy, some of which involve the supernatural. *Babushki* gather dried herbs and sell them on the street as medicine. List your symptoms and they'll mix a tea infusion that can – they say – cure anything. Mustard plants, powder or plasters are also effective for soothing chest colds.

COLD WEATHER Ukrainian winters are colder than might be expected, so bundle up with lots of layers and make sure to cover your hands, ears and head, from where you lose the most heat. After a while, you'll find your body gets used to the cold, but pay attention to signs like chattering teeth. After being outdoors, drink hot tea or eat hot *borsch*, for it can help prevent you from catching a cold.

Frostbite is a serious condition where the flesh has actually frozen. The first signs include a 'pins and needles' sensation and white skin. Go inside and warm the affected area with lukewarm water and slowly increase the temperature until feeling returns. Be smart about walking on frozen rivers and lakes. Ukrainians will not step on ice unless the temperature has been continuously below 0°C for at least five days. You can usually see which ice is safe for recreation by all the footprints and fishing holes there. If you do fall through, get indoors, remove the wet (but frozen) clothing and treat for hypothermia.

CRIME AND SAFETY

In general, Ukraine is a very safe place to travel, and much safer than most of its neighbouring countries. The anarchy of the 1990s seems to have settled down to a semblance of law and order; however, whenever riches are flaunted in the midst of poverty, there will be crime. No matter how hard you may try to belong in Ukraine, you will stick out as a wealthy foreigner and be the desired target for petty criminals.

Muggings, pickpocketing and robbery are the most common threats. Such things tend to happen in train stations, bus stations and marketplaces where there are lots of people continuously moving about and cash and belongings are shifting hands. Be especially alert when you are in any of these places. Also, people have been known to have their bags slashed while riding crowded subways or trolleys.

Capitalism has not been around long enough to divide cities into 'good' or 'bad' areas so potential for both exists everywhere. Bear in mind that public places are badly lit and that people are often mugged at night or in dark stairwells. Bring a small torch (flashlight). Local crime also tends to involve alcohol and money. If you are drinking with people you have just met, be on your guard. People have been robbed when they are drunk; or worse, they have been drugged and then robbed. Don't engage with drunk people who approach you, simply get away.

Trains are quite safe, so don't believe the horrid tales people tell. They normally forget which country it was in the first place. In any country, people usually only get robbed on trains when they are alone and vulnerable, so travel in groups or else close the door to your compartment with multiple locks. Taxis are also safe, but beware of any dodgy behaviour. If the driver demands you pay up front, get out of the car. If they pull over midway for petrol or to change a tyre, get out of the car and watch them from the roadside. If you feel suspicious, simply walk away. Pay a taxi driver only after you have stepped out of the car and have your bags with you.

Organised crime (the mafia) gets a lot of talk, but is of no real interest to tourists and vice versa. Mobsters in Ukraine fill a very different niche than they do in the West and will not bother you unless you are purposefully trying to undermine their business. Donetsk and Dnepropetrovsk both have reputations as gangster towns but seem to be moving from the shadows into legitimacy.

If you are a victim of a crime, think before you act. If you are staying in an upmarket hotel or are travelling with a tour agency, report it to them first. If your passport has been stolen or the crime is of a serious nature, be sure to make a report at your embassy. Also be sure to call the police and file a report, as this will help you in the long term. Corrupt policemen seem to be passé in the 'New Ukraine'. Let's hope it lasts – back in the 1990s, the slang term for the police was *musor* ('rubbish').

SCAMS AND SWINDLES Ukrainians freely admit that they don't trust their own countrymen, a general fear which contributes to nationwide tension. Remember that Ukraine is a relatively poor country with high unemployment, so that foreign tourists with hard cash in hand are the sought-for prey of a few con men. Swindles can take many forms. Offering services for cash, or demanding special fees, are common, and there has been an increase in staged scenarios to attract your attention and then take your money without you being aware. A tired scheme (but still tried) involves someone finding a large wad of money within your view and then forcing you into confidences or using sleight of hand to take or switch real money for fake. Ignore anyone who approaches you with a plan or blocks you from others' view. Extortion and intimidation are often used to get money from foreigners. Use your logic and just say no. There is no legitimate reason to open

DATING/MARRIAGE SERVICES

In Ukraine, there are more companies that market women to Western men than there are travel agencies. Luring older single men (and their money) over to Ukraine has become a booming, yet unregulated business, and sadly 'romance tourists' are a common sight in the country. Most dating services charge a yearly fee and allow you access to women's pictures, profiles and addresses so that you can pursue a long-distance courtship. Men are then encouraged to send flowers and gifts and spend as much as they can on having letters translated from their Ukrainian girlfriends. Eventually, you are expected to travel to Ukraine to meet the woman, although most men plan an itinerary to visit a dozen or so girls and pick one to marry. Typically the woman will offer to make all the travel arrangements, adding a 200% mark-up on price to any service you require. It is not for me to question how any two people expect to have a meaningful marriage when they don't speak the same language, but if this is your intent, there are some things you should know:

- Very few of these marriage services are legitimate businesses but instead are temporary internet scams collecting the credit card details of naïve men and milking them for all they're worth. I've known people to lose thousands of dollars.
- Obviously, a Western–Ukrainian romance has much more to do with economic disparity than any mystical connection between Western men and Ukrainian women, as is advertised.
- Ukrainian women are not as desperate to get out of the country as they once were. Too many men show up in Ukraine and find they are at the complete mercy of their 'date,' who proceeds to spend all their money for them, or else simply robs them and disappears. Set-ups involve multiple accomplices who will know what to do with your wallet and will successfully cover their tracks.
- Bear in mind that unless you marry her in Ukraine, getting a visa for her to accompany you in order to pursue a relationship in your own country will be extremely difficult, if not impossible.
- Ukrainian women may be very beautiful, but they do not make good souvenirs. Many a newly wed husband has been divorced once his wife has her new passport.
- Today, Ukrainian women make up a significant majority of (white) prostitutes in European capitals, most of whom are victims of human trafficking. Travelling to Ukraine in pursuit of women is of the same genre. Remember that an estimated 50% of prostitutes working in Ukraine are HIV positive or infected with syphilis.

your wallet for anyone, unless there's a real threat of violence. Many travellers use fake wallets filled with cancelled credit cards and stuffed with valueless cash. This can be a wise precaution.

Visitors are often shocked by the Ukrainian belief that if a crime has been done to you, it is your fault for not preventing it. Be streetwise. For example, Ukrainians will never simply open a door without asking '*Kto tam?*' and checking who's there. You may find that people seem always to be asking you the time or requesting a cigarette. This is a way for them to confirm your status as a foreigner. Their curiosity may be innocent, but it is acceptable to ignore the question and continue walking; that's what Ukrainians do. Avoid fortune-tellers who always leave with much more money than you intended them to have. Also, don't underestimate Ukrainians – they are smart bunch who've made do with very little for a long time.

When it comes to money, they can be quite cunning. Internet scams are rife. When making travel arrangements with any Ukrainian company, check their website to see when it was last updated or call them, and refrain from wiring money or sending credit card details. Most dating and marriage agencies are high-profile set-ups and romantic meetings often turn into big scams. Emails from complete strangers demanding you send cash by Western Union should be a red flag to most, and yet every year, a whole new group of people get taken in. Realise you are taking a large risk by getting involved with any of these organisations.

Having been warned, know that Ukrainians have a frightfully honest nature and are above all very kind and hospitable. People in the market will refuse to sell you something that isn't fresh, compliments are sincere and sarcasm non-existent. Don't let unnecessary fear lead to a rejection of everyday Ukrainian hospitality.

BRIBERY Paying someone a little extra to make sure something gets done became a way of life when a collapsed legal framework offered no guarantees. Things have changed a lot in a very short time, however, and now most fees come with receipts. Some bribery still exists on a very informal level, but the practice should not be encouraged by foreigners. These days, a sly slip of American cash rarely solves any problems, but it will draw undue attention and be taken as an insult by many.

ON THE STREET Driving in taxis can be plain scary, but most survive the experience by looking out the side window. Cars often drive down sidewalks, so be aware when walking. Pedestrians must be doubly alert in big cities. Be vigilant when crossing the street, even if you think you have the right of way. Also, always look both ways when crossing tram tracks in the city, even if they appear old and unused. Take care with pot-holes, and never step on a 'manhole' cover. They tend to be loose and people are always tripping on them. Also, in crowded public transport, it is fairly easy to get shut in the doors. Simply yell, and others will alert the driver to stop.

WOMEN TRAVELLERS On the surface, Ukraine's many decades of communism erased sexism to the point that women doing anything on their own – including travel – is now the norm. Females may find that they feel more vulnerable as a foreigner than as a woman. It would also not be facetious to say that a certain solidarity exists among women in Ukraine so that you should feel protected when other women are around. The most obvious risk is travelling alone on overnight trains, where even in first class you may be sharing a compartment with an unknown traveller. Nine times out of ten, you will befriend the stranger and it will be a great experience, but the odd smarmy passenger is not unheard of. You always have the option of buying out the tickets for an entire compartment, which is still a rather cheap way to travel, if also a slightly lonely one. Otherwise, there is safety in numbers, and travelling in a four-person *coupé* will increase your odds of someone else looking out for you. If you find that you are expected to share a train compartment with three men and they all give you the creeps, simply ask the conductor (almost always a woman) to change your place. You will find, however, that most men follow train etiquette, allowing women privacy to change clothing and offering the lower berths for sleeping.

Overall, follow your intuition and take the same precautions you would in your own country. Don't walk alone in dark secluded streets. Think ahead and have a contingency plan for ways out of various situations (ie: alternative means of transport, alternative accommodation). Professional taxis (with signs and phone numbers listed) are normally safe for women. Let others know where you will be travelling and if you are planning on going out at night, tell them when you hope to be back.

Ariadne Van Zandbergen

EQUIPMENT Although with some thought and an eye for composition you can take reasonable photos with a 'point-and-shoot' camera, you need an SLR camera if you are at all serious about photography. Modern SLRs tend to be very clever, with automatic programmes for almost every possible situation, but remember that these programmes are limited in the sense that the camera cannot think, but only make calculations. Every starting amateur photographer should read a photographic manual for beginners and get to grips with such basics as the relationship between aperture and shutter speed.

Always buy the best lens you can afford. The lens determines the quality of your photo more than the camera body. Fixed fast lenses are ideal, but very costly. A zoom lens makes it easier to change composition without changing lenses the whole time. If you carry only one lens, a 28–70mm (digital 17–55mm) or similar zoom should be ideal. For a second lens, a lightweight 80–200mm or 70–300mm (digital 55–200mm) or similar will be excellent for candid shots and varying your composition. Wildlife photography will be very frustrating if you don't have at least a 300mm lens. For a small loss of quality, tele-converters are a cheap and compact way to increase magnification: a 300 lens with a 1.4x converter becomes 420mm, and with a 2x it becomes 600mm. Note, however, that 1.4x and 2x tele-converters reduce the speed of your lens by 1.4 and 2 stops respectively.

For photography from a vehicle, a solid beanbag, which you can make yourself very cheaply, will be necessary to avoid blurred images, and is more useful than a tripod. A clamp with a tripod head screwed on to it can be attached to the vehicle as well. Modern dedicated flash units are easy to use; aside from the obvious need to flash when you photograph at night, you can improve a lot of photos in difficult 'high contrast' or very dull light with some fill-in flash. It pays to have a proper flash unit as opposed to a built-in camera flash.

DIGITAL/FILM Digital photography is now the preference of most amateur and professional photographers, with the resolution of digital cameras improving the whole time. For ordinary prints a 6 megapixel camera is fine. For better results and the possibility to enlarge images and for professional reproduction, higher resolution is available up to 16 megapixels.

Memory space is important. The number of pictures you can fit on a memory card depends on the quality you choose. Calculate in advance how many pictures you can fit on a card and either take enough cards to last for your trip, or take a storage drive on to which you can download the content. A laptop gives the advantage that you can see your pictures properly at the end of each day and edit and delete rejects, but a storage device is lighter and less bulky. These drives come in different capacities up to 80GB.

Ukraine's dating protocol is mysterious, although acting helpless and flirtatious will attract men who will expect more than you may be prepared to give. Accepting drinks from strangers is always a bad idea, as is going back to their apartments. Telling a persistent man that you are Orthodox Christian (*Ya Verushaya*) will get him off your back.

RACIAL MINORITIES Racism is another unfortunate aspect of life in Ukraine, although cities like Kiev and Odessa appear to be rather multi-cultural on the surface. In Ukraine, racist mindsets are linked to the general animosity of the poor towards the rich as some find it hard to grasp that someone of a different race earns more and lives better than they do. If you are not the same colour as they are, you

Bear in mind that digital camera batteries, computers and other storage devices need charging, so make sure you have all the chargers, cables and converters with you. Most hotels have charging points, but do enquire about this in advance. When camping you might have to rely on charging from the car battery; a spare battery is invaluable.

If you are shooting film, 100 to 200 ISO print film and 50 to 100 ISO slide film are ideal. Low ISO film is slow but fine grained and gives the best colour saturation, but will need more light, so support in the form of a tripod or monopod is important. You can also bring a few 'fast' 400 ISO films for low-light situations where a tripod or flash is no option.

DUST AND HEAT Dust and heat are often a problem. Keep your equipment in a sealed bag, stow films in an airtight container (eg: a small cooler bag) and avoid exposing equipment and film to the sun. Digital cameras are prone to collecting dust particles on the sensor which results in spots on the image. The dirt mostly enters the camera when changing lenses, so be careful when doing this. To some extent photos can be 'cleaned' up afterwards in Photoshop, but this is time-consuming. You can have your camera sensor professionally cleaned, or you can do this yourself with special brushes and swabs made for the purpose, but note that touching the sensor might cause damage and should only be done with the greatest care.

LIGHT The most striking outdoor photographs are often taken during the hour or two of 'golden light' after dawn and before sunset. Shooting in low light may enforce the use of very low shutter speeds, in which case a tripod will be required to avoid camera shake. With careful handling, side lighting and back lighting can produce stunning effects, especially in soft light and at sunrise or sunset. Generally, however, it is best to shoot with the sun behind you. When photographing animals or people in the harsh midday sun, images taken in light but even shade are likely to be more effective than those taken in direct sunlight or patchy shade, since the latter conditions create too much contrast.

PROTOCOL In some countries, it is unacceptable to photograph local people without permission, and many people will refuse to pose or will ask for a donation. In such circumstances, don't try to sneak photographs as you might get yourself into trouble. Even the most willing subject will often pose stiffly when a camera is pointed at them; relax them by making a joke, and take a few shots in quick succession to improve the odds of capturing a natural pose.

Ariadne Van Zandbergen is a professional travel and wildlife photographer specialising in Africa. She runs the Africa Image Library. For photo requests, visit www.africaimagelibrary.co.za or contact her on ariadne@hixnet.co.za.

may suffer double the attitude, but rarely aggression. Expect to be stared at a lot and periodically stopped by the police for passport checks.

WHAT TO TAKE

It is difficult to pack light for Ukraine, where a wide range of situations demands different things. However, Ukraine is not so barren these days. In big cities you can find most consumer goods, so leave the contingency items at home and bring extra money. Some things you can't get in Ukraine are: quality sunscreen, a Swiss army knife (with screwdriver head – you'll use it), powdered milk for your tea or coffee, nail clippers, and hand sanitiser or packaged wet-wipes. You can buy all toiletries in Ukraine, including designer razor blades. Contact lens solution is just hitting the big shops in Kiev, but is non-existent elsewhere, so bring what you need with you. If you are travelling during the coldest part of winter, you may find your contacts (especially hard ones) have a hard time staying in and you'll wish you had your glasses. If you normally wear glasses, bring an extra pair. Many people also find they need sunglasses in summer. Bring a small first-aid kit with you; see page 64 for details on what to include. Instead of the pre-packaged travel sewing kits, make your own: bring one spool of dark thread (blue or black), a pack of needles and a fair number of buttons (it is uncanny how often they fall off in Ukraine). Depending on which part of the country you are going to, bring a small Russian dictionary, a Ukrainian one, or both. Also, Ukrainians love business cards and use them passionately. If you have them, bring lots.

LUGGAGE The nicer your luggage, the more people will have their eye on you. Having scruffy bags makes you less of a target for theft. A hard-sided suitcase with wheels is best as large soft-sided bags can be (and have been) slashed open. Much depends on the nature of your trip. If taking to the road independently, pack light and inconspicuously. Dark duffle bags, simple backpacks, or a small, wheeled suitcase are best. The giant, brightly coloured backpacks you see all over western Europe are still too loud for Ukraine and you will only draw attention to yourself. The exception would be a planned hiking trip. Army/navy surplus stores always sell a good variety of heavy canvas bags, and their colour scheme will help you blend in better in Ukraine. Padlocking bags is also a good idea. When touring during the day, refrain from using a 'fanny pack' ('bum bag') or fancy camera bag. Carry your belongings (including camera) inside a simple plastic shopping bag like you see all the Ukrainians using. It's all you need and a thief won't think to grab it.

Leaving luggage at a train or bus station, or a hotel, is perfectly safe. The symbol for left luggage is a suitcase inside a box. Follow the signs, pay your money and receive your ticket. While left luggage offices are open 24 hours in bigger cities, in smaller towns check their working hours – sometimes they close at 17.00.

CLOTHING You are judged by what you wear in Ukraine, and Ukrainians will wear their very best clothes and shoes in public no matter how intense their poverty. The Western impulse to dress down on the road comes as a shock, since Ukrainians assume all Westerners are rich and therefore should be travelling in designer clothes and diamond bracelets. At the other unnecessary extreme, many travellers are loaded down with pre-conceived images of a desolate land and pack for Ukraine as if they were going camping. Comfort should be your main aim, but men should bring at least one pair of nice trousers and a shirt, and women should have one 'semi-nice' outfit (ie: skirt and blouse or dress). You will be surprised how a change of clothes will bring you increased respect when needed.

Bring comfortable and sturdy walking shoes, but avoid flashy white trainers which are coveted merchandise. Sturdy clothes are best for daytime activities. Even if it's normally not your style, bring a pair of loose-fitting pyjamas to wear on overnight trains, or a T-shirt and running trousers. You will be more comfortable and it's de rigueur. Keep in mind that you can buy any kind of clothing you will need in most large Ukrainian cities.

Ukraine gets fairly hot in the summer (+30°C) and people's clothes come off. Women tend to dress skimpily and a lot of men will work in the fields wearing nothing but their underwear. Travellers in public are still expected to keep covered, except on beaches and in parks. In other seasons, you will be amazed at how women in high heels never fall on the ice and how men keep mud off their trouser legs, two feats that set the Ukrainians apart.

Winter wear Ukrainian winters are bitterly cold, with temperatures down to −25°C, or lower if you factor in the possibility of severe wind chill. If you are travelling from November to March, pack warm clothes. The streets are never cleared when it snows so that thick ice forms on all roads and sidewalks which later turns to grey slush and gloopy mud in the spring. A pair of sturdy **insulated, waterproof boots** will prevent you from being cold, wet, dirty and miserable. A hat is also vital – bring something warm that covers your ears, like a woollen beanie. Ukraine knows its weather best, so a lot of travellers purchase their hat after they've arrived. You may have reservations about fur, but the classic Russian *shapka* is still the preferred head covering in winter, and it makes a lot of sense in the cold and wind. If you do choose to buy one, go with rabbit, mink or astrakhan wool – all made from farmed animals (and therefore not endangered).

Several layers will keep you warm inside and out (proper indoor heating has only just been introduced). A wool sweater is nice and warm unless it gets wet (hang it outside to dry, let it freeze and then beat out the ice crystals). Cotton dries quicker indoors. Wear a thick and heavy coat or parka that is extra long (and preferably water-resistant). Bring at least one pair of long underwear (or long johns) during the coldest part of the year and wear long thermal socks that come up to your knees. To keep the wind out, wear a long scarf that you can wrap several times around your neck.

If you are going hiking in the Carpathian or Crimean mountains, bring layers of clothing that can be easily added or removed to match the erratic weather. A waterproof windbreaker is also a good idea, even in summer.

MAPS Fortunately, Ukraine has inherited the talent of Soviet cartographers, although the process has taken awhile to adapt and modernise to the demands of such quick transformations. Finding the right kind of map for your needs can be tricky, especially with the added complexities of Cyrillic place names and varied transliterations, as well as the continued habit of changing street names to fit current political trends. Probably the most professionally printed maps are those of Kartografiya (*www.ukrmap.com.ua*), affiliated with Ukraine's Ministry of Ecology and Natural Resources. They produce a very good but basic foldout political map of Ukraine (1:1,000,000) in either English or Cyrillic, as well as an accurate topographical map (1:500,000) and the *Ukraine Road Atlas* (Russian and Ukrainian only). *Kartografiya* also publishes a series of quality maps for nearly every major city in Ukraine (over 500,000 inhabitants), and tourist hotspots (eg: Yaremche, Crimea), typically at a scale of 1:20,000.

Available online and in most major travel bookshops, travellers can find the very recent title *Ukraine* (1:1,000,000; 2006) from ITMB (International Travel Maps & Books; *www.itmb.com*). They also have a separate map for Crimea (1:320,000).

Nowadays, you will also find that more and more high-quality maps are widely available for purchase in Kiev, along with cheaper, advertisement-focused maps that are beginning to be distributed free at the airport and other tourist spots.

ELECTRICITY

AC is 220 volts and outlets fit the same (two-pin) plugs used in continental Europe. Unless you are staying in very posh hotels (which have their own power systems), make sure to unplug appliances that you are not using. Frequent electrical surges can destroy your television, iron or hair dryer. The electrical outlets on trains are for small razors only. Frequencies are also different (50 hertz), so in certain cases you will require an adapter as well as a converter. Keep in mind that certain electrical appliances will cost much less in Ukraine than in your home country. I've never had any problems plugging in laptop computers with a regular converter, although some people favour buying a local cord and plug that attaches to their own computer's adapter.

TOILETS

Funny how we always judge a country based on the quality of a trip to the bathroom. According to that measure, Ukraine falls somewhere below Sweden, but somewhere above western China. If you're lucky, you'll get to use some of the old-fashioned Ukrainian toilet paper – a tribute to recycling, with rough chips of pulp still visible (and tangible). That said, there is no need to stuff your suitcase with toilet paper from home, as soft, fluffy (and scented) toilet paper is now widely available in Ukraine. Nine times out of ten there will be no paper in your public toilet stall so saving paper napkins from restaurants in your pocket is still a worthwhile precaution. If you are in search of a toilet, think like a socialist (train and bus stations, large public parks, city squares). Most of the country's newer restaurants also feature public toilets today. The letter (M) is the Gents and (Ж) is the Ladies. Be aware that most public toilets are of the stand or squat variety with raised porcelain footsteps. The cost ranges from 50 kopecks to a hrivna, so always keep a single hrivna ready to pay the attendant. Ask for *bumaha* (paper) if you see that the attendant has some, and be prepared to fork out some kopecks for the privilege. Each wagon on a train has its own toilet at the end of the car, although it is better to use it closer to the beginning of your journey while the floor is still dry. Long bus rides will stop at least once every two hours for a break. In some rural areas, most 'outhouses' are a clumsy brick or cement shack without any heat and a deep and dangerous hole in the ground. If you tend to be fussy about clean toilets and you are only travelling in bigger cities, McDonald's almost always guarantees a hygienic experience and they are open to the public. Having visited several hundred public restrooms in Ukraine, I can report that the very best toilets are in the business class lounge at Boryspil Airport; the very worst can be found in the basement of Chernivtsi train station.

$ MONEY AND BUDGETING

Ukraine still has a cash economy, but credit and debit cards are making headway. Typically you can tell the economic state of a city by how accepting they are of plastic. Travellers' cheques are often more of a pain than their security warrants in Ukraine, although some banks and most luxury hotels accept them. Diversifying is the best method of carrying your money: bring a fair amount in cash, use a debit card for withdrawing more cash, and bring a credit card for certain hotels and as a safety measure. Cash means US dollars or euro. British pounds are usually accepted by banks only and will not give you a competitive exchange rate. Go to the bank in your home country and ask for crisp, mint condition bills printed after 1995, as Ukrainian moneychangers often refuse a bill showing any sign of wear. Foreign citizens bringing more than US$5,000 in cash (travellers' cheques included) must fill out a special declaration form. These days it is not necessary to carry that much and you only increase your chances of being robbed if you do. US$500–700 is more than enough. Wearing a hidden money-belt is wise, but don't keep all your cash, cheques and cards in one place. Spread them on your person and in your luggage and don't forget where you've put it all. Stuffing bills into shoes or socks is a bad idea as they often tear or get sweaty. Smart travellers will always carry an emergency stash of a US$100 bill or euro equivalent. If you do have old or damaged money, some large banks will take it, but for a lower rate.

Paying with credit cards is becoming more widespread. Visa, MasterCard, Maestro and Cirrus are generally accepted, Diners Club and American Express less so; simply check the stickers in the window of the establishment. When paying with plastic, be patient. Sometimes you may even need to show the attendant how to process a credit card transaction. Credit card fraud used to be a big concern in Ukraine, so be conservative in your payments and hold on to all receipts as a precaution. It is best to reserve your credit card for big transactions with reputable businesses. Instead, use debit cards to draw cash from machines (and keep your statements). This gives you the best exchange rate and limits the amount of money you are carrying on your person at any one time.

When needed, money transfers are convenient. Western Union has been in Ukraine for ten years and now has literally hundreds of offices all over the country. Call 8 800 500 1000 from anywhere in Ukraine to find the closest point. The main office is in Kiev at Prorizna 15 (\f 044 228 1780; e office@westernunion.org.ua; www.westernunion.org.ua or www.westernunion.com).

CURRENCY The hrivna (abbreviation UAH, plural hriven), was chosen as the new currency because the soft 'h'/hard rolled 'r' diphthong can only be pronounced by the most nationally astute of Ukrainians. Hrivna bills come in denominations of 1, 2, 5, 10, 20, 50, 100 and 200. One hundred kopecks make one hrivna (kopecks are the very cute coins that jingle in your pocket). Inflation has stabilised to the point that for the past year (2007) the US dollar has been worth about 5.3UAH and the euro worth slightly more. In hotels and some very expensive shops, prices are often listed as *y.e.* (standard equivalent) which is Ukraine's politically correct term for the US dollar.

Exchange booths are ubiquitous, recognisable for the daily rate chalked in next to the various flag symbols. It is illegal, unwise and unnecessary to change money anywhere else. Gone are the days when foreigners could pay for things in small US bills: people prefer hrivna (or euro!). Even though everyone deals in it, though, there seems to be a perpetual lack of small change. Always carry a fair stash of 1, 2 and 5 hrivna notes for buses, toilets and entrance fees (taxis normally have change). The couple of hundred hriven you are carrying in your pocket may not seem much to you, but it is a month's pension for some. Save the big bills for big purchases. Kopecks often seem a nuisance, especially when you consider their worth, and shop attendants will sometimes round up to the nearest hrivna. Always keep at least 50 kopecks just in case; it is better to have some coins in your pocket than to rummage through your bills trying to determine if that's a 1, 10 or 100 note.

HOW MUCH? This is a question only you can answer as only you know your spending habits and the level of comfort you demand. Ukraine can be incredibly cheap without too much effort. Train, plane and bus travel are all very inexpensive, going to a museum or to the opera is cheap, and nice restaurants cost so little that the poorest travellers can eat well. In fact, Ukraine is arguably the only country left in Europe where travelling can be cheaper than staying at home. Travellers can get by on US$25 a day, by choosing the cheapest hotel rooms (without individual plumbing), buying food in markets, eating in cafeterias and travelling on trains. Most independent adult travellers I've met (who don't speak any of the language) budget for around US$75 a day.

Accommodation and extra services (taxis, interpreters) will eat up most of your budget, as many hotels charge per person and a lot of 'tourist' services intentionally overcharge. Ukraine's tourist industry now caters for US$100–300-a-day budgets and you can easily spend that much per day on hotels. Travelling by aeroplane and chauffeured car will increase the price tag further. Organised tours usually charge US$500–700 a week and include hotel accommodation, meals, transport and guide.

TIPPING Tipping is not a traditional practice, but it's slowly making headway within the emerging market economy. In restaurants, a service charge of 10% will be included in your bill. If the service was good, 15% is the unwritten rule. Taxi prices are usually negotiated beforehand, so a tip might be defeating the purpose of bargaining. You might find that you have a hard time convincing some people to accept a tip as they don't see why they should accept extra cash for just doing their job. Explain that it is *na chai*, which is the Russian/Ukrainian expression 'for tea' from the old days, when servants were given a little extra to spend on meals. Anything up to 5UAH is enough. Tipping with US dollars is simply gauche.

5

Travelling in Ukraine

Even after 15 years of independence and a recent revolution, foreigners are still something of a novelty in Ukraine outside of Kiev. To avoid frustration, it's a good idea to consider the local mentality regarding travel and tourism and don't discount recent history.

SOVIET INFLUENCE For nearly 70 years, people living in Ukraine were subject to totalitarian management of their lives. Individuals were told where they could and could not go, what they could experience and what was forbidden. All citizens were issued 'passports' that served as a control mechanism to keep people in place. These documents marked which city a person was allowed to be in and what they were allowed to be doing there. Travel within the USSR was highly restricted and holiday opportunities were usually granted through a person's workplace. This did not mean that people never travelled but rather meant that travel was purely functional. The Soviet Union spanned 12 time zones, and its citizens were jostled from one end to the other in order to make socialism work. Ukrainian geologists were sent to research Kamchatka's volcanoes, while an Estonian family in the north would be given work in a Zaporizhzhya factory in the southwest. The gigantic Soviet military was the largest mechanism of travel, where new recruits were given assignments that usually tended to be very far from home. (Ask any man over 35 where he served in the army and you'll get a lesson in Eurasian geography.) Besides the military, only the party élite and very few others were permitted to make trips beyond the border. Soviet citizens showing interest in foreign countries were under suspicion of wanting to defect and all Westerners were dubbed spies. Needless to say, the concept of independent travel was non-existent.

INTURIST 'Inturist' was the established government section in charge of all tourist affairs both for incoming foreigners and Soviet citizens. As the ultimate award for work or political achievements, Ukrainians could go on specially designed tours to other parts of the communist world such as Bulgaria or, in very rare cases, Cuba, and only after completing intense background checks. For the few foreign visitors that did get into the Soviet Union, Inturist acted as an 'anti-travel agency' to prevent them from actually travelling. Tours, hotels and itineraries were set up to let foreigners see as little of the country as possible and go home with decent (albeit fake) impressions of the Soviet Union.

A two-tier system evolved that kept foreigners and locals segregated in their leisure. Foreigners paid six to ten times the price for any tourist service, despite the false exchange rate of the command economy. There were plush 'foreign' hotel rooms, restaurants and fancy shops where only foreigners could go, and train tickets for higher, foreign prices. Most of the country was completely off-limits. Today, this two-tier system is slowly crumbling, and most proprietors now pride themselves in charging foreigners the same price as Ukrainians. Still, the unfortunate belief pervades that foreigners need to be catered for separately. For that reason, travellers will feel confined if they do only what is expected of them. This also means luxury treatment at luxury prices, and at first you may be refused a budget room simply on the pretext that you are a foreigner and should pay more.

In addition to keeping the outside separate from the inside, Inturist served to keep track of foreigners' movements. Visas were issued for individual cities, not the whole country. Upon arrival in a city, registration with the local authorities was mandatory and checks were put in place to trace the traveller's path. You had to show your visa and have the details copied before being issued a room key or buying a train ticket. Many of these protocols still remain but have more to do with ticket sellers being able to read your name in Cyrillic than having a bored bureaucrat in Kiev tracking your moves.

The most unpleasant leftover of the Inturist days is the mentality that travel only exists in an institutional medium granted from above. According to this mindset, there are no travellers, only tourists; and tourists only go and see what is offered them. Group tours still reign supreme, and Ukrainians still travel en masse. You will often be quoted an excursion price based on a group of 40 or more. Ask how much it costs for just one or two people and your tour guide will consider the question as if it's the first time they've ever heard of the concept. According to Inturist, experiences are either purchased or permitted and there is little room for free movement or free interpretation. Much of Ukraine's tourist industry still caters to this philosophy out of bad habit, and independent travellers will get lots of quizzical looks. You may be told that what you are doing is *nelzya* ('forbidden'!) or just impossible. It *is* possible, and legal, and everyone else is missing out.

UKRAINE UNVEILED Beyond the Soviet experience, Ukrainian traditions are closer to a traveller's heart. Historically, Ukraine's *kobzari* roamed freely across the land singing long ballads and reciting poetry to villagers in exchange for their hospitality. Pilgrims spent lifetimes walking the thousands of miles between the sacred sites of Orthodoxy, the very voyage becoming a spiritual act. These are traditions that deserve remembrance today as more people travel to Ukraine and more Ukrainians begin to travel in their own country. Ukrainians have a growing curiosity about what lies inside their own borders and beyond – they are travelling more and are far more interested in travellers. People who stop you are far more interested in chatting with a foreign visitor than causing you problems. Indeed, the sudden interest of the outside world in Ukraine is a continual boost to national self-esteem following a slump of bad press. Ukraine is Ukraine's best advertisement – in response to fellow Ukrainians dreaming of the tropics, one Ukrainian traveller said, 'Why go and see sand? We have everything here: forests, rivers, lakes, fields, mountains, and the sea.'

ORGANISED TRAVEL VERSUS INDEPENDENT TRAVEL This may be an easy choice for some to make, but it is worth pondering seriously. If you want to see the main tourist sites in a short time, or if you are looking for a specialised itinerary to include, say, Jewish heritage sites, an organised tour would be better. If you are keen to wander across the countryside and enjoy the process of discovery, do it yourself. Keep in mind that preconceived notions about either form of travel do not apply in Ukraine because 'travel' is still so young. The new group tours on offer have not been around long enough to be cheesy, and if you pick the right tour agency, the trip will definitely prove adventurous. Most people choose organised tours for the convenience of having someone else deal with the language barrier and internal transport arrangements. Ukrainians will tell you that Ukraine is much more ready for foreigners travelling in a group than it is prepared to deal with independent travellers. And yet, the real Ukraine – the hilariously rude women behind counters, the all-night train rides, and picnics in the forest – are beyond the coach's windows and tour guide's umbrella. Independent travel ensures intimate interaction with the people, which is easily Ukraine's greatest attraction. There are still certain activities that will require someone else's help, eg: a trip to Chernobyl or serious hiking in Crimea, and these are probably best arranged prior to your trip. If you are travelling on your own, remember that you are a pioneer of sorts, reinventing a lost concept. Move wisely and enjoy the bumps.

GETTING AROUND

✈ **BY AIR** Flying between cities in Ukraine can save a lot of time and is usually quite cheap (around US$60–100 one way). Forget all the horror stories and jokes about Soviet-era jets. Domestic flights may be loud and bumpy, but Ukraine's aviation industry is just fine. Lviv, Donetsk, Dnepropretrovsk, Kharkiv, Odessa, Uzhgorod, Luhansk and Simpferopol all have convenient year-round air connections to Kiev. Often, travellers going from one point to another in Ukraine will have to change in Kiev, but gladly, the trend is changing as more regional airlines open up. Remember that some domestic flights go through Kiev Zhulyany Airport and that if connecting to an international flight, you will have to transfer to Borispol.

Even though many other cities will boast an airport, they may not actually have any flights, and schedules depend on the season. The summer months offer a wide range of flights, and during the tourist season in Crimea there are direct daily flights between Simpferopol and all major cities. Most local travel agencies can book and sell tickets, as can any of the upscale hotels in cities where there is a functioning airport. Take note that domestic flights have a much lower service standard than international flights and stricter luggage requirements.

Keeping up with Ukraine's domestic airlines of the day can be difficult. Here are the big ones:

Aerosvit Main booking office: Vasylkivska 9/2, Office 7A, Kiev; ☏ 044 490 3490; f 044 490 5872; e kev@aerosvit.com; www.aerosvit.com. An established domestic carrier with internal flights between Kiev, Ivano-Frankivsk, Lviv, Uzhgorod, Kharkiv, Simpferopol, Odessa, Donetsk, Dnepropretrovsk and Zaporizhzhya (many of these flights are code shared with smaller regional airlines).
Kiy Avia Horodetskoho, Kiev; ☏ 044 490 4949; f 044 490 4924; e info@kiyavia.com; www.kiyavia.com. Offers the widest range of destinations (including Ivano-Frankivsk and Chernivtsi). Of late, they have become the de facto booking agent for nearly all of Ukraine's domestic airlines. They have offices at nearly every airport and in nearly every major city in Ukraine, and quite a few in Kiev.
Ukraine International Airlines 14 Prospekt Peremohy, Kiev; ☏ 044 461 5050; e uia@ps.kiev.ua; www.ukraine-international.com). Has domestic flights between Kiev and Lviv, Dnepropretrovsk, Donetsk, Odessa, and Simpferopol.

Most regional airlines are listed in their respective chapters. Here are a couple that tend to have a nationwide outreach.

Ukrainian Mediterranean Airlines Kiev, Shulyavskaya 7; ☏ 044 238 2002; f 044 238 2043; e info@ umairlines.com; www.umairlines.com. The main charter airlines for Ukrainians going to Turkey on holiday. They also fly to Kharkiv, Odessa, Luhansk and Chernivtsi.
Donbassaero Donetsk, Artyoma 167; ☏ 0623 345 6761; f 0623 345 6763. The regional airline for Donetsk, with connections across Ukraine, the Middle East and eastern Europe.

Charter airlines Not so much for the budget traveller, but if you want to jet around Ukraine quickly and conveniently, there are a number of private jet services. This can be convenient for business travellers and small groups.

ACR-Aero Charter Airlines ☏ 044 207 0828; f 044 297 0827; e Aero-charter@acr-air.com; www.acri-air.com

Volare Airlines Kiev, Polevaya 24; ☏/f 044 537 5296; e office@volare.kiev.ua; www.volare.kiev.ua

🚃 BY RAIL While most Soviet institutions dissolved in a flash, the trains kept running. Ukraine has inherited its own portion of the vast rail network that once connected the entire Soviet Union (at its height it was the largest railroad in the world), and although it is often the slowest way to travel, it is the most reliable and romantic way to criss-cross the country. Trains are comfortable and cheap, and Ukraine's present rail system is far more efficient than those of Britain or America.

Technically, you can get almost anywhere by train, but it is best for long distances between larger cities. Train routes were built towards Kiev and Moscow as focal points, so north and south lines tend to be quicker than the east–west trains which have to zigzag across the country. Schedules were designed so that a journey between two major cities would last the night and travellers could awake at their destination. As distances vary, these overnight trips may have to leave in the early afternoon or else closer to midnight in order to make travel time end closer to morning. Thinking in terms of train travel time, Ukraine is 'two days' wide, with Kiev in the centre. Lviv–Kiev is one overnight journey, and Kiev–Kharkiv is another night's journey. Dnepropetrovsk and the Black Sea cities are overnight journeys from Kiev, while far eastern Ukraine (Luhansk) and Crimea are one and a half days, meaning a long night and then a half-day more.

Every large city has at least one train with a daily connection to and from Kiev. These 'company' trains are a little nicer and faster than the regular trains and christened with cute names to represent the region of Ukraine they serve (the train to Donetsk is called 'The Little Lump of Coal'). The Capital Express is a series of new 'European' trains that speeds between regional towns and Kiev; for instance the express train runs to Kharkiv twice daily in only five hours. Cities closer to Kiev can be reached on daytime trains, or else you can wake up in the middle of the night to quickly get on or off during a two-minute stop.

Smaller *elektrichki* connect rural areas to regional urban centres and leave from a smaller *vokzal* usually located next door to the main station. These trains are used primarily by people who live in the country and come to trade in the town markets, or else during the summer when they are packed full of city dwellers brandishing hoes who faithfully tend their individual plots. This is a completely separate rail system with its own ticketing. The trains are dismally slow and, even with their tight rows of upright wooden benches, the cars are crowded. *Elektrichki* are hot and airless in the summer and absolutely freezing in the winter. If you want to go out to the countryside, you may be better off taking a bus, although you'll be missing another bright bit of the real Ukraine.

In the station The вокзал (*vokzal*, station) embodies all the excitement of travel under one great roof. The buildings tend to be more grandiose than the functional Soviet style since many of them were built by the Germans during the occupation. Inside, the commotion never stops. Hustlers and pickpockets are always at work in the larger stations, so be on guard.

Довідко (*dovidko*, Ukrainian), **Справочная** (*spravochnaya*, Russian), is the information booth, which may or may not be marked with the little 'i' symbol. It is more identifiable as the window where the woman has a microphone. Finding out about train timetables and prices has to be done separately from the actual buying of the ticket, and your sincerest question at the **КАССА** (*kasa*, ticket counter) may be met with a finger pointing you to the information counter. If you require any information to be written down they will charge you for it (around 2UAH).

New to many refurbished *vokzal* are plush first-class lounges with an entrance fee of around US$1. Passengers rest here after arriving in the middle of the night or before leaving sometime before dawn. This closed-in lounge is guarded, heated in winter, air conditioned in summer and there are lots of big cushy chairs to sleep on. If you can sleep sitting up and don't mind the TV blaring all night, it's a cheap night's rest.

Some remodelled stations also have flashy 'Service Centres' which were designed as a separate information/ticket booth for Western tourists. In some cities, foreigners are required to buy their tickets here. The attendants rarely speak English but can be helpful. If nothing else, it allows you to jump the longer queues elsewhere.

In every station there is a secure room where you can leave luggage for up to 24 hours and sometimes longer. Look for the **камера схову** (*kamera skhovu*, Ukrainian); **камера хранения** (*kamera khraneniya*, Russian) with the symbol of a suitcase in a box with a key above it. (Sometimes it is a short walk to the side of the station.) Larger stations will have automatic lockers that work with tokens purchased at a booth nearby. Set your own combination on the inside, drop in one token and shut the door. To open, set the combination on the outside, drop the token and pull. If there are no automatic lockers or your bags are too large, the left-luggage room with shelves is perfectly safe. You may be horrified at the thought of leaving your things with seemingly impoverished strangers, but I have never heard of anything being stolen from these attended rooms. The service costs up to 5UAH a bag and you'll be given a flimsy bit of paper that you need to show when you come back.

Train schedules/buying tickets Kiev's main station is the only one in Ukraine that posts both Cyrillic and Latin spellings for its train schedule. This should be a strong incentive to learn the alphabet. If you can read the cities and know the words **відправлення** (*vidpravlennya*, departure) and **прібуття** (*pributtya*, arrival), you should be able to understand the timetables. Only final destinations and origins are listed so think regionally. Find the closest city to your desired goal or else look at a map. Trains leave **щоденно** (*shchodenno*, every day), or perhaps on even **парні** (*parni*) or odd **непарні** (*neparni*) days. Remember that you can get almost anywhere on a train, but it will take time. Ukraine's national rail schedule is now available online (*www.uz.gov.ua*) but only in Ukrainian.

There are generally three different class tickets for a train. **CB** (*es-vay*) is luxury class and means the compartment will have only two bunks inside. Not all trains have these first-class spaces, but most do. **Купе** (*coupé*) is still considered comfort class with four bunks inside. **Плацкарт** (*platskart*) is the lower-class car packed full of rows of small bunks and not too different from a cattle car. Most people prefer travelling *coupé* because it is the better option that is most widely available. A typical overnight ride in a *coupé* costs US$10 to US$30, while a luxury (**CB**) ticket from Lviv to Kiev will be under US$50.

Some train stations will have only one functioning ticket counter, while others seem to have a hundred, all with different specifications as to who is allowed to buy tickets there (eg: war veterans, parents with children, invalids, etc). Go to the longest queue, or ask which *kasa* sells to foreigners. If you do not speak any of the language, say the city, or else write down the date you want to travel, your destination and which class. You will have to show the visa page of your passport in order to be issued a ticket, and you must pay in cash. Outside of the station, there are central offices selling rail tickets in larger cities, and some of the former Inturist offices located in hotels can also do bookings. It is best to buy tickets a few days in advance, but if you are an impulsive traveller, you will most likely be able to get tickets on the day of departure. You may be told there are no more tickets and to come back later. Last-minute free spots only show up on the computer a few hours before the train leaves and may cost a little bit extra. Some travellers want to buy out a whole compartment either for privacy or security. This works sometimes, but you cannot prevent the conductor from sticking somebody in with you when they see your *coupé* is empty. Your belongings are probably safer when there are other people around. Don't ever buy from touts, even though they rarely approach foreigners. In the early post-perestroika days it was easy to bribe your way onto a train, even across a border. Those days are long gone and a foreigner without a legitimate printed ticket will pay heavily.

Spaces are usually assigned. Lower bunks (*nyzhniy*) are considered more favourable than the upper (*verkhniy*) and it is normal to request your preference when you buy the ticket. In principle, your luggage is more protected under the lower bunks, but it really doesn't make a difference. *Coupé* train cars have seven compartments, and No 4 in the middle of the car has the most sought after tickets. If you end up in the upper right-hand bunk in No 7 you will know that you did not make a flattering impression at the ticket counter or else you were the last one to buy a ticket. The toilet is on the other side of the wall and the door bangs all night long. Going *platskart* is hardly worth the few hrivna you save, but if you want to try it out, take extra precautions. Travel with someone else and don't carry valuables with you. The people in *platskart* are not significantly more dishonest, but there are so many people in one space that it is more difficult to keep a watch out for the one thief that may be lurking.

Train schedules seem to be the one thing that never changes in Ukraine and trains always run on time. If the train is originating from your location, board early, around 15 minutes before departure. Platform numbers are listed no more than 20 minutes before the train leaves. If the train is only stopping by, be ready to get on fairly quickly. Read your ticket to know which car (*vagon*) you are in and be standing near where you judge that car will arrive.

On the train A rush of legs and bags will follow the train's shining headlight down the platform, even though there may be plenty of time before it leaves. Early boarders get to stake out the better storage spaces and tend to roost supreme in the *coupé*. Each *vagon* has a uniformed conductor who checks your ticket before letting you on, distributes bedding, and serves tea (*chai*) and coffee (*kofye*). These conductors are usually young women who work a gruelling schedule. Get on their good side and your trip will be nicer.

Don't expect to 'see Ukraine' from your seat on the train. Years of dirt and smoke have misted up the windows, causing the view to be more obscured than mystical. In addition, the Soviet government planted trees along the major rail lines to prevent travellers from seeing politically sensitive bits of the country. In summer, it may seem you are riding in a green tunnel. Still, there will be gaps when a glance out the window will meet a fantastic view of golden sunflower fields or an ice-encased forest.

Where you will see Ukraine is *inside* the train. Life on the train car is as real as it gets, and you'll find that trains are a great way to become intimately acquainted with people. A range of customs sets the atmosphere on Ukrainian trains. For the duration of travel, the stress and hard work of daily life have ceased, and the mood is laidback and celebratory. If you are sharing a *coupé* it is polite to introduce yourself early on and participate in the conversation. Food is shared, stories are swapped and the party will drag on late into the night. This is a great time to practise your language and interact freely. In almost every case the other passengers will be excited to have a foreigner in their car and they will look out for you. A *coupé* generates a sense of solidarity and befriending your fellow travellers is the best way to ensure you don't get anything taken and that you feel safe. In these circumstances, it is generally fine to leave your things while you explore the rest of the train.

Early in the trip, the conductor will come by to check tickets and distribute bedding. She will normally take your ticket and return it to you as you leave the following morning. Bedding is mandatory for overnight journeys and costs extra (around 15UAH). The conductor also serves coffee, tea or mineral water upon request, each for a handful of kopecks. It's a good idea to bring an extra bottle of water with you as the windows are permanently screwed shut and the air gets rather warm. Restaurant cars are present but rarely serve the lavish cooked meals they once did. Things are quick and casual now: soup from a packet, instant coffee, dry rolls, etc. The train will stop at many towns along the way, and *babushki* jump at the doorway to sell you *pirozhki* (stuffed rolls), hot *varenniki* (dumplings), drinks, or even whole smoked chickens and piglets.

Each car will have a WC at one end, equipped with a toilet and small sink. Push on the lever under the tap to make the water run. When you flush, you'll catch a glimpse of the tracks whizzing beneath you. This is the very obvious reason that the WC is locked when the train is not moving. Smokers must use the small space at the end of the car right before the coupling joints that connect the cars. Watch your fingers and toes when crossing from one car to the next. Before going to sleep, lock the door of your compartment. One lock is the turning handle and the conductor can open this with a key. The other lock is a metal clip on the upper left-hand side of the door. This sticks out and blocks the door from opening all the way and is not entirely necessary.

If you are on an overnight train and your stop is not the final destination, the conductor will make sure you are awake. Be ready to hop off quickly. In the smaller stations, trains stop for one to two minutes. Otherwise the whole train wakes up together with lights and loud pop music. You'll find that mornings are busy with people brushing their teeth and shaving in the corridor, changing clothes and re-packing bags. It may have taken you 12 hours to go just 300km, but you will have slept most of the way and experienced Ukraine's grandest travel tradition.

BY BUS Much quicker, much less expensive, but a little less comfortable is the *avtobus*, which can be a plush coach, a bouncy 1960s bus or a claustrophobic minivan. The bus travels at about 100km/h so it cuts train times in half (Odessa to Kiev takes only six hours). The bus also allows a great view of the countryside, and this is how most people travel to the rural areas. It is the main form of transport around Crimea, as well as the preferred method of travel between the many mountain villages of the Carpathians. You can go literally anywhere on the bus, but schedules change frequently so it becomes a task of going to the station and finding out how soon you can leave. The main *avtovokzal* (bus station) is located on the far outskirts of town in big cities or else right next to the train station in very small towns. When there are multiple bus stations, locate the one closest to the direction of your destination. Tickets can be bought in advance, or on the bus. Tickets are normally tiny slips of paper that look much like a receipt that you would throw away. Sometimes there are assigned seats, sometimes not, and sometimes seats are assigned but people sit wherever they want anyway. Hold on to the minuscule bit of paper that is your ticket. Buses and minivans will stop and pick up every person that flags them down so things can get fairly claustrophobic, if not chaotic. In the dead of winter, buses can be extremely cold and you'll pray for a large *babushka* to come and sit next to you. In the summer, you'll want a window seat. When the bus does make a stop, keep a sharp eye out for your bags. Theft on buses is uncommon, but then, so are you.

The exception to the above is a new range of private companies that charge a little more than the train, but will get you there quickly and in relative comfort. **Avtoluks** is the largest, quality coach company offering regular daily service throughout all of Ukraine (NB: not to be confused with Autolux, the anarchist rock band of the same name). They have offices in almost every regional centre of the country. In Kiev, they can be found at Chistyakovskaya 30 (\f *044 536 00 55;* e *info@autolux.com.ua; www.autolux.com.ua*). **Gyunsel** is another coach company with good reliable nationwide service. They are based in Kiev and have daily services to and from Dnepropetrovsk, Donetsk, Khar'kiv, Kherson (via Uman) and Kosiv (via Vinnytsya and Chernivtsi). There are additional lines to Crimea in summer. In Kiev, they're at Bubnova 15 (\f *044 258 0438;* e *office@gunsel.com.ua; www.gunsel.com.ua*). Both bus companies make a mandatory stop at Boryspil Airport in Kiev as they come and go to their ultimate destination, making it convenient to travel directly from your flight into the regions of Ukraine.

BY CAR There are not enough pages in this book to list the reasons you should not want to drive in Ukraine, and yet people do it all the time. Yes, touring the vast expanses behind the wheel is a great adventure, but it can also be very stressful and is known to cause heart murmurs in otherwise healthy adults. If you are driving your own car, have every possible bit of paperwork and registration with you, especially your customs declaration form. You must also have an international driver's licence, which can be readily obtained at home through the AA, or AAA in the US. A very solid anti-theft device (eg: steering-wheel lock) is mandatory, and a car alarm is highly recommended. Foreign cars are known targets for break-ins and car-jacking. Park only in guarded, fenced-in car parks and avoid driving between cities after dark as this is when most car-jackings occur.

Realise that no matter how good a driver you are, you are pitting your defensive driving skills against some of the most offensive drivers in the world. In principle, Ukraine has a zero tolerance policy for drunk driving, and yet most everyone drives as if they were drunk. Everyone speeds, everyone overtakes on one-lane roads, and everyone ignores pedestrians, road signs and stop lights. If you can accept those generalisations, then drive on. Also, Ukrainian roads are abominable, something that is not likely to change too soon. Often there are more holes than there is road and it is common to get stuck doing 30km/h just to keep the suspension (shocks) intact. Every season has its perils: deep sticky mud in spring, ice in winter and dust and pebbles in summer. Cracked windscreens are very common. Fortunately, petrol stops, road-stop cafés and motels are regular, although many only accept cash. International road signs apply and most Ukrainian bookshops sell good-quality road atlases, some with Roman spellings.

Highway roadblocks are not uncommon. Drivers in the other lane will flash their headlights to warn of an upcoming block and to slow you down. A patrol will signal you to pull over by holding out a black-and-white stick. If you do get pulled over at a roadblock, the best strategy is shrugging your shoulders and speaking only in English. Usually this gets you waved on. If not, be co-operative in showing them the requested documents and don't try anything silly like bribing them.

Car rentals are coming into wide use and are available in a number of larger cities. Prices are two to three times higher than what you would expect at home, and this is not including the additional, higher-than-average insurance. Professional auto thieves target rental cars so take every precaution for security. Rental companies offer chauffeur-driven cars as well, which can be a much less stressful option. **Europcar** (*www.europcar.com*), **Hertz** (*www.hertz.com.ua*) and **Avis** (*www.avis.com.ua*) are the most established. Specific information is given in the regional chapters.

HITCHING There is no such thing as a free ride in Ukraine. Waving down a car for a ride is normal, but the driver is stopping in the hope of getting some cash from you. Out in the country this is sometimes the better way to travel. In cities, hitching works as an informal taxi system. Stop a car by sticking your right hand out palm down. Many drivers will take whatever you give them, but it is best to make a deal beforehand. Near the bus station there will always be a few men trying to fill their cars up with passengers going to the same destination. This way they cover their gas costs and can make a bit of money on the way. You may sit for a long time until the car is absolutely crammed before you leave. Still, it can be a quicker way to travel and usually costs the same as the bus. Make sure the price is understood and don't pay until you've reached your destination and stepped out of the car with your bags. Women travelling alone should obviously avoid hitching.

TRAVELLING IN CITIES

Taxis Taxis are generally easy to find and use, but keep in mind that in Ukraine taxi drivers have the reputation of being minor league con men so it pays to be savvy. They are doing it for the money and some will double the price when they encounter a foreigner. It never pays to be too paranoid about getting ripped off, but bargain all the same. Excluding Kiev, a trip anywhere inside a city should never be over US$5–7. (Kiev, followed by Simpferopol, Zaporizhzhya and Chernivtsi are infamous for their overpriced taxis). If you have the choice, go for the little guy – meaning the beat-up Lada and Zhigulii with self-positioned taxi signs. These are entrepreneurial taxi drivers who must still pay off a higher hand for the privilege to be working. They cost less than the larger taxi companies and tend to be of more honest character. Always agree on a price before sitting in the car and don't get talked into paying more. If you are planning on taking a taxi on a long trip outside the city, the general rule is about 3UAH per kilometre. Often the driver will offer to wait, or else you will have asked him to make the return journey. He will charge you extra for the wait so make sure you have agreed on the price.

Public transport within towns and cities Communism granted Ukraine an exceptional system for moving lots of people around quickly. Decades of wear and tear have slowed things down a bit, but it will always be the best way to go from A to B in a bustling city. Most people travel only by public transport and you'll be amazed at the number of bodies squeezed into a single bus or carriage. Things can get very cramped during rush hour (*07.00–10.00, 16.00–19.00*) so keep your purse or backpack against your chest and breathe slowly. Before a stop, individuals inch their way to the door, asking each person in their way if they are getting off. If someone taps you on the shoulder and mutters something, move out of the way or else nod if you are getting off. At times you will have no choice but to be ejected. Learn to be pushy and fight your way on and off transport.

Subway Kiev, Kharkiv and Dnepropetrovsk each have a metro, open from 05.30 until midnight. Tokens cost 50 kopecks and can be bought in a booth at the entrance or sometimes from the small orange machines hanging on the wall. One token buys one trip to any other station. Drop the token in, and the metal gates open up. When things get really crowded, make sure to allow the doors to close after the person in front of you before dropping your token and walking through. Getting shut in the doors really hurts.

Ability to read signs is helpful, especially when changing lines, but a good map will do the trick. There are maps in this guide and most subways will have maps posted at the entrance and in the vehicles. If in doubt, follow the largest crowd.

Trolleys, trams and buses The *tramvai* and trolleybus are an eastern European institution and good for going short distances in town. Signs mark the stops. People are usually packed on too tightly for you to just walk on and pay. The best method is to hold a 1UAH note in your hand as if you are ready to buy a ticket. The conductor will come and sell you one for between 40 and 60 kopecks. Otherwise, people pass money hand-over-hand all the way to the driver, and the change is passed all the way back. A ticket is ripped or hole-punched to show that it's been used. Hold on to it in case of random checks by the controllers. If you are carrying heavy luggage, you may be expected to pay extra. It is safest to buy one ticket per bag and avoid the likes of big-city controllers who enjoy fining foreigners. The word for fine is *straf* and if it's over US$2 they are making it up.

Marshrutka taxis are both public or private minibuses that run maze-like routes through the city, or around town. They use the regular bus stops, but you can also flag them down anywhere you see them. In smaller towns, these will be the most reliable way to get between city centres and train and bus stations. The number and route are usually posted in the window, but always check with the driver by stating your destination and waiting for a *da* (yes) or *nyet* (no). The cost is usually 1–2UAH. They can get crowded and your view may be blocked. Ask someone next to you to let you know when to get off or just call out *na ostanovkye!* ('next stop!').

🏠 ACCOMMODATION

HOTELS Ukrainians like shiny things, namely glamour, glitz, and signs of affluence. Many of the great new hotels you'll encounter show blatant evidence of the local penchant for perceived luxury. An attitude of 'out with the old, in with the new' seems to dominate the hospitality industry, and you happen to be part of the 'new'. Count yourself lucky to be arriving at this later phase of transition, but do appreciate the challenges of the past. Not so long ago, the majority of Ukraine's hotels were either bawdy hangouts for the Soviet *nomenklatura* or basic dormitories to house the travelling proletariat. In the early years of independence, a push to change everything into *Yevro* (European) standard generated inflated room prices and introduced some saccharine décor, while often overlooking the very essentials. Now that new hotels are opening left and right, there's some real competition and standards are increasing everywhere. Just keep in mind that many Soviet-era hotels are in the midst of staggered reconstruction.

What that means is that many older establishments have six or seven different classes of rooms with an illogical pricing system to match. At the top of the pile are the 'lux' or luxury suites, which are sometimes truly luxurious, and other times not (foreigners are prime targets for the 'lux' category rooms). At the bottom end of the spectrum are pokey little rooms that have remained unchanged since the Komsomol convention of 1974, although these can be great deals if you don't like spending money on hotels. Variations and combinations of the two extremes exist throughout the country, and what's on offer will tell you how far off the beaten track you are travelling.

In Ukraine, it still pays to be flexible and a little tough. Awareness of the following realities will help you grin and bear it.

Plumbing was never a Ukrainian forte, and enquiries about water can incite a frank display of optimism. ('No, we don't have hot water, but we *do* have cold water!') In the luxury and most middle-range hotels listed, there will always be hot water, but in budget hotels, be sure to check, even if it means visiting the room and turning on the tap. Certain cities – like Lviv and Odessa – are infamous for their water problems, which is why many upscale hotels have their own systems. In rural areas and in many cities, hot water is usually turned off sometime in late spring and then comes back on in early October. During the winter months, most budget hotels will post hot-water schedules in the lobby (usually early morning and late evening). 'European' showers are often perceived to be classier than bathtubs, and so remodelled rooms will often have showers. Budget rooms also sometimes have a 'shower' which is nothing more than a drain on the bathroom floor and a hose coming out of the wall.

The concept of double beds is a new concept for many lower-standard hotels, although nearly every 'lux' room now offers you the option. In the past, a 'double' room meant twin beds that may or may not have been pushed together. Nowadays, more and more hotels are differentiating between twins and doubles. Requesting a queen-size or king-size bed will get you confused looks. Instead, insist on a *bolshaya kravat* (big bed) or a *frantzuskaya kravat* (French bed). Traditional Ukrainian bedding consists of a sheet covering a thick woollen blanket, much like a duvet, and most pillows are filled with goose down. During colder months, you can always find extra blankets stuffed in the cupboard.

Central heating and air conditioning are now common enough that nicer hotels will advertise a class of room with *konditsioner* If travelling in winter among the humblest of hotels, you can stay warm by stripping the bedclothes and mattress and making your bed next to the heater on the floor.

Ukrainian rooms are traditionally classified as *odnomestny* (single, *one place*), *dvukhmestny* (double, *two places*), *pol-lux* (junior suite) and *lux* (suite). Suites can be much nicer, or simply more complex, with multiple rooms, multiple television sets or multiple toilets; however, in terms of value-for-money, it is sometimes better to get a *lux* or *pol-lux* in an average hotel than to get the double room in a more expensive hotel. This may have something to do with the fact that Ukrainians rarely stay in a hotel for functional reasons, but usually hold parties in larger suites.

Classification Establishing a fixed system for grading Ukrainian hotels is practically impossible since price, quality and service vary so much from place to place (and even from floor to floor). Ukraine's star-rating system should be totally ignored since it is inconsistent, irrelevant and often self-awarding. Never trust the outside appearances of a hotel: the entrance may sport a gold-emblazoned 'Reception' sign (in English) over smiling uniformed staff, while two floors up the rooms lack hot water. At the same time, the dingy grey concrete block down the road may turn out to have outstanding luxury rooms for half the price. In this book, hotels are classified to some extent by price, but more so by personal experience and room standard. In many cities, there are not enough hotels to classify them, or else the rooms in one hotel will cover the whole gamut of classifications. The general rule is to always see a room before you agree to take it, even if you've booked it well in advance.

Luxury Most of Ukraine's poshest hotels have been open for less than five years and range from an élite corporate standard to very opulent palaces that could easily classify as four- or five-star in the west. Ukrainians expect all foreigners to stay only in luxury hotels, and will always steer you towards the very best. Anything upwards of US$150 a night is considered luxury, although the locations of the very best hotels in the country (Kiev, Yalta, Odessa, Lviv, Donetsk, Kharkiv and Dnepropetrovsk) are also those places where the value you get for US$100 is highly variable. Don't expect prices to correlate to the standards of rooms back home for the same price. A room in a luxury hotel will be light and spacious and the beds fitted with luxury posture-enhancing mattresses. Bathrooms tend to be newly tiled with still-shiny pipes and uphold the highest standards of hygiene. All luxury hotels have their own private source for hot water and electricity and usually feature gourmet restaurants, an English-speaking staff, in-room internet access, and all the amenities that you would have in your typical business hotel back home (bathrobe, slippers, satellite television, minibar, and chocolates on the pillow). The country's latest trends in hospitality tend to trickle down from the luxury hotels via Ukraine's very unique mafia culture.

Middle range The nebulous in-between means anything that fails to attain the superiority of a luxury hotel but still maintains a habitable standard, based on a strong commitment to cleanliness and comfort. Prices range from US$45 to just over US$100 per night, and these are often the kind of large-scale hotels that house tour groups. The majority of middle-ranges are recovering Soviet-era hotels that happen to be blessed with good management. That means gargantuan reinforced-concrete construction, cell-like rooms and minuscule bathrooms; it also means friendly, unpretentious service and sincere attempts to make your stay enjoyable. Most middle-range hotels are in flux, meaning that while some rooms have been remodelled, many have not, instilling a tiered pricing structure for lower quality rooms versus refurbished, higher-standard rooms. These newer 'lux' rooms tend to employ an embellished style best described as 'post-Soviet chic': frilly embossed curtains, zany print carpets, big poofy couches, misty-eyed artwork and giant Korean television sets in every room. IKEA brand furniture often fills out the middle-range décor. Middle-range rooms will always have their own, en-suite bathrooms that usually feature dependable hot water. Since many of the older versions were former Inturist hotels, they also offer convenient in-house travel services to visitors.

Budget The majority of hotels in Ukraine used to be fairly inexpensive, but the push to modernise has allowed wealthier markets to take over. Ukraine's budget hotels mainly consist of the few old Soviet hotels that have not been bought up by business developers, and charge US$10 to US$40 for a very basic room. Budget means that the bed is most likely of Soviet construction with a bit of a thin mattress on top. Bathrooms can range from the pretty decent to the downright abysmal. Things can get damp or cold or draughty, and rooms tend to suffer from severe smoke damage. The floors will be kept spotless through constant scrubbing by diligent grannies, but many other aspects will be left in a more dismal condition. In many smaller towns, this will be all that is available, and you should relish the experience. The exceptions to all this are the rare modernised hotels that target the average Ukrainian traveller, such as train station hotels or hostels. These tend to be clean and efficient, and cost between US$20 and US$30 a night. A lot of middle-range hotels will also have cheap budget rooms which are simply not yet remodelled, so if you are trying to stick to a budget, don't assume a middle-range hotel is out of your price range. Budget travellers can also knock a fair amount off the room price by differentiating between a room with *udobstv* ('conveniences') or *bez udobstv* ('without conveniences'). Getting a room with sink only and no toilet or shower means sharing a communal facility in the hall for which you normally pay US$1 each time for a hot shower. Smaller budget hotels will also clean clothes and shine shoes for minimal fees.

Security Nearly every middle-range and luxury hotel will have a security guard posted at the entrance or near the lift to prevent non-residents from entering. Upon checking in, you will be asked to present your passport, which is required in order to fill out your registration. Don't worry if they keep your passport for a while; they tend to get backed up with registrations and will make sure you get it back. Hotel management also keeps a secure safe, and most upmarket rooms will also have their own personal safes for your use. Leaving things in your room is normally fine – the cleaners will dust underneath the wad of bills you left on the night table and put them right back as they were, but like anywhere, hotels won't take the heat when the diamond bracelet you left by the open window sill suddenly disappears. Stash valuables (money, passports, jewellery) away in a safe or in different places in your room. The real threat is people from outside the hotel who know you are staying there. Always lock the door behind you when you enter the room. If someone knocks, ask who it is (*Kto tam?*) and if it is not room service or a sweet old lady with cleaning supplies, then don't open up. Equally, it may seem obvious, but don't bring strangers back to your room.

Payment Making a reservation (*bronirovaniye*) usually means contacting the hotel ahead of time and paying a non-refundable fee equal to half the price of the room upon arrival. While this is a less desirable feature of Ukrainian hotel culture, it comes in handy in the summer, when popular tourist sites tend to fill up fast. As yet there is no norm for hotel pricing: some will charge per person, others charge per room. In some budget hotels, all amenities are considered added extras and will be included in your bill: telephone, refrigerator, television. Hotels usually specify if breakfast is included in the price (in nicer hotels it normally is) and most lower-standard hotels will charge you in advance for the whole duration of your stay. Credit cards are making headway, so that most hotels that charge more than US$50 a night will offer you the chance to play with plastic. There is the rare exception, but in these cases, the hotel lobby normally features a cash machine.

OTHER OPTIONS Most train stations have small sections of rooms with beds that function like a hotel. Follow the bed signs, normally up to the second floor. In small towns a room costs around US$8 while in the biggest cities, the standard is much nicer and rooms cost around US$25. Another good way to save money is to rent a private **apartment**, for one night or for a month. The quality of accommodation is often much more comfortable than any budget hotel (hot water, bathroom and kitchen) and can cost around US$30 and up a night. Private companies will advertise short-term apartment stays, or you can find women outside the train station who are yelling *kvartira* (apartment) or *komnata* (room). Ask the price, see the apartment, and then make a deal and get the keys. Arrange beforehand if you will pay up-front or pay per day.

Ukraine's youth hostel culture is just taking off and with great success. The Ukrainian Youth Hostel Association (*www.hostel.org.ua*) offers great opportunities for cheap sleeps in Kiev and Lviv, and a few places in Crimea, all of which can be booked in advance on line. If you really want to delve deep into Ukraine's rich tapestry, try to stay at a monastery or convent. Most of these services are only available to true Orthodox pilgrims, but as long as you are willing to pitch in with the prayers and daily tasks, you will be welcome, sometimes for free, sometimes for a small donation.

Country homestays Inspired by foreign development projects, 'rural tourism' is evolving in certain regions of Ukraine (eg: the Carpathians and Crimea) allowing a bed-and-breakfast-style stay on rural farms for between US$5 and US$15 a night. Keep in mind that these programmes are in their earliest stages of development, so the experience can be raw but invigorating. If you want to see life on a farm and make friends with the people who live there, it should be encouraged. Information on green rural tourism is found in the appropriate chapters.

Camping Camping in Ukraine can be more institutionalised than travellers wanting to camp are used to. Often signs for camping will bring you to hotel-like accommodation with hotel-like prices. The only difference is that you are 15km from the city centre as opposed to five. In the Carpathians, most campsites include a *kolyba* (mountain hut), be it an authentic mountain hut or a fake that sells souvenirs; in Crimea, campsites tend to be near caves of some sort. If building a fire near prescribed sites, always use the metal rings provided. Camping in the wild should not pose a problem, but keep in mind the general mindset of suspicion towards foreigners (see page 78) and check beforehand to make sure you are not entering a restricted area. Otherwise, if you are staying in certain budget hotels, it will feel a lot like camping. Employing the services of a guide or adventure travel agency can be helpful in really getting out to Ukraine's wilder places. They also normally offer inexpensive camp-gear rentals so that you don't have to lug it all from home. The websites www.adventurecarpathians.com and www.mtcrimea.com are good places to start.

✖ EATING AND DRINKING

DRINK Drink is synonymous with alcohol in a country where drinking vodka is the national pastime and a cultural rite. All holidays, birthdays, weddings (and funerals) are celebrated with *horilka* (vodka). Business dealings are done over a vodka toast, and new friends are made to feel welcome with '100 grams'. In the dead of winter, a stiff swallow at breakfast keeps workers warm as they set off into the cold, but only when followed by frequent doses throughout the day. Without a doubt, vodka is imbibed in alarming quantities in Ukraine. Hetman is the most refined brand, but there are more brands of vodka than there are first names in Ukraine, and vodka takes up the most shelf space in food shops. *Samogon* is a homemade vodka brew and each family has its own special method for distilling it. Drink *samogon* (literally 'self-made fire') only if it is offered to you in someone's home or in a restaurant. The stuff sold in the open-air market is not regulated and is often laced with lethal ingredients (like anti-freeze) to increase its volume and potency. *Pyvo* (beer) is the most widespread 'soft' drink in the country, with varying degrees of alcohol content (up to 12%). Chernihiv and Slavutych are the most beloved Ukrainian brands, although travellers in Britain may be familiar with Obolon. Non-alcoholic beer is also widely available in Ukraine and more popular to drink than it is in the west. Foreigners take differently to Ukrainian wine, but if wine-tasting is your thing, there are a few Crimean and Tavrian wines with a good reputation, in particular those from Massandra. Georgian and Moldovan wines are next in popularity and Sovietsky champagne is uncorked at the slightest allusion to festivity.

The national non-alcoholic beverage is *kvas*, made from old black bread and sugar. It has a malted flavour and tastes best cold, homemade and bubbly. Ukrainians also bottle *kompot*, a light drink made from their home-grown fruit and boiled water. Cherry is the best. A very wide selection of fruit juice (pear, peach, plum, grape, etc) is available in restaurants, kiosks and shops.

Mineral water is always available, and it is a good idea to become acquainted with the Ukrainian springs and choose one you like. Evian and Volvic are sold in the fancier marketplaces, but locals will insist you benefit from the healing qualities of their own mineral water. Ukrainian brands tend to be a bit saltier than you may be used to. Mirhorod and Truskavets are some of the most well known, but if you want plain water with less mineral taste and no fizz, just ask for Bon Akva Negazova (the light blue bottles). They sell it everywhere.

Coffee (*kava* in Ukrainian, *kofye* in Russian) will be on offer in the humblest of circumstances; instant flavoured coffee seems to be the latest fad, along with chi-chi coffee houses that serve Italian espresso and double machiattos, etc. *Chai* (tea) is revered in Ukraine almost as much as it is in England, and is usually served with lemon and sugar. Having milk with your tea is a totally foreign concept and may be treated as an impossible request; bring your own milk powder if it is that important. Herbal teas (*chai iz trav*) make a nice hot drink, and for every ailment Ukrainian *babushki* have collected some twig or flower that will cure you. Every Ukrainian collects *lipa* from the flowering lime trees after which the month of July is named. The taste is both refreshing and bitter, and its positive effects are tried and true. Mint (*myata*) and camomile (*ramoshky*) are also popular. In homes, homemade jam or natural honey is served with tea to be stirred into the cup or else eaten plain by the spoonful.

Bread is life in Ukraine, and you'll find it an important staple on your travels, by itself or else with cheese, *smetana* (a type of sour cream) or sausage. Buy bread in the morning as all bakeries are sold out by early afternoon. Baton are the short white loaves that resemble oval French bread except much heavier. You can also find sourdough (square loaves) and all kinds of braided varieties for festivals. The traditional Ukrainian loaf is black bread (*chorni khlib*), made with buckwheat and rye flour and tasting slightly of vinegar. As a rule, one round loaf should weigh exactly one kilo. Black bread was the main staple of peasant diets far into the 20th century (and again during the last stretch of national poverty). The rallying cry and slogan of the first Russian revolution was 'Bread, Peace and Land' and the central role of wheat in Ukraine means that bread has always been a symbol of food, independence and wealth. Ukrainian tradition welcomes guests of honour in a ceremony of 'bread and salt' where a decorated loaf and a small bowl of salt are presented on an embroidered cloth. Originally, guests were meant to break off a piece, dip it in the salt, eat and nod. Nowadays, the loaf is usually spared for a later meal, so simply nod or bow in recognition of the ceremony.

FOOD Ukrainian cuisine is such an honest expression of the land itself, and a traditional meal can teach you more about Ukraine than any guided tour in a museum. The richness of natural ingredients comes from centuries of growing things in fertile soil and an intimate relationship with the woods and steppe. Poverty, shortages and political turmoil prevented store-bought goods from being used in recipes. The heavy workload of the peasant lifestyle, combined with the added stress of severe winters and repeated famine, meant food's main function was to fill empty bellies and keep bodies warm. This it does.

Borsch is the mainstay of the Ukrainian table and is probably the number one connotation foreigners make with Ukraine. It is not simply 'beetroot soup' as it tends to be known, but rather an important staple made with anything that grows in Ukraine. The bullion base is boiled with meat or vegetable stock, and then the various ingredients are slowly added one by one to bring out each flavour. Cabbage, potatoes, onions and dill are a must, and the beetroot is added to give colour. Everything else is thrown in at the discretion of the cook. A good bowl of *borsch* will consist of more vegetables than liquid and have a strong tangy aftertaste that hits the back of your throat. The proven rule of a good bowl of *borsch* is that your spoon won't sink when placed in the centre of the bowl. As the ultimate comfort food, *borsch* is boiled in massive proportions in Ukrainian homes and served for breakfast, lunch, and dinner. It always tastes better after a day in the pot. In restaurants, the soup will usually come with soft buns called *pampoushki* to dip into garlic sauce, or else the more common black bread and *smetana*, a rich and flavourful cream.

Varenniki are large stuffed dumplings and are considered *the* national dish of Ukraine. Generally, they are filled with potatoes and smothered in fried onions and *smetana*. They can also be filled with meat or farmer's cheese, and in spring they are stuffed with cherries, apples or strawberries and served for dessert. *Holubtsi* is another traditional dish of meat and rice rolled up in cabbage leaves and covered with a creamy tomato sauce. The name means 'little doves' and they are simply addictive. Technically from Siberia, *pelmeny* are meat-filled ravioli popularly served in cafés and eaten with vinegar and cream. Meat is still treated as a luxury even though most people can afford it now. The traditional Ukrainian recipe is to stew it in little clay pots with potatoes, freshly picked mushrooms and black pepper, then topped with cheese and baked. On menus, the dish is often called *zharkoye* or hot pots. Pork dishes tend to be the most popular. *Balyk* is smoked pork tenderloin with very little fat that is great for travellers, though it's not to be confused with *salo* – pure smoked pork fat carved right off a pig's back. Ukrainians love the stuff and there are many jokes about how wonderful a thing it is. (When a beautiful woman lands on his desert island, a stranded Russian calls to a stranded Ukrainian on another island telling him to come quickly, the thing he wants has just arrived. The Ukrainian jumps into the sea and swims furiously, gasping 'Salo, Salo!') The lard is usually cut in thick slices and served as a snack with bread or whole raw garlic cloves. As a foreign visitor, friends and strangers will shove *salo* upon you at any given chance, delighting in your repulsion. It seems as though the Ukrainian word for cholesterol (*kholesterol*) has only just come into common useage in the last six months or so. 'Trans-fat' is still lost in translation. Sausage tends to also be very fatty and usually eaten cold with bread, but somehow Ukrainian hot dogs just taste better than they do back home.

Chicken Kiev is a legitimate Ukrainian dish but ordered only by foreigners. Fish abounds on restaurant menus, but skip anything from Ukraine's polluted rivers. Also, do not order *osetrina* (sturgeon) or black caviar. Sturgeon is an endangered species, and both of these Russian delicacies kill its chances for survival (note that the United States has allowed the import of all caviar). Still, you'll see sturgeon on a lot of menus, and caviar is pretty much ubiquitous. Sardines and anchovies on toast are also popular party fare, and traditional drinking parties centre around dried and salty fish that you tear with your teeth and suck on.

What food you eat in Ukraine depends largely on the time of year you are travelling, although imported produce is quickly becoming the norm for the new élite. Generally, market tables are laden with fresh fruits and vegetables – sweet peppers, cucumbers and every form of squash imaginable. All summer long, Ukrainians work in their country plots and then preserve the food for the barren winter months. These bottles of fruit, relishes and pickles spruce up the potatoes and soured cabbage. If you don't pucker up when you bite into a Ukrainian pickle, then it isn't Ukrainian. Fistfuls of salt, home-grown garlic and hot peppers give the piquancy. Ukrainians also take their mushroom and berry collecting seriously, using them in all kinds of traditional dishes (mushrooms sold in the market are safe and tasty).

Vegetarians need not fear as abstaining from meat has been a necessity for Ukrainians during lean years, and is also a religious practice for faithful Orthodox believers fasting for Lent and other holy festivals. Keep in mind that eating and serving meat of some sort is perceived as a sign of status, while a lack of meat at a dinner table is a reluctant admission of poverty. If you do turn down meat offered by a host, make sure to sincerely compliment another part of the meal. Traditional vegetarian staples include *deruny* (potato pancakes), buckwheat (*kasha*) and various vegetable stews and soups. As Asian food becomes more popular, it is easier to order. Nearly every restaurant will offer a diverse salad menu. About half of the choices will have meat, so just make sure that the one you order is *byez myaso* (without meat). *Mlyntsi*, or *blyni* in Russian, are pancakes, sold like crêpes in outdoor stands with either jam or savoury meat and cheese. If you want truly good Ukrainian cuisine, do what you can to be invited into someone's home for a meal. No restaurants can imitate the cooking of a Ukrainian *babushka*.

Street food Food sold on the street is usually safe and very tasty (if it's steaming or smells fresh, it won't come back to haunt you). *Babuskhi* are always selling hot *pirozhki* filled with potatoes, seasoned cabbage, or meat, and you'll soon recognise their universal call and learn to buy a few of these stuffed buns for the road. Hot dogs, sunflower seeds, kebabs and poppy seed rolls are also common. Different kinds of breads and pastries are sold in different parts of the country, so go on and be adventurous. Odessa takes the prize for best street food, hands down. Modern street cuisine reflects the 'friendship of the nations' or multi-culturalism of Soviet days. Originally from Crimea and the Caucasus, *chebureki* pastries are stuffed with spicy meat and onions but their nourishing value comes from the heavy grease left on your fingers. In restaurants and homes you'll also taste *plov*, a rice and mutton dish from central Asia, and *adzhika*, a spicy Georgian sauce made of herbs and tiny peppers served with meat or potatoes.

It is a sin to travel without food in Ukraine and people you've just met may pack elaborate hampers for the next leg of your journey, even if it's only just a two-hour bus ride. Train and bus stations sell more and more candy and alcohol and fewer staples, but a stop at any food shop (*gastronom* or *produkty*) can stock you for a journey. Fresh fruit, yoghurt, cheese, sausage, rolls, juice and water make good reserves for train trips. For long hikes, Ukrainians normally pack canned goods, chocolate, bread and bottled water.

Thank goodness the fall of the Soviet economy did not end Ukraine's faithful sweet production. The brightly wrapped candies are sold in bulk on the street, in shops, and even from restaurant menus. Try *byelochka* (chipmunk), a delicious hazelnut cream chocolate, or the crunchy *metior*, little balls of nuts and honey covered with black chocolate. Ukrainians like ice cream year-round, and it is sold and eaten on the streets even on the most frigid of January days (if it doesn't melt in your mouth, chew it).

Restaurants and cafés Dining out is still a rare entertainment for the average Ukrainian, which explains the exotic flair of many restaurants, as well as the kind of food and presentation that is often available. Traditionally, Ukrainians prefer long banquets, interrupted by drawn-out toasts and frantic bouts of dancing. Because of the perceived luxury of eating out, you may find that you're one of the few patron(s) in an upscale restaurant, or that the only other guests are there for a wedding, birthday or business deal. As with everything, Kiev is the exception to the rule, with hundreds of restaurants to choose from, and for any budget.

An exuberant free market has promoted an explosion in themed dining that would put Disney World to shame. Folksy Ukrainian-themed restaurants are pervasive and range from the very cheesy (animatronic cows and singing Cossacks) to the more rustic and refined (waiters in hand-embroidered shirts, and authentic Ukrainian cuisine). Participants in organised tour groups tend to suffer from Ukrainian themed restaurant fatigue by the third or fourth day and wonder out loud where to find 'regular' restaurants. Alas, themed restaurants are generally 'in' so the alternatives offer little respite. Do as the 'Romans' do and enjoy the crazy glitz; you'll be amazed at what's out there. Overall, menus and themes are less than original as the country's restaurant developers chase one trend after another en masse. The late 1990s witnessed a nationwide discovery of Mexican food, followed by sushi (the must-have credential of any upmarket establishment), then Thai, and now believe it or not, 'British pub cuisine' (bangers 'n' mash in Dnepropetrovsk anyone?). The upshot of Ukraine's wave of migrant workers to Italy is the introduction of real Italian pizza in Ukraine and the regular charter flights to Egypt have resulted in a new appreciation for Middle Eastern cuisine.

It's becoming quite normal for restaurants to offer their menu in English, and it is always worth asking for one, even in a small café. Otherwise, never let the fact that you can't read the menu be a deterrent. Ask what something is, sound it out or take a stab in the dark. Restaurant menus will appear incredibly inexpensive at first glance, which they are. The budget-conscious can still eat elaborate dinners

Out of principle, fast-food or chain restaurants are not included in the dining recommendations for regional chapters, and yet they are fast becoming part of Ukraine's culinary landscape. While many bemoan the cultural degradation of such establishments (regional monotony, mediocre food, teenage employees, mass marketing), Ukrainians are eating it up, quite literally (meals for under US$1, jobs that pay, clean bathrooms, smoke-free dining, service with a smile).

Here's a quick guide to Ukraine's favourite fast-food franchises:

✘ **Potato House** www.potatohouse.biz. Baked potatoes, Tex-Mex grill, and fried things from US$1–2, all served under the guise of a native American, country and western theme.

✘ **Shvydko** www.shvydko.ua. The Ukrainian McDonald's translates as 'quick' and serves doughy machine-made *varenniki* in little plastic containers, watery *borsch* in a styrofoam tub, and even a hand-held version of Chicken Kiev. Thank goodness you can still get real *varenniki* for about the same price.

✘ **Dva Gusya** www.dvagusya.ua. 'Two Geese' is slightly more upmarket than Shvydko, with hearty, cafeteria-style Ukrainian food and a 3-course meal for under US$5.

✘ **Pan-Pizza** www.pan-pizza.com.ua. Quick Italian fare in more locations than you can count. Personal pizzas, pasta, and meat dishes for about US$5 pp.

✘ **Celentano** www.pizza-celentano.com. Make your own pizza for under US$5. Surprisingly tasty and a popular student hangout in any Ukrainian city.

for practically nothing; however, the accepted restaurant tactic is for bills to add up quickly. Old-fashioned (Soviet-era) restaurants usually state the price of a food next to its allotted quantity (in grams) – you pay separately for any extras, and everything is extra, including the sauce. Also, you may often find that the menu is several dozen pages long, but when you start ordering you are told that everything you want is unavailable. In such a case, find out what the kitchen is prepared to make or ask about the house specialities (*firmeny blyuda*). Also, quite a few restaurants will offer a set, three-course *beezness lanch* from the hours of 12.00 to 3.00 for a very reasonable price. A new series of discount restaurant cards have emerged, offering the holder an automatic 10% discount at selected restaurants. For more information, check out **Kozyrna karta** (*www.2k.com.ua*) and **Mirovaya karta** (*www.kartamir.com.ua*). If you are staying in Ukraine for a good while, it's a smart investment.

The best way to judge a restaurant is by the price of a bowl of *borsch*, a universal common denominator in Ukraine. US$1–2 should be standard. Anything more than US$3 means the restaurant is upmarket or downright pretentious and if it costs below one dollar, the general food standard may be lower than your stomach can handle. Travellers with small pockets or the simply curious can get a hearty and affordable hot meal at the *stolovaya* (cafeterias). If you are afraid of getting a bug, stick to hot staples like *borsch* and avoid the cold fried breaded bits of meat.

There exists no traditional concept of breakfast and Ukrainians eat much the same food in the morning as they do for lunch and dinner, only less of it. Hotels generally offer a 'Swedish table' in the spirit of a smorgasbord with smoked meats or sausage, cheese, cereals, yoghurt, bread, coffee and tea. In recent years, European-style cafés have become popular, with continental-style coffee and croissants.

THE BANYA

Ancestral tradition and a lack of hot water helped to make public bathing a favoured pastime in Ukraine and a cultural institution. A sauna is a dry sweat-bath of the Finnish variety, usually accompanied by a small pool of freezing water for intermittent dips followed by much yelping. The Russian *banya* is more traditional in Ukraine, and resembles a Turkish bath. A stone oven in the *parilka* generates incredibly hot steam and people stand or lie down on the varied levels. Once your body is running with sweat, bunches of lime, birch or oak branches (depending on what effect you want) are used to whip and beat you until the green gel of broken leaves, bark and dead skin cells stands out against your red back. Traditionally you are supposed to scream for more (*yescho!*) until you almost pass out. Stepping out of the *parilka*, you should immediately immerse yourself in cold water, rest a bit, and then go back for more. Typically, you repeat the process six or seven times over the space of a few hours. Going to the *banya* also includes taking a series of showers at various temperatures, scrubbing yourself with soap, getting a massage, shaving, drinking lots of fluids (non-alcoholic) and engaging in vigorous conversation with the lads (or the girls). The experience is very communal, not least because people must partner up to beat each other. You emerge feeling clean inside and out, revived and ready to take on anything. In winter, regular visits to the *banya* will prevent catching colds.

Entrance normally costs less than US$10, although private rentals cost much more. The experience is meant to last several long hours, if not the whole day. You'll be given a white sheet as a wrap, and you can buy *veniki* (branches) there. Traditionally, the ritual is performed nude, hence men and women visit on separate days or there are two separate sections. That's changing now that many *banya* are affiliated with hotels where swimsuits are worn. Most hotels will also have a Finnish sauna, some of which are rented out privately by the hour. In Ukraine's large cosmopolitan cities, authentic communal baths have given way to élite or tawdry private clubs, but in the outskirts, people still follow a weekly tradition of going to the *banya*. Simply ask around or get your friends to take you to the real thing.

Here are a few of the more traditional baths in the capital, Kiev:

Solomenskye Bany (Solomon's Baths) Urytskovo 38; ☎ 044 244 0198. Communal and historic. *Open 09.00–22.00, closed Mon.*
Troitskye Bany (Trinity Baths) Krasnoarmeiskaya 66; ☎ 044 227 4068. Private and luxurious. *Open 10.00–22.00.*
Tsentralnye Torgovye Bany (Central Trade Baths) Malaya Zhytomyrskaya 3; ☎ 044 228 0378. Huge, gritty and famous, right off of the Maidan Nezalezhnosti. *Open 08.00–22.00, closed Mon.*

☕ ARTS AND ENTERTAINMENT

The Ukrainians are passionate about art in all its forms (theatre, dance, music, painting, etc) and right now, the entire country seems overtaken with a creative buzz that appears limitless in its outreach. Shop window displays, television commercials, fashion, food, theatre, music, graphics – everything seems to be touched by art and experimentation.

Nobody should go to Ukraine without taking in a performance at the opera or ballet. Tickets are incredibly cheap (a private box in the Kiev Opera will cost under US$10), whereas the show's quality is always outstanding. The long-standing traditions of Russian and Ukrainian ballet have not faltered and many a traveller who thinks ballet is not his/her 'thing' gains a new fascination with dance. Opera is just as invigorating, and most theatres will rotate a very large repertoire over the course of the season.

Even if you don't understand what a play is about, there is something about watching Chekhov performed in the country where he wrote. Many of the smallest towns will have a local theatre troupe that is quite talented. Also, part of

Kodak Express and other camera shops are on the high streets in even the smallest of Ukrainian cities, so getting film developed anywhere quickly is not a problem. City camera shops also sell quality digital equipment in case you lose a lens, but it's all a lot about double the cost of what you find back home, the exception being batteries and flash (memory) cards, which are readily available. Digital cameras are hot property, so take extra precautions in keeping yours close. Sadly, the old Soviet photographic implements are gone for the most part, meaning you can no longer buy or develop the ultra-grainy black and white film. In fact, generic 400 ISO colour film is all you'll find. Slide film, unusual speeds or any form of black and white are still almost impossible to buy in Ukraine. Photographers should remember that brilliant white snows and the slant of winter light can drastically affect the exposure. Pay close attention when spot metering off of a subject's face, or, if you are simply taking landscape pictures, then take care to compenssate by increasing the film exposure value.

Many Ukrainians still cannot afford cameras and have very few pictures of themselves or their families. Random strangers generally have no concerns about having their picture being taken, but you should be sensitive and ask permission first. Offering to take pictures, getting their address and then sending or emailing them your shots is a kind gesture. Keep your word. Also, you'll find that the minute you put an adult in front of a camera, their smile will fall into a serious grimace, presenting the ever-solemn 'Soviet passport' face. If you want to get someone to smile, hold the camera and aim, but talk to them for a long while until they do smile, or pretend you've already taken it, say vsyo (that's all), and when they smile in relief, click the shutter. The trick doesn't work so well with digital since they will usually demand to see the picture afterwards, but by then it will be too late anyway!

Also bear in mind that under-funded churches, museums and tourist sites supplement their revenue by charging photographers per frame shot. This can cost from US$1 to US$5 and seems slightly ridiculous, especially when the lighting is so bad. Even so, don't try to get away without paying. They will follow you. Although this is really not an issue any more, don't run around taking pictures of military subjects (tanks or marching soldiers) unless there's a parade. You'll only appear suspicious. Overall, enjoy all the great subject matter that's out there. As of yet, Ukraine still lacks a strong and honest photographic narrative in the world's eye. Hopefully you can help change that.

the fun is watching all the families and young children who come dressed up for an affordable night out. Ukrainians of all ages enjoy even the most serious of plays, and to be seen at the theatre is a sign of one's cultural prestige. To complete the experience, eat canapés during the intermission, bring flowers for the ballerinas and shout 'bravo' louder than anyone else. Ukraine's experimental theatre is also invariably spectacular.

In larger cities there's always an opportunity to experience live music, be it Ukrainian folk songs, classical, or showy rock bands. Ukraine's national philharmonic (*www.filarmonia.com.ua*) is definitely worth catching, as is their national folk choir (Dumka), both of which tour around the country. Folk bands, organ recitals and single-singer concerts are always available. Most upscale restaurants will also offer live music in the evenings or on weekends, which is either somewhat pleasant or totally annoying. Ukraine's modern and pop music scene is a lot of fun, and whether or not you want to participate, the music will reach your ears in a number of ways.

Films are always badly dubbed into Ukrainian or Russian, with the very rare exception of a Russian film. Cinemas can be found in any town, and watching movies is cheap. Of late, Ukrainian filmmakers have been turning out some epic monuments of historical fiction dealing with Ukraine's more controversial heroes. Several film festivals also take place throughout Ukraine, the most famous of which is Molodist (*www.molodist.com*), held in Kiev in the autumn and dedicated to young Ukrainian and East European filmmakers. Most viewers come away vastly impressed.

Ukraine's visual artists are also busy expressing themselves, and in larger cities it pays to check out some of the private (and public galleries) selling paintings, sculptures and photography. Incredible talent and undiscovered names have made cities like Kiev and Lviv centres for avant-garde art collectors.

An inner appreciation for high culture doesn't prevent a more depressing cultural void from spreading widely. Lowbrow mafia mores are still highly influential: casinos and slot machines have invaded the country like cockroaches, striptease joints and prostitution are commonly advertised, and all the kids spend their free time blowing each other up on computer screens. Hopefully this is just a phase.

MUSEUMS The majority of Ukrainian museums are run by pleasant ladies and old men who normally did some related degree at a Soviet university and now earn kopecks managing the displays. Ask a question and you'll be astounded by the knowledge you gain. You'll find that the same authoritarian attitude about travel exists within museums and you'll be vehemently commanded where to go and what to look at. Free wandering is a no-no and if you skip a room or go in the 'wrong' direction you will face the wrath of a *babushka*. Because of a lack of money, there is rarely any heat inside museums and the attendants will not turn on the lights until you walk into a room. The phenomenon of lights switching on and off according to your movements feels rather empowering.

Nearly every town has a natural history museum that tells the socialist version of the history of the town from prehistoric times to the revolution and on to the Soviet era with displays on local achievements in agriculture and industry, as well as natural history, local dress and regional arts and crafts. Many people write these off as derelict and anachronistic (which they are), but a deeper look is always quite entertaining and educational. Some museum attendants will be selling their own souvenirs or museum booklets which help to supplement their meagre incomes. Smaller towns rarely get foreign guests, so you may be asked to sign a guest book with your impressions of their museum.

A new wave of original private museums is popping up in some of the larger cities, with more user-friendly displays, the best example of which is the Museum of One Street in Kiev (see page 146).

SHOPPING

Capitalism conquers and you can buy absolutely anything in Ukraine. That's quite a statement seeing that not so long ago, many shops were empty. Posh shopping centres now grace the streets and underground passages of Kiev where people buy things like crocodile handbags and US$2,000 shoes. In smaller towns, you will still have no difficulty finding whatever you need in any number of local shops. At the other end of Ukraine's economic spectrum are grannies who sell shoelaces or sunflower seeds on the street. During the early transition years, the commerce that was not conducted on the street corner was based in temporary metal kiosks, which you still see in residential neighbourhoods. Everything that's for sale will be

Travelling is always a two-way experience, where visitor and visited make all sorts of exchanges, both intended and subconscious. As you take in all that Ukraine offers, consider how your presence affects this country and what you can give back to it during your travels, as well as after you have returned home. Just being in Ukraine and spending money at local businesses helps, even if it is only sunflower seeds from a *babushka*. And yet, there are always opportunities to do more to help. In the regional chapters I have listed certain opportunities where travellers can actively participate in local projects and offer their support. I also ask that you please contact me with your experiences and any future suggestions of organisations or means for giving something back (see page IV for contact details).

At present, one of the most crucial nationwide efforts is being led by **Ukraine 3000**, a foundation which manages a wide variety of charity and community programmes to improve the future of Ukraine and to benefit the daily lives of its citizens, particularly its children. The foundation was established in 2001 and is currently chaired by first lady of Ukraine, Kateryna Yuschenko. Of the many initiatives already launched, the foundation's Hospital-to-hospital programme has seen particular success in matching up foreign hospitals with Ukrainian hospitals to improve techniques, resources and care. Get in touch and see how you can help (*Ukraine 3000 Foundation, Borychiv Tik 22A, Kiev;* \ *044 467 6780;* f *044 467 6783;* e *info@ukraine3000.org.ua; www.ukraine3000.org.ua*).

hung in the window so you only have to point and pay. You can still buy magazines, drinks and snacks in kiosks, but most have been phased out in favour of normal shops. Large-scale food supermarkets are becoming part of the regular shopping culture, while the traditional Ukrainian *rynok* (market) should be a part of the travel experience: taste-testing honey or cream on your knuckle, tumbling through rutabagas and sniffing smoked chickens. Don't start bartering for something simply because it's an outdoor market. Fixed pricing is more and more regular in Ukraine and the tag will usually tell you how much it costs. Food is the exception, and if you are indecisive, you may be offered a discount, or you can request a deal.

SOUVENIRS With the new rise in tourism comes the advent of mass-produced 'Ukrainian' goods, many of which are not Ukrainian at all. Everyone thinks first of the *matryoshka* doll, the wooden personage inside another inside another inside … These days, *matryoshka* have turned into a comic venture, and are often painted with the faces of foreign politicians, but traditional dolls are painted with family faces and flowery designs (there should always be an odd number). Ukraine's traditional hand-embroidered clothes – *narushniki* – should be made of long white linen or cotton with ornate stitching on the ends. Those in the know can tell the difference between machine-spun and authentic hand designs. Red, brown, orange, yellow, black and blue are traditional colours, although this varies in some regions. *Petrikivka* is the pure form of Ukrainian folk painting where bright brushstrokes depict ornate bright flowers or fairy-tale themes on a black lacquered surface, usually on a bowl, platter, round jewellery box or wooden egg. Traditional *petrikivka* is beautiful, reflecting repeating patterns of natural design (feathers, leaves and flower petals). Alas, much of what's for sale is a cheap imitation. Carved woodcraft is also genuinely Ukrainian: combs, ornate spoons, pipes, plates and bowls. Pottery is also quite Ukrainian, the most traditional of which is the fragile and rustic-looking charcoal-black version, made into bowls, candlesticks, pots, pitchers and dishes. Such black pottery is one of the most ancient art forms in

Ukraine, originating in the west of the country and being fired by hand outdoors. Small red clay pots are very authentic and are used in cooking. Religious **icons** are also very authentic and some very beautiful modern examples can be purchased at most churches. Just remember that it is illegal to export any antique icons. Check the date and be sure your purchase is legal. Ukraine enforces very strict laws about retaining national art treasures, historic coins and medals. Make sure and ask the buyer if you will be allowed to take your purchase outside of the country, as they are somewhat responsible under the law. Old Soviet curios are also a common sight in antique and souvenir stands. Silverware, statuettes, and cultural icons of the Stalinist era are particularly hot property. A lot of Soviet military leftovers are also for sale, but only about half of it is real. The stuff in the markets emblazoned with red stars is all made in China.

Buying fur should be discouraged all round; however, if you really must have that Russian fur coat or *shapka* (cap), choose wisely as buying fox, beaver, lynx or sable will further deplete endangered species. Ukraine's (and Russia's) red and silver fox population is slowly disappearing due to unregulated trapping for the cash foreigners will spend. Know what you are buying: you can always find *shapkas* made of farmed rabbit and mink, or even dog. Fewer and fewer Ukrainians are wearing the traditional fur hats as it's perceived as old-fashioned among the younger generation.

C MEDIA AND COMMUNICATIONS

NEWSPAPERS, MAGAZINES AND TELEVISION Ukraine's media reflect a highly active civil society and a nation that likes to read. There's also quite a lot out there in English. In Kiev, the English-language magazine *What's On* (*www.whatson-kiev.com*) details everything that's happening in the city that week, much like TimeOut in London or New York. Nearly every large city in Ukraine also has a glossy magazine named *Afisha* (*www.afisha.ua*) which details the local goings-on for that week with lists of restaurants and entertainment. *Welcome to Ukraine* (*www.wumag.kiev.ua*) magazine is a unique monthly, English-language travel magazine with well-written stories and artistic photography focusing entirely on Ukrainian destinations and local culture and history. The publication is sold in most bookshops in Kiev. In-flight magazines are also good for getting up-to-date information on travel to Ukraine: *Meridian* (Aerosvit) and *Panorama* (Ukraine International Airline) are among the best. Practically every magazine available in the West is on the shelves in Ukraine, both in English and in translation.

In Kiev, there are more newspapers than there are political parties. They range from shameful tabloids to highbrow publications with highly intellectual news analyses. The *Kiev Post* (*www.kyivpost.com*) rules supreme as the most balanced, English-language newspaper. *Correspondent* (*www.korespondent.net*) is the *Newsweek* of Ukraine, and *Zerkalo Nedeli* (*www.mirror-weekly.com*) is offered online in English, Ukrainian and Russian.

Ukraine's television is constantly embroiled in scandal and mud-slinging over which oligarch owns which channel. Channel 5 (*www.5tv.com.ua*) was the channel that broadcast the original Orange Revolution and is still riding high on the street cred this afforded. Another very popular news channel is 1+1 (*www.1plus1.net*).

TELEPHONE Ukraine's country code is 38; a zero is included with the city code. Public pay phones only take electronic cards which can be purchased at any post office, tobacco shop or kiosk, normally in amounts of 20, 50 or 100UAH. Dialling landlines is incredibly cheap, but dialling mobile phones will chew up your minutes quickly. Most hotels will let you make international phone calls from your room, but tend to charge a fair amount (at least US$2 a minute to Britain and Europe, US$1 to USA and Canada). Most post offices will also have a series of international phone booths, where you pay a deposit, make a phone call at regular rates and then retrieve your balance. Some international phone cards are now sold in big cities, but the least expensive way to call internationally is to find any internet café that offers web phone access. Such phone shops are very popular, remarkably cheap and the connection is far clearer.

To call within Ukraine, dial 8 (for long distance), then the city code (eg: 044 for Kiev) and then the number. In this book, all phone numbers are listed with their city codes (if you are dialling from within the same city, drop the first group of numbers). When calling internationally, dial 8, wait for the tone, then dial 10, followed by the country code, city code and so on. Sometimes it takes a few tries.

Mobile phones make a lot of sense in Ukraine, and if you're going to be in the country even for more than a week or so, and need to make calls, you might consider buying a chip to use in your own phone. You can buy them for relatively little (under US$20) in any phone shop you see. Try Kyivstar (*www.kyivstar.net*) or UMC (*www.umc.ua*).

POST Traditionally, the *poshta* (post office) was for paying electricity bills and receiving pensions. Travellers can get confused by the dozens of queues and windows. If you want to buy stamps and mail a letter, go to the window with all the colourful envelopes and cards. Always send letters *avia* (airmail). Ukraine now addresses letters in the standard European fashion (name, address, city and postcode, country). The sender's address goes in the upper left corner and the recipient's in the middle. Note that postcards can be sent as open cards only within Ukraine; if you are sending them internationally you must put them inside a red-and-blue-striped airmail envelope with a stamp on the outside. Receiving letters in Ukraine by *poste restante* has become a less secure option in recent years, but is still available to those who ask. Simply look up the postal code and post office of the city that you want to receive mail in (*www.poshta.com.ua*). Retrieval can sometimes be a bit of a hassle if your name is not in Cyrillic. If you are going to be in the country for a while, getting a post office box is cheap and reliable. Otherwise, it's better to use email on your travels. Letters from Ukraine to Europe take around one week to arrive and to North America up to two weeks.

In addition to letters, stamps, cards and post office boxes, most Ukrainian post offices now offer internet and telecommunications services, including domestic and international calls.

PARCELS Every big global shipping corporation has an office in Ukraine these days, typically in Kiev and in a surprising number of regional cities. Ask at your hotel or check the local yellow pages. Check with DHL (*www.dhl.com.ua*), FedEx (*www.fedex.com/ua*), TNT (*www.tnt.com*) and UPS (*www.ups.com*) for their local office listings. Inside Ukraine, you can send parcels on trains or buses for very small fees. The process is a lot more secure than it sounds, as long as you have someone picking it up at the receiving station. Ask at the train station, or approach the Avtolux and Gunsel bus companies about sending a package.

INTERNET Ukraine's such a wired country, you should never have to worry about not having access to the internet. Several hotels have installed wi-fi and Ethernet systems and even some of the McDonald's in Ukraine offer wi-fi. In big cities, you'll have your pick of internet clubs and cafés to choose from, but you may have to contend with pre-teens playing blood-splattering video games. Most are either underground in basement properties, or up on the second floor. Just follow the signs for **интернет**. Attendants tend to be younger, and many of them speak some English and can get you set up. In very small towns, just find the central post office, which almost always has at least one computer available for public use. In both internet clubs and post offices, charges range from US$1 to US$2 per hour. Cyrillic letters are printed beneath the Latin letters of the QWERTY keyboard, and you can change the typing language by clicking the language prompt at the bottom right-hand corner of the screen. I've listed a few internet locations in Kiev (see page 139), but most cities have so many clubs as to render separate listings pointless.

BUSINESS

Business hours are normally 09.00 to 18.00 with a lunch break between 13.00 and 14.00. That said, you'll find many places are open until very late, and many food shops, hotels and stations are open 24 hours. Museums and other tourist spots usually have one or two 'days off' when they are closed. Check before you go somewhere.

Whole separate guides are written on how to do business properly in Ukraine, but the only thing they agree on is that it's quite a different experience to back home. Even the word 'business' has its own separate connotations in Ukraine (historically quite negative and involving sharp objects). In Ukraine's highly corrupt past, honouring contracts was quite arbitrary, but suddenly, being an honoured businessman has new prestige and anti-corruption is in. A vigorous free press is helping the transformation, as is the lure of the Ukrainian market and the 50 million buyers awaiting new products. Ukrainians are also hungry for foreign investment and eager to show off their business savvy and their appreciation for good marketing. If everyone in Los Angeles is secretly working on a screenplay, in Kiev it's a business plan. MBAs are hot property, business books are bestsellers and entrepreneurship is cool.

In actuality, business culture is not so different in Ukraine. There's the question of cultural nuance followed by very long dinners and displays of mutual admiration. In certain fields, you'll find the 'stab you in the back before you stab me' vibe is still a reality. But overall, that culture of apprehension is giving way to a more serious breed of Ukrainians who are well travelled, speak foreign languages, have a very global outlook, strong technical educations and an appreciation for the bigger game.

TRAVELLING WITH CHILDREN IN UKRAINE

I have yet to meet a child who has travelled to Ukraine and not loved the experience. On the flip side, parents may feel apprehensive due to fears about hygiene, safety or their own sanity in coping with a child on the road in a strange new country. Yet these days, conditions in Ukraine have improved to the point that it's a pity to leave a child behind and have them miss out on such a rich adventure. First off, children travel at half the cost in Ukraine with significant discounts for museums, trains, planes and entertainment. Furthermore, kids often pick up the Cyrillic alphabet a lot quicker than their parents and will learn to speak conversational Russian and Ukrainian just by meeting other children their own age. Finally, travelling with a young child in Ukraine can be a pass-key to goodwill and kind treatment by all you encounter.

It always pays to ask what discounts are available to children and families. Most medium to upscale hotels will allow an additional person in a double room for a small fee (US$5–10). Slightly larger 'family rooms' will normally have the option

During the Soviet era, children were revered as the bright socialist future and thus somewhat coddled into a prolonged state of innocence. Such government policies evolved into some wonderful public services and entertainment programmes designed specifically for children, many of which have held over to the current era. The following amusements can be found in almost every major city in Ukraine.

CHILDREN'S PARKS In addition to the requisite botanical garden, Shevchenko statue or war memorial, almost every large Ukrainian city boasts a park dedicated solely to children. The colourful play areas vary widely in their state of repair but in the summer they may have functioning rides, such as small trains, Ferris wheels, etc. In addition to the many children that swarm the park, there will normally be a team of photographers with live animals (donkeys, monkeys), costumes or child-sized props who will take your picture for a price, or allow you to take your own, also for a price.

THE CIRCUS The Russian **цирк** (*tsyrk*) tradition is centuries old, and year-round circuses perform in practically all the major cities. Smaller towns will almost always have a travelling circus passing through. Alas, there is no tent – most cities have a permanent indoor stadium built exclusively for the circus. The cost of tickets to these shows is negligible, while the quality of entertainment is superb. Come prepared for dancing bears, slinky contortionists, death-defying acrobats and unfunny clowns.

ZOOS Ukraine's three best zoos are located in Kiev, Kharkiv and Mikolayiv. Be warned that standards of animal maintenance tend to be much lower compared with those back home, and the experience can sometimes be more troubling than entertaining for children (and their parents). Even so, if a child suffers from sightseeing fatigue, the zoos are worth checking out. The wildlife park Askania Nova (see page 295) is another attractive option if you plan on being in the south.

PUPPET THEATRES A great Ukrainian tradition lives on in the fanciful puppet theatres where traditional fairy tales are acted out in elaborate shows using custom-built *kukly* (meaning dolls or puppets). Schedules vary from town to town, but the best shows normally run in the early afternoons on weekends and run for an hour or so. Ask for the *kuklny teatr* and try to buy tickets a day or two before as the theatres typically get packed with energetic young children. The theatres in Kharkiv and Lviv are both award winners, but you should be able to find a good show almost anywhere.

MILK BARS AND KIDDY CAFÉS Designed expressly for the impressionable young Soviet child, Ukraine's milk bars actually do serve milk, as well as milkshakes, fruit juices, ice cream, cakes, pastries and tea. The walls are usually painted with brightly colourful murals and there is normally some form of entertainment offered. Going to the milk bar was once a grand event, with parents dressing up their children in polished shoes or giant hair bows and sending them off with a jingly coin purse and the command to have fun. The trend is lessening as many milk bars are slowly transforming into cafés that serve lunches and cater to both children and adults. Ask around or search for shops and cafés titled **детския харчувания** (*detskye kharchuvaniya*).

Travelling in Ukraine **TRAVELLING WITH CHILDREN IN UKRAINE**

5

of a fold-out sofa bed that sleeps two, and a few hotels have begun the practice of adjoining rooms. If travelling with several children together, you may prefer the three and four single beds per room, which can be a real bargain. Many upscale hotels will offer babysitting services on-site, with a separate room allotted for full-time childcare. In Crimea and other touristy areas of the country, many of the resorts and hotels will have day programmes for children or recreation camps.

Almost every new restaurant in Ukraine carries a children's menu for those under 12, often in English. Children are often more prone to the ill effects of new germs and bacteria, so it pays to be extra diligent with their hygiene. Be religious about giving them only bottled water to drink and only from bottles on which you have broken the seal yourself. This includes when they are rinsing out their mouth or brushing their teeth. Carrying individual-sized bottles of hand sanitiser with you is a good idea – help your children get into the habit of sanitising their hands before every meal and after using the toilet. For young children and toddlers, it's also a good idea to bring along a children's detachable plastic toilet seat (sold in department stores), which can facilitate the use of the country's more dreadful toilets, particularly those of the 'hole-in-the-ground' variety or on trains. For infants, you can buy disposable diapers/nappies in almost any major shop in Ukraine (just say 'Pampers' with a Russian accent).

Stating the obvious, children that travel should be covered by good medical insurance. In case of emergency, there are several good private hospitals and clinics in Ukraine that can address children's needs with quality, high-tech care; however, your insurance will give you peace of mind and far more options if needed.

Even the most astute parents end up swearing by portable DVD players as blessed tools of diversion, especially for very long train and road trips. If you give in to the temptation, bring along a healthy collection of DVDs, as those in Ukraine are either pirated or fall into a different programmatic zone (or both). That said, there is plenty in Ukraine to wow even the most attention-deficient child.

Part Two

THE GUIDE

6

Kiev
Київ

First impressions count – Ukraine's capital and largest city tends to wow its visitors with a winning display of stateliness and energy. Truly, Kiev's freeform skyline is one of a kind: towering granite buildings along Khreschatyk, colourful cathedrals with golden domes, the glories of Byzantium and Stalinism side by side, burgeoning shopping centres beneath back-lit advertisements and the flashy commotion of no-holds-barred, 24-hour business. And all of this rising up from the midst of an ancient forest, with the sprawling hilltops of the city sloping down to the wide channel of the timeless Dnepr and its islands. Flowering chestnut trees line the streets and riverbanks for half of the year, and during this time no other city could seem so green and full. Indeed, this is a beautiful city. Despite a growing population of over three million, Kiev feels very natural, and for now, it seems that everything that can happen, is happening here.

Kiev occupies a strange mental space in the world's mind: those who know the city feel an intense affection for the place; those who don't still associate it with a revolutionary zeal, along with a vague reference to pop culture. Otherwise, 'Kiev' denotes a distant Eastern capital or else a buttery piece of chicken. Alas, few songs or stories romanticise Kiev (in English, yet) and so most people still hark back to Soviet recollections when Kiev completed the triad of great Slavic capitals – placed third after St Petersburg and Moscow. Sadly, too many travellers still 'do' Kiev as an add-on, as if it were the optional dessert after Russia's meal. They soon discover that Kiev has experienced a far more tasteful resurrection than the other two cities, and today the Ukrainian capital stands alone as the most ancient and least politicised of the three.

In fact, while Kiev boasts a millennial history of reinventing itself, the Orange Revolution gave the city cause to undergo yet another makeover, so that even the most sophisticated *Kievlyanini* have a tough time keeping up with the changes. Travellers should enjoy the sheer hubbub and miscellany of the moment.

Targeted wandering should be your mantra. There is the Kiev of monuments and vistas, churches and statues – all of which fits nicely into a bus tour or a few days of walking. Then there is Kiev the new Ukrainian capital – a realm of power and change that has welcomed a whole new wave of foreign visitors. Last, there is the *real* Kiev – composed of several highly individualised neighbourhoods, some of which are over a thousand years old, others of the brick-and-mortar variety just now reaching their thirties, and those which are still under construction. Each and every quarter preserves its very own personality, defined over the years by who has lived (and died) there and what has happened on those streets.

Kiev is still the easiest city to travel to in Ukraine and the capital has become the number one tourist destination in the country. For organised group tours, Kiev is included on almost every itinerary, even if it seems out of the way or out of context with the subject of the visit. For individuals, Kiev should be a priority – there is an amazing amount to see and do in this city and it would be a pity to come all this

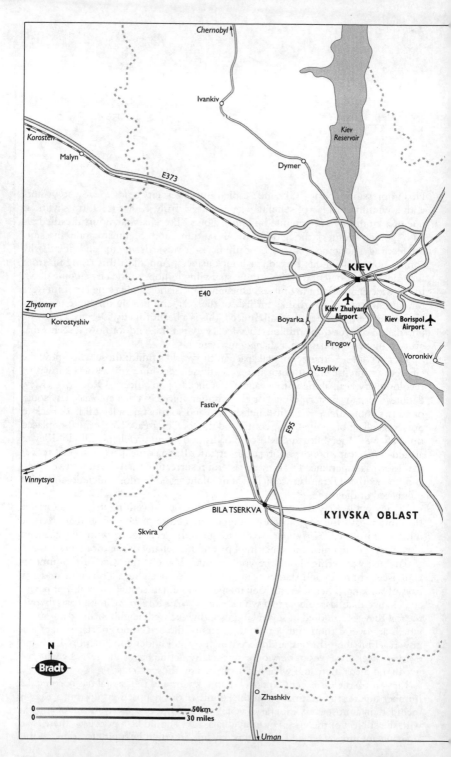

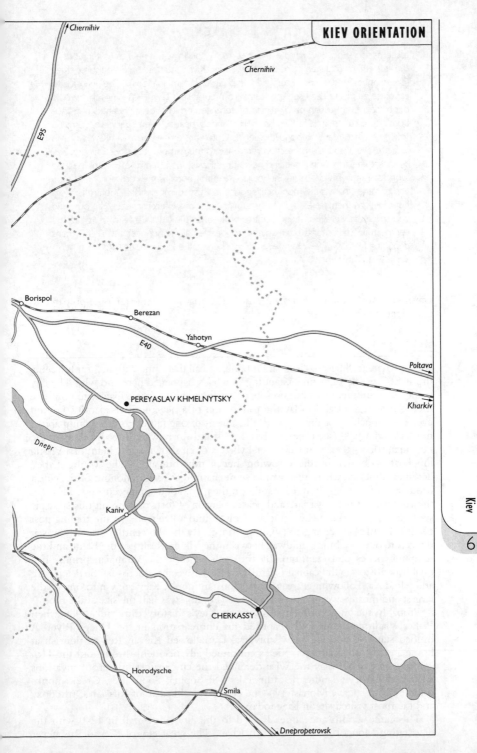

way and miss the place Ukrainians enjoy showing off the most. Come prepared to participate in the fray.

HISTORY

Kiev is where it all began – Russia, Ukraine, and all that came with it. Simply 'seeing the sights' reveals a fair understanding of what's happened here and why. The city confesses a turbulent past but uses its colourful and impressive history to reinforce the right to respect and to lay the foundation of a new, positive identity. Legend presents a touching beginning with the advent of one family to these uninhabited hills around AD560 (see page 15). Kyi, Schek and Koriv were three brothers of the Polianian tribe – their younger sister Lybed is often shown at the helm of a Viking longboat with her brothers rowing her gently onwards. The young Lybed designated the site where they would settle, naming it Kyiv in honour of the eldest brother. Today, three hills in Kiev still bear the names of its first occupants. Through the centuries of tribal warfare and peace, a group of forts rose up on this strategic spot on the Dnepr and Kiev quickly evolved into a lively and secure trading post eventually ruled by Varangian (Viking) princes. By the 9th century AD, Kiev was at the centre of everything – midway between the Viking Realm of the Baltic and the tempting riches of Byzantium. By the 10th century, the Varangian princes had established Kiev as the capital of all the lands between modern-day St Petersburg and Moldova. Following a treaty with Constantinople, Kiev grew into one of the largest and most powerful cities in Europe (London was half the size at the time).

Probably the most influential event in Kiev's history came in AD988 when Prince Vladimir dramatically baptised his entire nation in the Dnepr River. A unified state religion and new universal law allowed Kievan Rus to flourish at home and abroad, leading to Kiev's continued advancement throughout the 11th century: Prince Yaroslav the Wise defended the city against numerous invasions and erected Kiev's landmark cathedral of St Sophia. Soon after, Greek monks founded Kiev's Cave Monastery – the ecclesiastical centre of Russian Orthodoxy and the most visited site in Kiev today.

This same wealth and fame also led to the city's downfall in 1240 with the devastating Mongol invasion of Batu Khan. The great city of Kievan Rus never fully recovered, and was eventually annexed to the Lithuanian principality in 1362. At the beginning of the 15th century, Lithuania granted Kiev the Magdeburg Law, a Germanic legal code which granted autonomy to prominent cities. Under self-rule, Kiev benefited from a strong urban development and vibrant cosmopolitanism similar to the cities of western Ukraine, but alas, the Mongol invasion of 1482 cut the city down once more.

Poland began ruling Kiev after the Union of Lublin in 1569, which changed the demographic of the city with a large influx of Poles and Jews. Meanwhile, the age of the Ukrainian Cossacks was coming into full force, and the towns just outside Kiev began to witness periodic uprisings against the Polish nobility. Cossack Pyotr Sahaydachny is remembered for supporting the Ukrainian and Orthodox community in Kiev, all the while keeping peace with Poland, but it was the Cossack *hetman* Bohdan Khmelnytsky who finally drove the Poles out of the city in 1648. The moment of freedom was short-lived for Kiev's inhabitants, since Khmelnytsky signed the Pereyaslav Agreement in 1654 and the city immediately fell under the jurisdiction of Russia. At first Moscow's influence was minimal, a fact attributed to Cossack *hetman* Ivan Mazepa who had formed strong ties with Russia but guarded the city's autonomy. Mazepa funded a plethora of constructions in Kiev (including the walls and towers of the Pechersky Lavra) and donated the rest of his wealth to the Kiev Academy.

Kiev's Russian fate was settled at the Battle of Poltava in 1709 when Tsar Peter I beat Mazepa and his Swedish allies, ending any hopes of Ukrainian autonomy. The culture and language of St Petersburg were the signs of the new élite and Russians were added to Kiev's diverse population. When Russia took control over 'right bank' Ukraine in 1793, Kiev was no longer the peripheral city of other empires, but a central metropolis, albeit in 'Little Russia'. The Magdeburg Law was revoked only in 1835 and the autocratic government introduced the centralised legal system. Despite present-day anti-Russian sentiments, the period of Russian rule during the 18th and 19th centuries turned Kiev into a beautiful and booming modern city. Ukraine's sugar trade was the first of many large industries to be based in Kiev, and the fever of industrialisation spread quickly. In 1900, the population had reached 250,000; ten years later, it had doubled.

Kiev's intellectual tradition and large labour population made it an important city in the dissent and popular revolt against the tsar. With both nationalists and workers challenging St Petersburg's authority, Kiev was targeted by the Black Hundreds and made an example of. During the Russian Revolution and subsequent civil war, Kiev changed hands 18 times until the final Bolshevik victory in 1921. The capital of the Ukrainian SSR was moved from Kiev to Kharkiv, where there was greater support for the Bolsheviks, but then moved back to Kiev in 1934. As the capital of the second-largest republic in the Soviet Union, Kiev wielded significant political power, but this was severely curtailed by Stalin's purges of the Ukrainian communist leadership, followed by the Nazi occupation in June 1941. The defence of Kiev in World War II was perhaps less heroic than is portrayed in the city's memorials. Over half a million Red Army troops immediately surrendered to the Germans, and this was soon followed by the ordered execution of 180,000 civilians at nearby Babi Yar. When the city was liberated in November 1943, it was estimated that nearly half of Kiev's population had been killed.

Kiev's real heroism lies in the city's ultimate survival and total reconstruction following the war. Of all the cities in the USSR, Kiev was revered for its beauty, art, culture and especially people. Famous Kievans include Mikhail Bulgakov, Golda Meir, Mikhail Hrushevsky, Sholom Aleichem, and more recently statesman Yevgeny Primakov and actress Milla Jovovich.

The last great tragedy to take place in Kiev was in 1986, with the explosion of the Chernobyl nuclear power plant 90 miles north of the city. The citizens of Kiev were not informed until more than a week after the event, and the patterns of chronic illness are only now being recognised. At the height of *perestroika*, the catastrophe widened the split between Kiev and Moscow. The city witnessed many active protests on the Maidan Nezalezhnosti in the final months of the Soviet Union, including a 1990 hunger strike of students calling for an end to military service outside Ukraine.

After independence in 1991, Kiev quickly established itself as the prosperous capital of a rather inert leadership whose corruption was legendary the world over. Such mafia-style governance ensured Kiev remained the static capital of a self-serving economy, guided by the not-so-invisible hand of big brother Russia. In November 2004, a handover of presidential power from Kuchma to Donetsk clan boss Viktor Yanukovych was disrupted when tens of thousands of opposition supporters gathered on the Maidan Nezalezhnosti and began protesting what was clearly a fraudulent election. The crowd in Kiev soon grew into the hundreds of thousands, who closed down the main street of Khreschatyk and surrounded parliament and government buildings in an effort to nullify the results. Brandishing the emblems of the opposition movement, the Orange Revolution brought up to a million Ukrainians out into the wintry streets of Kiev in a non-violent stand-off against decades of corruption and oppression. It was a watershed moment for the city and the country it leads, resulting in a newfound confidence for the capital.

The transformation of a newly uninhibited but slightly more law-abiding Kiev is both odd and monumental. In one great swoop, a Europe-conscious capital unveils a progressive vision of the future while recovering the rights to its long and clouded past. A host of impressive renovations continues to amaze, and the renewed gaze of international scrutiny has helped bring general guest services to international standards. Be sure to enjoy the Slavic sense of glamour in its heyday, but know that beneath it all, Kiev remains soulful and timeless.

GETTING THERE AND AWAY

BY AIR Obviously, Kiev is the main entry and exit point for air travel to Ukraine and *Chapter 4* details more information on particular routes. Kiev has now joined the integral network of inter-European and transatlantic flights, and is also the convenient central hub for all domestic flights in Ukraine.

Airline offices in Kiev

✈ **Aeroflot** Saksahanskovo 112A; ✆ 044 245 4359; www.aeroflot.ru

✈ **Aerosvit** Chervonoarmiyska 9/2, No 7A; ✆ 044 490 3490; www.aerosvit.com

✈ **Air Baltic** Khmelnytskovo 52; ✆ 044 238 2668; www.airbaltic.com

✈ **Austrian Air** Chervonoarmiyska 9/2; ✆ 044 244 3540; www.aua.com.ua

✈ **British Airways** Yarsolaviv Val 5; ✆ 044 490 6060; www.britishairways.ua

✈ **Czech Airlines** Ivan Franka 36; ✆ 044 288 1064; www.csa.com.ua

✈ **Delta Airlines** Chervonoarmiyska 9/2, No 17; ✆ 044 287 3595; www.delta.com

✈ **El-Al Israeli Airlines** Lesi Ukrainky 34; ✆ 044 230 6993; www.elal.co.il

✈ **Estonian Airlines** Chervonoarmiyska 9/2, No 14; ✆ 044 289 0520; www.estonian-air.ee

✈ **Finnair** Chervonoarmiyska 9/2, No 6; www.finnair.com

✈ **KLM** Ivana Franka 34/33, 2nd floor; ✆ 044 490 2490; www.klm.com.ua

✈ **KyiAvia** Peremohy 2; ✆ 044 490 4902; www.kiyavia.com

✈ **LOT Polish Airlines** Ivana Franko 36; ✆ 044 288 1054; www.lot.com

✈ **Lufthansa** Khmelnytskovo 52; ✆ 044 490 3800; www.lufthansa.com.ua

✈ **Malev Hungarian Airlines** Pushkinska 45/2, No 22; ☏ 044 490 7342; www.malev.hu
✈ **Transaero** Chervonoarmiyska 9/2, No 1; ☏ 044 490 6565; www.transaero.ru
✈ **Turkish Airlines** Pushkinska 19; No 1; ☏ 044 281 7322; www.thy.com
✈ **Ukraine International Airlines** Khmelnytskovo 63A; ☏ 044 461 5050; www.flyUIA.com

Boryspil Airport БОРИСПІЛЬ (KBP)

Kiev's Boryspil Airport is a very modern, efficient and busy airport with the same degree of amenities and chaos found at airports everywhere else in the world. There are three main terminals: most international flights arrive and depart through terminal B; domestic flights use terminal A, and C is reserved for charter flights. Arrival, immigration and customs are typically painless and quick. All incoming travellers are required to fill out an 'information card' which proves date and place of entry. Keep it with your passport and don't ever lose it. Customs declarations are filled out at baggage reclaim. When departing from Boryspil, note that there are security checkpoints before and after checking into your flight. For those who demand personal attention, Boryspil still offers a VIP service (US$100), which includes being met at the plane with a personalised placard and circumventing general immigration and customs. These days it seems a bit redundant. For more information about the airport, check out the website (*www.airport-borispol.kiev.ua*).

Communist logic dictated that a city's international airport should be built incredibly far away, and Boryspil is no exception – it's located 40km east of the city centre. Fortunately, the road into the city is the very best in the country (eight lanes, newly paved), thus making the transfer into the city a grand introduction to Ukraine itself, with birch forests melting away into high-rises, the river and the golden domes of the Pechersky Lavra in the distance. Unfortunately, the vulture-like taxi drivers that hang around Boryspil are busy hunting out unassuming first-timers. Expect to be quoted fairs of US$50–100, although you should never pay more than US$30–40 to be brought right to the doorstep of your destination in Kiev.

Catching a bus is just as easy and much less expensive. The **Polit** airport bus travels from Peremohy Square in the centre of Kiev to Kharkivska metro (green line) and to Boryspil and back, leaving every 15–20 minutes from 05.00, with the last bus leaving at 23.15 (☏ *044 296 7367*), cost US$5. The journey takes about one hour. In Kiev, travel to and from the bus terminal at Peremohy Square is a quick and easy ten-minute transfer (on taxi or bus) to Kiev's railway station and the metro station Vokzalna. There are also several new private bus companies with regular and direct services between Kiev's train station and Boryspil Airport. Most have signs in English and wait to fill up the bus before setting off. The service costs US$7–10 and gets you there in about 35 minutes.

Another option is the ubiquitous private bus company Avtoluks (*Boryspil Terminal B;* ☏ *044 230 0071; www.autolux.com.ua*). Every single one of their transit journeys to and from the rest of Ukraine makes a stop at Boryspil. If travelling to Kiev, you can take the 40-minute ride to the central bus station. If going elsewhere in Ukraine, you can buy your ticket and board directly at the airport.

If you're travelling light or on the cheap, you can also take a minibus from the airport to the city. Right as you exit the main terminal, you'll see a queue of *marshrutkas*, most of which make a stop at Boryspilska or Kharkivska metro stations on the Pechersk (green) line, or go directly to the train station. The cost is normally around US$5–7.

Boryspil Airport also offers two airport hotels to facilitate travellers coming and going. Both are reasonably priced and convenient. The **Boryspil Airport Hotel** (☏ *044 281 7105;* f *044 281 7953; www.airport-borispil.kiev.ua/hotels/airport*) is right at the airport and offers generic rooms from US$30–50. The newer **Boryspil Hotel**

(*Frenkl 3;* ✆ *044 281 7376;* ✆ *044 281 7679*) has inexpensive, but very nice, modern rooms from US$15–40, although it is not particularly close, being situated about five miles away from the airport, although a shuttle is provided.

Zhulyany Airport ЖУЛЯНИ (IEV) The lesser of Kiev's two airports is located just 7km from the city centre and makes a very convenient entry point. Normally, Zhulyany deals primarily with domestic air traffic, although there are notable exceptions like Czech Airlines and Aeroflot. For more information, contact the airport (*Povitroflotsky 92;* ✆ *044 242 2308; www.airport.kiev.ua*).

Taxis between the city centre and Zhulyany Airport take about 12–20 minutes and should cost less than US$10. On public transport, take trolleybus No 9 (the ride feels rather long) to Peremohy Ploscha, or much better *marshrutka* No 568 which goes to Prospekt Shevchenka and costs close to the same price as a taxi. Transferring between Zhulyany and Boryspil is not terribly difficult. A taxi between the two should cost around US$40; during the day there are also some bus services which connect.

The **Zhulyany Airport Hotel** (*Povitroflotsky 92;* ✆ *044 491 2023*) is rather basic but remarkably cheap, with rooms from US$10.

BY RAIL All train tracks lead to Kiev, making it the easiest destination to get to in Ukraine and the easiest place to leave. In fact, even if you don't want to come to Kiev, you may have to stop over here in order to get somewhere else.

Arriving in Kiev by train feels far more authentic than simply dropping in at the airport, and anyone who has the time should consider the journey. On any given day, you can get a train to almost anywhere and come to Kiev from anywhere in Eurasia. Without fail, Ukraine's trains run on perfect time and go to any city that you need to get to. Whether or not there are any spaces is the catch – especially during holiday seasons. The earliest you can buy tickets is one month before you travel, but many people wait until a few days before, the morning of travel, or even five minutes before departure. You should also check times and duration of travel, since this can vary a great deal depending on the train. Trains to Crimea either go to Sevastopol (2 daily; 18 hours) or Simferopol (4 daily; 16 hours). There are also plenty of trains to Lviv (5 daily; 11 hours) and Odessa (5 daily; 11 hours). Travel to and from Kharkiv (5 daily; 5 or 9 hours) has recently become easier with the advent of Ukraine's first luxury trains, the Capital Express, which makes two daily connections to Khariv (5 hours; with stops in Poltava and Mirgorod) and two connections to Dnepropetrovsk (5½ hours). There is only one overnight train to and from Donetsk (12 hours) and one to Dnepropetrovsk (8 hours), although many other trains pass through Dnepropretrovsk on their way to Kiev. The train's departure platform number is posted in English and Ukrainian 20 minutes before departure.

International routes to and from Kiev are numerous and rather inexpensive. Russian destinations are usually listed as domestic routes, with around 15 daily connections to Moscow (14 hours) and just one to St Petersburg (via Chernihiv; 24 hours). A few cars leave from Kiev every other day to be connected to Ukraine's Trans-Siberian railroad all the way to Vladivostok (via Kharkiv; 7 days). Other trains come and go from Minsk (twice daily, via Chernihiv; 12 hours) and Kishinev (twice daily; 14 hours), while train schedules to Riga (24 hours) and Vilnius (18 hours) constantly change. The most popular international routes are between Kiev and Warsaw (1 daily; 20 hours; US$80), Berlin (1 daily; 24 hours; US$100), Prague (1 daily; 34 hours; US$150), Budapest (1 daily; 30 hours; US$120) and Vienna (every second day; 34 hours, US$150). There are also various trains to central Asia and the Caucasus, but these schedules change much more frequently, depending on current political situations.

Kiev's main railway station is probably the most exciting place in the entire city. The station actually comprises two stations joined by a causeway crossing all the tracks and platforms. Vokzalna metro station is the closest public transport access. The imposing Stalinist façade is the main entrance of the 'Central' station, while the modern glass-and-steel building on the other side is the 'South' station. If you have a talented taxi driver who knows the trains, he will drop you off at the side closest to your point of departure; otherwise, it's a matter of walking over the long causeway terminal to your platform. Impressive renovations have transformed the interior of Kiev's station into the most modern and user-friendly station in Ukraine and visitors will be grateful for the English signs and listings.

There are over 100 ticket counters in Kiev's main station, all for different purposes. Counter numbers 40, 41 and 42 (*2nd floor of the South Station; open 07.30–20.00*) are designated to sell to foreigners and the attendants speak limited English (have your passport with you). You can still buy tickets elsewhere, but it is to your advantage to use these attendants since they are more flexible, have special access to better seats and give foreigners priority on full trains. Plastic is making some headway, but come prepared to pay in cash.

The other ticket office in central Kiev is located on the first floor of the Express Hotel (*Prospekt Shevchenka 38/40; open daily 10.00–21.00*). Dialling 005 on any Kiev phone will put you through to the train station, but if you don't speak Russian, the nice lady on the other end is not much help. Most tour companies and Kiev hotels will have agents who can also book tickets for you, but they tend to slap on a US$10 service fee.

Kiev's train station also features very nice overnight hotel rooms and service stations, situated at either end (listed under *Where to stay* – see page 125). On the south side, follow the signs up to the fourth floor. On the north side, exit the main doors, turn right and find the entrance on the corner. There are also left-luggage offices in both basements (look for a sign with a suitcase). The central station will just take your bag and give you a token. At the south station, pay your money to the nice old woman and you'll get two tokens – one that locks the locker and another to open it later. Set your own combination on the inside (and write it down somewhere), drop in the token, and shut it firmly while it's buzzing. To open, set the outside combination to match, drop in the token and carefully yank it open. You are allowed to leave luggage for 24 hours before it's cleaned out. The lockers are safe and well guarded and using them can give you some peace of mind. This helps if you want to check out of a hotel and spend the day around Kiev before boarding a night train to somewhere else.

When not salivating at the airport, Kiev's vulture taxi drivers congregate outside the train station, quoting wild prices. If you're tired and don't care, just pay whatever they want to take you to your hotel, knowing they're charging you double. If you are trying to save money, take the metro one stop to metro station Universitet and you'll be able to catch a cab there for much less.

BY BUS Like the train, you can catch a bus from anywhere to get to Kiev and vice versa. Schedules change frequently for the smaller lines and public buses, but several larger, private companies offer comfortable and reliable services.

Bus routes spread out in a radial pattern from Kiev, divided into five directions: Zhytomyr (west), Chernihiv (north), Uman (south), Cherkassy (southeast) and Poltava (east). The Central station (*3 Moskovskaya Sq;* \ *044 526 5774*) is best reached by travelling to Lybidska metro station (blue line) and then taking a bus (No 4 or No 11), taxi, or walking to the next junction. Buses to western destinations leave from Dachna terminal (*Peremohy 142;* \ *044 444 1503*); to eastern destinations from Darnytsya terminal (near the metro station Darnytsya)

(*Gagarina 1;* ☏ *044 559 4618*); to northern destinations from Polissya terminal (*Shevchenka Square;* ☏ *044 430 3554*); and to southern destinations either from Podil Terminal (*Nyzhny 15A;* ☏ *044 417 3215*) or Pivdenna terminal (*Glushkova 3;* ☏ *044 263 4004*). If in doubt, go to the central bus station where most long-haul routes still originate. Ticket windows 8, 9 and 10 are more accustomed to selling tickets to foreigners. Bus tickets can also be purchased at the central bus office (*Lesi Ukrayinki 14,* ☏ *044 225 2066*).

Regular buses are cheap, slow and bumpy. The most popular routes go to Zhytomyr (3 hours) and Pochayiv (12 hours). Shorter bus rides visit the tourist sights just outside of Kiev, such as Kaniv or Pereyaslav Khmelnytsky. The newer, private bus companies are based out of Kiev's central bus station and travel as fast or faster than the train, are very comfortable and charge about the same amount as the train. **Avtoluks** has the most widespread and dependable service, with brand-new buses that go to and from Lviv (10 hours), Yalta (17 hours), Odessa (8 hours), Kharkiv (7 hours), Zaporizhzhya (9 hours) and every city in between. Besides their office at the station, there's a central office (*Chistyakovskaya 30; info@autolux.ua;* ☏ *044 536 0055; www.autolux.com.ua*). **Gyunsel** has good connections between Kiev and the east (Kharkiv, Poltava, Dnepropetrovsk, and Donetsk) as well as Crimea and the Carpathians (*Novopolevaya 2;* ☏ *044 488 8801/ 044 265 0378;* e *office@gunsel.com.ua; www.gunsel.com.ua*).

International bus routes to and from Kiev include Paris, London, Rome, Amsterdam, Antwerp, Berlin, Brussels, Naples, Prague, Rome, the Baltic capitals, Vienna and Warsaw. For now, one of the best international coach lines in Ukraine is **Lviv Inturtrans**, offering weekly connections with Italy, France and the Netherlands (*Reitarska 30, No 23;* ☏ *044 272 3340;* e *kyiv-lviv@ukr.net; www.lviv-inturtrans.com*). **Ecolines** is a Latvian company with routes all across Europe. They have an office right at Kiev's train station (*Privokzolna 2;* ☏ *044 245 0352*) and a central booking office (*Mikhayilivska 16, No 2;* ☏ *044 279 2462; www.ecolines.lv*). **Kiy-Grand** offers regular connections across Germany and the Czech Republic for about US$80 single/US$100 return (*Zolotoustivska 20, No 3;* ☏ *044 468 5908;* e *kiy-grand@ukr.net; www.avtobus.kiev.ua*). While 48-hour bus rides may tempt the tried and true traveller, it seems downright masochistic in these days of budget airlines. Inside Ukraine, the only real advantage to taking the bus is that sometimes it's much quicker, and if you travel by day, you'll get to see the countryside. If the trip is over six hours though, consider the train as a more comfortable, albeit slower, option.

GETTING AROUND

METRO You haven't seen Kiev unless you've been underground. Because Kiev is built on top of the Dnepr's ravine, the metro stations are dug extremely deep, and this may be the longest escalator ride you've ever been on. During the five minutes it takes to descend, everyone stands and stares at everyone else before zooming off in different directions.

Construction of the Kiev metro was begun only after World War II, in 1949, and many of the oldest stations (on the red line) exhibit classic examples of Socialist Realist design, some of which are remarkably beautiful. Currently, there are 44 stations divided into three separate lines, coloured blue, green and red. The routes were designed to transport people from home to work, and so the metro is not always the best way to go from one tourist attraction to another; however, it is the quickest way to get around the city, especially during rush hour.

The metro is open from 05.30 until midnight every day, with constant and frequent trains all day long. During rush hour (from 07.30 and 16.30), things get

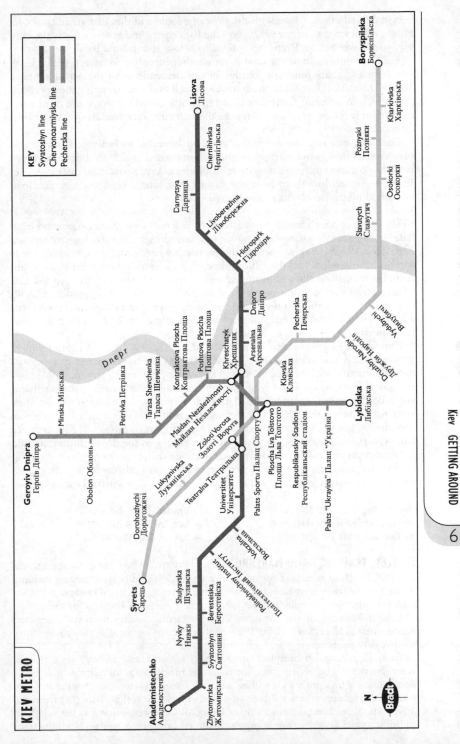

KIEV METRO

KEY
Syatoshyn line
Chervonoarmiyska line
Pecherska line

Boryspilska Бориспільська
Kharkivska Харківська
Roziyaki Позняки
Osokorki Осокорки
Slavutych Славутич
Vydubichi Видубічі
Druzby Narodiv Дружби Народів
Pecherska Печерська
Klovska КлOBCbki
Lybidska Либідська
Palats "Ukrayina" Палац "Україна"
Respublikansky Stadion Республіканський стадіон
Ploscha Lva Tolstovo Площа Льва Толстого
Palats Sportu Палац Спорту

Lisova Лісова
Chernihivska Чернігівська
Darnytsya Дарниця
Livoberezhna Лівобережна
Hidropark Гідропарк
Dnipro Дніпро
Arsenalna Арсенальна
Khreschatyk Хрещатик
Poshtova Ploscha Поштова Площа
Kontraktova Ploscha Контрактова Площа
Tarasa Shevchenka Тараса Шевченка
Petrivka Петрівка
Minska Мінська
Geroyiv Dnipra Героїв Дніпра
Obolon Оболонь

Maidan Nezalezhnosti Майдан Незалежності
Zoloti Vorota Золоті Ворота
Lukyanivska Лук'янівська
Teatralna Театральна
Universitet Університет
Vokzalna Вокзальна
Politekhnichny Instytut Політехнічний Інститут
Berestelska Берестейська
Shulyavska Шулявська
Nyvky Нивки
Syatoshyn Святошин
Zhytomyrska Житомирська
Akademistechko Академістечко

Dorohozhychi Дорогожичі
Syrets Сирець

Dnepr

N Bradt

very tight and pushy. Move with the flow of people and don't be afraid to shove. Politeness never got anyone very far on the Kiev metro and at times this is the only way you'll ever get on. Keep bags and wallets close at hand and be alert.

Finding your way underground is yet another incentive to learn Cyrillic. Look at a map and think out your journey before descending. In the actual tunnels, arrows show the direction the train travels as well as the remaining stations on that line. When transferring from one station to another, read the signs, ask, or in some cases, simply follow the crowd climbing the stairs from the middle of the platform rather than moving to the ends.

For now, one ride on the metro costs 50 kopecks, including transfers. The orange machines in the entrance of the stations take 1 and 2UAH notes and give you plastic tokens in return, but these machines always seem to be out of service. Wait in line and buy them from the cashier. For longer stays you can purchase unlimited metro travel on a monthly card.

TAXI Riding in Kiev's traffic cures atheism – sidewalks can become an extra lane, lanes can suddenly change direction, and taxi drivers like to drag race down Khreschatyk. Alas, the city's beautiful hills, narrow streets and quaint cobblestones were not intended for the automobile. Kiev's horrendous traffic jams are completely unavoidable and put most drivers in a foul mood at least twice a day. Blaming traffic is the quintessential (and forgivable) excuse for being more than 45 minutes late to anything. There are times when it is better to walk, and then there are times when a taxi can zip you from one end of the city to another in less than ten minutes.

Taxi fares are the equivalent of Kiev's stock exchange – there's no pinpointing a good fare, and 'good fares' change by the hour. It's a secret language that you will never know, and as a foreigner you will always be expected to pay more. US$3–4 is normal for hopping around the city centre. Hail a cab outside your hotel and you'll be charged a flat rate of US$10 plus whatever else they want to add on. Stick your hand out on the street, and anyone can stop and offer you a lift for a fee. Negotiate a fixed price prior to getting in. Most freelance cabbies in Kiev are very fair, especially those driving beat-up jalopies. Talking to the driver during the ride (or even trying to) can teach you more about Kiev than most tour guides. Dialling 058 on any phone will give you a voice that can get you a cab. Or for a no-nonsense pay-and-just-get-there ride, try one of Kiev's numerous private taxi companies:

🚖 **Radio Taxi** ↘ 044 249 6249	🚖 **Kyiv-Taxi** ↘ 044 459 0101
🚖 **Taxi Blues** ↘ 044 295 1444	🚖 **Swift Taxi** ↘ 044 459 0439
🚖 **Euro Taxi** ↘ 044 249 4040	🚖 **Twist** ↘ 044 238 2030

TROLLEY, TRAM, BUS AND MARSHRUTKA Rickety trolleybuses and clanging trams add to the web of transport options above ground. If you're travelling or residing in the farther corners of Kiev, it's well worth learning the numbers and paths for each bus and tram. Popular transits include the tram from Podil to the upper city, and the trolleys out on the left bank. Tram and trolley routes are usually depicted on city maps, albeit very badly. Pure trial and error or local advice make more trustworthy references.

Following years of complete apathy, Kiev's trams and trolleys now feature vigorous ticket controllers that seem to be making up for all the lost time. Recognising a foreigner, they will be especially keen to check your ticket and fine you for something or other. Make an effort to buy a ticket (50 kopecks) from the driver upon boarding, or keep some change out and ready for a ticket seller. In addition, buy a ticket for every large suitcase you may be carrying. Nodding your

Taking the funicular or the metro to the station Poshtova Ploscha brings you to the River Terminal (☎ 044 416 1268). Pleasure cruises originate and end here, many of which travel all the way down the Dnepr to Crimea. There are also basic passenger services available to other Dnepr towns and short boat tours of Kiev, as well as short transits to some of Kiev's islands and beaches in summer. Ice covers the Dnepr for about three months a year, and the river terminal is in full swing only from May until October. Schedules change all the time; either check out the terminal, or else contact one of the tour agencies that organises river tours.

head and saying you don't speak Russian won't help the situation. A *straf* (fine) costs around US$2 and you'll wish that you'd just taken a taxi.

There are over 400 official *marshrutka* (minibus) routes through Kiev and not one of them goes in a straight line. These minibuses are the cheapest and fastest way to move above ground, once you get the hang of it. A major central pick-up stop is in front of Universitet station (and all other metro stations) although you can flag one down just about anywhere. If you can't read the destination sign in the windshield, simply ask. Fellow passengers tend to be very helpful as well. Costs range from 1 to 3UAH.

CAR RENTAL Kiev is leading the way for Ukraine's new car-rental industry. Until very recently, driving on your own in Kiev (especially in a rental car) has always been perceived as foolhardy. That said, many still do it and things may be changing with the advent of so many international companies. Here are a few reliable leads:

🚗 **Avis** Hospitalna 4; ☎ 044 490 7333; f 044 490 0410; e avis@avis.kiev.ua; www.avis.com.ua
🚗 **Europcar** Gorkovo 48A; ☎ 044 238 2691; f 044 238 2692; www.europcar.ua

🚗 **Hertz** Zdolbunivska 7D; ☎ 044 494 4935; f 044 494 4938; www.hertz.com.ua
🚗 **Sixt** Dmitrivska 46; ☎ 044 490 8158; e info@ol.com.ua; www.sixt.ua

Most upmarket hotels will also offer some sort of car-hire services, although usually with a chauffeur. These are two of the best companies in the city, both with 24-hour service:

🚗 **Alles Business Auto** Khvoiki 21; ☎ 044 586 4929; e info@alles.com.ua; www.alles.com.ua

🚗 **Limousine Service** Institutskaya 19B; ☎ 044 407 4246; e limo@limo.kiev.ua; www.limo.com.ua

LOCAL TOUR OPERATORS

Kiev now does a roaring business in guided group tours, fixers and other travel services, many of which are semi-reliable. City tours in several languages (including English) are announced and depart from outside the central train station. In summer, you can also find guided tours from the Maidan Nezalezhnosti. If you want something a little more concrete, here are a few of the more reputable companies that have a proven record and English-speaking guides:

Olymp Travel Shovkovychna 24; ☎ 044 253 7108; f 044 253 8329; e welcome@olymp-travel.kiev.ua; www.olymp-travel.kiev.ua. Very professional English-speaking staff and one of the more established nationwide package tour providers in the country. They also have an array of services for visitors in Kiev.
Artex Hrushevskovo 28/2; ☎ 044 253 0009; f 044 253 0663; e incoming@artex.com.ua; www.artex.com.ua. Traditionally for youth and children, now with a broader professional clientele.

Bytsko Chokolovsky 33, No 21; ✆ 044 452 4411;
f 044 450 3833; e incoming@bytsko.kiev.ua;
www.bytsko.kiev.ua. Newer company.
Mandrivnyk Poshtova Ploscha 3; ✆ 044 463 7604;
e mandrivnyk@adam.kiev.ua;
www.mandrivnyk.com.ua. Strong, Euro-conscious travel
agency based in Podil.
New Logic Mikhayilivska 6A; ✆ 044 206 3322;
e incoming@newlogic.kiev.ua; www.newlogic.com.ua.

Young and vibrant, with good sightseeing packages
in Kiev and low-cost trips to Chernobyl.
Ukrzovnishintour Khmelnytskovo 26; ✆ 044 279
3240; f 044 279 8208; e incoming@uit.com.ua;
www.uit.com.ua. Don't be put off by the
unpronounceable name; this company gives good
tours of Kiev and specialises in day trips to Kaniv,
Uman and Chernihiv.

🏠 WHERE TO STAY

In the last decade, the capital's delusions of grandeur have helped churn out a pile
of super swish hotels that smell of new money and fresh paint. Nearly everyone
who comes to Kiev complains of the outlandish hotel prices and wonders how it
can be so when not so long ago nobody would have dreamt of coming here. Yet
high demand continues to outstrip the limited supply, putting the visitor on the
outs. The competition has become quite fierce as several new hotels open up.
Travellers should be encouraged to shop around; there's no other city on earth
where a US$100 bill can mean so little.

LUXURY Every hotel in Kiev likes to think of itself as a luxury hotel, which is simply
not the case, unless you count having a bed in Ukraine's capital to be a luxury.
Nevertheless, luxury rates are charged all around, regardless of the condition of
that bed, or if buying a nicer bed would be cheaper. The following represent Kiev's
new élite circle, all bona fide 'luxury' hotels; all take credit cards.

🏠 **Premier Palace** Shevchenka 5–7; ✆ 044 537
4500; f 044 279 8772; e info@premier-
palace.com; www.premier-palace.com. Truly the most
elaborate hotel in the city, the 'Palace' takes its
refined inspiration from the early 1900s, when much
of the original building was part of the finest hotel
in the city. The resurrection of one of Kiev's more
luxurious traditions has evolved into an entire city
block that rises up from the crossroads of the city's
two most impressive boulevards, Kreschatyk and
Shevchenko. Few superlatives need be spared. The
newer and larger wing of the hotel features floor
after floor of spacious, personal suites, with elegant
high ceilings and thoughtfully lavish décor. The
rooms in the heart of the hotel are slightly smaller,
but no less perfect, featuring the most comfortable
and luxurious beds in the city, hands down. Devotion
to detail and the unrelenting customer service are
reinforced by the hotel's Latin creed reminding
visitors that their 'name says it all'. Wi-fi and high-
speed internet are a given, as is anything else you
may demand. The Palace's panoramic restaurant
'Empire' on the 8th floor offers a pleasant setting
for opulent meals and a breathtaking view of Kiev
morning and night, while the first-floor Sumosan
restaurant breaks through the tired cliché of Kiev's

other Japanese restaurants and delivers an elegant
and modish private dining experience. The Premiere
Palace also features the very best swimming pool
and fitness centre in the city. If you are royalty, a
celebrity, on someone else's account, or aspire to any
of the above, then don't hesitate to come and stay
at the 'Palace'. *The least expensive 'economy' room
costs US$400; sgl standards are US$475; king-size
dbls are US$500; and business suites cost US$550.
A series of mirthfully decorated 'club' suites
(US$700) commemorate various moments of
Ukraine's past and future. B/fast for a king inc.*
🏠 **Radisson** Yaroslaviv Val; ✆ 044 492 2200; f 044
492 2210; e reservations.kiev@radissonsas.com;
www.kiev.radissonsas.com. A close second to the
'Palace', the Radisson SAS feels more modern and
élite, and is becoming a regular with the established
foreign business crowd. Located in a belle époque
building in the heart of Kiev's ancient upper city,
the interior of the Radisson is plush, yet simple and
Scandinavian. Standard rooms start at US$300, with
US$350 for business suites which are larger and a
little more tricked out (all rooms feature wireless or
high-speed internet). The junior and executive suites
have 2 or more rooms and much more spacious
bathrooms and go for around US$400/night. There's

a fine Italian restaurant in-house, as well as a jazzy downstairs lobby bar where business happens around the clock. The Radisson's conference centre is also one of the best and largest in town. B/fast is inc for some (but not all) rooms.

🏠 **Dnipro** Khreschatyk 1/2; ☎ 044 254 6777; f 044 254 6737; e reservation@dniprhotel.kiev.ua; www.dniprohotel.kiev.ua. Once upon a time, this was the only hotel foreign visitors were allowed to stay in, meaning the Dnipro has a slight advantage in working with group tours and taking care of all travel arrangements. The location on European Square (on the far end of Khreschatyk) is also convenient. Attempted grandeur makes it a nice enough hotel to stay in, but it is difficult to mask the Soviet construction, meaning rooms tend to be very small and narrow, except for the few larger and overpriced suites. Only dbl superior rooms or those of a higher standard have baths; otherwise, all rooms are equipped with showers. Although the Dnipro presents itself as Kiev's ultimate luxury hotel, there is no real comparison to the first two. The fitness centre is small and lacking, and the internet is patchy. A highly ambitious Ukrainian chef keeps things gourmet in the second-floor restaurant. The division between superior and standard rooms further complicates the pricing structure: superior sgls US$140–190; dbl (queen size) US$180–225; suites US$300–400. B/fast inc.

🏠 **Natsionalny** Lypska 5; ☎ 044 291 8888; f 044 291 8997; e natsionalny@ukrsat.com; www.natsionalny.kiev.ua. This very exclusive hotel favours official state visitors and government delegations, and is located within walking distance of the Verkhovna Rada and the presidential residence, all inside Kiev's ultra-swanky Pechersk neighbourhood. The 'National' also offers some of the nicest rooms in the city, but getting a reservation is not always as simple as calling. The officious Euro-Baroque interior is offset by the fantastic bathrooms. Sgls US$225, the incredibly plush junior suites cost US$300, and suites start at US$350. B/fast inc.

🏠 **Domus** Yaroslavska 19; ☎ 044 490 9008; f 044 462 5145 e postmaster@domus-hotel.kiev.ua; www.domus-hotel.kiev.ua. Located in the heart of Kiev's historic Podil neighbourhood, the pale pink Domus hotel is thoroughly quaint and favoured by the solitary businessman who seeks escape from the noise of the city. A modern and tactful renovation deserves mention, as does their dapper Italian restaurant downstairs. Sgls/dbls US$150/$210, suites US$300.

🏠 **Hotel Impressa** Sahaidachnovo 21; ☎ 044 239 2939; f 044 463 7902; e impressa@

happydays.kiev.ua; www.impressa.com.ua. Small, private and quiet, the boutique Hotel Impressa is located on one of the main streets in Podil, offering a more intimate alternative to the larger city hotels. Features fewer than 20 rooms; each is clean and spacious enough, with simple but elegant décor. There are internet services, but not in every room, and the authentic pizzeria is tempting. Standard sgls US$185, junior suites US$220, suites US$290. B/fast inc; special w/end rates.

🏠 **Hotel Rus** Hospitalna 4; ☎ 044 294 3020; f 044 220 4396; e reservation@hotelrus.kiev.ua; www.hotelrus.kiev.ua. Considered upmarket in Kiev, the Rus is a behemoth hotel tower with hundreds of clean, orderly and compact rooms, used frequently for conferences and group tours. Visitors will probably find that the service and standard are just about average compared with back home, but staff are very professional, and are especially good at dealing with high-maintenance groups. The location is somewhat central, although there is no public transport close by, leaving you at the mercy of the hotel's random taxi service if you don't want to walk down the hill. Prices are per room, meaning sgls or dbls cost US$130, while the 'remodelled' suites are US$160; suites US$200 and up. B/fast inc.

🏠 **President Hotel Kyivsky** Hospitalna 12; ☎ 044 256 3256; f 044 256 3254; e info@president-hotel.com.ua; www.president-hotel.com.ua. Sister to Hotel Rus (and just across the street), the Kyivsky is another towering high-rise chock full of respectable rooms and plenty of hallways to get lost in. Beloved by mid-range bureaucrats and mafia, the pool and fitness centre make the whole experience a little more special, as does their racy nightly cabaret. Sgls US$140; dbls US$170–200; suites US$300. B/fast inc.

🏠 **Lybid** Peremohy 1; ☎ 044 236 0063; f 044 236 6336; e info@hotellybid.com.ua; www.hotellybid.com.ua. Within fair walking distance of Kiev's main railway station, and St Vladimir's Cathedral, Lybid's location is fairly convenient and very conducive to getting around the rest of the city. The higher up you are, the more intense the view. Incredibly tourist-friendly and well managed; the Lybid's sensibly stylish rooms are modern and comfy. Sgls US$120, dbls US$155, suites US$225 and up; b/fast inc.

🏠 **Vozdvyzhensky** Vozdvyzhenska 60; ☎ 044 531 9900; f 044 462 5748; e info@vy.kiev.ua; www.vozdvyzhensky.com. Small and quiet, this endearing hotel is tucked away just off Andriyivsky Uzviz, making it the perfect hotel for first-time visitors to Kiev. It's a great way to be in central

Kiev, but hidden from the central rush. Vozdvyzhensky is also the rare Ukrainian hotel where you actually get what you pay for. Professional management and big, brand-new, fully equipped bathrooms put this hotel a step ahead of the rest so that the 'luxury' is not just in the price. Personal attention to guests is everyday policy. *Dbls (with king-size bed) US$180; large suites US$290, but there are a few 'tourist class' rooms that are much cheaper (around US$70) in their Andreyevsky wing. B/fast inc.*

🏠 **Hotel Sonya** Volodymyrska 77; \/f 044 228 5878; e info@hotelsonya.kiev.ua; www.hotelsonya.kiev.ua. Comprising 8 well-furnished apartments in an absolutely perfect location in Kiev's city centre, this 'alternative hotel' is a great option for private couples or families with small children. Each secure apt comes with a private kitchen and bathroom, and any level of service that you may require. *Prices range from US$100 for basic sgl to US$180 for first-class suite – much better value than most hotel rooms for the same price.*

🏠 **Dniprovsky** Naberezhno Khreschatytska 10A, No 2; \/f 044 490 9055; e info@capitan-

club.kiev.ua; www.capitan-club.kiev.ua. The wackiest of Kiev's already-vintage 1990s mafia hotels is now available to the paying foreign customer. This 2-storey, permanently anchored barge on the Dnepr features a series of 'luxury' suites made famous by the has-been celebrities who have slept in them. Most rooms feature queen-size beds with mirrored headboards, while the suites sport jacuzzi tubs, obviously. There's a sauna, restaurant, and internet in some of the rooms. Their motto also demands mentioning … *where everyone is 'capitan'. All this can be yours for only US$150 (sgls); US$240 (dbls); and suites US$300.*

🏠 **Camelot** Melnykova 4; \ 044 455 9467; e kamelot@kamelot.in.ua; www.kamelot.in.ua. Having travelled all this way to Ukraine, why shouldn't you spend your time at a jaunty themed hotel devoted to 13th-century Britain and the Knights of the Round Table? Rooms are brand new, spacious, and extremely comfortable, though the restaurant 'Lancelot' is a little too gimmicky, even for Kiev. *Sgls US$160, dbls US$220, suites US$300.*

MIDDLE RANGE Kiev's vague sense of 'middle range' hotels runs the gamut of price and quality. Assume nothing (eg: breakfast will probably not be included) and be picky. In this mix, your tourist dollar suddenly becomes rather undefined. All accept credit cards unless otherwise stated.

🏠 **Andriyivsky** Vozdvyzhenska 60; \ 044 425 8730. Paired with the more upscale Vozdvyzhenky Hotel, the Andriyivsky is right off of Andriyivsky Spusk and features remodelled and fairly comfortable rooms. This is probably the best choice for independent tourists that like to walk around and explore the city on their own, although keep in mind you are staying only halfway up Kiev's steepest hill (on a pedestrian street). *Sgls US$60–80; dbls US$70–90.*

🏠 **St Petersburg** Shevchenka 4; \ 044 279 7364; f 044 279 7472; e s-peter@i.kiev.ua. Across from the Premier Palace, the spacious and old-time St Petersburg has undergone a tremendous renovation, pulling it into the heady competition of Kiev's hotels. Travellers on a budget may still want to venture this way as it is truly a bargain for the address; there is no better location for the price of their few remaining 'unrenovated' rooms. Staff are warm and friendly, room conditions comfortable, and plumbing reliable. *Spacious remodelled rooms US$80–100, 'unrenovated' rooms US$35.*

🏠 **Adria** Raisy Okipnoi 2; \ 044 516 2457; f 044 517 8933; e researvations@eurohotel.com.ua;

www.eurohotel.com.ua. A Polish–Ukrainian joint venture, the Adria offers the same quality and comfort as any of Kiev's 'upmarket' hotels in the city centre, but is located further from the centre on the left bank. Basic rooms have a strong IKEA vibe to them, and the Soviet floorplan makes some of them feel awkward and small, yet this 'Euro-hotel' is the private 'luxury' wing of the giant Turist complex. *Rooms US$90–100, with suites US$150.*

🏠 **Turist** Raisy Okypnoi 2; \ 044 517 8832; f 517 6243; e hotel-tourist@uprotel.net.ua; www.hotel-tourist.kiev.ua. Officially Kiev's largest hotel (it's right next to the Adria), this 27-storey building is not unlike the millions of Soviet apt blocks that house most of Eurasia today, although it's slightly nicer inside. The left bank location may seem dissuasive, but the Livoberezhna metro station is literally next door, the river and Hydropark are close by, and after all, this is true, residential Kiev. *Regular budget rooms are US$55–65 pp, whereas the remodelled rooms cost US$85 and up.*

🏠 **Salyut** Sichnevoho Povstannia 11A; \ 044 494 1420; f 044 290 6130; e hotel@salute.kiev.ua;

www.salutehotel.kiev.ua. Like a rejected piece of the *Star Wars* set that got dropped in one of Kiev's more beautiful neighbourhoods, the Salyut's main attractions include (ironically) the Caves Monastery (just down the street) and the hotel's very own flashy casino lights. The cylindrical concrete construction does offer myriad views of the capital, and the interior is far more appealing than the exterior. Still, the hotel feels a little old. *Sgl rooms with dbl beds US$120, dbl suites 2 beds US$130.*

🏠 **Ukrayina** Instituska 4; ☎ 044 229 0347; f 044 229 1353. Towering opposite the Maidan Nezalezhnosti, the 'Ukraine' is the most visually prominent hotel in Kiev, so if it's a room with a Stalinist view you want, this is it. Rooms are comfortable for the most part, about half of which have been remodelled to international standards. The second-floor restaurant is vintage Soviet, as is the complimentary b/fast. *Sgls US$65–90, dbls US$80–120.*

🏠 **Hotel Kiev** Hrushevskovo 26/1; ☎ 044 253 0155; f 044 253 6432; e marketing@htl.kiev.ua; www.hotelkiev.com.ua. Located directly across from the *Rada* (parliament), the president's house and the Marinsky Palace, Hotel Kiev is operated by the presidential administration and is often used by those government employees and guests who aren't VIP enough for the Natsionalny. The structure and atmosphere is not unlike most renovated Soviet buildings, with some rooms feeling very luxurious and pleasant, and others that feel a little drab and bureaucratic. *Sgls from US$100; dbls from US$120.*

🏠 **Express** Shevchenka 38/40; ☎ 044 239 8995; f 044 239 8947; e hotel@railwayukr.com; www.railwayukr.com. From the outside things look abysmal, but a massive remodelling has really turned things around on the interior of this Soviet skyscraper. Like most Kiev hotels, the Express charges room rates that are entirely inflated for what it is, but boasts its prime location between the train station and the city centre as reason enough to part with big cash. The ground floor is also the central office for booking rail tickets, and the train station is a direct walk down the boulevard. *A few economy standard sgls/dbls US$55/75, while nicer rooms cost US$115/130, up to US$170 for 'suites'.*

🏠 **Hotel Kozatsky** Mykhailivska 1/3; ☎ 044 279 4925; f 044 279 2709; e kozatsky@ukrnet.net; www.kozatsky.kiev.ua. There is no better location than the Kozatsky, looking right out on the action of the Maidan Nezalezhnosti just below. While the rooms have the layout of a Soviet apt building and reception feels a tad dingy, most of the luxury

rooms are comfortable and convenient. There's also a number of sgls and dbls that are not bad at all, especially for the location. The Kozatsky is owned and operated by Ukraine's Ministry of Defence, so your neighbours will always be interesting. *Luxury rooms US$120, sgls and dbls US$65–80.*

🏠 **Sport** Chervonarmiyska 55A; ☎ 044 220 0252; f 044 289 7620; www.h-sport.kiev.ua. Yet another impersonal towering Soviet-era high-rise with semi-decent rooms and a wild casino up on the top floor. It's also an easy walk to the Respublikansky Stadion metro station. *A few US$30–40 rooms, but they're pretty lacking, while the nicer rooms, complete with remodelled bathrooms and new furniture, are US$50–90.*

🏠 **Slavutych** Entuziastiv 1; ☎ 044 555 3859; f 044 555 5637. This hotel has both standard (old) rooms and new (refurbished) rooms. One must decide if the cost of the cab ride offsets the money saved for a somewhat mediocre hotel, although this is precisely the reason that the Slavutych is so popular with groups travelling by coach. The left bank location is no treat in terms of access, but from this side there are some great views of the Pechersky Lavra and all of Kiev, especially in the summer. *Old rooms US$30–50, refurbished rooms from around US$70.*

🏠 **Bratislava** Malyshka 1; ☎ 044 559 6920; f 044 559 7788; e market@bratislava.com.ua; www.bratislava.com.ua. This is one of the better deals on Kiev's left bank, with modern rooms that feature new bathrooms with showers. A few of the older rooms also remain — the standard sgls which cost around US$40. Darnitsya is the closest metro station. *Remodelled sgls US$55, dbls US$60–90, suites US$120 and up.*

🏠 **Alexandria** Peremohy 62A; ☎ 044 455 6362; f 044 446 2128; e hotel@alexandria.com.ua; www.alexandria.com.ua. Inhabiting a Khrushchev-era Soviet gem of an apt building, the Alexandria has transformed itself into a homely and personal hotel with chintzy décor and kindly staff. The quality of stay is fine, and the Alexandria is a particularly good deal for groups of travellers. Alas, payment is by cash or bank transfer only. *2-room suite for 3 costs around US$95, while a 3-room hotel suite is about US$120.*

🏠 **Mir** (300 rooms) Holosiyvisky 70; ☎ 044 524 9646; f 044 524 9651; e hotelmir@ukrnet.net; www.hotelmir.kiev.ua. This is not exactly a bijou hotel, but it is the most beloved high-rise of the city's southernmost park and conveniently close to the central bus station. Even after some remodelling, most rooms feel coffin-like, with vintage 1970s Soviet bathrooms. *Cheap rooms US$40–50, while slightly improved rooms cost more (sgls US$75; dbls US$85)* or spend another US$5 and stay in a plush junior suite. Hotel guests also get an automatic 20% discount at 'Peace', the in-house strip bar.

BUDGET Trying to get a cheap place in Kiev is a battle you may never win, especially if you are looking for a plain hotel room. Not only are all the hotels in Kiev grossly overpriced, as of yet there is no appreciation for a business model that would offer foreigners somewhere 'cheap' to stay. Some of the mid-range hotels will still hang on to a few of their older rooms, which they may or may not be comfortable allocating to you. Typically, these can be had for US$30–40. Otherwise, most 'budget' hotels are far away from the city, which opens the question of travel time being money. For those who swear by youth hostels, if there's a group of you it may be far cheaper to share a three- or four-person room in a fancy hotel near the city centre than to try to get into one of Kiev's hostels. Anyone who knows Kiev well will tell you to get an apartment, which gives you the biggest bang for your buck.

⌂ **Druzhba** Druzhby Narodiv 5; ⧄ 268 3406; f 044 268 3387; www.hotel-druzhba.com.ua. A good find for budget travellers, Hotel 'Friendship' is located right next to Lybidska metro station and offers typical non-nonsense rooms hidden beneath a colourful veneer, and all for a rather fair price. The Druzhba feels much like the rest of Ukraine's offbeat hotels, providing a healthy dose of reality and local interaction. The rooms seem pricey, but feel budget. *Sgls US$45, dbls US$55, suites US$80.*

⌂ **Holosiyivsky** Holosiyivsky 93; ⧄ 044 259 7672; f 044 259 7646; e rezerv@hotelgolos.kiev.ua; www.hotelgolos.kiev.ua. Far from the madding crowds and everything else in Kiev, but pleasant in both price and setting – the leafy expanses of Holosiyivsky Park make a very nice walk in summer. The cheapest rooms are very bare beds and not much else. *The hotel still functions in un-remodelled post-Soviet glory, with the very worst sgls US$16; US$35 for 'slightly improved'; and US$40–50 for dbls. They do have a few 'lux' rooms, but then you're back to paying US$100.*

⌂ **Park Hotel** Tsyurupynska 2; ⧄ 044 422 0344; f 044 422 0355; www.park-hotel.kiev.ua. Aptly named for its location in Nyvky Park, this small, unpretentious hotel is within walking distance of Nyvky metro station. Rooms are well kept, and the staff are very personable, making this more of a B&B-type place. The higher priced rooms can be ideal for families or groups. *Sgl US$40, 'business-class' dbl US$50, junior suites US$65, suites up to US$100.*

⌂ **Prolisok** Peremohy 139; ⧄ 044 294 3020; f 044 220 4396. Kiev's main 'motel', the Prolisok is located on the far western outskirts of the city, and it can take 30–45mins to drive into the centre. If you're already driving to Kiev, this is a logical stop off the main road in. Rooms and the little cottages are nice and low-priced. *Sgl US$48, dbl US$58.*

⌂ **Sunflower Guesthouse** Travneva 12; Hotiv, ⧄ 044 406 3500; f 044 989 3315; e info@tourkiev.com; www.tourkiev.com. Run by a friendly couple, this B&B-style accommodation is peaceful and quaint, and favours those who prefer the country to the big city. Keep in mind that you are a good 30–45-min drive from the city centre and thus a captive buyer to all the various extras that your kindly hosts will be offering you, although they offer quite a lot, including picking you up at the airport. This is one of the only Western-style B&Bs out there, and is very reasonable. *US$25/night pp, or US$45 for a room with a queen-size bed.*

⌂ **Perova Hotel** Perova 16B, No 3; (no phone). This family-run left bank 'hotel' is equivalent to a homestay, where you can either have free range of the 3rd-floor house, or pay a little more to be treated like a guest and waited upon hand and foot. A popular residence on the backpackers' circuit, things are always busy here, and it's far easier to book a place in advance on any number of the hostelling websites online.

YOUTH HOSTELS A series of youth hostels in Kiev are managed by the **Youth Hostel Association of Ukraine**, an emerging youth hostel co-operative with good intentions that's associated with Hostelling International. All bookings and contacts are made through their central office in Kiev (*PO Box 156;* ⧄ *044 331 0260; f 044 219 2297; e info@hihostels.com.ua; www.hihostels.com.ua*). The association is very friendly, features many English-speaking staff, and offers convenient and competitive services like airport pick-ups.

⌂ Yaroslav Hostel Yaroslava 10; metro: Kontraktova Ploscha. Probably the cleanest and most popular; it's located right in the heart of Podil and – following comprehensive renovations – it has the newest beds and reliable hot water. Places are rather limited though. *Prices hover around US$22 pp with discounts for IYH card holders.*

⌂ Kiev Youth Hostel Artyoma 52A, 2nd entrance, 8th floor; metro: Lukyanivska. On the northwest side of the city; it's slightly bigger and dingier, but 'historic' and a little cheaper. *US$18–20.*

⌂ Olympic Youth Hostel Marshala Zhukova 3; metro: Lisova. Located near the final left bank metro station, and therefore near the forest and a good 30mins from the city. Rooms are a little more spacious, and amenities include a sauna and a cheery café. *US$18–20 pp.*

⌂ Vydubychi Hostel Promyshlennaya 4; metro: Vydubychi. Recently opened and conveniently located right at the exit of the metro, with big modern rooms and a lively atmosphere that feels a lot more like the hostels in the rest of the world. This is by far the biggest hostel in Kiev, with praiseworthy rooms. *From US$20 (some beds for as little as US$10).*

RAILWAY STATION For rail passengers, Kiev's central railway station now offers an upscale **Service Centre** (*Privokzalna 1;* ☎ *044 233 2080;* f *044 223 208; a double room with private bathroom costs US$40–50; a single room without bathroom costs US$16. If you've just come in from an overnight journey, you can also simply leave your luggage and take a hot shower (towels provided) for about US$6*). The centre is a business centre with internet access, a nice café and spacious, comfortable rooms at a great price for such a central location.

The southern end of the station *(Pivdenny Vokzal)* also features clean hostel-type rooms up on the fourth floor – just follow the signs with the bed on it. Everything is in good shape, and the rooms are heated in winter and cooled in summer. None of the rooms are en suite, but the shared bathrooms are new and clean with continuous hot water. (*US$20 a night pp, b/fast inc; no reservations.*)

RENTING APARTMENTS An oft-preferred option for reasonable accommodation in Kiev is renting a private apartment, and if you plan on staying more than three or four days, you might well consider it as an affordable alternative to the city's over-priced hotels. Traditionally, the square in front of the central train station is busy with female agents who either advertise their own apartment or arrange rentals for a range of accommodation. Recognise them by their call: *kvartira* (apartment) or *komnata* (room). For now, the going rate in Kiev is about US$30 a day for a semi-decent one-room apartment with double bed, kitchen and bathroom, or US$50 for anything that's within walking distance of Khreschatyk. If making arrangements on your own, ask the price, see the apartment, and then make a deal and get the keys. Arrange beforehand if you will pay up front or per day. Use caution, since prices will already be jacked up a bit and this is a black market trade where foreigners can be targeted for swindles.

Much better is to go the legal route and use one of Kiev's many licensed and trustworthy apartment rental agencies. A good company can do all the hard work for you and meet you at the airport with keys in hand. This is rarely the cheapest option, but it is much less expensive than staying in hotels, while the housing situation is often much nicer and more secure. Expect to pay around US$50–60 a night for a clean, somewhat centrally located one-bedroom apartment, and up to US$100 or more for one with lots of whistles and bells (internet, satellite television, jacuzzi baths, etc). Be sure to shop around until you get exactly what you want – the options are limitless. The following are tried and trusted agencies, the majority of which accept credit cards.

🏠 **Albion** Lesi Ukrayinki 9; ✆/f 044 295 9860;
e albion@ukrpost.net; www.albion-hotel.kiev.ua
🏠 **Apartments in Kiev** Sofiyivska 10, No 7; ✆ 044 279 2232; e info@apartment.com.ua; www.apartment.com.ua
🏠 **Arkadia** Gorkovo 156, No 3; ✆ 044 521 6903; f 044 528 3041; e office@apartments-arcadia.com.ua; www.apartments-arcadia.com.ua
🏠 **Avanti Apartment Services**; ✆/f 044 247 0558; e hotel@avanti.kiev.ua; www.avanti.kiev.ua
🏠 **Star Rent** ✆ 044 561 0467; e starrent@ukr.net; www.starrent.com.ua
🏠 **Absolut** Tsvetayevoyi 10/87, office No 17; ✆/f 044 530 1310; e hotel@hotelservice.kiev.ua; www.hotelservice.kiev.ua.
🏠 **Predslava** Gorkovo 100, Apt 30; ✆/f 044 268 6283; e predslava@nbi.com.ua;

www.predslava.com.ua
🏠 **Senator Apartments** Pirogova 6; ✆ 044 200 7755; f 200 7733; e office@senator-apartments.com.ua; www.senator-apartments.com.ua
🏠 **Sherbourne Apartments** Sichnevy Provulok 9; ✆ 044 490 9693; f 044 490 9699; e reservation@sherbornehotel.com.ua; www.sherbornehotel.com.ua
🏠 **Kiev Apartments** ✆ 044 492 0618; f 044 492 0619; e info@apt.kiev.ua; www.kievapartment.com
🏠 **Kiev Apartment Service** Yankarvsky 9; ✆/f 044 496 0762; e info@kievapartmentservice.kiev.ua; www.kievapartmentservice.kiev.ua
🏠 **Teren Plus** ✆ 044 289 3949; f 044 284 3561; e info@teren.kiev.ua; www.teren.kiev.ua
🏠 **UKR Apartments** Hospitalna 2; ✆ 044 234 4824; www.ukr-apartments.kiev.ua

✖ WHERE TO EAT

Kiev has more restaurants per capita than any other city in Ukraine, a record inspired both by the general demand for nice places to eat and an entrepreneurial explosion that introduced a lot of gaudy décor (like mermaid waitresses, and motorcycles hanging from the ceiling). While chasing the comically exotic is already somewhat passé in the capital, the remnants of the crazy 1990s still remain. Now that Kiev has got over the joys of sushi and Tex-Mex, there seems to be a push for the truly refined, the classic and the creatively culinary. Most first-timers to Kiev are astounded by how well they eat and how diverse the choices. Though far from being comprehensive, the following choices all come with recommendations. All take credit cards unless otherwise noted.

UKRAINIAN

✖ **Za Dvoma Zaitsiamy** Andriyivsky Uzviz 34; ✆ 044 416 3516. Truly a fun and sophisticated restaurant that is quintessentially Kiev in style, passion and the vintage antiques that surround the diners. 'The Two Hares' features a rare rendition of old Slavonic cuisine and a welcome twist to the everyday Ukrainian cuisine. *Mains from US$12; open 11.00–23.00.*

✖ **Khutorets** Naberezhno-Khreschatytska (Pier No 1); ✆ 044 463 7019. Occupying a giant wooden riverboat still afloat on the Dnepr, this old-time Ukrainian restaurant makes for a very fun lunch or dinner. Wood-burning hearths and a live folk band add to the rustic country style, and the food is hearty and delicious. *Mains from US$10; open 12.00–midnight.*

✖ **Monastyrskaya Trapezna** Vydubytska 40; ✆ 044 451 4256. Part of the ancient Vydubychi Monastery, this monastic refectory aims for the atmosphere of earliest Kiev, decorated with local antiquities and serving a menu of unorthodox classics, washed down

with heady herbal liquors. The food feels heavy, the atmosphere Victorian, and yet the experience is highly recommended, especially if you're already visiting the monastery. *Mains from US$10; open 10.00–01.00.*

✖ **Hunter (Myslyvets)** Saksahanskovo 147/5; ✆ 044 236 3735. A wild mountain theme is reinforced by lots of fur and dried plants hanging from the walls. The cuisine is Carpathian, specialising in wild bird and game, and cups of delicious hot mulled wine. *Mains from US$15; open 12.00–midnight.*

✖ **Kozachok** Kyrovogradska 118; ✆ 044 250 9352. Traditional Ukrainian cabin-style restaurant/pub with singing Cossacks that serve all the Ukrainian basics and dozens of different vodkas. Food is pancakes, grilled kebabs, famous fruit *varennyki*, homemade pickles and potatoes, of course. *Mains from US$7; open 24 hours.*

✖ **Kozak Mamai** Prorizna 4; ✆ 044 228 4273. One of Kiev's better Cossack-themed restaurants, reliving the 17th century in a series of tastefully decorated rooms just off Khreschatyk. The Ukrainian food is exceptional and fresh, while the atmosphere more peaceful than would be expected if the uniformed waiters really were Cossacks. *Mains from US$12; open 09.00–23.00.*

✖ **Budmo!** Mykhailivska 22A; ✆ 044 229 6193. A rather new spot for Kiev, 'Cheers' is located on one of the busier central streets and strikes a happy medium between prim European café and old Ukrainian tavern. The food is solidly Ukrainian and is already acquiring quite a following. *Mains from US$5; open 11.00–23.00.*

✖ **Pechersky Dvorik** Krepestnoi Pereulok 6; ✆ 044 253 2667. Upscale restaurant in Pechersk, not far from the Lavra. Representing a turn-of-the-century Kiev salon, the light and open space of the Dvorik offers a relaxed atmosphere and a very creative menu. The cuisine is mainly Russian/Ukrainian, with a few recipes borrowed from the earliest Slavic chronicles. *Mains from US$10; open 11.00–midnight.*

✖ **Pervak** Rohnidynska 2; ✆ 044 235 0952. Cute and quirky, Pervak's nostalgia for the bourgeois Kiev of yesteryear leads to frilly waitresses and a Disney-type effect. The food includes good salads and traditional Russian and Ukrainian favourites. *Mains from US$8; open 11.00–midnight.*

✖ **Tsarskoe Selo** Sichnevoho Povstannya 42/1; ✆ 044 280 3066. Located right between the Pechersky Lavra and the giant motherland statue, this complex of Ukrainian huts goes all out to create the ultimate Ukrainian themed-dining experience. Meat is

THE AMERICAS

✖ **Sam's Steak House** Zhylyanskaya 37; ✆ 044 227 2000. There is some novelty in watching Kiev imitate a bawdy American restaurant. When that wears off, there's steak and wine. *Mains from US$20; open 11.00–01.00.*

✖ **Soho** Artyoma 82; ✆ 044 244 7351; www.soho.kiev.ua. Kiev's secret desire to look and act just like New York City. If you like red wine with a giant T-bone, this is the place. *Mains from US$25; open 11.00–midnight.*

✖ **Steak House** Chokolovsky 16A; ✆ 044 241 0597. A name that says it all: big steaks and lots of meat. Besides pork, fish, chicken and lamb, there's a big salad bar and rich desserts. *Mains from US$20; open 11.00–01.00.*

✖ **Cantina Azteca** Vorovskovo 31A; ✆ 044 486 8656. Better than average expat Mexican food. *Mains from US$8; open 10.00–22.00.*

grilled on a brick fireplace, and waiters keep your glass filled with authentic *uzvar, kvas* and vodka. A fun place by day, things turn jazzy and boisterous at night. *Mains from US$10; open 11.00–01.00.*

✖ **Taras** Park Shevchenko; ✆ 044 235 2132. Right in the park (by Universitet metro station), Taras has an advantage over other country-style restaurants in that it doesn't have to fake the forest. This 2-storey wooden hut is surrounded by real live trees and greenery. The food is pretty typical Ukrainian. *Mains from US$8; open 10.00–22.00.*

✖ **Gostinny Dvir** Kontraktova Ploscha 4; ✆ 044 425 6876. A quaint restaurant in Podil with typical home-style Ukrainian food and decorated with traditional arts and crafts. *Mains from US$5; open 12.00–midnight.*

✖ **Samobranka** Bogatyrskaya 26A; ✆ 044 592 9929. Dedicated to Kiev's rustic roots, this decked-out cabin offers a maze of fireplaces in which meat is grilled. *Mains from US$10; open 24 hours.*

✖ **Varenychnaya No 1** Esplanadnaya 28; ✆ 044 227 1539. A fun and homely restaurant that serves up 25 different kinds of delicious *varennyki*, the ultimate Ukrainian dish, along with a buffet of creative *hors d'oeuvres*. *Mains from US$7; open 24 hours.*

✖ **Vulyk** Chervonoarmiyska 40; ✆ 044 230 2642. A pretty friendly and down-to-earth Ukrainian restaurant with Western-style 'booths' and a great menu. Honey-roasted meats are a prominent feature, and the potato pancakes are superb. *Mains from US$5; open 11.00–01.00.*

✖ **El Asador** Nyzhny Val 29; ✆ 044 425 44 02. Steaks and other hearty South American favourites prepared by a vivacious Argentinian chef. *Mains from US$10; open 12.00–23.00.*

✖ **Tequila House** Spasska 8A; ✆ 044 417 0358. Did you really come all the way to Kiev for a poor imitation of Tex-Mex? If you really love tequila, then come and try one of the dozens of varieties served. Otherwise, leave the locals to enjoy the novelty of guacamole and tortillas. *Mains from US$10; open 11.00–01.00.*

✖ **Mambo** Druzhby Narodiv 5; ✆ 044 522 8224. One of Kiev's crazier venues, inspired by a Ukrainian take on Brazilian and Caribbean cuisine, but with some sushi and oddly authentic Peruvian food thrown into the mix. Salsa lessons every night and, at weekends, they sponsor art classes for kids. Hey, it's Kiev. *Mains from US$8; open 12.00–02.00.*

EASTERN BLOC

✗ **USSR Sichnevoho** Povstannia 42/1; ☎ 044 290 3066. Rightfully next to Kiev's most Soviet monuments (and part of Tsarskoe Selo), 'CCCP' is a delightful take on the Soviet era, and the jovial cuisine only adds to the atmosphere of good-time nostalgia. Enjoy specialities from each of the former Soviet republics. *US$20 for dinner; open 11.00–01.00.*

✗ **La Russe** Mezhyhirska 1; ☎ 044 467 7517. The gourmet play on words (Larouuse) invites a fresh approach to the classic heavies of Russian cuisine, illustrating Tsarist glory with grilled fish and meat served with yummy reduction sauces. A must for Kiev's 'foodies'. *Mains from US$20; open 12.00–23.00.*

FRENCH AND ITALIAN

✗ **Bistro Coté Est** Yaroslaviv Val 22; ☎ 044 492 2250. The Radisson's in-house bistro is truly French in its devotion to regional cuisines and the diverse wines of France. Expect lots of fresh herbs, dainty dishes and Parisian flair. They also serve a wonderfully decadent b/fast. *Mains from US$15; open 07.00–23.00.*

✗ **Osteria Pantagruel** Lysenka 1; ☎ 044 229 7301. Italian gourmet restaurant, with blissful pasta dishes, creamy risotto, and a renowned Italian wine list. Also features one of Kiev's more convincing versions of tiramisu. *Mains from US$15; open 07.00–23.00.*

✗ **Marché** Chervonoarmiyska 13; ☎ 044 451 4050. The French grandeur gets laid on thick, but the provençale-style cooking, exquisite French cheeses and diverse wine list transcend the sunny surroundings. A very popular venue in Kiev for the time being. *Mains from US$30; open 08.00–midnight.*

✗ **Mille Miglia Ristorante** Yaroslaviv Val 22 (inside the Radisson Hotel); ☎ 044 492 2200. Any upscale restaurant born out of a love for Italian race-car driving can't be all that bad. Traditional northern Italian cuisine and matching wines that deserve some extra time to be enjoyed. *Mains from US$20; open 12.00–midnight.*

✗ **Fondue Bar** Maidan Nezalezhnosti (Globus shopping centre, 1st floor); ☎ 044 238 2072. Exactly as the name suggests, offering morsels with melted cheese, *bourguignonne* (with meat), and rich chocolate. A very fashionable place to be seen. *Mains from US$5; open 11.00–02.00.*

✗ **Capucin** Chervonoarmiyska 81; ☎ 044 531 1378. Gregariously French cuisine served with

✗ **Oli** Ilinska 18; ☎ 044 425 2979. Tasty Yugoslavian cuisine served in an ambient hall or out on the covered terrace (011 is the telephone code for Belgrade). Quite a popular dining spot for the late evening. *Mains from US$18; open 11.00–midnight.*

✗ **U Hromgho Pola** Suvorova 4; ☎ 044 280 5007. Lots of what the Czechs do best: pork products and goulash galore. *Mains from US$10; open 10.00–midnight.*

✗ **Porto** Chervonoarmyiska 72; ☎ 044 206 8387. Traditional seafood recipes from the former Yugoslav republics of Montenegro, Croatia and Slovenia. A choose-your-own-fish-or-lobster-out-of-the-tank kind of place. *Mains from US$35; open 12.00–midnight.*

medieval flair. *Mains from US$8; open 11.00–midnight.*

✗ **Svitlytsya** Andriyivsky Uzviz 13B; ☎ 044 416 3186. This rustic French café and crêperie is right off Kiev's major tourist street and serves wonderful meat fondues, delicious crepes and light meals for generally low prices. *A full meal will cost around US$12.*

✗ **Gavroche** Mezhyhirska 3/7; ☎ 044 416 5524. A bit of a hole in the wall in Podil that looks a lot like the set from *Les Misérables*. Hearty French fare but good-natured enough to be Ukrainian. *Mains from US$5; open 10.00–23.00.*

✗ **Gorchitsa** Shovkovychna 10; ☎ 044 253 7691. Laidback French restaurant in Pechersk, serving Ukrainianised French food, with *gorchitsa* (mustard) of course. *Mains from US$15; open 12.00–23.00.*

✗ **Fellini** Gorodetskovo 5; ☎ 044 229 5462. Obviously named after the famed Italian film director, as Fellini's b&w movie stills cover the walls of this upscale, all-day, all-night supper club. Cooking blends French and Italian elements to new heights of pretentiousness, including frog's legs and the like. Right off Kiev's busiest street. *Mains from US$20; open 24 hours.*

✗ **L'Amour** Naberezhno-Khreschatytskaya 17/18; ☎ 044 451 50 80. A quaint French cottage, propped next to the Dnepr, serving stylish French cuisine prepared lovingly by a talented gourmet chef. The grilled tuna is *magnifique*. *US$20–30.*

✗ **Il Patio** Bessarabska 5A; ☎ 044 246 4327. Kiev's finest pizza and pasta in a gimmicky Italian setting right off Khreschatyk. *Mains from US$8; open 11.00–23.00.*

ASIN

✕ **Lun Van** Khmelnytkovo 26; ☎ 044 229 8191. One of Kiev's earliest Chinese restaurants, now serving classy Asian food (including some Japanese specialities). A royal atmosphere with a well-designed interior and a dedicated chef. *Mains from US$10; open 11.00–midnight.*

✕ **Mandarin** Naberezhno Khreschatytskaya (Pier No 6); ☎ 044 459 0877. Asian fusion served on a Han Dynasty-style riverboat on the Dnepr. Great Chinese and Japanese food. *Mains from US$12; open 11.00–midnight.*

✕ **Asahi** Saksahanskovo 1Г; ☎ 044 244 2237. Very authentic Japanese cuisine made by a real Japanese chef: sashimi, sushi and Japanese beer. *Mains from US$12; open 11.00–midnight.*

✕ **Nobu Shota** Rustavelli 12; ☎ 044 246 7734. Minimalist sushi joint and Asian drinks bar. *Sushi from US$4 apiece.*

✕ **Planet Sushi** Khreschatyk 12; ☎ 044 270 6679. Exactly like the name implies – a gigantic sushi smorgasbord right on Kiev's main drag. *Sushi from US$5 per roll; open 11.00–02.00.*

✕ **San Tori** Sahaydachnoho 41; ☎ 044 462 4994. Kiev's most perfect Asian food: delicate sushi, incredibly fresh fruit, all served in a first-class setting. On one of Podil's central squares. The masterful combination of Thai and Japanese should outlast current fads. *Mains from US$25; open 11.00–01.00.*

✕ **Tampopo** Saksahanskovo 55; ☎ 044 289 2999. Kiev is still going crazy over the discovery of sushi,

and this modern dainty features a sushi conveyor belt that continues to wow Ukrainians. Good if you have Ukrainian friends or clients. *Mains from US$20; open 11.00–midnight.*

✕ **Vostok** Naberezhno-Khreschatytskaya; ☎ 044 416 5375. A tribute to Eastern exoticism, this Chinese restaurant stands out from the rest for its sense of style and authenticity. Diverse chefs from various regions of China serve up unique and unfamiliar dishes. If you order fish, you'll be asked to pick it out of their small pond before it wriggles off to the kitchen. *Main dishes US$10–20.*

✕ **Murakami** Naberezhne Shosse; ☎ 044 428 7224. What with a Chinese riverboat next door, Kiev added this 2-storey Japanese restaurant atop its very own river barge. The kind of place you go to at 2 in the morning for sushi and cocktails. *Mains from US$10; open 11.00–06.00.*

✕ **Great Wall** Kostiantynivska 2A; ☎ 044 230 6027. No-frills Chinese food that's fit for the pickiest, most culturally insensitive tourist out there. *Mains from US$3; open 11.00–23.00.*

✕ **Himalaya** Khreschatyk 23, ☎ 044 462 0437. Kiev's main Indian restaurant for the time being. The location on Khreschatyk is convenient and visible, the atmosphere pleasant enough, and the chef is really Indian. *Fixed lunches around US$8.*

✕ **Yakitoria** Lesy Ukrayinky 42; ☎ 044 295 8161. Kiev's early introduction of Japanese cooking – the antithesis of Ukrainian food. *Mains from US$10; open 10.00–midnight.*

THE TURKS AND CAUCASUS

✕ **Alazani** Saksahanskovo 1Г; ☎ 044 205 4467. One of Kiev's Georgian greats, renowned for its overflowing wine and incredible grilled food (temporarily sharing space with Asahi). *Mains from US$15; open 13.00–02.00.*

✕ **Antalya** Fedorova 10; ☎ 044 220 6157. Refined and authentic Turkish food just outside Kiev's centre. *Mains from US$10; open 11.00–midnight.*

✕ **Caravan Klovsky** Uzviz 10; ☎ 044 290 9577. Uzbekistan's unique culinary tradition hallmarked the most exotic cuisine during the Soviet era. Caravan highlights central Asia's diverse cuisine with dumplings, grilled meat, *plov* (aromatic pilau rice dishes), kebabs and spicy vegetables. *Mains from US$8; open 12.00–midnight.*

✕ **Mimino** Spasska 10A; ☎ 044 417 3545. Georgian food is like no other, and if you're uninitiated, this is the right place to start with somewhat authentic cuisine, great service and good wine. One of Kiev's

most beloved restaurants, this cosy venue (complete with crackling fireplace) is located right in the heart of Podil. *Mains from US$15; open 11.00–01.00.*

✕ **Gorets** Vorovskovo 9; ☎ 044 272 1549. If only the real Caucasus were so amiable. Georgian-themed restaurant with shish kebabs, fresh khachipuri cheese pastries, and spicy sauces, along with some more Persian-influenced Azeri favourites. *Mains from US$15; open 12.00–01.00.*

✕ **Kavkazkaya Plennitsa** Khreschatyk 12; ☎ 044 278 1852. A tribute to a popular Soviet film, featuring Armenian ambience and cuisine. Grilled meats, tasty soups and breads. *Mains from US$4; open 10.00–23.00.*

✕ **Kazbek** L. Ukrayinki 30A; ☎ 044 285 4805. Upscale Caucasian dining experience leaning towards Georgian cuisine. Great décor and arguably the best Georgian wine cellar in the city. *Mains from US$10; open 11.00–midnight.*

✖ **Shirvan Shah** Ihorivska 5; ☏ 044 463 7572. Authentic Azerbaijani cuisine in the heart of Podil. Scented with rose oil and exotic spices, this elaborate palace of a restaurant is deservedly popular. *Mains from US$15; open 11.00–23.00.*
✖ **Mangal** Pankivksa 11; ☏ 044 244 1990. A hearty and feelgood kind of place, this open restaurant

VEGETARIAN/KOSHER

✖ **New Bombay Palace** Druzhba Narodiv 33A; ☏ 044 285 8708. Atmospheric Indian restaurant right next to the motherland statue serving traditional fare typical of Indian restaurants the world over. *Vegetarian dishes galore; mains from US$10; open 12.00–23.00.*
✖ **Haiffa** Kostiantynivska 57; ☏ 044 417 2512. In the far north of Podil, this Jewish restaurant not only serves Israeli cuisine, but several favourites from the Ukrainian Jewish tradition. A good pick for the pickiest of vegetarians. *Mains from US$10; open 13.00–23.00; closed Sat.*
✖ **Maccabee** Shota Rustavelli 15; ☏ 044 235 9437. 'Kosher food for kosher prices' says the slogan. Located next to Kiev's central synagogue and serving authentic Israeli fare, grilled meats and delicious vegetarian food to both Jew and Gentile. *Mains*

grills fish, poultry and beef over an open fire. *Mains from US$5; open 11.00–23.00.*
✖ **Tiflis** Shota Rustavelli 22; ☏ 044 235 6101. Yet another Georgian restaurant, but conveniently located near the city centre. *Mains from US$7; open 11.00–midnight.*

from US$4; open 11.00–01.00; closed Sat.
✖ **King David** Esplanadna 24; ☏ 044 235 7436. The central synagogue's very own restaurant, featuring an all-kosher menu, several vegetarian staples and a clientele from around the globe. *Open 10.00–23.00; closed Sat.*
✖ **Tzimmes** Ihorivska 5; ☏ 044 428 7579. Reclaiming one of Kiev's older Jewish neighbourhoods in Podil, Tsimmes celebrates the old east European Jewish tradition, with Yiddish music, paintings by Marc Chagall, and authentic Ukrainian Jewish cuisine. *Mains from US$15; open 11.00–midnight.*
✖ **Non-Stop** Prospekt Peremohy 6; ☏ 044 216 4073. As the name implies, this lively bar and grill is open all the time, offering a broad vegetarian menu, a fantastic barbecue, and lots of colourful drinks. *Mains from US$1; open 24 hours.*

GOURMET Although all of Kiev's restaurants evoke the gourmet, there are only a few that are the real thing.

✖ **Lypsky Osobnyak** Lypska 15; ☏ 044 254 0090. If you're in search of 'real Ukrainian food' but think it's all peasant fare, sit back and be regaled. True, Ukraine's tradition of haute cuisine has been stifled by decades of famine and oppression, but Kiev's finest restaurant counters history by delivering the natural comfort food of Ukraine with an exquisite native style that blends the highly Baroque with the creative genius of a star chef. Beautiful 19th-century interior, first-class service and an incredible wine collection. *Mains from US$30; open 11.00–01.00.*
✖ **Pena** Yaroslaviv Val 30/18; ☏ 044 234 1701. Elitist and super pricey, Pena caters to those with a hankering for impossible dishes. This is most likely the restaurant responsible for introducing the word 'fusion' into Kiev's culinary lexicon. Fresh Japanese

fish (flown-in daily) and exotic veggies in teeny salads. *Mains from US$40; open 12.00–midnight.*
✖ **Annabelle** Chervonoarmiyska 57/3; ☏ 044 287 7374. This ultra-fancy French restaurant is the first restaurant in Ukraine to receive a Michelin star, marking a real crossover. The food is exceptional – even the roasted pigeons. For dessert, try the marinated pears or the mango mousse. *Mains from US$25; open 11.00–02.00.*
✖ **Empire** Shevchenka 5–7/29, 8th floor; ☏ 044 244 1235. One of Kiev's first real gourmet restaurants, up on the top floor of the Premier Palace Hotel. The Empire serves a mature and sophisticated version of Ukrainian and European cuisine with one of the best panoramic views of the city. The b/fast buffet is legendary. *Mains from US$30; open 07.00–23.00.*

CHEAP EATS IN KIEV Kiev has become a great city for eating lots, even if your pockets aren't that deep. Fast-food and pizza joints polka-dot the city and you can find a cheap meal in just about any neighbourhood without having to look too hard. Despite an abundance of options, here's a few of the more popular non-chain spots for a quick and inexpensive bite.

✕ **Puzata Khata** Basseina 1/2; ☎ 044 246 7245. Both thrifty and nifty, this jolly corner cafeteria offers delicious Ukrainian classics with zero pretence. Located just behind the Bessarabsky Rynok, the hotel is packed both day and night with students and workers. *Mains from US$1; open 08.00–23.00.*

✕ **Gourmet** Krasnoarmiyska 12; ☎ 044 287 7363. Owned and run by some of Kiev's entrepreneurial Turks, this upscale cafeteria serves up healthy portions of Turkish cuisine on one side and a smorgasbord of delectable Middle Eastern pastries and cakes on the other. Try the baked eggplant with fresh airyan yoghurt sauce, then sample the dozens of different *baklavas. Mains from US$3; open 09.00–22.00.*

✕ **Pid Osokom** Mikhayilovska 20. This small café caters mainly to the Ukrainian business set during lunch hours, seating people together on long wooden benches. It can get crowded because it is so popular, but the aromatic food is worth it. Authentic and inexpensive Ukrainian cuisine is served hot by matronly staff. *Mains from US$3; open 10.00–21.00.*

✕ **Kyivska Perepichka** Khmelnitskovo 3. My favourite place to eat in Kiev and the only permanent foodstand to have remained open since independence. The *perepichka* is a quintessentially Kiev snack similar to a sausage roll; hot dogs are covered in Pirozhki pastry and then deep-fried (yum!). This hot, hand-held treat costs about 50 cents and you'll need to buy one for each fist. *Mains from less than US$1; open 09.00–21.00.*

DESSERT Going out for dessert – day or night – suddenly seems a necessary Kiev tradition.

✕ **Éclair** Artyoma 82; ☎ 044 484 1668. Coffee, teas and cakes galore. A gourmet coffee house lacking nothing. *Desserts from US$5; open 10.00–01.00.*

✕ **Surprise** Pirogova 3; ☎ 044 246 4828. While this is actually a fancy French tea salon serving things like oysters and quail's eggs, 'Surprise' is best known for its painstakingly hand-dipped chocolates, all made right in front of you in the open kitchen. The glass counter of deluxe pastries displays all that is gooey, sweet and delicious. The best dark chocolate in Kiev? *Desserts from US$3; open 09.00–01.00.*

✕ **Marquise de Chocolat** Prorizna 4; ☎ 044 235

4546. This dessert café has already made its name in Kiev with an advertisement of a woman covered in melted chocolate. Besides all things dark and delicious, the menu offers colourful cocktails and a range of stylish coffee. *Desserts from US$5; open 11.00–01.00*

✕ **Semadeni** Chervonoarmiyska 68; ☎ 044 289 6380. Dipped chocolates and creams, tea, coffee and cakes inside a serene, 19th-century Kiev café, inspired by the original Swiss establishment of the same name. *Desserts from US$3; open 08.00–22.00.*

CAFÉS Kiev café culture is as eclectic as its restaurant scene, but it nevertheless offers a whole different experience. Meals and coffee come with certain brands of live music, themes and attitudes. Enjoy discovering the ones that suit you best.

⌷ **Pret à Café** Andriyivsky Spusk 10A; ☎ 044 425 1297. Cool, counter-culture bar and café popular among Kiev's poets and theatre types. Right on the artsy Andriyivsky Spusk. *Open 11.00 until very late.*

⌷ **Le Grand Café** Muzeiny 4; ☎ 044 228 7208; www.legrandcafe.kiev.ua. Both pricey and elitist, this French-style café is Kiev's flashiest hangout, dressed in fin-de-siècle Parisian décor and offering dramatic highbrow dishes. The menu explores some interesting Ukrainian–French hybrids (like *vareniki* with foie gras) while the drinks are more sturdy and conventional – the pastry cart is highly recommended. *Mains from US$20.*

⌷ **Baboon** Khmelnytksovo 39; ☎ 044 234 1503; www.baboon.kiev.ua. Bookish café for Kiev's bookish types. Great coffee and desserts, as well as light

meals and chilled-out live music. *Open 09.00–02.00.*

⌷ **Charme** Khmelnytskovo 50; ☎ 044 224 9065. This tiny underground café and bar presents a much more honest picture of Kiev's café life. A good refuge on rainy days and snowy evenings, the food is straightforward, with a range of Ukrainian beers on tap and inexpensive, warm meals. *Mains from US$4; open 10.00–21.00.*

⌷ **Chayny Club** Mezhyhirska 22; ☎ 044 416 1877. Kiev's ultimate tea house, serving dozens and dozens of different global teas and all the cakes and sandwiches you need to go with it. Inexpensive. *Open 09.00–21.00.*

⌷ **Dobra Chainova** Shota Rustavelli 10; ☎ 044 270 5824. Just tea (no alcohol, smoking or coffee allowed!), and tea it is, from all over the world. Open 11.00–23.00.

Coupole Sichnevoho Povstannya, 27B; ☎ 044 290 6650. An intimate circular café near the Caves Monastery, Coupole serves 'original meals for loyal prices'. Good for quiet, leisurely lunches and dinners. *Mains from US$10; open 12.00–22.00.*

Deja Vue Khmelnytskovo 30; ☎ 044 235 9802. Although it bills itself as a restaurant, this underground café goes way beyond its peculiar Chinese/European menu. Imagine motorcycles on the walls, stolen street signs and Soviet memorabilia, with great live music (from talented local bands) every night. If it's midnight and you need tea, cake and a sad song, this is the place. Quickly becoming a chain across the rest of the country. *Mains from US$15; open 12.00–02.00.*

Dno Peremohy 45; ☎ 044 456 4505. Popular with Kiev's younger set, this tribute to the Beatles recreates the psychedelia of *The Yellow Submarine* and is aptly named 'bottom' in Russian. The food is unique, hip and Slavic, meaning it mixes well with alcohol. The 'beat café' is very close to Shulyavksa metro station; a good place if you're young and want to meet locals your age. *Mains from US$10; open 11.00–midnight.*

✗ **Dva Gusya** Khmelnytskovo 46B; ☎ 044 221 1231. 'Two Geese'. A simple, pub-like atmosphere right in the centre of Kiev. Good for a quick, mid-

BARS AND PUBS

♀ **Sunduk** Shevchenka 36A; ☎ 044 244 3941. Action-packed cowboy bar that's always moving. They serve 30 kinds of beer, and an eclectic mix of Ukrainian and American food. *Mains from US$3; open 11.00–23.00.*

♀ **The Wall** (Stina) Bessarabska Ploscha 2; ☎ 044 235 80 45; Next to Bessarabsky Rynok. The heavy influence of Pink Floyd, East Berlin and old-school rock offer a foggy glimpse at the former angst of Soviet Ukraine's once youthful generations now happily feasting on a bizarre Mexican/Ukrainian menu. *Mains from US$5; open 11.00–02.00.*

♀ **Belle Vue** Saksahanskovo 7; ☎ 044 220 8780. Belgian beer bar for all those EU expats awaiting Ukraine's accession. *Open 11.00–23.00.*

♀ **Bier Stadt** Chornovola 12; ☎ 044 592 3872. Lots of German beer and big-screen sports. *Open 10.00–02.00.*

♀ **Bierstube** Chervonoarmiyska 20; ☎ 044 235 9472. Upscale beer hall for professionals and expats, also serving filling sandwiches. *Open 08.00–02.00.*

sightseeing lunch. *Open 10.00–23.00.*

Dveri Reitarska 13; ☎ 044 229 5168. Open bar and urban café not far from the Golden Gate that's fast becoming a Kiev regular. *Open 10.00–midnight.*

Fruktopia Shevchenka 2; ☎ 044 235 8347. Billed as a 'fashion café', this colourful downtown venue serves fresh, inexpensive meals that challenge the grey of the streets. *Mains from US$2; open 10.00–23.00.*

✗ **Massandra** Naberezhno-Khreschatytska 19/21; ☎ 044 416 0440. Ukraine's most famous wine is served with custom-made dishes to bring out the best of this Crimean favourite. *Mains from US$8; open 11.00–23.00.*

House of Coffee (Passazh) Khreschatyk 15; ☎ 044 229 1209. Viennese-style coffee house and pastry shop that serves delicate cream cakes, hefty patisseries and delectable truffles. One of Kiev's better escapes during teatime (go under the archway to get there). *Open 08.00–23.00.*

Nouvelle Khreschatyk 15; ☎ 044 231 4549. Next to Passazh, but slightly more upscale. Deadly hot chocolate and espresso, flaky pastries and cakes. *Open 09.00–23.00.*

Time Out Gorkovo 50; ☎ 044 248 73 90; e timeout@timeout.com.ua. Nothing too different from back home: European and American food served with gusto 24 hours a day. *Around US$10.*

♀ **Double Bass** Kostyantynivska 34; ☎ 044 467 6018. Live jazz and blues played late into the night; the chef who works this creatively decorated 'bar' happens to go in for the gourmet – not a bad choice for a late-night repast. Good vibes, good music and considerate staff offer a low-key night out. In Podi. *Open 12.00–midnight.*

♀ **Fiji Bar** Sahaidachnovo 14B; ☎ 044 425 5578. We're proud to announce the very first underground Polynesian tiki-huts in the former Soviet Union. Featuring exotic food, drink and dancers. *Open 24hrs.*

♀ **English Pub** Raisy Okypnoyi 2; ☎ 044 552 5091. Part of the out-of-control funfare that is Hotel Tourist's Joss nightclub. Come and enjoy Ukraine's take on how the English have fun: lots of beer, pub games, big-screen footie and live music. *Open all night.*

♀ **Le Cosmopolite** Volodymyrska 47; ☎ 044 228 7278. Jazzy continental bar that serves Belgian beer and all that tastes good with it: French fondue, German sausages and heavy bread. Also serves a full vegetarian menu. *Mains from US$20; open 11.00–23.00.*

♀ **Golden Gate** Volodymyrska 40/2; ☎ 044 235 51 88. Kiev's other Irish pub (not O'Brien's) that differs little from any other Irish pub anywhere else in the world, except this one has a kids' menu. Draught beer and plenty of whiskey. *Open 11.00–01.00.*

♀ **Korona Club** Rohnidynska 4; ☎ 044 220 0216. A zany interior that features the east European hybrid of bar/restaurant/casino, the 'club' reflects the outlandish tastes of Kiev's early mafia set, but feels most comfortable when you go there to drink. Corona is served as well. *Open 11.00–02.00.*

♀ **Lounge Bar** Muzeyny 4; ☎ 044 228 7208. Just as the name implies, the piano bar is a place for kicking back and having a cocktail. As part of the Grand Café complex, élite attitudes soar as high as the prices, letting you feel suave. *Mains from* US$20; open 10.00–02.00.

♀ **O'Brien's** Mikhaylovska 17A; ☎ 044 229 1584. Knowing it wasn't a part of the global community until its capital sported an Irish pub, Kiev quickly adopted O'Brien's as its own. If you like hearing English all around you, come watch sports here (good food!). *Open 08.00–02.00.*

♀ **112** Chervonoarmiyska 5; ☎ 044 230 9631. Kiev's most original cocktails served all night (112 different kinds), with a steady stream of entertainment kept lively by super-energetic staff. *Open 21.00–04.00.*

♀ **Pilsner** Pushkinska 20; ☎ 044 225 2101. A Czech beer hall in Kiev that serves Czech beer and Czech food. Comfy and casual. *Mains from US$4; open 09.00–midnight.*

ENTERTAINMENT AND NIGHTLIFE

It's utterly impossible to keep up with Kiev's party that seems to do battle in the city night after night. Unassuming visitors to the capital often find themselves being dragged in a taxi down dark streets, usually from one 'cool café' to 'this crazy casino' and on to strip bars or blinking disco barges out on the Dnepr, either finishing up in a US$100-per-plate, all-night supper club or a basement packed with beer-drenched head-bangers. It's all part of the fun that's Kiev. To make your own choices about what you do, check out *What's On*, the *Kiev Post*, or any number of free English-language publications that are given out at hotels and restaurants.

☆ **Orangerea** Basseina 4; ☎ 044 230 9500. Funky dancing and drinks for the 20–30-somethings. Typically featuring visiting European DJs. *Open 21.00–06.00.*

☆ **Art Club 44** Khreschatyk 44; ☎ 044 229 4137. A pretty hip place in Kiev of late, the '44' serves US$5 cocktails from an ultra-long bar and provides the venue for all of Kiev's rocking-est bands. *Open 10.00–02.00.*

☆ **Pa Ti Pa** Muzeiny 10; ☎ 044 235 0150. Absolutely crazy nightclub with Latin music and dancing. *Open 11.00–06.00.*

☆ **Decadence House** Shota Rustavelli 16; ☎ 044 2064920. Baroque decadence at its most extravagant, packed with Kiev's wealthiest and most self-important hipsters. *US$20 cover minimum; open 12.00–02.00; weekends until 06.00.*

☆ **Sound Planet** Dmitrivska 18/24; ☎ 044 486 0300; www.soundpla.net. Not unlike London's Ministry of Sound, this raver's delight plays great DJs all night long. *Open 21.00 until dawn.*

☆ **Fabergé** Rybalska 22; ☎ 288 7129. Ritzy and exclusive, this new-ish nightclub is heavy on attitude, which is probably why it's become so popular. Gourmet *hors-d'oeuvres* and snooty cocktails. *Open 24 hours.*

☆ **Opium** Saksahanskovo 1Г; ☎ 044 205 5393. This is the club you're bound to come to without even knowing it. A Kiev staple, 'Opium' welcomes all, playing dance and pop favourites. *US$10 cover; open 23.00–04.00.*

☆ **Moda Bar** Naberezhno-Khreschatytska, Pier No 6; ☎ 044 416 7388; www.2k.com.ua. Already passé but still known for its outlandish parties, daily fashion shows and bartenders who perform dazzling tricks to brain-shattering techno music – all on a Dnepr river boat. *Open 20.00–06.00.*

THEATRE Ukrainians love a good drama, so it should come as no surprise that Kiev's world of theatre thrived through world wars, repressive regimes, and total poverty. The capital's recent cultural renaissance was lead in large part by Kiev's unofficial acting guilds, and it is on the stage that the real drama of Ukraine's present cultural and political experimentation unfolds with passion.

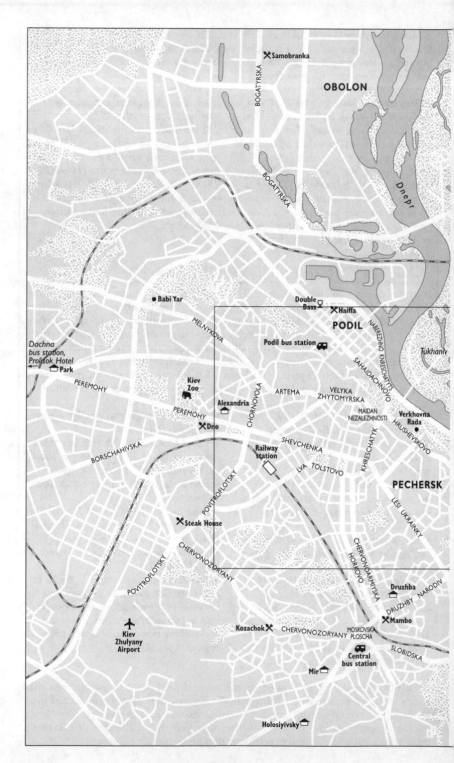

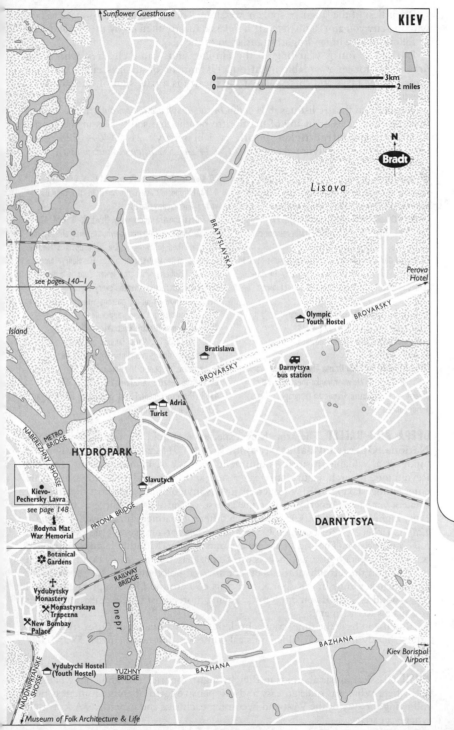

KIEV

0 ———————— 3km
0 ———————— 2 miles

N

Bradt

↑ Sunflower Guesthouse

Lisova

BRATYSLAVSKA

see pages 140–1

Island

Perova Hotel →

Olympic Youth Hostel

BROVARSKY

Bratislava

BROVARSKY

Darnytsya bus station

Adria
Turist

NABEREZHNY SHOSSE

METRO BRIDGE

HYDROPARK

Slavutych

Kievo-Pechersky Lavra
see page 148

↑ Rodyna Mat War Memorial

PATONA BRIDGE

DARNYTSYA

Botanical Gardens

Vydubytsky Monastery
Monastyrskaya Trapezna
New Bombay Palace

RAILWAY BRIDGE

Dnepr

BAZHANA

Kiev Borispol Airport

NADDNIPRYANSKE SHOSSE

Vydubychi Hostel (Youth Hostel)

YUZHNY BRIDGE

BAZHANA

↓ Museum of Folk Architecture & Life

Regardless of the language spoken, watching a play in Kiev puts you face to face with the city you aim to discover. If it's classic theatre then enjoy the visual drama or follow along with an English translation of the play.

Part of the fun is watching all the families and young children who come dressed up for an affordable night out. Ukrainians of all ages enjoy even the most serious plays and to be seen at the theatre is a true sign of one's cultural prestige.

You can find theatre listings in *What's On* (*www.whatson-kiev.com*), at the various theatres themselves or in any of the theatre booths that sell tickets in the centre. Also try the **central ticket booth** at Khreschatyk 21 (↘ *044 228 7642; www.ctik.kiev.ua*) or **Olvia** ticket agency (↘ *044 247 5523; www.olvia.com.ua*).

☺ **Actor Theatre** Velyka Zhytomyrska 40; ↘ 044 219 1048. Some of the latest in Russian and Ukrainian playwriting, along with lesser-known classics.

☺ **Bravo Drama Theatre** Honchara Olesya 79; ↘ 044 216 4022. Highbrow drama and stark romanticism by Ukraine's leading professionals.

☺ **Drama and Comedy Theatre** Brovarsky 25; ↘ 044 517 1955. On the left bank, specialising in dark comedies that only Ukrainians could get away with.

☺ **Lesya Ukrayinka Russian Drama Theatre** Khmelnytskovo 5B; ↘ 044 224 4223; www.rusdram.com.ua. Kiev's renowned Russian-language playhouse.

☺ **Ivan Franko National Drama Theatre** Ivana Franka 3; ↘ 044 229 5991; www.franko-theatre.kiev.ua. Diverse and innovative Ukrainian-language performances.

☺ **Kiev Youth Theatre** Prorizna 17; ↘ 044 235 4218. European classics produced by the capital's young and creative artists.

☺ **Kolesa Theatre** Andriyivsky Uzviz 8; ↘ 044 416 04 22. Small avant-garde playhouse that already has an established following in Kiev. The upstairs theatre produces more well-known pieces (ie: Henry James, Ionesco, Flaubert) while the lower floor is a working café with interactive theatre every night of the week. Somehow or other, patrons will get roped into the performance art and vaudeville.

☺ **Podil Drama Theatre** Kontraktova Ploscha 4; ↘ 044 416 5489. World famous and very entertaining, doing everything from adapted Shakespeare to poetic Ukrainian pieces.

☺ **Suzirya Theatre** Yaroslaviv Val 14B; ↘ 044 212 4188. The experimental and traditional mixed right before your very eyes.

OPERA AND BALLET The true Kiev experience should include a show at the **National Opera and Ballet** (*Volodymyrska 50;* ↘ *044 224 7165*). Not only is the building a valuable historic monument to Kiev, Ukraine and the Russian Revolution, its architecture amazes (inside and out), and the shows are truly entertaining. Taking in Kiev's opera is just as invigorating, and most theatres will rotate a very large repertoire over the course of the season. There is something every night (*starting at 19.00*), and often a different matinee show as well (*starting at 12.00*). Tickets sell for between US$5 and US$25 for a range of classics like *Swan Lake* and *Rigoletto*. The shows are always outstanding. Monthly listings are posted outside the opera house, and tickets can be purchased in the small booth (through the door) on the left side of the main entrance on Volodymyrska. Take special care to avoid ticket touts in this spot. Good seats cost around US$5, a private box will cost around US$10. If you don't mind paying more, most hotels can arrange to get you tickets to the opera.

Also, if you have the time, come check out Kiev's **Theatre of Operetta,** which offers slightly lighter and sillier musical comedies (*Chervonoarmiyska 53/3;* ↘ *044 428 2630*).

MUSIC Classical music abounds in Kiev by night; the trick is finding out what's on and when. What was once an easy and inexpensive form of entertainment is now following the way of the West and becoming exclusive and expensive. Ask around when you arrive.

National Opera You can often find symphony concerts with available tickets here; see above for details.
National Philharmonic Volodymyrska Uzviz 2; ✎ 044 229 6251, 044 228 1697; www.filarmonia.com.ua. Featuring one of the country's most beautiful architectural interiors, the Philharmonic provides Kiev with stunning classic and folk performances almost every night.
House of Organ and Chamber Music Chervonoarmiyska 75; ✎ 044 268 3186; www.organhall.kiev.ua. Like many churches during the Soviet era, St Nikolai's was transformed into the respectable 'Organ Hall'. The respectability continues with stalwart performances of chamber music and powerful organ recitals.
National Conservatory Arkhitektora Horodetskovo; ✎ 044 229 0792. This venue also makes good with its broad European classical repertoire.
Palats Ukrayina Chervonoarmiyska 103. For something slightly more peppy, try here. Pop stars from across the former USSR like to show their stuff at the Palats, or you might be lucky and catch an evening with one of the burned-out stars from the West.
Soho Artyoma 82; ✎ 044 244 7351. For Kiev's best and brightest live rock bands; see page 41.

CINEMA In Kiev, cinemas are nearly always showing American films that are badly dubbed into Ukrainian or Russian, with the very rare exception of a Russian film that isn't, and some subtitled movies. Prices can be as low as US$2 to get in, and up to US$10. More important than the film, and definitely unique, are the big Soviet-style movie houses throughout Kiev. These were purpose built for the masses before Hollywood came along, and can still be enjoyed as such.

Butterfly Moskovsky 6; ✎ 044 531 3977
Kino Palats Institutska 1; ✎ 044 228 7223
Kinopanorama Shota Rustavelli; ✎ 044 227 3041
Kyiv Chervonoarmiyska 19; ✎ 044 221 0881

Kyivska Rus Artyoma 93; ✎ 044 251 6051
Ukraina Horodetskovo 5; ✎ 044 229 6301
Zhovten Kostyantynivska 26; ✎ 044 251 6095

SHOPPING

Never fear, these days you can find anything in Kiev. All along Khreschatyk, the formerly dingy underground passages have been transformed into sparkling luxury and high-tech shops that sell perfume, teeny bathing suits, diamonds and laptops. The largest of these 'malls' occupies the space beneath the Maidan Nezalezhnosti, offering two floors of wealth and glamour year-round. The old Soviet state department store ЦУМ (for *Central Universal Store; Khmelnytskovo 2*; ✎ *044 224 9505*) once offered everything the USSR produced; now it's looking more and more like Harrods of London.

For a more traditional (yet upscale) Ukrainian shopping experience, try the **Bessarabsky Rynok** at the corner of Khreschatyk and Prospekt Shevchenko. This is the way people have been shopping in Kiev from the beginning, only now the products have changed. All the vegetables and fruit are imported and picture perfect, as are the flowers and jars of caviar. The name of the market comes from the Bessarabian (Moldovan) merchants who lived and worked in this section of town. Lots of noise and free samples are part of the act. Everyday open-air street markets are more commonplace by the metro stations further outside the city.

If you're looking for souvenirs, a lot of vendors congregate on the Maidan Nezalezhnosti with their music, books, flags and Ukrainian-themed knick-knacks. The other most obvious souvenir marketplace is on Andriyivsky Uzviz, where the upper section is rather cheesy and mass-market, while the lower sections focus on local antiques. A number of high-quality souvenir shops are opening up all over the city though.

SOUVENIRS
UKRSOV Pushkinsa 31A; ✎ 044 235 7383; www.ukrsov.kiev.ua. One of the most comprehensive
souvenir shops in Kiev: traditional embroidery, national dress, high-quality art and every kind of

Kiev's got plenty of home-grown alternatives to the 'dinner-and-show' options for an evening out. A classic form of local entertainment is the **Kiev Circus** (*Tsyrk*); (*Peremohy 2;* ☎ *044 216 3856*). You don't need to speak the language to enjoy the animals, sequins and death-defying feats. Shows normally start at 19.00 on weekends and at 13.00 and 17.00 on weekends, costing US$2–5. Call ahead to get tickets, buy them from the theatre ticket booths, or from the people standing next to the circus posters in the subway. Your hotel concierge should be able to hook you up as well.

Kiev dearly loves its several puppet theatres, which provided common kiddie entertainment during the Soviet era, and which continue to serve as a revered art form for all ages throughout Ukraine. Try the **Marionette Theatre** in Podil (*Sahaydachnovo 29/3;* ☎ *044 417 3058*). The theatre is known for its artistic puppet renditions of classic Ukrainian fairy tales. The **Kiev State Puppet Theatre** (*Hrushevskovo 1A;* ☎ *044 278 0499*) is more traditional, with giant-sized puppets and cool lighting. For a little more rhythm and energy, try the **Children's Musical Theatre** (*Mezhygirska 2;* ☎ *044 416 4280*) with lively song and dance numbers.

Ukrainian craft. *Open 09.00–20.00.*
Ukrainian Folk Art Khreschatyk 27A; ☎ 044 228 8332. Authentic souvenirs, wonderful beaded jewellery and ceramics. *Open 10.00–21.00.*
Gonchary Andriyivsky Uzviz 10A; ☎ 044 416 1298. High-quality decorative craft and ceramics. *Open 10.00–19.00.*
Kristina 4 Kostyolna; ☎ 044 228 7950. A more down-to-earth Kiev souvenir shop. *Open 09.00–21.00.*

ANTIQUES
Antique Salon Horkovo 11; ☎ 044 297 3758. *Open 10.00–19.00*
Antique Centre Andriyivsky Uzviz 3; ☎ 044 416 1237. *Open 10.00–19.00*
Belle Époque Andriyivsky Uzviz 34; ☎ 044 228

Perlyna Khreschatyk 21; ☎ 044 228 1773. Fine jewellery, some of which is Ukrainian-designed. *Open 10.00–20.00.*
Silk Route Suvorova 4; ☎ 044 295 0324. Elaborate and artistic shop in Pechersk, selling beautiful things. *Open 10.00–19.00.*
Sia Khreschatyk 46A; ☎ 044 235 9231. Upscale gift and souvenir shop. *Open 11.00–20.00.*
Suveniry Khreschatyk 32; ☎ 044 235 4134. Selling classic Ukrainian souvenirs and lots of books. *Open 11.00–17.00.*

3955. *Open 11.00–18.00.*
Chef d'oeuvre Horodetskovo 12; ☎ 044 229 6274. *Open 11.00–19.00*
Relikviya Baseina 21; ☎ 044 235 9123. *Open 11.00–19.00.*

OTHER PRACTICALITIES

NEWSPAPERS AND MAGAZINES The *Kiev Post* (*www.kyivpost.com*) is the capital's English-language free press weekly, offering great political and business insight, as well as up-to-date listings for city events. The newspaper is available free in most upmarket hotels and restaurants or for sale at any newsstand. The other English-language newspaper is the more stodgy *Kiev Weekly* (*www.kyivweekly.com*), also widely distributed for free. The *Ukrainian Journal* (www.ukrainianjournal.com) is an online English publication with more in-depth analysis. The *Ukrainian Observer* (*www.ukraine-observer.com*) is more expat and business focused, while *What's On Kiev* (*www.whatson-kiev.com*) is a colourful English-language weekly in the style of *TimeOut* guides, detailing restaurants, nightlife and entertainment. For more general newspapers and magazines, see page 100.

INTERNET More and more hotels (and apartments) in Kiev are offering wi-fi and high-speed internet access as part of their normal service. If not, they will feature a 'business centre' that caters for business travellers, for a price. If you want to cut down on costs, choose among a plethora of Kiev's high-tech, 24-hour internet cafés, few of which charge more than US$2–4 an hour. English-language signs will point the way, and the staff are typically younger and English-speaking. If you're panicked and disoriented but need email badly, go to the central post office (the entrance on the Maidan Nezalezhnosti) and go up to the second floor, where there is a real café with lots of internet connections. Otherwise, here are a few centrally located cafés:

📧 **Pentagon** Khreschatyk 15; 📞 044 228 2182; www.pentagon.kiev.ua
📧 **Bunker** Artyoma 11A; 📞 044 212 4860; www.bunker.kiev.ua
📧 **Cyber Café** Prorizna 21; 📞 044 228 0548

📧 **MI6** Pechersky Uzviz 3; 📞 044 235 3840
📧 **Orki** Khmelnytskovo 29/2; 📞 044 228 1187
📧 **Orbita** Khreschatyk 29, 2nd floor; 📞 044 234 1693
📧 **Vault I3** Chervonarmiyska 19; www.vault13.com

POST Kiev's behemoth **central post office** is on the Maidan Nezalezhnosti (*Khreschatyk 22; open 08.00–21.00 every day, closing on Sun 19.00*). Besides enabling you to buy stamps and mail things, there is an internet café and a number of international phone booths that charge about US$0.60 a minute for calls to North America and US$1 to western Europe. You can also fax things here, and it is one of the few places to buy postcards, although sadly, no-one has had the enterprising vision of making quality photographic prints of Kiev. (There are great alternatives though, such as Happy Red Army Day cards). Mail letters in the little yellow boxes with dark blue writing marked ПОШТА that hang from the sides of buildings and outside post offices. There are 232 post offices in Kiev and each is named as it is numbered. Naturally, Kievans are still more likely to know 'their' post office by its number. Ask the concierge at the hotel where you're staying, or ask a stranger on the street '*de poshta?*'

BANKING So many banks have popped up around Kiev that you will have no problem getting cash or finding out your bank balance in hrivna. There are also banking facilities at the central post office, and most middle to upmarket hotels will have an ATM in the lobby. Finding a place to change money is even easier than finding a bank. Just look for the signs with American, Russian and European flags, with corresponding currency rates listed. Currency exchange booths are normally open from 9.00 to 21.00, some later. Banking hours in Ukraine normally run from 9.00 to 16.00.

Listing all of Kiev's banks would be like listing all of its fire hydrants. You shouldn't have any trouble finding one if you're in Podil, the centre or Pechersk. Things are tougher in more residential areas, although cash machines are becoming ubiquitous in smaller restaurants and shops. Here are a few leads:

$ **Citibank** Dymytrova 16Ё; 📞 044 490 1000. South side, by metro station Respublikansky Stadion.
$ **Diamantbank** Kontraktova Ploscha 10A; 📞 044 490 8383. In Podil, at the bottom of Andriyvsky Uzviz.
$ **Nadra** Khmelnytskovo 4; 📞 044 462 0001. In the centre, off Khreschatyk, next to ЦУМ.

$ **Parex Bank** Striletska 16; 📞 044 244 6715. Behind St Sophia's Cathedral.
$ **Raiffeisenbank** Mykhayilivska 2; 📞 044 490 0526. The north side of the Maidan Nezalezhnosti.
$ **Western Union** Prorizna 15; 📞 044 228 1780. In the city centre, a block up from Khreschatyk.

TELEPHONE Kiev's city code is 044 and all city phone numbers are seven digits. Within Kiev, just dial these seven digits; from outside Ukraine, drop the 0, dial 38

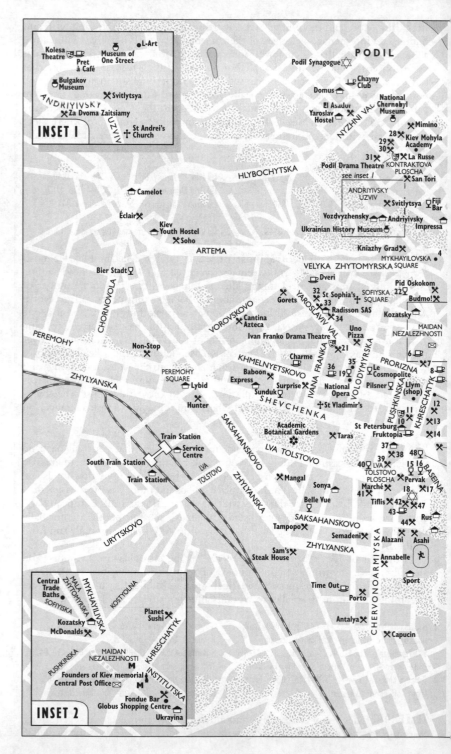

INSET 1

Kolesa Theatre
Pret à Café
Bulgakov Museum
L-Art
Museum of One Street
Svitlytsya
ANDRIYIVSKY UZVIV
Za Dvoma Zaitsiamy
St Andrei's Church

PODIL

Podil Synagogue
Chayny Club
Domus
National Chernobyl Museum
El Asador
Yaroslav Hostel
NYZHNI VAL
Mimino
28
29
30
31
Kiev Mohyla Academy
La Russe
KONTRAKTOVA PLOSCHA
Podil Drama Theatre
see inset 1
San Tori
ANDRIYIVSKY UZVIV
Svitlytsya
Fiji Bar
Vozdvyzhensky
Andriyivsky
Ukrainian History Museum
Impressa

HLYBOCHYTSKA

Camelot
Éclair
Kiev Youth Hostel
Soho
ARTEMA
Kniazhy Grad
MYKHAYILOVSKA
VELYKA ZHYTOMYRSKA SQUARE
4

Bier Stadt
Dveri
Pid Oskokom
22
Budmo!
CHORNOVOLA
32 St Sophia's
SOFIYSKA SQUARE
Gorets
YAROSLAVIV VAL
33
Radisson SAS
34
Kozatsky
MAIDAN NEZALEZHNOSTI
VOROVSKOVO
Cantina Azteca
Uno Pizza
PEREMOHY
Ivan Franko Drama Theatre
21
6
PRORIZNA
7
Non-Stop
ZHYLYANSKA
PEREMOHY SQUARE
Lybid
KHMELNYETSKOVO
Charme
36
35
19
Le Cosmopolite
8
Baboon Express
Surprise
Sunduk
National Opera
Pilsner
Llym (shop)
12
Hunter
SHEVCHENKA
St Vladimir's
11
10
13
Taras
St Petersburg
Fruktopia
14
Academic Botanical Gardens
37
38
48
Train Station
Service Centre
39
40 LVA TOLSTOVO PLOSCHA
15 16
Pervak
South Train Station
LVA TOLSTOVO
Mangal
Marché
41
18
17
Train Station
Sonya
Tiflis
42
47
Belle Vue
43
44
Rus
SAKSAHANSKOVO
Tampopo
Semadeni
Alazani
Asahi
ZHYLYANSKA
Sam's Steak House
Annabelle
URYTSKOVO
Time Out
Sport
Porto
Antalya
CHERVONOARMIYSKA
Capucin

INSET 2

Central Trade Baths
MALA ZHTOMYRSKA
MYKHAYILIVSKA
KOSTYOLNA
SOFIYSKA
Planet Sushi
Kozatsky
McDonalds
PUSHKINSKA
MAIDAN NEZALEZHNOSTI
KHRESCHATYK
Founders of Kiev memorial
Central Post Office
INSTITUTSKA
Fondue Bar
Globus Shopping Centre
Ukrayina

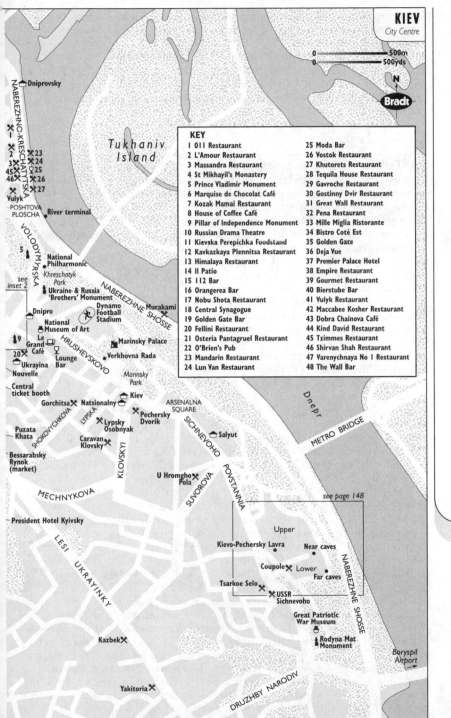

KIEV
City Centre

0 ——————— 500m
0 ——————— 500yds

N

Bradt

KEY

1 011 Restaurant	25 Moda Bar
2 L'Amour Restaurant	26 Vostok Restaurant
3 Massandra Restaurant	27 Khutorets Restaurant
4 St Mikhayil's Monastery	28 Tequila House Restaurant
5 Prince Vladimir Monument	29 Gavroche Restaurant
6 Marquise de Chocolat Café	30 Gostinny Dvir Restaurant
7 Kozak Mamai Restaurant	31 Great Wall Restaurant
8 House of Coffee Café	32 Pena Restaurant
9 Pillar of Independence Monument	33 Mille Miglia Ristorante
10 Russian Drama Theatre	34 Bistro Coté Est
11 Kievska Perepichka Foodstand	35 Golden Gate
12 Kavkazkaya Plennitsa Restaurant	36 Deja Vue
13 Himalaya Restaurant	37 Premier Palace Hotel
14 Il Patio	38 Empire Restaurant
15 112 Bar	39 Gourmet Restaurant
16 Orangerea Bar	40 Bierstube Bar
17 Nobu Shota Restaurant	41 Vulyk Restaurant
18 Central Synagogue	42 Maccabee Kosher Restaurant
19 Golden Gate Bar	43 Dobra Chainova Café
20 Fellini Restaurant	44 Kind David Restaurant
21 Osteria Pantagruel Restaurant	45 Tzimmes Restaurant
22 O'Brien's Pub	46 Shirvan Shah Restaurant
23 Mandarin Restaurant	47 Varenychnaya No 1 Restaurant
24 Lun Van Restaurant	48 The Wall Bar

Dniprovsky

Tukhaniv Island

NABEREZHNO-KRESCHATYTSKA

1
2 23
3 24
45 25
46 26
27

Vulyk

POSHTOVA
PLOSCHA · River terminal

VOLODYMYRSKA

5
National
Philharmonic

Khreschatyk Park

see inset 2

Ukraine & Russia
'Brothers' Monument

NABEREZHNE SHOSSE

Dnipro

Dynamo
Football
Stadium

Murakami

National
Museum of Art

9
Le
Grand
20 Café

Marinsky Palace

HRUSHEVSKOVO

Verkhovna Rada

Lounge
Bar

Ukrayina
Nouvelle

Marinsky Park

Central
ticket booth

Kiev

Gorchitsa Natsionalny

ARSENALNA
SQUARE

Pechersky
Dvorik

LYPSKA

Lypsky
Osobnyak

SHOKOVYCHKOVA

Caravan
Klovsky

KLOVSKYI

Salyut

SICHNEVOHO

Puzata
Khata

Bessarabsky
Rynok
(market)

MECHNYKOVA

U Hromgho
Pola

SUVOROVA

POVSTANNIA

Dnepr

METRO BRIDGE

see page 148

President Hotel Kyivsky

LESI UKRAYINKY

Upper

Kievo-Pechersky Lavra

Near caves

Coupole Lower

Far caves

Tsarkoe Selo

USSR
Sichnevoho

NABEREZHNE SHOSSE

Great Patriotic
War Museum

Rodyna Mat
Monument

Borispyl
Airport

Kazbek

Yakitoria

DRUZHBY NARODIV

Kiev OTHER PRACTICALITIES

6

141

(the country code), 44, and then the seven digits. All pay phones in Kiev take Utel cards only, which you can buy at the central post office or at any number of city kiosks for denomations of US$5, US$10, and US$20. If you are planning a short-to long-term stay in the country and need to be calling frequently, you should just buy a pre paid Ukrainian SIM card for your own mobile phone. Try **Kyivstar** (*Sichnevoho Povstannya 24;* ⟩ *044 466 0466; www.kyivstar.net*) or **UMC** (*Leiptsizka 15;* ⟩ *044 500 0500, www.umc.com.ua*) or any of the dozens of mobile phone shops around town.

WHAT TO SEE AND DO

CITY CENTRE The first place you'll be shown, or the first place you'll find on your own, is Kiev's most central north–south boulevard **Khreschatyk**. The road was one of Kiev's very first and once followed a clear stream flowing into the Dnepr. During World War II, the retreating Soviet army booby-trapped most of the street so that it would blow up after the Nazis had entered the city. The violent welcome was answered by the systematic shooting of tens of thousands of Kiev's citizens. Everything you see today has been rebuilt – people may criticise the pomp of post-war Stalinist architecture, but these monumental structures define Kiev today. The central focal point of the boulevard is the **Maidan Nezalezhnosti** (Independence Square) that seems to be moving in the direction of Times Square in New York or Piccadilly Circus in London, with its large-scale electronic advertising and billboards. This used to be the Place of the October Revolution but is now remembered as the focal point for the Orange Revolution of 2004. Some of the original 'Orange' graffiti has been preserved on the panelled pillars of the central post office. Today, the Maidan continues to be the throbbing heart of Kiev, with the city's largest shopping centre (underground), a chic McDonald's, the central post office, and lots of friendly Ukrainian patriotic entrepreneurs selling flags, books and music. On the opposite side of the street is Kiev's newest **Monument of Independence**, a white and gold pillar erected in 2001 to celebrate the first ten years of freedom from the Soviet Union. Down below, on the left side of the square is another recent bronze sculpture showing the **Founders of Kiev**: 'Kyi' the elder brother, for whom the city is named; Lybid, his sister, who was reported to have chosen the spot; and their two younger brothers, Schek and Khoriv.

Where Khreschatyk begins its descent to the river stands a giant titanium arch over the brawny statues of two 'brothers' – Ukraine and Russia – raising fists in a joined union. Of course, the monument to the '**Friendship of Nations**' is controversial today, but the space has remained, probably for its wonderful view of the river and the city. The park continues south all the way to the Caves Monastery, *Rodyna Mat*, and the botanical gardens.

Volodymyrska runs parallel to Khreschatyk and is the historic 'backstreet' for Kievans. Central to the boulevard is the **Golden Gate** (Zoloti Vorota), a replica of the last remaining portion of Kiev's original ramparts prior to the 13th-century Mongol invasion. Kneeling in front of the gate is a **Monument to Yaroslav the Wise**, who defended Kiev from the Pecheneg invasion of the 11th century and founded St Sophia's Cathedral in thanks (his statue holds a model of the church in his hands). Further down the street (on the corner of Khmelnytksovo and Volodymyrska: *50 Volodymyrska*) stands the **Ukrainian National Opera** – an incredible building from Kiev's fleeting belle époque, completed in 1901 and named after Taras Shevchenko (his bust has been added to this national monument as well). The building's luxurious hall reflects the typical Viennese style for an opera house, and is one of the most well-preserved historic interiors in the city,

If you take the time to visit each place mentioned, this itinerary will take a day.

- Starting at Universitet metro station, cross the street to **St Vladimir's Cathedral** (see page 151).
- From St Vladimir's walk down Leontovycha to Khmelnystkovo, turn right and walk one block.
- Cross the street and you are in front of Ukraine's **National Opera House**. Book tickets for a night performance.
- Walk up Volodymyrska (north) to the green park where you see the remaining 'Golden Gate' (Zoloti Vorota) of Kiev's pre-Mongol fortress and a monument to Yaroslav the Wise (see page 152).
- Continue down Volodymyrska to **St Sophia's Cathedral** (see page 151)
- In the middle of Sofiyska Square is the monument to Bohdan Khmelnytsky. Cross the park/thoroughfare to the opposite St Mikhayil's Square and the bright blue **St Mikhayil's Monastery of the Golden Domes** (see page 152). On the way you will pass the monuments to Princess Olga, saints Cyril and Methodius and the Apostle Andrew, and near the entrance to St Mikhayil's you will see the monument to the victims of the Ukrainian famine.
- The stately white building across St Mikhayil's Square is Ukraine's **Ministry of Foreign Affairs** (see page 431). Walk past it and down Desiatynna, to the ruins of Desiatynnaya Church, the History Museum and the ancient tree.
- Continue down Desiatynna past the art galleries and to the turquoise St Andrei's Church. Begin your descent down **Andriyivsky Uzviz** (which can take a whole day if you want to see everything). At the base of the hill, walk one block into the heart of Podil at Kontraktova Ploscha. Take the metro or a taxi back.

If your time in Kiev is really limited, you can take transport to Podil, or to the Caves Monastery, which should not be missed. The simplest, fastest and most common walk for those who live in Kiev starts at the Maidan Nezalezhnosti and goes all the way down (south) Khreschatyk past all the government buildings, city hall, the shops and restaurants, and ends at Bessarabsky Rynok. The street is closed for pedestrians only on Saturdays and Sundays.

thanks to its everyday use during the Soviet era. The opera house is also renowned for the 1911 assassination of Pyotr Stolypin, prime minister to Tsar Nikolai II during the first attempt at reforming the St Petersburg government. He was shot at point-blank range during the second intermission of Rimsky-Korsakov's *The Tale of Tsar Saltan*. Nobody has died here since, and it is quite easy to get tickets for any of the shows – the ballet and opera boast an amazing repertoire (see page 136). Few things in Kiev compare to an evening spent in this building, and for now, tickets to a show are the only way to get inside.

UPPER CITY At the opposite end of Volodymyrska is **Sofiyska Square,** with the landmark tower of **St Sophia's Cathedral** and the mighty statue of Bohdan Khmelnytsky on horseback, the Cossack *hetman* who liberated Kiev from the Poles and subsequently handed the country over to the Russians. From here it is an easy walk across the park to Mikhayilovsky Square, and **St Mikhayil's Monastery of the Golden Domes**. Behind the monastery is Kiev's most fun form of public transport – the funicular, which takes passengers down from the 'upper city' into the lower Podil. Rising behind the monastery is Vladimir's Hill, where the famous

Statue of Prince Vladimir holding a cross still stands above the river as he did in legend when all of Kiev was baptised.

At the end of Volodymyrska and Desyatina are the ruins of Kiev's oldest stone building, the **Desyatina Church,** first constructed as the Mother of God Church under the rule of Prince Vladimir. 'Desyatina' means 'tithing' in Russian, and following Kiev's conversion to Christianity, the prince ordered that one-tenth of the city's tribute be granted to the church. Walking among the floorplan-like ruins of the church today, you can appreciate that for the time, this was a sizeable church. The original church was crushed by the Mongols. (The ancient tree providing the shade for the ruins is a linden that was most likely planted around the 13th century.) Further down from the church, Desyatina meets the very vibrant and artsy street Andriyivsky Uzviz.

OFFICIAL KIEV The seat of the Ukrainian government is based along the blocks of Hrushevskovo that runs south from Khreschatyk. The street is named after Mikhail Hrushevsky, a renowned Ukrainian academic, who was elected as the first president of independent Ukraine in 1918 (sadly, his presidency lasted only three months). At the intersection (now called European Square), you will see the round white **Ukrainian House**, once home to the Ukrainian Communist Party. On the other side, moving up Hrushevskovo, is the playing field and stadium of Kiev's famous **Dynamo** football team which has a huge following in the West and throughout the former Soviet Union.

Of Ukraine's government buildings, the rococo **Marinsky Palace** is one of the prettiest, built in 1752 as a royal residence fit for the Russian aristocracy, after they had complained there was nowhere decent to stay in Kiev. Today the blue and white building is used only for the president's private state functions, but in principle tourists may walk the grounds (although at times you will be hurried along by the guards that stand on every corner). Next door to the palace is the **Verkhovna Rada**, the national parliament of Ukraine. All of Ukraine's representatives meet beneath the big rounded glass dome and it is in this building that Ukrainian independence was declared on 24 August 1991. Life within the Rada today is as exciting as ever, as Ukrainian's *deputaty* (parliamentarians) wage war with one another.

Further down Hrushevskovo, in the park by the river, stand a few key monuments in Kiev's history. Askold and Dir were the first of the Varangians (Vikings) to raid Kiev, boasting of their spoils to the northern principality of Novgorod. Jealous, their older brother Helgi plotted, attacked and killed the pair. Askold was buried on this hillside in Kiev, and the small round church added in 1810. Sadly, Askold's actual grave (and many others in this same place) did not withstand Stalin's wave of destruction, which wiped the area clean in the mid-1930s.

ANDRIYIVSKY UZVIZ АНДРИЇВСЬКИЙ УЗВІЗ According to the Bible, Andrew was the first apostle to be called to follow Christ, and according to legend the saint sailed up the banks of the Dnepr and landed in this particular spot – prophesying that on these hills a great city would rise up (legend also claims he landed in Crimea). The saint supposedly climbed this particular hill in Kiev and fixed a cross in the ground – a curved and narrow lane now twists from this spot and follows St Andrew's path down to the Dnepr. After Kiev adopted Christianity, the great pagan idol Perun was tied to a stag and dragged down 'Andrew's descent', beaten with sticks, and shoved into the river.

Today the sea-green and dark teal **St Andrei's Church** (*Andriyivsky Uzviz 23;* ✆ *044 278 5861; open 13.00–18.00, closed Wed; entrance 5UAH*) crowns the top of

Kiev's favourite street with spindly turrets and a fanciful Baroque dome. The unique design is the work of Italian architect Rastrelli who had already built St Petersburg's most famous buildings, the Winter Palace and Tsarskoe Selo. The church in Kiev was his last masterpiece, completed in 1762, after which he was fired by Catherine the Great. The church was turned into a museum of architecture to avoid the wrath of Stalin and remains a museum today. The interior has only just been renovated and is still rather empty, except for the two very interesting paintings of St Andrew and Prince Vladimir.

By the time you get to St Andrei's, someone will have tried to sell you something to remember Kiev by. In the 19th century, Andriyivsky Uzviz was the proud domain of artists and writers and since then the street has harboured Kiev's more bohemian elements. Today, souvenir markets and so-called art shows run along the entire length of the street and this is where most tourists are directed to buy gifts. Most of the stuff for sale is mass-produced, but it is what most people want: matroshka dolls, fake Soviet paraphernalia, machine-stitched Ukrainian embroidery or T-shirts with Lenin making obscene gestures. Further down the street the bits and bobs become more varied with woodcarving, home-knit wool, old prints, books and coins. The festive antique and souvenir bazaar is kept alive with the help of musicians, street poets and mimes. Much of the art consists of rows upon rows of kitsch paintings, but there are still a few authentic galleries on the descent. Have a look in **Gallery 36** – a private gallery that features quality work by contemporary Ukrainian artists (*Andriyivsky Uzviz 36;* ✆ *044 228 2985;* e *infor@Gallery36.org.ua; www.Gallery36.org.ua*). Next door, the gallery **Triptych** also deserves a serious browse (*Andiryvsky Uzviz 34;* ✆ *044 229 8385; www.triptych-galler.org*). For more traditional Ukrainian themes and Socialist Realist painting, try the very professional **L-Art** at the bottom of the hill (*Andriyivsky Uzviz 26;* ✆ *044 416 0320; www.lartgallery.com*).

From the top of the street, you will spot the modest white **Statue of Apostle Andrew**. This marks the beginning of the old residential area, and most of these homes are architectural monuments, including the wooden house at No 34, known as **Noah's Ark** for its wooden exterior and a history of cramming lots of poor starving artists onto its floors. Every building has a story – the seven-storey yellow edifice with one single tower (No 15) is known as **Richard's Castle**, named after King Richard I in *Ivanhoe* by the children who once played on the street. These were once the favoured flats of Kiev's more prestigious artists.

The famous Russian writer Mikhail Bulgakov was born in Kiev, and moved to house No 13 with his theologian father at age 15. Here he attended high school and medical school and then worked as a doctor during the revolution. The **Bulgakov Museum** now occupies the home (*Andriyvksy Uzviz 13;* ✆ *044 416 3188; open 10.00–18.00, closed Wed; entrance 5UAH, 20UAH for a guided tour in English*). The ghostly surrealist exhibit incorporates ideas from all of his well-known works, but mainly from his autobiographical first novel *The White Guard*, which recounts his experiences in Kiev during the Russian civil war. Any object that is not painted white is an original object from the Bulgakov family. Enthusiasts of *The Master and Margarita* may find fewer allusions to this book than might be hoped for, but a general knowledge will help for understanding some of the stranger features in the house. Bulgakov spent most of his writing career in Moscow but published very little in his lifetime due to harsh censorship.

It's not too hard to find food on the Uzviz, but if you want to sit down for a bit, the place next door to Bulgakov's house is worth trying out. The restaurant has no name so as to reinforce its mysterious nature, but the building is recognised for the black metal cat outside, with the tail of a snake – a character remembered from Bulgakov's *Master and Margarita*. The chef is Armenian so of course the food is wonderful, and live piano and violin music adds to the semi-spooky atmosphere (*Andriyivsky Uzviz 11;* ☎ *044 416 5123; mains from US$8; open 11.00–01.00*).

Across the street is the **Kolesa Theatre**, a small avant-garde playhouse that already has an established following in Kiev (*Andriyivsky Uzviz 8;* ☎ *044 416 04 22*). The upstairs theatre produces more well-known pieces while the lower floor is a working café with interactive theatre every night of the week. Somehow or other, patrons will get roped into the performance art.

Last but in no way least is the delightful **Museum of One Street** at the very bottom of the descent (*Andriyivsky Uzviz 2B;* ☎ *044 416 0398; open 12.00–18.00, closed Mon, entrance 6UAH*). Breaking away from the stifling mould of Soviet museums, the ingenious display recounts the story of this one street through a meticulous collection of objects gathered over the ages from each address. Simple treasures like old clothes, spectacles, dishes and books are arranged in artful installations to represent all that has happened in these homes during the past century. Visitors need not speak Russian to enjoy the visual history of the lives of this neighbourhood: the circus performer, the Orthodox priest, the Jewish rabbi, the composer, the writer and the soldier. A second room is dedicated to temporary exhibits, always thoughtful and pertinent to Kiev's intriguing history (truly, this is my favourite museum in the whole country).

PODIL ПОДІЛ Adnriyivsky Uzviz and Kiev's funicular join the original 'upper city' with Podil, the Dnepr floodplain turned residential neighbourhood. To get there, take the funicular: the ride is fun, the view is good and it only costs 50 kopecks. Pick it up behind St Mikhayil's Monastery of the Golden Domes or near the boat terminal. Otherwise, take the metro to Kontraktova Ploscha or Poshtova Ploscha, walk down the Uzviz, or take a taxi.

Long ago, Podil was the nitty-gritty part of Kiev where foreign merchants and craftsmen lived and laboured far away from the more refined churches and palaces on the hill (hence the river port, contract house and large market spaces). The cosmopolitan flair of yesteryear is still in place and a visit to Podil allows an honest impression of what the rest of Kiev used to look like before all the turmoil of the 20th century. What was once Kiev's fringe quarter now features some of its best architecture and most candid street scenes. Walking around Podil with the intention of sightseeing is a worthy endeavour. In addition to the historic buildings (including the Podil Synagogue, merchants' homes and several smaller churches), there is the riverfront close by and a fury of human activity.

Kontraktova Ploscha (Contract Square) is the central space in Podil. As in centuries past, this area is still an open market of sorts and is becoming a popular focal point for restaurants and clubs. On the south side stand the white colonnades of **Hostiny Dvor**, or Hospice's Court. The long shopping arcades are very similar to those you see on Nevsky Prospekt in St Petersburg, and were built at the very beginning of the 19th century. Further up Mezhigirska is the **Contract House**, once the offices of the marketplace where annual 'contract fairs' were held, which took the form of large-scale swap meets between merchants from throughout the Russian Empire.

Podil is also home to **Kiev Mohyla Academy** (*Kontraktova Ploscha 4; www.ukma.kiev.ua*), probably the most prestigious place of learning in Ukraine. Founded in 1615, it was Kiev's first university, but was only reopened in the 1990s as a private liberal arts academy. Student life is vibrant around the main building and throughout Podil. However, as with all city quarters made famous by the students, few students can actually afford to live here anymore. Artsy and historic, Podil is becoming a gentrified neighbourhood for Kiev's newest professionals.

Detailing Kiev's hundreds of churches would require a multi-volume set of guidebooks, and then a few years later there might very well be a hundred more to write about. Even if churches are not your thing, it would be a pity to miss what Kiev does best. For now, these are the sites that fascinate the majority.

KIEVO-PECHERSKY LAVRA The 'Caves Monastery' is Kiev's number one tourist attraction both for Ukrainians and foreigners. Really, no-one should come to Kiev and not visit it. The enormous ensemble of white church halls with green and gold rooftops has come to represent the spiritual heart of the country and symbolises Kiev's survival throughout a millennium of adversity. Officially, the monastery is defined as a government Historical-Culture Preserve, but this area – and the caves in particular – is a national religious shrine and the headquarters for the Ukrainian Orthodox Church (Moscow Patriarchate). Over 200,000 pilgrims come every year to pray and worship and tourists should visit only in the spirit of reverence and modesty. That said, the Lavra is beginning to show signs of tourist-trap development that already detract from the mood, including abundant souvenir shops and multifarious money-making devices.

The history of the Lavra dates back to Prince Vladimir's introduction of Christianity as the new state religion of Rus. Following this event, St Anthony of Lyubech left Mount Athos in Greece and settled in Kiev in 1051. He lived on the banks of the Dnepr in a manmade cave where he became known for his strict asceticism and spiritual powers. With the help of his devoted follower St Theodosius, Anthony was able to expand the caves by a series of tunnels and cells to accommodate more disciples, leading to the formation of an extensive underground network where monks spent entire lifetimes meditating, praying and writing. Ukraine's (and Russia's) earliest historians, scholars and icon painters were all attached to Kiev's Lavra, including the author of the *Chronicle of Bygone Years*, Nestor. This heritage, and the advent of a printing press in 1615, made Kiev the intellectual centre of Christian thought for all Slavic lands.

The stunning buildings on the surface were begun as early as the 11th century, and while a few exhibit the simple rounded domes of Byzantium, most of the architecture reflects mid-18th-century Baroque styles employed to rebuild the monastery after a devastating fire in 1718. (The Mongol invasions of 1240 and 1480 – as well as an earthquake in 1620 – had already destroyed the older portions of the monastery in stages.) The area was made a cultural preserve in 1926 after the Soviet takeover, but long periods of neglect and the destruction of the war left a series of odd museums surrounded by rubble. Gorbachev returned the monastery and Far Caves to the Church in 1988, followed by the Near Caves a year later, while the Ukrainian government gained control of the upper churches after independence. Most of the glistening structures you see today have only just been restored.

A visit to the monastery and caves can be as short or as long as you want. The ticketing system is as Byzantine as the architecture. General admittance to the Upper Lavra is 20UAII, but every church, exhibition and museum sells separate tickets – it does not take long to collect a pocketful of ripped paper. On occasion, foreigners are charged about ten times more and the right to take photographs costs an additional 15UAII. If you find this troublesome, you can sometimes avoid the maze through a personal guided tour, which will cost around US$45. Freelance tour guides will approach you with lower prices upon entering, or you can make prior arrangements (\ *044 290 3071*). To get to the Pechersky Lavra, take the metro to Arsenalna, then cross the road and take trolley No 38 or bus

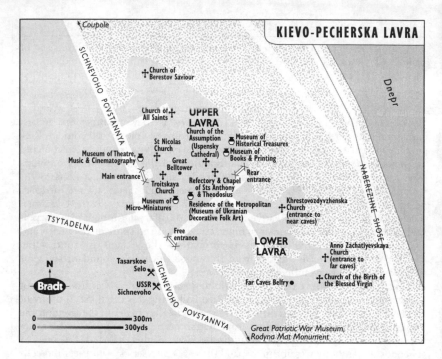

Coupole

SICHNEVOHO POVSTANNYA

Dnepr

Church of
Berestov Saviour

Church of
All Saints

**UPPER
LAVRA**

St Nicolas
Church

Church of the
Assumption
(Uspensky
Cathedral)

Museum of
Historical Treasures

Museum of
Books & Printing

Museum of Theatre,
Music & Cinematography

Great
Belltower

Main entrance

Rear
entrance

Troitskaya
Church

Refectory & Chapel
of Sts Anthony
& Theodosius

Museum of
Micro-Miniatures

Residence of the Metropolitan
(Museum of Ukranian
Decorative Folk Art)

Khrestovozdyvzhenska
Church
(entrance to
near caves)

NABEREZHNE SHOSE

TSYTADELNA

Free
entrance

**LOWER
LAVRA**

Anno Zachatiyevskaya
Church
(entrance to
far caves)

N

Tasarskoe
Selo

SICHNEVOHO

USSR
Sichnevoho

Far Caves Belfry

Church of the Birth of
the Blessed Virgin

Bradt

0 ——— 300m
0 ——— 300yds

POVSTANNYA

Great Patriotic War Museum,
Rodyna Mat Monument

No 20 to the fortification walls at Ivana Mazepa 21. *Marshrutka* No 163 also travels between the Lavra and Khreschatyk. A taxi from the city centre should be US$5–10.

If you are in a taxi or with a tour group, you will most likely get dropped off outside the light blue **Troitskaya Church**. Now used as a gatehouse, the original church was built in 1108 but now features classic examples of Ukrainian Baroque. Before rushing inside, be sure to enjoy a long look at the murals of the outer walls, painted in 1900. The main path leads to the **Great Bell Tower**, the tallest Orthodox structure in the world at 96.5m. For 6UAH you are allowed to climb to the third-highest level and take in a fantastic view of all the domes, the park and the river. Directly across from the bell tower is the **Church of the Assumption** (Dormiton Cathedral), which is technically the oldest church (above ground) in the Lavra, completed in 1077. The original structure was blown up by retreating Soviet forces in 1941 and was rebuilt only in the year 2000 with its seven gold turrets and marvellously detailed design. A photograph of this stunning church, typically snapped from the birds'-eye height of the bell tower, has become Kiev's must-have 'Eiffel tower' shot. To the north is the **Church of All Saints** built at the end of the 17th century by the Cossack *hetman* Ivan Mazepa. It's known best for its vivid interior of gold and painted portraits. To the south of the Dormiton Cathedral is the **Refectory**, built at the end of the 19th century when the community of monks was sizeable enough to require such a large dining hall. The accompanying Byzantine dome is astounding both outside and in. While the interior **Chapel of Saints Anthony and Theodosius** is faded, some of the original and very beautiful 19th-century frescoes remain.

The rest of the Upper Lavra comprises several remarkable buildings housing slightly less remarkable national museums (*each is open 09.00–17.00, most are closed on Tue, and entrance is 5UAH*).

♦ **Museum of Historical Treasures** In the far rear of the Lavra and shows all the jewellery and metalwork from the Scythians to the present.

♦ **Museum of Books and Printing** Directly behind the Dormiton Cathedral is the early 17th-century print shop that now houses this museum which exhibits some unique illuminated manuscripts dating back to Kievan Rus.

♦ **Museum of Theatre, Music and Cinematography** Located at the back of St Nicholas Church with the star-studded blue dome. The exhibit is mostly nostalgic paraphernalia from Kiev showbiz days.

♦ **Museum of Ukrainian Decorative Folk Art** Directly south of the bell tower is the Residence of the Metropolitan where the head of the Ukrainian Church once lived. Today it is a museum that is slowly accumulating its collection of national costume and craft.

♦ **Museum of Micro-miniatures** Directly across from the Museum of Decorative Folk Art is this remnant of the Lavra's Soviet period. There is little historical value in this off-the-wall display except maybe to better understand the Soviet cultural mentality of the 1970s. Through a row of microscopes visitors can view things like a chessboard on a pinhead, the word 'Peace' written on a human hair, the portraits of famous Soviet heroes etched into poppy seeds, or golden horseshoes on a dead flea. Several other halls are open and advertised as art galleries; however, the exhibits consist largely of conveyor-belt paintings churned out and sold to tourists.

Visiting the caves *(The caves are open to the public from 09.00–16.00; there's no admission fee, but it is customary to purchase a beeswax candle at the entrance to use as your light in the tunnels)* Sadly, most tourists wander for hours in the Upper Lavra looking for the caves and seeing everything but. What your guide won't tell you is that you can visit the caves on your own for no charge, since the entrance to the tunnels and the present-day monastery (the Lower Lavra) are holy sites that exist outside the realm of entrance fees. To get to the caves from the Upper Lavra, walk under the white flying buttresses of the old print shop and descend to the right and through the gate. This brings you to the Lower Lavra. To get to the caves from the street, walk down the long descent outside the fortification wall – this is where most of the Russian-speaking crowds will be headed.

Visitors are asked to whisper only, and women are asked to cover their heads and not to wear heavy make-up. Few places in Ukraine grant a better view of Orthodox spirituality than these caves. Both church and lay people come to pray, to sing, to meditate and to pay homage to the oldest saints of Ukrainian Orthodoxy, whose bodies are preserved in the tunnels. Darkness, gold, incense, icons and skulls add

MONKS ON LINE

Before visiting the Lavra, it's a good idea to check out their official website: www.lavra.kiev.ua. Not only is the site informative, but its layout and choice of information will grant you a much clearer understanding that the Lavra is not merely Kiev's most touristy of sites, but rather a sacred centre for the Orthodox world, and a leading destination for serious Orthodox pilgrims for almost a millennium. Amazingly, traditions have changed little. Besides a lengthy history of the monastery and its importance to Slavic and Christian civilisation, the website gives very clear instructions on what items a pilgrim must bring on his of her voyage:

- Icon of the Mother of God (the Virgin Mary)
- Icon of St Nicholas the Miracleworker (patron saint of travellers)
- Prayer books
- A bottle to collect holy water from healing wells

To be received as a pilgrim at the monastery (meaning a free, but cold room, and all the soup and bread you care to eat) you should also wear a cross around your neck and come with a written introduction from your home parish.

After the monastery moved above ground, many of the caves became virtual necropolises – underground cities with marked 'streets' where the dead were laid. While some of these saints died nearly 1,000 years ago, their bodies have been preserved without any form of embalming. The Church claims this to be the miracle of saints, and pilgrims still come to touch the shrouded bodies and partake of this life power.

Soviet scientists were employed to disprove the miracle and deride any supernatural belief in the caves. Their studies concluded that the caves' total lack of moisture prevented organic decay. Now in the post-Soviet era, these same studies are being used to support the mystical power of the saints' relics. Supposedly, the Soviet scientists had also found that radiation from the bodies was emitted in elliptical patterns somehow linked to the magnetic poles of the earth. An experiment with wheat plants then proved the saints emitted a 'bio-physic' power that directly influenced the nuclear level of living matter. This research was especially useful following the Chernobyl disaster, when it was 'scientifically proven' that this holy radiation protected against atomic radiation, especially when prayers were offered to the saints.

Many other miracles are attributed to the bodies of the saints, but the biggest miracle is that the bodies are still there. Seventy years of atheist Soviet rule did much to destroy the Ukrainian Church, but somehow the caves survived with their saints. There is evidence that many of the bodies were moved or hidden to confuse the authorities, though the accepted story is that the Soviet government tried to empty the caves and failed. After piling all the saints into the back of a truck, the driver found he could not start his engine. The officials tried everything, but they could not move the vehicle. The patriarch was summoned and told of the dilemma, to which he responded that, try as they might, the saints' bodies would never leave the monastery. After three weeks of sitting outside, the bodies were brought back into the caves, the truck's engine started, and there was no more meddling with anything subterranean.

to the solemn and mystical aura of the caves. As the popularity of this holy site increases, certain sections of the tunnels and underground chapels have been barred off, for the use of pilgrims only. These are usually the most beautiful and interesting parts of the caves, so be a pilgrim if you want and enter through the wooden doors; just be silent and circumspect.

The caves are divided into two separate networks, Blyzhny (Near) and Dalni (Far). The **Near Caves** date from the 11th century and contain the very sacred Vedenska Church with its gold iconostasis. St Anthony built these tunnels for himself to find solitude from his original community that had expanded in the older caves. His tomb lies in these caves, as does that of Nestor the chronicler. Once your eyes get used to the darkness, you can see the fragments of original frescoes above most of the tombs. The entrance to the Near Caves is slightly hidden, since the real entrance is used for guided group tours only. If you are on your own, go to the **Khrestovozdvyzhenska Church** (18th century). The entrance to the caves is in the fore chamber, the exit is in the chapel.

The **Far Caves** comprise the original underground monastery from 1051 and centre around the **Church of the Annunciation** with its immaculate gold doors and incredible painting. St Theodosius is buried in his own chapel, as well as many other saints and those church leaders killed during the Russian Revolution. The Far Caves also join up with the legendary Varangian cave, where the Vikings hid their booty back in the 10th century. If you think you suffer from claustrophobia, think long and hard before entering the Far Caves. Most tunnels are fairly deep underground and barely measure six feet high and two feet wide. The influx of large tour groups can easily place over a hundred single-file people between you and the surface.

Entrance to the Far Caves is through the **Annozachatiyevskaya Church** at the furthest southeast corner of the Lavra. The green-roofed walkway connects the exit of the Near Caves to the entrance of the Far Caves. The towering gold-domed church across from the Far Caves exit is the **Church of the Birth of the Blessed Virgin**. Built in 1696, the only remaining painting dates from the 19th century, while the exterior uses examples of traditional Ukrainian folk art. Nearby is the **Far Caves Belfry**; with its sharp spires and classic Ukrainian Baroque style, this is one of the better restored buildings in the Lavra.

ST VLADIMIR'S CATHEDRAL (*Shevchenka 20;* ↘ *044 235 0362. Located across from Universitet metro station, just a five-minute walk up from Khreschatyk. There are daily services at 8.00 and 17.00, and on Sun at 7.00, 10.00 and 17.00*) Kiev's most artistic church is also one of its youngest constructions, built to commemorate 900 years of Christianity in Rus. Started in 1862, the cathedral took over 30 years to complete due to some overly ambitious architects and designers who continued to think bigger and better until this small project became one of Kiev's masterpieces. In one of his last displays of public duty, Tsar Nikolas II presided over the cathedral's christening in 1896. The final design reflects the basic Byzantine style of seven black domes, but the lemon-yellow exterior and colourful interior make this a much lighter and more decorative church than is typical in Orthodoxy. Stepping inside will trigger some very sincere 'oohs' and 'aahs'. Colossal paintings depicting Kiev's spiritual history cover much of the walls and ceiling, guaranteeing fulfilling moments and epiphanies. On your right, upon entering, is the painting of Prince Vladimir's baptism in Chersoneus in Crimea. On the left is the baptism of Kiev, with the citizens of Rus descending into the Dnepr, and the prince presiding with his cross. Facing backwards exposes a rather dark and ominous representation of Michael the Archangel in the Final Judgement. Most of the interior of St Vladimir's was painted by the Russian artist Viktor Vasnetsov who belonged to a 19th-century circle of artists known as 'the wanderers' (*peredvyzhniki*). Impressed by the political adventurism of the time, the wanderers broke from the famed St Petersburg Academy, disenchanted by the rigid Western classicism advocated by aristocratic culture. They sought realism and contemporary culture in art, two things which they felt had been denied to subjects of the Russian Empire. The paintings of St Vladimir express this search in sincerity, but do so using very spiritual themes. The faces and human figures reflect a strong Art Nouveau and Pre-Raphaelite influence, but the themes and composition are expressly Slavic (the dark colours look best in winter sunlight). One can spend hours crooking one's neck up at the walls and ceiling, moving from icon to icon, fresco to fresco.

St Vladimir's is the church most frequented by the citizens of Kiev and therefore the best place to experience an Orthodox service with the most beautiful music.

ST SOPHIA'S CATHEDRAL (*The cultural reserve is located at Sofiyska Square; open 10.00–18.00, closed Thu. Tickets to get in the grounds are 3UAH, everything else is priced separately, although the main church is really the only building worth touring, entrance 5UAH; all access tickets are 15UAH*) Kiev's oldest standing church is also the most visible landmark in the city centre, thanks to the giant gold bell tower added in 1752. The original structure (through the Baroque gates and to your right) was built in 1037 by order of Kievan Rus Grand Prince Yaroslav the Wise, who sought to thank God for defending Kiev against the Pecheneg invasion of 1024. As Prince Vladimir's son and heir, Yaroslav's wisdom is attributed to his knack at diplomacy, honest judgement, cultural leadership, and his ability to join the varied principalities of Rus together. He modelled and named the church after the greater Hagia Sophia in Constantinople, although today, the resemblance is slightly hidden beneath the external trappings of the Baroque era, and the vast central compound which it inhabits. The original church was brought into the monastery during the 17th century, and later became the ecclesiastical centre for the Orthodox metropolitans (similar to archbishops). Miraculously, it was under Comrade Stalin's command that the place was turned into a 'cultural reserve'. In that same era, St Mikhayil's Monastery (just down the street) was blown to bits. St Sophia's was most likely preserved for its political connotations with a centralised 'Rus', allowing the Soviets to present their rule as a rightful continuation of Yaroslav's just autocracy. Not a consecrated house of worship, St Sophia's still retains its political symbolism today.

Visiting the 13-domed structure of St Sophia's requires attention to detail. Unlike many of Kiev's churches, which embody complete renovation and modern aesthetic appeal, St Sophia's is more of a museum-temple, preserving the city's past in layers. Pay close attention to the bare patches of the original church beneath the white-plastered buttresses, the glass panels in the floor showing the foundations, the ornate metal foot tiles inside, and the method of stone construction, with alternating layers of stone sizes (a feature clearly transported from Byzantium). Standing inside the central apse of St Sophia's offers the visitor the physical presence of the Kievan Rus that existed one thousand years ago. Hundreds of original frescoes and some very well-preserved Byzantine mosaics have somehow withstood the ages, giving small clues about the spiritual and everyday life of Kiev's first royal family. The sarcophagus of Yaroslav the Wise is located in the north chapel (along with his bones) and both Russians and Ukrainians visit his grave with the reverence owed a model statesman. At one time, many other Kievan princes were buried here, including Vladimir Monomakh, seen as the last just and kindly ruler of Kiev.

ST MIKHAYIL'S MONASTERY OF THE GOLDEN DOMES This sky-blue sanctuary rises up in a pyramid of bright domes directly east from St Sophia's bell tower. Several different monasteries stood on this spot from the 12th century onwards, but this newest version was only just completed in 2001. During Stalin's destructive wave of 1937, St Mikhayil's was completely blown up and the lot left empty until President Kuchma supported its reconstruction. The complex is now owned by the more nationalist Ukrainian Orthodox Church (Kiev Patriarchate) meaning this is one of the few places in Kiev where you'll actually hear Ukrainian being spoken. Both architecture and artwork are true to Ukrainian style and few churches in Kiev are so delicate and bright.

Outside the monastery walls are two meaningful monuments. The iron and stone cross that forms the shadowed outlines of humans remembers the victims of the Ukrainian famine of 1932–33. The larger white marble sculpture shows Princess Olga in the centre with the Apostle Andrew on her right-hand side, and the founders of Slavonic literacy on her left, St Cyril and St Methodius. None of these characters were ever alive at the same time, but the figures represent Kiev's spiritual, political and artistic forebears.

VYDUBYTKSY MONASTERY According to legend, Vydubytsky was founded upon the spot where the pagan effigy of Perun floated to the surface after having been dumped into the water upriver. After baptising Kiev into Christianity, Prince Vladimir had cut down the idol and ordered it dragged by horse into the river, where it should have sunk. Despite their newfound faith, the Christian converts ran along the Dnepr banks following their pagan god downriver, until Perun floated to shore. They declared this a place of holy remembrance, for which the monastery was built. Others claim the monastery existed far earlier than the 10th century, and that the monks kept themselves and their religion hidden away in the caves. As this was the narrowest spot of the Dnepr, and the chosen spot for crossing the river, the monastery is named 'Vydubytksy' a word that incorporates the roots for 'sailing' and 'oak tree', from which skiffs were once fashioned. Throughout much of Kiev's history, the monastery controlled the Dnepr ferry that crossed here, and was an important centre for writing the chronicles from which all of early Russian/Ukrainian history is known.

For a period during the 16th century, Vydubytsky was handed over by the Poles to the western Ukrainian Greek Catholic faith, which led to intense protest from the Ukrainian Orthodox branch. After the Cossacks drowned the monastery's superior, the Poles closed all of Kiev's churches, but finally returned the monastery to the Orthodox community.

Like many of Kiev's churches, the monastery suffered destruction by fire, flood and political turmoil. During the Soviet era, the buildings were used first to house a carpenters' union and workshop, followed by the Soviet Institute for Archaeology. At the height of Stalinist repression, the famous 17th-century linden wood Vydubytsky iconostasis was ripped from inside of the main cathedral and burned to ash by communist youth activists. It was only in 1998 that the monastic community returned to full activity; the monastery now houses fewer than a dozen Orthodox monks who prefer the quiet hillside retreat to the larger and busier Cave's Monastery.

Lovers of art and architecture should definitely take the time to visit Vydubytsky. Even with all the destruction that has taken place, this small cluster of buildings and gardens reveals a far more undisturbed piece of Ukraine's history and religious life than many of the city's recently renovated examples.

St Michael's Church was built in 1070 and features some stunning mosaics and early frescoes. The rough-hewn doors, intricately formed doorknobs and ancient architecture are like none other in the city. Look carefully, as some of the walls hold inscriptions (a holy graffiti of sorts) that date back to the 12th century.

St George's Cathedral features a more classical design of the Kiev renaissance, built in 1701 and resembling many of the churches you'll see at the Caves Monastery. The white walls, green roof and gold domes are also typical throughout Ukraine, as are the odd number of towers and domes, five for St George's. Sadly, the interior does not reflect the artistic glory attributed to this cathedral in historical accounts, but some original frescoes remain.

The **Refectory** is next to the main entry gate to the monastery, built at the time of St George's in a clear Neoclassical form, and painted inside with exquisite, Baroque depictions of the Final Judgement and the Second Coming of Christ, as well as St George's triumph. Funnily enough, the clarity of the paintings dates to their timely restoration during the Brezhnev era of the Soviet Union.

Vydubytsky is a little outside the main tourist circuit, so you may just want to take a taxi straight there (*around US$5 from the centre; Vydubytsky 40;* ☎ *044 295 4713*). You can also take the metro to the Druzhby Narodiv station, although this is a long walk – or you can take a shorter walk from the Caves Monastery/Motherland complex. In the thick green forest of the summer, you can spot the monastery on the banks of Dnepr by searching for the dark blue bell tower painted with seven-pointed gold stars.

JEWISH SITES One of the oldest documents to come from Kiev, which makes reference to the city in the 9th century, was written in Hebrew. It is impossible to estimate the exact percentage of the city that was Jewish, but it is safe to say that the community was large and prominent, and that like most minorities Kiev's Jews became easy targets in times of turmoil. Prior to World War II, there were over 150,000 Jews in Kiev who made up 20% of the city's population. Before the Nazi advance reached Kiev in 1941, some 100,000 of Kiev's Jews had already fled deep into the Soviet Union, many of them into central Asia and Siberia. It was the Nazi *Einsatzgruppe* who ordered all Jews to report for relocation on 29 September 1941. Kiev's older generation clearly remember the papers posted on telephone poles and glued to walls, demanding Jews report with their belongings to one of the outer train stations. Non-Jews were made to believe that the Jews were simply being deported to Israel. Instead, thousands were brought to a forested ravine that lies just outside the city limits, called **Babi Yar**. After digging long pits at gunpoint, the captives were ordered to undress and line up in groups, after which they were shot en masse.

On that first September day, 33,771 Jews were shot, and throughout the occupation, Babi Yar continued to be used for executing Ukraine's Gypsies, nationalists, communists and more Jews. Few outside of occupied Europe knew of the tragedy until after liberation. During the 1950s a solemn Soviet monument was erected to the 'Soviet citizens' who perished, and the massacre was remembered in the famous poem by Yevgeny Yevtushenko 'Babi Yar'; however it was only in 1991 that the construction of a Jewish memorial was allowed to be built, followed by another monument in 2001 dedicated to the children who perished there. Visiting Babi Yar today is a sobering experience. To get to the area, take the metro out to Dorohozhychi metro station (at the end of the green line). Crossing Melnikova and walking south across the park will bring you to a shallow meadow and the austere Soviet memorial. Or, exit from the north side of the metro station (which goes right into the park) and you will see the very sad-looking **Children's Memorial**. Walk two park blocks north, then take the path to the right, and continue to the **Menora Monument**. The memorial is placed at the top of Babi Yar ravine, and marks the spot where the actual massacre took place.

Not far away from Babi Yar is the largest (formerly) **Jewish cemetery** in Kiev, although it is not so commonly known as that today. Continue down Melnikova (about 600m) and the gates will be on your left side. Today there are an estimated 100,000 Jews living in Kiev, who make up about 40% of Ukrainian Jews, but only about 3% of the city's population. There are no longer any marked Jewish neighbourhoods, but some key properties have been returned by the government to the community, and are now open as places of worship. The **Central Synagogue** was built in 1898 in the very heart of the city (*Shota Rustavelli 13;* ✆ *044 235 9082*). The building is often referred to as the Brodksy Synagogue, named for one of the city's key sugar magnates, Lazar Brodsky. For the duration of the Soviet regime, the building was used as a puppet theatre, and it was only reopened in the year 2000. Next door to the synagogue is a popular kosher restaurant and market where Jews from all over the world seem to mix. This area of the city once housed one of the strongest Jewish communities in all of Ukraine.

The slightly older **Podil Synagogue** is on Schekavytska 29 (✆ *044 416 2442*). Completed in 1885, the façade was built to look like a semi-detached duplex home with a clandestine entrance in the rear. Like many of Kiev's synagogues, the one in Podil was gutted and partially destroyed during the Nazi occupation, but it was the first (and only at the time) to be rebuilt immediately.

Closer to the central synagogue is the birthplace of **Golda Meir**, the former prime minister of Israel; Basseina 5A. Her father and mother had rented a set of rooms in this building, but left Kiev for America in 1903. A plaque and bust of the politician marks the home. Not far outside of Kiev is also the birthplace of **Sholom Aleichem**, famed Jewish writer and storyteller, whose stories inspired the Broadway musical *Fiddler on the Roof*. A sympathetic statue of him stands on Rohnidynska. (And see *Outside Kiev*, page 158.)

MUSEUMS

Kiev has plenty of wonderful museums. In addition to these, don't forget to check out the Museum of One Street, the Bulgakov Museum (see page 145) and those at the Lavra (page 149).

THE GREAT PATRIOTIC WAR MUSEUM (*Sichnevoho Povstannya 44;* ⟍ *044 295 9452; entrance 5UAH; open 10.00–17.00, closed Mon*) In Russia, World War II is remembered as the great patriotic struggle for the motherland. The **Rodyna Mat** (the 'Nation's Mother', or 'The Motherland') is the titanium goddess that towers above Kiev's right bank with a sword and shield in hand, bearing the hammer and sickle and commemorating the defence of one's country. Don't even think about comparing it to the Statue of Liberty, although there are elevators going up inside and a staircase to a viewing platform in her right hand (Brezhnev built it). The museum is located inside the pedestal and an adjoining hall, telling the story of Soviet Ukraine's victory over the Nazis in panoramic displays that transcend the need to understand the Russian-language descriptions. A separate exhibit details the struggle of socialism in the Soviet wars of the Third World, including those in Angola and Afghanistan. The letters, pictures and old uniforms are sobering.

The surrounding park is a popular place for strolling and offers a great example of vast Soviet public space and Socialist Realist statuary. Paths lead past the Eternal Flame, in remembrance of World War II, the Tomb of the Unknown Soldier, and two heavily graffitied tanks tied together in peace. An underpass brings you past larger-than-life sculptural depictions of Kiev's defence and liberation. Over-muscled men (and women) carry cannons and machine guns, throw grenades and charge the enemy. Outside the underpass is a display of Soviet aeroplanes, tanks and rocket launchers. Another trail leads down to the ruins of the **Pechersk Fortress**, the main Tsarist defence for Kiev in the 19th century, and its own museum today (*Hospitalna 24A;* ⟍ *044 224 1970*). Much of this original fortress area has been built over in the Soviet style, but some of the original ramparts are still in place. The military function of this part of the city granted the closest metro station its name – Arsenalna – for the tsar's arsenal that was located here.

Getting to the *Rodyna Mat* is just a few more bus stops from the Caves Monastery. Go to Arsenalna metro station and take bus No 20 to the very end, or else a *marshrutka* or taxi to 'Rodyna Mat'. Grand tours of Kiev will normally include this area in their tour of the nearby Caves Monastery.

THE MUSEUM OF FOLK ARCHITECTURE AND LIFE (*Pirogov;* ⟍ *044 266 2416, open 10.00–18.00; entrance 10UAH*) Of all the recreated village-museum preserves in Ukraine, the assembly near Pirogov is the largest in size, the broadest in culture and the liveliest. Over three hundred original pieces of folk architecture have been gathered to represent every traditional region of Ukraine and now comprise a national 'village'. Visitors are allowed to roam freely and enter the wooden churches, windmills, thatched cottages and barns. The attention to detail on the inside is impressive, as are the craft displays. Costumed peasants play the part and answer questions. During warmer months traditional craftsmen work in the open and sell wild honey, woodcarving, pottery and embroidery. The outdoor fairs (in late spring and early fall) are a lot of fun if you can time it right.

Kiev MUSEUMS

6

Visiting the outdoor museum should be a priority, as Kiev is Kiev, but 'the real Ukraine' is a strikingly different world of rural survival. The wooden wells, windmills, ancient churches and thatched huts were Ukraine's reality until very recently, and in some parts of Ukraine what you see here continues to be reality. Wandering through the fields, you will pass through 'villages' from Galicia, the Carpathians, Podillya, Polissya and other regions of Ukraine, ending with the 'socialist village' showing grand examples of modern regional adaptations on the traditional Ukrainian *khata* (cottage). Perhaps not so intended these days, the museum still functions as an example of Soviet efforts to meld Ukrainian traditions into the communist logic.

Most people visit the museum with a group tour ordered through any local company. Plan on at least four hours to really enjoy the place. Pirogov (Pyrohiv) village is directly south of Kiev on the right bank of the Dnepr, and thus outside the reach of most public transport. On your own, take bus No 27 from metro station Libidska to the village of Pirogov (Pyrohiv in Ukrainian). Or take the metro to Respublikansky Stadion and then take *marshrutka* No 156 for a 20-minute ride to the village. All together, the trip takes about 30 minutes. Otherwise, you can choose to spend your money on a cab or an organised tour (around US$15 either way).

THE NATIONAL MUSEUM OF ART (*Hrushevskovo 6;* ❨ *044 228 6429; open 10.00–18.00, closed Fri; entrance 5UAH*) This classical building was once the Museum of History, and any art on display was a mere illustration of the past. Later, all artwork was nationalised by the Soviet government, leaving the museum with the largest collection of Ukrainian art in the world. Establishing a well-rounded display that defines the country's art has been difficult. For now, you can see medieval icons, 18th- and 19th-century romantic art (some Shevchenko sketches) and some of the most well-known pieces of Soviet-era socialist painting, including original poster art from the revolution.

THE ART MUSEUM OF BOHDAN AND VARVARA KHANENKO (*Tereschenkivksa 15;* ❨ *044 235 0206; open 10.00–17.00, closed Mon and Tue; entrance 5UAH, English tours US$10*) Another bourgeois mansion-cum-art-museum, the Khanenko gallery includes a vast collection of post-Renaissance, western European painting. Recognisable portraits by Rubens, David, Reynolds and Velasquez hang on these walls, and the house and furniture are an exhibit by themselves.

MUSEUM OF RUSSIAN ART (*Tereschenkivska 9;* ❨ *044 234 6218; open 10.00–17.00; entrance 7UAH*) Filled with beautiful Russian artwork from the age of icons to the impressionists and Soviet mosaics. The museum is slightly controversial due to its categorisation of several prominent Ukrainian artists (like Repin) as 'Russian', although visitors tend to be wowed by the treasures on display.

NATIONAL CHERNOBYL MUSEUM (*Provulok Khorevy 1;* ❨ *044 417 5427; open 10.00–18.00, closed Sun; entrance 5UAH*) One of Kiev's newest museums, the Chernobyl display in Podil explores the human side of a most devastating nuclear tragedy. Probably the most haunting sight in the museum is the hundreds of old signs from cities that were made ghost towns after evacuation. A model of the reactor and a detailed pictorial account of the accident help explain the event to non-Russian speakers. The rest of the exhibit deals with the pain and trauma of Chernobyl in a series of highly surrealist art installations.

NATIONAL MUSEUM OF UKRAINIAN HISTORY (*Volodymyrska 2;* ❨ *044 228 6545; open 10.00–18.00, closed Wed; entrance 6UAH*) Ukrainian independence is the prominent

Christy Quirk

It's hard to find a finer early summer climate than the one in Kiev. The temperature hovers around 25°C (75°F) and afternoon breezes toss the canopy of chestnut leaves. The days are long, the workdays short and the supply of pork limitless.

Out of such favourable conditions a new English verb has emerged: to *shashlyk*. *Shashlyk* as a noun is simple: it's cubes of meat on a skewer cooked over fire and served outside. The meat can be marinated or not, served with sauce, dill and *lavash* (flat bread), or unadorned. It is almost always accompanied by a plate of summer tomatoes, cucumbers, parsley and green onions.

Shashlyking as a lifestyle is simple, too. It is the essential summer dining experience in Kiev. Purists argue that self-*shashlyking* is the most legitimate way to enjoy Kiev's summer. Ukrainians flock to the woods and islands around the city, back seats full of children and *babushkas*, trunks packed with firewood, skewers and vodka. Shirts come off, toes disappear in the warm sand and the sluggish Dnepr dissolves the week's worries. Fires crackle from makeshift rings and columns of pork-scented smoke meander skyward through the trees.

But for the lazy, the cafés on Kiev's Tukhaniv Island offer paradise on a stick. Everyone is welcome beneath their umbrellas: locals and foreigners; kids and dogs; oligarchs and the proletariat. In much of expat life, happiness is a function of lowered expectations. Satisfaction comes from appreciating what you get rather than getting what you want. Don't come to Tukhaniv expecting variety, complexity or luxury. Sometimes the beer is warm, the service leisurely and the mosquitoes aggressive, so leave your high-maintenance friends at home.

Never mind. Pay attention to the care with which the *shashlyk* master sprays the skewers with water to keep the meat moist; note how carefully he stacks wood in the fire to keep the heat even; marvel at his sense of timing, how he knows exactly when the fat has caramelised around the meat like the crust on crème brûlée. It may be the best pork you've ever eaten.

Perhaps the waitress will offer you raki (the freshwater crayfish, not the Turkish liquor) in addition to your *shashlyk*. Briefly consider the pros and cons of eating shellfish freshly harvested from the Dnepr, but don't dwell on the decision. Drink a Slavutych beer from a clear plastic cup, then get another. Listen to the wind in the trees and absorb the sun. *Shashlyk* as often as you can. Winter will be here soon enough.

There are several *shashlyk* cafés on Tukhaniv Island. One of the most popular is Kafe Bogatil, located about 100m down the road to the boat houses (the first road to the right just over the pedestrian bridge). It, and other island *shashlyk* joints, are open from late May to early September.

theme of the main exhibit, from pagan Slavic times to the political struggles of the last decade. In the open square next to the museum lie the foundation stones outlining the first stone church in Kiev. The Desyatina (Tithing) Church was built in AD989 in honour of Prince Vladimir's promise to give one-tenth of the state income to the new church, but the building was razed by the Mongols in 1240 and never rebuilt. Shading the ruins is an 800-year-old *lipa* or lime tree, a plant revered by Ukrainians who use the leaves and flowers as a cure-all.

PARKS

So many parks to choose from, and all of them so nice. **Krheschatyk Park** between the street and the river makes a good beginning for a walk above the

Kiev PARKS

6

Dnepr. The road and path connect to over five different parks, including the exquisite **Marinsky Park** once used for Tsarist military manoeuvres. In the lower end of the city (right bank) are the expansive **National Botanical Gardens** near Vydubytsky Monastery, with broad chestnut forests and diverse species. Another public, forested space closer to the centre is the **Academic Botanical Gardens** behind the metro station Universitet.

The feel-good Soviet recreation zone **Hydropark** can be reached by the metro station of the same name. Spanning two long islands, the park is composed of small forests, marshes and natural sand beaches, constantly reshaped by the Dnepr. Plenty of trails allow for some interesting walks and views of the city, and in summer the place is filled with sunbathers, swimmers, and ice cream vendors. In winter, the islands are an offbeat but strategic spot to see the gold-domes of Kiev, to watch the ice-fishing and to step out onto the ice yourself. For a more rustic adventure, head out to Kiev's **Tukhaniv Island** – a country oasis in the middle of the Dnepr River.

OUTSIDE KIEV

There are plenty of interesting destinations just outside the city limits, and a few that are a bit further but can be fitted into one day. **Pereyaslav-Khmelnytsky (Переяслав-Хмельницький)** was a vital city in Kievan Rus and a seat of its own principality. However, the town went down in history in 1654 when Bohdan Khmelnytsky came to this spot and swore allegiance to the tsar, fatefully tying Ukrainian lands to Moscow. Today the town brings in tourists interested in the Cossacks, ancient Kiev and the Pereyaslav Agreement. The entire town and adjacent countryside now make up the Pereyaslav Historical Preserve, which includes the Museum of the History of Ukrainian Folk Architecture, similar to the one in Kiev (Pirogov), and St Michael's Church. In contrast to big urban Kiev, a day trip to this left bank settlement offers a fair introduction to the old country.

Pereyaslav is also the birthplace of Jewish writer **Sholom Aleichem** (Solomon Rabinowitz) whose famous stories candidly portrayed *shtetl* life in Tsarist Russia. A principal character in these tales was one Tevye the dairyman, and collectively these writings formed the plot for the musical *Fiddler on the Roof*. The home where the writer was born is part of the preserve and now houses a museum of his life. On the road to Pereyaslav from Kiev, you will pass near Voronkiv, the village where Sholom Aleichem attended school and on which he later based his fictional town of Kasrilevke (Anatyevka in the musical). Travel to Pereyaslav takes about one and a half hours and is best done by bus or taxi. Most tour agencies also offer Pereyaslav as a day trip.

Bila Tserkva (Біла Церква) is another town made famous by Bohdan Khmelnytsky when he signed his treaty of Bila Tserkva with Poland in 1651, cutting back on Cossack rights and allowing Polish gentry to regain their lands. Khmelnytsky broke the treaty within the year, eventually driving the Poles out. Bila Tserkva (literally 'White Church') is a popular day trip for its quaint churches and pleasant tree park. Travelling to Bila Tserkva is easy since it falls on the well-travelled southern route from Kiev to Uman and Odessa. Joining an organised tour of the town can be done with any Kiev agency and there are plenty of direct buses from the central bus station. The drive takes about one hour.

7

Polissya
Полісся

The north-central region of Ukraine is clad in thick forests, hence its name Polissya, literally 'in the woods'. Ironically, these wilder regions that are so close to the country's capital also tend to be some of the least visited. The Chernobyl nuclear disaster of 1986 led to the creation of a restricted zone which still impedes travel in certain areas and added a stigma to some of the most beautiful landscapes in the country. At the same time, the lack of people and cars means that Polissya's natural world is simply pristine compared with the rest of Ukraine. Gigantic trees, numerous lakes, plenty of birds and mammals, and the rare quiet of undisturbed woods attract both nature lovers and your average urban escapee from Kiev. Because of its proximity to the capital, most independent travellers can venture north in a series of day trips from Kiev, escaping from the city for this rare bit of true wilderness.

The very first Slavic tribes settled among Polissya's trees and rivers and were brought under Kiev's jurisdiction during the 7th and 8th centuries. Some of Ukraine's most ancient towns and villages stood between these mixed oak and spruce forests. Tour operators most often highlight the ancient churches and pre-Christian fortress of Chernihiv, while of late, a more popular excursion takes in the barren shell of Chernobyl's nuclear power station and the quietest miles of Ukrainian countryside.

GETTING AROUND

The capital Kiev is technically a part of Polissya and acts as the central transfer point for each outlying area. Frequent trains and buses run to Zhytomyr and Chernihiv, both of which are close and accessible. The 'controlled zone' around Chernobyl presents more difficulties to those who are really looking to get off the beaten path, especially around the lovely Kiev reservoir and the mysterious border with Belarus. Getting to Chernobyl itself involves more precise plans, usually with a tour company.

CHERNIHIV ЧЕРНІГІВ

For its grand past, along with its unparalleled concentration of ancient churches and holy sites, Chernihiv tops UNESCO's impressive list of World Heritage Sites in Ukraine. Referred to as Ukraine's 'open-air museum', the golden cupolas and towers of several cathedrals and monasteries come into view from over 20km away, so that even from a train, you're hit with the same sense of wonder that Orthodox pilgrims feel as they approach such a glorious and historic destination. Chernihiv offers a fascinating and primeval retreat from the modern noise of the big city, and the countryside surrounding Polissya's Desna River warrants long meandering walks.

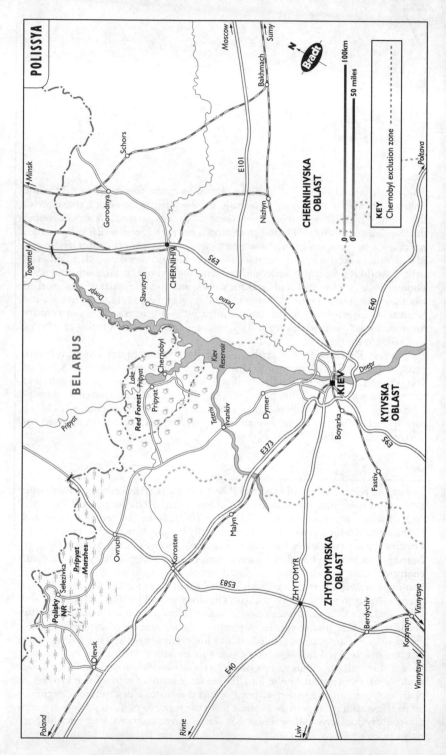

Most people believe the city's name comes from either the black forest surrounding the original settlement – hence *cherny* ('black') – or from Cherniga, the prince of the Severian forest tribe who lived here. By the 7th century, the Polissyan tribes had already joined with Kiev to form the basis of the Rus civilisation, and the line of Chernihiv princes became instrumental in the political process. Chernihiv became an official Kievan principality in the early 11th century and covered a territory almost the size of Texas. Large tribute payments and trade with Byzantium funded the several churches built in honour of Kiev's new religion. Prince Svyatoslav (son of Yaroslav the Wise) was the first Kievan prince to rule this region permanently, but the city's golden age was cut short by two hundred years of Mongol attacks. After brief Lithuanian rule, the lands and city came under the jurisdiction of Moscovy. As the closest Ukrainian city to Moscow, Chernihiv played only a minor role in the struggle between Russia, Poland and the Cossacks but thanks to these uneventful years, Chernihiv preserved its best architecture when other cities were decimated. It also escaped the industrial development instigated by the Russian Empire and the USSR. During the Soviet age, Chernigov was the brand name of the country's best beer, and the breweries still make the stuff today and sell it under the Ukrainian label Chernihiv.

Independent Ukraine reveres Chernihiv as a lost and royal city that honestly conveys the country's proud imperial past and that provides a stately reminder of the way the whole country once looked. While so many Ukrainian cities have suffered their churches being destroyed, only to have them replaced by the unromantic façades of Soviet industry, Chernihiv has kept its original countenance of Orthodox reverence and Slavic sensibility. Pilgrims have begun to pay homage en masse and the secular tourists have matched their numbers, travelling to Ukraine's hidden north to personally witness the provincial glory of Kievan Rus. Chernihiv makes a wonderful day trip from Kiev, allowing visitors to tour most of the churches and all the historical sights they care to see. However, spending the night in Chernihiv is a pleasant and peaceful alternative to rushing back to Kiev. Despite its recent popularity, and its proximity to the capital, Chernihiv remains far beyond the normal tourist circuit, so a trip this way becomes rather intentional or, for the brave few, an intriguing point of transit to and from Belarus.

GETTING THERE AND AWAY A brand-new speed train jets off to Chernihiv every morning and evening from Kiev's central station, a journey of about two hours compared with the three- and four-hour journeys on the less-than-speedy old train. Other rail connections do exist en route between Kiev and Minsk, but the stop at Chernihiv tends to be either very late in the evening or quite early in the morning. On these trains, it takes about four hours to get to Kiev, and depending on the border, Minsk is nine hours away. Upon arrival, few visitors can resist photographing the cherry-red train station. Driving to Chernihiv is far more scenic and a lot quicker. You can probably convince a taxi driver to take you there for US$50 or so, or you may just want to rent a car for the day. The drive should be under two hours and should take you through some gorgeous forests, a drive that is particularly beautiful in the autumn. In addition, several *marshrutka* run from Kiev's Polissya (north) bus station on Ploscha Shevechenka which take about 2½ to 3 hours.

WHERE TO STAY AND EAT The sudden interest in Chernihiv has seen a rise in the number of services offered. Each hotel has its own restaurant, and there are a number of cafés and tea shops near the main square.

Pridesnyansky Hotel Shevchenko 99A; 0462 954 802; f 0462 954 958; e reception@ chernigivhotel.com.ua; www.chernigovhotel.com.ua. Chernihiv's most corporate and 'European' hotel, with remodelled rooms and very nice suites in a very self-contained atmosphere. A small café serves spruced-up Ukrainian food. They also have a great in-house tourist office that can fix you up with an English-speaking guide for the day. Credit cards accepted. *US$35/US$60 sgl/dbl, plush suites US$75 (tpls for US$100).*

🏠 **Gradetsky Hotel** Mira 68; 🔾 0462 245 025. The biggest hotel in the city, this 18-storey high-rise falls within walking distance of most of the city's churches, and guides can be arranged at the main

desk. Some rooms have been renovated, meaning a whole range of rooms, prices and comfort levels is available. The restaurant on the top floor is a popular point for its panoramic view and is still considered one of the best dinner options in the city. Credit cards accepted, b/fast inc. *Typical dbl with bath US$55, sgl US$30; the nicer rooms run up to US$70.*

🏠 **Slavyanksy** Mira 33; 🔾 0462 274 604. Quite basic rooms. *US$20–35.*

WHAT TO SEE The oldest part of the city lies in the 'Val' next to the Desna riverbank, surrounded by earth mounds once used to defend the settlement in prehistoric times. These ramparts and the complex of churches make up the **Dytynets** stronghold and present-day cultural preserve. Remnants of the fortress date back to the 16th century, although the original structure was built in the 12th century and subsequently destroyed by the Mongols in 1240. The **Cathedral of Boris and Hlib** commemorates Ukraine's first Christian saints, the two brothers of Yaroslav the Wise who were killed by their eldest brother, Prince Svyatopolk. This small white church was built in 1123, and features the stunning, pure silver Tsar's Gate, doors recast from a single pagan idol that was found near the church in the 17th century and melted down. Next door is the first building of the **Chernihiv Collegium**, founded in 1701 and one of the first secular schools in Ukraine. Across the green on Pidvalna stands the **Cathedral of the Transfiguration of Our Saviour** (Spaso-Preobrazhenskya), Chernihiv's oldest and most visited church, built in 1036. Most of the early Kievan princes are buried here, including the son of Yaroslav the Wise, Svyatoslav (note the highly Baroque iconostasis). South of the Dytenets is the 18th-century gold-domed Katerynynska Church, funded by a Cossack colonel in thanks for his victory against the Turks. The building now houses a small museum of Polissyan folk craft and a souvenir shop. The **Chernihiv Historical Museum** is next to the small art museum in the Neoclassical building by the river. An informative exhibit tells the history of the town in pictures and objects, and displays some remarkable religious treasures.

The city branches out from its own **Red Square** in front of the Chernihiv Theatre (citizens now refer to the square as *krasna* in Ukrainian, which means 'beautiful', instead of the Russian *krasnaya* for 'red'). In the park behind stands **St Parasceve's Church**, fashioned from brick in the most basic of Byzantine styles during Chernihiv's 'golden age' of the 12th and 13th centuries. The chapel is famous for its perfect acoustics, a feat attributed to early craftsmen who placed overturned clay chamber pots in the corners of the church and periodically rang them to test resonance. The interior is still quite bare, since the church was closed for much of the Soviet era.

The **Yeletsky Uspensky Convent** is on the southern side of the town, centred around the flowing towers of the **Uspensky Cathedral**. Founded by Prince Syatoslav in the 11th century, the first Christian monastery in the provinces of Kievan Rus has become a popular pilgrimage site. The nearby mound is the **Chorna Mohyla** (Black Grave), an early Slavic burial mound, much like the barrows of Celtic civilisations. Most of what's in the museum was found here. The hills continue with **Boldyna Hora** (old Slavic for 'Oak Hill') that covers the Caves of St Anthonius, built by the same St Anthony who founded the Kievo-Pechersky Lavra. This underground city of monasteries, catacombs and churches is the largest of its kind in Ukraine, with an intricate floor design on four separate levels. The perfect white, green and gold turrets of the miniature **Ilyinska Church** mark the entrance to the caves (*open every day from 09.00 to 16.00*). Following the winding path leads to the **Troitsky Monastery**, the best preserved of Ukraine's religious buildings, often used as the model which so many other structures follow in their present-day renovations. The murals inside the **Trinity Cathedral** are rare originals from the 18th century.

Nearly every tourist agency in Kiev offers some sort of Chernihiv package, which is either a day trip, or an overnighter with walking tours of the riverbank.

CHERNOBYL ЧОРНОБИЛЬ

The site of the world's worst nuclear accident now piques the curiosity of tourists who probably knew about the event long before most Ukrainians ever did. For all of the wonderful things there are to see and do in Ukraine, Chernobyl is on its way to becoming the country's leading 'I was there' destination. Practically every Ukrainian tourist agency offers a day trip into the 'zone', trading the would-be environmental attractions of Polissya for a post-apocalyptic view of a tainted landscape.

The town of **Chornobyl** (in Ukrainian) lies 20km south of the Belarus border on the Pripyat River. Few foreigners realise what a giant operation Chernobyl was and how central a role it played (and still plays) in the region. A massive artificial lake was formed to cool the four reactors and nearly everyone living in the nearby town of Pripyat was somehow connected to making the nuclear energy that kept Kiev's metro running and street lights aglow.

Unfolding the fateful events of 26 April 1986 now sounds like a too-often told campfire tale: the number-four reactor of the Chernobyl nuclear power plant was to be shut down for routine maintenance and it was decided to test the electrical system to determine if it could keep the reactor's regular cooling system running in the event of a power loss. Obviously, the experiment failed, and this was exacerbated by the fact that the emergency cooling system had been shut off, allowing the overheated system to continue to overheat. The initial explosion at Chernobyl was actually pressurised steam in the cooling system, followed by a genuine nuclear detonation a few seconds later. Two plant workers were immediately killed by the blast. Open to the air, the burning reactor shot nine tonnes of dematerialised waste a mile skyward, followed by a giant radioactive cloud of xenon and krypton gases.

Chernobyl's real heroes were the very first firemen sent in, many of whom were young conscripts. A lack of preparation and a general failure to grasp the seriousness of this type of accident led to the firemen receiving lethal doses of radiation within a couple of minutes. For two weeks, the reactor continued to burn while workers tried to counteract a myriad of chemical fires. A modern monument to the 31 firemen who died in this initial struggle was recently erected in the town.

The double tragedy of Chernobyl was the Soviet Union's attempt to keep it quiet. The towns close to Chernobyl were only evacuated two days after the explosion, and the Ukrainian public was not notified until nearly a week after Swedish scientists had identified the radioactive cloud blowing north. Contaminated rain fell on southern Belarus soon after the explosion, so that this and the environment around Pripyat are considered the worst-hit areas. Soviet logic deemed Polissya a safe place for a nuclear plant due to its low population density and relative proximity to Kiev. The Pripyat marshes and woodlands of Belarus and Ukraine are still considered an exceptionally rare ecosystem, but the woods around Chernobyl will be forever poisoned. The famous 'red forest' surrounds the southern and western sides of the site and forms a creepy landscape

7

of barren trees sprouting from thick sand that was imported to stop ground radiation. All the small mammals died within the first year after the accident and new fauna has only recently ventured into the area. Still, many biologists are now realising that voiding a region of people for two decades has done far more to benefit local wildlife than radiation has damaged it. As Chernobyl's cooling system once flowed directly into the Dnepr, the water has higher than average radiation levels that decrease as you move downstream (this is the real reason you shouldn't eat river fish from the markets).

For Ukrainians themselves, the most direct consequence has been a jump in thyroid cancer among children, as well as the thousands of stillbirths and deformities in newborns in the first year after the accident. Since then, thousands more deaths have been blamed on the nuclear disaster, but it is hard to prove any correlations and equally politically incorrect not to beat one's breast upon invoking the word 'Chernobyl'. The government supports involved compensation schemes with discounts and regular health treatments for registered 'invalids', but sadly Chernobyl has become the national excuse for any form of malaise that has evolved over the past 20-odd years. Ukraine continues to battle between two sensitivities: the sober recognition that Chernobyl was a terrible event from which the country has recovered (but not forgotten) versus a mass paranoia that all of Ukraine's ills stem from the plague of Chernobyl. It's still a touchy subject for many.

After repeated requests and cash payments from the EU and the United States, Chernobyl's last reactor was shut down permanently in the year 2000. Thousands remain unsettled or unemployed, and with the continual struggle with Russia over energy issues, the question of Ukraine's nuclear energy future lingers on. Over 120,000 inhabitants were permanently evacuated from the Chernobyl region, and to house them the government built the planned community of Slavutych on the northern banks of the Dnepr. For those keen to see Ukraine's youngest town, **Slavutych** is not in the 'zone' and can be easily reached by bus from Kiev or Chernihiv.

Chernobyl is still very much an open wound for Ukraine, so that many Ukrainians still don't know how to react to a rise in travel interest. Ukrainians are eager to veer away from the negative associations that Chernobyl brings (danger, incompetence, radiation), while still confronting those issues that remain (energy, illness and environmental revitalisation). April 2006 saw the 20th anniversary of the Chernobyl disaster, with much hullabaloo from the international media and a fair bit of nostalgic fanfare in Ukraine. International agencies and the government now hope that frank and open tours to the site will take away some of the stigma at home and abroad.

VISITING CHERNOBYL You will not become sterile or get cancer by visiting Chernobyl. In fact, you get about three times as much radiation from an aeroplane on a regular transatlantic flight than you do from a visit to Chernobyl. Even so, the restricted exclusion 'zone' is cordoned off by two concentric circles 10km and 30km from the plant, and visitors are allowed in with proper documentation only. The only thing to see in the zone is that there is nothing to see. Landscapes are barren and wildly overgrown, and the villages feel eerie and empty. A few die-hards have returned to their country homes and live brazen lives in ghost towns. For the most part though, things have remained as they were left at the time of evacuation. The real excitement of the journey comes from entering an area that's frozen in 1986 USSR, a trip that feels remarkably similar to time travel.

Anyone is allowed to contact the appropriate government ministry and apply for the necessary passes to get into the 'zone', but going through a private tour agency is a lot less hassle, as getting to Chernobyl is not so tricky if you're with a group.

The drive from Kiev takes about two hours and passes checkpoints at the 30km and 10km circles (the guards' posturing and flustered paper checking is a bit of show to recreate that special Soviet mood). Although it's clearly unnecessary – except for the obvious dramatic effect – visitors are sometimes fitted with special jumpsuits and shoes at the 10km checkpoint, then periodically checked with a Geiger counter during the tour.

Tours to Chernobyl have become little more than street theatre for tourist thrills. Good guides will constantly wave a Geiger counter about, hoping to spook you with the scratchy beeps that speed up only when the counter is pointed at the reactor itself. Some tours even offer an 'ecologically clean lunch' prepared with Geiger counter in hand and magically waved over every dish. After lunch, visitors are expected to feel good and overwhelmed, and therefore willing to spill their guts about the benefits of nuclear safety and world peace, perhaps even hugging afterwards.

Typically, a visit comes down to staring at the giant concrete sarcophagus that supposedly stops the 100 tonnes of festering nuclear fuel from harming anyone. As a rule, you must stay at least 100m from the building. Many tours will include the very Soviet monument to the firemen, and the junk pile of contaminated vehicles that have been left to rust. A proper tour should also include a sobering visit to the ghost town **Pripyat** and other nearby villages, where radioactive buildings were buried under mounds of earth, and children's toys still lay abandoned in the streets. The village of Chernobyl itself still sports a few working bars and cafés and even a hotel, mostly for the use of workers and visiting scientists and UN officials. They won't let me publish their information, but if you can convince them to let you stay the night, then you can.

Organised trips leave out all the bureaucracy, and make it a lot easier to plan from abroad. These days, nearly every tour agency in Kiev offers a Chernobyl tour, typically done as a one-day trip that leaves right after breakfast and returns at about 19.00. As demand to see Chernobyl increases, so do prices.

SAM In Kiev: Ivano Franka 40B; ☏ 044 238 6959; f 044 238 6952; e Ukraine@samcomp.kiev.ua; www.sam.ua. The best-known trip provider for Chernobyl and charges around US$350 for a one-on-one private guided tour, decreasing in price as group numbers increase (a group of 4 cost US$90 each).

New Logic Mikhailivska 6A; ☏/f 044 206 3322; e inc@newlogic.com.ua; www.newlogic.com.ua. Caters to young and professional travellers, and offers a similar day trip with a bit more spunk. Prices began at US$450 for 1–2 persons, with the price decreasing as the group numbers increase.

If you are one of these fiercely independent types who wants to discover Chernobyl on your own, you are free to go the government route, although it takes much longer and you will be without your passport for a few days while you are 'processed' (document clearance can take up to seven days). **Ukraine's Ministry of Emergencies and Affairs of Population Protection from the Consequences of the Chernobyl Catastrophe** (*Honchara 55;* ☏ *044 247 3211;* e *main@mns.gov.ua; www.mns.gov.ua*) is the longest name for a Ukrainian bureaucracy and is based in Kiev. They have an official mandate to process all requests to visit the 'zone' and the site. These days they are becoming more of a formality, as **Chernobylinterinform** is the official government-sponsored organisation that actually organises tours into the zone (*Chernobyl, Khmelnytskovo 1A;* ☏ *044 235 5014; f 044 935 2205;* e *m_orel@mail.ru*). For the most up-to-date information on visiting the site, and to get answers for any of your questions, check out the English-language website (*www.chernobyl.info*). Recently, the site has also become a de facto meeting place for individual travellers who co-ordinate group visits, allowing for much cheaper tour prices. There is no public transport to

Chernobyl, so independents will have to arrange their own (which can mean additional documentation for drivers, etc). An alternative to all the trouble is to visit the Chernobyl Museum in Kiev (see page 156).

ZHYTOMYR ЖИТОМИР

Zhytomyr pinpoints the 'in between' zone of changing landscape where the forests of Polissya turn into the fields of Podillya, and the suburbs of Kiev are traded for the rural existence of the wide expanses of western Ukraine. The name Zhytomyr reflects the poetry of Ukrainian folklore: *zhyto* is rye, *myr* is peace. A large rock in the main park commemorates the founding of the city in AD884, when local tribes joined with Kiev, albeit reluctantly. Wedged between Kiev and Polish lands, Zhytomyr was never one or the other, but in 1804 the city was made the capital of the new Russian province Volyn, which incorporated all the land between western Volhynia and Kiev. Today the city is still the primary point of transit to and from the west and is a predominantly Ukrainian-speaking area.

As average and uneventful a Ukrainian town as this may first appear, those who visit Zhytomyr tend to fall in love with the city immediately. The area around town is very beautiful, the people are hospitable and the atmosphere remarkably laidback. It is the quiet, normal city that so many people long to live in. Visiting tourists should not be in a rush to take in the sites: the old city feels small and contained around the castle square and the list of 'noteworthy sites' is an ill guide from which to truly enjoy Zhytomyr. This is a town for picnics, friends and long walks by the river. On another note, this region of Ukraine is also famous for growing the hops from which most Ukrainian beer is made.

GETTING THERE AND AWAY As the closest western city to Kiev, the road to Zhytomyr is fairly busy and travelling in either direction is quick and convenient. The central bus station is at Kyivska 93 and buses to Kiev (2 hours) and Vinnytsya (2 hours) are the most obvious choices. The private company Avtoluks (*at the bus station;* \ *0412 360 257*) has three daily buses back and forth from Lviv (7 hours) Rivne (3 hours) and Kiev (2 hours). *Marshrutka* zip back and forth to Kiev all day long and in under two hours, usually dropping off at Kiev's Dachna bus station. A taxi to or from Kiev should cost around US$50.

The Zhytomyr train station is on the eastern side of town at Privokzalna 3. Contrary to logic, the main railroad from Kiev does not come straight to Zhytomyr, so that getting back and forth to the capital by train usually takes much longer than by motor transport. Still, Zhytomyr is a railway junction and there are trains to almost anywhere, eg: daily connections to Vinnytsya (2½ hours), Odessa (12 hours) and Zaporizhzhya (15 hours).

WHERE TO STAY

 Hotel Zhytomyr Ploscha Peremohy 6; \ 0412 228 693; f 0412 226 772. The city's nicest hotel, refurbished in 2001, and located right near the city's central square. There's also a helpful in-house tour agency and one of the city's better restaurants. Credit cards accepted and b/fast inc. *Remodelled rooms with real dbl beds and hot water US$50–80,* more basic 'Soviet' rooms US$20.

 Hotel Ukrayina Kyivksa 3; \ 0412 472 999. The more stolid hotel in town, but things are not all that bad. Location is somewhat central and room standards somewhat average. Also, the hot water is sporadic. Still, rooms are cheap. The in-house Georgian restaurant is fantastic. US$20–$30.

WHERE TO EAT
A lot of new and inexpensive restaurants make for a pleasant night out in Zhytomyr. For some reason, the Ukrainian food tastes particularly authentic in these parts.

✗ **Polisyanka** Dombrovskovo; ✆ 0412 420 653. Serves traditional Polissian dishes, made with local ingredients, especially mushrooms and berries. *Mains from US$3; open 11.00–23.00.*

✗ **Korchma Chumatsky Schlyakh** Kotovskovo 26; ✆ 0412 228 768. Slightly more theme-driven, but just as Ukrainian and delicious. *Mains from US$5; open 10.00–22.00.*

✗ **Dom Polski** Chernyahovskovo 34B. Serves a unique blend of Polish and Ukrainian specialities in a very down-to-earth setting. *Mains from US$3; open 11.00–22.00.*

✗ **Stare Misto** Stary Bulvar 10; ✆ 0412 420 660. A nice and peaceful café with light meals, coffee, sandwiches and desserts.

✗ **Venezia** A popular Italian bakery serving pizza and incredible pastries.

✗ **Pirosmani** (see *Where to stay* for contact details, page 166) Another favourite, is the Georgian restaurant on the first floor of Hotel Ukrayina. *Mains from US$6; open 10.00–23.00.*

✗ **Shanghai** Mikhayilivska 14; ✆ 0412 354 848. For sound Chinese fare. *Mains from US$5; open 10.00–22.00.*

WHAT TO SEE AND DO The city's main historical sights are concentrated on the **Zamkovy Maidan** (Castle Square), including the pastel-coloured **St Sophia's Cathedral** and the **Natural History Museum**, which is more of a centre for local folk arts. A definite highlight is the **Cosmonauts Museum** (*Maidan Korolenka 1A;* ✆ *0412 372 030*), a curious tribute to Soviet space travel with a focus on Soviet space hero Sergey Korolov, who was born in Zhytomyr and lived in this house. The exhibit is fairly modern and rather interesting, and includes the original *Soyuz* spaceship which Yuri Gagarin travelled in, as well as the very first Soviet satellite. They also offer pre-recorded English-language tours (*open 10.00–17.00; closed Mon; entrance 2UAH*). The **Cathedral of the Transfiguration** (*Ploscha Peremohy 12*) is a popular sightseeing spot, built in 1874, as is the city's 19th-century **magistrate** (*Kafedralna 5*).

Park Gagarina is a popular attraction among visitors and locals, most particularly the giant Ferris wheel, which looks rather shaky but offers a great view of the surrounding forests. While practically every city in Ukraine sports a **Hydropark**, the one in Zhytomyr is especially beautiful. On the banks of the Teteriv River (southwest from the city), the park cuts through a steep channel of rocky cliff formations before it curves through the tree-lined fields of Polissya. In summer, the beaches and rocks above the city dam are a popular place to swim and sunbathe (and jump!). To get there, take *marshrutka* No 45 from the bus station, or a cab for about US$4.

The countryside around Zhytomyr is ripe for the curious explorer: big, climbable cliffs, empty fields and forested hills. There are few organised tours in this area, nor any typical travel infrastructure, but that should be encouragement to those who seek to discover a natural and under-appreciated corner of Ukraine. For those hardcore wanderers who seek the unknown path, the **Polisky Nature Reserve** is in the farthest northern corner of Zhytomyr region and encompasses beautiful virgin forest near the village of **Selezivka**. Bird lovers will see some rare owls and the area has been home to known populations of wolves and lynx.

BERDYCHIV БЕРДИЧІВ

This quaint country town marks the border between the leafy forests of Polissya and the vast fields of Podillya. The story of Berdychiv is the same sad story told by hundreds of similar western Ukrainian towns and villages – a town that was born from various religions and cultures, thrived under free enterprise, became a centre of wealth, culture, art and philosophy, and was systematically destroyed in the mayhem of the revolution, civil war, Stalinist repressions and then World War II.

Berdychiv officially appeared on the map in the 16th century while this part of Ukraine was under Lithuanian and Polish rule. With the influx of the Poles came

Catholicism, and in 1627 a group of barefoot Carmelites completed a monastery that looks more like a castle – a factor that has helped it remain intact throughout Berdychiv's turbulent history. The common symbiosis of Polish landowners with Jewish trading and banking was a recipe for success and by 1861, Berdychiv boasted the second-largest Jewish population in the entire Russian Empire (Berdychiv was also the first city in Ukraine to conduct its city court proceedings in Yiddish). A French writer visiting the town wrote 'the place is thoroughly Jewish. Jews are everywhere!" That French writer was none other than Honoré de Balzac, who had travelled to Berdychiv to further an illicit affair with the haughty Polish Countess Evelina Hanksa of Zhytomyr. The two had met in Switzerland and Balzac travelled to Ukraine after news that his lover's husband had died. The pair married in a Berdychiv Church, but Balzac died three months later, in Paris.

Few people also know that Joseph Conrad – the famous British/Polish novelist – was born in Berdychiv in 1857, christened Jozef Teodor Konrad Korzeniowski. His father was a member of the Polish *szlachta*, or landowner class, but was later exiled to Siberia.

Berdychiv remained a prominent and influential town until the 20th century: business prospered and a liberal brand of Hasidism flourished among the religious community. Then the political upheaval of Russia saw numerous backlashes inflicted upon this and similar Jewish towns. Pre-revolution pogroms were followed by White Army massacres in the civil war – all focused on Berdychiv, a very Jewish target within easy reach of Kiev. Stalin continued his legacy of oppression, outlawing Yiddish and Jewish and arresting and executing Jewish intellectuals. The Nazis arrived in June 1941. Because of its majority Jewish population, the whole town of Berdychiv was fenced into a ghetto with its own extermination unit. Within three months, the Nazis had killed all of Berdychiv's Jews and closed the camp. It is estimated that close to 39,000 people were shot.

If the tale of Berdychiv was somehow unique, there would probably be more visitors today. Recent years have seen an influx of Hasidic tourists, as well as some nostalgic Poles, but very few organised tours take in Berdychiv. Still, the town is close enough to Kiev for an easy visit, and while it is melancholic, it is completely different from what you will experience in the bigger cities.

GETTING THERE AND AWAY Berdychiv is midway between Zhytomyr and Vinnytsya (in Podillya). You will most likely have to travel through Zhytomyr to get there. *Marshrutka* and taxis run between the two towns in less than an hour, while only a few trains stop in Berdychiv. From Kiev, it is also feasible to catch either a *marshrutka* or a taxi from Kiev's Dachna station.

🏠 **WHERE TO STAY AND EAT** Berdychiv is still blessedly free from chain hotels and franchised restaurants.

🏠 **Mirabela** Lenina 20; ☎ 0414 340 970. The nicest hotel with fancy suites at US$50, and a basic twin is US$30. The Mirabela café serves Ukrainian food and good salads.

✖ **Kazka** Zhovtneva 3. This restaurant has a menu of hearty Ukrainian dishes and a live folk band on weekends. *Mains from US$5; open 10.30–midnight.*

WHAT TO SEE AND DO The **Carmelite monastery** is well worth visiting, although the interior is quite bare (*open 10.00–17.00, closed Mon; entrance 4UAH*). The peach church of **St Barbara** is where Balzac was married; a brass plaque commemorates the event. To get in touch with the small but resilient Jewish community, contact synagogue **Shabad Lubavitch** (*Yanova 9;* ☎ *0414 320 235*) or the other **synagogue** (*Soborna 9;* ☎ *0414 322 062*). To visit the very sombre site of the

Berdychiv massacre and the **mass grave**, one may take a taxi or *marshrutka* No 104 out to the village of Ivanivka. Follow the dirt road into the forest about 300m, and the graves can be seen on the left, marked by a black obelisk. Berdychiv also has its very own brewery, but you must ask around in order to sample the local beer (most is shipped away for sale).

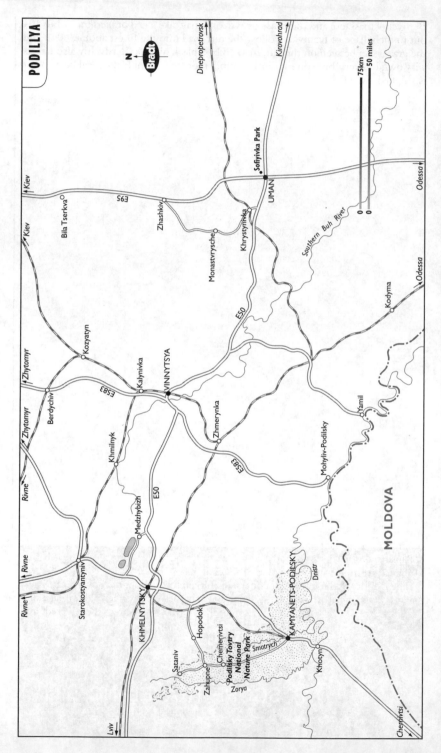

8

Podillya
Поділля

Discovering the 'real Ukraine' is an elusive goal, but Podillya will most likely satisfy any such longings. This traditional region fills in a comfortable distance between Kiev and the far western fringe and also represents the happy medium of an honest but moderate cultural revival without the political edge. The cities hold some historical importance but are pleasantly run-of-the-mill, while the active rural areas are less tainted than average. It is no strain to wax romantic about these lands – for all that has transpired here and the simple natural beauty of the place. In the southwest the hills of the Carpathian plateau begin to flatten out into one eternal field stretching all the way across the country. The landscape appears monotonous at first glance but unique to this area are the river gorges that cut through the low hills and expose the layered bedrock under grassy bluffs.

Historically, Podillya has been the centre of 'right bank' Ukraine – the land between Galicia-Volhynia and the Dnepr River. On the edge of both Poland and Muscovy, Podillya developed on the fringe and was therefore never very Polish nor very Russian. This borderland existence led to two phenomena: firstly, the long war between Poland and Turkey inspired a ring of fortresses to be built which in turn demarcated Podillya as a region. These medieval castles are still a common sight around the larger towns and their architecture reflects a continual change in ownership. Secondly, lawlessness characterised the shifting periphery. Bohdan Khmelnytsky began his campaign in Podillya and liberated the right bank from any overrule before marching on to Poland. Minorities suffered tremendously, especially the local Jewish population. Later, Russia returned the area to Poland's jurisdiction, but repeated peasant uprisings prevented the Polish nobility from gaining any firm foothold in the region. The *haidamaky* movement continued in Podillya until the mid 1770s, with small peasant bands violently attacking landlords and merchants. The largest rebellion in 1768 had the peasants in complete control of the fortress and city of Uman. When the *Rzeczpospolita* (Polish Republic) finally collapsed, the western parts of Podillya came under the control of the Austro-Hungarian Empire and Russia took the rest.

The identity of these lands did not change, even throughout the Soviet era. Wheat made Podillya what it was for the Poles and what it is today. Here, the image of a golden field under a blue sky (as promised by tourist brochures) is delivered, and wheat is still the focus of so many traditions. During the Podillyan harvest, the labourers hold work contests and present the winners with elaborate necklaces, bracelets and crowns braided from blades of wheat, and a symbolic sheaf of wheat is usually displayed in the home. A little-known fact is that most of the wheat covering the great plains of Canada is a hybrid from a single plant brought over from Podillya; local farmers swear that Podillya has the best soil in Ukraine and a walk through any field will reveal mucky black *chyornozom* waiting to stain your hands.

Podillya's greatest appeal is that it has stayed so average. As one of Ukraine's traditional regions it has kept its own customs, dress, dialect and *pysanky* (decorated eggs) designs which now set it apart from the surrounding areas. In addition, the Jewish heritage sights and castles make it an intriguing destination and a worthwhile stop between Kiev and the west.

GETTING AROUND

Vinnytsya, Khmelnytsky and Uman represent the major transport hubs in Podillya. Major train lines to the west (Galicia and the Carpathians) and to Odessa all pass through Podillya and several trains originate in each of Podillya's cities. Still, getting around Podillya is best done by motor transport, since the trains are quite slow and usually run only during the night on their way to a long-haul destination. There are buses and *marshrutka* to many of the smaller villages, but if time is of an essence, you'll most likely find yourself haggling over taxis.

VINNYTSYA ВІННИЦЯ

Podillya's unofficial capital and largest city spreads out along the banks of the Southern Buh River as it winds through the outlying hills and turns south towards the Black Sea. Friendly and open, Vinnytsya represents a hospitable gateway to the west, and as a rising symbol of the boundless Ukrainian heartland, the city has quickly evolved into an important region both culturally and politically. Composed of small individual cottages and a hotchpotch of old and new buildings, Vinnytsya is a down-home kind of place, lacking all pretences, but quite rich in its Ukrainian-ness. Due to severe damage during the war, the aesthetic is sporadic, but the parks and churches hold an undeniable appeal while the surrounding villages are rather endearing. Podillya may be known for its wheat, but Vinnytsya built its reputation on sugar refining and even today the fields outside town still feature mile after mile of leafy green sugar beet. A keen commitment to agriculture, and its status as the home of the Ukrainian air force provide staple jobs for the locals.

Once a fortress of Kievan Rus, the city was founded in the 14th century by conquering Lithuanian princes. A few small castles were built, raided and reinforced; the latest was constructed in the 16th century on the small island that is still visible in the middle of the river. In Ukrainian history books, Vinnytsya is best remembered for its role in the Ukrainian 'liberation' movement led by Bohdan Khmelnytsky. Here, in 1651 the Cossack regiment defeated the Polish troops for which the obelisk monument stands today. The scene was repeated during the *haidamaky* uprising when the city's Polish and Jewish infrastructure was taken over by the Ukrainian peasants. Regardless, Vinnytsya's Jewish population flourished up until the Holocaust and the Polish Catholic church is still open for business. When Podillya was declared a Russian province in the 18th century, Vinnytsya was designated the capital and quickly assumed its role in providing the empire with sugar. The railway from Kiev to Odessa was built in the 1870s, linking the city to the rest of urban Ukraine and developing the local economy towards light industry. In the turmoil of 1917, Vinnytsya was the spot where 'first' Ukrainian president Mikhayil Hrushevsky declared independence, only to be drowned out in the civil war that ensued. Vinnytsya only came back to Russia's attention during World War II after the Nazis quickly occupied the city in July 1941 and began construction of their eastern front command centre. The 'Wehrwolf' compound was visited twice by Hitler during his campaign and the ruins of the sizeable underground base can still be visited just outside the city. In Soviet times Vinnytsya's population nearly reached 400,000 but has been declining since independence. Today, Vinnytsya stands as a downtrodden memorial to lost empires, the Jewish past and as a gateway into the timeless villages of the surrounding Ukrainian countryside. Although lately it's evolved into a perky little Ukrainian city with plenty of small businesses. More and more travellers are working in a visit, as it's a major transit point between destinations.

GETTING THERE AND AWAY As the major railway hub for the south and west, trains to and from Vinnytsya are very frequent but all are passing through to another location. Train schedules for more prominent destinations will usually list Vinnytsya as a stopping point on any particular route but it pays to be picky about which one you take. In the worst case you will be on a very slow train that leaves or arrives in the middle of the night. From Kiev, the evening train to Odessa is best, arriving in Vinnytsya at around 21.30. Travel time from the capital is over three hours and a little less by bus. The luxury bus companies also stop in Vinnytsya on their long-haul routes to and from the Carpathians, and this is the quickest and most comfortable ride to and from Kiev. Avtoluks has an office on 50 Rokiv Peremohy (↘ *0432 554 078; open 09.00–20.00*). In any case, getting a bus to Kiev, Zhytomyr, Khmelntysky, Uman, Chernivtsi or Odessa is never a problem from the central bus station on Kievskaya 8 (↘ *0432 351 269*). The east (*Batutina 18*) and west (*Khmelnytske Shosse 107*) stations are more likely to service the local villages. There are regular flights to and from Vinnytsya's airport (located in the nearby village of Gavryshivka), but the schedule is new and not without changes. Currently, there are occasional flights to Kiev and in the summer there is a flight to Simferopol every other day. Check with the local airport office of Vinavia (↘ *0432 324 875; e tur@vinavia.com; www.vinavia.com*) or at Kiyavia (*Soborna 101;* ↘ *0432 355 022; e vinnitsa@kiyavia.com*).

GETTING AROUND The train station is located on 1 Ploschad Geroyiv Stalingrada on the far eastern side of the city (↘ *0432 271 631*). Trolleys, trams and several dozen *marshrutka* run down Kotsyubinskovo then Soborna to the city centre. Taxis in Vinnytsya are still remarkably inexpensive, for US$3–5, you can go anywhere, and for US$20–25 you can take a return trip to most nearby villages.

WHERE TO STAY Vinnytsya's hotels remain in a phase of transition despite changes elsewhere in the country. Room standards can be hit or miss, so be sure to check your room before agreeing to take it.

🏠 **Podillya** Pushkina 4; ↘ 0432 592 233; f 0432 524 870; e vintur@nest.vinnica.ua; www.vintur.vinnica.ua. In the very city centre, right off the Maidan Nezalezhnosti (Independence Square). This modern building has smallish rooms but they are all refurbished and everything functions. The staff also tend to be slightly more professional in service. Credit cards accepted. *US$40 regular sgl (the same price for a dbl); US$60 for 'improved' sgl; US$80 for 2-room apt. B/fast inc.*

🏠 **Savoy Hotels** Consisting of two different buildings, the **Ukrayina** (Kozitskovo 36; ↘ 0432 321 771) and the **Vinnytsya** (Soborna 69; ↘ 0432 321 771; f 0432 359 060); e hotel_savoy@vn.ukrpak.net; www.vn.ukrpark.net./~hotel_savoy. Owned and managed jointly and located just across the street from one another, both hotels occupy some of the few historical buildings left in the city centre. The

light blue Baroque Ukrayina was once the very posh Savoy Hotel of the early 20th century, whereas today's version is only a distant reminder of its former glory. Accepts credit cards. The refurbished rooms are nice enough, all with private bathrooms. *US$40 sgl, US$60–80 dbl. Older rooms (US$15–30) vary in standard.*

🏠 **Zhovtnevy** Pirohova 2; ↘ 0432 326 540. Within the city centre, and just across from Park Gorkovo, 'the October' has undergone a reasonable renovation of all its rooms so that guests can expect clean bathrooms, hot water and a comfortable stay. *Sgl with dbl bed US$35, twin US$45, 2-room suite US$80.*

🏠 **Gostynniy Dvir** (15 rooms) Pirohova 135; ↘ 0432 352 482; f 0432 325 729. Located on the city's outer limits, but close to the Pirogov Museum and botanical gardens, this newly constructed boutique hotel incorporates a decent restaurant, a sauna and billiards room, a guarded parking lot, a bar and spacious rooms. Credit cards accepted. *US$40–60; b/fast inc.*

🏠 **Pivdenny Buh** Ploschad Zhovtnya 1; ✆ 0432 323 876; f 324 535. The 'Southern Buh' is a short walk from the central bus station and right on the banks of the river. A standard post-Soviet hotel with simple rooms and spotty hot water. The all-night disco is not terribly conducive to a good night's sleep. *US$15–30; a few upscale rooms are available from US$50.*

✗ **WHERE TO EAT** Some of the hotels have restaurants: The **Podillya Hotel** has a passable restaurant with typical modern Ukrainian food (fried meat, 'fancy' salads), while the cafés in both Savoy hotels have minimal offerings. The cafeteria-style restaurant **Yizhko** operates on the the first floor of **Zhovtnevy** hotel and serves real Ukrainian food for real Ukrainians. **Gostynniy Dvir** has a much nicer restaurant with a conscientious chef.

✗ **Tête à tête** Soborna 58; ✆ 0432 351 122. Friendly new European café serving cakes, pastries and good coffee with full meals in the larger restaurant downstairs. Tasty salads, rich soups, and stable entrées that are both delicious and inexpensive (under US$5). *English menus; open 12.00–midnight.*

✗ **Art Deco** Hrushevskovo 30; ✆ 0432 616 400. Upscale restaurant centrally located in a quaint pink building facing Kozytkovo Park. Art appreciation seems to be the central focus: local artists display their work and musicians play their music in the adjoining jazz club. A calm and refined atmosphere predominates; the menu consists of salads, typical meat and vegetable dishes, and a rare house specialty: fondue. *English menus; open from 12.00–midnight.*

✗ **Kolyba** Sverdlova 109; ✆ 0432 352 574. Much like the Carpathian-style lodges seen elsewhere in the country, this themed restaurant serves up delicious Ukrainian food, grilled meats and stuffed deruny. Quite a popular place for locals. *Mains from US$8; open 13.00–23.00.*

✗ **Celantano** Soborna 43; ✆ 0432 320 580. For the time being, Vinnytsya's lack of dining spots makes this nationwide pizza chain a little more attractive to travellers. *Order the toppings you want and eat a whole pizza for about US$4; open from lunch until midnight*

✗ **McLaud Pub** Sverdlova 3A; ✆ 0432 354 314; This Scottish-themed pub/restaurant was most likely inspired by a badly dubbed version of *The Highlander*, but serves good meals and attracts a large clientele. The mundane world of shish-kebabs and pork chops spans into the more exotic calf's testicles and beer-fried cheese. *English menus; open 12.00–midnight.*

✗ **Café Arnem** Soborna 53A; ✆ 0432 352 717. Where Vinnytsya's youth seem to congregate. Loud, smoky bar and café that serves full meals. *Open 09.00–midnight.*

WHAT TO SEE AND DO Vinnytsya is a pretty straightforward town without too many frills. A good walk around town will take in most of the local sights and gives a good feel for what kind of place Vinnytsya is today versus the city it once was. Unfortunately, due to heavy bombing in World War II, there is no 'old city' left *per se*, but certain sections of the city's past life do remain. The white and grey Polish **Cathedral of the Angelic Mother of God** (*Soborna 12*) was completed in 1745 in the style of 'Tuscan Baroque' and still effects an Italian feel. Today, the building is the home of a Capucin monastery and the local Roman Catholic congregation who resent the gold-domed church across the street – the peach-coloured Ukrainian Orthodox **Church of the Transfiguration** (*Soborna 23*). Completed in 1758, this Baroque cathedral was built by Polish Dominicans as a monastery only to have it fall into Orthodox hands during the Soviet era. The interior has been remodelled with modern paintings, but houses some very beautiful icons. Next door is the **Natural History Museum for Podillya** (*Soborna 19;* \ *0432 322 673; open 10.00–18.00 every day except Mon; entrance US$2*). For the most part, the museum has remained unchanged from its Soviet origins, and yet there are a few real treasures within the local narrative, including a mounted mammoth skeleton, silver and glass jewellery from Samartian burial mounds, Cossack weaponry, 18th and 19th century Torah and other Jewish artefacts, and haunting photographs from the tragic span of the 20th century. It's definitely worth a walk through, and a recent addition at the end of the visit celebrates Podillya's multi-cultural heritage: Jewish, Russian Orthodox, Polish Catholic, Lithuanian, German and Roma (Gypsy). On the other end of Soborna is the **Ukrainian Drama Theatre** (*Teatralna 13*), one of Ukraine's better playhouses which has a varied repertoire of entertaining shows even if you don't understand the language.

Soborna may be the main street and the busiest, but making a detour of one or two blocks reveals a quieter side to the city. A few faint remnants of the former **Jewish quarter** (known as 'Yerusalimka') still stand in the corner between Soborna and the river. To see some of these older brick buildings, walk downhill on the street 1 Travnya, and among the cross streets of Mykhailchenka and Chervonokhrestovska. The Orthodox **Church of St Mikola** (*Mayakovsy 6*) is probably the last remaining example of Podillyan wooden architecture, completed in 1746 and still open to visitors.

Vinnytsya's parks are particularly pleasant. A monument to the dead of World War II and the Afghan conflict stands in the centre of **Kozytsky Park**, while the tall brick **Veteran's clocktower** is the dedicated memorial to all Vinnytsya war veterans (built in 1911). Visitors may climb up to the top for a better view of the town (*open daily 10.00–18.00 except Sun*). **Gorky Park** (Soborna and Pirohova) is much larger and covered with tall trees, and during the summer months this is where Vinnytsya congregates to enjoy the good weather in the outdoor cafés, among the fountains and park benches. On the very edge of town (at the end of Pirohova) are the **Vinnytsya Botanical Gardens** which consist of a single trail through a large forest. Be it winter or summer, those in search of the natural Ukraine should take a walk through the deep birches, for this is quite typical for the more remote areas of the country.

On the other side of the forest is the **Pirogov Museum**, the home and hospital of the world-renowned medical doctor Nikolai Ivanovich Pirogov (*Pirogova 155; open 10.00–18.00 daily; museum entrance US$2 for a guided tour*). Seeing as this is Vinnytsya's main tourist attraction, any taxi driver can take you for US$3 (just say 'Pirogova') and any hotel will be happy to arrange a visit.

In the summer, the city offers short river excursions by boat on the Southern Buh. For only US$2, passengers may ride from the city centre (by the bridge) upriver to lovely Sabarov Park, with its pleasant hiking trails and beach. The boat runs from 10.00 until 17.00 every day from May until the end of August.

TOURIST INFORMATION Podillya is ripe for self-exploration, but if you aren't sure about the language or have limited time, there are several tour operators that can arrange visits for you in the area. **Vinnytsya Tourist** is based in hotel Podillya (*Pushkina 4;* \ *0432 592 244;* f *0432 592 243;* e *beauro_vintur@ukr.net; www.vintur.vinnica.ua*) and does many local tours to Brayilov, Pirogova,

Vinnytsya is very proud of its museum and church dedicated to the surgeon Nikolai (Mikola) Ivanovich Pirogov, the father of modern medicine. Nikolai was born in 1810 in Moscow as the last of 13 children. As a child, he showed an early interest in medicine after watching a doctor heal his elder brother from a terminal illness. To encourage these leanings his parents purchased a fake birth certificate that allowed 13-year-old Nikolai to enter Moscow University. At age 17, he graduated from medical school among the top ten students in the Russian Empire, then went on to complete his doctoral degree at age 21 in Tartu, Estonia. His published dissertation on heart surgey (written in Latin) is on display, along with several of his early anatomical drawings. At age 25, Dr Pirogov was already teaching the practice of surgery to doctors in Germany based on his philosophy that a good surgeon must also be a good anatomist. He continued to write and draw books on surgical anatomy while experimenting with anaesthesia, often on himself. After perfecting the use of ether in Russia's military campaign in Dagestan, he bought the practice of general anaesthetic into wide use during the Crimean War. The battlefield provided ample opportunity for surgical experimentation, and Pirogov pursued his cause for humanitarian medicine by inventing the Pirogov method of foot amputation (leaving the heel bone as a walking support) and introducing the plaster cast. Recognised by many as the founder of modern medical practice, Pirogov designed a wide array of surgical tools that are still in use today

After retiring just outside Vinnytsya, in the small village of Vyshnya (which means 'the cherry tree') Pirogov opened a free hospital to treat all the local peasants. The small wooden building still stands and now makes up part of the larger museum complex, filled with wax-figure displays inspired by paintings in St Petersburg's Tretyakov Gallery. Pirogov's home, where he spent the last 15 years of his life, is right across the pathway and makes up the longer section of the tour. It was here that Pirogov wrote his final medical books, and where he entertained his good friends, including the composer Tchaikovsky. When Pirogov died, his wife built a church in his honor, which can be visited today in the small village of Pirogova, just 1km away. His body is still on display, embalmed by a method that the doctor invented himself. In Vinnytysa, there is a memorial statue to Pirogov on Pirogova, and the visibly bright lavender building on Pirogova is now Ukraine's most prominent medical academy.

Medzhybizh, Wherwolf, and Uman. There's also a wonderful English-language information website, maintained by local volunteers (*www.vinnytsatourism.com.ua*).

OUTSIDE VINNYTSYA Getting to Hitler's bunker, **Wehrwolf**, is easiest by taxi. The 8km journey north to the village of Stryzhavka should cost around US$3. Otherwise, several tour agencies and hotels in Vinnytsya can arrange a guide and transport. The local government and private investors have been debating as to the status of the site, so access inside may or may not be limited although visitors are welcome to visit above ground. Not much is visible from the roadside, but due to some heavy explosives, pieces of the 4m-thick concrete wall are jumbled about the surrounding fields. Hitler designated this spot as his secret command centre and over 14,000 Ukrainians were shot and buried here after they were used as slave labour to build the complex, a feat they accomplished in just six months (1941–42). The exact structure of the bunker remains a mystery, although it is rumoured to be seven storeys deep with state of the art communications technology for the time and even an underground train depot. Hitler visited the complex only twice due to the instability of the eastern front, and it was Stalin who took a real interest in this prime hideout and ordered it to be studied by leading Soviet engineers and architects so as to construct something similar for himself. Another local village of interest is **Brayilov**, once the estate of the Baroness Nadezhda Filaretovna Von Mekk. Having befriended the composer Tchaikovsky, the baroness sponsored many of his works and invited him to escape the bustle of St Petersburg in favour of the quiet idyll of the Ukrainian countryside. Tchaikovsky visited regularly, and the shimmering lake nearby is supposedly that which inspired his legendary ballet *Swan Lake*, parts of which he wrote here. The famous opera *The Maid of Orleans* was also composed here, in its entirety. The Von Mekk estate is now a college, but one room is dedicated as the Tchaikovsky Museum (*open 10.00–16.00; closed Wed; entrance 5UAH*). A return taxi will take you to Brayilov (30km away) for about US$20. If you would like a guided tour, best to go with one of the local tour agencies.

Another interesting trip from Vinnytsya takes you to the village of **Nemyriv**, from which was born the world famous **Nemiroff** vodka. Today the town is centred around the old estate of a Russian princess, set in the midst of the 'crystal lakes' from which water was initially taken to make vodka. The palace is in a state of disrepair, but is open as an 'art museum' (*10.00–16.00, closed Mon; entrance 4UAH*). Getting to Nemyriv is about a 45-minute taxi ride, about one hour in a *marshrutka*, from the train station. While in town, you can also visit the **Nemiroff Vodka Company** (*Gorkovo 31;* ✆ *0433 120 559;* f *0433 120 466; www.nemiroff.ua*).

UMAN УМАНЬ

It is sad to think that some travellers take in Ukraine's largest cities but miss the very heart of the country. Uman is the right place to come and get a glimpse of small-town Ukraine without going through the business of getting stranded in a tiny village. The strange-sounding town is considered the gateway between west and central Ukraine and is named for the Umanka River which crosses the Kamyanka River and forms a natural barrier against the south. The natural landscape inspired the Polish *rzeczpospolita* to station a regiment here in the 1600s that proved effective in warding off the Tatar invasions but failed to stop the Ukrainian Cossacks and the rebel peasant bands of the 18th century. Taras Shevchenko's famous poem *Haidamaky* tells the story of the 1768 Uman massacre in which 20,000 people were killed – most of them Jews seeking protection from the Poles. The extremely wealthy Pototsky family ruled Uman until 1834 and their greatest contribution was the extravagant garden covering the northeast side of the town. The contrast of boundless luxury in such common environs has made the exceptional park a major attraction for Ukrainians. The town itself is honest, if not slightly bare. If you find you're trying to kill time in Kiev, Uman makes a distinctive day trip into rural Ukraine. The central location also makes it an ideal quiet stop for any cross-country itinerary.

GETTING THERE AND AWAY Uman's fame means several Kiev-based tour agencies run day trips from Kiev with return coach travel included (see below for details). The same goes for tour agencies in Vinnytsya, Khmelnytsky and Odessa. For the sake of convenience, these pre-arranged tours are the best option for visitors.

Uman is the primary junction for road trips to Odessa from Kiev, so the quickest and most comfortable way to get here on your own is by long-haul luxury bus. A Kiev–Uman ticket with a company like Avtoluks should cost US$6.

The train station is located at Maidan Gagarina in the southwest corner of the town. There is a daily train to Kiev, but the other trains to Cherkasy and Vinnytsya are very slow and inconvenient. Instead, regular buses come and go from Vinnytsya (1½ hours), Cherkasy (2 hours) and Kirovohrad (2½ hours) at least twice a day. From Kiev's central *avtovokzal* there are two daily buses and the trip takes three hours. Uman is the primary junction for road trips to Odessa from Kiev so the long-haul luxury buses are the quickest and most comfortable way to get here on your own. A Kiev–Uman train ticket should cost US$10.

🏠 **WHERE TO STAY** The influx of cultured Hasidic travellers has resulted in a few very nice hotels for such a small Ukrainian town. This now makes staying in quiet Uman an attractive option and a nice way to break up any cross-country trips. Each hotel has a range of prices and rooms. The annual influx of pilgrims has also opened up quite a business for apartment rentals. Ask around for anyone offering a room or flat. For more up to date information, check the town's website (*www.uman.org*).

🏠 **Fortetsya (Fortress)** Chapayeva 54; ☎ 0474 450 041; f 0474 452 383. A great new hotel right in the centre of Uman and close to everything: good service, big sturdy dbl beds and a nice restaurant. *Economy sgl with shower less than US$20, small dbl US$25, slightly larger rooms US$40–60. Credit cards accepted and b/fast inc.*

🏠 **Shaarei Zion** Pushkina 27A; ☎ 0474 431 772; f 0474 431 672. The most Jewish and largest of Uman's hotels, the Zion caters to large groups of pilgrims, with high international standards, affordable rooms that sleep 1–4 people, and a fantastic kosher restaurant. *US$20–60; credit cards accepted.*

🏠 **Budinka** Sadova 53; ☎ 0474 433 527; f 0474 432 210. Fancy, modern chateau-like hotel on the outside, with spruced-up IKEA-style interiors. The economy twins, larger dbls and plush 2-person suites all have their own bathrooms with shower or tub, but you can also opt for the simple room with a shared bathroom. There's also a restaurant and sauna; credit cards accepted. *An economy twin is US$30; a dbl is US$45 and a suite is US$60; room with shared bathroom US$15.*

🏠 **Uman** Ploscha Lenina; ☎ 0474 452 632. A basic, Soviet-era hotel right in the centre where some rooms have been renovated to a degree, but most have not. Hot water is sometimes an issue. *Prices range from US$15 to US$75 for the 'luxe', which are not even close to the standard of the other two hotels.*

✖ **WHERE TO EAT** A few cafés line Sadova on the way to the park and for food essentials there is the central market (*rynok*) at the bottom of Radyanska. The hotels all have good restaurants (listed below).

✖ **Serge** Lenina 57; ☎ 0474 433 111. A family-run bar and café with staple Ukrainian food, beer on tap, and a kids' menu.

✖ **Shynok Kadubok** Radyanska 7; ☎ 0474 459 016. A lively Ukrainian restaurant decked-out as ye olde Ukrainian village. The food is pretty authentic, but the menu is almost identical to all the similar places you've eaten in Ukraine. During certain hours, the music is quiet and not annoying. Credit cards accepted. *Mains from US$2; open 12.00–01.00.*

✖ **Fortress** Chapayeva 54; ☎ 0474 450 041. The hotel's medieval-themed restaurant, complete with occasionally live disco music. The kitchen is sincere and the food tasty. Pretty much the same *borsch* and *varennyki*-style meal. *Mains from US$3; open 08.00–23.00.*

✖ **Budinku** Sadova 53; ☎ 0474 424 366; f 0474 430 550 Modern Ukrainian restaurant near Sofiyivka Park, and a popular stop for tour groups. Russian and Ukrainian food predominates, with the exception of their rather tasty beef stroganoff speciality. *Mains from US$2; open 08.00–23.00.*

SOFIYIVKA PARK Back when Imperial Russia had an inferiority complex against France, a common expression stated that 'Sofiyivka is no worse than Versailles!' The lavish gardens occupy a quarter of Uman and bear no resemblance to French symmetry and splendour. Instead Sofiyivka is designed in the romantic style aiming to imitate natural landscapes. Trees, rocks and water are the prominent media and the original architects redirected the Kamyanka River in order to fill the artificial pools and miniature waterfalls that cut through the gardens.

Count Felix Pototsky began construction of the gardens in 1798 as a gift to his new bride, the legendary beauty Sofia. Greek by birth, Sofia had been sold into slavery by her parents as a 12-year-old girl. The Polish ambassador to Turkey bought her in Istanbul as a present for the Polish King Stanislaw August; however, while travelling back through Ukraine she met the son of the Polish army commander Jozef Witte, who fell in love with the 15 year old and bought her from the ambassador. The newly married Madame Witte quickly became a celebrated society figure among the Polish gentry. She soon took up delivering diplomatic mail and was rumoured to use the opportunity for spying for the Polish king as well as Catherine the Great. Sofia eventually left her husband and two children but was soon remarried to the Polish Count Pototsky in Uman. He adored Sofia and designed the park as a memorial to her beauty incorporating the mythology of ancient Greece: the 400-acre park has its own Isle of Lesbos, a terrace of the muses, red poppy 'Elysian' fields, a Cretan labyrinth and an underground stream called Styx. Sadly, long before the park was finished, the count uncovered an affair between his son from his first marriage and his young wife. Broken-hearted, he grew seriously ill. Sofia supposedly spent two days on her knees begging to be pardoned but the count died without forgiving her. She finished the park herself during a brief affair with the Russian Count Potemkin, then lived out her days in melancholy. The fact that a freak earthquake actually pushed her grave out of the Uman churchyard has the locals convinced that she was a witch.

The park is well maintained and it is easy to spend up to a day walking the paths. The best time to visit is in September, when the colours are extraordinary and the white swans are still about, but the park is open all year and is still worth a trip even in the dead of winter. Horseriding tours can be arranged at the park, and there are boat tours through the river Styx and on the largest lake. A taxi from the train station is US$2 and the park entrance is an easy walk from the bus station. Entrance costs US$1.

UMAN'S RABBI The Breslov movement of Hasidism was inspired by Rabbi Nachman who was himself the great-grandson of the founder of Hasidism. Born in Medzhybizh in 1772, the rabbi spent most of his life in the village of Bratslav (near Vinnytsya and from which comes the term 'Breslov') where he preached a religion based on radiant joy and spiritual freedom. Modern-day Breslov Hasidic Jews follow a principle of living life to the fullest and practise a unique form of free-flowing prayer where the devotee 'chats' openly with God for one hour each day. Rabbi Nachman died young of tuberculosis having expressed the desire to be buried in Uman, next to the victims of the 1768 massacre. In his writings he promised to pray for the success of any pilgrim that came to his graveside and recited the ten psalms of the *Tikkun K'lali*. Breslov Hasidic Jews feel the need to make the journey to Uman at least once in their lifetime, which usually takes place on the Jewish new year and the commonly heard Breslov chant is 'Uman, Uman, Rosh Hashanah'. Uman's local Breslov community has quickly recovered in spite of decades of near extinction and the yearly pilgrimage is now the crowning event for the town. The rabbi's grave is located in the Jewish cemetery on the corner of Belinskovo and Pushkina.

KAMYANETS-PODILSKY КАМЯНЕЦ-ПОДІЛЬСЬКИЙ

The 'museum city' is renowned for its diverse historic architecture but the real 'wow' factor is the immense canyon that completely encircles the old city. Nature's sense of strategy could not have been more deliberate: the rocky island is high and inaccessible, except for one very tiny causeway leading to the site of Podilya's largest medieval fortress. Down below flows the narrow River Smotrych, so named because the transparent water allows you to see the bottom (*Smotry* is the Ukrainian imperative 'Look!'). Most of the new city is covered with thick tree cover and the castle faces west so the sunsets are spectacular. Kamyanets represents the historic and cultural heart of Podillya and in terms of things to see and do, the city is Podillya's main attraction.

Nobody knows for certain when Kamyanets came into being, but the valuable stone landscape was already protecting humans in the first millennium. Supposedly, Ptolemy the Greek geographer, travelled this far and was also inspired by the stones enough to dub the area Klepidav (or Petrydav). Another legend states that after Kievan Rus lost Galicia-Volhynia, a Lithuanian prince passed through this area and shot three deer within minutes. Three plaster-like deer by the gorge commemorate the event that convinced the Lithuanians to move here. They were followed by 350 years of Polish rule (less 25 years of Turkish occupation). The massive stone fortress with pointed towers replaces the original 11th-century wooden structure which had burned down. Changing ownership and numerous reconstructions have turned it into a sprawling fortification and none of the seven towers resemble each other (the Turks built the square-shaped ones, the Russians built the round ones).

Because the fortress and town were made of stone instead of the usual wood, the town was called Kamyanets (from the Slavic *kamen*, stone); the suffix Podilsky was added when the city was made the capital of Podillya by the Poles. The castle made the city an impenetrable safe haven and a developed centre for trade. Since Kamyanets fell under the Magdeburg Law, each ethnic community could have its own legal authority and all religious traditions were self-ruled. Cosmopolitanism became the norm and today the locals will state a different number for how many nationalities claim Kamyanets as their home (I've heard between seven and seventeen). The Armenians, Jews, Poles, Romanians, Azeri, Greeks, Bulgarians, and every other group each built their homes and places of worship so that Kamyanets looks like no other place in the world or every place in the world depending on how close you are standing. UNESCO declared the old city a World Heritage Site because of its high concentration of preserved architecture styles and the Ukrainian government has ranked it third in cultural importance after Kiev and Lviv.

Rankings aside, Kamyanets is a fascinating exhibit of history and culture not to be missed. There are currently 25 working churches, which is a record in this country, while the legacy of defence remains with the prominent Kamyanets-Podilsky military academy. On weekends the streets and parks are filled with camouflaged soldiers strolling under the chestnut trees. At any time of year, visitors will hear diverse languages being spoken. Nostalgic Poles and curious Ukrainians currently comprise the tourist legions, but to most, Kamyanets remains a well-kept secret (come and visit before the place becomes overrun). Intense renovations have beautified the old city and the tourist infrastructure is one of the best in Podillya. Overall the city is a refreshing destination with a very individual take on Ukraine's past and present. (In case you were wondering, the odd smell in the air comes from the city's largest industrial enterprise – the vodka factory.)

GETTING THERE AND AWAY There are two overnight trains to and from Kiev every day. The later Bukovina train starts in Chernivtsi and arrives in Kiev at a more reasonable hour, and vice versa. These and a number of other trains go through Khmelnytsky, which is three hours away. Travel to Chernivtsi is five hours (!) by

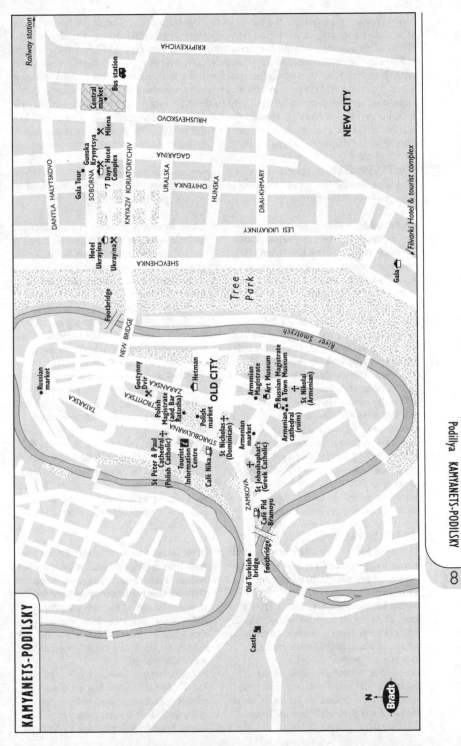

KAMYANETS-PODILSKY

Castle

Old Turkish bridge •
Footbridge

ZAMKOVA

Café Pid Bramoyu

St Jehoshaphat's ✝
(Greek Catholic)

Armenian
market

St Nicholas ✝
(Dominican)

Café Nika □

Tourist
Information
Centre

STAROBULVARNA

St Peter & Paul ✝
Cathedral
(Polish Catholic)

TATARSKA

• Russian
market

TROYITSKA

Gostynny
Dvir ✕

ZARVANSKA

Polish
Magistrate
(and Bar
Ratusha)

Polish
market ✝

OLD CITY

Hetman

Armenian
Magistrate

Art Museum

Russian Magistrate
& Town Museum

Armenian
cathedral
(ruins)

St Nikolai ✝
(Armenian)

River Smotrych

*Tree
Park*

SHEVCHENKA

Hotel □
Ukrayina ✕
Ukrayina

Footbridge

NEW BRIDGE

DANYLA HALYTSKOVO

Gala Tour •
SOBORNA

Gunska
Krynytsya ✕

'7 Days' Hotel
Complex

KNYAZIV KORIATORYCHIV

HRUSHEVSKOVO

Milena ✕

**Central
market**

Bus station 🚌

KRIPYKEVICHA

Railway station ↑

GAGARINA

URALSKA

OHIYENKA

HUNSKA

DRAHI-KHMARY

LESI UKRAINKY

NEW CITY

✈ Filvarki Hotel & tourist complex

Gala □

N
Bradt

Podillya **KAMYANETS-PODILSKY**

8

rail so motor transport is the better option going south. The train station is on Pryvokzalna in the far northeast corner of the city; a taxi into town should cost US$1–2. Kamyanets is much more conducive to bus travel. The station is right behind the central market on Pershotravneva Vulitsa in the new city. There are four daily buses to Kiev, and frequent, quicker links with Khmelnytsky and Vinnitsya. Routes to western Ukraine and the Carpathians are also plentiful but long; a better option would be going to a larger city first, like Chernivtsi. By bus or car the trip to Chernivtsi (via Khotin) is under two hours and a shared taxi from either bus station will cost under US$5. In the city, the bus No 19 and frequent *marshrutka* run between the old and new cities.

WHERE TO STAY

With the amount of constant tourist interest in Kamyanets Podilsky, the city supports a wide range of good hotels with a high standard of hospitality, and everything so inexpensive. All accept credit cards.

Gala Hotel Lesi Ukrayinki 84; \/f 0384 928 106; e galatour@kp.topnet.ua; www.hotelcomplex-gala.com.ua. One of the more 'Western' hotels in town, with very classy, minimalist rooms, and pristine modern en-suite bathrooms. Service is flawless, many of the staff speak English, and the café is quality. They also feature a unique fresh mineral fountain from which guests can drink the local Podillyan springwater. *Their very best rooms can be had for a mere US$40, and some sgls go for as little as US$15.*

Hotel Ukrayina Lesya Ukrayinka 32; \ 0384 932 300; f 0384 939 148. The fundamental Inturist hotel of the city, right near the bridge over to the old city. The cheapest rooms come with bed and sink while a limited number of refurbished rooms have hot water and individual bathrooms. Credit cards accepted. *Cheapest rooms US$15, refurbished rooms US$20–30, the very nicest rooms US$40.*

Hetman Polsky Rynok 8; \ 067 588 2215. Occupying an 18th-century house in the heart of the old city, Hetman invokes the Ukrainian side of Kamyanets, taking its inspiration from Cossack Bohdan Khmelnytsky (perhaps a tongue-in-cheek retaliation against the town's distinguished Polish and Jewish minorities). Extravagantly 'lux' décor predominates. A boutique restaurant and sauna complete the complex. *Lavish sgls US$80, jacuzzi suites US$100/night.*

'7 Days' Hotel Complex Soborna 4; \ 0384 930 322; f 0384 930 322; e sevendays@kp.topnet.ua. Undergoing a slow but deliberate reconstruction, this high-rise hotel in the middle of the new city (and close to the bus station) is open to several possibilities. At the time of writing, the rooms were basic, but new and comfortable; things are likely to change once renovations are complete. *Sgls less than US$20 pp with en-suite bathroom, more upscale rooms US$60.*

Filvarki Hotel Lesi Ukrayinky 99; \ 0384 933 231; e fcenter@kp.topnet.ua; www.filvarki.km.ua. A large complex on the southern side of town, and not conducive to walking around the old city. The rooms and bathrooms are of average standard, but the price is right. *Sgl/dbl US$20–25, suites US$45.*

WHERE TO EAT

Gostynny Dvir Troyitska 1. Right in the heart of the old city, this upscale dining room serves classic Russian food by candlelight. Credit cards accepted. *Mains from US$8; open 11.00–23.00.*

Café Nika Starobulvarna 4; \ 0384 923 252. Proud of the city's strong Polish heritage, this cute little café serves hearty, authentic Polish cuisine. In addition to a wide range of salads, the soup, dumplings and 'zhadkoe' all come highly recommended. The staff are multilingual and friendly, and the outdoor patio is a perfect place to sit back and experience the old city. In summer, it's packed with Poles. *Mains from US$2; open 09.00–22.00.*

Pid Bramoyu Zamkova 3; \ 0384 921 588. Perched directly facing the castle, this medieval café needs no dressing up as it occupies the original 17th-century stone gatehouse to the castle bridge. With a perfect view of the castle and plenty of outdoor dining space, it's a definite stop for tourists. Shish kebabs are prominent, along with grilled steak and fish, and lots of fresh salads. *Mains from US$2; open 09.00–midnight.*

Gunska Krynytsya Soborna 12/1; \ 0384 950 022; f 0384 932 562. Very clean and friendly cafeteria-style restaurant serving delicious, high-quality Ukrainian food. Salads, soups, poultry, meat and traditional dishes. A great place for lunch and bound to be a favourite among tourists. Cash only. *Mains from US$1; open 09.00–21.00.*

✗ **Milena** Soborna 16; ☎ 0384 931 596. Russian food in dark, smoky café. Cash only. *Mains from US$2; open 11.00–23.00.*

✗ **Bar Ratusha** (basement of the Polish magistrate, Polsky Rynok 1); ☎ 0384 924 300. Where K-P's disaffected teenagers hang out by day and everyone else drinks by night. Light meals served at any time;

cash only. *Open 09.00–midnight.*

✗ **Restaurant Ukrayina** On the ground floor of the Ukrayina Hotel (Lesya Ukrayinka 32) and is treated as the most luxurious of the city with its gold and scarlet décor while its menu and prices tend towards the typical: *borsch* is 50 cents and most of the larger dishes are under US$2. You'll find the chef friendly and willing to make anything you ask for and they do accept credit cards.

TOURIST INFORMATION AND LOCAL TOUR OPERATORS

Gala Tour Soborna 23/4 (2nd floor); ☎ 03849 300 805; f 0384 936 777; e galatour@kp.topnet.ua. As a new and energetic local tour company, Gala are passionate about their city. US$20 buys a one-on-one guided tour of the city in English by young, intelligent guides, but they also offer a whole range of fascinating excursions around Podillya, including

several castles and the crystal cave. *Open 09.00–18.00; Sat 09.00–13.00.*

Filvarki Also has a very professional agency (see hotel telephone and address above) offering excursions outside the city and outdoor activities including mountain-bike rentals and fishing.

In the old city you will find plenty of smaller tourist agencies that offer guided tours of the old buildings and churches. The official tourist information centre is on the main square (*Polsky Rynok; open 09.00–18.00 May–Sep*). They offer tours in English, German and Polish, and all the information you need (sigh, if only some of the other cities in Ukraine had the same thing). The city also runs a progressive informational website (*www.kam-pod.net*).

What's more, Kamyanets is fast becoming the unofficial capital for Ukrainian bungee-jumping, due in part to the perfect cliffs and the narrow bridge that crosses the gorge. The supposedly 'safe' jump from the centre of the bridge is recorded at 54m, while the bridge itself is about 700 years old (*chacun à son goût!*) The company works by individual request: Attraction Bungee Jumping (☎ 0384 934 774; *bungee@kp.rel.com.ua*). You may also arrange a jump through the above-listed tour agencies.

WHAT TO SEE AND DO The **castle** (*open 10.00–18.00 every day; entrance 4UAH (2UAH for children); a guided tour in Ukrainian costs 30UAH. For English, Russian or Polish, one must arrange something with a private tour agency*) is the focus of the city's attractions and a walk from the new city will take you past most of the sights. The castle was begun in the 11th century but most of what we can see today was built between the 14th and 18th centuries (the wooden version burned down). The greatest thing about Kamyanets-Podilsky Castle is that you can climb on everything freely, but take caution with the steep stairs. All the towers and ramparts are open as well as the various dungeons and the incredibly deep well. The ascents can be a little precarious but allow some lofty views of the fortress and city, as well as the surrounding landscape. The castle was first defeated by the Turkish invasion in 1672 and in their short reign, the Turks added some stylistic changes that are still in place. Peter the Great visited the castle after the Russian takeover and the beloved bandit Ustym Karmalyuk (one of many Ukrainian Robin Hoods) was a prisoner here on three different occasions. But the castle is best remembered as the set for the old black-and-white film version of *Ivanhoe*. A museum of folklore occupies one side of the castle with a permanent exhibit of local crafts, traditional objects and artwork displays about life in Podillya. From the turrets, one is treated to a panoramic view of the dramatic landscape that makes Kamyanets so unique. The white church with blue cupolas atop the hill is **St Nicholas Church**, a working monastery.

The bridge connecting the castle with the old city is one of the oldest in Ukraine and can be crossed only on foot as it is structurally unsound for cars. It was the Turks who filled in the arches and pillars with stones. Be it rumour or history, when the Turks finally found themselves fleeing from the castle, a cart filled with gold was overturned spilling over the bridge into the Smotrych. Treasure hunters have dug deep into the riverbed but nothing has been found. Now, the deep hole is a popular fishing spot.

The **old city** is confined to the very steep central island and serves as an effective display of the Magdeburg Law: each ethnicity has its own quarter, magistrate and churches. Every building has several different names and changing histories, so it can be hard to keep track of what is what. The Poles lived in the central part of the island, defined now by the tall tower of the central **Polish magistrate** (the yellow building with a red roof) and the steeple of the nearby **Church of St Nicolas** or the Dominican Monastery, built in a style known as Poznań Baroque. Climb up the steps of the Polish magistrate to enter the old city's three one-room museums: the Museum of the History of Money; the Museum of the Magdeburg Law; and the Museum of Medieval Kamyanets (*entrance to each is 1UAH; open 10.00–18.00*). Each is interesting and filled with artefacts, old coins, and old prints of the city, but the entire visit can be completed in under 30 minutes. The most prominent church in the old city is the pale pink Polish Catholic **St Peter and Paul Cathedral,** first built in the 15th century. Take note of the remaining minaret, incorporated after the city's Islamic past – now topped with a golden Virgin Mary. The triumphal arch at the entrance was built in 1781, and the church's black and gold interior also features the rare statuary of Christ sitting with his head in his hands.

The Armenian Square is situated further south, and the white gabled building, with the metal dragon is the **Russian magistrate**, housing the **town museum** (*open 09.00–17.00, closed Mon; 3UAH entrance*). The exhibit is small, consisting of religious paintings and a collection of weapons used by each army that has passed through Kamyanets; the museum's greatest piece is the Soviet-era statue of a monk carrying a basket. When plugged in, the statue turns to reveal an unclad girl inside the basket – at one time these were mass-produced as atheist propaganda but now appear as rare curios. The town's small but sincere **Art Museum** is located just across the street at Pyatnytska 5 (*open 10.00–17.00, closed Mon; entrance 3UAH*). South of the square is the **Armenian magistrate** with its remaining 16th-century white-and-black square bell tower. The small yellow Armenian **Church of St Nikolai** (built in the 14th century) is behind the ruins of the much larger Armenian cathedral (visitors can walk down into the cross of the original crypt). The Greek Catholic **St Jehoshaphat's Church** is closest to the bridge and was the central building of the old Ruthenian community.

Sadly, while much of the city has been spruced up for tourists, some parts are in a serious state of disrepair; the colourful buildings and bare parks make for a sobering but intriguing walk. One of the old synagogues has been turned into a flashy restaurant and most of the open empty cellars mark the former homes of Kamyanets-Podilsky's Jewish population. The main bridge into the new city is at the top of the island but a few small footbridges also cross the Smotrych and lead to a lot of winding trails through a shady park on the right bank. Above the new bridge is a waterfall seeping down the wall of the gorge and a long stone staircase descends to the river. From here, one could spend a day simply hiking up and down the cliffs and along the river. The new city is much less dramatic but just as quiet. Most activity surrounds the **central market** on Prospekt Hrushevskovo.

The **Podilsky Tovtry National Nature Park** covers the southwest corner of Podillya and is part of the **Medobory Ridge**, a 100km-long mound following the north bank of the Dnistr River outside Kamyanets. The scenic countryside is a blend of green forests and rocky steppe scattered with villages and several smaller parks. The term *medobory* means 'honey-drinking' since the area is a known spot for collecting medicinal herbs and flowers. The area is open for exploring, and the agencies in Kamyanets can help arrange specific visits and activities for the region.

KHMELNYTSKY ХМЕЛЬНИЦЬКИЙ

The capital of Khmelnytsky bases much of its glory in Kamyanets-Podilsky to the south and in the surrounding Podillyan countryside. On its own, the city of Khmelnytsky could very well be the least exciting place in western Ukraine. Most Ukrainians feel the same way, including those who live here. Travellers in Podillya will end up here on their way to Medzhybizh or moving south, but they will find the city fulfils a very functional role for the region's farmers and not much else.

In 1954, the city's name was officially changed in honour of the legendary Cossack *hetman* Bohdan Khmelnytsky but this was little more than a Soviet political gesture made in a town where such a fiery name would not matter that much. Before Khruschev came along the city was known as Proskuriv, a derivative from the name of the River Ploska which passes on one side of the city. The Cossack armies did in fact pass through here in 1648 taking the small wooden fortress on the Southern Buh from where they prepared further onslaught of the Polish army, and Bohdan Khmelnytsky made his base here in the summer of 1653, rousing the local peasants to fight with him. Excluding such moments of massive uprisings, the Polish noble family Zamojski ruled the territory until Russia annexed the city in 1793 along with the rest of the right bank. Hit particularly hard during the Russian civil war, Khmelnytsky has since followed the path of most industrial Ukrainian cities and was known best in Soviet years as the home of a pasta factory. Today, despite outside intervention Khmelnytsky remains in a somewhat depressed state.

GETTING THERE AND AWAY Khmelnytsky is the link between Ternopil, Vinnytsya and Kamyanets-Podilsky. Three daily trains connect with Kiev (7–8 hours), each along a different route, costing US$15–20 for a *coupé*. Most people travelling to Kiev from Khmelnytsky take the Kamyanets-Podilsky train that leaves in the middle of the night and arrives in Kiev in the morning. The Kiev–Khmelnytksy train runs in the daytime. There are also daily trains from Khmelnytksy to Lviv via Ternopil and Chernivtsi via Kamyanets-Podilsky. The train station is at the end of Shevchenka on the city's eastern side. The inter-city bus station is on Vinnytske Shose 23 with routes to every major city in Ukraine and beyond, but the east bus station (next to the train station at 66 Shevchenka) is somewhat more convenient for local travel and shared taxis gather here. Gyunsel private bus company has a twice-daily bus to Kiev (7 hours) for US$10; their office is at the east station but the bus departs from the inter-city station (✆ 0382 656 495). Avtolyuks also has an office on Kamyanetska 9 (✆ 0382 701 965). Vinnytsya and Ternopil are both around two hours away by car; Chernivtsi is five hours. It's better to take the train for anything farther.

GETTING AROUND Khemlnytsky could also win the title for the worst-planned city in Ukraine, stretching for miles in every direction with very little sense or purpose. Locals use *marshrutka* to get around, most of which start or finish their routes from the train station. Shevchenko, Proskurivska, Kamyanetska and Gagarina are the more lively streets in the city. Taxis are rather inexpensive here and will take you most anywhere for US$2–3.

WHERE TO STAY

Podillya Shevchenko 34; ☏ 0382 610 83; f 0382 762 611. Located midway between the train station and the city centre, this is the largest and most comfortable hotel in Khmelnytsky for now. A gargantuan Soviet construction, most of the hotel has been remodelled with sound beds and good bathrooms with non-stop hot water. There is also a bar, restaurant, and internet centre on the 12th floor; credit cards accepted. *Renovated sgls US$40, dbls US$60, suites US$100. There are some very nice apts on the top floor for US$200/night.*

Eneida Teatralna 8; ☏ 0382 795 957; f 0382 795 932; e eneida@hirup.km.ua. You can't beat the location of this tall-standing hotel right off the main square – hence its preference among foreign visitors despite being slightly shabby at times. Only one floor has been renovated while the rest of the hotel offers average rooms. Non-stop hot water, b/fast is inc for an additional US$5. The reception speaks English; credit cards accepted. *Renovated rooms US$80 per dbl; average rooms sgls US$25, twin US$45, dbl suite US$60.*

Lyubé This glitzy restaurant/hotel complex has two locations – far away (*Kurchatova 17;* ☏ 0382 559 253) and a little closer; e lube@ic.km.ua; www.lube.com.ua. The new establishment benefits from its recent construction with larger rooms, new carpets, etc, but watch your step (and your head). As a favourite among celebratory locals, the noise can be heavy at times. All rooms are equipped with private bathrooms with hot showers. B/fast inc; credit cards accepted. *US$40–80.*

If you are on a very tight budget and find yourself stuck in Khmelnytsky, there are two Soviet-era hotels that still function to a degree: **Zhovtnevy** (*Proskurivska 44;* ☏ 0382 647 23) and **Tsentralny** (*Gagarina 5*). Both follow Soviet protocol of low-budget hospitality (rooms under US$25). Otherwise, there are cheap rooms available at the train station – upon arrival from the street, turn left and follow the signs for Камера Відпочінку.

WHERE TO EAT
Khmelnytsky's major hotels continue to be the primary eateries in town and visitors can get hearty Ukrainian food at any three for under US$10. **Podillya** has more exotic flair, **Lyubé** has menus in English and **Eneida** is decorated in what I refer to as post-Soviet Baroque. All serve Ukrainian cuisine. Another Soviet-era restaurant is **Ukrayina** (*Proskurivska 73*) which has seen better days but serves full meals up on the second floor. Otherwise, Khmelnytksy prefers its bars to its restaurants. **City Pub** (*Proskurivska 13;* ☏ 0382 785 111) advertises itself as a beer hall/sports club with non-stop football on the television screens and 24 kinds of beer, 19 of which are on tap. They also serve tasty Ukrainian food and good snacks and appetisers. The VIP room is non-smoking. **Blinko** is the popular pancake stand at Proskurivksa 67 and there are several dingy cafés around the train station. If you get tired of eating in mediocre restaurants there is a large, modern and convenient food shop directly in front of Hotel Podillya, open 24 hours.

WHAT TO SEE AND DO
There isn't too much really. Two statues of Bohdan Khmelnytsky remind you that you are in Khmelnytsky, on Gagarina and by the train station. Buildings of note include the beige-coloured **Regional Parliament** on the Maidan Nezalezhnosti and the **Cathedral of the Holy Blood** (*Vladimirska 113*), which is interesting in that it was one of the first churches ordered rebuilt by Gorbachev at the start of *perestroika* in 1986. After viewing the cookie-cutter construction of houses and factories, it is pretty fascinating to see how the Soviet architects approached the subject of churches. The **Philharmonia** (*Gagarina 7*) still plays a few concerts. Otherwise, for help in arranging local excursions out of town (eg: Medzhybizh) contact Khmelnytsktourist (*Shevchenka 8;* ☏ 0382 655 065; e turcentr@rp.km.ua) next to Hotel Podillya.

OUTSIDE KHMELNYTSKY

Medzhybizh МЕДЖИБІЖ This tiny village is one of Ukraine's true gems and is rightfully becoming a more celebrated destination in Podillya. Those who long to see a real *shtetl* – the type of old Jewish country village that dotted the landscape from Russia to Poland once upon a time – may find it here. While urban Ukraine races towards global integration, villages like Medzhybizh seem truly lost in time. Most of the 1,200 inhabitants have no plumbing or electricity and live directly off the land, farming with the tools and methods employed here for the past 1,000 years. Horse-drawn carts (or sleighs) are still in prominent use and the quaint cottages are decorated with traditional Podillyan designs: tulips, wooden stars and colourful geometric tiles or bricks. The recent interest in Medzhybizh could very well ruin the undisturbed beauty of this tiny village, but an afternoon spent walking these unpaved streets offers more insight into Ukraine than any guided tour you may encounter in Kiev or Odessa.

Medzhybizh means 'between the 'bizh' – a combined form of Buh and Buzhok, the two rivers that meet here. On the high bank of the Buh River stands a stocky medieval castle dating from early Lithuanian times (16th century), now surrounded by quiet farms and the village below. **Medzhybizh Fortress** (*open daily except Mon, 08.00–17.00;* ✆ *0385 797 123. Entrance is 3UAH; guided tours are US$2*) was just one of a circle of castles employed by the Poles in their defence against the Turkish slave raids. From the 17th century onwards, the Sinyavsky family lived inside the walled palace and made their fortune from the rents on the surrounding land and by exporting Podillyan wheat to Poland. As members of the Polonised Ruthenian nobility, they ruled all of the local territory and were rumoured to be wealthier than the King of Poland himself. The impressive outer wall with its stone and brick ramparts has remained, along with portions of the palace, the stable ruins, a spooky dungeon, and a Polish Catholic chapel to which the conquering Turks added a minaret. The walls of the impressive pentagonal tower are over 4m thick and took 45 years to build. The view from the top is well worth the climb as you can see where the Buh and Buzhok mingle and the outlying Podillyan landscape. The nearby rivers and open fields are so idyllic and the villages so peaceful it seems appropriate that a spiritual movement was born from such a place. For over two centuries Jews made up over 90% of the population of Medzhybizh. At the time (18th–19th centuries), this was a wealthy centre of commerce and agriculture, boasting 14 synagogues. Today, most visitors are on a pilgrimage to see the grave of the BESHT (Ba'al Shem Tov), the founder of Hasidism who lived, worked and taught in this very place. The town's **new synagogue** (*Baal Shem Tov 24;* ✆ *0385 797 174*) is located at the end of the street recently renamed in his honour – visible by the Hebrew lettering on the street signs. The complex is surrounded by dormitories for visiting pilgrims with a kosher kitchen, dining room and a rainwater *mikveh*. The nearby **old Jewish cemetery** dates from the 17th–18th centuries and is the location of the tomb of the Ba'al Shem Tov (*open 24 hours*). Several other prominent Hasidic leaders are buried here. A short walk down the hill and up another (ask directions at the synagogue) will take you to the **new Jewish cemetery**, which dates from the 18th–19th centuries. During Soviet times, this was a forest, which was only recently cleared to allow for the restoration of over 1,000 graves. The **old synagogue** is situated closer to the fortress on Zhovtneva 8/1 and is well worth a visit. Rebuilt with Hasidic exactness, this *beth midrash* looks exactly as it did in the 18th century, complete with interlocking wooden crossbeams, ornately hand-carved woodwork and the pulpit from which the BESHT preached to his followers. Behind the building are the 700-year-old ruins of another synagogue.

Yisrael Ben Eliezer was born in 1700 in the Podillyan village of Okopy. Orphaned as a young boy, the local Jewish community took charge of his education and welfare. He was a dedicated student but also a dreamer who disappeared into the forests and countryside for weeks at a time. Widowed at a young age, he was married a second time to a rabbi's daughter and the pair moved to the Carpathian Mountains where, legend states, he spent most of his time meditating in the forest. He enjoyed interacting with the poorer people whom he claimed were 'limbs of the divine presence'. By the time he had moved to Medzhybizh he had gained a reputation as a healer and holy man and was called the Master of the Good Name, or Ba'al Shem Tov (BESHT is an acronym of the Hebrew letters). He dedicated his life to spiritual work from which modern-day Hasidism was born. Denouncing self-mortification in favour of rejoicing, the BESHT taught of the divine presence in all things and that performing the normal tasks in life was a form of devotion. Song and dance became important rituals of worship and he loved simple stories as the primary means for spiritual learning. He died in 1760 leaving many followers but none of his own writings. He is buried in Medzhybizh and the tiny village has become an important site for Hasidic pilgrims – over 20,000 visit each year.

When the Nazis invaded Ukraine in 1941, they swiftly entered Medzhybizh and in just one night massacred over 3,500 Jews. This was a story that was repeated throughout all of eastern Europe, and many Ukrainian villages were wiped completely from the map. Four mass graves are marked with four very sobering monuments – about a 20-minute walk from the village centre.

Getting to Medzhybizh is an easy one-hour bus trip from Khmelnytsky's east bus station (next to the train station). Take any bus going to the towns of Letychiv, Mytkivtsi, Synyavka, Zapadyntsi or Ivki and let the driver know you want off at Medzhybizh. If you choose to go by taxi, bargain beforehand. The general rule is around 2UAH per km, and Medzhybizh is about 35km away from Khmelnytsky. There are also buses to and from Vinnitsya, and a taxi to Medzhybizh from Vinnytsya will set you back around US$40.

Where to stay and eat

Medzhybizh ✆ 0385 797 111; f 0385 798 619; e medzibizh.ic.km.ua; www.medzibizh.ic.km.ua. Medzhybizh is both small and remote, yet just 2km outside the historical village stands a giant new roadside complex bearing the same name. You can't miss it coming in from the main road (E-50), as it is taller than any of the buildings in Medzhybizh itself (including the castle) and situated at the crossroad of the E-50 and the turn-off to Medzhybizh, or the 277km mark from Lviv. A cheery stop for weary travellers, the complex includes everything from a pharmacy to a gift shop to several restaurants, cafés, a small grocery shop, an outside grill and hotel rooms that are rented for 12hr segments. *A totally decked-out apt, complete with jacuzzi for 2 US$50, smaller sgls US$20 and warm dormitory-style beds US$5. The taller bright yellow hotel offers rooms for US$30–60.*

9

Galicia & Volhynia
Галичина & Волинь

Known for its fiercely independent nature and quirky traditionalism, 'Halychyna' (Galicia) sounds like 'Wild West' to the Ukrainian ear and is regarded with both wonderment and suspicion. At heart though, Galicia is a curious relic of old Europe, both sophisticated and nostalgic. Travelling in this region is a delight; the landscapes are picturesque and the people's mentality is markedly different here from in the rest of Ukraine. In some ways, that means things tend to work better and make more sense, while in other ways travelling in Galicia is like being in a whole different country.

The two regions have been paired since the 12th century, but each is distinct: Volhynia is covered with tall forests and dotted with lakes; Galicia is a blend of soft brown fields and little green knolls. Polish influence marks both areas, but Volhynia in the north was more oriented towards Prussia and Lithuania, while some of Galicia's charm stems from its provincial role in aristocratic Poland and the Austro-Hungarian Empire. The architectural leftovers make Lviv a highly decorative regional capital and everyone I've met agrees that this is Ukraine's most beautiful city. The growing popularity of tourism in the west seems to be based on its proximity to Europe and the mistaken belief that dipping across the border into Lviv will fulfil the traveller's urge for a taste of the once-forbidden USSR. Any such desires are hopelessly outdated, not to mention slightly misdirected, since Galicia has always been a place unto itself. Entering Galicia feels more like dropping back a few centuries into a world where people still live close to the earth, and where custom and superstition rule (the evil eye is a common affliction in these parts). The countryside here is especially rustic and quaint: tin-roof farms, churches made of hand-cut logs, split-timber fences, and ducks waddling through vegetable patches. This was the one part of Ukraine that was never really collectivised by the Soviets, so the life and landscape are more rugged and unchanged.

Ukrainian nationalism burns brightest in the west. The oldest Slavic traditions are still followed religiously and it's worth planning a trip to coincide with a local holiday to witness the vivid spectacles and haunting music that accompany such an occasion. Outside most villages is a steep mound topped with crosses of tied tree limbs, flags and banners; these are burial sites to mark the graves and memories of partisan fighters who died in the struggle for Ukrainian liberation. A heritage of resistance has Galicians thinking they are the most Ukrainian of all Ukrainians, but the rest of the country pokes fun at their Polish accents. (With the commercialisation of Poland, the region has seen a massive influx of Polish tourists coming to see what their own country used to be like.) Group tours are likely to include some time in the west since Lviv is such an attraction, and individual itineraries should sway westward for the cultural riches and the simple fact that Ukraine is not Ukraine without Galicia.

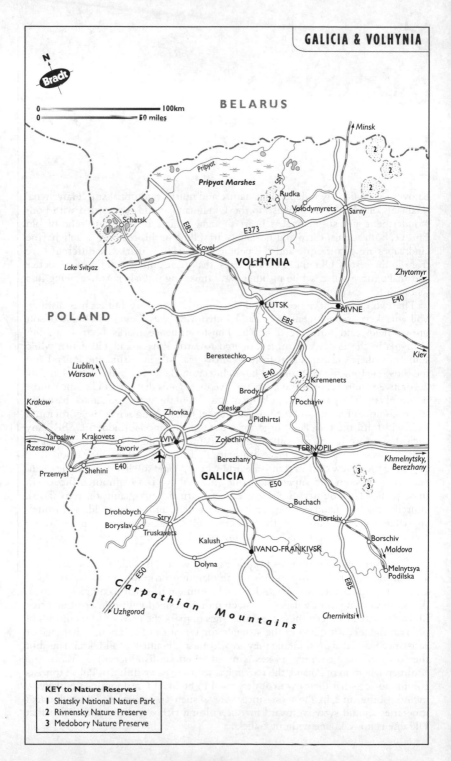

N

Bradt

0 |————————————| 100km
0 |————————————| 50 miles

BELARUS

↗ Minsk

2

2

2

Pripyat

Pripyat Marshes

Styr

2 Rudka

Volodymyrets

Sarny

Schatsk

E85

E373

Kovel

VOLHYNIA

Zhytomyr

Lake Svityaz

POLAND

LUTSK

E85

RIVNE

E40

Kiev

Berestechko

Liublin,
Warsaw

E40

3 Kremenets

Krakow

Brody

Pochayiv

Zhovka

Oleske

Yaroslaw

Krakovets

Pidhirtsi

Rzeszow

Yavoriv

LVIV

Zolochiv

TERNOPIL

Khmelnytsky,
Berezhany

Przemysl

Shehini

E40

Berezhany

3

Drohobych

GALICIA

E50

3

Boryslav

Stry

Buchach

Chortkiv

Truskavets

Kalush

Borschiv

Drohobych

Dolyna

IVANO-FRANKIVSK

Moldova

Melnytsya
Podilska

C a r p a t h i a n   M o u n t a i n s

↗ Uzhgorod

Chernivtsi ↘

KEY to Nature Reserves
1 Shatsky National Nature Park
2 Rivnensky Nature Preserve
3 Medobory Nature Preserve

In a historical context, Galicia and Volhynia have always been the exception to the rule, which is why they feel so different from the rest of the country. When Kievan Rus began to weaken in the 13th century, the joined principalities (based in Halych and Volodymyr) became an autonomous kingdom that endured the Mongol invasion in 1240 and continued for over a century as an independent polity. Many consider this brief interlude as the first true Ukrainian state. Poland occupied Galicia in 1349 (Lithuania had already invaded Volhynia) and introduced the Magdeburg Law in 1356 as a set of rights by which a city was self-governed. Beneath the princes and boyars, the 'burghers' evolved as a new social class of wealthy leaders that regulated Lviv's growing trade. Economic opportunity attracted Jews, Germans, Greeks and Armenians to Galicia's cities, while the Ruthenians (Ukrainians) had limited access to urban areas by law. Polish language and culture dominated and the Greek Catholic Church was born as a compromise between papal authority and Ukrainian Orthodoxy.

After the collapse of the Polish *rzeczpospolita* (see page 19) in the 18th century, Galicia found itself a part of the Austro-Hungarian Empire, while Volhynia was annexed to Russian right-bank Ukraine. 'Galicia' is actually the Austrian name given to the province that stretched from Krakow (in present-day Poland) to Kolomiya in the Carpathians. Austrian rule proved politically and financially beneficial and as in most of central and eastern Europe at the time, Ukrainian national consciousness was sharpened. The uprising of 1848 solidified a new ideal for the Ukrainian people and their petition for more recognition and cultural freedom was granted. (This was a noted difference from the rest of Ukraine, where use of the Ukrainian language was officially banned under Russian rule.) Great Britain was the only country to support the idea of an independent Western Ukraine forming in the Treaty of Versailles in 1918 and so the following year Galicia found itself once again a part of independent Poland. This ended with the Ribbentrop–Molotov Pact which sanctioned the German invasion of Poland in 1939 and subsequent Soviet occupation of the eastern half of Galicia. Stalin's attempt to help the area 'catch up' with Soviet Socialist Ukraine was a murderous disaster brought to a halt by the Nazi invasion in 1941. Jews made up 10% of Galicia's population and those who did not flee to central Asia were the first to be killed. Like the Baltic states, Galicia became an official part of the Soviet Union only after the war in 1945 and there are stories of Ukrainian partisan bands still fighting 'the Russians' in the hills of southern Galicia until the 1960s. Active cultural resistance never ended and the final push for Ukrainian independence was kindled in Galicia with the demonstrations in 1988.

The utterly turbid and separate history of the far west is a primary source for Ukraine's divided self-image today. Galicia is praised for the way it has protected the Ukrainian language and culture, but is resented for its militancy. Even while Ukraine tries to orient itself towards the EU, the European traditions of Galicia conflict with the post-Soviet ways of the east. Travelling in this area, you cannot help but notice the nationalist fervour, as well as the difference in attitude and service.

GETTING AROUND

Lviv is the largest city in western Ukraine and the central transport hub for getting anywhere in Galicia and Volhynia. From Lviv there are separate train lines and bus routes to all major cities: Lutsk, Rivne, Ternopil, Ivano-Frankivsk and Uzhgorod. Keep in mind that these cities also have their own direct links to Kiev and other Ukrainian cities. Lviv has an efficient local transport system with frequent minibuses to all the villages and regular routes to the Carpathians. As in most of Ukraine, getting around in Galicia is a question of supply and demand: for US$10–20 you can go anywhere. Volhynia is a little less easy to reach since the main rail line is the route between Kiev and Warsaw. Travelling between Galicia and Volhynia, you might want to take the quicker motor transport because you'll miss the dramatic scenery on the train.

LVIV ЛЬВІВ

As Ukraine's most elegant city, Lviv is a promised cure for any sceptics still entrenched in negative images of post-Soviet cities. Instead of rusted smokestacks, Lviv stands as a beautiful and eclectic monument to art, history and all the fortitude of European culture. Each building is like a fossil of Lviv's past reincarnations and artful developments have made this city a fashionable destination among Europeans from outside Ukraine, as well as those who live there. Among Lviv's open squares and wide boulevards, visitors will recognise bits of Paris, Florence, Krakow, Vienna and old St Petersburg. Attention to detail is everything in this city: the relief on door panels, the shaped iron gates, the graceful balconies and ornate stonework – all reflect centuries of luxurious craft. In keeping with notions of romantic decay, Lviv looks a bit rough and unpainted, yet the breadth of art and architecture here makes such an attractive ensemble that people should feel a sense of urgency to see Lviv in its natural state before the city gets covered in billboards and neon (locals insist that Lviv is immune to tastelessness).

Prince Danylo of Halychyna (Galicia) founded the city in honour of his son Leo, hence the name Lviv from the Slavic root for 'lion'. The symbol of the city is a lion, and those interested in symbolism could spend weeks discovering the thousands of lions that feature on doorknobs, cornices, gates, keystones and just about every façade in the city centre. The prince built his castle at the top of a conical-shaped hill, known today as Vysoky Zamok ('High Castle'), which is also the name of the leading Ukrainian-language newspaper. With Galicia's annexation to Poland, Lviv grew into a vital metropolis of very wealthy foreign merchants and churchmen as well as Ruthenian and Polish labourers. Polish rule contributed the cobblestoned streets and Baroque architecture as well as the still-present Polish language and Roman Catholic faith.

Lviv's real building boom took place in the 16th and 17th centuries and was heavily influenced by the Italian Renaissance. Architecture students from Europe and America are now coming to Lviv for its wealth of pure Italian design. Under the Hapsburg Empire Lviv (then known as Lemburg) developed into a more progressive, intellectual and artistic city. The university was founded and architects from Vienna and Prague introduced Art Nouveau to the city's collage. Lviv soon defined its own style and was the birthplace for various artistic and literary movements largely unknown in the West. The rise of Ukrainian national consciousness in the 19th century was centred in Lviv and a whole new set of monuments are dedicated to the writers who spread the word. Lviv's buildings (though not its people) emerged relatively unscathed from the wars of the 20th century, and since Ukraine's independence the city has developed in leaps and bounds. UNESCO has just designated the entire city as a World Heritage Site and the Ukrainian government claims that over half of Ukraine's recognised architectural monuments can be found in Lviv. The recent praise is well deserved, but says little about Lviv's wonderful and brooding personality. Whether or not you believe in the supernatural, there is something very mysterious and Gothic about the city, something dark but curious. That medieval quality seems to be part of the attraction of Lviv.

Lviv is the gateway for most European traffic into Ukraine and is less than an hour from the Polish border. With the range of budget flights to eastern Poland, this is becoming a popular entry point into the country. Due to the good relations between the two countries, the Poland–Ukraine border is probably the easiest one to cross. The biggest nuisance is the wait, which if you come at the wrong time can last more than four hours; a 'quick crossing' is anything under an hour. If you are travelling to or from Warsaw, it is often better to just go on the train, but if you are simply crossing the border, take one of the short bus connections to Rzeszów (*Zheshov*) or Przemyśl (*Permishl* in Russian, *Pshemys* in Polish). These can take between two and three hours to do the whole trip, and since they are regular and frequent, there seems to be a more established protocol with the checkpoints (sometimes).

Without any real competition from the capital or Crimea, Lviv is also Ukraine's most tourist-friendly town. The hotels are great, the café and restaurant culture highly service-oriented, and the people tremendously cosmopolitan and multilingual. As the city confirms its role as Ukraine's number one tourist destination, organised tours will normally stop here for a minimum of two full days. I would recommend even more, and if you are on your own, you should take advantage of being in such a vibrant European city that just happens to be in the throes of a reawakening. You'll find it difficult to pull yourself away, simply because of the quantity of things to see and the richness of aimless urban exploration; a person could easily spend an entire two-week holiday in Lviv and still feel all the contentment of travel.

GETTING THERE AND AWAY Lviv is Ukraine's European gateway and for obvious historical reasons the major routes are oriented towards Poland, meaning this is a good place to begin or end a trip. It is also an important stopping point between Kiev and the Carpathians.

By air Lviv's airport is just 4km to the southwest of the city centre – about a 20-minute taxi ride in traffic. There are also regular *marshrutka* and trolleybus No 9 will take you from the airport to the city centre. For airport information call 0322 692 112, otherwise most upscale hotels have their own air-ticket booking office.

These days, flying to Lviv is convenient, cheap and quick – more people should do it. Currently, there are several daily flights to and from Kiev on Lviv Airlines (*www.avia.lviv.ua*) who code share with Aerosvit (*Lubinska 168;* ✆ *0322 298 024;* e *lviv@aerosvit.com; www.aerosvit.com*). Domestic routes vary widely, with more options in summer, so check things out online beforehand. The most regular booking agent is Kiy Avia (*Prospekt Shevchenko 11;* ✆ *0322 743 027;* e *lvov@kiyavia.com; www.kiyavia.com*). Internationally, daily flights connect Lviv with Warsaw (LOT) and Frankfurt (Lufthansa), with periodic flights to and from Vienna (Austria). Other European connections are more sporadic.

By rail Lviv has the largest train station in western Ukraine and an important hub between domestic cities and international (mainly central European) destinations. The train station is at the end of Chernivetska (✆ *0322 748 2068*). A taxi to and from the city centre should be around US$4, or take tram No 6 or *marshrutka* No 2, which also connect to the city centre.

There are five daily trains between Lviv and Kiev, each along a different route, some of which are very indirect and long. The trip should take around 12 hours.

Galicia & Volhynia LVIV

9

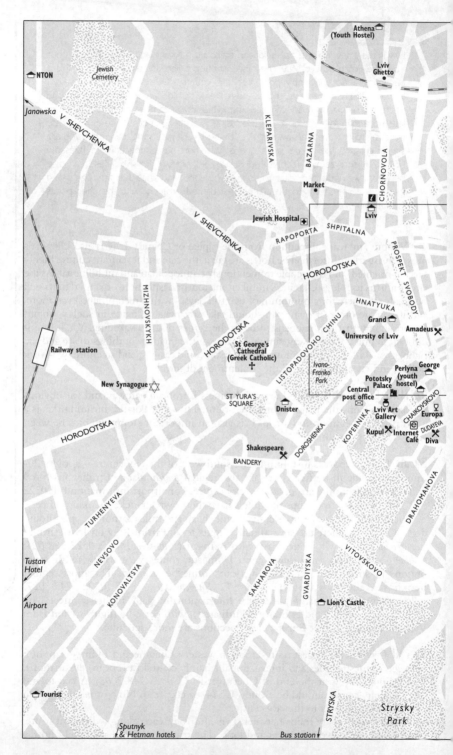

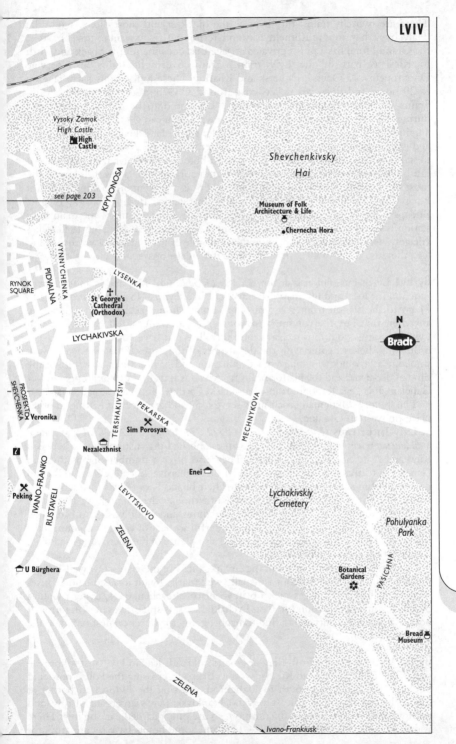

Vysoky Zamok
High Castle
High Castle

see page 203

Shevchenkivsky Hai

Museum of Folk
Architecture & Life
Chernecha Hora

KPYVONOSA

VYNNYCHENKA

PIDVALNA

RYNOK
SQUARE

LYSENKA

St George's
Cathedral
(Orthodox)

LYCHAKIVSKA

N

Bradt

PROSPEKT
SHEVCHENKA

Veronika

TERSHAKIVTSIV

PEKARSKA

Sim Porosyat

Nezalezhnist

Enei

MECHNYKOVA

Lychakivskiy
Cemetery

Pohulyanka
Park

Peking

IVANO-FRANKO

RUSTAVELI

LEVYTSKOVO

ZELENA

Botanical
Gardens

PASICHNA

U Bürghera

Bread
Museum

ZELENA

Ivano-Frankiusk

There are two city trains: the 'Lviv' is the quickest and most direct, while the 'Halychyna' has stops in Khmelnytsky and Ternopil. (If you want to travel in style, the Grand Hotel has a plush private carriage that does the journey back and forth to Kiev as part of the Lviv train.) Daily overnight trains also service Dnopropetrovsk, Odessa, Donetsk and Kharkiv. These longer routes can take up to 20 hours and first-class tickets cost around US$25; a *coupé* is under US$15. Trains to Ivano Frankivsk (4 hours) and Uzhgorod (6 hours) normally travel during the day and cost under US$10. As always, you can get to any other city on a train from Lviv but you need to find out the particular schedule, time and route and make sure it's worth your while. Admittedly, Lviv is a great place from which to start a rail adventure across Ukraine. Most hotels in Lviv have travel offices that can book train tickets, or at least give you the current timetables. Otherwise the most convenient place to buy railway tickets is the central booking office at Hnatyuka 20. From Lviv, international routes service Berlin, Warsaw, Prague, Budapest, Rzeszow, Przemysl, Kosice and Bratislava. Just south of the main train station is the local train station with the small *elektrichki* branching out to Galicia's villages. Here it's a matter of reading the timetable or finding a trustworthy soul to lead the way, but it's a lot easier to stick to the village buses.

By bus Lviv's bus station is at Stryska 189 (☏ *0322 632 473*) and is another busy junction for local and international travellers. Trolleybus No 5 and *marshrutka* No 71 go to the station from the centre and a taxi should cost US$3. You can go anywhere on a bus, but you must ask yourself if you want to. It does not help that Lviv's station is notoriously chaotic and travellers can have a really hard time co-ordinating their schedule with the departures of the buses. Don't hesitate to ask someone at a window, stating your destination and having them write down the time of departure and the platform. From Lviv, bus travel is best for going to other Galician cities (eg: Ternopil, Ivano-Frankivsk, Pochaïv) and the Carpathians.

The 'luxury' Ukrainian coach lines serve Lviv and are nice for getting to other places in western Ukraine.

Lviv-Inturtrans (*Kuznevycha 2/4;* ☏ *0322 971 168;* f *0322 926 114;* e *intu@ mail.lviv.ua; www.lviv-inturtrans.com*) has an established international route between Kiev and Antwerp, Paris and Rome. They also offer a number of bus tours in Galicia. **Avtoluks** has two offices in Lviv: on Sakharova 42 (☏ *0322 345 021*) and next to the bus station (☏ *0322 632 464*). Their bus to Kiev travels through Lutsk, Rivne and Zhytomyr and takes the exact same time as the train (about 10 hours). Longer routes on an overnight bus can be tedious and you'll wish you had a bed on the train, but if you want to see the wonderful scenery of western Ukraine, take the bus and travel during the day. There are also plenty of buses crossing the Polish border all day long (see below).

The local *marshrutka* buzz about the city like flies but there are a few well-known pick-up spots and each minibus is usually well marked with its destination. Buses to western Galician villages pick up in front of Shevchenko 24; eastern Galicia buses pick up at bus station No 6 on Lychakivska. It is still often safer (in terms of both confusion and success) to find transport going to your local destination at the main bus station.

By car If you're driving from Kiev or Poland, all roads lead to Lviv; just follow the signs. The E-40 goes east to Kiev or west to Brussels, crossing the Polish border at Shehini. The E-50 goes south to Uzhgorod, crossing the Hungarian border at Chop; the T-1402 goes southeast to Ivano-Frankivsk. Lviv's streets are narrow (and bumpy) and auto-theft is not uncommon, so use only guarded parking lots. There is one in the city centre (☏ *0322 974 114*) and some hotels have secure areas for cars. Negotiating your own long-haul taxi is not difficult. You can try to flag someone down, or ask at the hotel. Car rental is new to Lviv but the nicer hotels sometimes offer chauffeur-driven rental cars, or you can go with any of the international companies. Try Europcar *(Ivana Franka 28/3; ʌ/f 0322 967 550)* or Hertz *(Horodotska 62; ʌ 0322 947 488)*.

GETTING AROUND Even the locals seem bewildered by Lviv's public transport system, but compared with most, it's a good place for first-time foreigners to give it a go. A wrong move is easily forgiven since Lviv is really a walking city. Trams run along the larger boulevards and to the train station. You are most likely to use Nos 1, 6, 7 and 9. A central tram station is behind the theatre, diagonally across from the opera. From here, most cars go along Horodotska to the main train station. Trolleys have a tough time on Lviv's cobbles and so few venture into the centre, but there is the No 5 that goes to the bus station. Lviv's taxis are user-friendly and more honest than in other cities in Ukraine, so this is really the best way to see the parks and city sights that are farther out. A ride to anywhere in the city, including the airport and train station, should be about US$3 or less.

TOURIST INFORMATION AND LOCAL TOUR OPERATORS Being the progressive city that it is, Lviv has a central **tourist information centre** *(open every day 10.00–18.00; write to Lviv Tourist Board, Pidvalna 3, 79006 Lviv, ʌ/f 0322 97 57 51/67;* e *ltb@mail.lviv.ua. They have an exceptional website: www.tourism.lviv.ua)* that offers very useful information to visitors about hotels, restaurants, attractions and everything that is going on in Lviv (theatre, festivals, exhibitions, etc). This is the best place for city maps and brochures and they can also co-ordinate walking tours, and arrange English-language guides and local excursions. A private guided tour of the city in English costs around US$12 per hour, and there are two group tours every day except Sunday.

Lviv has more tour agencies and services than any other city in Ukraine, so there's no lack of help in this town.

Lviv Inturtrans Kuznevycha 2/4; ʌ 0322 971 168; f 0322 926 114; e intu@mail.lviv.ua; www.lviv-inturtrans.com. One of Lviv's most professional agencies, specialising in incoming tourism and featuring diverse tours throughout the country that specialise in Galicia, with Lviv as the gateway. In addition to their expertise in putting together affordable and interesting package tours, they are also one of the few local companies to welcome the requests of individual travellers. They can custom build any trip in the country, and are quite helpful even after you're on the ground. Their staff speak any number of languages and are very accommodating.

Meest-Tour Prospekt Shevchenka 34; ʌ/f 0322 970 852; e office@meest-tour.com.ua; www.meest-tour.com.ua. A well-known international travel company based in Lviv, specialising in outdoor pursuits in Ukraine and throughout Eurasia. This Ukrainian–Canadian joint venture has been around longer than most and has built a strong reputation for local knowledge and adventurous tours. This is a

good company to contact when planning a trip from outside Ukraine since they are comfortable communicating in English and are capable of taking care of lots of particulars in advance (hotel, transport, visas, etc). Besides offering unique tours in Lviv, they do a variety of local excursions to Galicia's monasateries and castles, and if you want to head to the Carpathians, these are the right people to contact for organising long treks, mountain biking and river rafting.

Adventure Carpathians Kyivska 25/3; ʌ/f 0322 372 727; e contact@adventurecarpathians.com; www.adventurecarpathians.com. A young and ambitious tour operator focusing on Lviv and adventure outdoor activities in the Carpathians. The staff speak impeccable English and their service is especially good for serious climbers and hikers. They also run their own rural home-visit programme, arranging inexpensive accommodation in the homes of mountain villagers. As a side project, they run the very informative travel website www.travel.inlviv.info.

Yunta Prospekt Shevchenko 23; ✆ 0322 728 710; e yunta@mail.lviv.ua; www.yunta.lviv.ua. A private company run by former members of Inturist, so they have access to much of the infrastructure for dealing with incoming tourists. They arrange more relaxed trips to the Carpathians, as well as local

excursions in Galicia.
Piligrim Kopernika 24; ✆ 0322 970 551; e travel@pilgrim.lviv.net; www.piligrim.lviv.ua. Not as in 'pilgrim', but as in *pili-grim*. Established tour firm based in Lviv, with several combination tours that start or finish in Lviv.

🏠 **WHERE TO STAY** Lviv's hospitality industry is a step ahead of the rest of the country in terms of quality, but it's managed to avoid the rash of overpricing that afflicts Kiev. Take note that the water situation has never been good in Lviv, so the more plush hotels will advertise their separate water systems, and lower-end hotels will post schedules predicting when the hot water will be flowing. Also, Lviv is not exempt from the general rule in Ukraine regarding accommodation: price rarely indicates quality, making it difficult to rank Lviv's very individualistic and competitive hotels. If you're trying to make your money stretch, don't write off 'luxury hotels' that may have a variety of rooms, some at lower prices. If you don't mind spending over US$100, then don't settle for the many sub-standard rooms that are offered – in Lviv you have very nice alternatives. All except the budget hotels accept credit cards.

Luxury

🏠 **Hotel Opera** Prospekt Svobody 34; ✆ 0322 259 003; f 0322 2259 001; e skuratoko@hotel-ukraine.com,web: www.hotel-opera.lviv.ua. Lviv's newest hotel boasts the polished quality of international hotels and dependable service. You can't beat the location across from the opera house, nor can you beat the view of Lviv (ask for something on the 4th floor or higher facing the rear). Besides the luxurious king-size beds (for dbls) and comfortable bathrooms, there's high-speed internet in every room, interactive TV, and centralised heating and AC. The staff also represent a new generation of Lviv's prodigious polyglot youth. The sgls are a good deal, whereas couples might consider upgrading from the standard rooms to the superior dbls. The tasteful suites are definitely worth a splurge. B/fast inc in the quaint basement restaurant. *Sgl US$80, dbl US$130–150, suite US$300.*

🏠 **Grand Hotel** Prospekt Svobody 13; ✆ 0322 724 042, 727 665; f 0322 769 060; e grand@ghgroup.com.ua; www.ghgroup.com.ua. This classy hotel deserves its sumptuous name and is one of the most upscale hotels in Lviv, not forgetting that they also have wonderful beds that are very comfortable. The 'grand' company works as a conglomerate of luxury services in Lviv, including an indoor pool, health spa, private clubs, a private train car, a business centre, and an in-house tour agency that can arrange any kind of trip to anywhere. Somehow the place avoids being too snobbish: the walls feature changing exhibits of local art and the staff speak impeccable English. Best of all is their

elegant ground-floor restaurant with live harp music every evening. Wired for internet. B/fast inc. *Sgl US$110–130, dbl US$145–170, larger suite US$180–250.*

🏠 **Hotel Dnister** Mateiko 6; ✆ 0322 974 305/06; f 0322 971 021; e reservation@dnister.lviv.ua; www.dnister@lviv.ua. The outside structure reveals this to be Lviv's former Inturist hotel, but now the Dnister functions as a quality corporate-style hotel for business travellers and large tour groups. The refurbished rooms are comfortable and clean, though a little small. The 'business' suites reflect the standards of a normal, Western hotel, but you could buy a much nicer room elsewhere in town for the price. All rooms have showers, except for the suites, which have baths. The Dnister does have a good view of the city and has kept all its Inturist connections, meaning they can book air and train tickets and offer private tours. The large restaurant on the second floor serves typical Russian fare with a separate vegetarian menu, and offers a b/fast buffet that is included in the price of the room. *Economy room US$80, larger room US$100, 'semi-luxury' room US$150, business suite US$200.*

🏠 **Lion's Castle** Glinki 7; ✆ 0322 971 563; f 0322 351 102; e lions_castle@org.lviv.net; www.lionscastle.com. If my parents were coming to Lviv, I would want them to stay in this converted Austrian mansion. Situated in one of Lviv's quiet and traditional neighbourhoods, the Gothic hotel characterises the city better than most. Visiting dignitaries from the Hapsburg Empire used to stay here and it was the first to be opened after independence. There are only 14 rooms (each very individual and spacious) and the hotel functions as a B&B. There are 5 categories of rooms. They also co-ordinate airport and train station pick-ups, have

Middle range

⌂ **Wien Guest Rooms** Prospekt Svobody 12; ⟍/f 0322 444 314; e wienhotel@mail.lviv.ua; www.wienhotel.lviv.ua. Newly renovated, this European-style guesthouse is safe, clean and affordable, with good beds, hot water and cheery multilingual staff: a good deal in the heart of the city. Credit cards accepted. *US$60–70 with b/fast inc in the downstairs café.*

⌂ **George Hotel** Mitskevycha Square 1; ⟍ 0322 974 255; f 0322 971 144; e info@ georgehotel.com.ua; www.georgehotel.com.ua. This pink and white Baroque hotel is in a fantastic location in the heart of the city and is becoming more popular with foreign tourists, particularly Germans. The grand staircase, high ceilings and chandeliers pay tribute to a distinguished past, but the years have left some of the rooms looking slightly tattered and smoky. Things have improved greatly in the last few years, so that now the hotel offers 3 distinct classes of rooms for all budgets. Second-class rooms come with a shared bathroom; first-class rooms have private bathrooms and are not bad at all; there are also larger, more comfortable dbl suites. Most of the bathrooms are just average, but there is always hot water and through constant effort the hotel stays clean. *Second-class rooms US$30–40, first-class US$70–80, dbl suite US$80–100.*

⌂ **Enei** Shimzeriv 2; ⟍ 0322 768 799; f 0322 965 031; e eney@mail.lviv.ua; www.eney.lviv.ua .This boutique hotel is on the southern side of town (towards Lychakivsky Cemetery). Built in a renovated Lviv home; some of the rooms are a bit oddly shaped, and decorated largely in IKEA style. Small and cosy, it also offers a rare outdoor pool and a guarded parking lot. B/fast inc. *Superior standard room with a queen-size bed US$70, and with a king US$95.*

⌂ **U Bürghera** Ivano Franko 73; ⟍ 0322 761 251; f 0322 966 569; e info@burger.com.ua; www.burger.com.ua. Modern and cosy, this luxury complex is named after the old burghermasters that ruled Lviv in Magdeburg times, though the lurid décor is aimed at the new business élite ruling Lviv today. This is honest-to-goodness

a guarded car park and a nice garden in the back. Their ground-floor restaurant is a bit glitzy but the sumptuous b/fasts are famous. It's just a 10min walk to the city centre. *The nice rooms (in the older building) are US$80–150; regular dbl US$95.*

Western-standard accommodation, but service is mixed; there are very comfortable dbl rooms and rooms with real dbl beds. All rooms have internet access and there are some really amazing luxury suites with private swimming pools and/or jacuzzis. The restaurant and bar are known party areas. Outside the city, the hotel owns a luxurious country resort with the unfortunate name of 'Burger Club'. The hotel staff can arrange rooms and transport if you fancy getting out of town. *Dbl room US60, room with real dbl bed US$75, luxury suite US$100–150.*

⌂ **Sputnyk** Knyahinya Olha 116; ⟍ 0322 645 822; f 0322 641 523; e suputnyk@mail.lviv.ua; www.suputnyk.com. An old Soviet building, this concrete high-rise is far from the city centre and a little drab on the outside. Inside, the rooms are renovated in a style that's best described as post-Soviet chic, but they feel very cramped. In classic Inturist style, they don't really want to deal with individuals, favouring large groups of over 20 persons. *If you show up by yourself or as a couple, a sgl will cost US$50, a twin US$65, dbl US$75 and a 2-room business suite US$100.*

⌂ **NTON Hotel** Shevchenka 154; ⟍/f 0322 333 123; e hotelnton@mail.lviv.ua; www.hotelnton.lviv.ua. If you are driving from Europe, this is a good motel to stop at, since it is right off the main road, has a large guarded parking lot and is only a short tram ride into the centre. From the centre, take tram No 7 to the end. Everything is new here, including the furniture and plumbing (meaning 24hr hot water). It's also very family-friendly and good at accommodating children. *US$45–50 with individual showers, US$60 with a bath, US$70/$90 for a suite.*

⌂ **Hetman** V. Velykovo 50; ⟍ 0322 649 981; f 0322 648 472; e hetman@mail.lviv.ua; www.hetman.lviv.ua. Though not at all central, the Hetman is good value for money, with comfortable rooms each remodelled (to a degree) with a private bathroom. The hot water is also independent and reliable. *Standard sgl US$35, dbl US$40. 'European'-style rooms are much nicer, a twin costing US$55; large suites US$80.*

Lviv is proud of its citizens, both the wicked and the holy. Leopold von Sacher-Masoch is remembered best for the clinical term for morbidly obsessive behaviour, and is one of the darker characters of the Hapsburg Empire. While he studied and wrote in Prague, Germany and Italy, the novelist's own persona is symbolic of Lviv: his father was Spanish by birth (but from Austrian Prague) and worked as the chief of police in Lemberg (Lviv); his mother was a dainty Ruthenian noble who had her child Leopold nursed by a Russian peasant woman to give him vigour. He studied and practised law but turned to writing stories that dealt with his own childhood fantasies. His novel *Venus in Furs* is a marked expression of masochistic behaviour, as was his violently bizarre marriage – he beat his wife whenever she refused to whip him. The actual term 'Masochism' was coined by the German neurologist Dr Richard von Krafft-Ebing, who referred to the novelist in his scientific work *Psychopathia Sexualis* and defined Leopold's mentality as that of someone with an unbearable urge to be controlled by the will of another. Today in Lviv people are more pleased than ashamed that their city was the birthplace of such a famous psychopath.

Budget

🏠 **Hotel Lviv** Prospekt Chornovola 7; ☎ 0322 792 270; f 0322 728 651. Hotel Lviv is a soot-covered, Soviet-style hotel offering a straightforward crash pad for travellers in the city centre behind the opera house. The rooms are small and beds are solid; you pay for any extras (eg: hot showers cost US$0.50). The clientele tends to be Ukrainians 'doing business' in Lviv and large Polish tour groups. Prices vary depending on whether or not you have 'a view' and how many stairs you have to climb to get to your room. Hot water is available 06.00–11.00 and 17.00–midnight, and the sauna is US$5 for a 2hr session. The ground-floor restaurant is open 08.00–midnight and serves inexpensive but filling meals. *Sgl without a view US$10–12; with a view it's US$15–20; dbl US$20–30. A group of 3 or 4 sharing a room US$8 pp.*

🏠 **Hotel Nezalezhnist** Tershakivtsiv 6; ☎ 0322 757 224. On the eastern side of the city, this hotel appears perpetually closed from the outside, but in fact it is always open; sneak through the many doors until you get to the administrator. The interior atmosphere is reminiscent of an early 1970s TV show, but the rooms are inexpensive and the hotel is secure. Their 'lux' room is a good deal and is an honest replica of the apts that most Soviet citizens used to live in. For a Soviet leftover, the staff are uncharacteristically friendly. Hot water runs in the early morning and late evening. The best deals are for couples: *sgl US$15, dbl US$20, 'lux' room US$40.*

🏠 **Tourist Hotel** Konovaltsya 103; ☎ 0322 352 391; f 0322 351 065. A self-contained Inturist-style hotel, with tour services, sauna, hairdresser and the works, all in-house. Not all rooms are scruffy, just some, and hot water is reliable for the most part. *Bare sgl room US$12, nicer dbls US$25, the most expensive suites US$50.*

🏠 **Tustan Hotel** 168A Lubinska; ☎ 0322 692 882; f 0322 692 881. Right near the airport, the Tustan has become the de facto airport hotel for those on a budget. The trolleybus takes you right into the city centre in under 10mins. *A sgl bed under US$10, 'first-class' rooms with private bathrooms around US$25.*

YOUTH HOSTELS Lviv's proximity to the backpackers' circuit in eastern Europe makes it an increasingly inviting destination for the huge influx of younger travellers that will surely spill across the border in the next few years. Being the progressive town that it is, Lviv was the very first Ukrainian city to establish a bona fide youth hostel. When looking or booking, note that several accommodation providers may advertise themselves as hostels, but are in fact seasonal residences or private apartments. For the time being, Ukraine's Youth Hostel Association manages the city's three actual hostels.

Perlyna Voronovo 3; ✆ 0322 965 734; info@hihostels.com.ua; www.hostel.org.ua. Right off of Halytsky Square, and the main reception office for all of Lviv's hostels. The central location makes this a coveted place to overnight, so book ahead. The shared bathrooms are clean, and the beds incredibly cheap. *Under US$10.*

Athena Khimichna 49A (contact through the office at Perlyna). Situated in a slightly older section of Kiev, but just as central, each room has 3 beds. The more expensive rooms feature their own bathrooms. 24hr check in. *US$15–20 pp.*

Banking Academy Youth Hostel 14, Kopernika St (contact through the office at Perlyna). At the time of writing, this is still a seasonal hostel (May–Sep), but with an unbeatable location. *Beds US$15–20.*

✖ WHERE TO EAT

Dining in Lviv is typically a more refined experience than elsewhere in Ukraine. The strong tradition of hearty Galician cuisine takes on an air of the aristocratic past, allowing most restaurants to feel both laidback and elegant. What's more, they'll bend over backwards to please. Nearly every establishment has an English menu and accepts credit cards.

'Having coffee' in Lviv involves the kind of ritual that one might expect to find in the coffee houses of Vienna. The colloquial expression for coffee shop (*kavyarna*) has an even richer meaning in Lviv, and whether it's mid-morning or mid-afternoon, you will find tables full of students, professionals and fancied-up old ladies all huddled over teeny cups of medicinal Turkish coffee and plates of sugared pastries – surely a fine local tradition in which to indulge oneself.

Restaurants

✖ **Oselya** Hnatyuka 11; ✆ 0322 721 601. You're bound to eat at a lot of Ukrainian themed restaurants on your trip, but this one stands far above the rest; the dishes, tables, waiters' clothes, antique decorations and drying flowers build an authentic representation of an old Ukrainian cottage. What's more, the food is genuinely Ukrainian as well as sophisticated. If you are not lucky enough to be invited to someone's home for dinner, this will do. The menu is true to tradition. *2-course meal with drinks around US$15 pp; open 11.00–23.00.*

✖ **Kupol** Chaikovskovo 37; ✆ 0322 744 254. Run by 3 sisters who love all things old, this restaurant is fashioned as a quaint Polish tea salon. In fact, this hilltop house was once the home of a famous Lviv art salon, and many of the relics on display belonged to the renowned Volsky family. The antique collection is as impressive as the exquisite food; a good look at the walls and artefacts tells you much about Lviv's history. The atmosphere is warm (candlelight, lace and framed Polish love letters) and the cuisine is a mix of Polish and Austrian dishes; the chicken and bacon rolls are a popular choice. In warmer months, the flowery outdoor patio is a nice place for tea and a romantic view of the city. This restaurant tends to be a favourite of visitors and should not be missed. *Mains from US$US15; open 09.00–23.00.*

✖ **Amadeus** Katedralna 7; ✆ 0322 978 022. Already famous for its grilled food and big servings, Amadeus is a very cosy upscale restaurant right next to the Latin Cathedral near Rynok Square. The clientele leans towards the young, hip and artistic, with dishes like 'the hungry husband' (a hefty portion of grilled meat and potatoes) and flame-broiled salmon. Live performances of romantic jazz every evening. *Mains from US$9; open 11.00–23.00.*

✖ **The Grand Restaurant** Prospekt Svobody 13; ✆ 0322 724 029. On the main level of the Grand Hotel, but with a separate entrance around the corner, this restaurant is both simple and very classy, with refined food and a gentle atmosphere. It specialises in European dishes and pasta. Despite appearances, it caters to nearly every budget. *Mains from US$7; open 08.00–23.00.*

✖ **Penthouse** Svobody 45; ✆ 0322 259 003; www.hotel-opera.lviv.ua. The top floor of the brand-new Opera Hotel is dedicated to this contemporary dining space, featuring an open-air rooftop with a panoramic view, slanted skylights and high-tech décor. The creative blend of French, Ukrainian and Asian cuisine offers welcome respite to those who've already had their fill of borsch. *US$10–$20 entrées; open 11.00–midnight.*

✖ **Shakespeare** Lyubinska 144; ✆ 0322 955 295. Inspired by the bard of England, this quaint brick and timber building is on the road to Lviv's airport or a short taxi ride from the city centre. A diverse menu includes some hearty British favourites such as leek soup and roast beef, along with Ukrainian classics, all served up by waiters in Macbeth-like kilts. A live medieval chamber orchestra playing Beatles songs adds to the camp atmosphere. Enjoy the indoor fireplace in winter; in summer eat outside. *US$5–12 per entrée; open 12.00–midnight.*

✕ **Sim Porosyat (Seven Piglets)** Bandera 9; ☎ 0322 975 558. A crazy, Ukrainian-farm-themed restaurant with live folk band. The food is fantastic, making it a popular stop for tourist groups. *Mains from US$7; open 11.00–midnight.*

✕ **Diva** Dudayeva 5; ☎ 0322 745 022. The menu is chic Ukrainian, the décor an almost-convincing imitation of Art Nouveau. Salads, soups and pasta dominate; they also do b/fast and some hearty dinner dishes. *Mains from US$8; open 11.00–23.00.*

Cafés
Meals

✕ **Wiener Kaffeehaus** Svoboda 12; ☎ 0322 722 021; e wienkaffe@mail.lviv.ua; www.wienkaffe.lviv.ua. Sip coffee outside or inside at this Viennese-style café, known for its rather luxurious desserts. Another section serves as a smoky bar with pool tables and sports TV. The restaurant area leans towards finer dining with tablecloths, candles and hearty Ukrainian meals. *Mains from US$6; open 10.00–23.00.*

✕ **The Milk Bar** Corner of Kopernika and Svobody; no phone. This is the place to come if you are really eating out on the cheap, or if you want to see where the real Lviv hangs out. The city's labour force and students come here for lunch and after work for drinks or meals so the atmosphere tends to be relaxed and jovial. Besides milk and ice cream, the café serves a variety of soups, pancakes and homey food that suits the local income. Nothing

✕ **Stary Tiflis** Pekarska 28; ☎ 0322 766 111. Old Tblisi is one of Lviv's very best Georgian restaurants, serving such staples as *khachapuri* cheese pastries, homemade stews and soups, vegetarian dips and great kebabs. *Mains from US$8; open 11.00–23.00.*

✕ **Vezha Kamariv** Svobody 16; ☎ 0322 965 627. Occupying a medieval fortress on Lviv's main drag, this is not the bawdy tavern that one would expect from the outside, but instead a rather upscale, banquety-type establishment. The Ukrainian food is good and grandiose, and (what a relief!) the band plays classical music. *Mains from US$6; open 11.00–midnight.*

✕ **Peking** Hrushevskovo 8; ☎ 0322 742 107. Classic (and yummy) Chinese food, served with chopsticks. *Mains from US$4; open 11.00–23.00.*

on their menu costs more than US$1 and if you can't read it, then pointing works well. *Open 08.00–22.00.*

✕ **Europa** Shevchenka 14; ☎ 0322 725 862. This is not just a bar serving Ukrainian beer, but a very personal place serving b/fast, lunch and dinner. The menu is diverse and inviting, and this is a popular meeting place with a large TV that attracts football fans. *Mains from US$5; open 10.00–midnight.*

✕ **Kilikia** Virmenska 13; ☎ 0322 726 201. Tasty and unpretentious Armenian cuisine, inspired by the city's rich past and set in a quiet alleyway. *Mains from US$7; open 11.00–23.00.*

✕ **Leonardo** Slovatskovo 5; ☎ 0322 727 140. A popular eatery for both foreigners and locals, inspired by the Italian inventor and serving a tasty blend of Italian and Ukrainian cuisine. A great place for lunch. *Mains from US$5; open 10.00–22.00.*

Coffee and cakes Just try saying 'no' to coffee in this town. There are hundreds of cafés and every one of them is normally a delight. Some of the more popular ones already have a following.

⬛ **The Italian Yard** Rynok Square 6; ☎ 0322 720 671. Mid-morning to late evening coffee inside Lviv's most memorable building. Go through the museum entrance into the courtyard. *Open 10.00–21.00.*

⬛ **Veronika** Shevchenka 21; ☎ 0322 978 128. This candy-striped café not only feels like a Viennese coffee house, but serves Turkish coffee, Austrian cakes and its own delicate chocolates and truffles. Sweet and savoury pastries draw crowds at all times of the day. The baked apples with raspberry sauce come highly recommended. A dark and smoky bar welcomes

visitors who come downstairs. *Open 10.00–midnight.*

⬛ **Svit Kavy** Katedralna 6; ☎ 0322 975 675. A new favourite in Lviv, the 'World of Coffee' serves an absolutely incredible cup of whatever kind of caffeine (or non-caffeine) jolt you're looking for, be it from Africa or South America. *Open 11.00–22.00.*

⬛ **Tsoukerina** Staroyevreiska 3; ☎ 0322 740 949; www.cykiernia.com.ua. Delicious and freshly baked pastries, cookies, candies and giant cakes – and all with coffee or chocolate. A decadent corner of Lviv that's not to be passed by. *Open 10.00–20.00.*

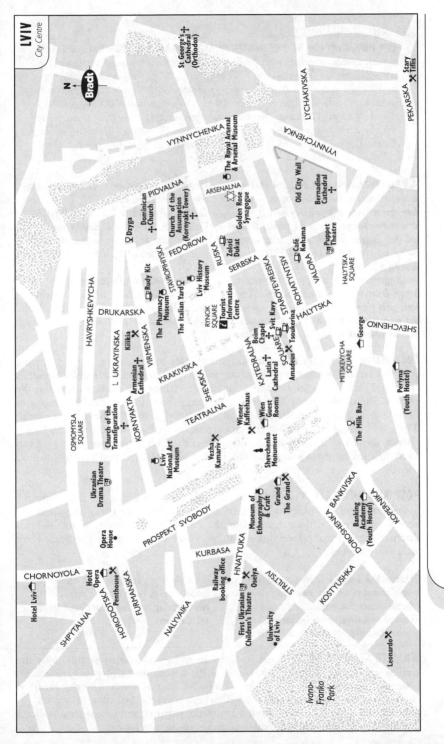

LVIV FOUNDATION FOR THE PRESERVATION OF ARCHITECTURAL AND HISTORICAL MONUMENTS
Lviv's architectural wealth is indisputable, and a fair amount of foreign investment has allowed some level of restoration work to go forward, but the work is never-ending and costly. The Lviv Foundation is a non-governmental, non-profit organisation with a mission to preserve, restore and popularise Lviv's monuments of culture, history and architecture. Donations are obviously appreciated, as is any form of assistance to promote Lviv's greatest resource. Contact Lviv Foundation, 1 Rynok Square, Office 104; ☎ 0322 975 852; e foundation@mis.lviv.ua.

Rudy Kit Drukarska 4; ☎ 0322 296 5914. Yet another patisserie of the decadent variety – be it flaky, creamy, crusty or sugary, they make it and serve it. They lure you in with the promise of coffee and then announce that they're also an ice cream parlour and cake shop. *Open 09.00–22.00.*

Dzyga Virmenska 35; ☎ 0322 752 101; www.dzyga.com.ua. Part café, part art gallery, part antique dealer, this is the commercial side of Lviv's avant-garde scene. The café inspires some interesting and vivacious gatherings and also features regular local art exhibitions, installations and photography.

The building is at the end of one of Lviv's oldest alleys. *Open 10.00–22.00.*

Café Kohama Valora 13; ☎ 0322 744 229. Friendly little café just off of Halytsky Square. Most come for coffee and dessert, but they also serve great lunches (and salads). *Mains from US$3; open 09.00–21.00.*

Zoloti Dukat Fedorova 20; ☎ 0322 298 623. Underground wine cellar turned into a cool little café, serving light meals, drinks and traditional Lviv coffee. *Open 10.00–22.00.*

Food markets If hotel restaurants and quaint cafés become a drag there are plenty of food markets and food stands throughout Lviv. The one at Halytska Square is small and central and sells mainly fruit and vegetables; the main market is at the end of Shpitalna/Bazarna and sells everything from frozen chicken thighs to pantyhose and prescription glasses (and this used to be the Jewish cemetery). There are also plenty of all-night grocery stores that sell fresh produce, bread, cheese, meat and bottled drinks. Like the rest of Ukraine, Lviv has also been overwhelmed by pizza joints and fast food. They will find you before you find them.

POST AND INTERNET The impressively large beige building on the corner of Slovatskovo and Doroshenka is the central post office (see map), but there are several other post offices throughout the city. Lviv also boasts more 24-hour internet/international phone shops than any other Ukrainian city I've seen. Here are a few good ones:

Internet Klub Dudayeva 12; www.internetclub.lviv.ua. A lot of computers and their international phone rates are cheaper than normal.

Nazgul www.nazgul.lviv.ua. Two separate locations: Chornovola 101 and Krushelnitskoi 1

(follow the signs). Schoolboys flock here to play computer games but the club is very accommodating for those seeking other services, and they serve drinks.

WHAT TO SEE AND DO The best thing to do in Lviv is to get lost and enjoy the aimless wandering in the streets. Many of the streets are narrow and there is no better way to appreciate oak cobbles than by walking on them. The city centre is compact, so the 'sights' are close together and there's even more to see and do between these sights. If you're not a fan of the urban adventure or long walks, a guide can be helpful and it is easy to pinpoint some target areas.

Architecture Lviv is synonymous with beautiful buildings and this is what most people come to see. You can spend weeks just staring at each and every structure, doorway, and even every door hinge – everything in Lviv is art. **Rynok Square** is bound to become the city's tourist hotspot, with the city administration building in the centre and statues of Adonis, Neptune, Diana and Amphitrite marking the four corners. This 'Market Square' has always been central to Lviv's trade, and wealthy merchants built their homes and shops on its edges. The city fire of 1527 burned the original Gothic structures to the ground so that today the square's colour and style reflect Baroque and renaissance design from the 17th and 18th centuries. The buildings' uniform width stems from a statute of the Magdeburg Law that permitted three windows tax-free. Larger houses belonged to merchants who were willing to pay the extra fee in order to impress. Each of the 44 buildings has a unique history and there are separate guidebooks (none in English yet) that give the individual backgrounds of each and every one. Most beloved by Lviv's citizens is the **Italian Yard** (*6 Rynok Square; entrance fee 1UAH*) which was the home of the wealthy Greek wine merchant Kornyakt. The courtyard's simple arches and columns reveal Lviv's romantic past, and during the summer there's a small café on the terrace. The upper floors house one of the city's many historical museums. No 3 Rynok Square is built in late Baroque style and comes with a tale. A poor labourer fell in love with the merchant's daughter who lived here, but her father disapproved and promised her to a man of higher standing. To celebrate the engagement, he threw a ball in the upper floors of the house and the young pauper slipped in uninvited to see the girl. The merchant attacked the boy but he fought back and severely injured the older man in the fight. The merchant grew ill but before he died he forgave the young suitor and gave his blessing to the two lovers. No 4 Rynok Square is known as the **Black Mansion** and features an uncomfortably small stoop at the front door that prevented the guard from falling asleep while sitting at his post. The **Venice House** is at 14 Rynok Square; the Venetian merchant who lived here added the St Mark's coat of arms; house number 32 displays some elements of Lviv's austere Art Nouveau. The **'House of the Seasons'** (*Virmenska 23*) is another popular stop, painted pink and decorated with the signs of the zodiac.

The square is but one example of Lviv's architectural wealth and there are some real discoveries to be made in every neighbourhood. These are just a few favourites: the red and grey **Kornyakt Tower** on Pidvalna was built by Lviv's wealthiest benefactor and has been the city's symbol through the ages; Pidvalna 13 is an astonishingly pure example of 19th-century Austrian 'Secessionist' architecture with its brightly painted leaves and carvings (alas, it is now a dentist's office). The peach-coloured **University of Lviv** (*Universytetska 1*) occupies the old Galician Sejm (parliament) and was founded in 1661. The statue on the top represents Mother Galicia blessing her two children, the rivers Dnistr and Vistula. Traditionally, lectures were given in Ukrainian, Polish, Latin and German. This is the right place for young travellers to meet people their age since the area is buzzing with students and there are some nice cafés in the vicinity. Everything about the building at 6 Listopadovoho Chinu is eye-catching, down to its highly decorative doors; the structure was intended as a casino but is now home to the **Lviv Inventors' Club**. The grandiose **Pototsky Palace** (*Kopernika 15*) was used for wedding ceremonies during the Soviet era; across the street (*Kopernika 22*) is the birthplace of Leopold von Sacher-Masoch (who gave us the term 'masochism'; see box, page 205). **Prospekt Shevchenka** underwent a major renovation in 1997 and the white and red towered building was designed by the poet-hero Taras Shevchenko himself. Every Ukrainian city has replaced its Lenin statue with a **Shevchenko monument**, but the one in Lviv is exceptional. Behind the standing poet is a sweeping relief depicting Ukrainian history using religious folk art. The statue was a gift from the vast Ukrainian community in Argentina and stands in the park on Prospekt Svobody, and like all beautiful monuments, it is still considered to be controversial.

Churches Not only is the number of Lviv's churches absolutely astounding, so is the diversity of faith and style represented. Indeed, church fatigue is a common ailment of all visitors to Lviv, even among those of us who gleefully rush from cathedral to cathedral. Hopefully you'll be in town long enough to limit your intake to two or three churches a day. If not, be choosy or else your trip will lead to not much more than a muddled Baroque memory. Identifying a church can be difficult since each is known by many different names (for the sake of convenience they are listed by their colloquial names in English).

Armenian Cathedral (*Virmenska 7*) This beautiful cathedral is one of the oldest in Lviv, built in the 14th century by the still-present Armenian community. The church is open only for services and on rare occasions, but the courtyard is usually open, and is paved with headstones (they say it is good luck in Armenia to have many people walk over your grave). A large wooden sculpture of Christ stands outside which is in pretty good shape after 150 years of snow and rain, and the colourfully painted vaults inside the church are worth coming back for.

Dominican Church (*organ concerts every Fri, Sat and Sun at 15.00; entrance 5UAH*) At the end of Ukrayinka, with the very visible big green dome, it is the legendary site of Prince Lev's palace (son of Danylo, see page 192). This was built by the monastic order in the 18th century using a toned-down Baroque, but now belongs to the Greek Catholics. The interior is beige, decorated with gold-covered wooden statues. Downstairs is the very gloomy **Museum of Religion** (*entrance 1UAH*) which used to be a museum of atheism in Soviet times.

Bernadine Cathedral The Greek Catholic cathedral is behind the city wall on Vynnychenka. The black and gold interior is both majestic and foreboding; the frescoes will be a sight to see when they are finished.

Church of the Transfiguration (*Krakivska 21*) This church once belonged to a Trinitarian monastery, as can be seen by the structure, but the violet and blue interior is decorated with traditional Ukrainian embroidery and features an impressive gold iconostasis. This is one of Lviv's better-preserved churches, and staring up into the cupola, you can see the frescoes of the writers of the four Gospels. There is a sung prayer service (*Wed to Sat at 19.00*) which is a good initiation into the strong Galician religious tradition.

St George's Cathedral (*5 St Yura's Sq*) A canary-coloured assembly of high Baroque buildings that make up the ecclesiastical centre of the Greek Catholic Church. It was here that the pope began his controversial visit to Ukraine in 2001. Before his arrival, the church underwent a costly but tasteful renovation and is now an important spiritual site for many western Ukrainians and the faithful diaspora from around the world. The interior is best seen during daylight hours when natural yellow light gives the walls a bright and surreal glow. The view from the hilltop is simply marvellous.

Latin Cathedral Occupying Cathedral Square (Katedralna), this is Lviv's largest Roman Catholic church, although here they are called Polish Catholics. The building is 18th-century neo-Gothic with a fresh pink and blue Baroque interior.

Supposedly three bombs landed inside the church during World War II but none of them exploded. This was a repeat miracle from a much earlier battle when cannonballs were unable to penetrate the church (one of these balls is hanging outside the church today).

Boïm Chapel Right next door in the corner of Cathedral Square and is a small and dark Gothic building dating from the early 17th century, with a highly detailed exterior. The church is topped with a rare statue of Christ sitting next to his cross above the Latin inscription 'He who passes by, let him ponder if his sorrows are greater than mine.' This is probably one of Lviv's most famous churches, and was also built by a family of wine merchants, the Hungarian Boïm family.

Lviv's Orthodox churches are fewer in number, but rich in history:

Church of the Assumption Incorporating the Kornyakt Tower (*the entrance is through the gate at Pidvalna 9; open for services every evening at 17.00*). Directly across from the church are the foundations of the first medieval city wall and the statue of Fedorov, who was a prominent figure in Lviv's famous 'brotherhood', a society associated with the church. Fedorov brought printing to Ukraine by publishing the very first Ukrainian Orthodox books in the 16th century. The work of the brotherhoods continued throughout the next century, dedicated to preserving Orthodox learning and tradition under Catholic rule. It now belongs to the Ukrainian Autocephalous Church. This legacy of literacy in Lviv is still much in evidence: in summer months, a vigorous antique book market takes place right on this square (Pidvalna). Many a treasure has been found.

St George's Cathedral (*Korolenka 3*) Across the square, St George's was built in the mid 18th century and is now the single symbolic stronghold of the Russian Orthodox Church in Lviv. There are over 50 more churches in the city centre, each featuring extraordinary architecture, and they're all open to visitors.

Museums Some of Lviv's museums have retained the dry Soviet approach for presenting art and history, but the collections are large, money is sparse and most exhibits are under-appreciated. Each institution is still relishing being able to print its material in Ukrainian, so English labelling is the exception rather than the rule.

Lviv History Museum (✆ 0322 720 671; open 10.00–18.00, closed Wed) Occupying three separate buildings on Rynok Square: numbers 4, 6 and 24. each separate museum requires a separate ticket that costs a few hriven and a few more if you want a guide. The exhibits have recently been improved to display all the finery of Lviv's older, aristocratic days. House number 6 is the best choice simply for the interior looking out on the Italianate yard. Note the parquet floor, one of the last true examples of traditional Galician woodcut design.

Pharmacy Museum (✆ 0322 720 041; open 10.00–17.00, closing early on Sat and Sun; entrance 3UAH; displays in English) On the corner of Rynok Square at Drukarksa 2, the pharmacy has been working non-stop for the past 250 years – a real feat considering Lviv's history. The shop in front still works as a chemist and looks like it must have looked three centuries ago, with coloured bottles and wooden herb drawers. The tour is self-guided, taking the visitor through the history of early chemistry with collections of old pill presses, balances, mortars and pestles, and alchemy equipment. Things turn a bit Gothic towards the end (follow the green arrows to find your way through the cellars and upper floors) but it is a good way to see the interior of an old Lviv house and there are some magnificent doors featuring Galician art. An interesting fact is that in Galicia (and throughout Poland) the old chemist shops were given names instead of numbered addresses, much like the pubs in England (eg: Under the Golden Deer).

Royal Arsenal (*In the rust-coloured stucco and stone fortress along Pidvalna*) This structure was once part of the earlier fortress that surrounded all of Lviv and was where the *haidamaky* rebels were imprisoned in 1768 (see page 21). The lower floor is an 'art gallery' that sells very large candlesticks and lifesize plaster statues of the Virgin Mary, while the upper floor is the actual **Arsenal Museum** (*open 10.00–17.00, closed Wed; entrance 2UAH*). Military enthusiasts will appreciate the diverse collection of swords, uniforms and antique guns. The weapons are not particularly Ukrainian (except for the Cossack war drums), but most of these are genuine artefacts left behind by Lviv's invaders: Hungarian battle axes, Austrian sabres, German crossbows, Tatar shields and glass maces.

Museum of Ethnography and Craft (*Svobody 15; open 09.00–17.00, closed Mon and Tue; entrance 5UAH*) For something more Ukrainian, visit this museum housed in an old 1920s Soviet bank (take note of the fabulous murals above the windows). The main floor exhibit is a hotchpotch of antiques from Ukrainian country life (animal traps, old beehives, woodcraft) but the larger room has a fantastic collection of regional Ukrainian costumes. The small shop at the entrance is a good place for buying artsy souvenirs and knick-knacks made by local craftsmen. In the upper floors, you may find more decorative arts (pottery and glazed tiles) depending on the current exhibits; however, simply ascending the staircase is worthwhile for all of its rococo elaborateness.

Lviv National Art Museum (*Svobody 20; open 10.00–18.00, closed Fri; entrance 5UAH*) A fine collection of early Ukrainian art, icons and 19th-century painting.

Lviv Art Gallery (*Stefanyka 3; open 10.00–18.00, closed Mon; entrance 4UAH*) Features a very large collection of European sculpture, decorative and graphic arts, and is quiet heavy on the Baroque. Sometimes the changing 'exhibits' are nothing more than moneymaking sales of bad modern art, but overall, this is a huge and high-quality museum.

Museum of Folk Architecture and Life (*Chernecha Hora 1; ✎ 0322 718 017; open 10.00–18.00, closed Mon; entrance 2UAH, children free*) Probably the most visited attraction in Lviv, this amazing outdoor museum-village was created from a wide collection of regional folk architecture and transported to the city's forested north side. Located in the Shevchenskyi Hai, it is more park than museum and it is best reached by taxi. The thatched cottages, barns and schoolhouses are all original structures, decorated inside and out with real artefacts and portraying rural western Ukrainian life over the past two hundred years. The wooden churches are most remarkable, and some are adorned with old-fashioned folk ornaments and are still open for worship.

Museum of Bread (*Pasichna 89; ✎ 03222 510 510*) Last but not least is this seldom-visited and quirky museum, an odd remnant of late *perestroika* years. They only open up for pre-arranged visits, but if you have the time and interest, it's worth a look. Artisanal bread has always been a staple of Ukrainian culture, but these naïve and outlandish three-dimensional installations reach beyond the traditions of bread-making and qualify as pure art.

Theatre

Opera House (✎ *0322 728 562*) Most visible, Lviv's grandiose opera house is situated at the end of Svobody (No 28), a true Viennese masterpiece, beautiful both inside and out, and the focus of community activity. Completed in 1900, the building has become a symbol of all that makes Lviv so refined. Tickets for the performances (typically classical ballet and opera) can be purchased inside at the *kasa* on your right.

Ukrainian Drama Theatre (*Lesya Ukrayinka 1;* ✎ *0322 720 762*) Across the street is this pale green theatre, supposedly the oldest theatre in Ukraine. All performances are in Ukrainian, but plays range from Shakespeare to Chekhov. Tickets can be purchased on site (*11.00–14.00 and 17.00–19.00*); the repertoire is posted outside.

Voskresinnya Theatre (*Hryhorenka Square 5;* ✎ *0322 741 160;* e *goldenlion@litech.lviv.ua*) Dabbling in the experimental, this theatre has built up a worthy reputation. With a name like 'Resurrection' they have become quite famous throughout the country and beyond for leading a bold cultural renaissance in Ukrainian-language theatre.

First Ukrainian Children's Theatre (*Hnatyuka 11;* ✎ *0322 740 025*) For the young at heart this is where you can hear the laughter on the street. A frequent performance is *King Lev*, a fairy tale about the founding of Lviv. They also do Ukrainian folk tales and some better-known classics, like *Cinderella*.

Puppet Theatre (*Halytskovo Square;* ✎ *0322 720 832*) This is also a must for kids.

Jewish sites The growth of Lviv's Jewish population correlated with the city's 'golden age' of the 16th and 17th centuries. The oldest **Jewish quarter** centres around the end of Fedorov Street and along Staroyevreiska (literally 'old Hebrew Street'). The bare park at the end of the street was commonly known as the '**Square of Weeping**' for the tragedy and violence suffered in this neighbourhood. The small houses look much like those in the rest of Lviv, except inside many of the doorways you can see a few remaining *mezuzah* (the encased scroll planted in the doorpost of faithful Jews when their homes are dedicated). At the end of Staroyevreiska and the beginning of Arsenalna are the ruins of the old city synagogue called the **Golden Rose**, built in 1582. For centuries, this was the centre of Jewish spiritual life until the larger city synagogue was constructed directly opposite (*Staroyevreiska 54*). Both were destroyed by the Nazis in 1941 – all that remains of the Golden Rose is the ghostly outlines of the northern back wall, the foundations and pillars, and the ritual baths now overgrown with grass and shrubs. Lviv's working **synagogue** is on the corner of Izhnovskykh and Korotka, built back in the 1920s but only just remodelled after decades of being used as a school gymnasium. The older **Jewish cemetery** was completely covered by the site of Lviv's largest market on Bazarna; at the top of the hill is the **old Jewish hospital** (*Rapoporta 8*), an expressive (and impressive) piece of Moorish architecture in brick, now used as Lviv's general maternity ward and as a military outpost.

As part of the initial Nazi takeover of Poland, most of Lviv's Jews were liquidated in local concentration camps during the early years of World War II. Prior to 1941, Lviv was about 45% Jewish (160,000 people); by 1943, fewer than 1,000 remained. Many Holocaust victims are buried in the **new Jewish cemetery** towards the end of the tram stop on Vulitsa Shevchenko, formerly known as the suburb of Janowska. Further down Shevchenko is the Kleparivska station from, where Lviv's Jews were deported during the war, as well as the remains of the

In 1875, Ukraine's most famous scholar came to Lviv to study philosophy at the university that now bears his name. Two years later he found himself in prison, falsely accused of being part of a subversive socialist plot against the empire. His published work was equally controversial, and he served another term in prison charged with encouraging the peasants' civil disobedience. Thus, the Soviet regime flaunted Ivan Franko as a martyr 'for the masses', while these days it is the nationalists who worship his brazen 'Ukrainian-ness'. Neither camp suits him really. Ivan Franko was a truly gifted intellectual with a talent for adapting his ideas to all forms of thought and letters. He is well loved for his vivid tales of peasant hardship, his satires, lyrical poetry and powerful essays. Ideologically, his real contribution to the country was his call for solidarity among all Ukrainian people, despite the foreign borders that divided them (his poem 'Moses' is a parable of the Ukrainian people in bondage). He also wrote in Ukrainian, which was a revolution in itself at a time when German and Polish were the only languages of the educated élite in Galicia. In spite of an additional arrest and time spent in prison, Ivan Franko managed to finish a doctorate, was awarded two more, ran for a seat in the Viennese parliament, and produce an astounding amount of published work (one piece for every two days of his life). He was nominated for the Nobel Prize in 1910 and it is a chip on many a Ukrainian shoulder that he did not win. He died in Lviv and is buried in Lychakivsky cemetery. His grave is easily spotted thanks to the abundant blue and yellow flowers on top.

Janowska concentration camp (marked by an engraved stone marker). The Janowska camp was notorious for its sadistic torture methods, including the formation of a prisoner orchestra which was forced to play the originally composed 'Tango of Death' as background music to the atrocities. The Lviv ghetto was one of five of the first Jewish ghettos in Poland, cordoned off at the same time as the Warsaw ghetto. Today, the site is marked by the railroad bridge over Chornovola. A modern-art monument commemorates the victims, along with a more sobering gated monument. Lviv's present-day Jewish community is based at Sholom-Aleichema 12.

Parks For all Lviv's manmade beauty, the natural elements have not been forgotten and dozens of parks break up the run of buildings. On the northeast side is the **High Castle** (*Vysoky Zamok*; built by Casimir the Great of Poland) and a climb to the top of the hill gives the best panorama of the city. Be aware that the walk is rather steep, but very green and lovely in summer. You'll be sure to get good pictures. **Ivano-Franko Park** fills a square hillside with very tall trees, right across from the university around the city's largest monument to the poet Ivano Franko. This is a popular forest for both elderly couples on a stroll, and passionate university students, who tend to occupy the benches. By far the most romantic of Lviv's natural zones is the extensive greenery of **Strysky Park**. By tradition, newlywed couples come here after the wedding ceremony to have their picture taken and dance under the trees, and the small lakes and shady lawns make it a relaxing place to escape from the city. Other than being a resting place for Lviv's past heroes, **Lychakivsky Cemetery** is a hilly forest with big ancient trees towering above the crosses and mausoleums. The park is serenely Gothic, with lots of crumbly statuary and giant crows leaping about the graves. A good look at the headstones gives a fair impression of Lviv's last one hundred years; Polish aristocrats, Soviet soldiers, Ukrainian freedom fighters, Jews and famous writers are all buried together. The entrance to the cemetery is at Mechnykova and Pekarska (*open 09.00–20.00 between Apr and Sep, 09.00–18.00 from Oct to Mar; entrance costs 6UAH and a guided tour of the 'famous' graves costs US$5. Ivan Franko is buried here – see page 210*). **Lychakivsky Park** is behind the cemetery (off Lychakivska Street) as are the botanical gardens and the much larger Park Pohulyanka ('Strolling' Park) made especially for long leisurely walks.

OUTSIDE LVIV The wonders of the Galician countryside deserve some attention since this is a 'happening place' in rural terms, and the villages are a more honest expression of what life is like in western Ukraine. Getting to and from villages is not difficult: buses regularly leave from the main station, and there are plenty of *marshrutka* that connect villages to the city (schedules and pick-up points can change – simply ask). Lviv's tour companies also specialise in short local trips, as do most hotels and some bus companies (eg: Lviv Inturtrans). It is also quite easy to negotiate a driver for the day.

Galician castles look more like chateaux than fortresses; most began as early medieval defence posts that were later turned into lavish palaces for the Polish aristocracy. These chateaux are now Ukraine's greatest claim to old European grandeur and they tend to be more popular with Ukrainians than foreigners. A rise in Lviv's tourism has sparked regional interest and you may hear talk of the mystical-sounding 'Golden Horseshoe' tour. The concept is rather affected, but it makes an interesting excursion all the same. Most organised tours will take in Olesko, Pidhirtsi and Zolochiv castles all in one day (*entrance to each is about 20UAH*).

Olesko Castle is situated just 70km west of Lviv and offers a fantastic panorama of the Galician countryside. The white citadel is perched upon a small knoll and is treasured by Ukrainians as the palace where the Cossack Bohdan Khmelnytsky spent his youngest years, this being Poland at the time. Founded in 1327, the castle is oval in shape, and features a moat and high castle wall, yet inside, the structure is palatial. By the late 15th century, this frontier outpost had become less of a fortress and more of a chateau for the nobility. Polish King Jan Sobieski III was born here in 1629, and later found fame by conquering the Turks in the Battle of Vienna. Today, the interior of the castle is an eclectic museum of medieval art, religious artefacts and late 16th-century furniture (the original furnishings of Olesko were all shipped to Pidhirtsi in the early 16th century). Some of the 15th- and 16th-century icons are worthy of note, especially the 'Final Judgement'. There's also a nice little café inside the old stables of the castle, with meals for under US$10.

Just a hop, skip and a jump from Olesko is **Pidhirtsi Castle** (Pidhoretsky in Russian). Part bastion, part palace, the bare interior is offset by the luxurious marble designs. Also worth noting is the sagging wooden church in Pidhirtsi which is said to have been divinely 'transferred' to the spot in 1720. The younger, more Baroque structure is the Church of St Joseph, built in 1766. The palace structure has hardly been touched since it was completely stripped and utilised as a hospital in the Soviet era.

Zolochiv Castle is directly west of Lviv, near the border with Ternopil oblast. Built in 1630, this was one of the less-cherished holiday homes of the Sobieski family of Poland, who later allowed it to become a Hapsburg prison. Stalin liked the idea, and continued to use the spot to hold and torture unrepentant Ukrainian separatists throughout the Soviet era. Today, the castle tour makes up for its lack of substance and renovation by relying heavily on legend and ghost stories, of which there are plenty (eg: Knights Templar, haunted tunnels, magic stones, etc). Still, this is one of the better preserved castles in the area and an interesting stop if you are travelling eastward anyway.

Only 30 minutes north, **Zhovkva** makes a good day trip from Lviv. The town's varied buildings have miraculously survived centuries of onslaught and now form a state historical site. **Zhokva Castle** was originally built in the 16th century but has been repeatedly changed by each Polish family that has reigned over this area. The city gates are impressive, as are the numerous churches that avoided destruction by the Soviets. The **Christmas Church** (on Ivan Franko) is a light wooden church built over 300 years ago, and this style is currently copied for all the local church reconstructions. The dark wooden **Trinity Church** on St Trinity is used by the local Greek Catholic community and has kept the original iconostasis from 1702. Another 'must see' is the ornate pink **synagogue** on Zaporizhka, built in the 17th century and one of the few still standing in Galicia.

DROHOBYCH ДРОГОБИЧ

About 50km south of Lviv lies historic Drohobych, a quintessentially Galician town that lives on as an undisturbed relic of western Ukraine's chaotic past. Established over 900 years ago as part of Kievan Rus, the area was renowned first for its salt mines, then later as the centre for oil refining in the Hapsburg Empire (some derelict pumps can still be spotted from the road). Walking the streets of Drohobych gives a good opportunity to break away from the modernity of Ukraine's bigger cities and get a sense of what life is like for many Ukrainians today. The old buildings are quaint and stylish, if not beautiful. **St Yura's** wooden church was built and improved between the 15th and 17th centuries – a miraculous structure of triple-tiered domes and traditional Galician ecclesiastical style. The remnant of an old Polish fort also stands in the centre. However the city's dominant feature is the giant pink Jewish **synagogue** that now stands as an empty ruin upon a forgotten hilltop. Declared the largest synagogue in Europe, the building highlights the city's melancholic air and provides a memorial to the prominent Jewish population that once lived here.

Visitors can get to Drohobych by taxi, *marshrutka* or car (1 hour) from Lviv, or on the train (2 hours) to Truskavets. **Tustan** is the town's only hotel (*1 Maidan Shevchenka;* ⟩ *0324 435 884*) with slightly renovated Soviet rooms. Singles are US$12 per night, doubles for US$30, whereas a three-room deluxe apartment will set you back US$50. There is hot water, but only during certain hours of the day. Tustan's restaurant serves meat from the grill and Ukrainian food – there are a few other establishments just off the Ploscha Rynok.

TRUSKAVETS ТРУСКАВЕЦЬ

Just south of Drohobych lies Truskavets, Ukraine's most famous spa town and once the coveted holiday destination of the Soviet élite. Back in the 1960s–70s you had to be someone to land a spot near these healing waters that bubble up from the foothills of the Carpathian Mountains. Throughout Ukraine, kiosks and restaurants sell Truskavetska mineral water, but this is only a commercial copy of the real thing, from two separate sources. Sodova and Naftusya, as the waters from the sources are known, are both are high in calcium and other minerals, though Naftusya is recommended for liver ailments, urinary infections and kidney stones, while Sodova works better to calm gastritis. Whether this is actually the case or whether it's just a list of common ailments during the Brezhhnev era remains unproven by Western medicine, but tens of thousands of people swear by the springs and visit every year for treatment. Visitors may drink water directly from the source at the *buvet*, the circular building with glass windows at the southeastern corner of the town. The springs run only during certain hours, and the sulphuric, salty taste is rather potent; however it is important to drink the water fresh – after three hours, Naftusya loses its beneficial effects.

GETTING THERE AND AWAY Truskavets is 100km (60 miles) southeast of Lviv. Taxis will take you for US$20–30 from Lviv, and there are plenty of *marshrutka* from Lviv (1½ hours) that leave and pick up from the bus station and Prospekt Svobody. Direct trains also run from Lviv and Kiev, but these take twice as long. If you plan to be a guest at any of the sanitoria and request it, they will pick you up in Lviv for an additional fee.

WHERE TO STAY AND EAT To get more into the spirit of the place, travellers can opt for the full sanatorium experience: checking into a health resort for a week, getting plenty of on-site medical attention, undergoing science-fiction-like spa treatments, and drinking plenty of water.

🏠 **Rixos** Horodische 8; ✆ 0324 771 111; f 0324 771 112; e info@rixosprikarpatye.com; www.rixos.com. The most elaborate of Truskavets spas, this newly opened, first-class Turkish-owned hotel takes the old Soviet-style spa vacation to new heights.. Their high-standard rooms are spacious, comfy and luxurious and b/fst is included in the price. Prices fluctuate upwards based on location (ie: corner penthouses), the degree of luxury desired and the season. The price includes full use of the gym, saunas and the elaborate hot pool. Meals are taken at either of the 2 restaurants – Dana (buffet) and Veles (*à la carte*). The number of medical procedures offered is staggering, and includes coloured light therapy, electric baths, water jet massages, microwave and speleo-therapy and the normal range of mud baths and Swedish massages. All medical treatments cost extra; normally around US$35 per procedure, with the option of an all-

inclusive package for US$100 a day. *Sgl US$150, dbl US$200.*

🏠 **Geneva** Sukhovolya 61; ✆ 0324 767 083; f 0324 767 082; e admin@sangeneva.com.ua; www.sangeneva.com.ua. The Swiss-owned resort offers a less expensive alternative, with all-inclusive package deals for a minimum 7-day stay that covers accommodation, meals and treatments. *Sgl US$90–150, dbl US$160–250.*

🏠 **Crystal Palace** Sukhovolya 35; ✆ 0324 751 540; f 0324 766 053. Seasoned travellers will prefer this enduring gem of an institution that functions exactly as it did back in Soviet times. Precious Soviet rooms remain unchanged, and prices are all inclusive to ensure your full anti-stress treatment; US$33 pp for accommodation, meals, diagnostics and treatments (remodelled 'Euro' rooms cost US$50 but lack the same spirit). Expect lots of water, strange procedures, and poundings from kindly, muscled grandmothers.

If you just need a meal, go to **Myslyvksy Rai**, the nicest restaurant in Truskavets, serving local Carpathian cuisine (*Halytskovo 2;* ✆ *0324 753 464*).

TERNOPIL ТЕРНОПІЛЬ

Nestled on the banks of the Seret River, simple Ternopil is the 'real thing' – a living caricature of red-blooded western Ukraine that the rest of the country only presumes to be out there, somewhere. There's very little show out on the streets of Ternopil, only the mix of old buildings, some of which are beautiful, and the people who live here – a people who harbour a Galician sensibility that copes well with the day-to-day versus the noise and power of Ukraine's larger cities.

Galicia's 'other' city has endured the same turbulent times as many of Ukraine's cities (five different countries have ruled over it in the last century alone) but this is still considered a young town, founded only in 1580 as a fortress to protect Poland's eastern border. Such a qualification was enough to make it a constant target for Turkish raids, after which came the vengeful Ukrainian Cossacks. Good old Bohdan Khmelnytsky razed the city to the ground in 1648, and in 1675 the Turks came back and tried to outdo him. Somehow the Poles returned, only to be attacked repeatedly from the north and have the city burned to the ground by the Russians. Despite the hideous violence and chaos that played out in Ternopil far into the 20th century, the people have somehow kept their heads held high. It's absolutely no coincidence that most foreigners who come looking for their ancestors end up finding their roots here. The villages of Ternopil oblast have always played a significant historical role in Ukraine's most turbulent history (eg: Kremenets, Duchach, Berezhany), and the thousands upon thousands who could simply fled the country. Renowned as the mother of so much of the Ukrainian diaspora, Ternopil is now famous for the number of Ukrainian celebrities who call it home.

Certainly, Ternopil lacks the glamour and show of some tourist attractions, but then this is also one of the purest regions in the country. As the borderlands between Galicia and Podillya, the area is virtually unknown to non-Ukrainians. And yet, the high hills, fields, rivers and forests all have a notably Galician charm to them. Anyone looking for an original outdoor experience would do well to include these small and serene national parks, one of which includes the country's largest caverns – a noted destination for international cavers. For organised tours, the glistening towers of Pochaïv Monastery seem to be the main attraction. For such pilgrimages, Ternopil is the most obvious stopover in terms of accommodation and transport.

GETTING THERE AND AWAY Most trains from Lviv going east pass through Ternopil; there are over 15 connections between the two cities every day and the trip can take from two to three hours. Khmelnytsky is about an hour and a half in the other direction with frequent train and bus connections; Chernivtsi is another close link to the south (usually around three hours). Many of the trains from Kiev use Ternopil as a junction for their international links and as the last stop before Lviv, so travel to and from the capital is fairly easy; the train station is on Khmelnytsovo. On the other hand, regional rail travel is not that simple, since the railroad tracks follow communist logic and miss all the places you want to go and see.

The main bus station is on Obolonya on the south side of the town. There is a convenient one-and-a-half-hour bus to Pochayiv that runs back and forth throughout the day. The route gets crowded with tourists in summer and with pilgrims on religious holidays (especially Ukrainian Christmas and Easter), but a constant supply of transport options appears to meet the demand.

WHERE TO STAY In spite of the city's wonderful appeal, Ternopil is not exactly brimming with tourist accommodation. The two main hotels are on opposite sides of the lake and are both owned and managed by the same company. Some might say a monopoly … Both take credit cards.

🏠 **Halychyna** Chumatska 1; 📞 03522 533 595; e reservation@hotel.te.ua; www.hotel.te.ua/gal_e.php. 'The' hotel for Ternopil is still not in great shape, even after major renovations. The Soviet-era concrete high-rise is next to the manmade Ternopil Lake, facing Hotel Ternopil on the other side. B/fast inc. US$35 for a bare sgl room to US$150 for the super-duper suites. High-class dbl or twin, with modern en-suite bathroom, US$60–70.

🏠 **Hotel Ternopil** Zamkova 14; 📞 03522 224 397; f 03522 229 360; e reservation@hotel.te.ua;

www.hotel.te.ua. This is the most centrally located hotel (it's by the castle) and for many it's a nice choice, with a view of Ternopil Lake. Still, many travellers have complained about the service. Most rooms are renovated to a degree and boast the basic amenities; however, most beds are sgls or twins and water problems are a common frustration. They also still hang on to an odd pricing scheme. The Ternopil does have one of the city's better restaurants. B/fast inc. Economy class US$30/35 sgl/dbl, standard twin US$40, 'higher' twin US$50, suites US$60–100.

✖ WHERE TO EAT

✖ **Ternopil** Zamkova 14; ☎ 0352 224 397. Hotel Ternopil's restaurant is very nice, if not fancy. For the most part, the food is upscale Ukrainian. *Mains from US$3; open 08.00–midnight.* (If you get bored with that one, you can always go over to **Hotel Halychyna** for something not too dissimilar).

✖ **Maidan** Slipovo 1; ☎ 0352 525 971. Themed restaurant along the lines of an old tavern, but with big submarine sandwiches and delicious brick-oven pizzas. *Mains from US$5; open 09.00–23.00.*

✖ **Rondo Bar & Grill** Chornovola 5; ☎ 0352 254 347. Steaks hot off the grill and lots of different beer on tap. A very popular and very noisy bar! *Mains from US$4; open 11.00–23.00.*

✖ **Bratislava** Budnovo 10A; ☎ 0352 432 277. Ukrainian food with a faint European touch (good holubtsi and varennyki). *Mains from US$3; open 10.00–23.00.*

✖ **Ternove Pole** Zhyvova 9; ☎ 0352 229 578. A fairly new restaurant for Ternopil with a diverse menu, including salads, lots of drinks, and delicious desserts. *Mains from US$3; open 09.00–23.00.*

✖ **Stary Mlin (Old Mill)** Old time Ukraine-themed restaurant in the city centre. *Mains from US$6; open 10.00–23.00.* In the centre (along Ruska and Shevchenka) there are few new cafés and nicer food shops.

WHAT TO SEE AND DO **Ternopil Castle** looks more like a Stalinist administration building, since it was remodelled in the 1950s (the battlements were removed back in the early days of Polish rule). Not to be missed are the twin towers of the city's **Dominican cathedral**, built in 1747 and now a place of worship for the Greek Catholic community. Also worth mentioning is the **Church of the Nativity**, built in 1608 and comprising several rough and rounded stone towers with pear-shaped cupolas. Ternopil's genuine quaintness includes a few gems of 'Podillyan' architecture among the very colourful streets. These are the main sights of the town most often touted during a city tour. However, the artificial lake is also quite lovely when the sun hits it just right. Known as 'the lake' locally, the body of water is the legacy of a team of Soviet engineers who dammed the tiny Siret. The concrete walkway along its shoreline is a popular place for summer strolls, and on occasion you can catch a romantic boat tour.

OUTSIDE TERNOPIL Lovers of small-town adventure can take buses out to a number of very old towns with castle ruins and numerous churches. **Berezhany** (**Бережани**) is one of the most famous in terms of its history, but is also a fascinating detour for the serious explorer. Quite a tiny town, for most of its existence it was known as the Polish outpost *Brzeżany*. Founded in the 14th century, the town evolved into quite a microcosm of the Galician economy: Jewish bankers, Armenian merchants and Ukrainian peasants all served the needs of the Polish landowners. The castle that is seen today dates from 1554, although all that remains of the ruins is the big round defence tower and crumbling Renaissance walls.

There are two semi-decent hotels in Berezhany: **Zolota Lypa** (*Ploscha Rynok 9; ☎ 0345 821 372*) and **Kolhospnyk** (*Miskyevicha 3; ☎ 0354 821 103*). Both have rooms for as little as US$7, but these can be a little drab.

Buchach (**Бучач**) is another little Ternopil village, claimed to have been founded both by the Poles (*Buczacz* in Polish) and the Ukrainians, either in 1397 or 1260. Whichever the case may be, the town is more noted for its large Jewish population, which qualifies Buchach as an authentic *shtetl*. Besides the many memorials and graves in the town, tourists will be pointed to the 16th-century **castle** and the **Baroque city hall**, constructed by a member of that ubiquitous family of Polish nobles, the Pototskys. Buchach is also the home town of Simon Wiesenthal, who miraculously survived each and every stage of the Holocaust to go on and become the world's most successful 'Nazi hunter'. Today, his organisation combats anti-Semitism worldwide (*www.wiesenthal.com*). Buchach docs have one hotel, but its standard is so abysmal that you'll wish you hadn't.

Around 80km north is **Kremenets (Кременець)**, one of Ukraine's oldest settlements, with remains of a 12th-century **castle** still standing on a windswept hilltop. Dating from the earliest Galicia-Volhynia principality, this fortress has served the area well – it is the only castle in all of Ukraine that Batu Khan failed to capture during the Golden Horde's first invasion in 1241. In fact, it was the Ukrainian Cossacks who finally conquered the site, but only after surrounding the hill for six weeks and starving out the Poles (the town continued to be known by the Polish name *Krzemieniec*). Only the castle's single-arch gateway and some of the outer walls are still standing, although the view from this conical hill is amazing. In town, there are quite a few examples of 17th-century Polish Baroque architecture, including the melon-coloured **Jesuit Collegium** and complex, and the **Bogoyavlensky Convent**. Several famous Cossacks who died in the battle at Kremenets are buried in the **Pyatnytske Cemetery**. Located on the northern border with Volhynia, Kremenets is the closest town of its size to Pochayiv, hence its increased importance as a stop along the pilgrims' path. Even so, as it's such a small town, it has very little tourist infrastructure.

At the southern end of Ternopil oblast lies the **Medobory Nature Preserve**, a national park of rocky bluffs along the high ridge overlooking the Podillyan steppe. 'Honey-drinking' park is made up of six different parts concentrated in two disparate areas: one is an hour southwest of Ternopil (by Khorostikiv), the other is in the north by Kremenets and is more frequently included in group tours. The protected spots feature indigenous Ukrainian hardwood trees and forest flowers as well as springs and caverns. It is also the best place in Galicia to see wildlife and birds. Getting there on your own is tricky, although it is an easy matter to take a bus to either place and simply walk from the village. Doing a day trip with a local agency is a lot less of a headache. Ternopil's Hotel Halychyna can arrange a visit, as can Lviv Inturtrans (see page 54) and the agencies in Kamyanets-Podilsky (see page 183) who are also experienced in arranging guides and transport for caving in Ternopil.

There are over 100 caves in the south of Ternopil region; **Optimistic Cave** is considered the longest in Europe with around 200km of gypsum tunnels. **Krystalna** and **Ozerna** are also very beautiful and unique. Most of these are close to the town of Borschiv (100km south of Ternopil) which can be reached by bus, or less conveniently by local train. At present, it is best to travel with an experienced guide as the caves are extremely long and maze-like, not to mention extremely difficult to navigate. In Lviv, the Fund of Support for Scientific and Creative Initiatives specialises in longer and more professional expeditions to 'Optimistic' cave (*Lviv, Ukraine; PO Box 9655;* ✆ *0322 404 624;* e *kursor@lviv.farlep.net or cave-ua@narod.ru www.cave-ua.narod.ru*).

POCHAYIV ПОЧАЇВ

Ukrainian Orthodoxy ranks the exquisite Pochayiv Monastery as Ukraine's most sacred site, after the Pechersky Lavra in Kiev (it seems a fierce competition). Both monasteries started as secluded caves that evolved slowly into towering Baroque edifices, and both monasteries greet hundreds of thousands (if not millions) of Orthodox pilgrims each year. The main difference is that Pochayiv lacks the political and touristic façade of its counterpart in Kiev; here, visitors can witness the sincere display of Ukrainian spiritual life in a quaint rural setting. Truly, the grandeur of Pochayiv is a grand sight to behold. The glistening complex stands high in the midst of the ordinary Volhynian countryside. If you're lucky, you'll arrive on a sunny day. Thankfully, Pochayiv was a more obscure target for the Soviet authorities and sustained much less damage than Kiev's Lavra. Today, Pochayiv's collection of ancient master icons is revered throughout Eastern Orthodoxy.

The 'holy mount' was first discovered by a group of refugee monks who had fled Kiev's Pechersky Lavra after the Mongol invasion in 1240. They were strict ascetics who envisioned this spot by the Pochayna River as a true wilderness, both physically and spiritually. The community grew and the cave chapels expanded into the complex of larger halls and churches above ground.

Today's pilgrim masses come to look upon Pochayiv's Holy Mother of God icon, a gift from the Greek Church to the local aristocrat Anna Hoiska in 1559. She discovered a healing power within the sacred icon when her blind brother was cured after he prayed to it. Astounded by the miracle, she handed the icon over to the local monks, along with a hefty gift of land and cash. (The icon was later stolen from the monastery by her grandson who had converted to Protestantism but was later returned by order of the court.) The other sacred relic is the leftover footprint of the Virgin Mary in a rock from which a holy spring now flows. The mark was left after the Virgin appeared in a pillar of fire to a monk and a local shepherd, after which the medieval church of the Assumption of the Most Holy Mother of God was built at the base of the mount. The assembly is mostly 17th-century Baroque, but for 100 years the church belonged to the Greek Catholic Church, and some Roman features remain. The monastery was returned to Russian Orthodox control in 1831, after which the high bell tower was added, followed by the Troitsky Cathedral, a rare example of Russian modernist design. The bright white and gold structures are stunning, and the religious excitement adds to the spectacle.

The monastery's legendary healing powers now draw bus-loads of the unwell (sufferers of migraines are promised a cure by praying whilst listening to the bell ring). Pochayiv's busiest times are during the summer and on Orthodox holidays, especially the day of St Iove (Job) on 10 September. Unless you are part of a larger pilgrimage tour, a visit to Pochayiv is best done as a day trip from Ternopil. Because of its beauty and importance, Pochayiv is a featured option of nearly every tour operator in Ukraine, and all the foreign companies that specialise in Ukraine. It makes a nice and convenient stop between Lviv and Kiev and should definitely not be passed by. A brand-new hotel has been constructed exclusively for pilgrims (*around US$20/night*), and Orthodox believers can often stay over at the monastery for a small donation. Foreigners are on their own trying to get in – most visitors will stay in Rivne or Ternopil. The villagers in Pochayiv are also known to rent out their apartments or a room in their house for a night or two, a general and safe practice that is far more interesting than staying in a hotel. Tourism is still developing here – enterprising tour guides will make themselves known to you (negotiate, but don't pay more than US$10 for a tour of all the chapels and grounds) and whenever indoors taking photos costs 5UAH per frame. The monastery's official website is www.pochaev.org.ua.

GETTING THERE AND AWAY The simplest way to get to Pochayiv is to take a direct bus from Lviv, Kiev or Rivne, although in principle you can also take the Lviv–Kiev train to Ternopil, then take a shorter bus north. The journey is about a 1¹/₂-hour drive from Ternopil. Many cross-country tours will stop in Pochayiv as a day trip. In summer and near religious holidays, there are much more frequent transport options.

VOLHYNIA ВОЛИНЬ

Traditionally lumped in with Galicia, Volhynia is the pretty little corner of northwest Ukraine that too often gets overlooked, mostly due to the fact that the very best spots in Volhynia are well off the beaten track. Getting here involves a lengthy journey into some of the most undisturbed areas of the country. The natural border with Poland and Belarus is characterised by the great northern forests, all that is left of the primeval European woodlands that were home to the earliest Slavic tribes. The trees and wetlands are remarkable, with dozens of giant lakes, quiet marshes and hundreds of rivers and streams that flow north. To visit these farthest corners is to travel beyond the normal vision of dry Ukrainian steppe and to gain a better understanding of the country's more pagan ties to nature.

The original principality of Volhynia was based in Volodymyr sometime in the 10th century and is recognised as one of the most ancient Slavic civilisations. The land was joined to Galicia in a shared kingdom (Galicia-Volhynia) in 1199 and the dual principality flourished until the 14th century. Even so, Volhynia always maintained a clear and separate identity, based first on the heavy Lithuanian influence that predominated after the fall of Kievan Rus, and then later on in 1795 when Galicia remained a province of Poland, while the Russian Empire controlled the Volhynia Gubernia from 1795. The area was one of many to which Catherine the Great invited hundreds of thousands of German settlers whose strong European consciousness still remains. The cities of Lutsk and Rivne did not escape the atrocities of the 20th century.

Today, Volhynia is quiet and remote, home to proud speakers of the Ukrainian language, but less prone to rabid nationalism. Overall, Volhynia is probably one of the most rural areas in Ukraine, still practising the everyday traditions and crafts that have been forgotten elsewhere, and maintaining a healthy distance from politics. Travelling to or from Poland can take you along the main rail and motor route between Kovel, Lutsk and Rivne, but these basic cities hold little interest compared with venturing outwards into the empty forests and meadows, namely up north. Such trips are easier said than done, but well worth the effort.

LOCAL TOUR OPERATORS AND TOURIST INFORMATION There are several firms willing to help arrange your journey for you. For more information contact the **Volhynian Tourist Information Office** (*Na Taborische 4;* ☏ *0332 240 051;* e *info@tourism.lutsk.ua; www.tourism.lutsk.ua*). Also, **Volhyntourist** (*Hrushevskovo 33;* ☏ *0332 230 411;* e *vturist@lutsk.utel.net.ua*).

LUTSK ЛУЦЬК

Volhynia's largest city is not that large: the ancient city is nestled into a bend in the River Styr and three castle towers and church domes give Lutsk its traditional skyline, while the newer Soviet suburbs appear less disheartening among all the greenery. A visit to Lutsk may be a break away from the average tourist logic; the city's thousand-year-old past is more tragic than heroic and not everybody finds the place entertaining. And yet, one may without hesitation describe this hamlet-like city as simply charming. Visitors find the mix of the old and the new quite attractive; likewise the very unhurried way in which people live their lives in this quiet corner of Ukraine. Lutsk is also destined to become the main base for river and lake excursions up north, a trend that is only just beginning to take hold.

Like all western Ukrainian cities, Lutsk (historically known as Luchesk) was originally a wooden fort. It was turned into a stone fortress sometime in the 15th century by Lithuanian leader Liubartas. His successor Vytautas the Great expanded the city, inviting both Turkic (Karaim) and Ashkenazi Jews to settle the area. For Ukrainians and Orthodox believers, Lutsk is revered as the home of an early icon-painting school of the 13th and 14th centuries from which survives the Volhynian Blessed Virgin Mary – considered a national treasure, and now kept in Kiev's National Museum of Art. Lutsk was also home to an established Ruthenian Orthodox 'brotherhood' that sought to protect local rights and promote their own faith and culture under Polish Catholic rule, hence the Ukrainian Cossacks targeting the city for liberation during Khemlnytsky's 17th-century uprising. Since that time, the city has been a crucible of Ukrainian religion, culture and art. Lesya Ukrayinka, probably the most famous of Ukraine's female writers, spent her most formative years in Lutsk, seeking to promote the use of Ukrainian language in literature. Jews also played an integral part in the city's history, once accounting for almost half of the city's population. Many were killed in the infamous Lutsk massacre, while thousands of others were gathered into the horrific but lesser-known Lutsk ghetto of World War II. Local Ukrainians suffered equal cruelty from the Soviets when over 5,000 were shot by the retreating Red Army. During the Soviet era, Lutsk was simply known as a production centre for construction materials, namely lumber gleaned from the surrounding forests, and linoleum. Today the city is a stalwart advocate of Ukrainian national consciousness and local environmental awareness. In a ploy of self-promotion, Lutsk recently celebrated its nine hundredth and something anniversary, a tradition that is likely to be repeated again with much medieval fanfare until its 150,000 citizens agree on how old the city really is.

GETTING THERE AND AWAY Most of the routes between Poland and Kiev pass near Lutsk, but do not always stop here since Kovel is the main railway junction. Presently, there is one direct Lutsk–Kiev overnight train every other day (12 hours) and two daily Kovel–Kiev connections that also takes passengers to and from Lutsk. The train station is at the end of Hrushevskovo in the northeast corner of the city.

The central bus station is not far away, at Konyakyna 23, and frequent buses pass through Lutsk on their way between Kiev and Lviv – this is the best place to find transport to the north and other surrounding areas. Driving on your own, the trip from Kiev to Lutsk takes about nine hours and is truly a splendid drive from the passenger's seat. Regular buses travel to and from Lviv (3 hours) and Rivne (1 hour), including the nicer 'deluxe' coaches – Avotluks has an office in Lutsk at Konyakyna 39 (✆ 0332 247 108).

If you are keen to fly, catch a flight to Lviv or to Rzeszow from Poland, both of which are a little over two hours from Lutsk by car.

WHERE TO STAY

Ukrayina Slovatskovo 2; ✆ 0332 788 1118; f 0332 243 320; www.hotelukraine.lutsk.ua. Newly renovated and located right near the main central square, the 'Ukraine' is considered the town's best all-round first-class hotel and is still quite affordable for those on a budget. Standard sgls are charged pp, per place, but spend double for an 'improved' room and let your imagination run wild with the extravagant décor (and murals) that truly give each hotel room a certain je ne sais quoi. Dbl luxury suites come with real queen-size beds. Credit cards accepted and b/fast inc; the well-known restaurant is still the most dependable place for meals and the in-house tour agency takes care of all your travel needs, including trips to the regional national parks. *Standard sgl US$20 pp, US$40 for an 'improved' room, dbl luxury suites.*

Hotel Luchesk Vidrodzhennya 1; ✆/f 0332 789 070; e luchesk@itt.net.ua; www.hotel.lutsk.ua.

Popular among tour groups as it is quite inexpensive, the Luchesk is much like every other Soviet era hotel you've stayed at in Ukraine, except that the location is not entirely convenient. Credit cards accepted. *Standard sgls US$10, twin US$20, improved 'upper class' rooms US$35–45, lush 2-room suite US$60.*

Svityaz Naberezhna 4; ✆ 0332 249 000. One of the closest hotels to the old city and not far from the banks of the River Styr. The white building underwent a Las Vegas-type renovation and now advertises a nightclub, swimming pool, sauna, and the all-too-familiar 'retro' restaurant. *US$45–90.*

Ameksim Dubnivska 99A; ✆ 0332 230 197; f 0332 243 596. A new 'luxury' hotel complex for Lutsk, with plush rooms, a small but perfectly good restaurant and a sauna. Credit cards accepted. *Rooms US$65–100.*

✖ WHERE TO EAT

Hotel **Ukrayina** has a very nice restaurant, as does **Svityaz**. There are also many nice, upscale cafés in the city centre. A few of the places most beloved by tourists are:

✖ **Korona Vitovta** Zamkova Ploscha (Plytnitsya 1); 📞 0332 227 114; ✉ info@kvrestoran.com; www.kvrestoran.com. Right next to Lutsk Castle on the castle square, this medieval-themed restaurant serves Ukrainian food with a side of local history. The 'crown of Vitovt' refers to the ruling Prince Vitovt who reigned back in the 15th century. Today the restaurant offers loads of yummy salads, grilled fish and meat and delicious desserts. *Mains from US$4; open 10.00–23.00.*

✖ **Krai** Vynnychenka 2. Eat, drink and be merry, for this lively bar and grill will never die. Think pork products and beer. *Mains from US$4; open 11.00–01.00.*

✖ **Edem (Let's Eat!)** Krylova 1; 📞 0332 724 516. A clean and shiny café beloved by students for its hearty and inexpensive fare. Salads, sandwiches, Ukrainian entrées and cute cakes on plates behind glass. *Mains from US$2; open 09.00–21.00.*

✖ **Vizantiya (Byzantium)** Lesi Ukrayinky 49; 📞 0332 224 170. Traditional Ukrainian food in an old world setting. Great *borsch* and killer *holubtsi*. *Mains from US$3; open 10.00–22.00.*

✖ **Stary Zamok (Old Castle)** Lesi Ukrayinky 24. A nice, 'sit-down' restaurant offering a huge number of diverse dishes (mainly Polish and Ukrainian). The grilled chicken comes highly recommended. *Mains from US$6; open 12.00–midnight.*

✖ **Maidan** Boika 2. 24hr bar with meals worth mentioning.

✖ **Cey Remo** Also recommended, near the city park and serving delicious, Italian-style pizza for about US$7.

WHAT TO SEE AND DO Lutsk Castle (*open to visitors 10.00–18.00, closed Mon; entrance 5UAH*), at the end of Kafedralna, is an intriguing triangular structure set within three square towers atop a craggy knoll at the city's southern end. The citadel you see was built in the 13th century and considerably touched up during Lithuanian rule. The blend of white and red stone is unique and much of the castle grounds represent an ongoing archaeological dig. The city's legacy of oppressive rulers and shifting borders defines one of the more curious sights, an underground **labyrinth** of old vaults and tunnels dating back to the 16th century, once used for clandestine activities and supposedly connected to nearby villages. The central old city makes a fascinating tour despite its ruinous state: old Polish monasteries and churches line Kafedralna, and the 14th-century **synagogue** can still be visited at Halytskovo 33. The **Pokrovska Church** on Halytskovo was the original home of the Volhynian Blessed Mother icon, and other examples from the Lutsk school can be found at the **Volhynia Museum of Iconography** (*Peremohy 4*) along with other exhibits of 16th- to 18th-century religious art. If you want to explore the underground vaults, one entrance is by the **St Peter and Paul Cathedral** at Kafedralna 19. Lutsk is also home to several monasteries; the one most often included in tours is the **Dominican Monastery** (*Dragomanova 16*).

The new city centres around the 'theatre square' in the shadow of the **Church of the Holy Trinity**, built in 1755. Modern Lutsk features a small but earnest **art museum** (*Lesi Ukrayinki 26*), the **Museum of the Volhynian Icon** (which is interesting despite 'the' icon being in Kiev; *Peremohy 4*) and the **Natural History Museum** (*Shopena 20*). There's also a good amount of antique shopping along Lesi Ukrayinky. After you've seen and done the sites though, try to get out into the countryside. If you don't have the time, take a walk in **Lesi Ukrayinky Park** which follows the contours of the Styr River.

OUTSIDE LUTSK

Berestechko БЕРЕСТЕЧКО After freeing Ukraine from Polish rule in a glorious rampage, the Cossacks suffered an exhausting defeat by the Polish army at the Battle of Berestechko in June 1651. The battle lasted for two weeks, during which time *hetman* Bohdan Khmlenytsky was abducted for ransom by his supposed allies. A black-domed church is built over the 'Cossack Graves' and the event is commemorated every year in June with ceremonies and festive re-enactments. Another sad memorial is the 17th-century Thekla's Chapel, built over a mass grave of the 500 maidens who were tortured to death by the Tatars. Getting to Berestechko is easiest on a bus, or by hired taxi from Lutsk or Rivne.

Shatsky National Nature Park ШАТСЬКИЙ НАЦІОНАЛЬНИЙ ПРИРОНИЙ ПАРК (*Shatsk village;* ✆ *0335 523 276 or check out the Russian-language website:* *www.svityaz.lutsk.ua*) Ukraine's 'Lake District' is one of the last true wetlands remaining in Europe, and one of the most threatened; the Pripyat River ends in far-away Chernobyl and local pollution has also proved problematic. The Pripyat marshes consist of the larger Shatsky Lakes, over a hundred streams and rivers, and scattered swamps along the Belarus–Ukraine border. This intertwining of river systems is where the Baltic Sea and Black Sea watersheds meet and by Ukrainian standards the plant and animal life is extraordinary. Svityaz is the largest lake and the serene home of abundant waterfowl and some incredible stands of tall forest. The tourist facilities are in a phase of transition: old resorts are closing down or attempting to spruce things up. Hopefully there will be some more established, long-term accommodation in the future.

A summer music festival is held on Lake Svityaz every year and camping is usually not a problem, but as regulations tend to be fluid, stay flexible.

Many will say that foreigners trying to get into Shatsky should just go with a private tour. This is the way that things have always been done and it may seem less hassle, but seasoned travellers will have no problem getting there on their own. Either take the train or bus to Kovel and then a bus (1 hour) to the village of Shatsk inside the park, or else go on the direct bus from Lutsk (once a day). Keep in mind that Shatsky is wedged between two international borders (Poland and Belarus) so that your presence can arouse some old-time fears and suspicions. If you are going to get lost in the woods and end up accidentally crossing into another country, make sure that it's Poland. For more information contact Shatsky National Park, see above for details.

Shatsky Park is only a small part of what's really out there. Too little is known about northern Volhynia and its ecology – explorers should take note. The Pripyat, Stokhid, Turiya and Styr rivers are inviting for kayaking or long canoe trips, and the miniature villages of the marshes are wonderfully obscure.

RIVNE РІВНЕ

Most visitors to Ukraine will pass through Rivne region, but almost none will stop and visit. The territory appears as tiny on the map, and the city of Rivne often provides nothing more than a bathroom break between the west and the capital. This faulty logic has more to do with the way the Soviets built the railway lines and highways than it has to do about about Rivne itself. The region's best lakes and forests were purposefully made inaccessible, but now the area is open, Rivne remains 'uninteresting' to most tour companies. This borderland between Volhynia and Polissya is the most heavily forested area of Ukraine today; the lack of development keeps the region pure but grossly unappreciated.

Rivne's history mirrors the history of western Ukraine. The region was imperative to Kievan Rus, so today many smaller towns feature castles and ruins. The city then lived under the Magdeburg Law, had its 17th-century peasant uprisings, and suffered occupation by both Poles and Russians (the town is known as Rovno in Russian). Hitler made Rivne the capital of occupied Ukraine and so the city was levelled by the end of World War II. A favourable Soviet leftover is the local candy factory that still makes most of Ukraine's sweets.

GETTING THERE AND AWAY There is an airport in Rivne, but flights are extremely rare. Rivne does not have its own train to and from Kiev, but the Lutsk–Kiev train makes a stop here, as do all trains that go to or through Kovel from Kiev, including the Warsaw train. This means that in either direction, the Rivne stop can fall at an awkward time during an overnight journey. Travel time to Kiev averages around six to eight hours; other train routes go to Lviv (around 4 hours) and Lutsk (1 hour). Train tickets can be purchased at the station located at the end of Prospekt Miru (at the north end of the city), or at the hotel travel agencies. North–south routes to Ternopil, Kremenets and Pochayiv are best negotiated by bus; the main bus station is at Kyivska 40 on the east side of town. Buses go to and from Kiev all day, including the plush coaches and international bus lines from western Europe. The trip from Rivne to Kiev takes a little under six hours via Zhytomyr.

WHERE TO STAY (all take credit cards)

Hotel Mir Mitskevicha 32; ☎ 0362 221 255; f 0362 290 212. The 'Peace' Hotel is located right in the city centre, and is therefore promoted as the top choice by travel agents. As it's a slightly renovated Inturist hotel, the majority of rooms are small, but new and comfortable enough. In addition to the classic sprawling restaurant, it's also home to the main tourist office for the city (on the first floor). You can book tickets and order excursions, or be set up with a guide in almost any language. *Rooms with showers US$55–75; luxury suites US$90+; very basic old-style sgl rooms US$12.*

Turyst Kyivska 36; ☎/f 0362 265 614. Further from the city centre on the road to Kiev, the Tourist is located conveniently close to the bus station. The high-rise complex has many rooms; about half have been remodelled and some are offered at a lower cost than those at Hotel Mir. Extra facilities include a restaurant and in-house tourist agency. *Rooms US$35–70.*

Ukrayina Soborna 112; ☎/f 0362 225 026. Recently renovated and housed in a more historic (read Stalinist) building, the 'Ukraine' is arguably the nicest hotel in the city, with new furniture and a comfortable standard maintained throughout. In addition, it also has a decent gym and an efficient tourist office.

WHERE TO EAT There's no shortage of cafés and restaurants in Rivne. The hotels all have decent restaurants, but in summer, everyone eats in small cafés that pop up in the parks.

Stambul Stepana Bandery 31A; ☎ 0362 236 092. Turkish and Tatar cuisine with atmospheric décor and live music. *Open 12.00–02.00.*

Khmil Soborna 17. Serves traditional Ukrainian food. *Mains from US$5; open 11.00–midnight.*

Mislivets (Hunter) Chernyaka 2; ☎ 0362 246 371. A wonderful themed restaurant with traditional Ukrainian food and 'Volhynian' ambience. Some of the dishes served are made from wild game. *Mains from US$7; open 12.00–midnight.*

Magnat Stepana Bandery 61; ☎ 0362 636 487. 'Elite' dining spot and bar that quickly erupts into the city's hottest night club. *Mains from US$4; open 12.00–02.00.*

Pizzeria Prikhodka 66; ☎ 0362 638 151. Thin crust pizza made to your liking. Popular with Rivne's college-age crowd. *Pizza from US$5; open 11.00–22.00.*

Ventotto 16 Lipnya 71; ☎ 0362 266 624. A very nice Italian restaurant with fresh pasta, delicious lasagne and fresh salads. *Mains from US$5; open 10.00–23.00.*

Kozatsky Zabavi Soborna 420; ☎ 0362 251 111. Far out on the western city limits, this raucous Ukrainian restaurant complex is a local favourite come weekends and holidays. The grilled meats are mouth-watering, as are the roasted potatoes and pots of handmade *varennyki*. *Mains from US$4; open 11.00–01.00.*

WHAT TO SEE AND DO While Rivne may not draw the same crowds as Yalta, those who end up here always find something quite special about the place. Much of Rivne was rebuilt after the war, so that tour guides are quick to point out the remaining gems from yesteryear, namely **St Antony's Cathedral** (*Soborna 137*), which miraculously survived its many facelifts and bombardments. Today it stands as the symbol of Rivne with its tight, red-brick, twin-towered construction. As in Soviet years, the church offers weekly organ recitals. Another stunning structure is the white and turquoise **Cathedral of the Holy Resurrection** (*Soborna 36*); this is a rare and beautiful example of turn-of-the century Ukrainian architecture. A standard tour also takes visitors into the rustic **Church of the Assumption** (built in 1756). Legend claims that Ukrainian *haidamaky* general Ivan Gonta prayed in this church during his rampage across western Ukraine. Rivne's **Natural History Museum** (*Dragomanova 19;* ↘ *0362 223 367*) is housed in an old lyceum, and while the exhibit may be weak, it recounts the history of a city that was never dull. The many parks offer another attractive diversion, and in summer, Rivne seems to take to the outdoors more than most.

Dubno and **Ostroh** are two nearby towns that make for interesting excursions as both feature very ancient castles. You can get to either city by bus or taxi in around 45 minutes. The castle in Ostroh used to be a magnificent palace with squat towers and ramparts atop a shaped 'castle hill'. Founded in around 1100, Dubno's old churches and many monasteries make for a fascinating visit, enhanced by the very small-town atmosphere. If you decide to overnight, **Hotel Dubno** was recently remodelled (*Halytskovo 53*), with rooms from US$20. For food, visit restaurant **Viktoria** (*Hrushevskovo 158;* ↘ *0365 642 450*). Every summer Dubno also hosts the country's biggest Ukrainian rock music festival – quite a show if you happen to pass through at the right time.

The northern part of the Rivnensky region is naturally beautiful but rather undeveloped (some areas were subjected to fallout from Chernobyl but are now considered safe). **Rivnensky Nature Preserve** consists of four protected zones in northern Volhynia, all part of the Pripyat marshes and only designated a preserve in 1999. These are great birdwatching areas, but getting to the parks is difficult since there are no major roads like in Shatsky. First take the train north to Sarny (from Rivne or Kiev); from here the far western zone can be reached by bus or hired taxi via Volodymyrets and the village of Rudka. East of Sarny, the town of Klesiv is within hiking distance of another zone, though the other two are extremely remote. The reserve's main office is located in Sarny (*Gogolya 34;* ↘ *0365 534 763*). The Rivne Inturist office at Hotel Mir organises limited local excursions; a local tourist company that may prove helpful is **Sport I Turizm** (*Zhukovskovo 39;* ↘ *0362 243 939*). Another is **Volhyn Tour** (*Masepy 4, No 1;* ↘ *0362 262 719;* f *0362 223 364;* e *volyntur@ukrwest.net*).

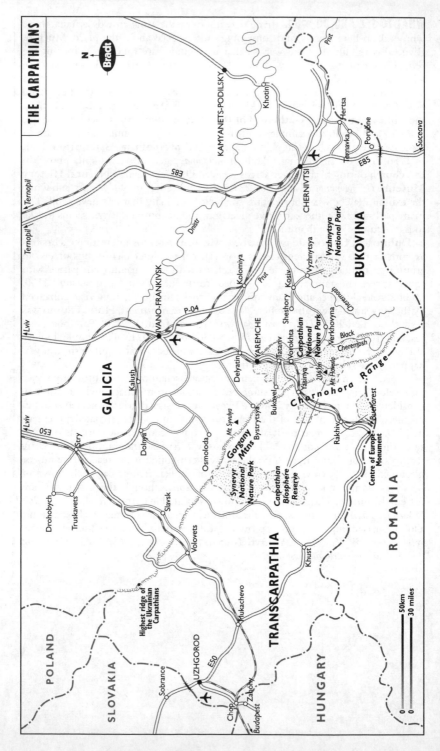

10

The Carpathians
Карпати

Untamed landscapes and the dramatic scenery of the Carpathian Mountains attract nature lovers and accommodate those of us who still savour the last remaining slivers of rustic, old-world Europe. Ukraine's most significant mountain chain arches across the southwest corner of the country and forms a natural border with Hungary, Romania, Poland and Slovakia. These are relatively low peaks (Ukraine's highest mountain, Hoverla, is only 2,061m high) but the unruly terrain has protected the area from so much 'development' and now the Carpathians form the greenest area in all Ukraine. It is also the cleanest – the most breathtaking feature is the taste of the mountain air, and the shallow braided streams running through the valleys are absolutely pristine. Anyone venturing away from Lviv or the capital should consider the Carpathians a top priority.

As it's so closed off from the rest of the world, travelling in the Carpathians feels a lot like going back in time. A rich and separate folklore makes this a truly rural setting where ancient tradition still dictates a pastoral life built upon the slanted landscape. Typically, a Carpathian 'town' is no more than a long stretch of disconnected farms in vague proximity to a minuscule tin-roof church. Horse-drawn carts are preferred over cars. It is a land of round haystacks, pine-log fences and vivid folk art – the place in the journey where you keep your camera gripped in one hand. In winter, everything seems to be shrouded in a white haze, fenced in by steep slopes and falling snow – only tiny puffs of woodsmoke indicate where to find a village of half-buried huts. In summer, nowhere seems so green and boundless as these open valleys and angled peaks.

Yet the Carpathians' largest cities deserve the same attention as the mountains. Three very distinct regions make up the Ukrainian Carpathians, each of which belonged to a bordering nation once upon a time: Southern Galicia (Poland), Transcarpathia (Hungary) and Bukovina (Romania). Nurtured by an independent heritage, the cities of Ivano-Frankivsk, Uzhgorod and Chernivtsi bear no resemblance to any of Ukraine's cookie-cutter Soviet towns. These three separate cultures are still evident in people's speech, their particular attitude, and the stylish architecture that attracts a rising number of tourists from around the country and the rest of the world. Herein lies the oldest of Ukrainian traditions, and the Carpathians represent the youngest part of the country, annexed only after World War II. Ukraine's most diverse ethnic groups (the Lemko, Boiki and Hutsuls) evolved in these valleys and still resist national assimilation today.

Unlike the rest of Ukraine, the Carpathians enjoy a solid tourist infrastructure that dates back to the Hapsburg monarchy and the romantic urge to seek out all vistas both wild and quaint. A tradition of hospitality sets the region apart and this is still the place to hike, camp, climb, raft, ski and simply relax. As a whole, the Carpathians are just now being rediscovered as the trendy alternative to Europe's more eminent mountain chains, but Ukraine's 10% of the range still attracts the least amount of visitors. That is likely to change as people discover the emerging wave of fine mountain resorts and as the intrepid 'no frills' backpackers venture in a little deeper. The utter remoteness of much of the region represents its very appeal, while its proximity to the more visited countries of Europe offers an adventurous detour to the worthy traveller.

THE MOUNTAINS

The mineral-rich Carpathians are considered Europe's youngest fold mountains, forming a landscape of pyramid-shaped peaks and pocketed valleys. In a country as flat as Ukraine, the elevation range of 500 to 2,000m is impressive. Mountain summits are considered sacred places here and most peaks are marked with crosses or patriotic monuments.

Three main recreational ranges make up the Ukrainian Carpathians: the lower hills south of Lviv that include the ski resorts at Slavsk and spa towns like Truskavets; the secluded Horhany range is the least accessible but truly spectacular; and the Chornahora Mountains are the highest, located directly south of Ivano-Frankivsk by the Romanian border. Someone visiting Lviv can very easily do a day trip into the northern Carpathians, but the heart of the Ukrainian Carpathians lies south of Ivano-Frankivsk. A popular mountain circuit starts here, passing through Yaremche, Tatariv, Vorokhta, Verkhovyna, Kosiv, Sheshory, Kolomiya, and finally ending in Chernivtsi and Bukovina. Train and motor transport are available all along the way, with opportunities for small hikes from each place. Alternative itineraries would allow for long walks in between, such as crossing the Chornohora by foot from Yasynya to Verkhovyna.

Hiking Carpathian peaks rarely involves an intense climb, but is very satisfying for its unique interaction of natural and human elements. Some areas are empty and forested, in others the mountain huts and wooden fences add to the romance (and view). The hills are also a collector's paradise with easy-to-find fossils (mainly flowers and fish), and relics from the first and second world wars such as helmets, bullets and bombshells. Remember that many people still harbour the mentality that individual exploration – or hiking without a guide – are not viable actions, especially by foreigners. That kind of caution is unjustified in the Carpathians, where there are plenty of well-worn trails and civilisation is never too far away. In the mountains, use only marked campsites and fire areas. *Kolyba* are traditional Hutsul shepherd lodges now built and used as accommodation for hikers; most of these are represented on maps and fall along the trail. All the same, bring a compass. Always travel with sufficient warm clothing. The people who get lost here rarely suffer from hunger or thirst, but from the intense cold at night or the damp that hits any time of year.

The Soviets were always skilful cartographers, but only now is the information from these maps trickling into the public realm. A few private companies have put together decent orientation maps and these are best bought in bookshops in Lviv and Ivano-Frankivsk (yet another incentive to learn Cyrillic). An over-abundance of Ukrainian travel companies are ready to unveil the secrets of the Carpathians for a price but keep in mind that the best aspects of these mountains are freely available. Adventure Carpathians (*www.adventurecarpathians.com*) is one of the best places to start (see page 197) for specialised activities and long group treks, as well as Outdoor Ukraine (*www.outdoorukraine.com*).

FLORA AND FAUNA

Carpathian plants and animals form a separate world to the rest of Ukraine and recent years have seen an increased recognition of the region's biodiversity as more people discover one of Europe's most pristine (and most threatened) habitats. The alpine environment and virgin forests form a familiar backdrop for mountain wildlife, but so far the Carpathian's eastern European location has prevented the over-development of ski resorts and other tourist industry projects that have been the bane of the Alps and Pyrenees. The Carpathians is the last place on the continent with large carnivores, including bears, wolves, lynx and other wild cats.

Ukraine's bear population is nominally small, with only about 1,000 left, but aside from those in Russia and Romania, this is the largest bear population in Europe. The Carpathian brown bear (*Ursus arctos*), a smaller and more docile relative to the North American grizzly bear, spends most of its time rummaging for food, which can include anything from roots and berries to rodents and grubs. (Ukraine's Hutsul shepherds sometimes complain of bears attacking their cattle.) Poachers kill a few dozen bears every year, but the real threat is the destruction of their habitat: Ukraine's small nature reserves are rarely contiguous, meaning that animals like bears, which need wide spaces for roaming and hunting, are forced to make precarious crossings into human territory. Seeing a bear in the Carpathians can't be guaranteed but it is a definite possibility if that is what you are looking for. Local guides, especially those affiliated with the national parks, tend to know where the bears are and when to see them. Midsummer is best for viewing the animals out in the open. In winter bears go into a state of dormancy; some guides have an uncanny ability to stake out bear dens in the snow and give tourists a peek at the slumbering beasts.

There are only about 500 wolves left but their presence is real in the southern national parks. If you are camping in remote places and are lucky, you will hear them. European lynx are rare, but other types of wildcat are occasionally seen. Ukraine's elk and bison populations are endangered in the Carpathians; most of them are in the tri-country biosphere reserve in Transcarpathia. The most visible local animal species is the Carpathian deer (*Cervus elaphus carpathicus*) which has a unique profile and is easily spotted on wooded slopes and mountain glens all over the area. Fox, marmot, mink and chamois are also prevalent but shy.

Birdwatching in the Ukrainian Carpathians is rewarding, with over 280 species represented, many of which can only be seen in this area. Keep an eye out for mountain wagtail, water pipit, golden eagle, the Carpathian two-tail owl and the white-back woodpecker. Ukraine lacks the organised birdwatching tours of its surrounding neighbours, but the parks support birding and can be helpful with locating prime spots and species identification.

Wildflowers and soft mosses cover much of the open mountain glens. Spring, summer and autumn each exhibit a changed cover of grasses and blooms; crocus, snowbell, violets and monkshood are characteristic of the Ukrainian hills. The symbol of the Ukrainian Carpathians is the edelweiss, or *pidlisniv* ('under the snow') in Ukrainian. You can still find it growing throughout the Chornahora, especially in early spring. The mountains on this side of the border are the most heavily wooded of the entire range: beech, sycamore and tall virgin pines make up the larger forests. The air smells so nice because of all the spruce trees, especially the squat and bushy Siberian juniper, and there are enough deciduous trees to colour things brightly during the autumn. Up in the mountains, many trees are over 30m high and over 400 years old. Only 8% of these forests are under protection, but it is not uncommon to see a swathe of trees cut down inside a reserve. Local tradition and present poverty levels require that the timber is used for building and fuel, and enforcement in Ukraine is generally weak. Efforts to protect the area as a whole are complicated by the fact that six different countries share the territory. The area has only recently come under focus from international conservation groups who seek to avoid the same destruction that happened to mountain environments in western Europe.

WHEN TO VISIT In general, the climate is much more mild than in the rest of Ukraine with a constant flux between sunshine and mist. Snow falls from late November and covers the peaks until May while the lowlands begin a turbulent spring in mid-March. Under snow cover, most peaks are too dangerous to climb, but midwinter (after New Year) is the best time to go skiing. The Carpathian summer is only two months long and this is also when the heaviest rain falls: Ukrainian and Polish tourists invade in August. Like most mountain climates the weather is always changing, so it is wise to wear layers of clothing and carry some

THE HUTSULS ГУЦУЛИ

Ukraine's mountain people create an alternative image to the scythe-wielding peasant of the broad Ukrainian steppe. In place of the sickle, Hutsuls carry ornate *toporets* (hatchets) for chopping down trees, defending themselves against bears and as a prop in their very specific style of folk dancing. Although Ukrainian in language, belief and custom, their unique lifestyle stems from a separate natural world of steep, wall-like mountains and dark pine forests. Felling trees provides lumber for tall-roofed houses that stay dry under the snow, while sheep herding in the mountain pastures offers food, clothing and income. The traditional Hutsul dress consists of red woollen jackets, red trousers or skirts, and wide leather belts and boots. Hutsul cuisine reflects a blend of wild mountain products and Romanian influence. A main ingredient is *smetana* (like sour cream), as are forest mushrooms, corn meal, wild blackberries and sheep and goat products. *Brynza* (a sharp and crumbly Carpathian goat cheese) is pressed fresh and eaten in large wedges, often as a salty snack with vodka, and mutton shish kebabs are sold in every roadside stand.

Pure Hutsul dialect is a mixture of old Ruthenian mixed with borrowed Romanian and Magyar, and a few of their own expressions – the average Ukrainian cannot understand it at all. Instead of the characteristic 'runs' seen in most Ukrainian folk dancing, Hutsul dances are a show of fierce jumping, made popular by Ukrainian pop singer and winner of the 2004 Eurovision contest, Ruslana. Hutsuls also play a long alphorn-like instrument called a *trembyta* that can be fashioned only from a pine tree that has been struck by lightning. The horn is held high in the air and when played (at births, deaths and marriages) makes a trumpeting bellow that echoes off the hills. Most revealing of Hutsul mentality are the details, especially in folk architecture: a building's front door is built at chest level so that guests must bow before the host when entering.

Modern Ukrainians will make proud reference to the Hutsuls but even in the Carpathians, they are still perceived as a caricature rather than a fact of present-day existence. Actually, most of the southern Carpathians are still populated by Hutsuls, whether or not they are on display as such, while the term 'Hutsul' is used as a broad reference to a collective of mountain ethnic groups, including the Boiki, Lemki and Pokuttians. If you are travelling with a group tour through the Carpathians, much of the journey will consist of pinpointed shopping trips for Hutsul souvenirs. Everything will be touted as genuine Hutsul craft, including embroidery genuinely imported from China. The real thing is not too elusive. Look for hand-knitted woollen socks, long-hair sheepskins, and simple woodcraft: plates, combs, pipes and utensils. Authentic Hutsul embroidery is recognisable for its simple repeated diamond or diagonal patterns and for its traditional colours: earthy reds, ochre, dark blue and black. Geometric animal and plant designs are also characteristic.

kind of waterproof jacket. Hiking is best in late spring or during the long warm autumn (until November).

GETTING AROUND Because of the mountains, local rail access is limited and going by train to those smaller Carpathian towns with stations is a slow and awkward process. Usually, it is better to take a bus, *marshrutka* or taxi from the larger cities to the rural areas. East–west travel is hampered by topography, so if you are going into the mountains, plan your trip along north–south routes. Travel in these parts is also fairly inexpensive: you can go to most places by train or bus for less than US$7.

Ivano-Frankivsk is the conventional hub for transport between the main mountain ranges and other towns, as well as Lviv. Comfortable trains also service Chernivtsi and Uzhgorod. Going into the mountains, there are three daily connections via Yaremche (2 hours) to Vorokhta, and two to Rakhiv (5 hours) via Yasynya. A train goes to Kolomiya four times a day (2 hours). The other Carpathian rail line travels from Stry to Mukachevo (and on to Uzhgorod), connecting with the Ivano-Frankivsk train at Dolyna. Despite all the rail connections, *marshrutka* traffic between all the Carpathian villages is much more convenient and frequent. The quickest way to and from Vorokhta, Verkhovyna, Kosiv and Yaremche is by minibus; there is usually one every hour. It is wise to pay attention to where the *marshrutka* stops, since Carpathian villages can easily occupy a 15-mile stretch of valley. Either specify your exact destination to the driver, who will stop nearby, or get off at the station (usually at the northern outskirts) and walk or take a taxi the rest of the way. Catching a taxi is pretty much necessary in rural situations. As always, decide on a price before getting in. Taking a taxi can also be a good way to get between towns, or if you are carrying a lot of luggage or equipment. The unwritten rule is about 1UAH per kilometre, but that is highly negotiable. The Carpathians is a locale where hitching is a generally accepted practice, especially in the mountains, though drivers usually expect a token payment (see page 85).

TOURIST INFORMATION Travelling in the Carpathians is such a relief because there's far more information available than in most parts of the country. Nearly every town features an information centre that's open during regular business hours, a plethora of tour firms keep busy all year-round, and then there's the Carpathian Tourist Board, which may very well be the most intelligent branch of the Ukrainian government. Their main office is in Ivano-Frankivsk (*Hruskevskovo 21;* \ *0342 551 856;* e *ctb@trade.gov.if.ua; www.tourism-carpathian.com.ua*). They have a very good English website and can provide current information and the right contacts for almost every kind of activity. They also have an information booth on the main square of Ivano-Frankivsk. The Ukrainian-language magazine *Karpaty* (*www.karpaty.net.ua*) sells at most local newsstands and details every aspect of travel for the region.

IVANO-FRANKIVSK ІВАНО-ФРАНКІВСЬК

'Ivano' is the gateway for most travel into the Carpathians and a magnificent city to visit. Thanks to a complete urban restoration everything looks so sleek and fresh that this could well be western Ukraine's most sophisticated town. A series of city squares, pedestrian-only boulevards and small urban trails make it a fun and accessible space, while the old Polish flair provides a romantic backdrop. Art, fashion and business seem to be the town's latest creed and the outer signs show a successful blend of old and new.

The oblast forms the southern reaches of Galicia, and is still marked by pre-World War I borders. Originally, this was the old Ukrainian village of Zablottya, but in the mid 17th century this land (and much of western Ukraine) came under the control of the Pototsky family, the super-wealthy Polish aristocrats who then 'founded' the city and named it in honour of their firstborn son, Stanislaw. The new construction spread out from a six-pointed, star-shaped fortress, bits of which can still be seen in the city centre today. Under Polish rule the town attracted a variety of monastic orders whose presence is still visible, as well as small merchant communities (namely Jews and Armenians). Stanislaw had a brief moment of glory at the collapse of the Austro-Hungarian Empire, when the short-lived Western Ukrainian People's Republic (ZUNR) proclaimed the city its capital in 1919. Alas, Poland regained control until the Yalta Conference when the USSR annexed Galicia. For its 300th anniversary in 1962, the Soviets changed the city's name to Ivano-Frankivsk in honour of the Ukrainian poet and scholar Ivano Franko whose sobering statue now stands in front of the Hotel Ukrayina. The change was a feeble attempt on the part of the Soviet government to appease local Ukrainian patriotism: it is in these southern mountains that the Ukrainian Insurgent Army and many other partisan groups resisted Soviet occupation well into the 1960s, the memorials of which are still the visible focus of Carpathian villages.

Many will prefer to simply get off the train in Ivano and directly board a bus for the hills. However, it's a real mistake to skip this glorious little city and miss out on the vivid contrast between the modern European buzz on the streets and the very rustic ways of the nearby mountains. Ivano is also a good base for getting organised, arranging tours, and enjoying some ease and comfort before and after an extended hike.

GETTING THERE AND AWAY As a former Soviet air base, Ivano-Frankivsk has a great little **airport** with at least one flight per day to Kiev, as well as the occasional flight to Moscow. More and more people are flying here for quick access to the mountains. In town, the airport is best reached by taxi (around US$3) and is located on Konovaltsiya 46. For tickets, check out Kiy Avia's local office (*Shechevikh Striltsiv 10;* ✆ *0342 552 331;* e *info@kiyavia.com; www.kiyavia.com*).

The **train** also remains a solid and efficient way to get into the Carpathians via Ivano-Frankvisk. There are at least three daily trains to and from Kiev; the one via Lviv is the shortest (14 hours) and offers the best time for overnight travel, whereas the link via Chernivtsi can take up to 21 hours. There are also other daily trains to and from Lviv (4 hours), Kharkiv (20 hours), as well as Uzhgorod (8 hours via Lviv) and Chernivtsi (4 hours). Please note that the rare 'internal train' – such as the daily train from Ivano-Frankivsk to Odessa – actually clips across parts of Moldova, and if you don't have a Moldovan visa you'll end up camping out in the woods with some surly Moldovan border guards (see page 274). Double check when you purchase the ticket. The Ivano-Frankivsk train station is a beautiful belle époque structure (built in 1908) located next to the central bus station at Pryvokzalna Square on the eastern side of the city.

Ivano's **bus** station is frenzied and hectic, which is what makes it so exciting. Small masses of villagers and their oversized bundles are hustled into compact buses and sent winding off into the mountains. Normally, you'd be clutching onto your bags and ignoring the people shouting to you, but the drivers here are noticeably helpful and honest. Tickets can be purchased inside the station (to the right when facing the train station) or from the driver. If you are simply taking a bus within the Carpathians, it's not worth buying tickets ahead of time; just show up at the station and you will never wait more than an hour for a departing vehicle.

There are dozens of daily buses and *marshrutka*, to and from every village in the Carpathians: Yaremche (1 hour), Polyanytsya (2½ hours), Bystrytsya (2 hours),

A few years back, scheming international development specialists dreamt of a self-empowering programme wherein Ukrainian villagers would open up their homes to tourists in a B&B-type situation, allowing an exchange of hard currency to the rural poor and a rare adventure for the traveller. Several public efforts have attempted similar programmes and Ukrainian government officials continue to refer to such 'Green Tourism' as their one and only policy plan for the poorest parts of the country. Yet, the entire idea and its execution have been fraught with disorganisation, bad bureaucracy and a lack of initiative. That means that most of the resources and the information on the web are out of date. For those who think that living in a villager's cottage in the Carpathians sounds cool, never fear. Governments will bungle, but Ukraine's entrepreneurial villagers and the private sector have run with the idea.

Almost everywhere you go in Ukraine, simply ask around and you'll quickly be set up with someone, typically on a small farm, who can offer a room in their house for less than US$10/night. (Beware of the term 'green tourism' though, as it's a common moniker for gargantuan hotels that have planted a few trees out front). Staying in a Carpathian home is a wonderful experience, especially in these very remote villages where there are more goats than people. Each individual home offers different services (pools, saunas, wildlife tours, skiing, hiking) and many hosts will gladly provide transport to and from larger towns. A few of these opportunities are listed here under their respective village locations. To book ahead, it is best to work through a private company as they tend to be more reliable than the national government agency (www.greentour.com.ua). Try Adventure Carpathians (www.adventurecarpathians.com/adv_greentour.php) or Meest-Tour (www.meest-tour.com) or ask at any of the tourist and information centres in each town, in particular Eco-Play (✆ 0343 421 157; e eco_play@ukr.net).

Vorohkta (2 hours), Verkhovyna (2½ hours) and Kosiv (4 hours); all travel times are approximate since much depends on the condition of the mountain roads and the number of stops the bus makes. All the long-haul bus services leave from here as well – to Lviv, Kiev, Uzhgorod, and so on – as well as many international buses to Poland and the Czech Republic: Warsaw, Brno and Prague (24 hours). A taxi to Lviv will cost around US$50.

GETTING AROUND Ivano is a compact town and most of the streets in the city centre are pedestrianised. Any taxi around town from the centre or the station should cost only US$2. The No 24 white minibus costs just a handful of kopecks and runs a circle between the train station, Hotel Ukrayina and the airport.

LOCAL TOUR OPERATORS AND TOURIST INFORMATION A central **tourist information centre** is located in a corner booth of the central Plosha Rynok (*Halytska 4A*) where they sell books, pamphlets and maps, and can arrange local guides (in English, Russian and Ukrainian). Most hotels will also provide local tours. Because most travel interest is in the Carpathians, Ivano has a plethora of 'agencies' that act as middlemen connecting travellers to tours. The travel agency at **Hotel Nadia** is highly professional and employs a number of good mountain guides for local excursions (*Nezalezhnosti 40*; ✆f 0342 537 042; e *tour@nadia.if.ua*; *www.karpaty-tour.com*). **BESHTAU Tour** (*Nezalezhnosti 33*; ✆ 0342 55 30 61; *open 09.00–18.00*) is a local agency that arranges smaller excursions in the mountains, and also does Jewish and Polish heritage trips.

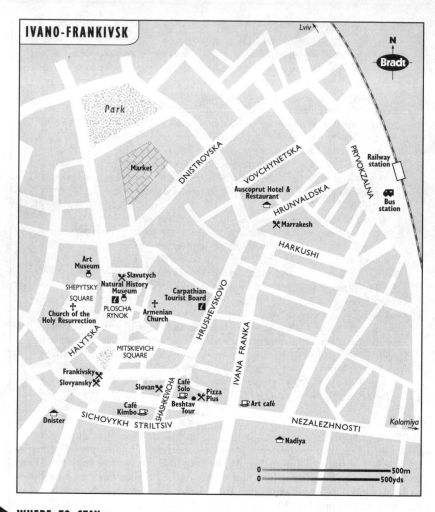

IVANO-FRANKIVSK

N

Bradt

Lviv

Park

Market

DNISTROVSKA

VOVCHYNETSKA

PRYVOKZALNA

Railway station

Auscoprut Hotel & Restaurant

HRUNVALDSKA

Bus station

✗ Marrakesh

HARKUSHI

Art Museum

SHEPYTSKY SQUARE

✗ Slavutych

Natural History Museum

Carpathian Tourist Board

Church of the Holy Resurrection

PLOSCHA RYNOK

Armenian Church

HRUSHEVSKOVO

HALYTSKA

MITSKIEVICH SQUARE

IVANA FRANKA

Frankivsky
Slovyansky ✗

Slovan ✗

SHASHKIEVICHA

Café Solo

Pizza ✗ Plus

Café Kimbo

Beshtav Tour

Art café

Dnister

SICHOVYKH STRILTSIV

NEZALEZHNOSTI

Kolomiya

Nadiya

0 ————— 500m
0 ————— 500yds

WHERE TO STAY Accommodation in Ivano-Frankivsk has that rare quality of matching diverse needs and budgets without being in a constant state of flux.

Auscoprut Hrunvaldska 7/9; ☎ 0342 231 401; f 0342 231 402; e auscoprut@ivf.ukrpack.net; www.auskoprut.if.ua. This light blue Hapsburg 19th-century mansion later became the favoured private residence for the Soviet *nomenklatura* who once visited Ivano. An Austrian joint venture has transformed the building into a relatively luxurious hotel where rooms have high ceilings, big beds and spacious bathrooms. Compared with much of Ukraine, this hotel feels enlightened: English-speaking staff, facilities for disabled travellers, and sparkling clean floors. A meal at their classy restaurant is incomparable; mains from US$8; open 07.00–midnight. Credit cards accepted. *Sgl*

US$45–65, dbl US$60–80, suites US$120; they also offer very reasonable group rates from US$35 pp.
Hotel Nadia Nezalezhnist 40; ☎ 0342 537 077; f 0342 537 076; e nadia@utel.net.ua; www.nadia.if.ua. The city's former Inturist has quickly evolved into a shiny, corporate-style hotel with a staff that speak exquisite English and German and take care of your every need. There is a wide range of rooms, some of which offer very high quality. 'Euro-standard' rooms face the park. The smaller (but better) rooms have real queen-size beds. All rooms have showers and not baths, except for suites. The cheapest 'Soviet' rooms remain in their original state, complete with 1970s furnishings and bad showers.

The hotel features 2 restaurants, one serving old-style Ukrainian food (the 'Ukraine'), the other more European food (the 'Nadia'). Both are a little conventional, with their synthesised music and overly grandiose menu, but they do deliver a good meal. Note that while the hotels accepts credit cards, the restaurants only accept cash. Nadia's ground-floor travel agency can be very helpful in meeting your every travel need. 'Euro-standard' rooms: dbl US$80, sgl US$75; smaller rooms with queen-size bed US$50–60; suites US$100; 'Soviet' rooms US$25.

🏠 **Dnister** Sichovykh Stilsiv 12; ✆ 0342 223 533. A bit dilapidated, this old building in the town centre caters mostly to cash-strapped Ukrainian visitors, but offers a comfortable and cheap night's sleep. The café and bar is extremely dingy but still serves home-style cooking late into the night. Obviously, it's cash only. Dbl with bathroom US$30, suites US$60; bed with shared facilities US$7 and the price goes down as the number of people in the room increases.

✖ WHERE TO EAT

Dining out seems to be the favoured pastime in Ivano, and a definite restaurant culture is emerging. Along Nezalezhnosti there is a string of brand new cafés and pizzerias that always seem to be full. Of the hotel restaurants, **Auscoprut** is the very best in town, serving a deadly cup of hot chocolate at teatime. All take credit cards unless noted otherwise.

✖ **Slavutych** Halytska 19; ✆ 0342 750 980. An upscale restaurant with a lot of local flavour, including some Hutsul recipes and some truly colourful salads. Mains from US$5; open 10.00–midnight.

✖ **Slovan Restaurant** Shashkevicha 4; ✆ 0342 712 594. Poised waiters in uniform serve ornate banquet dishes. The high-style atmosphere attracts the local élite and the 'modern European' menu means meals like grilled salmon, chicken-fried steak, and all kinds of crazy cocktails from the bar. Mains from US$7; open 11.00–midnight.

✖ **Slovyansky** Bachinskovo 2; ✆ 0342 553 000. Old-time Slavic fare served in one of Ivano's finest dining establishments. Mains from US$9; open 10.00–midnight.

✖ **Marrakesh** Hrunavaldska 4A; ✆ 0342 559 036. Steps away from the train station, this groovy underground café serves heaps of yummy Middle Eastern food, as well as hearty Ukrainian staples like borsch. Delightfully smoke-free, everything is under US$2; open 09.00–23.00.

✖ **Frankivsky** Bachinskovo 4; ✆ 0342 232 524. An underground dining club offering lots of real Carpathian cuisine. Be a true local and try the corn banosh with sheep's cheese, or opt for the tamer fruit varennyki. The live music is not always an asset. Mains from US$4; open 11.00–23.00.

✖ **Café Solo** Nezalezhnosti 25; ✆ 0342 232 859. One of the city's classier cafés, serving lots of dainty cakes, espresso, and the kind of light, intimate meals that are conducive to good conversations. Mains from US$3; open 09.00–23.00. Cash only.

✖ **Café Kimbo** Nezalezhnosti 10A; ✆ 0342 777 619. Coffee, tea and desserts. Mains from US$2; open 08.00–23.00.

✖ **Pizza Plus** Nezalezhnosti 43; no phone. A colourful student hangout with pizza for under US$5; open 09.00–22.00. Cash only.

✖ **Art café** Nezalezhnosti 53; no phone. Casual, light meals in the smokiest establishment in the city. This place is always packed with the art-aware crowd and serves incredibly inexpensive food. Mains from US$1; open 11.00–23.00.

If you want to avoid the attempted grandeur, there is a swanky delicatessen and grocery to the right of Hotel Nadia where you can buy fresh baked goods, meat, cheese and imported groceries. There is also a market at the end of Sheremety.

WHAT TO SEE AND DO

In many respects, Ivano-Frankivsk is a fairly common western Ukrainian city with the exception that it bears a stronger than average resemblance to towns in southern Poland. The streets are paved with cobblestones and the buildings are all painted in bright Easter-egg colours. Some of the architecture is simply grand. **Ploscha Rynok** is the old market square and the evident town centre dating back to the year when Stanislaw was granted the Magdeburg Law (see page 111). The art deco building in the centre used to be the city hall and now houses the regional **Natural History Museum** (open

10

10.00–16.00; entrance 2UAH). Mammoth bones, iron bits from local burial mounds, and collections from the old Galician kings help tell the story of the oblast, along with some rudimentary yet very sincere displays about local legends. The green and grey **Church of the Holy Resurrection** (*Sheptytsky Square 22*) is the very prominent and beautiful Greek Catholic cathedral built in 1753 – it's still quite an active church run by local monks and nuns. The original iconostasis is impressive and the glorious musical services attract crowds of townspeople every day (if you're lucky, you'll come inside when the pink neon 'Christ is Among Us' sign lights up). Outside the church stand the statues of Princess Olga and Prince Vladimir, founders of Kievan Rus. The **Armenian church** is the pale blue building facing the main square and is owned today by the Ukrainian Autocephalous Orthodox Church. It was first completed by the local Armenian community in the 1760s. The **Museum of Galician Sacred Art** (*Shepytsky Square 8; open 10.00–20.00, closed Fri and Sat; entrance 5UAH*) occupies the former collegiate church (built in 1703) and contains the country's largest collection of Galician iconography, sacred wood painting and sculptures, including the rare figure of Christ in Sorrows. This was the old museum of atheism during the Soviet occupation, and much of the art now on display was hidden from the Soviets in the crypt of the church. The original frescoes are just being uncovered and the ceiling is painted with six-pointed stars – an old Galician design. English-speaking guides are available. Another architectural highlight is the wonderful example at Halytska 2: the pink and lavender **medical school,** built in 1894. Across the street and under the bank passageway, you can see the old city wall and part of the original six-pointed, star-shaped **fortress.** If you are around for a bit longer, be sure to investigate the natural wonders of Ivano's **Park Shevchenko.**

YAREMCHE ЯРЕМЧЕ

Yaremche is the tourist centre for the Ukrainian Carpathians – some will be pleased by the relative amount of development, stable accommodation, ease and accessibility here, while others will find the gaudy signs and souvenir markets a little disappointing. Either way the surrounding scenery is beautiful and as the main entrance into the Carpathian National Park the town has become a requisite stop and a base for hiking into the Chornohora range. The longest trail to Mount Hoverla begins in Yaremche, and some of the more accessible natural spots are close by, such as the Dovbusha Cliffs. The Prut River runs rapid and green through the village, forming the gully that made it possible for the railway and the mountain road to pass through here – the latter is called Freedom (Svobody) Boulevard in the town limits. A series of bridges (and ruins of former bridges) cross the river at the southern end of town, and this is where most of the tourist attractions are centred, but there are also a few nice trails down to the river. Yaremche is a clear example of modern-day *Hutsulschyna* with its wooden buildings, red clay tiles and steep roofs for the heavy snow and rain of the mountains. The village survives due to tourism and sells itself as a folksy Hutsul backwater, which it actually is, despite all the holiday veneer. Traditional methods of herding continue to be the livelihood of many, and the customary hospitality comes with a heavy dose of suspicion and curiosity.

GETTING THERE AND AWAY If the mountains are your aim, all paths lead to Yaremche. The best way to get there is to drive or take a bus from Ivano Frankivsk or Kolmiya. The ride into Yaremche from Ivano-Frankivsk is a beautiful little stretch with long reddish wheat fields set before the dark blue of the distant mountains; duck ponds and horse-drawn ploughs are prime features. The bus

The Carpathians are the most 'natural' part of Ukraine and one of the most vulnerable to human impact. Eco-Play was started in Yaremche as a grassroots organisation that strives to promote ecotourism as an alternative to unsustainable use of the environment in the Carpathian National Park. They have regular project days where they clean and maintain the forests and rivers, or plant trees. A foreign visitor lending a hand can be affirming, and it is a fantastic way to see the park. Write, call, or pass by their office. Their English is limited, but they welcome visitors enthusiastically. The group's members are all volunteers who are truly passionate about their mountains and know the trails better than anyone else. They can tell you of planned activities, and are experts on local wildlife. Remember that even the smallest financial donation will help them to publish and distribute their environmental awareness literature. Several travellers have come and spent a few days to a week working with the local volunteers and in the process have seen some of the more hidden and spectacular sections of the mountains. Eco-Play is also deeply involved in the rural tourism program and will happily arrange an inexpensive homestay for anyone who seeks a true Carpathian adventure. (*Contact: Lidiya Fedorivna Hotsul, Eco-Play; Stusa 6, Yaremcha 78500; ☏ 03434 211 57; email: jaremche@ukr.net; eco_play@ukr.net*).

station is at the far northern end of the town and is nothing more than a two-room concrete block at the back of a parking lot; stay on the bus and go further along Svobody if you need to (just tell the driver where you're headed). Most motor transport continues south to Tatariv, Vorokhta and Verkhovina throughout the day. Less frequent buses travel south towards Yasinya and Rakhiv, a few of which go on to Khust and Uzhgorod. There is regular, on-the-hour transport back to Ivano-Frankivsk all day long. The train station is the adorable peach building near the rather vague town centre. Every day there are four trains to Rakhiv (3 hours, via Yasinya and Vorokhta), one to Lviv (5 hours), two to Ivano-Frankivsk (1½ hours) and two to Kolomiya (1½ hours). The train stops in Yaremche for two minutes only, and the station is open only when a train is passing through, complicating ticket purchases. Typically, the station is open from 8.00 to 12.00 and 16.00 to 19.00. *Marshrutka* and taxis pick up all along the central road and will take you anywhere. There are also plenty of trails and roads so that hardcore hikers can make their way to the next town without much effort.

WHERE TO STAY There is no shortage of places to stay in Yaremche, but even with a number of new hotels popping up, things can get crowded in summer. Bed and breakfast-style homestays are becoming more and more popular, and if you're adventurous, just show up in Yaremche and ask around for a free '*Sadiba*' or guesthouse.

Krasnaya Sadyba Ivasyuka 6; ☏ 0343 422 253; www.krasna-sadiba.nezabarom.com.ua. A red-brick, gingerbread-style house right on the banks of the river, which now functions as a luxury B&B. Amenities include heating, cooling, 24hr hot water and a high level of security. *Most rooms US$100, though they have a few rooms for US$50.*

Karpaty Dachna 30; ☏ 0343 422 134; f 0343 421 472. More of a resort than a hotel, the Karpaty

has adapted from its Soviet past into a thriving private enterprise run by Ukraine's (formerly public) gas company. The complex is built near the larger souvenir markets; swimming pools, saunas, spas and organised mountain tours attract conference guests and families on holiday. The beds and facilities are clean and comfortable, with varying standards of 'luxury'. *Foreigners are charged more than Ukrainians: sgls US$45–65, dbls US$60–80.*

🏠 **Hotel Prut** Svobody 275 (across from the train station); 📞 0343 422 237. Right across from the train station, this small, century-old Austrian hotel offers low-priced rooms. Most have shared bathrooms and hot water is a rare amenity. *US$5–10.*

🏠 **Hotel Ruta** Svobody 270; 📞 0343 422 017. In the vague city centre, the Ruta is a hotchpotch hotel with a few homey, self-contained rooms. They always have hot water and offer a decent b/fast, but the management do seem a little odd. *US$30–50.*

A few homey bed and breakfasts in the village offer a very personal stay:

🏠 **Karpaty Zatishok** (8 rooms) Halytska 22; 📞 0343 422 533; e jaremche@ukr.net. A wonderful cabin in the meadow as part of a very comfortable homestay with great hosts. They'll also cook for you if you want. *US$10–20 per night in*

summer (in winter you can stay for about US$4).
🏠 **Sadiba Xenia** Kupaka 28; 📞 0343 422 289. Another guesthouse with traditional Hutsul hospitality and cheap rooms. *US$5.*

The following personal homes all offer comfy rooms and great service; negotiate a fair price and agree on the number of days you will be staying beforehand. All have hot water, but only take cash.

🏠 **Hanna Yakivchuk** Kamyanka 48; 📞 0343 433 227. Open year-round. A very cheerful host!
🏠 **Olga Irodenko** Fedkovycha 9; 📞 0343 421 508. A small and typical Yaremche home not too far from

the bus station.
🏠 **The House at Pushkina 30B** 📞 0343 221 423. Has rooms from Apr to Oct.
🏠 **Halina Boiko** Pushkina 8; 📞 0343 421 662.

✖ **WHERE TO EAT** Authentic Hutsul cuisine may seem elusive, but in Yaremche this is what's advertised in most restaurants.

✖ **Kolyba** Svobody 275; 📞 0343 422 708. Housed in the wooden complex near the bridge and named after the traditional Carpathian mountain hut. The log interior and big fireplace make it cosy and there is live Hutsul violin music every night. Food is shish kebabs, fish and salads. Vodka is also cheap, and Kolyba appears to be the watering hole favoured by villagers. *Mains from US$6; open 11.00–midnight.*
✖ **Hutsulschyna** 📞 0343 422 378; e agenstso@ trade.gov.if.ua. This is the most recommended restaurant; another ornate log hut but a tad more

contrived: one can't miss the unique rooftop and signs on Dachna. The food is bona fide Carpathian fare and delicious: river trout, mushroom soup, pork ribs, *brynza* cheese, and berries dropped into everything from dessert to tea and salads. A wooden bridge leads from behind the restaurant over a waterfall and into the town's largest souvenir market. Roadside *shashlyki* stands are ubiquitous, and most cafés serve the Ukrainian staples *borsch* and *varennyki*. In summer, the number of *shashlyk* stands multiplies exponentially. *Mains from US$6; open 13.00–midnight.*

If you get tired of grilled meat and sheep's cheese, there's a reliable food store (Favorit) near the bus station on the north side of the village.

LOCAL TOUR OPERATORS AND TOURIST INFORMATION The **Department of Tourism and Recreation** in Yaremche is located at 266 Svobody (*2nd floor; Room 13;* 📞 *0343 422 606; open Mon–Fri 08.00–17.00*) and there are many tourist agencies that offer mountain excursions. One of the oldest private enterprises is **Zori Karpat Tourist Bureau** (*Svobody 246, Office 1;* 📞 *0343 421 182; open 08.00–17.00*). This is a mum-and-dad outfit recommended solely for their intimate knowledge of the mountains and its animals. They can arrange English-speaking guides and do special flora and fauna tours, and they often take groups out to collect mushrooms and berries.

WHAT TO SEE AND DO Enjoy the outdoors! There are plenty of trails to follow through forests and over the hills, and the Prut River is a common swimming hole.

A small nature park on the southwest side of town acquaints visitors with the mountains and wildlife of the national park; they always have a few Carpathian deer living on site. Yaremche has an interesting history of conflict and recreation. The **Carpathian Museum of Liberation** is on Svobody (across from the bus station) and tells the story of the partisans that fought in these mountains, though the museum is open irregular hours and only in season. Most activities centre around the tourist complex of markets and the **Hutsulschyna** restaurant near the short waterfall. Otherwise, Yaremche is the base from which people go out and explore the surrounding villages or take short day hikes into the mountains.

Walks near Yaremche The **Cliffs of Dovbusha** are a close and easy walk from the village, but are fairly representative of the higher Carpathian forests and offer quite interesting terrain. The trail is especially good if you are travelling with children or have any health condition preventing a longer hike: the largest loop is under 5km and a thorough slow walk through should take about three hours. From the bridge over the Prut River, walk about 1km south on the main road. The trail starts on the left-hand side and slowly rises up over the rocky drop towards the river. Beech and pine forest covers much of the ridge, and near the turn in the path there's a great view of the valley and the distant Chornohora. The main attractions on the walk are the sandstone 'caves' where the outlaw Oleksa Dovbusha once hid out. These are actually a series of gargantuan boulders tumbled over the summit, with lots of crevices to explore and rocks to climb on. Beneath the spindly trees are a variety of ferns and thick spongy moss. The wild raspberries and blackcurrants underfoot are indeed edible.

No doubt you will hear of the so-called **Ecological Trail** of the Carpathian National Nature Park, which is the popular route to Mount Hoverla for those who want to take buses between the towns with periodic hiking in between. Most of the 'trail' follows the road and allows a good view of the scenery while staying close to civilisation; go to Vorokhta, then continue on to the village of Zaroslyak until the end of the road, from where it's a 3km hike to the summit of Hoverla. Yaremche is much better for starting or ending long expedition-like walks into the eastern Gorgany and then south into the Chornahora.

CARPATHIAN NATIONAL NATURE PARK

Ukraine's very first national park was established in 1980 and is about 72km (45 miles) long and 20km (12 miles) wide. The park's western border follows the ridge of the Chornohora range south almost to the Romanian border and this area is the most popular place for hiking. Boundaries are marked by the park's painted edelweiss symbol. The park is the most accessible reserve of Carpathian animal and plant life, and the area of the mountains most frequently visited by Ukrainians. Serious hikers will find the trails stimulating and the natural setting is one of Ukraine's best.

The park's **central office** is located in Yaremche at 6 Stusa (\ *0343 421 157, 22 817; open Mon–Fri, 08.00–17.00*). This is the dilapidated white Soviet building with socialist stained glass at the top of the hill above the marketplace. It may appear uninhabited, but the inside is more lively than the exterior. Technically, all visitors need to register before entering the park, which costs 1.5UAH. This is just a formality, but perhaps a wise one to follow if you are going trekking for more than a few days and if you want to avoid an ugly run-in with bureaucracy. The office offers a fair amount of information about the park and they can sometimes organise individual guides for more specific aims (eg: finding bears). This is *not* the place to get detailed hiking maps: buy those in a bookshop in Ivano-Frankivsk or Lviv.

The park is divided into separate *lisnytsvo*, or wooded areas. Only 20% of the park is completely off-limits to industrial use, and there are certain periods when these protected areas are off-limits to hikers too (check at the office). As a rule, stay on the trails: some are dirt roads marked with unsightly cement telephone poles and others zigzag unmarked through the hills. Painted coloured stripes on posts indicate the level of trail you are on: green is the easiest, with practically no incline, blue trails are found in low mountains, and red indicates a more intense climb (the trail to Hoverla's summit is red).

The drive through the park goes south from Yaremche to Vorokhta, Rakhiv and beyond. The journey is definitely scenic, if completely otherworldly. Beyond the natural splendour of the mountain range and rushing river, the tiny villages that cling to the hillside (or roadside) are nothing short of magical.

TATARIV ТАТАРІВ

For most, Tatariv is simply a junction on the road to Vorokhta right on the banks of the Prut River. However, this amazing little village marks the real departure from 21st-century Ukraine and the gateway into the old world of the Carpathians. Besides the horse-drawn carts that begin to pass you by, look out for the single pole haystacks and the wooden cottages and churches decorated with traditional stamped metal designs (typically with the local edelweiss pattern). Tatariv is famous for its mineral water springs and the old Hutsul Church of St Dmytry, and many tourists come here to start the trail to the top of Mount Khomyak and Mount Synyak. The train from Yaremche makes a brief stop in Tatariv, as do all the *marshrutka*. Tatariv is also the turn-off to Bukovel and the village of Polyanitsya. **Hotel Pihy** (\ *0343 435 404;* e *pihy@jar.if.ua*) is a small bed and breakfast in the village centre with clean rooms and a constant hot-water supply, as well as a good restaurant. Another is the **Anastasiya Inn** (*Nezalezhnosti 10;* \ *0343 435 254*).

VOROKHTA ВОРОХТА

Vorokhta is right in the heart of the Chornohora and has a very alpine feel to it, with tall pine trees that seem to spring up from out of the rocks. The town was the winter base camp for Soviet Olympic athletes and the giant ski jumps are still in use. It's undergoing a slow conversion into a contemporary ski resort, but 'slow' is the key word – rumours still circulate that lift equipment is outdated and unsafe so skiers are skiing at their own risk. Those skiers with less gumption tend to head further on to Bukovel. In summer, Vorokhta marks the best base from which to hike to Hoverla in the shortest time, and few consider hiking from anywhere else. The 'town' is stretched over 20km (12 miles) and a steady flow of hikers has kept a few tourist facilities in business. In Vorokhta, be sure to take a peek inside the **Christmas Church**, one of the oldest surviving Hutsul wooden churches, first built in 1615 in Yablunitsya and moved to Vorokhta in 1780.

GETTING THERE AND AWAY Vorokhta is a one-hour *marshrutka* ride from Yaremche and 30 minutes from Verkhovyna; buses do a circle between the three cities throughout the day and there are longer direct buses to and from Ivano-Frankivsk and to Kosiv and Kolomiya. If you are trying to reach the mountains by train, Vorokhta is the final stop. There are no more than two trains daily to both Rakhiv and Ivano-Frankivsk.

WHERE TO STAY AND EAT Vorokhta was built as a winter sports camp and the hotels used to offer Spartan accommodation for Soviet athletes. Of late they have improved slightly and two ski resorts are still working: **Avangard** (\ *0343 441 140*) is at the entrance of the village and **Ukrayina** (\ *0343 441 270*) is in the village centre. Both have a wide range of rooms and prices, but they would rather sell you a week-long package. **Zaroslyak** (\ *0343 441 591*) is the complex closest to the base of Hoverla, with rooms for less than US$20 and equipment hire for climbing and camping. In addition to the many regular rural homestay options in the area, there are several new upscale cottages offering first-class accommodation either in the village or just outside. Most are within Hoverla's shadow, offering a unique opportunity for a day trip on foot to the summit and back again in time for dinner. For the time being, **Ruslana** (*Voitup 28;* \ *0343 441 940*) is the primary restaurant.

Vorokhta village homestays

Kermanych Halytskovo 188; \ 0343 441 082. Brand-new log home with very nice rooms. All rooms have big dbl beds and hot showers. Meals included for extra. Cash only. *US$30–80, and mega-suites for US$100.*

Sadyba Markiv Halytskovo 29B; \ 0343 441 350. Private home of the Markiv family. Hot water available. Cash only.

Sadyba Heredzhuka Lesi Ukrayinki 15; \ 0343 441 118. Private home of the Heredzhuk family. Hot water available. Cash only.

BUKOVEL БУКОВЕЛЬ

Ukraine's flashiest ski resort lies in the western Chornahora just above the miniscule village of Polyanitsya. While the town's altitude is not that impressive (just 900m), the snow is some of the best in the country, allowing people to ski well into the spring and even summer. Modelled after the world-class ski resorts in places like Aspen and St Moritz, Bukovel has set a new standard for the Carpathians and all of Ukraine. Backed by a US$125 million seed investment, this virgin Carpathian valley currently sports six top-of-the line ski lifts and attracts serious skiers from western Europe and all of the former Soviet Union (the language on the slopes is an odd mix of Slavic tongues and Euro-English). Plans are under way to make it one of the biggest ski resorts in the world. The dozens of ski trails link three important peaks, Mount Bukovel (1,139m), Mount Dovha (1,370m) and Chorna Klyva (1,241m). Obviously, the views are spectacular. Lift tickets are sold by ascent, but it works out to be around US$25 for one day, or US$120 for five days, an absolute steal compared with anything in the Alps. Ski rentals begin at US$15 per day. Contact the ski resort of Bukovel (✆ *0342 559 546;* f *0342 559 389;* e *info@bukovel.info; www.bukovel.com*).

Getting to Bukovel is becoming easier and easier as its popularity increases. Several buses now leave directly from Ivano-Frankivsk and make the journey in about two hours. Those who fly with their skis to Lviv end up taking a direct bus (about 5 hours).

Bukovel also features a fine chalet-style hotel that properly invokes a Ukrainian Hustul motif (many of the rooms are situated in comfortable private cottages). Rooms are warm and cosy, with all new European bathrooms. Doubles cost US$90–110 in winter, but prices double during the week of New Year. In summer, prices drop by almost half. The deluxe suites are truly deluxe and cost around US$400/night. To reserve, contact **Bukovel Hotel** (✆ *0342 559 546;* e *reserve@bukovel.info*).

Bukovel provides plenty of opportunities to **eat and drink**. Their most popular venue is Kozachok (✆ *0343 437 296*), a complex of several Carpathian-style dining halls (*open 10.00–midnight*) and a lounge bar that's open 24 hours. The food is authentic (if not gourmet) Hutsul cuisine, with entrées from US$8. A less traditional option is Pizzeria Feliccita, with great pizza from US$6. The Obzhora sandwich shop does a bang-up business right on the slopes (*mains for US$2; open 10.00–19.00*). The restaurant Grazhda serves Ukrainian food in a very fun little cottage, located in the village of Polyanitsya (*Vyshnya 4;* ✆ *0673 522 191; open 10.00–23.00*).

Those who don't stay at the resort have a number of options at private guesthouses in the valley below, in Polyanitsya or back in Tatariv and Vorokhta.

🏠 POLYANITSYA The village is so small the hotels have no addresses. Just follow the signs!

🏠 **Hutsulska Svitlytsya** ✆ 0343 437 223. Right next to the bus station, with plenty of comfortable beds, a great little café, good plumbing and horseriding. Sauna and barbecue a plus. *Rooms from US$20/night.*

🏠 **Urochysche Vyshnya** ✆ 0673 522 496. Slightly more upscale guesthouse, with grandiose 'lux' rooms, an in-house sauna and pool, outdoor barbecue, and yet another restaurant/café named 'Kolyba'. *Rooms from US$65.*

THE CHORNOHORA RANGE ЧОРНОГОРА

The Chornohora are literally the 'Black Mountains' of Ukraine, but under the shifting mist, the colours of the hills change from bright green to dark blue and steely black. These are Ukraine's highest peaks. **Mount Hoverla** (2,061m) is the highest, and therefore the most revered and most climbed. The summit is covered with snow from late August to early June so climbing later than early November or earlier than May is foolhardy for those without the requisite mountaineering experience. The popular trail up to Hoverla starts in Vorokhta and follows a road next to the Prut River to the village of Chornohora where there is a tourist base with unpredictable accommodation (take a bus, taxi or walk this first bit).

From here it is 11km to the summit, about a five-hour round trip if you drive all the way to the winter sports camp at **Zaroslyak** where there are camping facilities and an old hotel (☏ *0343 441 591*). Indeed, most tours drive the hikers right up to the parking lot in Zaroslyak, from where it's only two hours to the top. Most hotels will get you a guide for about US$25, but you really don't need one. The well-marked path goes through some grand bits of silver fir and birch forest with lots of wildflowers in the spring, and falcons are always swooping above the higher slopes. On a clear day from the summit a fantastic view displays Romania's Marmarosh Alps to the south, the Bila Tysa Valley in Transcarpathia, and the rest of the Chornohora range. Recently, Hoverla's peak has become a bit of a nationalist shrine with its big iron cross and giant Ukrainian flag. Beneath are the words *Ne Maye Natsii, Ne Maye Derzhavy* ('If you have no nation [people], you have no state'). Yet for all the hype of Hoverla, it is by no means the quintessence of the Carpathians: the paths can get crowded in summer, and the rest of the Chornohora is just as beautiful, and more peaceful. Hikers and climbers like this range because there are so many peaks so close together, forming a long straight backbone from Mount Hoverla to Pip Ivan. This line of mountains was the post-World War I border between Czechoslovakia and Galicia (Poland) and remaining boundary markers still bear the faded imperial Polish eagle. **Mount Breskul** (1,911m) is 1.5km south of Hoverla, and then it is another 1km to the stunning **Mount Pozhyzhevska** (1,822m) with a trail connecting the peak to Zaroslyak. Further south is **Mount Dantsyzh** (1,866m), followed by the imposing and rocky **Mount Turkul** (1,933m). Trails from Zaroslyak and Rakhiv meet at the peak. In Turkul's shadow is the pristine mountain **Lake Nesamovyte** (1,750m) with a spring from which clean drinking water flows. **Mount Rebra** (2,001m) and **Mount Brebeneskul** (2,037m) are less popular as they are farther away, but as Ukraine's second-highest peak, Brebenskul provides some exciting rocky terrain. Travellers go to the southern Chornohora to climb **Mount Smotrych** (1,894m) and **Pip Ivan** (2,028m). The old meteorological observatory at the top of Pip Ivan looks more like an abandoned castle and now attracts a fair number of hikers who want to check out this spooky Soviet leftover.

WALKS IN THE CHORNOHORA There are so many trails, mountains and possibilities, it is best to sit down with a good map and plan your own journey. If you are backpacking or simply want to explore the largest amount of terrain, it is best to begin in one town and hike/camp over mountain trails as far as the next village, from where it is usually quite easy to get bus transport onward. Trails leave from Vorokhta and Dzembronya (Verkhovyna) on the eastern side of the range, and from Yasinya and Rakhiv on the western side. Mountain paths tend to be well marked and not too rough except for rocks; however, a lot of lower trails have become overgrown. If you start to think that the trail has simply ended or faded away, walk on a little to see if it doesn't reappear. The main trail between the Chornohora peaks is well marked by the old Polish border posts. The following are some suggested itineraries that can be amended, cut down, reversed, or added to most of the other walks listed in this chapter (NB: these itineraries are meant as a guide only, and should not be attempted without a proper contour map).

From Vorokhta to Rakhiv An extensive, high-altitude walk with somewhat rocky terrain; feasible only in fair weather.

Day 1 (*13km; about 7 hours' walking*) Instead of taking the main path to Hoverla, leave on the southwest trail out of Vorokhta where you pass through the mountain glade and head uphill for about 6km. From here it is another 1.5km to the top of

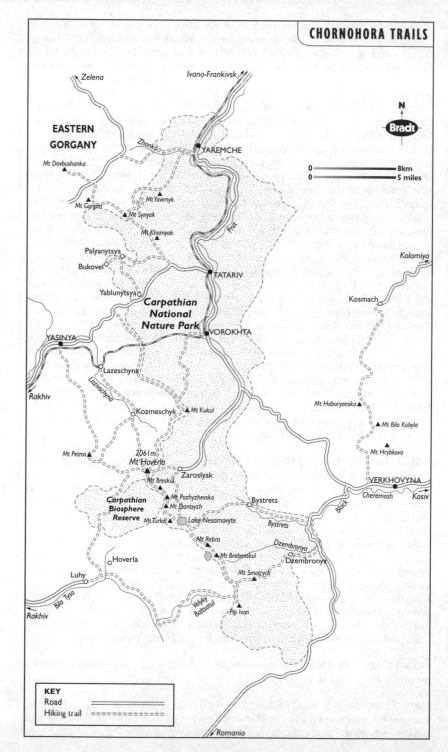

CHORNOHORA TRAILS

N

Bradt

0 ———— 8km
0 ———— 5 miles

Zelena

Ivano-Frankivsk

EASTERN
GORGANY

Zhonka

YAREMCHE

Mt Dovbushanka ▲

Mt Yavirnyk ▲

Mt Gorgan ▲

▲ Mt Synyak

Mt Khomyak ▲

Palyanytsya

Bukovel ○

Kolomiya ○

Yablunytsya

Carpathian
National
Nature Park

TATARIV ■

VOROKHTA ■

Kosmach ○

YASINYA ●

Prut

Lazeschyna

Lazeschyna

Rakhiv

Kozmeschyk ● ▲ Mt Kukul

Mt Haboryanska ▲

▲ Mt Bila Kobyla

Mt Hrybkova ▲

Mt Petros ▲

2061m
Mt Hoverla ▲

Zaroslyak ○

VERKHOVYNA ●

Cheremosh Kosiv

Mt Breskul ▲

Carpathian
Biosphere
Reserve

Mt Pozhyzhevska ▲

Mt Dantsyzh ▲

Bystrets ○

Mt Turkel ▲ Lake Nesamovyte

Bystrets

Mt Rebra ▲

Dzembronya ○

Dzembronya

Hoverla ○

▲ Mt Brebenskul

Mt Smotrych ▲

Luhy ○

Bila Tysa

Velyky
Ballsatul

Pip Ivan ▲

Rakhiv

Romania

KEY
Road ——————
Hiking trail ==========

Mount Kukul (1,539m). You are now on the ridge of the Chornohora and the border of the Carpathian National Nature Park. Take the right-hand trail for 5km; the path descends gently and slowly climbs back upwards towards the peak of Velyka Kozneska (1,571m). Spend the night nearby: there is an established campsite about 800m to the right

Day 2 (*7km; about 4 hours' walking*) Get back on the trail (you should pass the first old Polish border post) and ascend 2km to Mount Hoverla. After taking the requisite snapshots and enjoying the sights, follow the mountain trail south along the eastern ridge to the next three peaks, Breskul, Pozhyzhevska and Dantsyzh. Continue on to Turkul (5km from Hoverla) and on to Lake Nesamovyte. Stay the night here.

Day 3 (*14km; 8 hours' walking*) Continue south passing Rebra's summit and Lake Brebeneskul, then pass the peaks of Brebeneskul, Menchul and Dzembronya and on to the observatory at Pip Ivan. Descend on the western path into the valley. Camp in the glade at the base of Pip Ivan.

Day 4 (*13km to Luhy; 7 hours' walking*) Follow the path along the stream (Velyky Baltsatul) until the bridge at the confluence with the Bila Tysa, then take the road back to Luhy. Continue to Rakhiv by bus or on foot.

On Day 3 there is the option of turning off at Turkul: the right-hand trail will bring you back to Zaroslyak and Vorokhta; the left-hand trail will take you to the villages of Hoverla and Rakhiv.

From Vorokhta to Verkhovyna A lower path that skirts the mountains and then turns back into a cute rural area.

Day 1 (*from Zaroslyak: 10km, about 6 hours*) Journey from Vorokhta to Zaroslyak on foot or by bus, then take the southern path (by the chapel) up to the botanical research station and on to the eastern slope of the mountains. Follow it along the lower sides of Pozhyzhevska and Dantsyzh until Lake Nesamovyte. Take the southern path 1km, until border post No 30, turn left and descend to the next peak, Mount Shpytsy. Follow the trail east to the campsite.

Day 2 (*15km; about 7 hours*) Take the trail across the stream, to the bigger stream into the picturesque valley and village of Bystrets (7km). From here it is another 8km into Verkhovyna.

From Yaremche to Verkhovyna The proven hiker's route: a week of hearty hiking and mixed scenery in the eastern Gorgany and Chornohora.

Day 1 (*9km; about 5 hours*) Take the southern trail from Yaremche to Mount Yavirnyk, then head west/southwest to the camp at the base of Synyak.

Day 2 (*12km; about 6 hours' walking*) Climb to the top of Synyak, then head southeast to Khomyak's peak. Descend to the small road by the stream, turn left and walk to the village of Polyanytsya. Take the southern trail towards the village of Yablunytsya passing Hotel Berkut (✆ 0343 436 230). Stay in the hotel or camp at the site nearby.

Day 3 (*14km; 7 hours' walking*) Hike from Berkut to Mount Kukul; camp at the base.

Day 4 (*10km; 6 hours' walking*) Kukul to Hoverla; descend on the main trail and camp near or at Zaroslyak.

Day 5 (*12km; 6 hours' walking*) Hike from Zaroslyak to Mount Brebenskul; descend on the left for 3km to camp.

Day 6 (*14km; over 6 hours*) Circle back up to the ridge trail and on to Pip Ivan, then back and east towards Smotrych; 2km west of the peak of Smotrych in the clearing is a campsite.

Day 7 (*14km; 6 hours*) Hike from Smotrych to Dzembronya and back to Verkhovyna.

YASINYA ЯСІНЯ

Tiny Yasinya is a treasure of bucolic proportions, comprising traditional wooden architecture and hearty Hutsul peasants, and surrounded by a very beautiful spread of mountains, including the 'back' view of Hoverla. Yasinya offers the same delights as any other Carpathian town, including hiking, swimming, horseriding and fishing, but it also has a deeper poetry that's all its own.

Getting there is easiest by train from Ivano-Frankivsk to Rakhiv (2 daily, 3½ hours), although the trains really creep through the curving valleys. At night, the trains tend to arrive at odd hours and barely make a whistle stop. Regular buses connect to Rakhiv, Vorokhta, Yaremche and beyond; the bus stop is right in the middle of the town, consisting of two wooden benches and several goats. The Soviet ski holiday once made this town quite fashionable, but new tourist amenities are scarce. **U Stepana** is really just Stepan's house (*Kievska 9; 0313 242 099*). He has several clean rooms and sturdy beds costing US$15 per person; the **Zelinska** couple also run a small guesthouse in the village (*Vyzvolennya 243;* ✆ *0313 243 186*). For more information, contact the Proponue Tourist Agency (*Yasinya; Hrushevskovo 8/2;* ✆ *0343 242 428*).

WALKS FROM YASINYA The trail up to the mountains runs south from the nearby village of Lazeschyna. Follow the road by the bubbling River Lazivschyna for about 8km to the mountain base of Kozmeschyk (offering cheap beds in season). The path diverges into three here: the central path goes directly south and then rises up the northwest ridge to the summit of Mount Hoverla. The hike is only 7km but is relatively steep, with a gradual 1,000m climb; the small cluster of huts is the halfway mark. The left-hand trail is a low, forested walk that circumvents the base of Hoverla and ends in Zaroslyak (6.5km), with the option of two intersecting trails that also go up to Hoverla's summit from the northeast. The semi-paved road on the left from the bridge is a mountain path from Kozmeschyk to **Mount Petros** (2,020m). The walk is around 7km, first following a low valley, then winding back and forth before turning off the road and climbing straight up the eastern face of Petros (a 600m climb over 1km). A direct path between Mount Petros and Mount Hoverla completes the triangle from Yasinya and makes for a very tame two- or three-day walk:

Day 1 (*14km; 6 hours*) Walk from Yasinya/Lazeschyna following the river to Kozmeschyk; take the central path towards Mount Hoverla, passing through the low mountain meadows and into a forest of pine scrub. Set up camp in the clearing by the huts.

Day 2 (*10km; 6–7 hours*) Follow the trail almost due south for nearly 2km up to little Hoverla (1,850m), then 1km more over high rocks and shrubbery to the summit of Mount Hoverla. Backtrack past little Hoverla and then take the western trail towards Mount Petros. The path meets up with a mountain road and passes a spring. Set up camp at the base of Petros.

Day 3 (*12km; 6 hours*) Climb up to the summit of Mount Petros and get a nice view of eastern Transcarpathia: Rakhiv to the southwest and Yasinya to the north. Go back down the same way you came up but take a left on the mountain road and descend north along the winding back road to Kozmeschyk and Lazeschyna.

RAKHIV РАХІВ

The lucky few make it as far as Rakhiv, and many are surprised to find that this is not the kind of backwoods Transcarpathian village they were hoping for, but in fact a bustling little city. Packed along the banks of the roaring Tysa River, Rakhiv is first and foremost a market town where Transcarpathia's odd mix of mountain people come to swap goods and gossip. The languages heard on the street represent a town that's always been on someone else's border. Hungarians, old Ruthenians (or Rusyns) and Romanians predominate – add the local Gypsies (Roma) and things get colourful. Here in Rakhiv, some of the oldest traditions are still followed without much thought. If you are the kind of traveller that likes to sit back and watch the show played out on the street, come to Rakhiv.

Rakhiv marks the end of the Carpathian railroad into Transcarpathia, and you can feel the marked difference to the villages on the northern side of the mountain pass. The surrounding mountain areas have a good reputation for abundant wildlife and healthy air. This is also the headquarters of the Carpathian Biosphere Reserve, and an alternative starting point from which to hike Mount Hoverla. From Rakhiv, there are buses to the villages of Luhy and Hoverla (1 hour) where trails to **Mount Turkul** and **Pip Ivan** begin or end. Hikers wanting the more 'green' experience should start their trek from Rakhiv and choose from a number of longer paths into the Chornohora. For more information, contact **Village Rural Tourism** (*Rakhiv; Shevchenko 8;* \ *0313 221 292;* e *card@rakhiv.ukrtel.net; www.rakhiv.com.ua*).

GETTING THERE AND AWAY Three daily trains come to Rakhiv from Ivano-Frankivsk (5 hours), Lviv (9 hours) and Chernivtsi (8 hours); regular buses go to Uzhgorod, Ivano-Frankivsk and Kolomiya about twice a day. Flagging down the smaller *marshrutka* can get you to the next village and beyond.

WHERE TO STAY AND EAT

Hotel Europa Mira 42; \ 0313 221 345; f 0313 222 063; e admin@hotel-europa.com.ua; www.hotel-europa.com.ua. The latest and greatest hotel here. A very friendly and hospitable bunch run this local tour base, with access to ski lifts, and plenty of interesting hikes throughout the Chornohora. Rooms have been refurbished and all have private bathrooms with hot water. They also have a good restaurant and in-house tour agency. *Dbl 'luxury' suites US$60, smaller rooms from US$30.*

Tysa Ivana Franko 1; \ 0313 222 690; f 0313 221 162. Another popular resort in Rakhiv. Occupying an old Soviet-style chalet, the hotel complex is right in the city and offers Soviet-style holidays with a tendency towards rigid schedules and strong group dynamics. That said, you are free to participate or not. Rooms are very basic, but there's always hot water and prices are less than US$10 pp. Of the many tours they offer, one may visit the Centre of Europe, the local Museum of Mountain Ecology, or go with a guide to the top of Hoverla.

✗ **Stare Misto** Khmelnytskovo 1; no phone. Rakhiv's most exciting (although probably not best) restaurant. Imagine a dark and smoky café packed with real-live Hutsuls and Gypsies, all within a stone's throw of the Romanian border. The food is palatably Ukrainian. *Mains from US$1; open 08.00–22.00.*

THE CARPATHIAN BIOSPHERE RESERVE

As part of the UNESCO World Biosphere Project, this area falls under a different jurisdiction from most Ukrainian parks, but like most Ukrainian national parks, the territory is divided into six detached 'massifs', none of which are very close to one another. The largest section is adjacent to the Carpathian National Nature Park and protects the western slopes of Mount Hoverla and Mount Turkul. The collective was formed specifically to preserve Ukraine's threatened mountain habitats, and a large number of wild mammals live among these massifs. Attempts to develop ecotourism in the area will require a more active outside interest. For more detailed information, contact the reserve office in Rakhiv (*Krasne Pleso 77;* ✆ *03132 221 93;* e *cbr@rakhiv.ukrtel.net*).

VERKHOVYNA ВЕРХОВИНА

As a central hearth to the most rural mountain villages, Verkhovyna is a collage of old-time Carpathian imagery that, depending on your view, has either been well preserved or completely forgotten. This is what most tourists were hoping to see in Ukraine all along. Stretched out along the Black Cheremosh River the town

---

THE CENTRE OF EUROPE

Ever since Europe mattered to people, people have been trying to find its very centre. Much like defining those common 'European' values that will naturally unify the continent, the quest is ongoing, its target elusive. After having travelled vast distances across Europe and then crossing the rugged Carpathians to get to Rakhiv, you should breathe easier knowing that you have nearly arrived at the very geographical centre of Europe. Performing their duty to the Hapsburgs, a team of Austro-Hungarian geographers thus concluded in 1887: this otherwise unremarkable point on the banks of the Tysa River is, in fact, the centre of the whole continent. The Austro-Hungarians were disappointed that the centre of Europe was so far east, and not closer to Vienna. Shortly after erecting a pillar to mark the spot, the territory was lost to the empire. Long forgotten in the Soviet era, it was only after independence that someone brushed away the dirt and actually translated the Latin inscription on the single pillar monument. Ukrainians were elated and now visitors to Rakhiv are all taken down to the monument for a picture with one foot set upon Europe's centre. If you dare to follow tradition, be aware that the practice is highly controversial, as presently, no fewer than five different cities in five different countries also claim to be the geographical 'centre of Europe'. Apparently, having the centre of Europe in one's country justifies a wide range of political options, including accession to Europe (the Nazis claimed that Dresden was the actual centre of Europe). No matter that Lithuania now runs a theme park by that name, and that the Germans have recently re-issued their claim to the European Parliament – the Ukrainians have crowned themselves to be the centre and insist it is so. To visit the spot, just tell any bus driver or taxi driver to take you 'to the centre of Europe' and they will drive you 15 km south of Rakhiv to a speck of a village called Dilove. Standing at the monument today, one is quite literally a stone's throw from Romania (depending on the size of the stone, of course). While Romania is now an actual member of the European Union, the centre of Europe lies on the other side of a muddy riverbank where most homes lack plumbing and woolly sheep graze behind splint wood fences. There's a perfect Ukrainian expression for it all: *irônia*.

branches out into literally hundreds of dirt roads, paths and minuscule villages that extend from the town, dividing the pastures and forests. The mountain town is a good point from which to hike the lower Chornohora (Pip Ivan and Smotrych) and to head off on some long and rewarding walks across the most idyllic region of the Carpathian countryside. Although not inside the boundaries of the national park, Verkhovyna is the transfer point between buses and taxis to and from Yaremche and Ivano-Frankivsk with Kosiv and Kolomiya. Eight buses go to and from Yaremche every day (1½ hours) as well as Kosiv (1 hour). There is no rail link to Verkhovyna though.

WHERE TO STAY AND EAT As part of the Rural Green Tourism programme, Verkhovyna offers a prized opportunity to stay with locals. All have hot water and take cash only.

Nad Cheremosh Popovicha 15; ✆ 0343 222 270. Beautiful 2-storey cabin in the middle of a gorgeous mountain meadow. The accommodation is comfortable and inexpensive, and the hosts are real live Hutsuls who cook and serve great Hutsul cuisine. *US$15–20 pp.*

U Hanusy Dovbusha 13; ✆ 0343 222 579. Hostel accommodation.. Good for hikers beginning or ending a long walk, and a lot of fun during holidays. *Under US$10.*

Usadba Spaskykh Dovbusha 31; ✆ 0343 225 248. Family cottages. They also offer many services, such as pick-up from Ivano-Frankivsk. Good with groups and families. *Under US$10.*

Verkhovyna Popovycha 9; ✆ 0343 221 571. Soviet resort-type accommodation. *US$20/night.*

WALKS FROM VERKHOVYNA To head into the Chornohora, walk 9km southwest of Verkhovyna to the scattered village of Dzembronya (the road will follow the Black Cheremosh River; take a left at the Dzembronya tributary). Paths to the mountains also pass from Verkhovyna through Bystrets.

A circular hike

Day 1 (*12km; 6 hours*) Verkhovyna to Dzembronya; follow the trail towards Smotrych for 3km to the camp.

Day 2 (*14km; 7 hours*) Climb to the top of Smotrych, then continue on to the highest ridge of mountains. Turn right and climb Pip Ivan. Backtrack north, then proceed to Menchul, descending on the right for 3km to the camp.

Day 3 (*15km; 7 hours' walking*) Follow the trail back through Bystrets and on to Verkhovyna.

Verkhovyna to Kolomiya A less travelled, but highly refreshing walk over hills, passing virgin forest and rural homesteads.

Day 1 (*10km; around 5 hours' walking*) The path heads north from the centre of Verkhovyna past the first peak, Mount Hrybkova, and on to Mount Bila Kobyla (1,472m). Continue around the pyramid-shaped Mount Haboryankska (1,445m). Camp at the base.

Day 2 (*11km to Kosmach; about 5 hours' walking*) Follow the trail north all the way to the town of Kosmach. The trail descends slowly and cuts through some lovely forest for the first half, then enters an extended clearing. The minute wooden Paraskivska Church in Kosmach was built in 1718. From here it is a 1½-hour bus ride to Kolomiya. (There are also buses from Kosmach to Kosiv; 1 hour.)

KOSIV КОСІВ

The famous Kosiv bazaar has put this tourist town on the map for quite some time. It's built along the tumbling Rybnytsya River at the base of the Carpathian foothills. The locals make a living by selling Hutsul wood crafts and wool products to unsuspecting visitors. Before buying, compare the trinkets with the real thing in the **Museum of Hutsulschyna Folk Craft** (*Nezalezhnosti 101; open 10.00–18.00*); a super-decorated log hut houses the collection. The central pension-style hotel, **Karpatsky Zori** (*Nad Hukhom 15;* ↘ *0347 821 693*) has rooms for under US$45. The town is also part of the rural homestay programme, so it is easy to find a home nearby. Multiple buses travel to and from Ivano-Frankivsk (5 hours) and Kolomiya (1½ hours); an overnight bus travels between Kiev's main bus station and Kosiv every night via Chernivtsi (13 hours).

SHESHORY ШЕШОРИ

Sheshory is yet another small Hutsul village built on the Pistynka River – visitors will enjoy themselves wading in the many pools and waterfalls that feature throughout the village. Getting there is an easy 30-minute taxi or *marshrutka* ride from Kosiv and a nice diversion from the usual tourist crowds. Sheshory is also home to the annual Sheshory Ukrainian music festival, which is a lot of fun, if slightly crazy and chaotic (*www.sheshory.org*). There are plenty of opportunities for accommodation in nearby towns. In Sheshory proper, try **Sikitura** (↘ *0343 321 824;* f *0343 322 928;* e *sheshory@nato.ko.if.ua; www.karpaty-uriks.com.ua*). Built above the Pistinka stream, the cottage offers a pleasant mountain getaway. A double with queen-size bed (or a twin) is US$35. Singles are US$20 per person.

KOLOMIYA КОЛОМИЯ

Pretty little Kolomiya lies along the well-trotted tourist trail between the Chornohora range and Chernivtsi and is the place where many tour buses stop for a convenient half-day display of Hutsul life. The small town is nestled on the sloping plain beneath the distant but still visible mountains, the very special region of Ukraine known as Pokuttia. As Carpathian towns go, Kolomiya is unique on many counts, beginning with the delightful pastel colour-scheme adopted by nearly every house. The bright display leads you right to Kolomiya's real pride and joy: the museum of brightly coloured Easter eggs built in the shape of a brightly coloured Easter egg. The **Pysanky Museum** (*Chornovola 27B;* ↘ *0343 327 891; open 10.00–18.00, closed Mon; entrance 5UAH; tours for 10UAH*) is a monument to the most Ukrainian of Ukrainian crafts: the intricate, layered colouring of blown-out eggshells. Pysanky designs are drawn with melted wax, and then dyed in different colours for each design (usually red, yellow, orange, brown and black). Every region in Ukraine has its own specific colours and patterns and the museum displays them all, as well as some talented submissions from the Ukrainian diaspora in Canada. You may think that a pink egg-shaped museum filled with over 10,000 eggs sounds wacky, and you're right, it is. But I know of no other museum in Ukraine that can express the diversity of Ukrainian culture and art, as well as its most universal craft. Plus, the town is fairly down to earth and fun in spite of its quirky tourist attraction. A more serious (and perhaps more boring) collection of traditional Hutsul home craft is displayed in the **Museum of Hutsul Folk Art** (*Teatralna 25; open 10.00–18.00, closed Mon; entrance 2UAH*). Decorated stove tiles, hand-embroidered national dress, ornate wooden axes, rugs and wooden dishes exhibit the unique style of Ukraine's Hutsuls. Also, be sure not to miss the wooden **Church of the Annunciation**, which dates from the end of the 16th century and is said to be the very best example of Hutsul wooden architecture still standing.

GETTING THERE AND AWAY Kolomiya is on the main railroad between Chernivtsi and the west; the station is on the north side of town on Krypyakevycha. Daily trains service Ivano-Frankivsk (4 times a day, 2 hours), Uzhgorod, Chernivtsi (over 2 hours) and Lviv (6 hours), and there are overnight connections to Odessa and Kharkiv every other day. Kolomiya's excellent connections make it a good alternative base from which to venture into the Carpathians via Kosiv. The bus station is a ten-minute walk from the town centre at the end of Hrushevskovo and this is the more convenient way to zip quickly between the smaller towns. Buses make constant trips to Chernivtsi for around US$3 (2 hours), Ivano-Frankivsk (1 hour), Ternopil and Kamyanets-Podilsky. *Marshrutka* also make frequent runs to Yaremche, Kosiv and Verkhovyna. As always, from Kolomiya there is a daily bus to practically anywhere in the Carpathians; it is simply a matter of deciding if that is the best option. A taxi to Ivano-Frankivsk should cost US$15 maximum.

WHERE TO STAY For such a small place, Kolomiya is one of the most hospitable towns in the Carpathians, and that's saying something.

Hotel Pysanky Chornovola 41; 0343 320 356; f 0343 320 204; e hotel@ko.if.ua. Directly across from the museum is this aptly named hotel. The rooms are new, light and clean, with continuous hot water (showers) and top of the line service. As the hotel is only a 1hr drive from Bukovel, they offer special deals for skiers. Credit cards accepted. Prices begin at US$20 for a sgl, and US$40 for a 'luxury' dbl room with sturdy dbl beds.

Hotel Kolomiya Chornovola 26; 0343 333 905; f 0343 325 733; e hotel_kolomiya@mail.ru; www.kolomiya.com.ua. Just across the street, you'll find this brand-new and forward-thinking hotel; every room is clean and spacious and each has its own big bathroom. What's more, the staff speak English and they cater especially to the needs of families with children. B/fast inc, credit cards accepted. *Largest and most beautiful rooms US$85, slightly smaller rooms US$70, a standard US$30, which is a great deal. They also have dormitory-style accommodation for US$15 pp.*

On the Corner Hetmanska 47a; 0343 327 437. Another option is this cosy B&B; cash only. *US$18/night pp.*

WHERE TO EAT Hotel Kolomiya and Pysanky both serve great meals in their cafés. There are also many small cafés and bakeries along the main street.

✘ **Zgarda** Vidrozhennya 23; ✆ 0343 332 971.
Kolomiya's most popular restaurant: dark wood
furniture, candlelight, and truly traditional Ukrainian
food with a penchant for roast chicken. *Mains from
US$4; open 11.00–23.00.*

✘ **Hal-Prut** Chornovola 43; no phone. The restaurant
next door to Hotel Pysanky, serving 'high' Ukrainian
food. *Mains from US$5; open 10.00–23.00.*
✘ **Karpaty** Teatralna 15; no phone. Carpathian
dishes made for the tourist palate. *Mains from
US$2; open 11.00–22.00.*

THE GORGANY RANGE ГОРГАНИ

For all those travellers who feel they have yet to see the 'wild' part of the
Carpathians, the Gorgany range is a place of refuge and complete peace. Far from
the paved mountain trails and garish tourist markets (and far from everything
else), the Gorgany is Ukraine's most remote area. They are called the 'Gorgons'
for the fluorescent yellow-green lichens that grow on the rocky scree on the
highest parts of these mountains. Unscathed forests cloak the slopes with
hundred-foot pine trees where an active birdlife makes the only noise around.
The eastern Gorgany are more accessible to hikers from Yaremche and include
the angular peaks of **Mount Khomyak** (1,544m), **Mount Synyak** (1,664m),
Mount Gorgan (1,595m) and **Dovbushanka** (1,757m). The central Gorgany
are more remote and present splendid views of seemingly never-ending
mountains. The main peaks include **Mount Grofa** (1,752m), **Mount Popadya**
(1,740m), **Mount Igrovets** (1,804m) and the highest, **Mount Syvulya**
(1,818m). Ukrainian partisans fought on these very mountains and the summits
of Popadya and Syvulya are still marked by rocky trenches used in the eastern
front during World War I. Through this central valley flows the River Limnytsya
– a rare and unspoiled waterway that holds the unofficial title as Europe's
cleanest river (a taste of the water is convincing).

Access to the central Gorgany is through **Osmoloda**, a spread of houses over
10km. Osmoloda's name comes from an old Hutsul folk tale. An evil dragon
living in the Gorgany looked down in the valley at a young couple about to be
married. Jealous, he stole away the maiden and watched the heartbroken young
man searching for his *moloda* (betrothed). When he asked the dragon where she
was, the dragon turned her into a rock and said *Os* ('There!'). **Mount Moloda**
(1,723m) is the drooping peak directly east from Osmoloda. The dirt path into
the valley and up to the mountains starts after the entrance sign with the deer
on it.

GETTING THERE AND AWAY Getting to Osmoloda is part of the adventure; most
Ukrainians have never heard of the village. It is best to take a bus from Lviv or
Ivano-Frankivsk to Dolyna (the bus station is next to the bustling market). From
Dolyna there are rare but direct buses and taxis to the village of Osmoloda via
Yasen, along the Limnytsya River. The journey from Dolyna takes around two
hours. If you are going on a long hike with a fair amount of equipment, arranging
a car and driver from a larger city may be the best option.

WALKS IN THE GORGANY RANGE The best walks leave from Osmoloda, but going
into the eastern Gorgany is easier from Tatariv. Ambitious hikers can connect the
two and walk the entire range from one end to another over a week through the
village of Bystrytsya.

Three peaks A remote hike through the thickest of woods, with steep rises and
falls and some incredible vistas.

Day 1 (*11km; 5 hours*) From Osmoloda, take the western trail for 2km. Cross the river at the bridge and follow the trail on the right side of the stream into the forest and up into the hills. As the incline begins to level out at the ridge, there is a dingy mountain hut and campsite.

Day 2 Hike up the steep right-hand slope to the top of Grofa. From the top you can see through the twin peaks of Parenky. Go back down to the ridge and hike across towards the top of Parenky (1,737m). From here it is another 5km to the top of Popadya, marked by the old Polish border post from 1923. Return back to the wooded ridge that drops steeply; there is a camp at the top.

Day 3 (*17km; about 8 hours' walking*) A long day of getting back to Osmoloda. Descend from the camp and follow the wooded hillside for much of the way. About a third of the way you cross over the top of a small waterfall; loop around and follow the northern shore of the stream until it joins with the River Limnytsia and goes back to Osmoloda.

Syvulya and Igrovets Two mountains in two days.

Day 1 (*13km; about 6 hours' walking*) Walk south from Osmoloda along the eastern riverbank for 7km; take a left on the trail that follows the stream Bystryk up to the underside of Syvulya where there is a hut and campsite.

Day 2 (*15km; 7 hours' walking*) Climb to the top of Syvulya, then take the northern trail for 6km to the summit of Igrovets. The path then descends towards the northwest back down through the forest to the River Limnytsya. It is 2km to Osmoloda.

The Eastern Gorgany Long but fulfilling days.

Day trip to Mount Khomyak (*16km; about 7 hours*) From the train station at Tatariv, take the fork in the road towards Yablunytsya. Continue for 4km until a bridge turns the road to a hard left – there is a petrol station on the right. Do not cross the bridge, but continue on the right-hand path along the stream for 1km more. Before the next stream there should be a perpendicular trail on the right. Ascend here, eventually crossing over to the left-hand side and into a high mountain glade. Take this trail on the left-hand side up to Khomyak's summit. From the peak, there is a straight view of the three other peaks: Synyak, Gorgan and Dovbushanka. Continue along the opposite ridge towards Synyak, but then drop down on the right-hand trail which goes back to the Zhenets River and on to the main road where there is a bus stop to Tatariv.

To Synyak and Gorgon (*Add 7km one way from Khomyak; 3 hours*) Follow the same trail as to Khomyak, but continue on the ridge. You will have to split the trip into at least two days. There are campsites at the northern and western bases of Synyak.

To Dovbushanka (*The trail from Dovbushanka to Syvulya takes 2 days with a stop in or near the village of Bystrytsya*) The main trail is 21km from Yaremche, some of which is on uneventful road following the River Zhonka. It is possible to connect to the peak from Synyak by taking the trail that curves along the mountain ridge all the way around the valley and up the west side of Dovbushanka, a 14km hike from Synyak and an all-day feat.

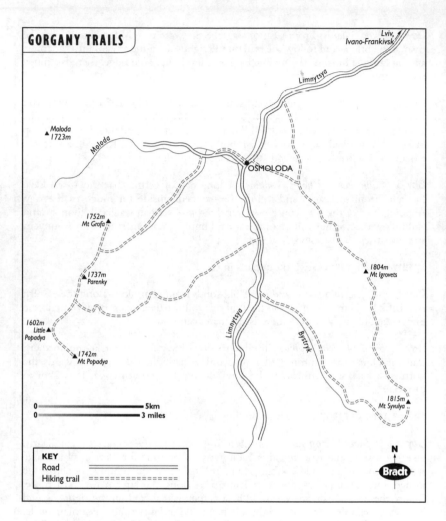

BUKOVINA БУКОВИНА

Charming and eccentric, tiny Bukovina fills the sliver of land between the Prut and Dnister rivers beneath the shadow of next door Moldova and Romania. The fortunate few who venture forth will be amazed at the quiet, enchanted nature of the countryside, dotted with old-fashioned windmills and wooden huts. Life passes slowly in this strange corner of Ukraine. Traffic is happy to wait for the conversations of old men to finish and there are more horses, goats, chickens and cows than there are people. Like most of Ukraine, giant fields surround the view, but here they seem to roll away from the road in deep waves, following the rhythm of the nearby mountains. The one exception to Bukovina's hand-to-mouth farm life is the regional capital Chernivtsi, which holds on fervently to its peculiar personality.

The territory's oldest castles were built by Kievan Rus in the 9th and 10th centuries, but after the Mongol invasions the area was incorporated into Moldovia – an event that has defined this land ever since. The Turks conquered in 1504 after which the region was ruled for nearly 300 years by the Ottoman Empire – the

Eastern flair of Khotin Castle dates back to this period. An Austrian victory in 1774 brought the area under the jurisdiction of Galicia and it was made a Hapsburg duchy in 1849, followed by a period revered as the height of Bukovinian culture and advancement. The shifting 20th century caused widespread emigration of Ruthenians and Jews, and it is these groups and their descendants who have mentally kept Bukovina on the map. World War I brought the eastern front right into Bukovina and in 1919 the 'Treaty of St Germain granted the territory to Romania. The inter-war period was marked by the dominant influence of Romanian language and culture, the remnants of which are still in place today. Northern Bukovina was then invaded by Soviet troops in 1940, but went back to the Romanians during the German occupation of 1941. In 1947 Stalin made a secret agreement, moving Bukovina into Soviet borders under the Ukrainian SSR and declaring Chernivtsi the capital. Today, Romania's northern region is still called 'Bucovina' and most natives regard the entire area as a single region divided by a false border. On the other hand, Kiev looks proudly upon Ukraine's youngest province as the birthplace of several national heroes and a home to Ukrainian patriotism. The reality is that Bukovina is still an odd mix of people and cultures that have more or less gotten along despite the constant shift of power. Variety is the region's most attractive feature, after the landscapes.

CHERNIVTSI ЧЕРНІВЦІ You will know when you have met someone from Chernivtsi because they will make sure to tell you right away – the capital and only real city of Bukovina deserves to be proud of its intricate and faded buildings and its diverse citizenship. Even after the direst economic crises, Chernivtsi has not lost the dignity of its past empire and few urban spaces in modern Ukraine offer such a remarkable visit. Tour firms may tout the town as a 'little Paris' but this is a weak comparison, if not utterly far-fetched. Chernivtsi is simply beautiful and mysterious, with lots of narrow streets and hidden views, and some incredible architectural gems.

The city began as a Galician fortress on the Prut River, soon destroyed by the Mongol invasions. Some say the black oak timber influenced the town's name, others say it describes the black soil of Bukovina. However, in old Ukrainian, *Chern-ovtsy* means 'black sheep' – an apt connotation for this city, whether or not the pun was intended. Among the family of Ukrainian cities, Chernivtsi still stands out as a bit of an odd place (seeing is believing). The city's Moldavian medieval existence was based in steady trade, a feature that attracted consistent ransacking from both friends and enemies and prevented any permanent structures. After gaining control in 1774, the Austrians scheduled Chernivtsi for a makeover. What had been a haphazard gathering of thatched cabins was quickly transformed into an ordered radius of streets lined with exquisite and colourful buildings, including a green opera house, stately pink and blue townhouses, and the magnificent brick residence of the Orthodox Metropolitans (the second highest-ranking officials in the Orthodox Church). Austrian rule over 'Czernowitz' lasted 250 years during which time an extremely cosmopolitan population developed. The city ranked third in size for the empire – after Vienna and Prague – and an independent stock exchange made many inhabitants wealthy. Granted its own university, Chernivtsi offered a home to the rising Ukrainian intellectualism of the late 19th century (this is the 'home' of the present Ukrainian national anthem). The movement suffered during World War I and was all but stamped out during Romania's control of 'Cernauti' from 1918 to 1940, followed by annexation to the Soviet Union. Due to its European past, Russian 'Chernovtsy' was far more advanced than the other Soviet cities in terms of technology (and ideas), and in a way the city was never designated a permanent role in communist society. During the lean years of post-Soviet collapse, Chernivtsi secured its reputation in free trade by starting the largest outdoor market in Ukraine, still booming today. It is no surprise that Chernivtsi was the first city in Ukraine to tear down its statue of Lenin on the main square and replace it with a sizeable effigy of Shevchenko.

Visiting Chernivtsi today is a purposeful venture into the unique persona of Bukovina and western Ukraine. The city still claims almost 100 nationalities as its own; Russians, Jews, Poles and Romanians are the most sizeable and influential minorities. General sightseeing is anything but average and lovers of art and architecture will find contentment in the many churches and museums. Conveniently situated on the route between the Carpathian Mountains and the Black Sea, Chernivtsi makes a gratifying stopover or allows an alternative connection to the mountains from Kiev. If you are entering or leaving the country from the south, the city is the most significant transfer point between Ukraine and Romania.

Getting there and away One flight per day connects Chernivtsi to Kiev Zhulyany (weekdays only), and there are two flights a week to Athens, Greece. The airport is small and located in the far southeastern outskirts; a taxi into town costs around US$4. During summer, flights serve Kharkiv and Simferopol as well. Buy tickets at Kiy Avia (*Holovna 96;* ↘ *0372 570 838; www.kiyavia.com*).

Chernivtsi train station, a noteworthy monument to belle époque architecture, was built in 1908 and is located on the northern side of town on Gagarina. Two overnight trains connect with Kiev, one in the early evening and the other around 21.30. The earlier train is longer (around 15 hours) but gets to Kiev the following morning. Both Kiev–Chernivtsi trains stop in Kamyanets-Podilsky, making it an obvious attraction along the way. Chernivtsi is situated at an odd rail intersection though, increasing travel time to its closest cities. Ovenight trains go to and from Odessa (almost 21 hours) and Uzhgorod (15 hours) once a day. Twice a day there are trains to Ivano-Frankivsk (4 hours) and Kolomiya (2 hours). International train routes leave every day for Sofia (via Bucharest), Moscow (via Kiev) and Kishinev (Moldova). A lot of smaller trains enter Romania throughout the day, as the border is just 40km away.

Chernivtsi's central bus station at the south end of Holovna offers the most options for connecting locally with two daily buses to Kamyanets-Podilsky (2½ hours), three to Ivano-Frankivsk (4 hours), two to Lviv (8 hours), three to Khmelnytsky (6 hours) and two to Uzhgorod (12 hours). An overnight connection travels back and forth from Kiev (via Zhytomyr) and local *marshrutka* go to Kolomiya (1½ hours), Yaremche and Truskavets. Buses into Romania and Moldova are frequent; Kishinev is nine hours away, Bucharest a day and a half.

Getting around The No 5 trolleybus runs up and down Holovna and will take you to most places you want to go. Much of the centre is more accessible on foot rather than rumbling down on cobblestones, but the hotels and some attractions are quite far and will require a taxi. For some reason, the wily taxi drivers of Chernivtsi think they are worth more than any others in provincial Ukraine and often charge Kiev-like prices. Around town, don't agree to over US$3–4; and going out to the countryside will be around US$15. Don't be afraid to barter a little, it's the way in these parts.

Where to stay While Chernivtsi has definitely been discovered, the accommodation is still pretty fair. All three hotels have rooms that range from very good to very basic and all three accept payment in cash only.

Hotel Bukovina Holovna 141; ☎ 0372 585 625; e bc_buk@hotel.cv.ua; www.hotel.cv.ua. Chernivtsi's business set claim this as their very own chintzy hangout, not too far from the city centre. Your eyes can't miss the cheery flowerboxes hanging along the bright yellow building, while inside a steady renovation has transformed some of the rooms into comfortable and modern rooms, usually with their own showers. What the hotel lacks in class, the restaurant makes up for in amusement (b/fast is inc). The largest dining hall is a memorial to Hapsburg glory, while the backroom is a converted Bukovinian farmhouse, complete with costumed waiters and lifesize, papier-mâché oxen. The food is traditional and inexpensive. On the second floor, there is a walk-in tourist bureau with good connections for making arrangements and guided excursions around Chernivtsi; ☎ 0372 585 636. New rooms US$60–80, a range of zany suites US$150–300. One floor has cheap, non-refurbished rooms from US$15.

Hotel Kiev Holovna 46; ☎ 0372 522 483. Kiev has the best location in the city centre and is also the least expensive, if not slightly delapidated. Some of the grand past still clings to the dingy carpets but about half the rooms have been renovated to a very decent standard, and the hotel now features 24hr hot water. Nice, remodelled dbls US$35; sgls

US$20; more basic rooms of the Soviet variety US$12.

Hotel Cheremosh Komarova 13A; ☎ 0372 247 518; f 0372 585 588; e cheremosh@chv.ukrpack.net; www.cheremosh.chv.ukrpack.net. The hotel stands as a rare product of mid-1980s *perestroika* when a Hungarian–Soviet joint venture embarked on a tragically premature investment. The final product is the finest in communist construction and visitors may feel like they are on a cruise ship with the high atrium, all the in-house amenities and smiley staff. Unfortunately, the Soviet feeling still lingers – nothing has changed here in the past 20 years. Plus, the location is typical of Inturist hotels, meaning that it is totally inconvenient for getting around on foot, as the modern, high-rise hotel complex stands on the far southern edge of town. Besides the normal swimming pool, sauna and live shows, the hotel does dry cleaning and supports a strong and creative travel agency that designs personal excursions on a local and national level. A very large restaurant is divided into 3 separate rooms, each with its own décor, music and cuisine: European, Bukovinian and Hungarian. (The Bukovinian menu is convincing and authentic.) Sgls US$45; dbls US$70; spacious and modern suites US$95–115.

Where to eat A wide spectrum of restaurants and a choice of lively cafés mean people in Chernivtsi can enjoy a night out. Yet despite the urge for glamour, Chernivtsi still deals in cash only (after all, this is still Bukovina).

10

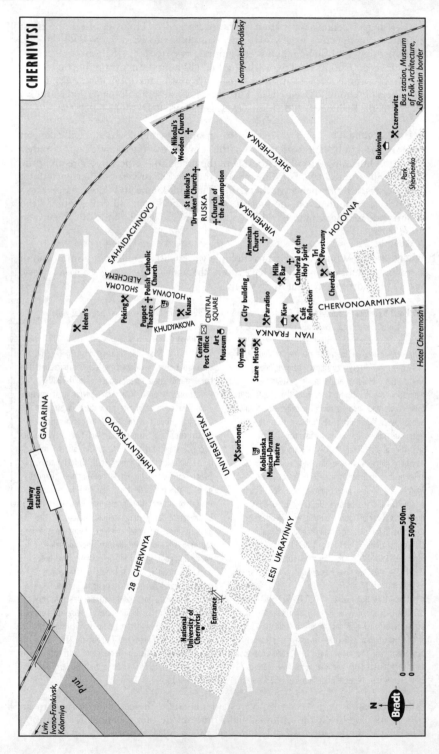

CHERNIVTSI

Lviv, Ivano-Frankivsk, Kolomiya

Prut

Railway station

GAGARINA

KHMELNYTSKOVO

28 CHERVNYA

National University of Chernivtsi

Entrance

UNIVERSITETSKA

LESI UKRAYINKY

Kamyanets-Podilsky

St Nikolai's Wooden Church

SAHAIDACHNOVO

SHOLOMA ALEICHEMA

Helen's ✗

Peking ✗

Puppet Theatre

Polish Catholic Church

HOLOVNA

Knaus ✗

KHUDYAKOVA

Central Post Office

Art Museum

Olymp ✗

Stare Misto ✗

Sorbonne ✗

Koblianska Musical-Drama Theatre

St Nikolai 'Drunken' Church

RUSKA

Church of the Assumption

Armenian Church

VIRMENSKA

City building

CENTRAL SQUARE

Paradiso ✗

Kiev ✗

IVAN FRANKA

Café Reflection ✗

Milk Bar ✗

Cathedral of the Holy Spirit

Tri Povstuny ✗

Cherdak ✗

CHERVONOARMIYSKA

SHEVCHENKO

HOLOVNA

Bukovina

Czernowitz ✗

Park Shevchenko

Bus station, Museum of Folk Architecture, Romanian border

Hotel Cheremosh

0   500m
0   500yds

N

Bradt

Restaurants

✗ **Peking** Sholoma Aleichema 1; ☎ 0372 512 147. The restaurant occupies the famous 'Ship' building (constructed to look like a naval craft) but features authentic Chinese cuisine served beneath red paper lanterns. *Mains from US$3; open 11.00–23.00.*

✗ **Café Reflection** Holovna 66; ☎ 0372 526 682. Upscale and European, this distinguished café is fast becoming a common expat hangout, featuring truly delicious Mediterranean, Italian and Lebanese cuisine. *Mains from US$7; open 09.00–23.00*

✗ **Cherdak (Attic)** Holovna 66 (2nd floor); ☎ 0372 556 006. Upstairs from Café Reflection, the 'Attic' is a more elegant and banquet-style restaurant, serving sumptuous meals and with the best wine list in the city. *Mains from US$10; open 11.00–23.00.*

✗ **Czernowitz** This restaurant is part of the Bukovina Hotel complex (see above) and is perceived to be the city's finest. Besides the super lavish fare, they serve a yummy version of *mamaliga*, the Bukovinian speciality consisting of a thick, savoury cornflour porridge, similar to Italian *polenta*.

✗ **Knaus** Khudyakova 4; ☎ 0372 510 255; e knaus@chv.ukrpack.net; www.knaus.com.ua. A little bit of Bavaria right in Bukovina: a lively ambience, real German food and an outdoor biergarten with waiters in *lederhosen*. The eating and drinking complex continues to expand and things stay rowdy all night long. *Mains from US$5; open 12.00–04.00.*

✗ **Olymp** Ivan Franka 1–3; ☎ 0372 542 979. A Greek restaurant by name and menu, but the Corinthian columns do little to hide the gangster touch. *Mains from US$5; open 11.00–23.00.*

✗ **Sorbonne** Universitetska 21A; ☎ 0342 578 987. Chernivtsi's schnazziest mafia restaurant complete with bowling, billiards, casino, and disco. There is some legitimate French cuisine on the menu, but most of the food is Russian. *Mains from US$12; open 12.00–02.00.*

✗ **Stare Misto** Ivan Franka 7. Old, Russian-style café with a pretty classic menu: borsch et al. *Mains from US$2; open 11.00–22.00.*

Cafés and bars

✗ **Helen's** Sahaidachnovo 2. This simple 'Christian bar' is universally known for some of the best cooking in Bukovina and is the right place to taste the real thing, especially *borsch*. The café also lacks the smoke and loud music that usually goes with the territory. *Open 09.00–22.00; closed Sun.*

✗ **Tri Povstuny** Holovna 63. Cafeteria-style Ukrainian food. *Mains from US$1; open 10.00–22.00.*

✗ **Paradiso** Ivan Franka 14. Italian pizza parlour. *Mains from US$5; open 10.00–23.00.*

▱ **Milk Bar** Holovna 53; ☎ 0342 524 113. No smoking and no alcohol, just pastries, milkshakes and pizza. *Mains from US$2; open 08.00–20.00.*

What to see and do

National University of Chernivtsi This fanciful brick complex should not be missed. Built between 1864 and 1882, the impressive chapel and halls were the official residence for the Orthodox Church leaders of Bukovina and Dalmatia, the two duchies in the Hapsburg Empire with strong Eastern rite populations. In this one structure, the Czech architect Josef Hlávka envisioned something remarkably different from his more classical buildings in Vienna, of which there are over 140. Working entirely with standard red bricks and brightly coloured tiles, his design blends elaborate geometric patterns with the traditional Byzantine styles of Orthodoxy into something that resembles a giant Lego castle with hundreds of playful chimneys and miniature turrets. The university was founded in 1875 making it one of Ukraine's oldest, though the school's headquarters was not moved to this location until after the Soviet occupation. Entering the chapel is a highlight of the visit, with its painted mosaics and lofty dome. Behind the main building is a nice garden of rare tree species tended by the university, including the squatty *platan* tree, endemic to Bukovina. For a guided tour (in English) of the church and gardens, go to the guardhouse at the main entrance gate (*at the end of Universytetska; open weekdays 10.00–17.00; US$4;* ☎ *0372 584 821*). On weekends, there are some organised tours.

Chernivetsky Regional Art Museum (*Central Square 10;* ☎ *0372 260 71; open 09.00–17.00; entrance 3UAH*) Chernivtsi's other true treasure is the stunning museum. Built in 1905, the glorious Art Nouveau façade with its tile mosaic inlay survives as a work of art in itself and was recently cleaned and restored to maximise its incredibly vibrant expression. It's amazing to find such a pure example of this art and time remaining in Europe today (sadly, much of the view is blocked by the town hall). The museum's interior reveals the same architectural wonderment, as well as some great exhibits, all labelled in English. Look for the woodcuts of Leon Kopelman, which portray the scenes and figures of Bukovinian Jewish life and legend; also, take note of Mikola Bylik's Soviet-era sculpture *Polit* (take-off). The third floor houses a broad collection of Bukovinian embroidery, as well as carpets, belts, vests, and other local craft.

Chernivtsi Museum of Folk Architecture (*Open 10.00–17.00, closed Mon; entrance 3UAH, guided tours 10UAH*) Resembles the outdoor museum villages in Kiev and Lviv but with a specific focus on preserving traditional Bukovinian houses and churches. To get there take the No 4 trolleybus to the end of the line, or even better, a taxi.

Kobylianska Muscial-Drama Theatre Housed in the green opera house on Ploscha Teatralna, the theatre is famed now for its first public performance of the Ukrainian national anthem, nearly one hundred years ago. Inexpensive tickets to very talented shows can be purchased on site, and the square out front is a busy centre for nightlife.

Puppet theatre (*Holovna 22*) The Chernivtsi Puppet Theatre is particularly well-known in Ukraine and is especially fun for children.

Churches The churches in Chernivtsi fortunately missed the wrath of the Russian Revolution and most have undergone recent renovation; a few merit closer investigation than a glance from the street. The **Cathedral of the Holy Spirit** was built in 1844 and stands today as a pale pink, Neoclassical cathedral topped with very Polish-looking cupolas. Austrian painters of the late 19th century painted the larger interior murals for which the church is known today. Chernivtsi boasts **two churches of St Nikolai**. The first (*Sahaidachnovo 89*) is an eight-sided log chapel built in 1607, with animal hair and hemp twine still wedged between the cracks to keep out the wind. This is one of the few original wood buildings in Chernivtsi and the city's oldest church. The other St Nikolai (*Ruska 35*) was built in the 1930s and boasts five bright blue domes with golden stars. The cathedral's twisted turrets create an optical illusion that has led to this being called the 'drunken church'. Another block down Ruska is the red-roofed Greek Catholic **Church of the Assumption**. The **Armenian church** (*Ukrayinska 30*) is another one of Hlávka's buildings, but was used as an organ hall throughout the Soviet years on the pretext that a suicide in the chapel made it unfit for worship. The Polish or **Roman Catholic church** (*Holovna 20*) is still a common gathering place for the local Polish community

If you are tired of looking at old churches and the crumbling beauty of the Hapsburg era, a more fresh and lively attraction is **Kalynivksy Market**, just a short trip outside the city. The expansive mile-wide outdoor shopping spread is a testament to the capitalist rudiments of human nature. After Moscow's economic collapse, Chernivtsi was left to fend for itself and would easily have gone the way of so many derelict Ukrainian towns if it had not been for some innovative locals who founded the grand-scale swap-meet in a farmer's field. Now much of Ukraine supplies its own bazaars with hard-to-get luxuries from Poland, Romania and Turkey, all exchanged in Chernivtsi's market. Here, anyone can buy anything,

Chernivtsi is Ukraine's main gateway to and from Romania, allowing travellers to go from one Bukovina into the next. If you're driving yourself, it's really quite simple – just take the E-85 south. If you want to get to the border on your own, there are regular *marshrutka* to the village of Porubne (45 minutes), from which it's less than 1km to the Siret/Porubne border post. Individuals are not allowed to cross by foot at this border, so if you want to be quick about it, take the daily bus that connects Chernivtsi to Suceava (3 hours). The border is actually marked by a swath of no-man's land that cuts through the soil of divided crop fields. About 2km into the Romanian side brings you to the village of Siret, from which there is regular transport to Suceava and Bucharest. Taking the train in or out of Romania is no problem – the entire ordeal takes less than an hour.

but the recent mood has become more pragmatic and sophisticated: fur coats, designer boots, high-tech kitchenware and *real* Barbie dolls. The change in goods does not detract from the chaos of over 50,000 daily visitors. (They're not kidding when they say they drove here from China, or Vietnam.) Kalynivsky is the easiest place to get to in Chernivtsi. Most *marshrutka* head to the *rynok* from all over town and the train station and a taxi costs US$1, or take the No 9 trolleybus to the end.

Outside Chernivtsi

Khotyn ХОТИН On the way to Kamyanets-Podilsky from Chernivtsi stands one of Ukraine's more famous castles, fortified by Moldavian Prince Stefan III in the 15th century and later occupied by the Ottoman Empire. The Moldavians rebelled against the Turks in 1621 and allied themselves to the Polish king, Sigismund III. Furious, the Turkish Sultan Osman II responded with an overwhelming attack that met its climax at Khotyn. As told, a quarter of a million Turkish troops charged Khotyn Castle on camels, mules and elephants during the famed Battle of Khotyn. The Polish prince, Sobieski, described the battle: 'More than 60 cannons were roaring without cease, the sky was burning, the air was darkened with smoke, and the ground trembled.' The Polish forces quashed the Turkish advance with a measly corps of 35,000 and today the Ukrainians claim it was the strength of 'their' fortress and the cunning command of the Cossack *hetman* Sahaidachny that granted the Poles a victory and sent the Turks packing all the way to Constantinople. In fact, the Turks conquered Khotyn in 1711 and the castle flip-flopped dozens of times between the Russians and Turks until 1812 when the Treaty of Bucharest secured its Russian ownership. Visitors can climb the highest towers and sturdy walls to enjoy the view of the Dnistr and the wide Podillyan plain. Almost every group tour in the region will stop at Khotyn, and each of Chernivtsi's hotels offers inexpensive day trips to the castle. On your own, Khotyn is a one-and-a-half-hour bus ride from Chernivtsi's bus station or one hour from Kamyanets-Podilsky.

Vyzhnytsya ВИЖНИЦЯ Bukovina's other town attracts nostalgic visitors seeking a glimpse of the poetic *shtetl* life in Yiddish folklore. Little imagination is needed to understand the past of this quaint and introspective village. However, modern-day Vyzhnytsya appeals less than the surrounding areas south of the Cheremosh River and in the nearby mountains. The bubbly streams, green walks and traditional Bukovinian farms led to the creation of **Vyzhnytsya National Park** in 1995. Still young and fragile, the protected areas are tough to get to on your own (*in Chernivtsi, try the tour agency **Navkolo Svitu** who offer some trips; Central Square 7/8;* ✆ *0372 585*

The Carpathians **BUKOVINA**

10

263; e ns@ns-tour.com.ua; www.ns-tour.com.ua). Over ten buses a day zip back and forth between Vyzhnytsya and the Chernivtsi bus station (2 hours) and offer a superb view of the 'real Bukovina'. An alternate itinerary is through Kosiv, just 15 minutes away by bus or taxi. The restaurant **Kolyba** in Vyzhnytsya is the regular touristy log-hut setting, similar to those seen throughout the Carpathians.

TRANSCARPATHIA ЗАКАРПАТТИЯ

Za-Karpattya translates from Ukrainian as 'Beyond the Carpathians', which it is, from Kiev's perspective. From Budapest, this is the borderland between the great Hungarian plain and the 'Russian Hills', an area that has constantly shifted ownership among history's more powerful players. It may very well be the most beautiful region of Ukraine, if not the most colourful. Purple mountains, green and yellow plains, and the spectacular red sunsets all warrant longing gazes, as do the lanky black storks and sensational wildflowers.

A visit to Transcarpathia also offers a distinct take on these mountains and its people, one that you won't get in southern Galicia or Bukovina. Culturally, the area is totally unique from the wider region and the many countries it borders. Purposefully left off the larger rail and road networks by the Soviets, Transcarpathia is too often dropped from itineraries through the west, usually because everyone simply passes through the regional capital on to the next place; or else they cross over to 'Ukraine' for a day before slipping back into Slovakia or Hungary. Although Uzhgorod remains forever the gateway from central Europe to Ukraine, the region deserves some deeper investigation than its largest city. Not long ago the towns of Mukachevo and Khust offered a picturesque 'European' tour to bemused masses of Soviet day trippers. Today, the really wild and wonderful landscapes stretch along the entire south side of the Carpathian range, just now entering a stage of discovery by foreign travellers and the locals themselves. In the far east of the region, Rakhiv and Yasinya are still known as Transcarpathia's mountain towns, but these are more accessible from (and closer to) Ivano-Frankivsk. The more remote spaces between the mountains and Uzhgorod are now open for exploration. A series of new national parks (the Carpathian Biosphere Reserve) and recent investment also mean there are countless fresh trails to be trodden through Transcarpathia.

After the Hungarians arrived in the 9th century, Transcarpathian history belonged to another country. The caprice of Hungarian nobles has granted the area a dark and mysterious past for which it is most proud. Under the Hapsburgs, it seemed that renewed treaties with the Austrians and consistent Ruthenian uprisings characterised the territory more than its natural treasures and the real Ruthenian traditions which set the region apart. World War I saw an end to Hapsburg rule, so that from 1919 Transcarpathian Rus fell under the jurisdiction of the fated inter-war Czechoslovak Republic. The confusion in Prague preceding Hitler's invasion allowed a brief taste of freedom when the independent Carpatho-Ukraine was established in 1938. For the non-Soviet Ukrainians of Romania and Polish Galicia, this was a vital step towards a joint Ukrainian state, but the thrill of self-government was ended with Adolf Hitler's support of the Hungarian invasion of Carpatho-Ukraine in the spring of 1939. The local Ukrainians were suspicious of the Red Army's 'liberation' of Transcarpathia and the subsequent 're-unification' to the Ukrainian SSR in 1945. However, as a late arrival on the Soviet scene, Transcarpathia has a completely different feel from the rest of the country. This is easily the least Slavic region of Ukraine, and many of the Ukrainian inhabitants can freely communicate in Hungarian, Slovakian or Russian, if not all three at the same time.

GETTING AROUND Moving about Transcarpathia is not easy. A lack of good roads has kept much of the region rural, remote, and natural, but also means that it takes less time to go to Kiev or Lviv than it does to get from Uzhogord to Rakhiv. Buses and *marshrutka* connect most towns and cities, but the trains are particularly long and slow. That's not much encouragement, but just be patient, and enjoy the view.

UZHGOROD УЖГОРОД Old Uzhgorod features all the ingredients of a romantic, central European city: narrow cobblestone streets, old stone bridges, Baroque cathedrals with bells that chime on the hour, and a crumbling castle on top of a barren hill. Those who know Hungary or the Czech Republic wonder what all the fuss is about, while those who know Ukraine find that Uzhgorod seems delightfully quaint and different in comparison with more 'Soviet' towns of the same size. As Transcarpathia's largest city and de facto 'capital', Uzhgorod has long served as the gateway between 'Europe' and the area now only described in euphemism: the Former Soviet Union, the Newly Independent States, the East, or the CIS. Having the EU right at one's doorstep keeps the town busy and fairly cosmopolitan, and ensures that this will become one of Ukraine's busiest entry and exit points. When eastern Europe went free market, Uzhgorod stepped to the head of the class and local *beezness* keeps a swanky attitude in the midst of the city's natural architectural charm – even the Soviet high-rises seem a bit more polished than normal. Walking around the town is a pleasure, especially along the *naberezhna*, or riverbank, and around the botanical gardens.

The town centres on the right bank of the winding Uzh ('Snake') River; 'gorod' is Slavic for 'city'. The *Gesta Hungarorum* ('Hungarian Chronicle') mentions the invasion of the Hungarian army into the city of Ung in 872, where the local Slavic prince was killed. Since then, the city has been known as Ongvar, Hungvar, Unguyvar and Ungvar – all references to the town's strong Magyar roots. Travellers doing a tour of Ukraine by land would do well to consider starting or ending their circuit in Uzhgorod and then returning home via Budapest, only seven hours away by train. Some excursions into rural Transcarpathia begin here, but the transport network means that Mukachevo and Rakhiv have better access to these southern mountains.

Getting there and away Catching a plane to and from Uzhgorod is easier than for most Ukrainian cities of this size and makes a lot more sense than travelling the huge distance overland to Kiev. Normally, at least one flight a day travels to either Kiev Zhulyany or Borispol (1½ hours) while links with other Ukrainian destinations vary; prices hover about US$65 for an advance purchase one way. The airport is at Sobranetska 145 but air tickets are best booked at the the Inturist agency at the Hotel Zakarpattya, or the Kiy Avia office in Uzhgorod (*Lva Tolstovo 33;* ☎ *0312 617 072*).

The train station is at Stantsiyna 9 at the south end of the town and not far away is the bus station at Stantsiyna 2. Four daily trains rumble back and forth between Kiev and Uzhgorod, always via Lviv, then through Chop or Mukachevo. Chop is only 30 minutes away by train, and the station then joins up with the Hungarian rail system. The rail journey to Kiev takes a gruelling 18 hours, and the slowest part is the last link to and from Lviv. Very slow trains also service Chernivtsi (14 hours), Vinnytsya (15 hours) and Kharkiv (30 hours) but Uzhgorod schedules frequently change. Travelling anywhere else in the Carpathians from Uzhgorod is best by motor transport; buses cross the mountains throughout the day to Ivano-Frankivsk (6 hours), Rakhiv (5 hours) and Chernivtsi (9 hours).

While the rest of Ukraine seems so far away, Uzhgorod is right next to door to Slovakia and Hungary. Regular trains service Budapest, Bratislva, Košice and Prague, and all the towns in between.

Where to stay

It's a pleasure to stay in Uzhgorod, where customer service is more of a way of life. All listed hotels take credit cards.

Hotel Uzhgorod Bohdana Khmelnytskovo Square 2; ☏ 0312 235 060; f 0312 612 070; e hotel@email.uz.ua. Right across the bridge from the central old city, this newly refurbished hotel features a sleek glass and steel exterior housing a range of rooms within, all with good value for money. The best suites are up on the 5th floor, true to international standards with nice comfortable furniture and modern bathrooms. Less expensive standard rooms are still of a higher standard than many rooms in other parts of Ukraine. An army of kindly multilingual staff is always on hand to help with anything, including pick-ups from either border. A luxurious b/fast buffet inc. *Sgls US$50; dbls US$75; elegant suites US$100; standards rooms US$20–40.*

Hotel Atlant Koryatovycha Square 27; ☏ 0312 614 095; f 0312 613 799; e reception@hotel-atlant.com; www.hotel-atlant.com. Probably the most 'European' of Uzhgorod's hotels, if not the best managed, and the best deal for your money. The Atlant is composed of about a dozen immaculate and modern rooms, all located right at the city centre. Some of the bathrooms might feel small, but they are especially nice in relation to the alternative. Some rooms have kitchenettes and they also offer good deals for families with children. There are a few rooms up in the attic, which are smaller, but feel slightly more romantic with their skylight windows that allow you to peer out over the rooftops. Hot water is a given and their restaurant is a cut above the rest. A very nice sauna and mini-pool are up on the top floor. *Dbls US$45, suites US$70, attic room US$30.*

Zakarpattya Kirila i Mefodiya Square 5; ☏ 0312 673 143; f 0312 671 467; e info@intur-zak.com; www.intur-zak.com. Not far from the train station, at the far southern side of the city, but it's only a small hike to the centre. As the former Inturist, there are lots of amenities; the in-house travel agency can be a big help with making arrangements and booking local excursions. The hotel favours groups, and beware, as the unrefurbished bathrooms bring a whole new meaning to 'mineral bath'. *Sgl US$22, dbl US$32, luxury suite US$50.*

Eduard Bachynsky 22; ☏ 0312 213 355; e eduard@eduard.utel.net.ua; www.eduard.com.ua. Private, upscale accommodation on the northeast side of the city. Besides very clean rooms and bathrooms with 24hr hot water, there's a good restaurant, a sauna and pool. *Rooms range from US$60 for basic dbl, to US$100 luxury suites.*

Hotel Druzhba Vysoka 12; ☏ 0312 237 233. Uzhgorod's other Soviet-age hotel, albeit a touch more classy. The great view from the north side of the city makes up for the long but pleasant walk into the centre and the quiet and wooded neighbourhood in the hills attracts Uzhgorod's business crowd for w/end conferences. If you are driving in your own car, this is a safe hotel to park. *US$25–70.*

Where to eat

All of Uzhgorod's hotels uphold a strong culinary standard and deserve recognition. **Hotel Atlant** (*open 08.00–23.00*) serves nearly gourmet Hungarian and Slovakian cuisine. **Hotel Uzhgorod** features an equally refined restaurant with epicurean taste, not to mention great steaks (*open 07.00–midnight*). The **Zakarpattya** is a little more Soviet, but is open all night long. For mid-morning or afternoon, stop by any number of the coffee shops along the Naberezhna that serve lethal little thimblefuls of Hungarian espresso. There's also an inordinate number of pizzerias in town.

Terrace Restaurant Uzhgorod Castle; ☏ 0312 614 609. Upscale restaurant located right at the medieval gate of the castle. Serving a wide and diverse menu of Hungarian and Transcarpathian favourites. Turkey filet with fruit sauce is their signature dish. *Mains from US$7; open 08.00–midnight.*

Budapest Slavyanksa 23; ☏ 0312 665 297. Hungarian food, of course, but served outside or in a giant Transcarpathian chalet, complete with outdoor swimming pool. *Mains from US US$6; open 10.00–midnight.*

Detsa U Notarya Gagarina 98; ☏ 0312 224 922. Uzhgorod's happiest restaurant. Traditional Transcarpathian food, average prices and lively ambience. *Mains from US$6; open 11.00–23.00.*

Da-Da Kapitulna 5/1; ☏ 0312 232 346. Very cool (and clean!) café with heavy hippy vibes, incense and delicious vegetarian food. In the evening, people

Uzhgorod feels so different from the rest of Ukraine, that many forget they are still in Ukraine; the familiarity also means Uzhgorod is fast becoming the most popular entryway into Ukraine for European travellers. Uzhgorod is right on the Slovakian–Ukrainian border and the willing can simply walk across by following Sobranetska Street all the way to the Slovakian border post in the direction of Sobrance. Otherwise, Kosice is the point of arrival and departure for most public transport (buses) between Uzhgorod and Slovakia; buses travel to and from Košice twice a day; the train from Kiev to Bratislava stops only in Chop.

The Hungarian border crossing is also located at Chop, 20 minutes (without traffic) south of Uzhgorod. From Ukraine, the daily rail services Kiev–Budapest and Kiev–Prague both pass through Chop, while most European trains coming into Ukraine also cross at Chop (the Hungarian rail system includes Chop as a final stop). Crossing this border by rail is far less hassle than the alternative – cross-border buses are also quick, as they can normally jump the queues. Not so for private vehicles. At the time of writing, the Hungary/Ukraine border at Chop was the very worst in the country, averaging a four-to-five-hour wait when crossing, with several drivers reporting waits up to 12 hours when leaving Ukraine to enter Hungary (coming into Ukraine is far easier). This has a lot to do with the amount of contraband that goes on in the area, the daily bread for many Transcarpathians who can sell cigarettes and other cheap goods for a profit in the EU. Buses and *marshrutka* run back and forth between Chop and Uzhgorod all day long; only a few actually cross into Hungary. The Hungarian border post is in the village of Zahóny, while the closest major junction is at Nyíregyháza; more than three buses a day go to and from these cities and Uzhgorod. The trip between Chop and Budapest takes about seven hours by rail and costs around US$45; Budapest's morning train will put you in Uzhgorod in the afternoon, while a later service arrives in Chop at odd times of the night.

gather to watch arty movies. Try the honey coffee. Mains from US$1; open 07.00–22.00.

✗ Sarmat Minaisaya 6A; ☎ 0312 221 443. A popular beer and banquet hall with lots of pork dishes and live music. Mains from US$4; open 09.00–23.00, closed Mon.

✗ Shafran Zolota 2; ☎ 0312 235 054. Oriental mystique and Middle Eastern cuisine. Mains from US$4; open 11.00–23.00.

✗ Kapitansky Mostik Sobranetska 56; ☎ 0312 242 340. The 'Captain's Bridge' is not much more than a bawdy hangout for businessmen, but the food is hearty. Mains from US$6; open 10.00–midnight.

What to see and do

Uzhgorod Castle (*Open 09.00–17.00, closed Mon; entrance 5UAH; guided tours for US$5; pictures cost an extra US$2*) Most attractions fill the old city and a walk down Kapitulna will take in Uzhgorod's most famous historical remnants, culminating at the hilltop Uzhgorod Castle above the bend in the river. The present ruins remain from the 13th century although the first construction began in the 9th century and continued well into the 1600s. Needless to say, the story of the castle is chaotic and rich with intrigue. The original Ungvar fortress stems from the Turkish *Ung* (for 'river') and the Hungarian Var ('castle'). Seeing as the castle is built on top of the 30m-high river bank, the name is appropriate. The original structure was simple: four towers, one in each corner, with walls in between and surrounded by a dry moat, built from a combination of basalt and andesite, hence its black colour. A deep (50m) and still visible well provided water to the inhabitants. In 1317, the Italian prince, Karl Robert Anjou, gave the castle to Count Phillip Drugeth, the patriarch

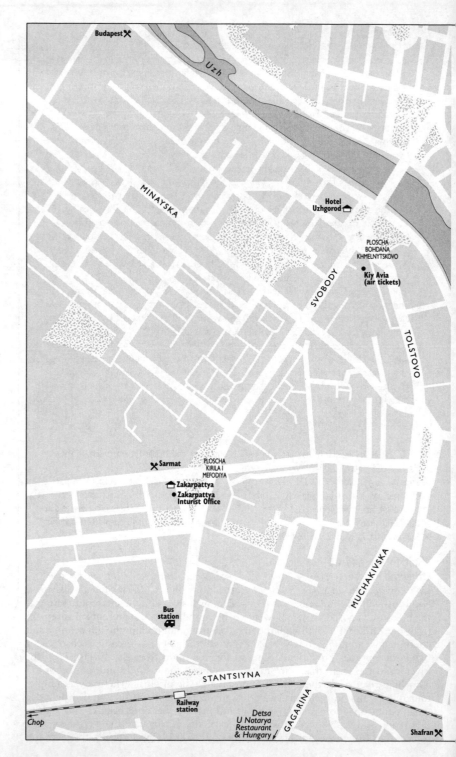

Budapest ✗

Uzh

MINAYSKA

Hotel
Uzhgorod 🏠

PLOSCHA
BOHDANA
KHMELNYTSKOVO

SVOBODY

● Kiy Avia
(air tickets)

TOLSTOVO

✗ Sarmat
PLOSCHA
KIRILA I
MEFODIYA

🏠 Zakarpattya
● Zakarpattya
Inturist Office

MUCHAKIVSKA

Bus
station
🚐

STANTSIYNA

Railway
station

GAGARINA

← Chop

*Detsa
U Notarya
Restaurant
& Hungary* ↙

Shafran ✗

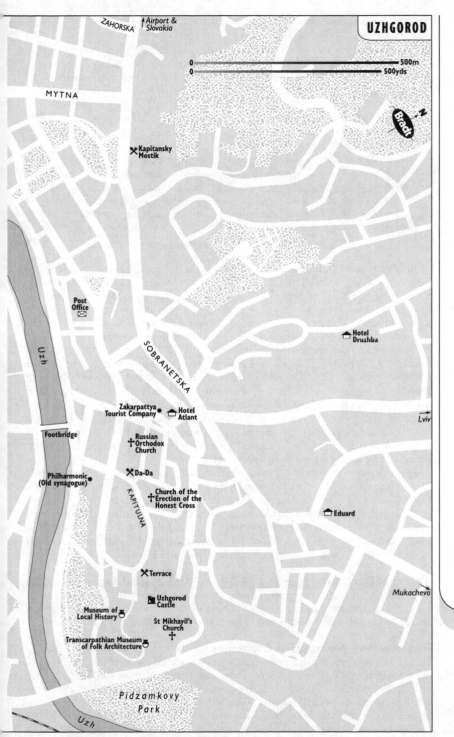

UZHGOROD

ZAHORSKA

Airport &
Slovakia

0   500m
0   500yds

MYTNA

Bradt

N

✗Kapitansky
Mostik

Post
Office ⊠

Uzh

SOBRANETSKA

▲Hotel
Druzhba

Footbridge

Zakarpattya
Tourist Company ● ▲Hotel
Atlant

Lviv

Russian
✝Orthodox
Church

✗Da-Da

Philharmonic ●
(Old synagogue)

KAPITULNA

Church of the
✝Erection of the
Honest Cross

⌂Eduard

✗Terrace

Mukachevo

🏰Uzhgorod
Castle

Museum of
Local History ⌂

St Mikhayil's
Church ✝

Transcarpathian Museum
of Folk Architecture ⌂

Pidzamkovy
Park

Uzh

of another Italian family which ruled the castle for the next 400 years, until the last male heir was murdered. The Drugeth family crest consists of seven birds (crows), a design which you see repeated throughout the castle. Miklós Bercsényi (of Hungarian fame) bought the castle from the Austrians as a gift to his intellectual wife, Christina Drughet. It was she who planted the lovely botanical gardens that still surround the castle ground today. She also invited the Jesuits, who built a chapel on site, which was burned to the ground in 1728 (the crypt and foundation remains). Unfortunately, Miklós was in league with the Hungarian and Ruthenian liberation movements, was betrayed, had his castle confiscated and was exiled with his wife to Romania. For a period, the fortress was used by the Austrians as a military garrison before Empress Maria-Theresa granted the complex to to the local Catholic bishop as his residence. In 1776, a seminary was founded for the Ruthenian Greek Catholic Church, and the castle's great hall transformed into a chapel. A few of the original frescoes remain from this era, painted in 1857 by Ferdinand Vydry. By far the most spectacular is the chapel ceiling, in which a rare image is depicted showing God the Father standing next to Jesus Christ, with the Holy Ghost above. The monastery functioned until 1945, when Stalin outlawed the Greek Catholic Church and killed every single monk on site. In 1946, the castle became the museum it is today, housing furniture, icons, and several exhibits on liberation from fascism. The statues in the courtyard date back to the mid 1800s, when the local metallurgy factories of Transcarpathia created iron statuary for much of central Europe (note Hercules killing the Hydra and Hermes).

Museum of Local History (*Kapitulna 33; open 10.00–17.00; closed Tue; entrance US$2*) Next door to the castle is the local history museum. Despite the outdated set-up, a tour of the museum's crafts and antiques is more stimulating than average, reflecting Uzhgorod's eventful past. This is also a good place to buy souvenirs.

Transcarpathian Museum of Folk Architecture (*Open 10.00–17.00, closed Tue; entrance US$1*) The outdoor Transcarpathian Museum spreads out just beyond the history museum, with over 30 examples of traditional Transcarpathian buildings, mostly reflecting the styles of Lemko and Boiki ethnic groups and including the 18th-century wooden **St Mikhayil's Church**, transferred from the village of Shelestovo, near Mukachevo. It is likely that you will see many wooden churches in your visit to Ukraine, but this is one of the more remarkably preserved ones. In the summer, frequent festivals and markets in the park play up the nostalgic peasant past.

Churches Uzhgorod's eclectic churches are famous throughout central and eastern Europe for their playful design and colour, and their active ethnic and religious communities. The twin towers of the beautiful yellow Catholic cathedral on Kapitulna are an Uzhgorod landmark. Locally, this is known as the **Church of the Erection of the Honest Cross** and was built in 1646 by Slovakian Jesuits. The Corinthian columns and early Baroque style on the outside say little of the wondrous interior. The fanciful pink and red **Russian Orthodox church** resembles a cheerful cake and what is now the very grand, albeit pink **Uzhgorod Philharmonic** (*the ticket office is inside and to the right; open weekdays 10.00–18.00*) was once the city's elegant **synagogue** (*Yevgena Fentsyka 10*), built of red marble in 1904. The philharmonic still offers regular concerts (almost nightly), and this is the best way to catch a glimpse of the interior.

Local tour operators and tourist information The tour office at Zakarpattya can be very helpful (*Hotel Zakarpattya;* ✆f *0312 671 370;* e *tour@intur-zak.com; www.intur-zak.com*). Don't confuse them with Sodis, or the Zakarpattya Tourist Company (✆ *0312 612 323;* f *0312 619 234;* e *travel@sodis.com.ua; www.sodis.com.ua*).

MUKACHEVO МУКАЧЕВО The medieval citadel of Mukachevo sits immaculately atop the city's single highest hill, overlooking the verdant Latorytsya river valley. Down below lies a small-town cultured oasis in the middle of rural Transcarpathia, a pleasant place to visit in spite of its relatively small size. The red-roofed Palanok Castle proved vital in defending the Austrian Empire from eastern invasion and it is one of Ukraine's most scenic. Founded during the earliest years of old Rus, the town was known as Munkacs during its long Hungarian existence, and sadly, is best remembered as the notorious Jewish shtetl from which so many were deported to the camps at Auschwitz. Today, visitors can tour the castle complex and roam through the quiet and colourful streets. Mukachevo still embodies all the quirks of a Transcarpathian town, complete with a typical blend of Hungarian, Ruthenian and Jewish people, culture, language, architecture and identity.

Getting there and away By bus, car or *marshrukta*, you are less than one hour from Uzhgorod; the Mukachevo bus station is at the far eastern side of the city. Once a day overnight trains from Kiev to Budapest, Belgrade and Zagreb all make their final Ukrainian stop in Mukachevo, and the reverse is true for the Hungarian and Yugoslavian trains that make their first stop here before heading to Kiev. This means the closest domestic connection is on these routes between Mukachevo, Lviv and Ternopil. Rail service between Uzhgorod and Mukachevo is usually once a day, usually in the middle of the day on the train from Kiev.

🏠 **Where to stay and eat**

🏠 **Hotel Star** Miru 10-12; ✆ 0313 132 008; f 0313 154 880; e star-ar@mk.uz.ua; www.star-ar.mk.uz.ua. As part of the élite circle of Premier Hotels, the Star favours old European charm with a touch of modern class. Formerly the urban residence of Austrian Count Con Sherborn, this may be the nicest hotel in all of Transcarpathia. The beds are magnificent and the fitness centre amazing. The in-house restaurant is also very suitable for languorous meals. They take credit cards. *Sgls US$45, which is a steal for the high standard room you get; dbls US$65, luxury suites US$125.*

🏠 **Alfa** Universitetska 78; ✆ 0313 152 010. A newly refurbished hotel of high, European standard. *Rooms US$50–70.*

🏠 **Inturist Mukachevo** Dukhnovicha 93; ☎ 0313 137 905. Like the name implies, Mukachevo's former intourist is still running strong. *Rooms from US$20.*

✗ **Traktir** Pushkina 12; ☎ 0313 151 057. For dining out, try this old-time restaurant.
✗ **Karpatsky** Mislevets ☎ 0313 141 462. Local cuisine.

What to see and do Definitely visit Palanok Castle, built in the 14th century and probably the best-preserved fortress in all Ukraine. Sitting atop an almost perfectly cone-shaped Lamkova hill, the conglomerate of towers, courtyards and dungeons reflects an honest to goodness castle that has seen many a real battle. The sheer size of the complex is impressive, as are the steep parapets. The Koryatovich family of Podillya owned and managed the castle for the first 200 years of its existence, followed by Francis II Rákóczy, the courageous leader of the Hungarian revolt against the Hapsburgs. He used the stronghold throughout his attempted overthrow of the Austrian monarchy, but eventually was forced into exile. From 1789 until the Soviet era, the castle was used as a prison, before it became an agricultural school, followed by its present reincarnation as a history museum (*open 10.00 to 17.00, closed Mon; entrance 5UAH; tours for US$5*). Other oft-visited sites include the wooden **St Nicholas Church** (*Pivnichna 2*) and the adjoining 18th-century monastery. The entire town is a delight to explore, but some of the grander Hapsburg-era pieces are located along Miru Street. For tourist information and help with local excursions, contact Tysa (*Miru 14 No 5;* ☎ *0313 123 923*).

11

The Black Sea
Чорне Море

Half land, half water, Ukraine's southern coastline surrenders vaguely to the Black Sea in a spread of wetlands, estuaries, wide river deltas, sandbar islands and beaches. The country's most diverse and abundant birdlife congregates here, as do a variety of Russian and Ukrainian tourists who flock to the coast in summer, mostly out of habit from Soviet days, when Odessa was still the balmy southern capital of a rather cold empire.

The south is still a very friendly place, where people are laidback and the sun shines year-round over grassy plains and the watery expanse. Ukraine's three largest rivers – the Dnistr, Danube and Dnepr – all empty into the sea here, so that small-scale farming on the deltas and traditional angling are still the accepted way of life in the country, while shipping has made the cities wealthy. Technically, this convergence of rivers designates the birthplace of human civilisation in Ukraine – a high concentration of prehistoric burial mounds and Scythian relics marks this as a central hub for early human migration from Asia into Europe. The ease of river transport and the fertile land attracted the ancient Greeks and much later brought the St Petersburg aristocracy to this 'New Russia', where they sought to raise a great navy. The grandeur remains – along with the Russian language – but the slower pace of life and the warm sky advocate little more than relaxation and a lazy dip in the water.

GETTING AROUND

Odessa is the largest and most obvious transport nucleus, with the fastest regional trains, buses and motor routes to Mykolayiv and Kherson. More rural routes towards the Black Sea coast and the Dnepr delta branch out from Kherson, while any travel towards the Dnistr and Danube deltas originates in Odessa. Note that rail and motor routes south towards the Danube are very long and slow. In many ways, this little stretch of land is a piece of deep Ukraine. Getting a taxi, going on an organised tour and being very patient can be the best way to access these more obscure destinations. The towns and villages north of Odessa tend to get overlooked by most travellers, but are easily accessible on public transport.

ODESSA ОДЕССА

Visitors fall in love with Odessa in about five minutes. All it takes is a warm sea breeze and one glance at the eager crowds moving up and down the shady, tree-lined boulevards. Never mind the elegant palaces with their peeling façades and the hint of squalor on every corner – like all southern cities, Odessa is beloved for its sunshine, colour and soul, and not its sense of order. Behind the busy port and frantic holiday zone lingers a childish energy unknown in the rest of Ukraine, paired with a rich legacy of poets, mobsters and dukes. The backdrop of grand

269

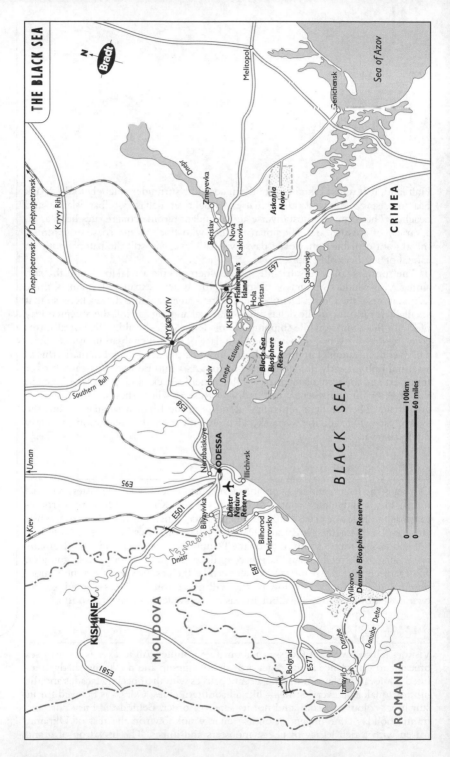

monuments and high culture only accentuates all the cheap amusements characteristic of seaside towns: jewellery stands, ponies, street clowns, balloon-sellers and dancing monkeys. Step away from the sidewalk theatre and you'll find a world of hushed courtyards, barking dogs and sleepy parks. Somehow it all fits together, making it Odessa.

The exact origin of Odessa's name is disputed, but it's most often attributed to the ancient Greek colony of Odessos (today's Varna in Bulgaria). In an attempt to bestow ancient Greek credentials upon her new Russian empire, Catherine the Great borrowed the name. Others believe she simply feminised the name of Homer's hero Odysseus and fancied herself as a classical heroine. For several centuries prior to this, the Crimean Tatars, followed by the Turks, controlled the natural harbour with their fortress Eni-Dunya. The Russians finally conquered the region in 1789, in the midst of the Russo–Turkish wars, envisioning a great commercial and naval port. At only 200 years old, Odessa is one of Europe's youngest cities, and yet it looks far more ancient than most of the other cities in Ukraine. The frilly Baroque architecture dates back to Russia's gilded age and the influx of European ideals and style. In 1803, Tsar Alexander I committed the governorship of the city to the Duke de Richelieu, in gratitude for his leadership of the Russians against the Turks at Izmaïl. The young Frenchman is now revered as the father of Odessa, and his statue stands at the top of the famed Potemkin stairs, draped in royal Greek robes and looking visionary. Committed to aesthetics and fast growth, Richelieu slashed trade duties and officially dedicated one-fifth of the port's income to 'making the city beautiful', a task in which he was highly successful. Granted the status of a free port in 1815, Odessa swiftly rose to third place for population and affluence in the Russian Empire, after Moscow and St Petersburg. Opportunity and very relaxed laws attracted a mixed crowd of political refugees and entrepreneurs: freed slaves, Christian dissidents, Ukrainian Cossacks, sailors, Germans, Marxists, Bulgarians, Greeks, Jews and Albanians. The mid 19th century witnessed a boom in Ukraine's grain exports, carried by rail to the loaded docks of Odessa. Rich ethnic diversity and plenty of jobs secured the city's independence from the otherwise highly centralised Russian Empire. Odessa remains fairly cosmopolitan today, boasting over 100 ethnicities.

Odessa's role in the Russian Revolution was not a small one since workers' unions had already been around for nearly 30 years before the famed uprising of 1905, led by the sailors from the battleship *Potemkin* (see page 281). Odessa was heavily bombed during World War I and suffered immense damage during the civil war. Still, the city's love for all things bourgeois allowed General Denikin's White Army to make Odessa its stronghold before finally succumbing to the Bolsheviks in 1920. The act of defence was repeated in 1941 when the city's inhabitants held out against the Germans for 73 days, after which the region was placed under Romanian occupation. By the end of World War II, Odessa's dominant Jewish population had been decimated. In the latter part of the Soviet era, Odessa was the country's busiest port and a popular holiday destination, hence its rows of hotels and beachside resorts.

Odessa's super-strong urban solidarity tends to supersede any national allegiance and that has changed little under independent Ukraine. By reputation, 'Odessites' are incorrigible jokesters, smooth talkers, and a little shifty – it is no coincidence that the city celebrates April Fool's Day like no other place on earth. People smile, laugh out loud, and talk with their hands – a common sight of two park benches turned to face one another reveals that lively conversation is this city's favourite pastime. Odessa also features its very own and rather specific Russian dialect that strikes the rest of the country as somewhere between the speech of a gangster and that of a comedian. With capitalism in its blood, local

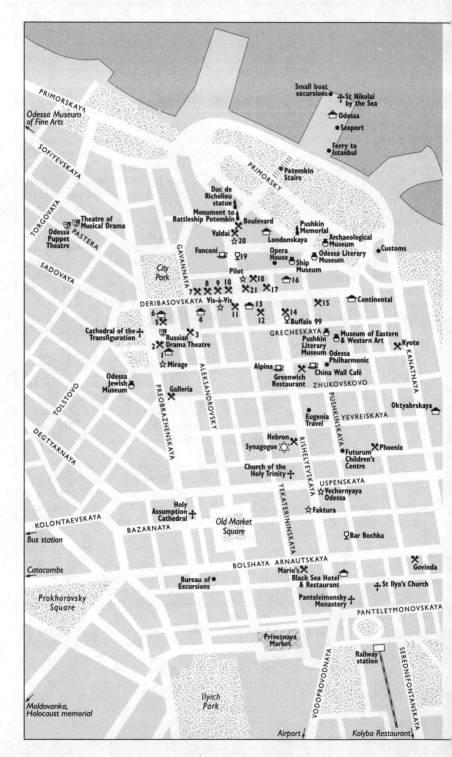

Primorskaya

Odessa Museum
of Fine Arts

Sofiyevskaya

Torgovaya

Pastera

Theatre of
Musical Drama

Odessa
Puppet
Theatre

Sadovaya

Gavannaya

City
Park

Deribasovskaya

Tolstovo

Degtyarnaya

Cathedral of the
Transfiguration

Odessa
Jewish
Museum

Preobrazhenskaya

Aleksandrovsky

Kolontaevskaya

Bus station

Catacombs

Prokhorovsky
Square

Bazarnaya

Holy
Assumption
Cathedral

Ilyich
Park

Moldovanka,
Holocaust memorial

Small boat
excursions

St Nikolai
by the Sea

Odessa
Seaport

Ferry to
Istanbul

Primorsky

Potemkin
Stairs

Duc de
Richelieu
statue

Monument to
Battleship Potemkin

Boulevard

Valdai

Pushkin
Memorial

Archaeological
Museum

☆20

Londonskaya

Fanconi

☐19

Opera
House

Odessa Literary
Museum

Customs

Ship
Museum

Pilot

☆ ✕18

☐16

8 9 10

✕21 ✕17

7 ✕✕✕

Vis-à-Vis

✕15

Continental

6 ✕

☆ ✕13

5 ✕

4

11

12

✕14

Buffalo 99

Grecheskaya

Pushkin
Literary
Museum

Museum of Eastern
& Western Art

Russian
Drama Theatre

Kanatnaya

2 ✕ 3

Odessa
Philharmonic

Kyoto

1

Alpina

Greenwich
Restaurant

China Wall Café

☆ Mirage

Zhukovskovo

Galleria

Eugenia
Travel

Pushkinskaya

Yevreiskaya

Oktyabrskaya

Hebron
Synagogue

Rishelyevskaya

Futurum
Children's
Centre

Phoenix

Church of the
Holy Trinity

Yekaterininskaya

Uspenskaya

Vechernyaya
Odessa

☆ Faktura

Old Market
Square

☐ Bar Bochka

Bolshaya Arnautskaya

Mario's

Govinda

Bureau of
Excursions

Black Sea Hotel
& Restaurant

St Ilya's Church

Panteleimonsky
Monastery

Panteleymonovskaya

Privoznaya
Market

Vodoprovodnaya

Railway
station

Serednefontanskaya

Airport

Kolyba Restaurant

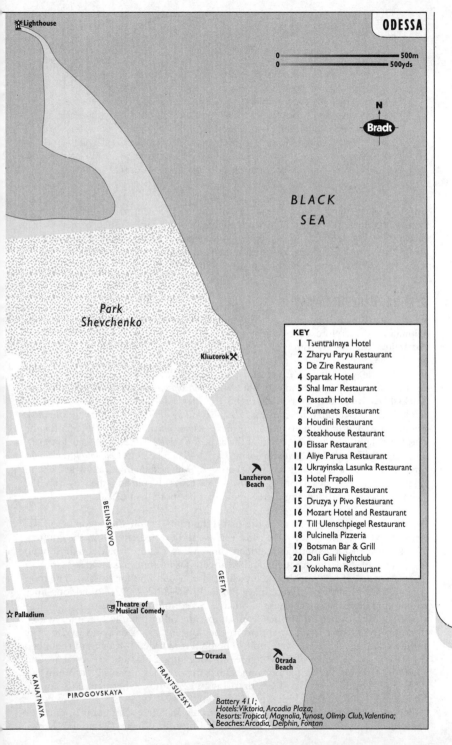

BLACK
SEA

N

Bradt

Lighthouse

Park
Shevchenko

Khutorok ✕

Lanzheron
Beach

KEY
1 Tsentralnaya Hotel
2 Zharyu Paryu Restaurant
3 De Zire Restaurant
4 Spartak Hotel
5 Shal Imar Restaurant
6 Passazh Hotel
7 Kumanets Restaurant
8 Houdini Restaurant
9 Steakhouse Restaurant
10 Elissar Restaurant
11 Aliye Parusa Restaurant
12 Ukrayinska Lasunka Restaurant
13 Hotel Frapolli
14 Zara Pizzara Restaurant
15 Druzya y Pivo Restaurant
16 Mozart Hotel and Restaurant
17 Till Ulenschpiegel Restaurant
18 Pulcinella Pizzeria
19 Botsman Bar & Grill
20 Dali Gali Nightclub
21 Yokohama Restaurant

BELINSKOVO

GEETA

☆ Palladium

🎭 Theatre of
Musical Comedy

KANATNAYA

FRANTSUZSKY

🏠 Otrada

Otrada
Beach

PIROGOVSKAYA

Battery 411;
Hotels: Viktoria, Arcadia Plaza;
Resorts: Tropical, Magnolia, Yunost, Olimp Club, Valentina;
Beaches: Arcadia, Delphin, Fontan

The Black Sea ODESSA

11

business is thriving, and instead of pronounced Soviet names, the ordered boulevards all hark back to Odessa's golden age – hence French Street, Polish Street, Greek Street and Jewish Street. Whichever one you walk down, and no matter the time of day, you will find buskers and businessmen out on the prowl. This is a city that never sleeps – it just takes intermission.

GETTING THERE AND AWAY

By air Apart from Kiev, Odessa is the most internationally accessible city by air in Ukraine, and therefore a convenient entry point from Europe and North America. **Austrian Airlines** has direct daily connections through Vienna (*airport office, 2nd floor;* ✆ *0482 490 079;* e *all-ods@aua.com; www.aua.com.ua*). **Malev Hungarian** has five flights a week to and from Budapest (✆ *731 2575, locally*), and LOT Polish airlines has a daily connection to Warsaw (*airport office, 2nd floor;* ✆ *0487 312 880*). **Turkish Airlines** also offers daily flights to Odessa and international connections worldwide via Istanbul (*Pushkinskaya 19/17;* ✆ *0482 347 906;* e *thy_odstztk@farlep.net*). Flights to Kiev are frequent and often inexpensive; usually around US$65 for the one-hour flight. Contact **AeroSvit** at the airport (✆ *0482 379 800;* e *aew@te.net.ua*). The office of **Kiy Avia** (*Preobrazhenskaya 15;* ✆ *0482 252 389;* e *Odessa@kiyavia.com*) can help with arranging internal flights between Odessa and almost anywhere else in Ukraine. The central airport is a 20-minute taxi ride outside the city (on the Ovidiopolskaya road); getting there should cost no more than US$6.

By rail A rush of warm sea air is the first thing to meet you after stepping off the train in Odessa, followed by the most earnest and excited crowds in the country. The fervour of movement and sudden sunshine is a grand finale for those who arrive by rail, and the frequent and relatively fast trains make Odessa an easy destination to get to from almost anywhere else in Ukraine (or Russia). The train station sits centrally on Privokzalnaya Ploshad (✆ *0482 224 242*). Avoid long lines by booking tickets at the central rail office at Serednofontansky 12A.

Odessa is an overnight journey from almost any other point in Ukraine. At least three overnight trains run to and from Kiev on any given day, and in the busy summer months there are even more. The preferred Odessa–Kiev train is dubbed the 'Black Sea' (*Chornomorets*) which leaves Kiev after 21.00 and arrives at around 07.00 or 08.00 the following morning. Other major Odessa trains go to Vinnytsya (7 hours), Dnipropetrovsk (12 hours), Lviv (12 hours), Chernivtsi (18 hours), Simferopol (13 hours) and Kharkiv (14 hours).

For international rail journeys, Odessa makes an interesting point of entry or departure. Daily trains connect to Kishinev (4 hours), Warsaw (24 hours), Minsk

(24 hours) and Moscow (25 hours). The Odessa–Berlin train departs three times a week – a dramatic 36-hour journey. As of now, there is no functioning rail connection from Odessa to Romania. Purchase international tickets in the first-class waiting room.

Finally, getting to the smaller towns in the lower Dnistr region and the Danube delta is quicker by bus or car; however the *electrichki* trains connect to all the villages on the way to Izmail and you'll be nestled amidst an army wielding gardening implements. A very slow train also travels to Kherson via Mykolayiv – take a taxi or bus.

By bus The main bus station is located at Kolontayevska 58 (✆ 0487 325 785). A number of nice, modern (and well-ventilated!) buses run between Kiev and Odessa. It's a seven–eight-hour journey with stops normally in Uman and Kiev Borispol Airport. Check with companies **Avtoluks** (*Raskydaylovksaya 18;* ✆ 0482 377 392) and **Gunsel** (*Balkovskaya 167;* ✆ 0482 326 212). Both also have offices at the bus station.

Like most bus stations in Ukraine, Odessa's is happily chaotic; however, one may travel to practically any destination in Ukraine on a bus for under US$10, including Dnepropetrovsk (14 hours) and Donetsk (16 hours). Buses and *marshrutka* are the best way to get to locations within the region, namely the coast, Bilhorod Dnistrovsky, Mikolayiv and Kherson. *Marshrutka* run all day long from the bus station to Mykolayiv (2 hours) and Kherson (3½ hours) – just find the person shouting out the city's name and climb on. A number of *marshrutka* to other parts of the Black Sea region leave from the front of the train station.

By sea Being the largest warm seaport of what was the world's largest country meant that at one time a traveller could take a ship to almost anywhere in the world from Odessa. It's hard to miss the towering seaport (*morsky vokzal*) off Suvorova at Tamozhnaya Ploshad 1. Customs and immigration are located inside the main building on the pier and anyone arriving by sea (including those in private yachts) is required to register. Passenger ships still come and go from Odessa, but they are few and far between. For the time being, the only year-round destination is Turkey, with once-a-week trips to Istanbul on **UKRFerry**; one way first class US$150; return US$300; 36 hours sailing (*Sabansky 4A;* ✆ 0482 347 995; e *welcome@ukrferry-tour.com; www.ukrferry-tour.com and www.ukrferry.com*). Boat tickets may be purchased directly at the seaport, through Eugenia Travel (see *Local tour operators*) or online. **London Sky Travel** maintains a regular summer route to Bulgaria, Odessa–Varna, from June through to the end of August (*seaport office;* ✆ 0487 293 196; f 0487 293 183; e *lstravel@te.net.ua; www.lst.com.ua*). In the past, a few sporadic services have linked Odessa to Crimea, namely Sevastopol and Yalta. It's worth checking at the beginning of each new season, but for now, foreign cruises seem to be the only ones plying these Black Sea routes.

LOCAL TOUR OPERATORS

Eugenia Travel Rishelyevskaya 23; ✆/f 0482 220 554; e janna@eugeniatours.com.ua; www.eugeniatours.com.ua. Southern Ukraine's largest incoming tour operator works out of Odessa and their office has become the de facto information centre for the city. The debonair Madame Zhanna arranges some of the best English-guided tours in the city and across the region, including combination tours with Crimea. She is absolutely passionate about Odessa, can cater for either big groups or individuals (in any language), and can get you good deals at the local hotels. She's also able to accept online credit card payments – a rare luxury in Ukraine.

Odessa Bureau of Travel and Excursions 113 Malaya Arnautskaya; ✆ 0482 252 874. Don't be put off by the peeling brown and green signs, for this corner office is a living relic from 1950s USSR. A roomful of smiling grannies can arrange English or Russian tours of the city and its outskirts, including the catacombs.

Ukrayinska Lakoma Deribasovksaya 17; ℩ 0482 258 412; f 0487 315 427; e lasunka@real-tv.net; www.lakomka.com.ua. Doubled up with a restaurant, this firm conducts English- and German-language tours with a few excursions to regional attractions.

The office is located inside the courtyard (follow the signs).
Unipress Travel Balkovskaya 120/2; ℩ 0487 860 516; f 0487 860 621; e travel@travel-2-ukraine.com; www.travel-2-ukraine.com. More of a hotel brokerage than a travel agency, this Odessa-based company can make local accommodation and transport arrangements and rent apts for a good price.

WHERE TO STAY Odessa's accommodation ranks high among Ukrainian hotels, with a rich past of entertaining newcomers to the city who arrived by sea. A range of new and refurbished hotels have opened up throughout the city centre, resorts and sanitoria line the beaches, and there are plenty of opportunities to rent grand and spacious apartments. Odessa picked up on credit cards quickly and any middle or luxury hotel will gladly accept plastic.

Keep in mind that this is vacationland for Russians and Ukrainians. During the first week of April (April Fool's), the first week of May, and all of July and August, vacancies can be rare. Book ahead to ensure a room. Also note that Odessa's public water system is notoriously bad. A few luxury hotels have their own private systems of heating and filtering, but even in the best of circumstances, be prepared for odd smells and momentary lapses in plumbing.

Hotels
Luxury Odessa's race towards opulence has resulted in a wide range of luxury hotels, most of which have awarded themselves four stars, regardless of widely varying standards and prices. Remember that these ratings are meaningless: the two boutique hotels Otrada and Continental are the ones most on a par with international luxury standards. All accept credit cards.

Continental Deribasovskaya 5; ℩ 0487 860 155; f 0487 860 550; e hotelcont@utel.net.ua; www.continental-hotel.com.ua. Occupying a tastefully remodelled 19th-century mansion, this intimate boutique hotel relishes simple elegance and boasts an incredible standard of service. Rooms feel open and tasteful (they're decorated with antique prints of old Odessa) and the large beds with real European pillows are heavenly. The location at the seaside end of Deribasovksaya is conveniently close yet quiet, and the young English-speaking staff are pleasant. A very *à propos* continental b/fast is inc. *Sgls US$130, dbls around US$160, semi-suites US$210.*

Londonskaya Primorsky 11; ℩ 0487 380 110; f 0487 380 111; e hotel@londred.com; www.londred.com. Built in 1827 and still dreaming of Victorian England, the 'London-ish' hotel is an important architectural monument for Odessa, rich in its repertoire of famous guests, which includes Isadora Duncan, Chekhov and Mayakovsky. Overlooking the city's scenic tree-lined promenade and the busy port, the building's grandeur cannot diffuse some of the Soviet undertones in style and

attitude. The very posh restaurant feels more liberating. The majority of rooms have been remodelled to international standard. *US$150–300.*

Mozart Lanzheronovskaya 13; ℩ 0482 377 777; f 0482 379 894; e office@mozart-hotel.com; www.mozart-hotel.com. Odessa's highly lavish 'Mozart' dreams of Old Vienna and has earned its high-class reputation following several years of luxury service. The location across from the opera house is unbeatable, the staff are professional and courteous, the beds are comfortable and the restaurant has become a local gourmet destination. *Standard sgls/dbls US$145/185; 4-person family room and suites with private jacuzzis US$350.*

Odessa Primorsky 6; ℩ 0487 294 808; f 0487 294 888; e hotel@hotel-odessa.od.ua; www.hotel-odessa.od.ua. This very visible 19-storey high-rise at the end of the pier (beyond the sea station) seeks to become an Odessa landmark in its own right. The setting high above the water is dramatic, yes, and the views looking out to sea or back towards the city are both superb; however, the location is not entirely conducive to relaxed strolling or sightseeing.

There is a nice fitness centre and a distinguished seafood restaurant; b/fast inc. Rooms can also be smallish. *Sgls US$200, dbls US$250.*

Otrada Uyutnaya 11; ☎ 0482 330 698; e contact@hotel-otrada.com; www.hotel-otrada.com. Well-managed, classy boutique hotel that favours a very personal touch for business travellers and tourists alike. The elegant rooms feel modern, while the luxurious 19th-century building is situated in a quiet and authentic Odessa neighbourhood not too far from the sea. The attention to detail is refreshing: features include high-speed internet in every room, a rare heated outdoor pool, a fantastic gym and a renowned in-house Italian restaurant. For the time being, this could be Odessa's best-kept secret. *Sgls US$130–180, dbls US$150–220, suites US$300.*

Middle range

🏠 **Black Sea Hotel** Rishelyevskaya 59; ☎ 0482 300 904; f 0482 300 908; e blacksea@te.net.ua; www.bs-hotel.com.ua. As a remodelled Soviet high-rise, the Black Sea is a sturdy, medium-grade hotel with refurbished rooms and a convenient location near the train station. Popular with groups, there are a few less expensive dbl rooms for US$50, while the nicer rooms range from US$60–150. The diligent staff speak English and an active in-house travel agency (on the second floor) offers small tours around the city and trips to the beach and countryside. B/fast is inc and dinner is served in the hotel's Japanese restaurant, next door to the hotel's jazzy nightclub.

🏠 **Hotel Frapolli** Deribasovskaya 13; ☎ 0487 356 800; e frapolli@te.net.ua; www.odessapassage.com/frapolli. Swanky private hotel right on Odessa's most exciting street. The first floor, all-glass café feels a lot like a Parisian brasserie and is great for people-watching. Functioning AC is a nice touch. B/fast inc. *Rooms US$65–160 depending on the level of luxury.*

🏠 **Viktoria** Genuezka 24A; ☎ 0482 619 038; f 0482 619 033; e okvictoria@te.net.ua; www.victoriya.com.ua. Although quite far from anything (except the world's most crowded beach), the Viktoria is good value for money and a quick taxi ride can fix the distance. *Done-up Soviet apt-style rooms cost US$40 and up, with the very best rooms US$60–80.*

🏠 **Oktyabrskaya** Kanatnaya 31; ☎ 0482 223 874; f 0482 228 494; e oktyabrskaya@odessaglob.com. Located near the city centre, right next to Park Shevchenko, this is a recently reformed Soviet hotel that's generally comfortable with a wide a range of room types. *US$45–100.*

Budget Finding a cheap place to stay is getting tougher in Odessa, but there are a few really terrific old places right in the city centre. There's always the risk that these gems will get bought up and developed, but for now, their popularity among Ukrainians keeps them cheap.

🏠 **Tsentralnaya** Preobrazhenskaya 40; ☎ 0482 268 406; f 0482 268 607. This old Odessa palace features simple yet refurbished rooms in a prime location. All rooms have showers. A lively café attracts an energetic evening crowd downstairs, and several in-house tour agencies are helpful to travellers. *Sgl US$30, dbl US$60.*

🏠 **Passazh** Preobrazhenskaya 34; ☎ 0487 285 500; f 0487 285 502. Odessa's best budget hotel was once its grandest. The pink and white exterior may be crumbling, and the staircase and halls are quite shabby, but the rooms are decent and most have hot water with their own toilets. *Standard rooms US$12–25, depending on the number of beds and the amount of plumbing. Their poshest suites – which are not that bad – cost US$60 for 2 people.*

🏠 **Spartak** Deribasovskaya 25; ☎ 0487 268 924; f 0487 298 900. Spartak translates as 'Spartan', which just about sums up this dilapidated classic on the main street. The staff are fun and friendly but the shared bathrooms are nauseating. *A bare room US$10; for US$20–30 you get your own bathroom.*

🏠 **Yunost** Pionerskaya 32; ☎ 0487 380 411; f 0482 633 377; e yunost@eurocom.od.ua; www.yunost.com.ua. An inspiring communist word like 'Youth' should attract anyone to this high-rise hotel on the Black Sea, closer to one of Odessa's cleaner beaches but quite far from the city itself. Bedrooms and bathrooms are clean and cosy. *Rooms US$35–80 (suites), with significant discounts for long-term stays (over 2 weeks).*

Renting apartments Odessa's innate knack for wheeling and dealing means you can arrange to stay in a private apartment for under US$20/night. As a rule, matronly women around the platforms of the train station will be advertising a *kvartira* (apartment) or *komnata* (room). Even if you don't speak a lick of Russian, try to negotiate lots before agreeing to go and 'have a look', which is considered close to a 'yes'. Renting a room can be a good option if you want to meet some locals, but if you value your privacy, get the whole apartment and the keys that go with it. Ask about hot water and check the doors to make sure they are secure. Pay in full at the beginning and then pay no more.

A few new companies arrange luxury apartment rentals on a more professional basis, which can be a far better deal for families and small groups. **Odessa Executive Suites** (*www.odessaexecutivesuites.com*) caters to more high-end visitors, with very nice apartments costing from US$90 and up. **Odessa Rent** (*www.odessarent.com*) has some less expensive options and offers 'fixer' services for getting situated in Odessa, and **Odessa Apartment Rentals** has a competent English-speaking staff and an office location (*Deribasovskaya 5;* \ *0487 771 400;* e *info@odessa-abc.com; www.odessa-apartment-rentals.com*).

Seaside resorts/Sanatoria After a year in the factory, tired proletarians migrated to Odessa's shores for a long break. The tradition of health holidays continues in dozens of sanatoria, though with a touch more elegance now. The seaside is mobbed with Russian tourists in summer, but communal joy is part of the fun.

🏠 **Arcadia Plaza** Posmitnovo 1; \ 0482 307 100; f 0482 307 104; e arcadia-plaza@com.od.ua; www.arcadia-plaza.od.ua. The poshest of Odessa's post-Soviet resorts, right on Arcadia Beach. The bourgeois fanfare can be a little overwhelming, but the rooms are very nice and the outdoor pool is great. *Rooms US$160–400.*

🏠 **Olimp Club** Frantsuzky Bulvar; \ 0482 356 080; e admin@olimpclub.com; www.olimpclub.com. Small and élite seaside resort, rich with delusions of classical grandeur. Caters to out-of-town mafia types. *Sgl US$120, dbl US$150.*

🏠 **Tropical** Krasnye Zori 4/6A; \ 0482 342 484; e administrator@tropical.odessa.ua. Advertised as a 'rest centre' by the sea, this brand-new resort offers high-end service with trendy perks, including a high-tech, full-sized bowling alley, a swanky billiard hall and the best private sauna in Odessa. Real king-size beds can be found in the rooms. Overlooking the

sea, a tastefully decorated restaurant serves delicious Italian cuisine and grilled seafood for around US$12 a plate. A 3min walk brings you to the beach. *Rooms from US$100, suites US$150–180.*

🏠 **Valentina** Kurortny 2; \ 0482 632 587; f 0482 681 542; e hotval@ukr.net; www.hotval.odessa.net. Refurbished Soviet-style high-rise sanatorium close to the beach. Rooms are small and basic with a good view of the Black Sea. *From US$40 pp.*

🏠 **Magnolia** Frantsuzky Bulvar 63/65; \ 0482 687 705; e magnolia@farlep.net. Flamingo pink and rather joyful, this flowery sanatorium might prove a cheaper alternative to a hotel for long-term visits. Meals, salt-water swimming pools, free massages and complimentary psychotherapy (really) are part of their package deals for the minimum week-long stay. Few rooms have real showers (rather, a hose from the wall) and hot water is sporadic. *Rooms US$30–60.*

✗ **WHERE TO EAT** Odessa's incredible range of restaurants reflects a southern appreciation for good eating and good conversation. Creative new dining opportunities keep popping up, and there is no better place for outdoor sidewalk cafés and street food. Authentic 'Odessit' cuisine offers an eclectic blend of French and Italian traditions applied to locally caught seafood and staple Jewish favourites. Nowadays, the sky's the limit food-wise, and for some reason this port city features more Chinese restaurants than anywhere else in the country. Vegetarians also fare well here – try Hebron, Govinda or Shal Imar. All listed establishments take credit cards unless otherwise noted.

Ukrainian

✗ **Khutorok** Park Shevchenko; \ 0487 353 873. A more commercial approach to Ukrainian cuisine,

right in the middle of Odessa's liveliest park above the sea. Grilled meats and a good bar. *Mains from*

US$10; open 12.00–midnight.
✖ **Kumanets** Havanna 7; ☎ 0482 376 946.
Ukrainian themed dining taken to the extreme.
Swashbuckling, country-style restaurant with hearty
servings of sausage, dumplings, and lots of fresh
vegetables. *Mains from US$6; open 11.00–midnight.*
✖ **Ukrayinska Lasunka** Deribasovskaya 17; ☎ 0482
258 412; www.lakomka.com.ua. This very Ukrainian
restaurant is decked out in Disney-esque props,
suddenly surrounding you with a friendly farm.
Besides doing convincingly authentic Ukrainian
cuisine, the chef prepares customary Odessa
favourites using fresh Black Sea products. Meals
begin with complimentary *samogon* (home-brewed

Fine dining
✖ **Aliye Parusa** Corner of Deribasovskaya and
Yekaterininskaya; ☎ 0482 253 438. Harking back to
Odessa's early days of tall ships and trade, with
epicurean food and lots of drink. *Mains from US$7;
open 11.00–midnight.*
✖ **Elissar** Deribaskovskaya 18; ☎ 0482 496 498.
Candlelit and quiet, this sophisticated Lebanese
restaurant makes a nice refuge from the hustle of
Odessa's main street. The food is authentically Middle
Eastern. *Mains from US$10; open 11.00–midnight.*
✖ **Galleria** Preobrazhenskaya 25; ☎ 0487 294 858.
Contemporary upscale dining in the heart of the
city: palm trees, good lighting, live music and a
robust gourmet menu. *US$20 mains; open
09.00–midnight.*
✖ **Greenwich** Bunina 21; ☎ 0482 347 401;
www.greenwich.com.ua. If after your meal you're
feeling enigmatic and snooty, it might have something
to do with the fact that you are sitting in an

Classic Odessa
✖ **Boulevard** Ekaterinskaya Ploschad 1; ☎ 0487 770
339. Harking back to Odessa's romantic past, this
sunny, belle époque tribute is located at the top of
the Potemkin stairs. The fish soup is famous, if not
authentic, and the luncheons aristocratic. *Mains from
US$5; open 11.00–midnight.*
✖ **Druzya y Pivo** (Friends and Beer) Deribasovksaya
9 (downstairs); ☎ 0487 601 998. This cool,
underground wine cellar is Odessa's most beloved
café among travellers and local bohemians, serving
beer and really delicious food. Decked out with
original Odessa antiques and forgotten books of the
Soviet era, the menu is thoughtful – do indulge in
the chocolate mousse. The very laidback atmosphere,
artsy film nights and striking waitresses add to the
café's allure. There's also a 20% discount if you eat

vodka), and proud waiters swish back and forth in
national dress. After a meal, consider taking a tour
of the city, since Ukrainskaya Lakomka doubles as a
tour agency. *Mains from US$10; open
10.00–midnight.*
✖ **Kolyba** Fontanskaya Doroga 32B; ☎ 0482
348905; ✉ kolyba@tm.odessa.ua. Kolyba recreates
the mood of the Carpathians with complete
earnestness. A talented chef cooks up fresh fish,
oversized shish kebabs and a variety of salads. The
large sauna can be rented out by the hour (US$15),
and if you eat too much, the restaurant/hotel has 9
rooms with beds, some with lofts. *Mains from US$5;
open 10.00–midnight.*

expensive Russian restaurant trying to be a posh
English restaurant posing as an artsy French
restaurant. Delicate seafood with complicated sauces
dominate the 'art menu'. *Expect to pay around
US$40 per head (a bowl of soup alone costs US$12).*
✖ **Houdini** Deribaskovskaya 22; ☎ 0487 261 569. A
tribute to the great magician and escape artist,
featuring European cuisine. *Open 10.00–midnight.*
✖ **Steakhouse** Deribaskovskaya 20; ☎ 0482 348
782; www.steak.od.ua. For those who love red meat
and wine – giant steaks done just right, lots of
wine and hearty sides in a rather distinguished
atmosphere. *Mains from US$5, open 11.00–23.00.*
✖ **Valdai** Ploschad Potemkintsev 3; ☎ 0482 226
737. Lavish Baroque banquet hall inside of an old
palace ballroom; famous for big b/fasts and
sumptuous feasts. The stuffed fish comes highly
recommended. *Mains from US$7; open
08.00–midnight.*

before 18.00. *Cash only; mains from US$6; open
11.00–midnight.*
✖ **Hebron** Rishelyevskaya 30; ☎ 0487 150 374.
Dedicated to old Jerusalem and the memory of
Odessa's Jewish emigration, this underground café
serves the very best Jewish food in the city. Located
beneath the synagogue, this totally kosher kitchen
offers staples like falafel, *latkes*, *knish* and *kugel*,
washed down with big goblets of kosher wine.
Mains from US$5; open 11.00–23.00, closed Sat.
✖ **Till Ulenschpiegel** Deribasovskaya 12; ☎ 0482 429
046. A great corner café that embodies the spirit of
Odessa. Warm and friendly locals gather round the
big copper fireplace for drinks (Russian and Dutch
beer) or to enjoy light, intimate meals by the
windows. Everything on the menu is made fresh in

the kitchen, including home-baked bread and hand-stuffed sausage. Other specialities include fishcakes,

Italian

✗ **Mario's** Bolshaya Arnautskaya 23; ☎ 0487 281 068. Cheery, modern pizza joint with a fresh salad bar, young and friendly staff, and big cosy booths. *Giant brick-oven pizzas from US$6; cash only; open 11.00–23.00.*

✗ **Zara Pizzara** Rishelyevskaya 5; ☎ 0487 288 888. Hipster pizza place favoured among the young and

Asian

✗ **Phoenix** Osypova 28/30; ☎ 0482 242 984. Classic Chinese restaurant, with big, dark and smoky halls decked out in red Chinese silk. Popular for lush Chinese banquets. *Mains from US$6; open 11.00–midnight.*

✗ **China Wall Café** Corner of Bunina and Pushkinskaya; no phone. Quite literally a hole in the wall, but with a real Chinese chef from Beijing and delicious food. *Cash only; mains from US$4; open 11.00–22.00.*

✗ **Govinda** Bolshaya Arnautskaya 45; ☎ 0487 773 033. Odessa's only all-vegetarian restaurant, true to Hindu tradition. A good range of Indian food, vegan salads and colourful desserts. *Cash only; mains from US$4; open 11.00 to 22.00, closed Sun.*

Cafés and bars

✗ **Alpina** Troitskaya 35; ☎ 0482 358 152. A sleek-looking, yet odd Swiss–Ukrainian hybrid café managed by teenagers who blare techno music from the organic juice bar. The food is good though, especially the chicken curry and homemade *varrenyki. Mains from US$4; cash only, open 10.00–22.00.*

⌷ **Bar Bochka** Pushkinskaya 76; ☎ 0482 223 853. Dark underground bar with lots of character and a silent but sturdy bartender. Serves a variety of beer on tap and very good food to go with it; cash only. *Mains from US$3; open 10.00–23.00.*

✗ **Botsman Bar & Grill** Ekaterininskaya 3; ☎ 0482 226 737. An Odessa favourite for beer and grilled meat and fish. *Mains from US$5; open 10.00–midnight.*

⌷ **Buffalo 99** Rishelyevskaya 7; ☎ 0487 288 899. Loud and busy sports bar with football playing on overhead TVs and fried food galore. *Open 11.00–23.00.*

omelettes and salads, and nothing is priced over US$10. *Open 08.00–23.00.*

mobile business set. Delicious wood-stove pizza and a very yummy dessert cart. *From US$10.*

✗ **Pulcinella Pizzeria** Lanzheronovskaya 17; ☎ 0487 773 010. Colourful pizza place right in the city centre. *Good pizza and pasta from US$5; open 10.00–23.00.*

✗ **Kyoto** Troitskaya 56; ☎ 0487 165 599. Upscale, minimalist sushi bar that caters to businessmen. Good, fresh sushi for around US$4/piece. *Cash only; open 11.00–23.00.*

✗ **Shal Imar** Grecheskaya 50; ☎ 0487 774 747. Real Uzbekistani cuisine in a relaxed central Asian setting with friendly service. Renowned for its *lagman* (noodles) and the yummy salmon in white rose sauce. I can honestly say that theirs is the best *plov* I've eaten in Ukraine. *Cash only; mains from US$7; open 10.00–midnight.*

✗ **Yokohama** Deribaskovskaya 26; ☎ 0482 356 600. Another sushi place, yes, but probably the most established in the city. The Japanese theme is taken to the extreme, with great sushi, sashimi and noodle dishes. *Mains from US$15; open 11.00–23.00.*

✗ **De Zire** Grecheskaya 3/4; ☎ 0487 384 478. Cute little French café with salads, good lunches and a quiet refuge from the streetside bustle. Salads, forgotten French cuisine, and a nice wine list. *Mains from US$7; open 10.00–23.00.*

⌷ **Fanconi** Ekaterininskaya 8/10; ☎ 0482 222 772. A very personal little place that specialises in dainty cakes and potent coffee – the kind of homey café where you stop for an afternoon beer when it's raining outside. Boasting several historical and literary references, this café is also probably the most authentic 'Odessa' establishment that's open right now. Drinks are inexpensive and the meals are also tasty and filling, with mains from US$5. *Cash only; open 10.00–22.00.*

⌷ **Passazh** Passazh Shopping Centre, 2nd floor. A good place for rich afternoon coffee and Turkish pastries. Light and savoury meals are also served. *Cash only; mains from US$4; open 10.00–20.00.*

Cheap eats You can already eat like a king in Odessa for under US$10, but if you are watching every hrivna, then try **Zharyu Paryu** (*Preobrazhenskaya 44;* ☎ *0487*

THE POTEMKIN STAIRS

Cities are usually known for their towers, statues, or buildings, but Odessa is best symbolised by the massive stone descent from Primorsky Boulevard to the pier. Designed by Italian architect Franz Boffo and completed in 1841, the original structure incorporated 200 steps that went right into the water but eight of the steps were covered after the lower port was built. Climbing up (or down) the 192 uneven granite steps can be a task, but it is worth seeing both ends, for the stairs were built as an illusion; the lower stairs are much wider than those at the top (by 7m), so that the width appears uniform when looking down them. If you want to cheat, there's a free funicular that runs up and down the hill, open from 08.00 to 23.00.

Outsiders may recognise the Potemkin steps from Sergei Eisenstein's immortal film, *Battleship Potemkin*, which recounts one of the more heroic tales from the first Russian revolution. In June 1905, sailors with the imperial navy mutinied and took control of the most powerful battleship in the Black Sea fleet, the *Potemkin*, named after General Potemkin (pronounced Pa-tyom-kin), Catherine the Great's sly suitor. In Odessa the workers' movement had already been leading a massive strike for over two weeks, and when the mutinied battleship sailed into the city's harbour, huge crowds gathered near the waterfront. The leader of the rebellion, Valenchuk, had been shot in the struggle, and his body was laid at the foot of the grand Odessa staircase. Thousands came to pay their respects and to support the sailors' uprising. In the film, the Tsarist troops descended the stairs, firing on the crowds below, while the people fled or jumped into the sea. Around 2,000 people died. Eisenstein's Odessa stairs sequence (filmed on site) is praised as the ultimate scene in modernist filmmaking, and despite the intended Bolshevik propaganda, the *Battleship Potemkin* is often considered to be one of the greatest action films ever made. The actual Potemkin rebellion was a turning point for the revolution since many of Lenin's sceptics had previously believed the military would never show solidarity with the workers' movement. Unrest in the military gave hope to the Bolsheviks and the rest is history.

224 430), a clean and spacious cafeteria that's popular with students. Everything is fresh and tasty, and the storefront bar sells freshly squeezed juice for US$1.

Walking down Preobrazhenksaya will bring you to several authentic 'Odessit' bakeries. The miniscule one on the corner of Uspenskaya and Preobrazhenskaya is a classic. Try the *agma* with *brynza* cheese, traditional Jewish honeycake, and the local version of *baklava*.

Hotel restaurants Every upscale Odessa hotel features a restaurant or café, and all of them are open to everyone. Otrada's **Casa d'Italia** (*Uyutnaya 11*) features an imaginative Italian chef and a fresh take on Odessa's culinary strong points. The main restaurant at **Mozart** (*Lanzheronsvskaya 13*) specialises in elegant and eclectic dishes, yet despite all the splendour, prices are comparable to back home (*US$20–30 per meal*). **Londonsky** (*Primorsky 11*) has long been considered a distinguished setting for a lunch or dinner of classic Russian cuisine, with an advantageous location for a stop during a walking tour of the city. The Black Sea Hotel's **Seven Samurai** (*Rishelievskaya 55;* ✆ *0482 300 937*) serves Japanese cuisine.

NIGHTLIFE Odessa plays harder and longer than any other city in Ukraine, with lots of flashy clubs and a whole culture surrounding underground basement pubs,

11

glitzy discos and all-night cafés. If you spend any time here, you'll quickly tune into the effervescent scene.

☆ **Vis-à-vis** Deribasovskaya 17; ☎ 0487 770 203; www.visavis.od.ua. Ultra-contemporary nightclub with glossy white and silver décor, lots of ambient lighting, and a hipper-than-thou clientele. The lounge, casino, disco, soundstage and supper club all fuse into the perfect all-night escape. The outdoor balconies are open for drinking and dining in the summer. *Open 24hrs.*

☆ **Dali Gali** Corner of Chaikovsky and Yekaterininskaya (no phone). Depending on when you walk through the doors, it's a restaurant, or a bar, or a nightclub. Like their Surrealist namesake, this place can get a little crazy. *Open 24hrs.*

☆ **Faktura** Rishelyevskaya 58; ☎ 0482 349 880. A rave-y dance club that's popular among the university crowd. *Open 08.00–06.00.*

☆ **Mirage** Preobrazhenskaya 36; ☎ 0482 220 310. Cheesy, Vegas-style casino and nightclub with an in-house Chinese restaurant and friendly, thick-necked bouncers. *Open 24hrs.*

☆ **Pilot** Yekaterininskaya 15/17; ☎ 0482 356 600. On the outside, it looks just like a sleepy sidewalk café, but go inside at night and things get pretty wild. *Open 10.00–02.00, weekends 24hrs.*

☆ **Palladium** Italyansky Boulevard 4. The flashiest dinner club in Odessa to date brings a bit of Las Vegas right into the city centre. Colourful shows and overpriced food secure the illusion. Don't say 'mafia' too loudly. *Open 17.00–06.00.*

☆ **Vechernyaya Odessa** Pushkinskaya 59; ☎ 0482 321 421. Pumping dance club, acrobatic bartenders and fashion shows. Quite a human circus. *Open 21.00–06.00.*

WHAT TO SEE AND DO When Mark Twain landed in Odessa in 1867, he rejoiced that there were 'no sights to see and that [he] had nothing to do but to idle about the city and enjoy [himself]'. The American writer reported sauntering through the streets, admiring the populace and eating ice cream. All three activities are still highly recommended in Odessa, and any traveller should start immediately after arriving by taking in the city's long boulevards and busy seaport. Odessa's streets form a slanted grid against the coast – each is remarkably distinct and action-packed. The main 'drag' **Deribasovskaya** is named for Spaniard De Ribas, who actually constructed Odessa's original stone harbour and secured its fate as a cosmopolitan port city. Deribasovksaya is by far the most lively of Odessa's cobblestone streets; it's packed with shops, restaurants, animals, people and movement. A large section is closed off for pedestrians, and it's a great place for dining and people-watching. Near the corner with **Preobrazhenskaya** is a gateway that leads into Odessa's most famous shopping spot, the extravagant 18th-century **Passazh** corridor where a vaulted glass roof shields the designer boutiques and posh cafés (entrance at Deribasovskaya 33) behind the elaborate Baroque façade. Continuing down Preobrazhenskaya takes you past several of the city's churches and parks, connecting to some of Odessa's quieter neighbourhoods. Built to resemble a well-mannered English promenade, the tree-lined **Primorsky Boulevard** stands high above the port and descends to the main sea terminal by way of the **Potemkin stairs**. Primorsky Boulevard is where locals prefer to stroll, and in the early evening there is truly no better place to take in the view of the Black Sea. From up high, one can spot the **Odessa Lighthouse**, thrice destroyed and rebuilt, but still guiding cargo ships into the harbour. As for eating ice cream, the options are limitless, especially in summer when it is sold on the streets and in every café and restaurant.

Monuments and memorials Odessa's collection of bronze statuary is impressive and sporadic. Little busts and memorial plaques dot the city, along with quite a few playful statuettes. Some are legitimate monuments to the city's grandest people and events, others are a little more obscure (e.g: the monument of the first water main; the bust of Dr Zamenhof, the founder of Esperanto who never lived in

Odessa's reputation for hard-nosed comedy was born with *The 12 Chairs*, a satirical novel that celebrates the absurd and carefree era of the late 1920's, when Lenin's New Economic Policy was in full force. The story opens with the penniless aristocrat Hippolyte Matveyevich bemoaning the Russian Revolution and his lost inheritance. He regains hope when his mother-in-law makes a deathbed confession that she has hid the family jewels inside one of the dining room chairs (upholstered in English chintz) that was taken from their estate by the Bolsheviks. Determined to regain his wealth, Hippolyte sets off on a crazy adventure across the Soviet Union and Europe, employing the sly Odessa conman Ostap Bender to track down a piece of bourgeois furniture in a nominally Communist society. One by one, the unlikely pair discovers each chair from the 12-piece dining room set, only to be disappointed by their lack of contents. Meanwhile, the Orthodox priest who overheard the mother-in-law's confession is also hunting down the same chair, as do others, until a whole army of treasure hunters are chasing one another. The book paints a hilarious picture of early Soviet society and is filled with very Odessa moments: bartering for foreign goods on the black market, scheming around bureaucracy, and a shower that cuts off, leaving the bather covered in soap suds. Odessites still quote such famous lines as 'all contraband is made on Little Arnautskaya street, in Odessa' and the book's very last sentence is a tribute to Odessa's fortitude in poverty or wealth: 'the city set off on its daily routine.' A bronze monument to the 12th chair is located where Deribasovskaya meets the City Garden, acknowledging the book's authors, Ilf and Petrov.

Odessa but who had quite a following in such a multilingual city). At the top of the Potemkin steps stands the **statue of Duc Armand de Richelieu**, known as the father of Odessa. As a descendent of the infamous French Cardinal Richelieu, the young noble fled revolutionary France and found his place within the Russian Empire. Granted governorship of the area, the duke invited other French and Italian aristocrats to expand their fortune in this New Russia. His short but effective tenure brought art, culture and wealth to Odessa. Legend claims that the duke was so beloved that when he accepted the post of prime minister of France and left Odessa, the citizens unhooked his horses and pulled the carriage themselves. At the base of Primorsky Boulevard (near the start of the promenade and just beyond the oversized bust of **Pushkin**) stands the **cannon** from the *Tiger*, an English frigate that was scuttled in Odessa's harbour in 1854, at the height of the Crimean War. (NB: In the history of the British navy, 12 ships have been christened HMS *Tiger*.) Next to the archaeology museum on Customs Square stands Odessa's most recent memorial (erected in 2004), the **orange monument**, which shows a giant bronze orange being pulled by horses. After Catherine the Great died, her son Paul I took over the throne for a brief and unsuccessful reign of five years. Contrary to his mother's vision for New Russia, he stopped construction of the port in Odessa and stripped the city of its privilege and subsidies. In response, Odessa's Greek community sent 3,000 oranges to St Petersburg as a gift to the young tsar and as a tasteful reminder of Odessa's role for importing fruit. The ploy worked, the subsidies were returned, and Odessa became a working port, saved by oranges. Odessits claim that this is a monument to the first bribe ever paid in Odessa and thereby the start of an important local tradition. The **monument to the sailors of the Battleship Potemkin** forms the roundabout on Ekaterininskaya Square, but as the name of the square suggests, the Soviet memorial replaced a much larger statue of Catherine the Great. A popular

Odessa photo-op takes in the **pair of Atlases**, holding a star-studded globe, beneath the palace where Gogol Street meets Primorsky Boulevard. The statue was a mere architectural flourish dating from the early 20th century, and the palaces were actually rented apartments for the visiting gentry. In the southwest corner of the city, on Prokhurovksy Square, is a small park and Odessa's **Holocaust memorial**, featuring an artistic rendition of emaciated victims. The monument recalls the first wave of 10,000 Odessa Jews who were deported to concentration camps in 1941. Another nearby memorial and the trees planted in the park recognise those citizens of Odessa who helped hide or free the city's Jews during the Nazi occupation.

Museums Odessa feels like such an exciting place that its museums pale in comparison with the streets. However, there are a few exceptions worth exploring on an overcast day.

Museum of Eastern and Western Art (*Pushkinskaya 9;* ❧ *0482 246 746; open 10.00–17.00, closed Wed; entrance 3UAH*) A small yet diverse art collection occupies this crumbling blue palace.

Along with a few works by Michelangelo and Rubens, there is a variety of oriental art on display from central Asia, Tibet, China and Japan.

Odessa Fine Arts Museum (*Sofiyevskaya 5A;* ❧ *0482 238 462; entrance 3UAH*) Far more impressive, the gallery is housed inside Count Pototsky's grandiose palace and features a superb collection of 19th-century Russian and Ukrainian art, including works by Shevchenko and Aivozovsky, and the Odessa school of early 20th-century impressionists.

Archaeological Museum (*Lanzherovskaya 4;* ❧ *0482 226 302; open 10.00–17.00, closed Mon; entrance 3UAH*) The oldest museum in Ukraine is Odessa's Archaeological Museum. A marble copy of the *Laocoön* from the Vatican stands in the front as a nod to the classical treasures within. Odessa's generous Greek Cypriot community refurbished an entire floor of the museum to modern standards with a striking array of locally found Greek antiquities. An English narrative is provided. The rest of the collection includes Scythian gold, Sarmatian swords, Greek amphorae, and early Slavic tools from Kievan Rus. The Egyptian room feels slightly irrelevant, however; it is the only one like it in Ukraine – a gift from the Egyptian Museum in Cairo.

Ship Museum (*Lanzherovskaya 6*) Across Customs Square, this museum recently suffered an unfortunate demise due to a destructive fire. The exhibit is closed for the time being, but will hopefully reopen soon. Once upon a time, the palace-like structure was Odessa's famed 'English club' where local Anglophiles and English diplomats gathered for dinners and conversation. During the Soviet era, the bourgeois club became a memorial to Odessa's main industry and the museum has changed little since. If you are a fan of model ships or Russian history, the vivid display will please. Intricate replicas and grand socialist paintings recount the 'natural' evolution from Viking ships to the mighty Black Sea fleet and Soviet merchant ships, all beneath the painted adage that 'Ships are like people, they all die differently'.

Pushkin Literary Museum (*Pushkinskaya 13;* ❧ *0482 251 034; open 10.00–17.00, closed Mon; entrance 5 UAH*) Practically every former Soviet city houses some tribute to Pushkin and this museum is dedicated to the poet's time in Odessa. In 1820, after

Odessa's most famous writer helped make Odessa famous with his brutally frank depictions of city life in the rough and tumble transition from civil war to Soviet society. Most of Babel's *Odessa Stories* take place in the Moldovanka, the city's Jewish ghetto in which he was born and grew up. As a young boy, Babel suffered repeated discrimination for being Jewish, being kept out of schools and universities due to government quotas on minorities. In 1905, his family survived the Black Hundreds (see page 25) thanks to neighbours who hid them in a basement. Babel grew up to fight in the Russian civil war and later wrote about his experiences in his very candid *Red Cavalry Stories*. He then went on to write about Odessa, painting the Moldovanka as a slum filled with grungy criminals, crafty street merchants and histrionic women. Ironically, this scant collection of stories has become the hearth of a warm nostalgia felt by Russians, Ukrainians, Jews and Odessit émigrés throughout the world. Failing to conform with Soviet ideals in art, Babel was arrested in 1939 and jailed at the infamous Lubyanka prison before being shot. One may visit Babel's '**home**' at Rishelyevskaya 17, although he only lived here later on in his life. If you are keen to venture into the real **Moldovanka**, head towards the southwest corner of the city, beginning at Privoznaya Market near the rail station. Many of the street names have been changed, but the traditional neighbourhood occupies the area from Prokhorovksy Square to Balkovskaya, along with Dalnitskaya, Melnitskaya (formerly known as Moiseenko; Ukrainian for *son of Moses*) and the eponymous Babelya off of Mikhayilovksa Square (formerly known as Polyamikov). The area makes for fascinating urban exploration, but bear in mind that the Moldovanka is slightly larger than Odessa's city centre. Either give specific instructions to a taxi driver or take a good map.

having published several politically charged poems, Pushkin was exiled to Kishinev. He was quite miserable in Moldova, but his friends finally succeeded in having him transferred to the more culturally astute Odessa. Pushkin fell in love with the area, beginning one of his books with 'And so, I lived a while in Odessa …' It is here that Pushkin wrote several chapters of the classic *Eugene Onegin*, as well as his famous poem, *The Bakhchisarai Fountain* (see page 316). The museum exhibit is rather sparse; it's limited to original books, sketches and scribbles, and some furniture.

Odessa Literary Museum (*Lanzheronovskaya 2;* \ *0482 220 002; open 10.00–17.00, closed Mon; entrance 5UAH*) A more worthwhile visit can be made to the Literary Museum. Located in a suite of galleries in Count Gagarin's palace, the museum remembers the works of Russian favourites like Pushkin, Gogol and Chekhov, as well as a large collection of Odessa's very own writers, including the beloved Isaac Babel.

Odessa Jewish Museum (*66 Nejinskaya, No 10;* \ *0487 289 743; open 13.00–19.00, closed Fri–Sat*) Private and petite but rich in local history.

Churches A diverse population brought many different religious buildings to Odessa, but communist activism and Russian history destroyed most and left the few remaining churches in pretty bad condition. Fortunately, the people of Odessa are slowly but surely rebuilding and redecorating. Coming in from the train station rewards visitors with a beautiful view of the **Panteleimonovsky Monastery** (*Panteleimonsovskaya 66*) with its floating silver domes. The inside will be magnificent once the refurbishment is completed. Used as a planetarium during

Soviet rule, the building is now a working monastery of the Russian Orthodox Church and an active centre of Odessa's spiritual life, teeming with believers, beggars and monks. Within walking distance is the light blue, Byzantine-style **St Ilya's Church** (*Pushkinskaya 75*), a somewhat more reserved cathedral. The Greek Orthodox **Church of the Holy Trinity** (*Yekaterinskaya 55*) is another Odessa architectural monument and a good place to catch lively Orthodox festivals and weddings. Preobrazhenskaya is Russian for 'Transfiguration', and runs up and down the west side of the city centre. On the corner with Bazarnaya stands the pale blue **Holy Assumption Cathedral**, which for the time being is the best-preserved church in Odessa, with lovely external mosaics and some beautiful natural lighting inside from the towering lanterns. Odessa's most famous cathedral was always known as 'the Cathedral', although it was officially christened the **Cathedral of the Transfiguration**. This is the very stately Neoclassical church with the giant dome on Sobornaya (Cathedral) Square, near the corner of Preobrazhenskaya and Deribasovskaya. The building you see today was constructed only in the last five years and follows the original plans, which include the uncommon feature of a second floor. Count Mikhayil Vorontsov (governor of New Russia from 1823; see page 344) and his wife were interred in the cathedral (she being famous for her very open affair with Pushkin). Prior to the Soviets blowing up the cathedral, some thoughtful citizens removed the bodies and buried them in a hidden Odessa graveyard. The Soviets used the stone from the cathedral to construct the two schools visible behind the square. Now that the exterior of the church has been rebuilt, the bodies of the count and countess have been replaced in a more respectable tomb. Another recent addition is **St Nikolai by the Sea** on the far end of the main pier, just below the monstrous Hotel Odessa. Small and modern, the church is dedicated to St Nikolai, patron of travellers and those making any type of voyage. It is to this church that Odessa's sailors come before going to sea, a common reality for tens of thousands of Odessits who are away for periods of six to eight months. Their wives and mothers also attend this church and light candles for their safe return.

Odessa's main working **synagogue** is at Yevreiskaya 25; it was only recently returned to the Jewish community after decades of Soviet occupation. A wonderful kosher restaurant is located in the basement, and the attendants upstairs can direct you to any of the Jewish sites in the area. A separate book could be (and indeed has been) written on the Jews of Odessa, who began settling following a decree by Catherine the Great. At one time there were 78 working synagogues here (today there are just two) and at its peak, Jews accounted for around 70% of Odessa's population. Jewish tradition still greatly influences this city, but following the violence of the revolution, World War II and major emigration since independence, Odessa's Jews now number only 30,000 out of the city's one million inhabitants. The second synagogue (which is not functioning) is the grey building at the corner of Pushkinskaya and Bazarnaya. The **Hasidic synagogue** is at Osipova 17. Odessa has several cemeteries, all of which are predominantly Jewish. The **Jewish cemetery,** as it is known, is located at Khimicheskaya 1 and dates mainly from the Soviet era. The flashy black headstones – some of them engraved with images of dice and semi-automatic weapons – often fail to impress. Travellers in search of specific gravesites in other cemeteries are often disappointed to find that they are no longer there. Often the older cemeteries are grown over, with only a few weathered stones beneath a deep forest.

Theatre A symbol of the city, the **Odessa Opera House and Ballet** was built by Austrian architects in 1887 and stands blossom-like at Teatralnaya Square. The previous opera house – completed in 1809 – was the very first in the Russian Empire, but sadly burned to the ground in 1873. The Viennese replacement has suffered additional misfortunes as the beauteous structure has been sinking into the ground, unevenly, for the past century. The proposed remedy involves using thousands of concrete pilings to alleviate the stress on the cracked walls, and for the most part, the building remains closed as long as the work continues. Even so, the Odessa Opera itself continues to perform, as does the Odessa Ballet Company – both of which are world famous and of incredible quality. The shows often take place at alternate locations, although opera and ballet tickets can still be purchased at the small booth next to the opera house (*corner of Lanzherovskaya and Chaikovskovo;* \ *0482 291 329*). Odessa's **Russian Drama Theatre** (*Grecheskaya 48;* \ *0482 227 250*) performs all the Russian classics and European favourites – like Chekhov – as well as some experimental pieces, while the **Odessa Ukrainian Theatre of Musical Drama** (*Pastera 15;* \ *0482 235 566*) presently hosts more ballets and classic musicals. For lighter operettas and more modern spectacles, visit the **Theatre of Musical Comedy** (*Panteleimonovskaya 3;* \ *250 924*). The **Odessa**

GIVING SOMETHING BACK

FUTURUM CHILDREN'S REHABILITATION CENTRE Walking down beautiful Pushkinskaya it's hard to miss the golden 'guardian angel' that hangs over house number 51. Nor is it easy to miss the children and parents that pour in and out of its doors. Dedicated to giving a future to children with cerebral palsy, the 'Futurum' rehabilitation centre offers a combination of therapies and medical treatment to help children develop sensory perception, stimulate muscles, improve motor skills and physical coordination, and train for a future career. On any given day, over 100 patients will be receiving treatment at the centre, and in total, over 15,000 children have already been treated here. Perhaps most miraculous is that all treatment is free of charge – almost unheard of in Ukraine.

The centre was founded by Boris Litvak, headmaster of the special athletic school next door. When his daughter contracted cancer, she questioned her father about why there were only such institutions for athletes and not for children with physical difficulties. After her death, he founded the centre in her honour, with the aim of improving the standard of living for children with cerebral palsy and their families. The centre functions completely on private donations and now boasts a gymnasium for wheelchair basketball and an extensive computer lab. Visitors are welcome to the centre any time and are free to donate funds or time.

Odessa Regional Charitable Rehabilitation Foundation for Handicapped Children Pushkinskaya 51, Odessa 65011, Ukraine; \ *0487 242 505;* e *referent@rc.odessa.ua; www.rc.odessa.ua.*

Philharmonic (*Bunina 15;* ✆ *0482 251 536*) first housed the busy Odessa stock exchange, and the Neo-Gothic, brick-patterned structure is worth visiting in its own right. Now home to Odessa's ever-famous philharmonic orchestra, few other evening activities could take precedence to a performance here. Tickets can be ordered by phone or bought at the booth inside the main entrance during the day (take the steps downstairs on Bunina). Last but not least, the **Odessa Puppet Theatre** (*Pastera 15;* ✆ *0487 601 970*) performs merry shows for children and adults right next to the Ukrainian theatre.

Parks Odessa's parks fall into two categories: the calm, quiet and often well-hidden city squares that offer a shady respite from the flurry of the streets, and the very rowdy and extroverted public areas where Odessits go to blow off steam. The **City Garden**, at the end of Deribasovskaya is very much of the latter type, with lots of souvenir stands and vigorous busking day and night, as is Sobornaya, the souvenir market surrounding the cathedral on Preobrazhenskaya. By far the largest park, **Park Shevchenko**, joins the industrial port to the long coastline of city beaches and has become an active centre for weekend and summer entertainment. The forest of trees competes with a bevy of beachgoers and the busy restaurants they patronise. The **Old Market Square** (*starobazarnaya*) on Aleksandrovsky is most representative of Odessa's old city parks, as is the green space below the distinguished promenade of Primorsky Boulevard.

Odessa's beaches As a rule, the further south you move along the coast, the better the beaches get, 'better' being relative to the murky harbour. Soviet families once made annual pilgrimages to these shores, and the tradition lives on with hundreds of thousands of visitors from all over Russia and Ukraine who come to enjoy the sea, sun and sand. If you haven't noticed, Russians prefer standing when they sunbathe and most of Odessa's beaches are standing room only during July and August. The sea is another matter, considering that untreated sewage for over one million people flows gently down to these shores (adding new meaning to the name 'Black Sea'). Both **Arkadia** and **Otrada** beaches are absolutely filthy, with more rubbish than sand in sight, and brown foam swilling through the waves. Arkadia is also the ultimate in post-Soviet beachside glitz, and if you enjoy semi-naked crowds, loud music and phoney tropical beach clubs, this is the place. Some clubs are private, allowing a bit more space on the beach for a price. Truly, some beaches are cleaner than others, but these also tend to be the most popular. **Delphin** and **Fontan** are relatively safe for swimming and have less garbage than normal, but the beaches are packed full from May to September. The best beach for cheesy amusement is **Lanzheron**, within walking distance of the city centre. The other beaches can be reached by taking the tram along Frantsuzky Boulevard from the train station in the direction of the sanatoria. The trip is long (and hot in summer), so you might want to consider taking a taxi.

OUTSIDE ODESSA For military and history buffs, a short excursion takes you from the city centre out to the memorial to the heroic defence of Odessa, better known as **Battery 411.** The former 1940s bastion has been converted into an outdoor park/museum featuring Soviet armaments, some of which were used in defending the city against the Germans. The collection includes Soviet aircraft, missiles, cannons, tanks and ships, as well as an intact World War II Soviet submarine. To get there, either take a cab (for around US$8) or jump on *marshrutka* No 194 by the train station and take it to the very end. A nearby museum tells the story of Odessa's role in World War II in pictures and Soviet-era commentary (*Dacha Kovalevskovo 150;* ✆ *0482 444 527; open 10.00 to 18.00, closed Fri*).

The Odessa catacombs About 10km north of the city is the back entrance into Odessa's more secretive past. The Odessa catacombs are unlike those in western Europe, as they are all manmade and relatively new (200 years old). Instead of piling up people's bones, these tunnels were used for all the city's clandestine activities, which have been numerous.

Before Odessa came into being, Russian Cossacks had settled in this area (which at the time was ruled by Turkey), due to Catherine the Great's policies outlawing Cossackdom in the empire after the Pugachev rebellion in 1773. As the Turkish sultan granted them asylum, the warriors made a pact to no longer fight, hence the village name, Nerubaiskoye ('no-fighting'). Many of these Cossack settlements line the Khadzhibeisky estuary, where easy access to soft limestone permitted the quarrying of unlimited building material for the glorious estates of New Russia. Most of Odessa's palaces are built from this rock. Through trial and error, workers in the late 18th century found that a horse and cart worked best in tunnels between 15–30m deep, and as the city of Odessa rose up, hundreds of level tunnels were cut through the bedrock. An extensive network was left beneath the city, totalling over 2,000km in length. In early years, the Russian gentry found that the constant temperature and humidity were perfect for storing wine, while Odessa's many smugglers found the tunnels to be convenient warehouses and exit channels in their private business of moving duty-free imports from the free trade zone into the heavily controlled Russian Empire. However the real glory days of the catacombs came to pass during World War II, when Romanian forces invaded Odessa. Unlike the Carpathians, where partisans could hide in forests and mountains, the Odessa resistance took over the catacombs and literally carried out their sabotage work from underground. Sleeping by day and going out at night, the resistance was successful in destroying several enemy buildings, as well as blowing up the Nazi headquarters. Throughout Odessa's occupation, the Romanians and German Nazis tried various tactics to find and empty the catacombs, and there are stories of dogs turning back from the darkness and the ghosts of lost soldiers still wandering, lost in the labyrinth. Whatever the case, the catacombs prevented 12 of Odessa's 13 partisan bands from ever being discovered.

A trip to the catacombs takes a little over two hours and is best done by organised tour; nearly all hotels and tour agencies listed in this chapter offer half-day trips that include a trip to the entrance in the village of Nerubaiskoye, an extensive guided tour through the tunnels and the underground partisan hideout, and entrance to the local Partisan museum (6UAH). Group tours usually cost around US$15 per person, individual tours with a guide and driver can run up to US$70. If you want to make the trip on your own, there are buses that leave from the train and bus stations to the village, but the schedule changes frequently. Visitors are not allowed inside the catacombs without a designated guide, and so you will be assigned one at the museum. I know it's stating the obvious, but never leave your guide or the designated path in the catacombs. Getting lost in a 2,000km maze can mean never being found. Some of the things to look for on the tour include graffiti from nationalist Slovak partisans (Gust Bezak), the memorial to slain partisan Ivan Ivanovich Ivanov, the secret entrance from the garden well, and the display of homemade weapons and bombs used against the Nazis. A personal taxi to the catacombs should cost around US$10 one way and the drive takes about 20 minutes.

BILHOROD-DNISTROVSKY БІЛГОРОД-ДНІСТРОВСЬКИЙ

The ancient town of Bilhorod rests on the southern shore of the Dnistr estuary, a strategic spot for entrance into both Moldova and Galicia. The Greeks built the city of Tira on this site back in the 6th century BC; however, visitors today come to take

11

in the mighty castle, most of which was built in the 15th century to defend Moldova from Turkish invasion. Alas, the Turks prevailed in 1484, and for the next 400 years the town and battlement were known as Akkerman. The Soviets renamed it the 'White City on the Dnistr', harking back to the days of early Kievan Rus and the Galician kingdom. The **castle** is open every day (*10.00–18.00; entrance 6UAH*). The structure's perimeter is over a mile in length and the fat walls and bulky towers are open for exploring. The gateway and minaret are pronouncedly Turkish, while the very square features date to the earlier Genoese era. In addition, the 15th-century **Armenian church** (*Kutuzova 1*) is worth a visit, as is the **Jewish cemetery** (*Laso 35*).

Some major trains connect Bilhorod with Odessa, but the *elektrichki* are far more frequent and quicker. By far the most convenient option is to sign up for an organised day trip that provides motor transport back and forth from the city. Most Odessa hotels and travel agencies can offer excursions to Bilhorod. If you decide to stay in town for a while, the best accommodation option is the Hotel Rus (*Shevchenko 1;* ☎ *0484 925 940; rooms from US$30*).

THE DNISTR AND DANUBE DELTA

Southeast from Odessa lie the convergent wetlands of the Dnistr and Danube rivers, a rich natural location that has only just come under international scrutiny. The Dnistr delta is closest to Odessa and provides some amazing natural scenery and plenty of wildlife for viewing. Covering a wide territory of marshes, lakes and natural canals, the **Dnistr National Park** is home to over 300 species of birds, including plentiful populations of egrets, cormorants, spoonbills and pelicans, as well as some very rare varieties like the glossy ibis and yellow-crowned night heron. Major campaigns to preserve the delta and expand the park into Moldova look towards outside interest and ecotourism to fund local education about the wetlands. Seeing the delta is nearly impossible without a boat, but if you want to travel down there on your own, take the bus from the Odessa station to the village of Bilyayivka. Make sure to get off before the border with Moldova and stay well on the Ukrainian side.

The Danube delta is even less accessible and feels extremely remote on the Ukrainian side, so that most visitors come up from Romania. Public transport from Odessa (on trains and buses) can bring you close to these northern wetlands, but it can take up to seven hours (!). It's far better to organise a tour to the **Dunaisky Biosphere Reserve.** Established only in 1998, this protected area takes in the very best wild spots on the Ukrainian side: the reeds and bulrushes, floating lilies, distinctive animal and bird life, and small islets, including the youngest island in Europe, *novaya zemlya*, or new land, from the accumulated silt of the delta. Interested travellers can contact the reserve directly in the village of Vilkovo (*Tatarbunarskovo Povstannya 132, No 4;* ☎ *04843 311 95*).

In Odessa, **Vilkovo Tour** specialises in ecotourism to both parks, with regular excursions planned from April until October. They offer a wide range of excellent programmes from group day tours that originate in Odessa to fishing and birding trips and much more exclusive ecotours that include a private boat and guide. Their Danube biosphere tours normally take travellers down to the absolutely remote riverside village of **Vilkovo**, where there are more canals and rivulets than streets, and where the local people live off the fish they catch. A three–four-hour boat tour takes you to all of the delta's 'sites', including fantastic birding, and the **0km** point from which the Danube is measured throughout Europe. Lunch is river-caught fish roasted over a fire on one of the delta's islands, accompanied by locally produced wine. The agency also offers fishing tours in the Danube delta;

the optimal season is September to October. Group tours start at US$12 per person, while individual VIP and special birding excursions cost around US$200/day. Contact Vilkovo Tour, Odessa (*Preobrazhenskaya 40, 3rd Floor;* e *v_tour_ad@ukr.net; www.vilkovo-tour.com*).

MYKOLAYIV МИКОЛАЇВ

Bridging the mile-wide mouth of the Southern Buh River, Mykolayiv (or Nikolayev) is home to over half a million people and stands as a visible testament to the ups and downs of the post-Soviet economy. Seeking to expand the empire seaward, General Potemkin ordered New Russia's shipbuilding centre to be constructed here in 1789. For the next two hundred years, skilled labourers hammered together Russia's navy and commercial fleet, until Ukrainian independence, when this massive port turned to rust overnight. During the late 1990s, Mykolayiv held the title of Ukraine's hard-drug capital and suffered all the problems that go with it – the city also went down in history as the official entry point of AIDS into Ukraine. Yet today, the mass of heavy industry and a population of skilled workers has attracted enough investment for the city to be making a slow comeback. Nearly all the mighty ships of the present Russian navy were built in Mikolayiv, including Russia's only working aircraft carrier, the *Kuznetsov*.

You will find locals use the city's two names interchangeably, as it is named after St Nikolai (Mikola in Ukrainian) for no other reason than the fact that the city was founded on or around St Nicolas Day (6 December). Almost all group tours will pass through Mikolayiv as they run between Odessa and Crimea overland, yet few – if any – stop. Thus, Mykolayiv separates the tourists from the travellers. It doesn't even compare to nearby Odessa, but it is no longer the depressing and dour port city that it was ten years ago. A swirl of new shops and hotels have sprung up from the ashes of the industrial meltdown, and the unemployed masses are plentiful and usually friendly. Ironically, this is where Trotsky went to school.

GETTING THERE AND AWAY The best part of Mykolayiv is actually leaving, for the landscape on the way to Kherson or Odessa is truly beautiful, with fields of wheat and gigantic marshes that are noisy with seabirds. Crossing the bridge from central Mikolayiv to Odessa takes you across the Southern Buh at its widest point – truly beautiful, and highly photogenic. The bus station is at Oktyabrskaya 8 (Zhovtnevy 8 in Ukrainian). The bus journey to Odessa takes around 2½ hours, while to Kherson it takes 1½ hours, and the train to either place takes twice as long. Regular *marshrutka* run all day between Mikolayiv, Odessa and Kherson. To catch a ride to Odessa, just go to the corner of Chingiz and Oktyabrksaya and climb into one of the many mini-buses waiting.

The train station is located at the end of Pushkinskaya, with regular services to Odessa and Kherson, but not an optimal choice. The direct overnight Kiev–Mykolayiv train comes and goes once a day (12 hours).

WHERE TO STAY

Hotel Kontinent Admirala Makarova 41; 0512 477 520; e kon@sp.mk.ua; www.continent.mk.ua. The city's most central and most popular hotel with a number of good rooms decorated in a charming fashion – mint green walls hung with Salvador Dali prints, with red satin couches to match. Dependable hot water. Credit cards accepted. *Rooms US$50–100.*

Hotel Imperator Moskovskaya 38; 0512 476 140; f 0512 362 123. This is more of a luxury complex for out-of-town Ukrainian businessmen, but it does have a few plush rooms, as well as a glittery restaurant. Tsarist grandeur reigns supreme. *Sgls US$70, dbls US$80.*

Hotel Ukraine Palace Lenina 57; 0512 582 700. Step away from dingy Prospekt Lenina and into a world of polished marble and sparkly chandeliers. Mikolayiv's flashiest new hotel affirms the city's chintzy new business profile but also offers high-quality accommodation to passing travellers. Roomy rooms, sturdy queen-size beds, good showers and staff that seek to impress. *Standard sgl rooms from US$75, US$80 dbl, business class US$110.*

🏠 **Hotel Tourist** Karpenko 46; ✆ 0512 349 521. Slightly soulless, Soviet-style high-rise on the far western edge of the city, next to the river and stadium but far from civilization. *Rooms US$25–70, but the best rooms are the 'remodelled' sgl/dbl rooms at US$50/$60.*

🍴 **WHERE TO EAT** Hotels **Kontinent** and **Imperator** both have very fine restaurants. The shopping district also has a number of small cafés and bars, and themed dining even seems to be making an entrance. Here are a few of the standards:

🍴 **Café Feliccita** Makarova 41; ✆ 0512 472 147. Happy little café right off the main square (next to the Kontinent) with an Italian-style menu and wonderful service. The chef specialises in light salads, pasta and Mediterranean meat dishes (eg: chicken in mustard sauce) and servings are rather substantial. *Mains from US$5; open 06.00–04.00.*

🍴 **Arka** Lenina 78A; ✆ 0512 476 655; f 0512 473 475; e restoran@arka.mk.ua; www.arka.mk.ua. Probably the fanciest dining experience in Mikolayiv, with its stylish setting, live piano music and gourmet interpretations of locally caught fish; credit cards

accepted. *Mains from US$10; open 11.00–23.00.*

🍴 **Gulyaka Tavern** Admiralskaya 41; ✆ 0512 358 533. A laidback café and bar known for its convivial atmosphere and good beer. They bake delicious pizza in their brick oven and the selection of grilled meat attracts a loyal clientele. *Mains from US$6; open 11.00–midnight.*

🍴 **Beirut** Bolshaya Morskaya 72; ✆ 0512 344 138. Authentic Lebanese food in a cosy café restaurant. Great kibbeh! They also have another location on Nikolayevskaya 346. *Mains from US$5; open 10.00–21.00.*

WHAT TO SEE AND DO The best thing to do in Mikolayiv is to walk along the river, which meanders nearly 180° and creates the peninsula on which the city is constructed. A good walk takes in all the colossal ships and the hangars in which they are built. Of course, Prospekt Lenina is the central thoroughfare on which the city itself is built, but the 'old city' and new, hip shopping district can be accessed on the now pedestrian Radyanska Street. Mikolayiv's **zoo** is famous Ukraine-wide, and recently celebrated its 105th anniversary (*Oktyabrksaya 2, within walking distance of the bus station*). No visit to Mikolayiv would be complete without paying homage to the **shipbuilders' monument** on Makarova Square, which features bold muscle-bound socialists surrounding a globe and carrying ships upon which the city's youthful graffiti artists have inscribed the word 'Titanic'. A visit to the Soviet-style **Shipbuilding Museum** is also closer to the city's pulse (*Admiralskaya 4; open 10.00–18.00, closed Mon*).

KHERSON ХЕРСОН

Because Kherson is neither Odessa nor Crimea, few Ukrainians or foreigners venture into this temperate south-central region or its capital. What they miss are the vast expanses of Ukraine's true steppe, some unique national parks and a good-natured town that still prizes its agricultural achievements with collective pride. The Dnepr's widest curves cut through the northern part of the region ending in the river's delta just below the city of Kherson, while the scattered sandbanks along the shores of the Black Sea and the Sea of Azov are recent tourist hideaways with lots of empty beaches and animated birdlife.

While Kherson has its own share of Scythian prehistory and Cossack folklore, the actual city came into being by decree of Catherine the Great in 1778, who hoped to use this final point on the Dnepr as both the Black Sea port and the shipbuilding centre for her new fleet. As with all of New Russia, the empress sought to reinstate the ancient Greek ideal, changing the original name from Alexandria to Kherson, believing that this was in the historical Greek colony of Chersonesus Heracleotica. Catherine's suitor, General Grigory Potemkin, is considered to be the founder of the city, and helped with the expansion of a colossal star-shaped fortress, of which now only the gates and arsenal remain. In a way, Kherson feels cheated of its birthright by its rival cities Odessa (which became the major Black Sea port) and Mykolayiv (which took over the shipbuilding industry). Kherson is now the smallest of the three, with 300,000 inhabitants and a predominantly rural focus, which also makes it the most appealing in terms of recreation. Nobody is trying to sell the town itself on the basis of aesthetics, but the sight of the broad blue Dnepr does inspire grand thoughts not unlike those of Ukrainian poetry. This love for the land is best exhibited in Kherson's bountiful summer markets and resilient farmers. Kherson-grown fruits and vegetables are famous all over Ukraine, especially the perfectly round and super sweet watermelons, ripe with 260 days of sunshine a year.

Kherson's tourist industry is rather highly developed for a town of this size and the nearby wetlands and prairies allow for some unconventional possibilities to see some of unconventional Ukraine.

GETTING THERE AND AWAY Kherson is a true crossroads between the north (Kiev), the south (Crimea and Odessa) and the east (Zaporizhzhya and Dnepropetrovsk). The train station is located at the very northern end of Ushakova. Two overnight trains come and go from Kiev every night (11 or 13 hours) via Kryvy Rih, while another overnight train travels to and from Simferopol (5 hours). There are also frequent trains to Russia from Crimea, a few of which travel through Kharkiv. Two daily trains also run to Odessa via Mykolayiv, but as the trip takes six hours by rail, it's far better to find a *marshrutka* near the bus station and cut your travel time in half.

Kherson's bus station is located at Novonikolayevskoye Shosse 6 (❜ 0552 249 403). Buses and *marshrutka* travel back and forth from Odessa all day long (4 hours or less), usually via Mykolayiv (1¹/₂ hours). Standard overnight buses to Simferopol (6 hours) and Sevastopol (8 hours) can be uncomfortably hot or cold depending on the season. However, the private bus company **Gunsel** offers a high-quality, twice-daily bus service to and from Kiev (10 hours) via Mykolayiv and Uman, as well as a quick, comfortable service to Simferopol (5 hours); their office is inside the bus station (*Zaliznychna 8;* ❜ 0552 264 729). Smaller buses also serve the Dnepr delta region, with several buses a day to Genichesk (2 hours), Nova Kakhovka (5 hours) and Berislav (1¹/₂ hours)

Trams, trolleys and *marshrutka* run up and down Ushakova from the train station to the river port – if you stay in the city for more than a day, you will figure out the simple pattern. Kherson is also a city conducive to frequent taxi runs – getting to most destinations costs around US$2.

Dnepr River cruises will often stop in Kherson for at least one day, and there was a time when regular boat services connected Kherson to other major cities. Nowadays, things are very much up in the air with boat services, so it's worth checking at the **river station**, located at Odesskaya Square No 1, at the end of Kommunarov (❜ 0552 488 339). Today, Kherson offers a seasonal ferry service to many of the towns and villages downriver, including Hola Pristan. The boat goes back and forth twice a day; the journey takes about one hour and costs US$1.

WHERE TO STAY

🏠 **Hotel Fregat** Ushakova 2; ❜ 0552 280 342; f 0552 241 321; e fregat@ukrincom.net; www.hotelfregat.com; www.hotelfregat.com. Named in honour of the very first frigate of the Russian navy

— built in Kherson — the city's fomer Inturist hotel preserves its Soviet look with cleanliness and disco-like charm. The majority of rooms have been remodelled to a decent standard. Showers only in all rooms, and hot-water supplies can be dubious, but the brand-new sauna and Turkish bath are large and inviting. As it's the highest building in town, and located right next to the Dnepr River, it offers the best views of the city, and sadly, it's the best hotel for large groups. Luckily, the 'Fregat' is Kherson's main base for all tourist information, and their second-floor travel agency will prove helpful for English-speaking guides and arranging excursions in the countryside or to any of the nearby nature reserves (e office@hotelfregat.com). Credit cards accepted. *Regular sgl US$30, remodelled rooms US$50; dbls US$70; suites US$100.*

⌂ **Angelina Guesthouse** Privokzalnaya 1; ☎ 0552 483 564; f 0552 266 275. A smallish but brand-new hotel right next to the train station and part of a whole 'complex' that includes a cute café and private sauna. Rooms are large and comfortable. Cash only. *Small sgl US$20, more elaborate dbls US$50, suites US$75.*

⌂ **Hotel Brigantina** Patona 4; ☎ 0552 273 551; f 0552 270 481; e brigantine@selena.kherson.ua. www.brigantinaua.com. This Soviet behemoth once benefited from its interesting location on the island in the river, but these days it seems more inconvenient than anything. Little has changed on the inside, so that room quality is slightly lower than the other options closer to town, although they are well heated in winter. Transport to anywhere in town is by taxi (US$2). *Sgls from US$20, 'semi-suites' US$50, full suites US$80.*

Train station If you happen to arrive or leave in the middle of the night, the Kherson train station has some welcoming accommodation on the top floor. Just take the stairs on the right, up to the balcony and the door with the sign *kimnata vidpochinku*. Rooms cost US$10–20, featuring new beds and hot showers.

✖ **WHERE TO EAT** Kherson's restaurant culture is still pretty dormant. Cafés come and go on Suvorova, but a few holdouts seem to have ridden the roller coaster of Ukrainian economics:

✖ **Krynychka** Ushakova 42; ☎ 0552 490 157. Considered Kherson's finest, this folksy Ukrainian café serves traditional dishes that by this point in your trip might seem a little repetitive; however, the quality of both food and service is very high and their *borsch* with *pampushki* is the finest around. *Mains from US$5; open 10.00–23.00.*

✖ **Café Favorit** Corner of Suvorova and Oktyabrskoi Revolutsii; ☎ 0552 496 072. Much to its credit, this hidden wine cellar is the only café that serves cold drinks cold, perhaps in all of Ukraine. This is also one of the oldest buildings in the city (200 years), dating back to the days of General Potemkin himself. Classic and filling Russian dinners (very 'meat and potatoes') as well as good salads and

lighter fare; the kindly service is also well above average and a large meal will still cost less than US$7. *Open 10.00–23.00.*

✖ **John Howard Pub** Ushakova 30/1; ☎ 0552 264 034. Expansive English-style pub complete with free-flowing beer and football on the big screen TV. Food ranges from very bland 'European' dishes to the unmistakable sausage and mashed potatoes. *Mains from US$6; open 10.00–midnight.*

✖ **Café Landa** Suvorova 19; ☎ 0552 265 013. Swanky new city café attracting a young crowd who come for tea, coffee, cocktails and cakes, as well as a diverse spread of savoury meals and sandwiches. Big poofy couches, tall draped windows and quiet music. *Mains from US$3; open 09.00–23.00.*

LOCAL TOUR OPERATORS The local Inturist is still your best bet for arranging tours in and around Kherson, including local Dnepr cruises, and trips to Askania Nova, Hola Pristan, Zmeyevka and Fisherman's Island (*Fregat Tour Complex; Uhshakova 2;* ☎ *0552 280 003, 0552 280 173 (English-speaking guide);* f *0552 496 087;* e *fregat@public.kherson.ua; www.hotelfregat.com*).

WHAT TO SEE AND DO The city offers no great single attraction, but this is the obvious base from which to visit a beautiful and lesser-known region of the country. Suvorova Street is, for the most part, pedestrianised. This is where Kherson's populace – most visibly sailors, soldiers and students – go for a stroll. Much of the city is in flux, hence the number of crumbling buildings around you. If you have a chance, take a walk down to the riverside and the port, where dozens of giant ships are being loaded or unloaded, or are simply rusting away. While you are in town, visit the **Kherson Natural History Museum** (*Lenina 9;* ❧ *0552 241 061; open 10.00–16.00, closed Mon and Tue; entrance 3UAH; 12UAH for a guided tour*). Besides the typical Soviet exhibits of industry and agriculture, the museum presents a comprehensive and interesting display on all the animals and plants that live in the region, including a special room dedicated to Askania-Nova. Quaint and informative, the **Kherson Art Museum** (*Lenina 34;* ❧ *0552 243 164; open 10.00–16.00, closed Tue and Fri; entrance 5UAH*) is dedicated to all Ukrainian art, but most specifically the work of Oleksi Shovkunenko, a Kherson native who made his name in the world of Socialist Realist painting. **St Catherine's Cathedral** remains one of Kherson's few old churches, built in Neoclassical form and incorporating parts of the original Kherson fortress foundation. (General Potemkin's body was first buried in this churchyard, but was later removed by Catherine the Great's resentful son.) Another key monument is **John Howard's Obelisk** (on Ushakova), dedicated to the man who is becoming more and more revered as a town hero. If you do come to Kherson during the summer, a trip to the outdoor market is imperative, if for no other reason than to see and smell the goodies that are on offer. Strawberry season (May and June) is best.

OUTSIDE KHERSON

Askania Nova АСКАНІЯ НОВА Although wildlife conservation was never a prominent feature of Soviet rhetoric, this 100km² of virgin Ukrainian steppe somehow missed mass cultivation and exists today as the only natural steppe landscape left in Europe. Askania Nova was set aside as a nature park over 150 years ago, but it was the son of local German settlers, Frederick Falz-Fein (1863–1920) who dedicated his life to preserving this spot and bringing in the animals that attract so much interest today. Today, the park consists of various zones, some of which remain completely untouched and inaccessible – relics of Ukraine's original steppe ecosystem.

Askania Nova is now the base for a Ukrainian research institute that seeks to preserve the dwindling steppe of Ukraine and maintains a vigorous breeding programme for endangered species, including the strange-looking and very rare Saiga antelope, as well as herds of Turkmeni Kulans and Przewalski horses, used to repopulate the species' former habitats in central Asia and Mongolia. This is the only place in Europe where you can see a Przewalski horse 'in the wild' – as such, it's the only remaining undomesticated Eurasian horse breed. The park's birds put on a better show than the mammals, and birders visiting Ukraine should make Askania Nova a priority. Extinct everywhere else in Ukraine, the steppe eagle (*Aguila rapax*) can be regularly spotted in the air and trees, while rarer steppe species include the famed great bustard (*Otis tarda*), Demoiselle crane *(Anthropoides virgo)* and long-legged buzzard (*Buteo rufinus*).

Askania's open zoo format follows a slightly 'world communist' mentality, advertising herds of animals from six different continents who share this single territory. Conservation purists may shudder, but watching how the free-roaming American bison distance themselves from the zebras who avoid the Indian zebus running from the South American rhea is bizarrely impressive. Also prancing across these plains is the genetically engineered (hence endemic?) Soviet 'steppe deer'.

Askania is usually offered as a day trip from Kherson, since travel there and back can take quite a long time, although watching the wild steppe grasses will keep you entertained. As of now, there is no place to stay in or near the park, and there are few amenities, since most people come on an organised tour. The reserve opens on 1 May and stays open until late October; entrance into the park costs only 6UAH, but a package tour from your hotel will cost a lot more. For additional information, contact the park directly (*Askania Nova, Stepova 3;* ❧ *0553 861 232;* e *bp_ackania-nova@chap.hs.ukrtel.net*).

Getting there and away

Askaniya Nova is 2½ hours away from Kherson, on a good day. Otherwise, the trip can take up to four hours. Two buses travel there from Kherson bus station, one in the morning and another in the evening (which will leave you stranded out there). Because Askania features on practically every national itinerary, most package tours will arrange transport, and the hotels in Kherson can prove very helpful in facilitating the journey, since this is really Kherson's main attraction.

Kherson's wetlands Entering the wilder regions of Kherson oblast is still not an easy process, and for the time being, it is wise to use a travel agency for arrangements. Popular day tours usually take in birdwatching spots or include fishing trips with a guide. Independent travellers are able to venture freely in **Hola Pristan** (Гола Пристань), the last town on the Dnepr delta and a grand finale to Ukraine's most central artery. Here, the cacophony of sea birds is invigorating and travellers are granted a glimpse of a people whose lives are connected to the river. Not far away is the **Black Sea Biosphere Reserve**, established to protect bird habitats and nesting grounds among the marshes and sea islands of Kherson's southern coast. Much of the reserve is permanently closed to tourists, but there are certain locations where visitors can see rare species in migration, including flamingos, black-winged stilts (*Himantopus himantopus*) and great white pelicans (*Pelecanus onocrotalus*). Contact the reserve's office in Hola Pristan (*Lermontova 1;* ❧ *05539 264 71*). Buses leave Kherson for Hola Pristan every hour and the journey takes about one hour, or you may arrange to take the hour-long ferry service in season (*Apr–Oct*).

Zmeyevka ЗМЕЄВКА When Sweden fell to Russia in 1790, the inhabitants of Dago Island in the Baltic Sea made a plea to be spared from serfdom. Catherine the Great granted their request with an empire-building twist: the Swedes would be sent south to settle part of New Russia. Over 1,000 industrious Scandinavians founded the village of Zmeyevka, and today, this display of Swedishness on the banks of the Dnepr attracts many cruise and land visitors. Once there, you will find a tiny Scandinavian colony where people still speak an old Swedish dialect and build very Scandinavian houses. If travelling from Kherson, the trip is about 120km; it's best done overland by bus to Berislav and then by taxi to Zmeyevka (around US$5). The Hotel Fregat in Kherson also offers an interesting day trip to the village.

Fisherman's Island Passengers cruising down the Dnepr will often be taken to the picturesque 'Fisherman's Island' – known locally as *rybalchi* – located just below Kherson and right before the wide delta of the Dnepr River. Here, a small group of families survive upon a tiny islet, completely isolated from the rest of Ukraine and totally dependent upon the food they fish out of the river. The tiny wooden huts and houses, makeshift docks and a swath of old-fashioned boats are all photogenic, and offer a pleasant respite from industrial-strength Ukraine. Making it to this very remote spot (accessible only by small boat) is a rare treat but well worth the effort to experience such an old world lifestyle. If you are taking a pre-organised cruise, simply check with the company about whether or not they are planning a stop. If you are in or around Kherson, the Hotel Fregat tour service can arrange a visit with some prior notice. The prescribed tour lasts about four hours and includes transport to the island, and a chance to purchase handmade island souvenirs (reed baskets, woodcarvings and fish). Very intrepid explorers may want to arrange their own motorboat transport to the island of *rybakov* (fishermen) or *rybalchi*, the price of which is highly negotiable. Staying for a while on the island is not impossible, but if that is your intention, please tread tenderly. Tourism is a rather new phenomenon for the villagers.

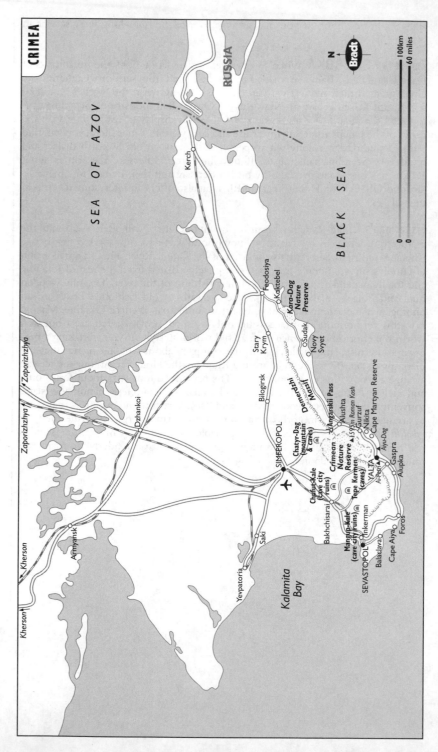

12

Crimea
Крым

Ukrainians believe Crimea is the most exotic place on earth and with good reason. This strange peninsula looks absolutely nothing like the rest of Ukraine. Instead of rolling wheat fields, the landscape is broken into deep canyons and jutting cliffs. Sharp mountains seem to pop up from nowhere, and if you stray from the road the noise of passing cars quickly turns to the roar of falling water. Here the hillsides are covered with a different kind of green and the warm breeze feels unmistakably Mediterranean. Little bays glow a turquoise blue that hints at the tropical, and the sea is impassive, with small waves that tumble onto black pebble beaches. The sun shines unclouded year-round, attracting tourist armies from the north, but the boardwalk crowds are fairly easy to avoid. The region's main appeal is in its natural diversity and its constantly changing scenery. The trekking is unique, mountain bikers are only just discovering the dramatic terrain, and underground caverns are spectacular and accessible.

No less exotic is the human element. Behind the neon glitz of the tourist traps are the leftovers of fallen empires that once laid claim to these seaports and mountains: Byzantine cave cities, Greek ruins, Russian palaces, Genoese castles and Soviet battleships. The oriental mystique attached to the peninsula is half-imagined, but the Crimean Tatars have returned from exile and are asserting a renewed cultural presence. With the wild rock-faces and poetic Turkish names, it is not surprising that so many legends are attached to the Crimea.

HISTORY

The prehistoric Cimmerians were the most prominent inhabitants of Crimea until the 7th century BC when the Scythians arrived. The Cimmerians retreated into the coastal mountains and were named the Tauri by the ancient Greeks – Crimea was called Taurica. The ancient Greek city states built numerous colonies on the Crimean coast, including Chersoneus (Sevastopol), Yevpatoria and Feodosiya. By the 1st century BC, most of these ports were being governed by Rome. Their energy and resources were largely devoted to blocking invasions from the northern steppe. In AD250 the Goth tribes invaded, and a century later the Huns arrived and decimated the local population. Another century later the Alan tribes invaded, but stayed and became allies to the now governing Byzantine Empire. The accepted legend states that the Apostle Andrew landed in Crimea (near Kerch) in the 1st century and raised the first cross on 'Russian' land. In the 5th century, saints Cyril and Methodius came from Constantinople to Chersoneus, bringing Christianity and the Cyrillic alphabet to Ukraine. The new religion began to spread among the smaller colonies, and one odd civilisation rose up from converted Alans, Goths and Greeks. This became the principality of Feodor, whose capital Mangup lasted until the Ottoman conquest. Its people were later known as 'Crimean Greeks', who left during the Russian Empire to settle Mariupol on the Sea of Azov.

From the east, the Jewish Khazar Khaganate spread towards Crimea. The Khazars reached Crimea in the 8th century and opened up the region to its first Turkic tribes. The handful of Karaim who live in Crimea today are descendants of the Khazars. Kievan Rus had expanded to the south by the 10th century and Slavic princes ruled over Tmutorokan at the eastern tip of Crimea. Prince Vladimir was baptised at Chersoneus in 988 before returning to Kiev to 'convert' his people. Prince Svyatoslav destroyed the Khazar Khaganate but this opened up Crimea to invasion by the Pechenegs who conquered it in 1050.

THE CRIMEAN KHANATE Crimea had always been linked to the romanticised Silk Road so attractive to medieval merchants. In return for not supporting the Crusades in the 13th century, Constantinople granted the Genoese a trade monopoly over the Black Sea region (it didn't hurt that they would provide a buffer from northern raids). In fact, there was much competition with the Venetian merchants and the many impressive fortresses built along Crimea's southern coast were not simply a defence against the Mongols but also a visible business presence. The main Genoese port was set up in Kaffa (Feodosiya) and for a time they controlled the entire coastline. These merchant towns lasted until the Ottoman invasions of the 15th Century and medieval Italian castles still stand at Sudak and Cembalo (Balaklava).

The Mongol's 1223 hit-and-run attack included a large raid on Crimea. After they conquered Rus in 1237 the peninsula became a comfy retreat for various tribes (the word Crimea stems from the Turkish name for the peninsula, *Kyrym*). When the Golden Horde evaporated, new khans struggled for control of the area. The Crimean khanate was established in 1441 by Haci Giray Khan and the capital was built at Bakhchisarai. The Giray dynasty ruled the peninsula for over three hundred years, with some help from abroad: the Ottoman Turks invaded in 1475 and the Crimean khanate was made a protectorate. As part of the Ottoman Empire, Crimea was granted its first ever 'autonomous' status, allowing Tatars enough independence to continue their own slave trade. As vigilantes, the Ukrainian Cossacks made frequent raids on the Turks.

The Russians and Turks have always been fighting one another, and Crimea is unfortunately located between the two. After the Pereyaslav Agreement (see page 21), Russian armies moved south in hopes of conquering their enemy's tributary. They were unsuccessful many times over but finally made an entrance in the early 1700s. This rivalry placed the Crimean Tatars in a difficult position and in 1772 they were forced to choose Russian 'protection'. Catherine the Great signed a treaty granting Crimea independence as a protectorate of Russia, but in 1783 the peninsula was simply annexed to the Russian Empire.

The Russians were not kind to the non-Christian Crimean Tatars and most left for Ottoman Turkey. Over a period of 100 years, these mass migrations decreased the Crimean Tatar population to less than a tenth of its original size. Meanwhile, Catherine was giving away Crimean estates to her favourites of the court, as well as inviting Russians, Ukrainians, Bulgarians, Germans and the Swiss to settle the area. Soon, the deserted Tatar villages were alive again and many Turkish names were preserved for exotic flair. Crimea was suddenly a place of sunshine for the Russian nobility, and many of the Neoclassical buildings in Sevastopol and Simferopol are reminiscent of St Petersburg's canal-side palaces. The strategic shape and location of the peninsula also made it a vital military outpost for Russia and the imperial navy soon came south.

THE CRIMEAN WAR Western Europeans know Crimea best for the infamous war fought in the years 1854–56. By 1853, international tensions were running high, but the spark that lit the fire was a dispute between Russian Orthodox priests and French Catholic clerics who both laid claim to Christian sites in the Holy Land. Russia and Turkey's centuries-old row was to provoke the first battles, and soon Great Britain and France had sent a joint force to the Black Sea. When the Russians destroyed the Turkish fleet in 1854, the European press went wild and the allies (soon joined by Sardinia) declared war on the tsar. The first fighting took place in Wallachia (Romania) and Bulgaria, and eventually the Russian army was forced into retreat. Fearing a new offensive from the powerful Black Sea fleet, the allies planned a siege on Russia's home port, Sevastopol. The remembered battles at Alma, Balaklava and Inkerman all took place around Sevastopol with great losses on both sides, but the port was not taken until 1856. The Treaty of Paris officially ended the war with conditions unfavourable to Russia, and Britain and France still hurting. Cemeteries and battlefields have remained in memoriam.

THE 20TH CENTURY By the turn of the century, Crimea had become the playground of Russia's wealthiest families, who built their summer palaces in the small seaside towns. Russian writers and artists also romanticised Crimea as an inspiring location for work and rest. However, these were short-lived days. Things quickly turned chaotic with governments rising and falling faster than the peninsula could be reoccupied. When Nikolai II abdicated in 1917, the Crimean Tatars raced to establish an independent Crimean state. They managed to form a national government but it was abolished one month later by the Bolsheviks. In March 1918, the Soviet Socialist Republic of Tauride was formed only to be abolished one month later by the Germans. The Germans then set up a regional government that lasted until the following allied occupation, but was consequently abolished by the Red Army. The Crimean Socialist Soviet Republic was formed at the beginning of the Russian civil war but went into exile at Kherson, while the White Army held the peninsula for a year and a half. Finally, the Red Army gained control in 1920 and the republic was made a part of the Russian Socialist Soviet Republic. In 1921, Crimea was granted the status of an Autonomous Soviet Republic and Lenin's campaign for *korenizatsya* ('making roots') allowed the Crimean Tatars to use their language and enjoy free expression of their culture. This changed at the end of the 1920s, when Stalin began targeting the non-Russian nationalities (although Stalin himself was Georgian, not Russian).

The Nazi invasion of Crimea was a separate occupation from the one in Ukraine, and the resistance in Crimea kept Sevastopol free until July 1942. The occupation ended two years later and the Crimean conference at Yalta marked a decisive end to World War II. After liberation, Stalin accused the Crimean Tatars of betraying the Soviet Union and deported them en masse to work in Uzbekistan. It was a calculated genocide that killed almost half of the deportees within the first year.

Crimea was simply reduced to a Russian oblast (province) until 1954, when the Crimean Autonomous Soviet Socialist Republic was transferred to the Ukrainian SSR in remembrance of the Pereyaslav Agreement between Russia and Ukraine. The 1960s and 1970s witnessed an improved standard of living in the Soviet Union and Crimea fast became the chosen holiday destination for those who could travel there. Young pioneers were sent to Crimea on holiday camps and a family might be awarded a week in one of the numerous seaside health resorts. Yalta and Alushta burgeoned into major tourist towns, while Sevastopol continued as the USSR's valued warm-sea naval port, closed to everyone but military personnel and their families.

In March 1991, Gorbachev held a referendum on preserving the Soviet Union. Around 88% of Crimeans were in favour, the highest in Ukraine and above average for Russia. That same year, Gorbachev was put under house arrest while on

12

holiday in Foros. Suddenly the world focused its attention on this small Crimean town while awaiting the fate of the coup.

When Ukraine gained independence, Crimea was the main object of dispute with Russia. The area was ethnically Russian and home to the treasured Black Sea fleet. If war were to break out between Ukraine and Russia, it would be a fight for Crimea. The Crimean Tatars were finally allowed to return from exile, but this further complicated an already complicated cultural friction. Crimea stayed Ukrainian on the maps, but the peninsula has kept is autonomy and the most Ukrainian thing one can find there is the money. Free enterprise has lessened the political tensions and hordes of Russian and Ukrainian tourists migrate yearly to the sunshine. The tourist pomp is quickly overriding this odd monument to Russian imperial glory, as well as the concerns of the Crimean Tatar refugee population.

THE AUTONOMOUS REPUBLIC OF CRIMEA

Ukraine has allowed Crimea to keep the autonomous status it has known for so long, but the Russian–Ukrainian divide is still a sensitive issue. Crimea's population is 2.5 million and comprises a record 80 ethnic groups, which makes their slogan 'Prosperity in Unity' appropriate. Russian, Crimean Tatar and Ukrainian are all official languages. There is a Crimean parliament and a separate constitution, and they have their own flag – a plain white field with a blue and a red stripe at the top and bottom respectively. Otherwise, the word 'autonomous' is still open to interpretation. For travellers, this means occasionally dealing with a whole new, discrete bureaucracy. Keep your passport with you at all times, but more importantly, keep in mind that you are in a separate land that's proud to be different.

GETTING AROUND Simferopol is the transport hub for all of Crimea and is very difficult to avoid if you are travelling from the mainland. Trains are slightly pointless for travel within the region, since the lines extend north only. Sevastopol to Simferopol is the most obvious rail link, while the line from Kerch to Dzhankoi sets a record for being the slowest train in Ukraine. Motor transport is the best option. Buses and *marshrutka* connect all the towns and popular sites. Major routes branch out to Yevpatoria, Sevastopol, Yalta and the southern coast, and eastern Crimea (Kerch, Feodosiya). The coastal road from Alushta up to Sudak and Feodosiya is very beautiful but very mountainous. The direct bus will take many more hours than travelling on the regular routes via Simferopol. A new 'lux' bus travels a constant circle (Simferopol–Alushta–Yalta–Sevastopol) in under four hours, while the world's longest trolley line goes from Simferopol to Alushta and Yalta, stopping at every bus shelter along the way. If you value elbow room, private taxis can always be negotiated for inter-city travel, although prices vary so widely based on season and mood.

GREEN RURAL TOURISM IN CRIMEA Getting out to a Crimean village offers a whole different experience to the hubbub of the coastal resort towns – travellers get to experience the peninsula's rare natural beauty and connect with the people who call it home. Such a practice of rural tourism also helps sustain the rural economy and encourages locals to preserve their natural surroundings. Yet while the campaign to get travellers out of the clichéd resorts and into local villages is indeed noble, the official governmental 'Green Rural Tourism' programme has suffered in the past from a highly bureaucratic system. Things are improving slowly, so that travellers should feel encouraged to give it a try (see *www.greentour.com.ua*). Luckily, most private travel companies and hotel booking agencies have met the demand with a far more inviting service. Try websites like www.travel2crimea.com and www.travel-to-ukraine.info/ruralgreen/index.php. Both offer rural accommodation for around US$10/night. EU-funded projects have helped catalogue and classify the homes of Crimean villagers who are willing to accept paying guests for short stays.

SIMFEROPOL СИМФЕРОПОЛЬ

The capital of the Crimean republic is a rather eclectic town of relaxed attitudes and quirky Russian officialdom, but an agreeable place all the same. The city was built for passing through, and its reputation relies on the recreational delights that surround it rather than on its own sunny streets of busy traffic. To its credit, Simferopol has something remarkably cosmopolitan about it, even though its 400,000 inhabitants appear by and large to be Russian. Fragments of Islamic architecture poke out occasionally and the ethnic mix is more diverse than meets the outsider's eye.

Above all, Simferopol is a great place to engage in the gentle Russian pastime of having a stroll (*gulyat*). With good weather for most of the year, the town's many parks, footbridges and boulevards make for an agreeable urban hike. The Salgir River flows through the centre with a lovely side path shaded in bending willows and giant cypress trees. The cobblestoned streets of the central quarter (around Pushkina and Gorkovo) make up a pedestrian-only zone lined with newly polished shops and cafés. As the transport hub of Crimea, any trip you plan will most likely put you here for at least half a day. This is also the best place to organise longer treks and other outdoor activities since so many tour companies are based here.

Simferopol is relatively young, founded in 1784 after Crimea was taken over by Catherine the Great. The ancient-sounding Greek name ('City of Use') was added to signify the purpose of the newer city to connect all the scattered settlements under a centralised power. Over two thousand years ago, the late Scythian civilisation built their 'Neapolis' as a hilltop fortress and a successful trading post. The ruins still remain on the eastern side of Simferopol. The conquering Tatars then built their own town of Akmescid (*Ak-mechet*), or 'White Mosque', of which the 16th-century mosque still remains. In the years of the Crimean War, Simferopol stayed well protected and was used primarily as a morgue and a base for the wounded. In contrast, the Russian civil war wreaked havoc on the city and its people as this was a stronghold for the over-eager White Army. The USSR granted Simferopol its greatest compliment by situating a perfume factory here while the rest of Ukraine was digging coal. A strong concentration of die-hard communists and Russophiles still looms large in Simferopol, along with everyone involved in Crimea's booming tourist industry.

GETTING THERE AND AWAY

By air Simferopol Central Airport is located on the far northwest side of the city (*www.airport.crimea.ua*) and is becoming the most popular international entry point into Ukraine besides Kiev. For quick and easy connections to Europe and North America, Lufthansa flies daily to and from Frankfurt (and sometimes Munich), although this is often a code-shared flight with Ukrainian International Airlines (*www.ukraine-international.com*). Another good option is the daily Turkish Airlines flight to and from Istanbul. Several daily flights also connect to Moscow Domodedovo, and there is a once-weekly connection to Tel Aviv. In Ukraine, regular flights connect to both Kiev airports (1½ hours), as well as Kharkiv and Lviv. For some inexplicable reason, flights to Odessa remain non-existent,

Crimea has been home to so many different ethnic groups it's hard to keep count; however, the Crimean Tatars actually formed their nation in this peninsula. As isolated descendants of the retreating Golden Horde, the Crimean khanate succeeded in unifying the people under one government. The Ottoman Empire made Crimea a tributary in 1475, but the relationship was quite free and the two worked very much as allies. For three hundred years this was their country and they developed a very individual religious and cultural identity. The population was 98% Crimean Tatar at the time of Russia's occupation. They began to emigrate en masse to Turkey when Catherine the Great deported the last khan and began the systematic destruction of every Tatar building and monument. The Tatar nobles who stayed were quickly assimilated into the Russian gentry and the people became a minority in their own country.

When Tsar Nikolai II abdicated, the Crimean Tatars came back to Simferopol in hopes of launching their independence campaign but the Bolsheviks had already taken control over the Russian navy. The Crimean government was quickly forced back into exile. During Lenin's regime Crimea's Tatar and Russian intelligentsia were targeted and 60,000 were killed in less than six months (another 100,000 died of starvation). A period of calm followed during the *korenizatsiya* (making roots) movement when Simferopol was symbolically called Ak-Mescid and Tatar schools and theatres were opened. Tatar language was making a comeback (the language has gone from Arab script to Latin and then to Cyrillic in a very short time), but then Stalin executed the leader of Tatar *korenizatsiya* and a new wave of oppression erupted.

Shortly after Crimea was liberated in 1944, Stalin made a declaration that the Crimean Tatar minority had conspired with the Germans and henceforth the minority nation was an enemy to the Soviet people. The entire Crimean Tatar population was deported in less than three days. Most were sent away in railway cars to central Siberia and Uzbekistan and thousands died in transit; one overloaded ferry was scuttled in the Black Sea and those who could swim were shot. In the Soviet east they were subjected to forced labour under harsh conditions, usually cutting down trees. It is estimated that nearly half of the Crimean population did not survive past the first year.

Despite a later apology from the Soviet government, the Crimean Tatars were given permission to return to Crimea only in 1989 and serious repatriation efforts took place only in 1995. The return of Crimean Tatar refugees into independent Ukraine has been highly problematic. Ukrainians and Russians are both fighting for their own nationalistic

although in summer months, the schedule expands to accommodate several other regional centres in Ukraine, like Uzhgorod and Donetsk.

In Simferopol, air tickets can be purchased at the airport or at the office at Sevastopolskaya 22 (✆ 0652 272 116). Lufthansa and Turkish Airlines have direct international connections to Simferopol. The Ukrainian Ministry of Foreign Affairs still runs a consular office at the airport, although for most travellers, their service is irrelevant (✆ 0652 295 740). A taxi is best for getting to the airport (around US$7), but trolleybus No 9 runs between the airport and Simferopol city centre. Several direct buses leave from the airport to nearly all of Crimea's coastal cities.

By rail Simferopol's elegant train station is the site most likely to be on a postcard of the city, and if you have the time, this is a far grander way to enter Crimea. The white walls, high arches and square tower blend Turkish architecture with socialist realism in a fitting style for the main gateway of the city. Most routes point towards Russia and pass through Zaporizhzhya, or go west to Odessa. There are at least two stance in Crimea, and many find a renewed Muslim presence unsettling, although movements in favour of repatriation have always been peaceful.

As the minority nation within a minority (Crimean) government, the Crimean Tatars must normally choose to side with the more powerful national government as the lesser of two evils. Unable to get dual Ukrainian citizenship due to their Uzbek passports, Crimean Tatars were forced to live a continued refugee existence in their own country. Most of their homes had been occupied or destroyed, so that now many Crimean Tatars are forced to live in shanty towns outside Crimean towns. But things have definitely improved of late. Ukrainian passports are being issued and there are now Crimean Tatar representatives in the Crimean parliament. Still, attitudes and opportunities are unsettled. The pro-Russian Crimean government publicly considers the Tatars a beneficial tourist attraction but an underlying racism is evident.

At the last count, a quarter of a million Crimean Tatars had returned and now make up 12% of Crimea's population. A few million Crimean Tatars still live in Turkey, the United States and throughout the world. Bakhchisarai is still recognised as the Crimean Tatar capital, but the returned refugees live throughout the peninsula, with larger concentrations in Yevpatoria, Feodosiya and Stary Krym. There is a Crimean Tatar Museum in Simferopol but it is empty and without money.

Visiting the Crimean Tatars in Crimea is a unique opportunity to witness such an ancient culture making its way in the 21st century. Most of the Crimean Tatars you will meet have returned to Crimea only in the last five to ten years. The older populations remember the deportations or can tell you stories of Siberian labour camps and long years of cutting down trees. The younger populations recall a very hard life in Uzbekistan and the upheaval of starting all over again in this homeland. As they are Sunni Muslims, the mosque is a centre for both cultural and religious activity, but most customs are preserved in the home. Three days after a baby is born, there is a naming ceremony, when the parents ritually bathe the child and then whisper the child's name into both ears. On the streets of Bakhchisarai you will also see young children greet their elders by kissing their hands and then pressing them against their forehead as a token of love and respect. Crimean Tatar food is a delicious alternative to Ukrainian fare, with its staples of rice pilaf, mutton, dumplings and honey pastries (be sure to try *lagman* and *köbete*). If your interest in the Crimean Tatar situation transcends the souvenir markets and food stalls, check out the site of the International Council on Crimea (*www.iccrimea.org*).

(and sometimes four) daily trains to and from Kiev (16–18 hours), and one to Kharkiv (10 hours), Dnepropetrovsk (9 hours), Donetsk (11 hours), Odessa (13 hours) and Lviv (24 hours). An average *coupé* ticket to or from Simferopol to any city on the mainland costs US$15–20. In the high season (July–August), the trains are packed and booked well in advance. Make reservations through a tour agency ahead of time or buy tickets right at the beginning of your trip. During the rest of the year, you can usually get away with buying your ticket on the day of departure.

By bus There are three main bus stations, central, east and west, and then a small depot by the train station. All are very active. The direction of your destination usually determines the station you should depart from, but the central *avtovokzal* is where most long-haul buses will come and go from. Simferopol is the most important destination in the south, so finding a bus to or from any Ukrainian city is rather simple. Finding a long-haul seat in the summer can pose more of a problem. The posh bus companies do run a good air-conditioned service between Simferopol and Kiev, but it is still a long overnight journey and you'll probably

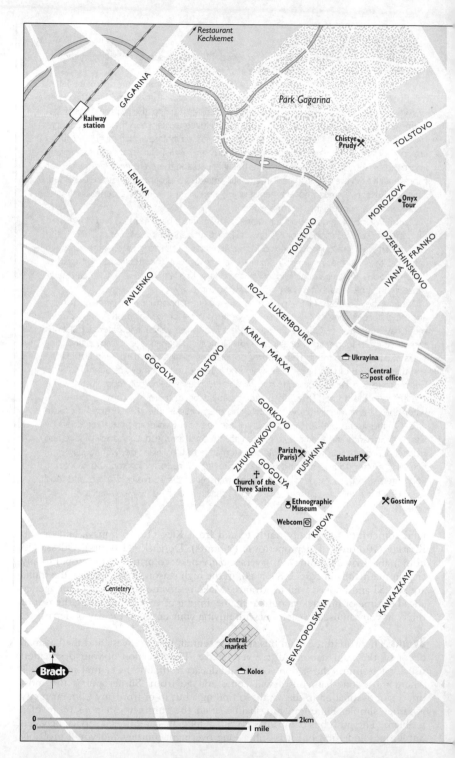

Restaurant Kechkemet

GAGARINA

Railway station

Park Gagarina

Chistye Prudy

TOLSTOVO

LENINA

MOROZOVA

Onyx Tour

DZERZHINSKOVO

IVANA FRANKO

PAVLENKO

TOLSTOVO

ROZY LUXEMBOURG

GOGOLYA

TOLSTOVO

KARLA MARXA

Ukrayina

Central post office

GORKOVO

ZHUKOVSKOYO

GOGOLYA

Parizh (Paris)

PUSHKINA

Falstaff

Church of the Three Saints

Ethnographic Museum

Gostinny

Webcom

KIROVA

KAVKAZKAYA

Cemetery

SEVASTOPOLSKAYA

Central market

Kolos

N

Bradt

0 ———————————————————— 2km
0 ———————————————————— 1 mile

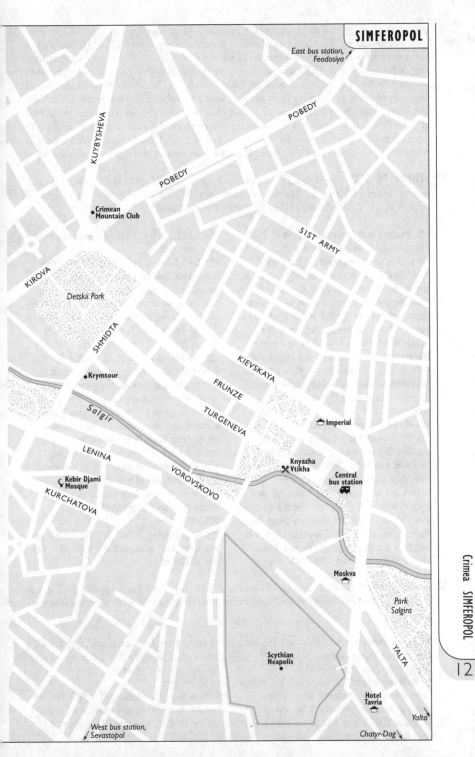

East bus station,
Feodosiya

POBEDY

KUYBYSHEVA

POBEDY

51ST ARMY

Crimean
Mountain Club

KIROVA

Detskii Park

SHMIDTA

KIEVSKAYA

Krymtour

FRUNZE

Salgir

TURGENEVA

Imperial

LENINA

VOROVSKOVO

Knyazha
Vtikha

Central
bus station

Kebir Djami
Mosque

KURCHATOVA

Moskva

Park
Salgira

Scythian
Neapolis

YALTA

Hotel
Tavria

Yalta

West bus station,
Sevastopol

Chatyr-Dag

prefer the bed on the train (*Autolux Simferopol Office; Kievskaya 4;* ✆ *0652 290 306; open 08.00–22.00*). The bus to Odessa is inexpensive (around US$15), but makes for a very slow and hideous journey (a whole day at least). For closer destinations (eg: Kherson, Zaporizhzhya) you can take a quicker day bus. *Zapadnaya* (west station) is at the end of Sevastopolskaya and has buses to Bakhchisarai and Sevastopol while *Vostochnaya* (east station) is at 243 Pobedy and has buses bound for Feodosiya and Kerch. A taxi to either bus station should cost under US$2. Remember that you can get a bus to anywhere from the central station, and there are plenty of regular *marshrutka* leaving from the train station (next to McDonald's) and travelling to every little town in Crimea. Just look at the signs or ask around.

🏠 **WHERE TO STAY** Simferopol does not have the same hotel development as the coastal cities of Crimea, but the available hotels do have a very wide variety of rooms at any price. All accept credit cards, except Kolos.

🏠 **Ukrayina** Rozy Luxemburg 7; ✆ 0652 510 165; f 0652 278 495; e jscukrcomp@ crimea.com; www.ukraina-hotel.biz. Simferopol's 'main' hotel has undergone a tasteful redecoration, leaving the entryway remarkably Baroque and grandiose, and the rooms clean and new. It seems they've achieved the dignified feel to which they aspire. The clear-cut 'business class' rooms for US$80–90 feel the most like those in a nice, Western hotel. The Ukrayina is very central and close to the train station. It also offers a sauna and hammam. B/fast inc. *Standard sgl with private bathroom US$50, US$150 for a zippy, fully accessorised suite.*

🏠 **Moskva** Kievskaya 2; ✆ 0652 232 113; f 0652 237 389; e moskva@utel.net.ua; www.moskva-hotel.com. This is the former Inturist hotel for Simferopol, built in the 1970s but newly remodelled with typical post-Soviet glitz. Its best asset is its location next to the central bus station and the Scythian Neapolis. All rooms have private bathrooms with a shower or bath and there is a decent Soviet-era restaurant on the ground floor. For people with cars, there is a guarded parking lot here. *Rooms range from the very cheap (US$20–30) to luxury*

suites (US$100). The US$60 business-class rooms are a good deal.

🏠 **Tavria** Bespalova 21; ✆ 0652 638 819. This former Soviet 'tour base' consists of 2 buildings, one remodelled to a much higher standard. A full meal plan can be added for US$10/day. *Suites (US$90) are spacious with real queen-size beds; standard rooms (US$30–45) have cramped bathrooms with so-so facilities. The US$70 'semi-suites' are not a bad choice.*

🏠 **Hotel Imperial** Kievskaya 22; ✆ 0652 547 488; f 0652 489; e info@hotel-imperial.crimea.ua; www.hotel-imperial.crimea.ua. Newly built, modern hotel that's well managed and super clean. The 5 separate categories of rooms are all show: while the standards make sense, the top 3 categories of suites are all within US$5–10 of one another and rather similar in terms of having queen-size beds, big windows and small TVs. Within walking distance of the bus station. The intimate restaurant sports an enthusiastic chef and classy table settings. *US$70 standard; the top 3 categories of suites US$110–120.*

🏠 **Kolos** Subkhi 4; ✆ 0652 272 384. A basic hotel with rather basic quality and very basic prices. Cash only. *US$20–40.*

✘ **WHERE TO EAT** To get a nice, sit-down meal, just walk into Simferopol's pedestrian heart, where there are plenty of small restaurants and cafés with a great choice of menus.

✘ **Knyazha Vtikha** Turgeneva 35; ✆ 0652 251 020. Fine Ukrainian country cuisine in a fun, themed setting. *Mains from US$7; open 10.00–23.00.*

✘ **Kechkemet** Gagarina 22; ✆ 0652 222 205. Perhaps Simferopol's most élite restaurant, serving a blend of traditional Hungarian food and rich European dishes, for around US$25 a head. A bit further out, but worth the cab ride to get there. *Open 11.00–midnight.*

✘ **Chistye Prudy** No phone. Located right at the main entrance to Gagarin Park and serves incredible Armenian food. *Mains from US$7; open 10.00–midnight.*

Gostinny Dvor Sevastopolskaya 4; ✆ 0652 299 744. Fine, French cuisine and rare dishes served with unbelievable flair. *Mains from US$15; open 11.00–23.00.*

✘ Falstaff Corner of Kirova and Karla Marksa; no phone. Next to the Central Univermag; English-style pub that's underground, with a big menu of hearty British classics and 15 kinds of vodka. *Mains from US$8; open 10.00–23.00.*

✘ Parizh (Paris) Corner of Pushkina and Gorkovo; no phone. Sophisticated little French café for pastries and bistro-style lunches. *Mains from US$7. Open 09.00–22.00.*

LOCAL TOUR OPERATORS AND TOURIST INFORMATION If you have specific needs, or just want somebody else to organise your travel to the rest of Crimea, Simferopol is the right place to start. Here are a few good contacts:

Krymtour Shmidta 9; ☎ 0652 250 350; f 0652 252 023; e info@krymtur.com; www.krymtur.com. This joint-venture company is the most established in the area and deals only with incoming tourists to Crimea. They offer a huge variety of package tours, and have the most comprehensive information on hotels, tourist sites and discounts, with helpful local branch offices in all major towns in Crimea.
Crimean Mountain Club Ul Kievskaya 77/4; ☎ 0652 249 528; e afk@crimea.com. This club was founded in 1890 and is the oldest of its kind in 'Russia'. The office is not easily accessible since they

share it with Ukraine's local branch of the Green Party, but they can be very helpful if you want to head off into the hills.
Onyx Tour Morozova 13; ☎ 0652 256 348; www.onixtour.com.ua. Crimea's caves are truly spectacular and worth a visit. Onyx Tour is the private caving club that owns access to the Mramornaya and Eminé-Bair-Khosar Caves and conducts excursions to several other local caverns. Professionals can set up a challenging underground tour, while first-timers can choose an easier group tour that is just as impressive.

ACTIVITIES

Mountain biking Crimea is just now being discovered by cyclists, but the terrain is perfect for the sport, especially if you crave really steep hills. There are also some unusual spots for off-road riding, but note that in other areas you will be dodging traffic much of the time. Bring as much of your own replacement parts and gear as you can, as there are no really great bike shops around. For more information or to join a tour, check out these two English-language websites: www.velosipeda.net and www.mt.crimea.com.

WHAT TO SEE AND DO There is no prescribed tick-list for Simferopol: the sights are there to see, but the city is more conducive to walking around and simply hanging out before or after your other Crimean travels. One of the oldest buildings in the city is the **Kebir Djami Mosque** (*Kurchatova 4*). Built in 1502, this is the Muslim exception that outlived both Catherine the Great and the Soviet Union. The old Karaite **Jewish Kenessa** (*Karaimskya 6*) was built in 1896 but is now a private residence. The **Church of the Three Saints** (*Gogolya 16*) is a beautiful white church with black cupolas built in 1871. During Soviet times the church was used as the city's archives, but now it belongs to the Moscow Patriarchate (*open every day 07.30–19.00*). Just down the street is the **Ethnographic Museum** (*Pushkina 18;* ☎ *0652 258 712*). The permanent exhibit presents 13 of the ethnic groups that have lived in Crimea, and each display was designed and donated by locals.

The **Scythian Neapolis** is an unfinished archaeological dig working to uncover what used to be the capital of late Scythian civilisation. These 'Royal Scythians' were heavily influenced by contact with the Greeks and flourished from the 2nd century BC to the 3rd century AD. The surrounding wall still remains, as well as dozens of half-excavated tombs and large palace ruins of stone rubble. Take a taxi to '*neapol skifsky*' or take the No 4 trolleybus to the end of the line or walk from the Hotel Moskva.

Simferopol's parks are its saving grace. A nice walk begins in **Park Gagarina** and criss-crosses the Salgir River through other small parks, ending in **Park**

Salgira (which then extends to the reservoir). **Detskii Park** (Children's Park) is a classic example of Soviet family entertainment and contains various amusements aimed at the youngest generation. Lastly, on Sunday afternoons there is a big outdoor book market across from the *vokzal* which is definitely worth browsing through if you are around.

OUTSIDE SIMFEROPOL

Chatyr-Dag ЧАТЫР-ДАГ This long, sloping plateau stands alone and is one of the highest in Crimea (1,527m), inspiring its Tatar name which transcribes as 'Roof Mountain'. The karst landscape is pockmarked but very green and open. On the lower eastern side of the mountain is the **Angarskii Pass** (**Ангарский Перевал**) which has its own bus stop on the M18 road between Simferopol and Alushta. This seems to be the base from which the popular hiking route goes to Chatyr-Dag (and Demerdzhi) and one of the few locations where it snows enough for winter sports. Another trail goes from Mramornoye on the road from Simferopol. Much of Crimea is visible from the top. Take care though, as this spot lies right between the rising steppe and the seaside mountain ridge and is prone to very high winds.

The caves of Chatyr-Dag **ПЕЩЕРЫ ЧАТЫР-ДАГА** Chatyr-Dag is more renowned for what lies beneath: all along its lower side are literally hundreds of limestone caves. Two of the largest have been set up for regular visitors and are located very close to one another. The caves are maintained by Onyx Tour (see *Local tour operators and tourist information*), who can arrange tours and transport from Simferopol. Otherwise, you can get there on your own by taking a bus/trolleybus to Zarechnoye or Mramornoye or simply by hiking. Next to Mramornaya Cave there are cabins for hikers (*US$7 a night per person/US$25 for the whole house*) as well as a café and a Russian *banya*.

Mramornaya МРАМОРНАЯ (*A maximum of five people can go to the lower level at one time and it costs US$15 per person, including equipment*) 'Marble' cave was discovered only in 1987 and is now one of the most visited caves in all of Europe due to its easy access and remarkable formations. It is a relatively shallow cave at 68m deep, but it is almost 2km long and filled with oozing geological shapes. The fat ochre pillars all seem to be melting and the glossy stalagmites are humorously statuesque, while deeper in the cave, white calcite 'moon milk' is still dripping ghostly forms onto the rocks and cave pools form tiny calcite pearls. The cave took its present shape sixty thousand years ago when a series of subterranean riverbeds collapsed one on top of another, leaving two 'floors'. The destruction created a massive room in the centre filled with house-size boulders, now jokingly called 'Perestroika Hall'. The air is so cool and so unpolluted here that things appear smaller than they actually are. Visits are by guided tour only. The normal one-hour tour costs US$4 and takes in the upper level and all its formations. If you really want to feel like you're caving, there is a three-and-a-half-hour tour through the lower levels where you'll get to wear a hard hat with a light on it. This is a bit more physically demanding but visits some truly incredible untouched spots.

Eminé-Ba'ir-Khosar ЭМИНЕ-БАИР-ХОСАР (*The tours vary in length and depth – the full tour costs US$4*) This cave's Tatar name translates as 'the Well of Maiden Eminé' and comes with a genuine Romeo and Juliet legend. Eminé's love was killed by her father's tribe and she began searching the mountains to find his lost soul. When told that he would be waiting in the heart of the earth, she climbed down into the bottom of the cave and found its deepest crevice. Staring into the darkness, she was overcome by grief and threw herself from the edge. The story matches the cave, which opens in a gaping hole and then spirals down to an incredible depth of 120m. The vivid colours and sheer size of this cave make it even more exciting than Mramornaya. Eminé is unique for its small crystal flowers, its absinthe-coloured lake and its stalagmite forests. The 'Hall of Idols' really does look like a jade shop and the caramel flows of clay are oddly inviting. There is also a small 'museum' inside the cave where the prehistoric finds of the cave are liberally displayed, including mammoth teeth, sabre-tooth tiger bones and onyx crystals.

YEVPATORIA ЕВПАТОРИЯ

Miles of natural sand beaches secured this town's fate as an escapist resort. Spread along the northern shore of Kalamita Bay, Yevpatoria is fast becoming a desirable destination – not just for Russian seaside holidaymakers, but for European spa junkies who are in the know. Things can get packed in the summer, but out of season there is no better place in the country for an affordable and relaxing spa holiday.

The port has gone through all the reincarnations of a Crimean town, starting with its Greek phase. Kerkinitida was a wealthy trading centre that even issued its own currency at one time. The Scythians seemed to attack this port more than the others and eventually took it over. Trade petered out and the city fell into oblivion for almost a millennium. Then Kievan Rus and the Genoese followed with brief appearances in the region, but only under the Ottoman Turks did the medieval Tatar city Gözlev establish itself as the centre of the Black Sea slave trade. Gözlev was surrounded by a thick 4km-long city wall and boasted 12 mosques. In their ongoing rivalry with the Turks, the Zaporizhzhyan Cossacks frequently raided the port. Later, Catherine the Great built a new Russian city and added the name of an ancient Slavic king Yevpator. Here the Russian aristocracy created a spa town along the lines of those they visited in Switzerland and Italy. During the Crimean War, the port was easily taken by the allied forces and occupied for the whole of the conflict. Sanatoria (health resorts) occupied the whole beachfront in Soviet times and the tourist/health industry now reigns supreme, with a special focus on children. Compared with the southern coast, this is still very much a quiet town and far less expensive. The boardwalk and high-rise hotels should not detract from the town's cultural relics: the Dzhuma-Dzhami Mosque, the Karaim Kenassa and the old imperial Russian resorts.

GETTING THERE AND AWAY There is a direct train to Kiev although its schedule tends to change frequently. There are regular trains to Simferopol, as well as buses, which take about 2½ hours. Less frequent buses travel to Feodosiya (4½ hours) and Yalta (4 hours). The train station is at the end of Frunze, while the bus station is just across from the train station on Internatsionalnaya. At one time, frequent ships ferried passengers to Odessa, other Crimean cities and Turkey, but this is a thing of the past.

⌂ WHERE TO STAY

⌂ **Liana** Kozitskovo 5; ☏ 0656 936 249; f 0656 928 174; e info@lianaevpatoria.com; www.lianaevpatoria.com. Probably the nicest place in town and recently-renovated. Fresh and homey, the Liana features comfortable rooms, good plumbing, a cute swimming pool (with sauna) and is just 100 yards from the beach. Prices are very reasonable for such a high standard of hotel. Credit cards accepted.

US$45–90 per room.
⌂ **Dolce Vita** Tokarova 6; ☏ 0656 960 729; e info@dolcevita.com; www.dolcevita.com. Slightly more centrally located with a private beach. The complex comprises a series of individual, 2-floor apartments and functions as a family-friendly beach club. Options for FB are also available, and credit cards are accepted. *In season, expect to pay*

US$70–80, while in the off-season, rooms cost as little as US$30.

🏠 **Yevpatoria** Pobedy 1/64; ☏ 0656 951 548. The largest hotel in town and with relatively high standards. Basic rooms US$15–35 based on a long-term stay, with better, hotel-style rooms from US$50–90.

🏠 **Planeta** Kositskovo 29/73; ☏ 0656 933 475; f 0656 960 320; e planetacom@evp.sf.ukrtel.net. A modern, higher-quality resort with a big swimming pool and several 'lux' rooms. B/fast is inc, FB is optional. Many of the other hotels and sanatoria stem from the Soviet era and haven't changed much since; some still require a minimum stay of a week

or more. Still, if you are keen to try out the local version of a spa vacation (complete with Russian concepts of medicine), Yevpatoria provides an authentic first time. Standard room US$35, junior suite US$45, full-size suite US$70.

🏠 **Krym** (Revolyutsii 46; ☏ 0656 910 549) and **Ukrayina** (Lenina 42/19; ☏ 0656 936 504) have rooms for US$10–50, with suites at US$70.

🏠 **Pobeda** Frunze 4; ☏ Kiev 044 220 66 50; e kurort@i.kiev.ua. Right on the beachfront and remaining true to the Soviet tradition that founded it; but that's not a bad thing. Intended for Ukrainian families with children. Rooms US$15–45.

If you're feeling adventurous, you may just want to show up and knock on doors – there's a sanatorium on every block.

✖ **WHERE TO EAT** All the hotels listed offer great restaurant options, especially **Yevpatoria** and **Planeta**. All along the beach there are food stands, and one shouldn't miss the opportunity to try some of the local Crimean Tatar cooking. **Atlant** (Frunze 20; ☏ 0656 930 087) does some seafood and typical Russian meals, and **Armenia** (Demysheva 160) serves its namesake's cuisine. The milk bar **Molochnoye** (Revolyutsii 51) is a fun café that serves milkshakes as well as very basic meals. Otherwise, try:

✖ **Mustafa** On Revolutsii, in the old city across from the mosque. In the old city, next to the mosque, this Crimean Tatar restaurant should be a high priority with its very authentic cuisine and lively atmosphere. Live Crimean music and dancing in the evening. Mains from US$6; open 11.00–23.00.

✖ **Hamlet** Corner of Frunze and Demysheva; near the Central Univermag. Yevpatoria's poshest restaurant, serving 'English' food (a curious, nationwide trend for the moment). Mains from US$20. Open 11.00–midnight.

✖ **Literature Café** Anna Akhmatova 21/16; ☏ 0656 944 307. A café that honours the great Russian poet Anna Akhmatova. Decked out in 1920s style, the menu ranges from quaint salads and yummy desserts to bistro-style meals. Mains from US$5; open 10.00–21.00.

✖ **Dulbert** Frunze 1 (where Frunze meets the seaside); ☏ 0656 936 684. A fancy French seafood restaurant (serving lobster bisque, frog's legs, etc.) with nice outdoor seating upstairs. Mains from US$18; open 11.00–23.00.

WHAT TO SEE AND DO Enjoy the beach! Kalamita Bay is one of the calmer spots on the Black Sea (in terms of waves, not people). Most transport goes to Solnyshko Beach but a long walk should take you away from the worst crowds (if you really want to get away, go to **Saki**, about 30 minutes away by bus or taxi). Yevpatoria's old city features the crazy winding streets of a Middle Eastern medina – definitely fun to wander through. The city also has several very nice parks and squares. On Yevpatoria's main street of Revolyutsii stands the **Dzhuma-Dzhami** – a working mosque returned to Crimean Tatar ownership in 1990. The original structure was built in the 16th century by Khodzha Sinan and it is here that the Crimean khans were crowned. The minarets and Sufi-inspired design are amazingly well preserved and it's the symbol of Yevpatoria today. Not far away is the **Tekiye Dervishes Monastery** (14th century) with a similarly distinctive spiritual architecture and mysterious past. The old **Turkish bathhouse** (Krasnoarmeyskaya 50) has remained from the days of the sultan and is open to visitors. Yevpatoria also contains one of the last remaining buildings of the Karaims, the non-Talmudic

Crimean Jewish nation. The **Karaim Kenassa** (*Matveeva 68*) is an assembly of holy buildings and arcades built by the Karaim in the early 19th century. For an insight into local history and culture, check out the **Museum of Yevpatoria** (*Duvanovksaya 11/12;* ✆ *0656 962 727; open 10.00 to 17.00; closed Mon*).

BAKHCHISARAI БАХЧИСАРАЙ

Crimea's extraordinary interior is a welcome destination all its own. Here, the windswept hills rise up into the broken outcrops of strange rock formations, and for the long spring and summer, the extensive fruit orchards and vineyards colour the landscape green, along with fields upon fields of wild flowers (mainly bright, orange-red poppies). Although the Crimean Tatars live all over Crimea, travellers seek them out in Bakhchisarai, remembering that once upon a time this sleepy little town was the eminent capital of the Crimean khanate.

During the past 15 years, Bakhchisarai has become the spiritual capital of Crimean Tatar repatriation, following their long and tragic history of exile. The 'return of the natives' has fuelled a steady regeneration of all that makes this place so distinctive: minarets grace the skyline and the crumbling tile-roofed buildings look anything but Slavic. Indeed, parts of present-day Bakhchisarai feel a lot like the Middle East, particularly as the old town stretches along the narrow canyon bed of the Churyuk-Su River. As you move upstream, the cliffs cut the upper plateau into deeper canyons and the mooing of cows echoes off the lumpy rocks. It was in these hidden, ancient spots that early believers first established their sacred cave cities, all of which are now popular hiking trails. Today, Bakhchisarai boasts the living remnants of three great world religions: Islam (the Khan's Palace and adjoining mosque), Orthodox Christianity (the Holy Assumption Monastery) and Judaism (Chufut-Kale).

Early Byzantine Christians settled in a nearby hillside some time around the 9th century, followed by the Golden Horde, who designated the area 'Eski-Yurt' (new town) in the mid 13th century. In the nearby cave city of Chufut-Kale, the Crimean khanate was separately established in 1427, prior to welcoming Jewish tradesmen to come and live, work and trade in 'the fortress of the Jews'. After the Ottoman Empire brought the khanate under its rule, the Crimean khan, Sahib Isahel Giray, officially moved his capital to the more centrally located valley, calling his new home 'the palace in the garden', or **Bağçasaray** in Crimean Tatar. The construction of the sultan's palace continued for three and a half centuries, with new halls and courts added to the palace by several descendant khans. Cosmopolitanism and vigorous trade led to the capital's prosperity – at the height of the Crimean khanate, there were 32 mosques in Bakchisarai, of which most were destroyed during the Russian occupation in 1783. While most of Tatar Crimea was knocked to the ground, Catherine the Great spared the Khan's Palace, supposedly for its romantic appeal and oriental mystique.

Today, Bakhchisarai is a resurrected ghost town with four working mosques and a thriving community of Ukraine's indigenous Muslims. The dry landscapes are just as dear to the heart of Orthodoxy, though, and many Russian and Ukrainian pilgrims still come to worship at these early Christian sites. Tourists have begun arriving in droves, yet while many group tours now make the nominal stop in Bakhchisarai, few stay more than a couple of hours – just enough time to tour the palace and bargain at the souvenir stands outside. Such hit-and-run visits seem a small abomination, as they bypass the real magic of the area – the dusty side streets, the evening *muezzin*, and the remnants of a 15th-century capital hidden beneath a blossoming shanty town of enterprising refugees. Bakhchisarai also boasts some of the most beautiful sunsets in Crimea, which it would be a pity to miss.

GETTING THERE AND AWAY Bakhchisarai is the main stop between Simferopol and Sevastopol and is often a convenient diversion en route to the southern coast. In summer, buses and *marshrutka* connect to either city all day long (an hour each way). In winter, there is an hourly bus but these run only until 18.00. Six inter-city trains pass through every day, two of which go on to Kiev, and another to Donetsk, yet their stop in Bakhchisarai is never longer than two minutes. The slower *elektrichki* do a back and forth run from Simferopol to Sevastopol but this is slow (over 1½ hours in either direction). With the usual caution, hitching a ride to and from Sevastopol is not terribly difficult. The *vokzal* and bus station are at the end of Ulitsa Rakitskovo. The *marshrutka* and buses leave from this square and go directly to the khan's palace, then up to the end of the main road, turning around at the base of the Assumption Monastery.

WHERE TO STAY This is still a small town with limited choices, which discourages larger groups, but also keeps Bakhchisarai rather peaceful.

🏠 **Prival** ✆ 0655 447 846; f 0655 447 235; e prival@tavria.net; www.prival.crimea.com. The largest hotel is this resort. Located high up on the hillside looking over the town below, the complex caters to families on holiday. Low-end rooms share a shower block (the hot water runs 24 hours) whilst private rooms come with en-suite bathrooms and b/fast inc; and separate individual cabins are quite plush. The camp comes with its own swimming pool, tennis courts and outdoor barbecue, and is a great base for hikers just starting out. *Low-end rooms with shared shower US$10 pp; private rooms with en-suite US$30 (b/fast inc); cabins from US$70.*

🏠 **Crimean Tatar Association of Local Tourist Initiatives** ✆ 0652 485 382; e ethnotour@crimean.biz; www.ethnotour.crimean.biz. Another highly recommended option, this local co-operative offers several opportunities for comfortable homestays with local Crimean Tatar families in Bakhchisarai, with meals inc. Guides can also be arranged for local tours — book online or call ahead.
🏠 **Bakhchisarai** Simferopolskaya 3; ✆ 0655 442 298; f 0655 442 658. Travellers have the option of this Soviet-era hotel with basic rooms. *US$10–40.*
🏠 **Avtomobilist** Krymskaya 12; ✆ 0655 426 872. A dingy motel for visitors travelling by car that is further away from the old city and its sites. *Rooms US$15–35.*

WHERE TO EAT Closer to the Khan's Palace are plenty of foodstands and cafés for the tourist crowds that pass through in summer. The *chebureki* and *baklava* sold on the street are delicious.

✗ **K'yavé Khané Gul'fidan** No phone. If you want a more formal introduction to Crimean Tatar cuisine, then take a walk across the palace moat to this lively restaurant that serves up the real thing. Cash only. *Mains from US$6.*
✗ **Karavan Sarai Salachyk** Bassenko 43A; ✆ 0655 452 220. For a much more relaxed setting and a far less touristy experience, travel up the road

(towards the monastery). Run by a hospitable young Crimean Tatar family, this outdoor restaurant is shaded by grapevines and the food is grilled in an open-air kitchen. If you're lucky, you'll be invited into the centuries-old cellar, where guests sit on sheepskin rugs and get served cups of thick coffee. *The restaurant is always open (really); cash only. Mains from US$6.*

Otherwise, there is a plethora of cheesier dining establishments lining the main street. All seem to cater to tourists but fail to capture the essence of the place, advertising with such oxymorons as 'Authentic Tatar Wine'.

WHAT TO SEE AND DO
The Khan's Palace (*Open 09.00–16.00, closed Tue and Wed (off season); entrance 15UAH. Signs are posted in Russian, Tatar and English. For more information, visit the official website: www.hansaray.org.ua; note that photography inside the complex is also charged*

per frame) Pictures of this building are in every Crimean tourist brochure and its high-domed mosque is *the* symbol of Crimea's oriental heritage. The lofty minarets and rows of Turkish chimneys clearly stand out from the rough-and-tumble look of the town. Here the Crimean khans once held court and kept a sizeable harem. The original structure follows the combined design of Persian, Turkish and Italian architects and spontaneous additions since 1551 made the ensemble an elaborate cluster of painted walls and lacy woodwork. The entire complex is a protected historic site that functions as a series of museums, but that also serves as a community centre and working mosque for the Crimean Tatars.

The palace is unique for a former Soviet museum since you are free to walk around and explore the various buildings and small gardens on your own. A self-guided walking tour gives you a small idea of what life was like for the khanate royalty. On the left of the main entrance is the original 'big' mosque from which the *muezzin* still calls prayers. It is not open to visitors. The other courtyards and buildings are open, although some are just used as storage space for unrelated exhibits. The **Divan Chamber** was the literal seat of government, where the khan and Ottoman emissaries discussed government affairs and made plans for war. The **Small Mosque** has remained in its original condition and stands as a monument to the liberalism of the Crimean Tatars – during restoration, frescoes were found with scenes of men, animals and flowers, all considered idolatrous images and shunned in mainstream Islamic design. The **Summer House** was a late addition to the palace and its latest renovation has a strong Soviet disco feel. The **Fountain Yard** is a collection of the fountains that have been moved from other parts of the palace, including the famous Fountain of Tears. Elaborate calligraphy over the doorways pays homage to individual khans, bestowing the Islamic blessing to 'Forgive him and his parents'. The **Harem** is in a separate building and is the one house remaining out of the four that belonged to the khan's wives. Apparently, women in the harem were allowed a peek of the outside world from the top of the **Falcon Tower** where the khan's hunting birds were kept. Also in the yard is the khan's **cemetery**, where 16 former Crimean khans are buried. Through the staterooms on the second floor of the palace there is a museum display of Crimean Tatar artefacts. There are beautiful examples of Islamic calligraphy in illuminated 13th-century Korans and original sharia books used in the Crimean khanate. The exhibit also features Crimean Tatar clothes, objects and utensils, as well as old photographs of Crimea and its people before deportation.

Somewhat more interesting than the palace complex itself is the activity that goes on around it. Out on the street, or in the main courtyard, the Tatar men in their black astrakhan hats gather to talk, and little Tatar grandmothers sell traditional Crimean Tatar food. On Fridays, the place is busy with families coming and going to prayer at the **main mosque** (which features the most prominent minaret in sight). Non-Muslim guests are encouraged to come inside and view the mosque's decorous interior, but are asked to show respect by removing shoes and covering heads (for women). If you take the time to stand and watch or else have a chat (Crimean Tatars are famously multilingual) you'll learn more about this small nation than any museum can show you. Visitors should also be encouraged to take a walk on the trails behind the palace (just follow the small stream). Walking through the old city takes you past many fascinating ruins – old palaces, mosques and homes, many of which date back to the period of Catherine the Great and much earlier. This is also the neighbourhood of greatest Tatar concentration and is a great place to meet people.

OUTSIDE BAKHCHISARAI
The Holy Assumption Bakhchisarai Monastery This tiny and very ancient church is built inside a cave so that its small windows appear naturally set into the face of

THE FOUNTAIN OF TEARS

In the corner of the Fountain Yard of the Khan's Palace stands a small marble fountain with a wistful history. Khan Krim Giray fell deeply in love with a Polish girl who was added to his harem as a war prize. When he first looked on her face he shouted out 'Dilara Bikech!' meaning 'Beautiful Princess'. The khan became obsessed with her but alas, his love remained unrequited. Unable to cope with harem life, the girl died after one year. The khan was grief-stricken and fell into a deep depression. He built a giant tomb for the girl and it is written that he cried day and night for years afterwards. His courtesans ordered a fountain be made that would 'contain' the khan's endless heartache so that he could begin to address the affairs of state. The fountain was built by the tomb of the girl and later moved by Catherine the Great into the fountain yard. Water is carried from shelf to shelf, tumbling out periodically like the overflowing tears of a grief remembered. The Sufi design brings the water to the bottom of the fountain where it trickles into a spiral, the symbol of eternity.

After visiting the palace, the romantic poet Pushkin was inspired by the khan's tragic love story and penned the famous poem *The Bakhchisarai Fountain*. He picked two roses from the garden, and placed them on the top of the fountain (red for love, and yellow for chagrin). The tradition is still followed with freshly cut palace roses. The popularity of the poem kept the palace from being destroyed during the Russian Empire and led to it becoming a museum during the Soviet era. The moral of the story is that if you want to preserve a place, write a poem about it.

the steep cliff from which it hangs. Diagonal stairs and open-air tunnels wind up to the single golden dome and the actual chapel, with its low ceiling, enforces a physical manifestation of humility. From this vertical churchyard you can see across the canyon to the cave city of Chufut-Kale. The monastery claims to be the oldest in Crimea, and was started in the 8th century by Byzantine mystics. The builders followed the natural contours of the cliff to construct a series of chapels and cells inside the rock. It was closed in 1921, but has now reopened and is home to an order of Russian Orthodox monks (in Soviet days the wide stone steps were used as a backdrop for a film version of *Hamlet*). The monastery is fast becoming an important pilgrimage site, not least for its holy fountain that brings health and blessings to those who drink from it.

Sincere travellers can approach the father of the monastery and receive his blessing to be a guest in the monastery for up to three days. During this time your food and accommodation are provided, but be prepared to get up very early, to pray lots and to work hard. The monks spend much of their day rebuilding their monastery by hand.

To get there take the No 1 or No 2 bus or any *marshrutka* on the main road (Rakitskovo) and go to the end of the line, or take a taxi. From the base, the trail curves up around the hillside for 500m; the hike should take 20–30 minutes. From the monastery it is 1km across the valley to the trail that goes to Chufut-Kale (not a trip to be underestimated).

Chufut-Kale ЧУФУТ-КАЛЕ The 'Fortress of the Jews' is a medieval ruin perched high on a plateau, and is the most-visited of Crimea's 16 cave cities. The Christianised Alan tribes were the first to use this strategic spot, and their many monasteries earned it the name Kyrk-Or (Forty Fortresses). The nations that passed through Crimea all left populations in this city, including the Armenians and the Karaim Jews, who were descendants of the Khazar khaganate. The Crimean khanate built its first capital here in the 15th century and ruled with tolerance, but many of the Greek Christians moved to Mangup. After relocating his capital to Bakhchisarai, the khan decreed that the Karaim Jews could trade freely in the city during the day, but then had to return back to their mountain home by nightfall. The Karaims predominated in Chufut-Kale for the entire reign of the Crimean khanate.

The city streets are still intact and the ruins make for interesting exploring. The 14th-century Karaim Kenassa is next to the southern entrance and there are countless homes hewn out of the rock. Hiking back down to the canyon bed brings you to the lower caves that run along the hillside. Among the grazing goats are new shrines to the oldest Orthodox saints. St Cyril, founder of the Russian alphabet, visited here in AD862.

Tepe-Kermen ТЕПЕ-КЕРМЕН
Called the 'Castle on the summit', this cave city is at the top of a mesa-like hill and is surrounded by a much less disturbed natural area. The knobbly grottos atop the plateau made a convenient base from which 240 cave structures were built into an impenetrable town. Founded in the 6th century, this is the oldest of Crimea's cave cities and was at one time the most populated. The king's palace is still recognisable on the southwest side, and the 8th-century cave chapel is a testament to human labour, with its altar and pillars carved entirely from the white rock. It is best to hike here from the eastern gate of Chufut-Kale. Follow the top of the ridge south for two miles. The only ascending path goes from the northeast side of the hill. There are no local springs here, so make sure you have some water with you.

Mangup-Kale МАНГУП-КАЛЕ
The ancient capital of the Feodor was the largest fortress and city in Crimea for about 500 years. A Turkish traveller writing in the 17th century remarked that Allah had used the rocks to build his own castle long before any people had come here. The twisted white cliffs rise straight up from the thickly forested slopes. The plateau is in the shape of a four-fingered hand with extremely sheer drop-offs on three sides – an obvious strategic advantage. The fort

---

REBIRTH OF CRIMEA FOUNDATION (RCF)

Due to Ukraine's already high unemployment and the difficult social conditions in Crimea, returning Crimean Tatar refugees have had little opportunity for work and self-support. Among the many projects to promote Crimean Tatar resettlement and self-sufficiency is the RCF Crimean Tatar co-operative, which secures international grants and uses them to re-educate the refugees in traditional Crimean Tatar craft to provide them with the means to earn an income. One of their centres, Marama, conducts short courses for Bakhchisarai women on traditional embroidery. These Crimean Tatar designs and handicrafts are applied to handbags, handkerchiefs and hats, then sold in the marketplace near the Khan's Palace during the long Crimean summer. Men are also taught traditional jewellery-making and beadwork. Buying something from the market is not your average souvenir shopping, but it helps to secure a place for the Crimean Tatars in their capital.

The RCF has also opened a House of Crimean Tatar Art in Bakhchisarai, at Rechnaya 125. For a small donation, guests visiting this preserved Crimean Tatar home are served a real Crimean meal, can enjoy a permanent exhibition, and best of all, can interact with Crimean Tatars. For more information on the foundation and opportunities to contribute, please contact Lutfi Osman at the Rebirth of Crimea Foundation (Pushkina 1; ✆ 0655 447 491; f 0655 447 491; e rcf@crimea.com or rcf@crimeastar.net; www.rcf.crimea.ua).

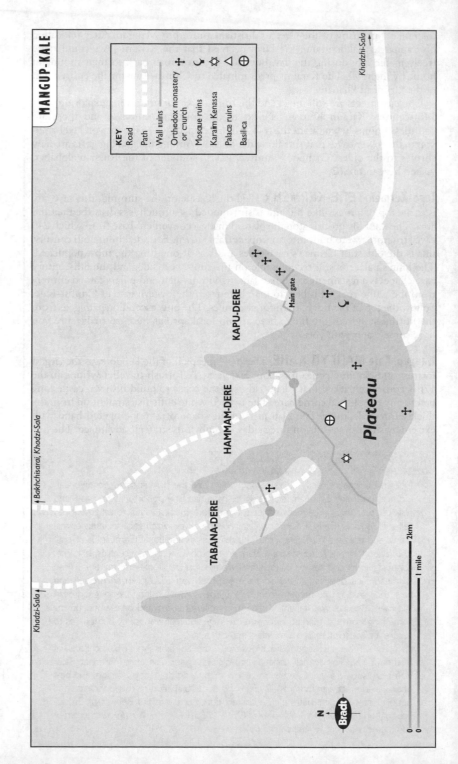

was built by Justinian I in the 6th century, but it was the independent Crimean Greeks who used this vantage point to establish a long-lasting regime in the southwest of the peninsula. Feodor was a medieval Orthodox Liechtenstein, carrying on its own diplomatic relations with Russia, Romania and Hungary. Its capital was its greatest strength – the Turks persisted in a six-month siege before taking the city in the 15th century, and then only through trickery: the Turkish army began marching away quickly, as if surrendering, leaving sentries hidden by the gates. When the Feodorites opened the gates and charged after the Turks, they found themselves quickly surrounded and their city was taken. The ruins today attest to its diverse use until the 1700s, when it was deserted. The original Byzantine ramparts, the citadel, the Orthodox cave churches, the mosque and the underground dungeons are all still intact and open for exploration.

In recent years, Mangup's challenging surface has become popular with rock climbers and mountain bikers. The ancient mystique has also attracted groups of Russian nonconformists and dabblers in the supernatural. Graffiti is rife.

Mangup is 20km south of Bakhchisarai. Take a bus from the *avtovokzal* most of the way through Krasny Mak to the town of Zalesnoye. On foot, turn left and follow the dirt road to Khadzhi Sala from which three separate trails go up to Mangup. (If you turn right at Zalesnoye, the path will go to Eski-Kermen, yet another cave city.) The first two paths go up through the fingers and are about a 2km hike, while the larger dirt road is less steep but extends 5km around the edge. A 4x4 taxi costs around US$10.

Hiking the cave cities If you are already in Bakhchisarai and have time to see only one cave city, Chufut-Kale is the closest, but Mangup-Kale is probably more interesting, and Tepe-Kermen is the most remote and least visited. A popular walk leaves from Bakchisarai, goes through Chufut-Kale and Tepe-Kermen, and all the way to Mangup via the town of Kuybyshevo. This is about a 30km hike and can be done in two or three days. In the height of the tourist season, Mangup-Kale can feel like Grand Central Station. There's a beautiful (and clean!) lake on the path from Mangup-Kale that lures dusty and tired hikers into its cool waters for a nice swim. Use a good contour map; you won't get lost, but you'll want to avoid the towns that can distract from the hike.

SEVASTOPOL СЕВАСТОПОЛЬ

The famous port city of Crimea's western coast is best known for being practically unknown. Sevastopol was a 'closed city' until 1997, when hyper-security around military areas was relaxed. Previously, nobody but the Black Sea fleet personnel and their families were allowed in the area, but the years of pampered isolation have worked in the city's favour: this is one of the cleanest cities in the former USSR and the latest trendy destination for Ukrainians. Those who venture here witness an unexpected shift from the humdrum of so many other post-Soviet towns. Orderly white buildings with bright red roofs dominate, all built in matching Russian Neoclassical grandeur and standing on rows of hills that seem to hover above the water. Squinting across any one of the bays brings visions of an ancient Roman port – the very intention of Catherine the Great when she chose the site to house her navy.

Sevastopol has a personal sense of chic unrivalled by any other 'Russian' city I know. Aesthetics matter here: Bolshaya Morskaya and Nakhimova Boulevard parade some classy shops and small pruned gardens surround the hundreds of monuments to generals, soldiers and citizens. All day long, single-file lines of short-haired sailors march back and forth in their ironed uniforms and shiny

- In summer, wear shorts, and light, airy hiking boots with very good grip. The rock can be very slippery, even when it's totally dry.
- The very best hiking map for Crimea is *Po Gornomy Krymu* (green background with red and yellow lettering), which is sold in most of the souvenir kiosks in Simferopol and along the southern coast. Drawn at a scale of 1:50,000, this contoured map shows the trails in incredible detail, so that even if you can't read the Cyrillic, you'll be able to orient yourself.
- Despite the need to take general precautions, it is practically impossible to get lost in Crimea. There are very few mountain locales that are not within a few kilometres of a town or village. Follow water or streams downhill, go to the highest place and look around, or simply listen for traffic.
- For simple, low-impact hikes, visit the cave cities (Mangup-Kale and Chufut-Kale); for more challenging terrain and serious rock-climbing, go to the upper portions of Demerdzhi, Roman Kosh or Ai-Petri. For a moderate nature walk along one of the peninsula's most pristine stretches of coastline, visit Novy Svyet (see page 354).

buckles. Military primness with a smile seems to be the unwritten city code. The general goodwill may have something to do with the fact that people in this city enjoy a sunny climate and a strong economy. Outside of the navy, most marine men have been commissioned by international shipping companies and are paid high foreign salaries. A virgin tourist industry has also taken off with only a few unfortunate results – the 'dolphinarium' fails to enhance the many natural and historical attractions.

Before Sevastopol, there was Chersoneus – the largest Greek port on the north Black Sea coast and a vital city for Kievan Rus trade. The importance of commerce allowed quick recovery following the Mongol and Ottoman invasions. Russia's interest in this strategic warm-sea port was a major incentive to their taking Crimea from the Turks in 1783. Catherine the Great was delighted with this crossover between her own empire and that of the ancient Greeks and ordered a city to be built around the ruins. She visited in 1787 with lots of oriental illusions in her head, claiming the city was straight out of the *Arabian Nights*. Succeeding rulers hoped that the Russian Empire's growing naval power would be launched from this port but in the end their aspirations brought the Crimean War to Sevastopol. Under the threat of a conclusive attack by the Anglo–French fleet, Admiral Nakhimov scuttled most of his ships, blocking the entrance to the bay. For 349 days, the Russian army fought on the terrain in and around Sevastopol, making the Malakhov mound a household name in Victorian Britain. Once the city fell in August 1855, the Crimean War was over and Sevastopol's identity has been branded ever since. War enthusiasts can visit a number of commemorative museums or walk the overgrown cemeteries and battlefields in nearby Inkerman and Balaclava.

People here are proud of their beautiful city in spite of the defeats it has suffered. Stalin granted Sevastopol the title 'Hero City' after it held out against the Germans until July 1942. Around here, nobody is spitting on memories of the Soviet Union and this may be the one place in Ukraine where you can still hear people address each other as *tovarisch* (comrade) and read slogans favouring a re-united USSR. Like all interesting places, Sevastopol is still wrapped in controversy. While the rest of Ukraine is trying to convince itself and the world that it is Ukrainian and not Russian, Sevastopol is doing the opposite. The

Russian tricolor is ubiquitous, as is the Tsarist St Andrew's cross sewn into the sleeves of black naval uniforms. The popular return to glorifying the Russian monarchy seems a bit more justified in this city once prized by the tsar, but Kiev does not appreciate these displays. When Luzhkov, the outspoken Mayor of Moscow, began making Russian claims on Sevastopol, the Ukrainian Department of Defence moved a number of its offices down here. The bureaucrats who transferred were the lucky ones; Sevastopol's coastline and countryside (not to mention climate) make this a very nice place to live.

GETTING THERE AND AWAY

By air Sevastopol's airport has only just opened for commercial business. It's located on the northern shore in the village of Belbek (↘ *0692 736 036;* f *0692 736 068*). To get to and from the airport, take *marshrutka* No 36 or No 37 from the city centre, or a regular taxi, which should cost around US$15. Flight schedules are still rather volatile, but it's worth checking with Kyi Avia in Sevastopol (*Lenina 13;* ↘ *0692 542 829*) for seasonal flights to and from Kiev. At present, there are regular daily flights to and from Moscow Domodedovo and flights to and from St Petersburg three times a week. As Sevastopol is a lot closer to Crimea's southern coast, it is likely that this will become a major entry point for travellers.

By rail Sevastopol station marks the southern terminus of the great Soviet railroad empire that stretches from the Baltic to the Black Sea to the Pacific Ocean. The long line of trains at the end of the track and among the giant battleships makes for an impressive sight. Two daily trains come and go from Kiev (18 hours), as well as one to and from Donetsk (12 hours). In summer, the number of trains to and from Russia doubles, including a daily St Petersburg train (32 hours), and a few from Moscow (24 hours). The frequency of the long-distance trains and the regularity of bus and taxi travel to the rest of the southern coast make it a good place to begin or end a trip in Crimea. All Sevastopol lines pass through Simferopol, which is between two and three hours away.

By bus Sevastopol's bus station is a busy little place from which frequent buses and *marshrutka* criss-cross all over Crimea and beyond; it's located right next to the *vokzal* (↘ *0692 488 199*). Buses are quickest for getting around the peninsula and are a better way to see the magnificent landscapes outside the city. All day long there are hourly services to Bakhchisarai (1 hour), Simferopol (2 hours), and Yalta (2 hours). Regular services to Balaclava (25 minutes) and Foros (1 hour) are normally included as a stop on the Yalta bus, but just ask the driver. There is one daily bus to Kerch (7 hours) and two to Feodosiya (5 hours). Taking buses any farther seems redundant, but there is a daily service to Nikolayev (11 hours), Odessa (13 hours), and an 'express' bus to and from Dnepropetrovsk (6 hours).

Those who travel by train or bus should take the time to look at the giant locomotive parked outside the station, attached to a rare train-mounted cannon that was used in the defence of Sevastopol in 1941. The words painted on the side mean 'Death to Fascism'.

By boat Sevastopol's *Morskoi Vokzal* (sea station; *Nakhimova 5*) provides a twice-weekly service to and from Istanbul – a 24-hour sailing that gives new meaning to the term 'party boat'. There are two competing ships with side-by-side ticket counters in the sea station, the *Geroi Sevastopolya* (↘ *0692 540 522*) and MV *Sevastopol 1* (↘ *0692 542 912*). The price for passage is US$100 one way, US$200 return.

Crimea SEVASTOPOL

12

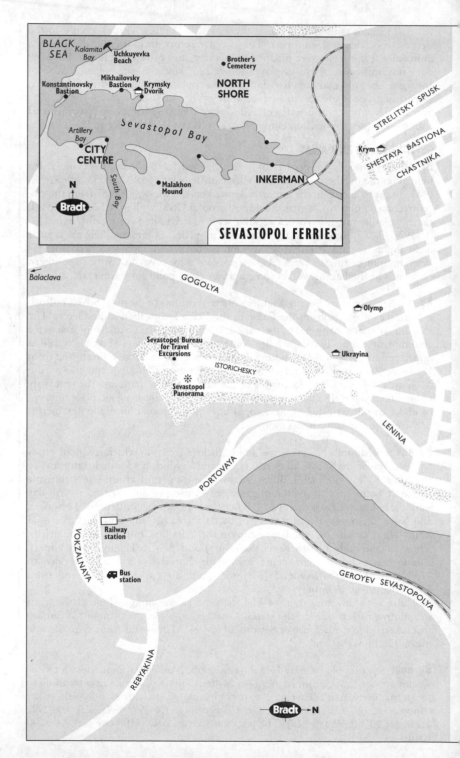

BLACK SEA

Kalamita Bay

Uchkuyevka Beach

Brother's Cemetery

NORTH SHORE

Konstantinovsky Bastion

Mikhailovsky Bastion

Krymsky Dvorik

Sevastopol Bay

Artillery Bay

CITY CENTRE

South Bay

Malakhon Mound

INKERMAN

N

Bradt

SEVASTOPOL FERRIES

STRELITSKY SPUSK

Krym

SHESTAYA BASTIONA

CHASTNIKA

Balaclava

GOGOLYA

Olymp

Sevastopol Bureau for Travel Excursions

ISTORICHESKY

Ukrayina

Sevastopol Panorama

LENINA

PORTOVAYA

Railway station

VOKZALNAYA

Bus station

GEROYEV SEVASTOPOLYA

REBYAKINA

Bradt ▸ N

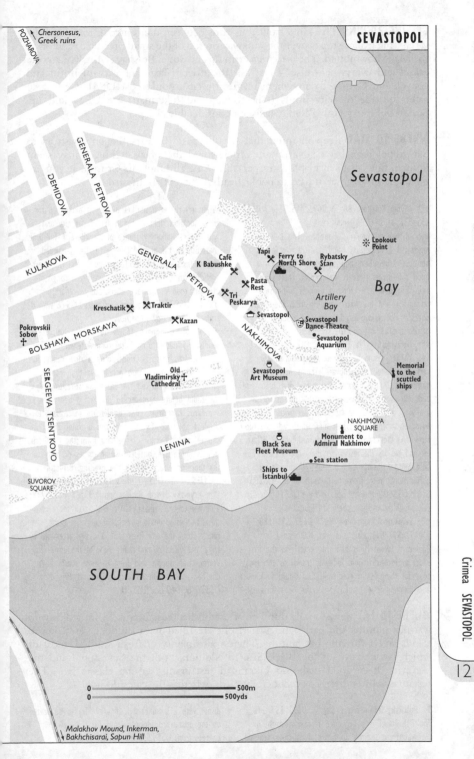

↑ Chersonesus,
Greek ruins

POZHAROVA

Sevastopol

☀ Lookout
Point

DEMIDOVA

GENERALA PETROVA

KULAKOVA

GENERALA
PETROVA

Yapi ✕
Café
K Babushke ✕
✕ Ferry to
North Shore

Rybatsky
Stan ✕

Bay

Kreschatik ✕

✕ Traktir

✕ Tri
Peskarya

✕ Pasta
Rest

*Artillery
Bay*

Pokrovskii
Sobor
✝

BOLSHAYA MORSKAYA

✕ Kazan

⌂ Sevastopol

NAKHIMOVA

Sevastopol
Dance Theatre

● Sevastopol
Aquarium

Memorial
to the
scuttled
ships

SERGEEVA TSENTKOVO

Old
Vladimirsky ✝
Cathedral

Sevastopol
Art Museum

NAKHIMOVA
SQUARE

Monument to
Admiral Nakhimov

LENINA

Black Sea
Fleet Museum

● Sea station

Ships to
Istanbul

SUVOROV
SQUARE

SOUTH BAY

0 ———————— 500m
0 ———————— 500yds

↓ Malakhov Mound, Inkerman,
Bakhchisarai, Sapun Hill

GETTING AROUND The No 9 trolleybus runs between the centre of town and the *vokzal* (the trolley stop is over the walkway on top of the small precipice) and on to the Malakhov mound. The *marshrutka* run up and down Bolshaya Morskaya, to the *vokzal* and everywhere else – just ask the driver. Taxis are very plentiful and convenient. Getting to anywhere inside the city should cost US$1. Getting to sights outside the city limits (Chersoneus and Inkerman) are US$4 and up. Sevastopol's very visible Radio Taxis are considerably cheaper.

🏠 **WHERE TO STAY** Keep in mind that for the past 70 years the only visitors to Sevastopol have been government officials and the Nazis. Choices may seem limited, but what's available is respectable. Like all hotels in Crimea, if you are travelling in summer, it pays to book ahead. All accept credit cards.

🏠 **Olymp** Kulakova 86; ✆ 0692 455 758; f 0692 455 736; e OLYMP@inbox.ru; www.olymphotel.com/eng/about.htm. This newly renovated 19th-century hotel is attractive for its boutique atmosphere and peaceful location on a quiet side street close to the centre. There's also a swimming pool and sauna, a friendly in-house restaurant, and the water running from their taps is potable! *Rooms are large, plush and modern, are priced at US$110, and the service is generous.*

🏠 **Ukrayina** Gogolya 2; ✆ 0692 542 127; f 0692 545 378; e ukrainehotel@stel.sebastopol.ua. This is a very clean hotel with renovated rooms, individual bathrooms, 24hr hot water, and a few real queen-size beds. However, the Soviet construction means rooms are small and there are far too many price categories based on amenities like balconies, which side the room faces, and the degree of luxury furnishing, etc B/fast is inc and besides the restaurant there are 3 cafés. *The best deal for the money is the US$70 upscale sgl. Other rooms range from the bare minimum (US$35) to the US$80 'improved' dbls and the US$140 luxury suites with extravagant themed décor.*

🏠 **Sevastopol** Nakhimova 8; ✆ 0692 591 188; f 0692 592 813. After the war, Nakhimova Boulevard lay in ruins and this hotel was the first effort at reconstruction. Today it stands as the most beautiful thing Stalin ever built and would fool most into thinking it was a Catherine the Great original.

What it lacks in upmarket quality it makes up for in its location right in the heart of the city and within easy walking distance of anywhere. A full-time masseuse on the second floor gives heavy-handed Russian massages for US$10 an hour. *The very best sgls/dbls are US$40/$60, but there are a range of cheaper rooms for budget-conscious travellers (ie: dbls for US$25). The lowest end costs US$18 with a shared shower down the hall.*

🏠 **Krym** Bastionnaya 46; ✆ 0692 469 000. The requisite Soviet Inturist hotel (complete with casino, bar and hair salon) is undergoing a slow renovation which means some rooms are better than others, although all are priced the same. Be sure to see the room before agreeing to take it – bed standards vary from good queen-size mattresses to single foam pads. Every room has a toilet and shower, and the view of the city from the northern side is impressive, but hot water comes on only in the morning hours and in the evening. B/fast inc. *Sgl US$30, dbl US$40, the very best rooms US$50.*

🏠 **Krymsky Dvorik** Razina Spusk 3A; ✆ 0692 718 260; www.dvorik.crimea.ua. On the north shore of the city, this intimate guesthouse offers a quiet refuge from the city itself, but is easily accessible by ferry and offers a panoramic view of the entire bay. Warm, clean, simple and friendly, most rooms have dbl beds, some with en-suite bathrooms. *Priced at US$20, US$40 and US$60.*

✕ **WHERE TO EAT** Sevastopol's number of established restaurants is limited, but in warmer months the parks and waterfront are filled with outdoor cafés, kebab stands and a thriving bar culture. There's also plenty of fresh seafood, most of which is right out of the Black Sea. In addition, both the Sevastopol and the Ukrayina have good in-house Ukrainian restaurants serving classic fare. The restaurants listed here do accept credit cards, whereas the cafés do not.

✕ **Rybatsky Stan** Artillery Bay; ✆ 0692 557 278. The 'Fish Stand' is a big open restaurant right on the waterfront serving an array of delicious seafood

dishes with a banquet-style flourish. Try to be seated on the upstairs outdoor balcony for the view. *Entrées from US$15; open 12.00–midnight;*

Sevastopol is home to Ukraine's most entertaining public transport – pedestrian ferries that connect the main peninsula to the north shore and all the various coves of Sevastopol Bay. Passage normally costs 1 or 2 hrivna and gives you the chance to see the city from the water. There are three main ferry docks in the city – the first is at the base of Artillery Bay, with ferries to and from the north shore (Mikhailsky Bastion); the second is located at the very tip of Lenina (just follow the pathway that everyone else is on down to the water) – ferries travel to the north shore and the other bays; the third dock is close by, near the steps that lead down to the water, next to the sea station – these ferries travel all the way down Sevastopol Bay to Inkerman, about a 45-minute ride away. As public transport is free for invalids and pensioners, you will often find clusters of elderly people riding the ferries as though on a pleasure cruise, playing cards or dominoes or just chatting.

✕ **Yapi** Artillery Bay; ☎ 0692 556 142. Upscale and modish Japanese sushi bar with very fresh sushi and the Ukrainian advertising slogan 'Isle of Sushi'. Attracts a rather swanky clientele. *From US$20; open 12.00–midnight*

✕ **Kreschatik** Bolshaya Morskaya 10; ☎ 0692 542 131. Still considered one of the finest restaurants in the city, specialising in grilled or fried fish and seafood. Still, the courteous staff will prepare most anything upon demand, and the daily specials are always interesting. *Entrées from US$8; open 11.00–midnight.*

✕ **Traktir 1854** Bolshaya Morskaya 8; ☎ 0692 544 760. Creative themed dining honouring the Tsarist military and remembering the Crimean War. The old Russian naval uniforms and thick wooden tables are fitting for Sevastopol and the waiters know their history. The menu sticks to old Russian classics and banquet-style cuisine, including *kurnik* (a Russian chicken pie) and roast duck stuffed with prunes. English menus are available. *A good-size meal will cost US$15; open 11.00– midnight.*

✕ **Pasta Rest** Artillery Bay; ☎ 0692 555 529. A new and rather authentic Italian diner right off the bay near the ferry dock. Incredibly fresh salads, creative appetisers and great pasta, plus a range of rich meat dishes, like rabbit-stuffed baked apple and grilled pork in blackberry sauce. There's also a good range of healthy, steamed dishes and a separate vegetarian menu. English menus available. *Entrées from US$7; open 10.00–midnight.*

✕ **Tri Peskarya** Nakhimova 12; ☎ 0692 555 581. This underground portside restaurant is a favourite among locals, serving tasty salads, clams, mussels and seafood kebabs, as well as pretty staple Ukrainian/Russian fare. They also have an 'exotic menu' which includes things like cuttlefish and frogs' legs. The set lunchtime menu of a 3-course meal for just US$3 is a popular choice. *Dinner entrées from US$7; open 10.00–midnight.*

✕ **Kazan** Bolshaya Morskaya 3; ☎ 0692 544 121. The owner hails from Tatarstan (in central Russia) and serves his national cuisine in a swanky Greek setting complete with Doric columns, fake ivy and waiters in dinner jackets. *Mains from US$12; open 11.00–midnight.*

✕ **Café K** Babushke Mayakovskaya 6; ☎ 0692 543 820. A happy little café not far from the port, owned and operated by a cheerful *babushka*. Hearty Russian staples make up the menu; the *plov* (meat and rice pilaf), *pelmeny* (ravioli) and cakes can all be recommended. *Entrées from US$2; open 09.00–20.00.*

LOCAL TOUR OPERATORS AND TOURIST INFORMATION The **Sevastopol Bureau for Travel Excursions** (☎ *0692 542 860;* f *0692 545 132;* e *sta@stel.sebastopol.ua; www.sevtravel.com*) specialises in short excursions of the city and surrounding areas (Mangup-Kale, Inkerman or Balaklava), but can also put together a nice package tour throughout all of Crimea. For Crimean war enthusiasts, contact **Battlefield Tours** (*27 Courtway Av, Birmingham B14 4PP, England;* ☎ *0121 430 5348;* f *0121 436 7401;* e *info@battlefieldtours.co.uk, www.battlefieldtours.co.uk*).

WHAT TO SEE AND DO A walk down to the end of Prospekt Nakhimova will give you a good feel of the city and bring you to one of the hearts of naval activity.

Crimea SEVASTOPOL

12

Nakhimova Square is 'the square' – a roundabout encircling the monument to **Admiral Nakhimov** and around which the parks descend to the waterfront. Down near the waterfront stands the very melancholic **memorial to the scuttled ships**, a lone pillar resting upon a rocky isle in remembrance of the port's tragic naval defence in the Crimean War. In the evening, this is a popular place for crowds to gather and for strolling couples. In the same vicinity you will find the **Sevastopol Art Museum** (*Nakhimova 9; open 10.00–17.00, closed Tue*) which is not particularly famous but which offers a few real gems: Korovin's *On the Shores of the Black Sea*, Aivozovskii's *Constantinople in Moonlight* and Kasatkin's *The Courtroom Hallway*. Besides the Hermitage in St Petersburg, the oldest museum in 'Russia' is the **Black Sea Fleet Museum** (*Lenina 11;* \ *0692 542 289; open 10.00–17.00, closed Mon and Tue*). The collection spans the entire history of the Russian navy, with nice exhibits on the Crimean War and a healthy dose of anachronistic Soviet propaganda. The **Sevastopol Aquarium** (*Nakhimova 2; open 10.00–17.00; closed Mon; entrance 25UAH*) is also advertised as the oldest aquarium in the country, with a good combination of local Black Sea fish exhibits and more exotic collections. For lively evening entertainment, try the dancing sailors at the **Sevastopol Dance Theatre** (*Nakhimova 4; shows Sat–Sun; cost 30–35UAH*).

By far the best museum in the city is the **Sevastopol Panorama,** located at the top of the hill at the end of the aptly named History Boulevard (*open 09.00–17.00; closed Mon (off season); entrance US$3, 85UAH for individual, English-language guided tours*). The round monument houses the gigantic 360° painting and lifesize model recreating the Battle of Sevastopol fought on 6 June 1855. Viewers watch from a central platform which is meant to be situated with the Russian forces on top of the Malakhov mound. It is truly an impressive display. Among the thousands of painted figures stand the likenesses of famous figures like Leo Tolstoy (who did fight at the battle), as well as Pasha Sevastopolskaya, the Russian equivalent of Florence Nightingale. The painting was designed by the French artist Roubaud and large pieces miraculously survived the German bombardment of 1941.

The Panorama's museum downstairs shows leftover artefacts from the Crimean War such as cannonballs, weapons and uniforms, as well as a detailed exhibit on the history of the war. The booth across from the Panorama sells tickets, but can also arrange English-language guided tours of the museum and the rest of the city.

The real Malakhov mound is covered with monuments to both the Crimean War and World War II. The original defensive tower has survived, along with some cannons and artillery guns. To get there, it's only a ten-minute taxi ride, or else take the No 7 or No 17 trolley. For a good view of the city and bay, climb to the base of the **obelisk monument**, built to commemorate the heroic defence of Sevastopol in World War II (on top of point Khrustalny). Another hilltop monument is the old **St Vladimir's Cathedral**, built in 1888 and the burial place of several famous Russian admirals. The church is on the hilltop in the city centre (off Marata Street). The more elaborate **Pokrovskii Sobor** is a uniquely designed old naval church, built in 1905 and reopened in 1992 (on Bolshaya Morskaya).

It's easy to suffer from monument fatigue in Sevastopol. For a break from the usual, go to the ancient site of **Chersonesus** (Khersones) – the largest Greek ruins in Crimea. Ukraine's first city was founded in 528BC and was unimaginatively named 'Peninsula'. It was independently governed as a democratic city-state until it became a Roman protectorate in the 1st century AD. Later, Byzantium took control of the port and it is here that Prince Vladimir was baptised a Christian in AD988. The very spot is shaded by a small gazebo and close by is **St Vladimir Cathedral**, built to commemorate the event in the 19th century and recently

The Black Sea fleet was founded in 1783 by Catherine the Great, who sought to expand and protect the Russian Empire's southern reaches with a mighty navy. Throughout the history of the Russian, then Soviet, then Ukrainian navy, the ships were built in Mikolayiv and harboured in Sevastopol. In the Crimean War, most of the wooden fleet was scuttled in a last ditch attempt to seal off Sevastopol's harbour, and following the break-up of the Soviet Union, the fleet of battleships and submarines was stripped of its nuclear capabilities. Even so, the Black Sea fleet is still revered with honour.

For Russia, probably the most contentious issue at Ukraine's independence was the future of the Black Sea fleet and the use of Sevastopol's port. For nearly a decade, Russia and Ukraine bickered back and forth ('Mine!' 'No, mine!') until the ageing fleet was officially divided in 1997 and an agreement was reached to 'share' the port. Today, Sevastopol remains in a situation whereby two antagonistic navies are using the same port, not unlike two warring siblings having to share a bedroom and drawing a line down the middle. Things remain amicable among the sailors, as not so long ago they were working side by side, yet the abundance of Russian versus Ukrainian flags is a clear case of one-upmanship and grandstanding. Russia uses energy cost and dependency to manipulate Ukraine, Ukraine uses the Black Sea fleet (with increased 'rents' for Sevastopol) to manipulate Russia in return.

From a facilities perspective, ownership of nearly everything in Sevastopol has been assigned to one navy or the other, including the historic white stone batteries on the north shore. Konstantinovskaya (closest to the sea) belongs to the Russians, Mikhayilovska belongs to the Ukrainians. For the sake of correct identification of ships and sailors in Sevastopol, the Russian naval insignia is a light blue St Andrew's cross on a white background, whereas the Ukrainian naval insignia is a light blue St George's cross on a white background with the Ukrainian blue and yellow in the upper left-hand corner. For a good show, come to Sevastopol on the last Sunday of July, the city's 'Navy Day', a two-toned celebration of a Soviet tradition.

rebuilt anew (not to be confused with the 'old St Vladimir's church' in the city, which is actually newer).

I suggest skipping the rather bare museums and walking straight to the Greek ruins by the seaside. These alone make a fascinating exhibit and the grassy streets and old temples cover an extensive space. Beware of open wells and deep holes. (*The grounds are open every day, 09.00–19.00; US$3 entrance.*) Chersonesus is about ten minutes away by taxi, or you may choose to go on a tour organised by your hotel. If you enjoy a good swim, be sure to bring along your swimsuit and towel. The Greek ruins go right down to the shore (and beyond) and have become a pleasant swimming hole in the summertime, as well as a fascinating diving site.

Sevastopol's **north shore** is well off the beaten path but provides the very best view of the city and is just a pleasant ferry ride across the bay. The hilltop memorial to the **30th battery** grants a superb view of the whole city and its outlying areas. The white stone **Konstantinovsky Bastion** (closest to the sea) and the **Mikhailovsky Bastion** (north shore) are functioning naval bases, and are therefore off-limits to visitors, but are some of the last remaining military buildings from Sevastopol's beginnings. The north shore's **Brothers' Cemetery** (Bratskoye Kladbische) holds the war dead from the Crimean War onwards, as well as some of the Russian sailors who perished in the recent *Kursk* submarine tragedy. Not far away is the shore of Kalamita Bay, and **Uchkuyevka Beach** is one of the nicer places to swim.

OUTSIDE SEVASTOPOL

Inkerman ИНКЕРМАН This small town lies at the mouth of the Chornaya (Black) River and is best known for its trademark bright white stone, which was used to build much of Sevastopol and the Livadia Palace in Yalta. Among the cliffs on the road from Simferopol you can't miss the windows and the miniature teal cupolas sticking out from the rock face. The **St Kliment/Clement's Monastery** was supposedly founded in the 1st century, after an impromptu visit by St Andrew in AD98 led to the discovery of a holy well that bubbled all the way up to the plateau above the cliffs. A community of monks was established and they begin to tunnel through the cliff face and establish a series of minuscule chapels connected by carved staircases. The two main cave churches were finished in the 8th century and the complex was named after a bishop from Rome who worked in the local rock quarries. The monastery prevailed for nearly two millennia, and today, the internal staircase leads up to the remains of a 15th-century Feodorite Kalamita fortress. Alas, the monastery was built unfortunately close to the stone quarry, a fact that led to routine blasting and the eventual destruction of the babbling holy well. Despite the loss, the monastery makes a very interesting and convenient side trip from Sevastopol – this is one of the oldest churches in the entire Russian Orthodox sphere, and the rocky landscape is fun to hike through. One should also note that the pristine lake up above the cliff is filled with the holy water.

The Battle of Inkerman was the last Russian offensive before the allied siege of Sevastopol and the greatest land battle of the Crimean War. On the morning of 5 November 1854, Russian forces marched to the British barricades but were unable to break through. The battle was incredibly intense but decided by midday: the British army had lost a quarter of its men while the Russians had retreated, leaving behind nearly 12,000 casualties. The actual battle was fought in the now forested plains west of Sevastopol and the ridges south of the Chornaya River. Most of the area is open for walking if you are keen; the top of St Kliment's ravine is the site of 'Shell Hill', close to where the barrier once stood.

To get to Inkerman, take a 15-minute bus or taxi from central Sevastopol. A more inviting option is the ferry, which runs from the waterfront on Nakhimov right to Inkerman – it's just a short walk up the hill to the monastery.

BALACLAVA БАЛАКЛАВА

Yes, the full hood that looks silly but keeps you very warm is named after this picturesque port. In the first winter of the Crimean War, British women read reports that their men were dying by the hundreds of exposure to the cold. They began knitting close-fitting covers that left only the eyes exposed, then sent the packages to 'Balaclava' where the British High Command had sheltered its warships and military. The Royal Navy was over-enthusiastic with the number of ships it harboured here, and in November 1854 a vicious winter storm sank a good portion of the naval force, including the prized *Black Prince*.

The legendary Battle of Balaclava (25 October 1854) was fought in the valleys above the entrance to the town. This was a surprise attack by the Russians who took the Turkish cannons and were then charged by the doomed Light Brigade. Aficionados of the Crimean War will recognise the terrain, and visitors are frequently finding historical mementos in the dirt. With a few exceptions, the area is open for walking. A small white pinnacle stands as a memorial.

The British were not the first to discover the calm inlet hidden behind winding sea cliffs. Homer's *Odyssey* mentions the hideout, where ferocious pirates lured sailors to its protected shores before attacking them. Curving

THE CHARGE OF THE LIGHT BRIGADE

Alfred Lord Tennyson's famous poem remembers the tragic events of the Battle of Balaclava. On 25 October 1854 the Russian forces succeeded in taking the Turkish cannons and it looked as if they would advance and take the port from the British. The 93rd British Highlanders kept the Russians from entering Balaclava in a defence referred to as the 'thin red line'; however, the causeway heights appeared open to attack. Through blunder or miscommunication Lord Cardigan was commanded to charge the Russian force at the far end of the valley, which can be seen today with its three high sides and its low flat centre. Surrounding this 'Valley of Death' was the combined force of the Russian infantry, artillery and cavalry; the command to charge was suicidal. The Light Brigade's 'noble six hundred' were precisely 673 cavalrymen who calmly mounted their horses and made the advance. Fewer than 200 survived the hail of cannonballs and bullets from all sides, and even now the debate continues as to why such a nonsensical command was given. In Victorian England the Light Brigade became a legendary example of unwavering obedience to orders, but also exposed a major weakness in the British military.

The 'Jaws of Death' or Tennyson's 'Valley of Death' is now a very peaceful meadow with a few scrubby trees and some lowly vineyards. To get a breathtaking perspective of the battlefield, visit the Sevastopol Diorama, which offers a panoramic view of the entire area from its outer ridge. For real Crimean war buffs, the humble memorial to the Light Brigade stands in the midst of a vineyard, just off the main road from Sevastopol to Yalta. The single white pillar marks the spot of the thin red line from where the Light Brigade charged. To get to the spot on your own, take a *marshrutka* or taxi to the '5km' stop, a junction of buses and taxis near the Yalta ring road. The monument is less than 1km further down the road from the junction.

Enthusiasts will also want to visit nearby **Sapun Hill**, from where Lord Raglan directed the battle. You can get to Sapun Hill by taking buses No 1 or 20 from Malakhova Square, or simply take a taxi, for around US$8, in the direction of Balaclava (12km from the city centre). The **Diaroma** museum has nothing whatsoever to do with the Crimean War: it was built as a Soviet monument to Sevastopol's defence in World War II but located instead atop a famous Crimean War site (*open 10.00–17.00, closed Mon; entrance US$2*). A monument church, and eternal flame stand near by, commemorating the Crimean War dead. The wide stone platform grants a fantastic view of the entire battlefield.

sharply from the sea, the back of the cove dips into an underwater cave before opening up into an underground 'harbour', a phenomenon that inspired the spot's Turkish name (*Balaclava* mean's 'Fish Nest') and later brought the Soviets, who built a secret, nuclear submarine repair station inside the cave, completely hidden from prying American satellites. Aside from Balaclava's notorious past, this is a very peaceful town to visit with its deep turquoise water and surrounding wide open hills. On top of the pyramid-shaped mound is the remaining tower and ruins of the Genoese fortress of Cembalo, a good starting point for a walk down the coast. Ukraine's rich and famous have recently discovered the port and have their eyes on making this their own élite hideout. Getting to Balaclava is an easy 12km trip by bus or US$10 taxi ride from Sevastopol.

WHERE TO STAY AND EAT Tiny Balaclava has quickly transformed from secret Soviet submarine base to luxury yacht club for the Ukrainian jet set.

🏠 **Golden Symbol Yacht Club** Nazukina 1A; e golen_symbol@souz.sevastopol.ua. Located right on the water, The Golden Symbol serves as a small hotel, tavern and upscale seafood restaurant. Rooms are simple but modern and with extra-long beds. There's hot water year-round and cable TV. The food and drink on offer downstairs is outstanding, and the VIP room has become a museum of local finds from under the sea, as well as historic prints of Balaclava during its British occupation; open all day; credit cards accepted. US$40 pp off season/US$50 in summer.

🏠 **Dakkar Hotel** Kalicha 13; ☎ 0692 637 763; f 0692 637 764; e info@dakkar-resort.com; www.dakkar-resort.com. Just opened, and much more of a hotel/resort is the Dakkar, clean and efficient; the English-speaking staff and incomparable customer service make all the difference. In summer, there are quite a few outdoor eating establishments and cafés, but many of these are seasonal. Credit cards accepted and b/fast inc. Standard dbl rooms and upscale business suites from US$75; luxury 2-room suites US$150.

✕ **Café Argo** Nazukina; ☎ 0692 530 233. For great Georgian food year-round. Open 11.00–23.00.

WHAT TO SEE AND DO Visitors to Balaclava should walk along Nazukina to get a glimpse of the trendiest tax havens, where Ukraine's millionaires can register their yachts. One can also hike up to the towers of **Cembalo**, the old Genoese fortress at the top of the highest hill. By far the number one tourist attraction in town is the **Balaclava Naval Museum** (*Mramorna 1;* ☎ *0682 535 990; 09.00–16.00; entrance US$5 with guide*). This originally very secret base was built at the onset of the cold war, from 1957 to 1961, and functioned as a submarine repair facility, in addition to a nuclear missile storage unit. The underground port made use of Balaclava's extraordinary geography to bring damaged vessels into dry dock, without them ever having to surface in view of enemy satellites. Tour guides take you from the old military quarters, past the underground arsenals where the nuclear missiles were stored and loaded, and on to the underwater docks where teams refitted nuclear submarines. The darkness and damp – not to mention the eerie 1950s Soviet architecture – make the whole experience rather spooky and delightfully sinister. The underground base doubled as a nuclear shelter, big enough to keep 3,000 people alive for 30 days with oxygen, food and water. Employees were sequestered to particular sections of the base, divided by 120-tonne steel doors. Indeed, the entire town of Balaclava was cloaked in secrecy until less than a decade ago.

Diving in Balaclava The underwater sites in this area are one of a kind. You are not likely to see pretty fish or coral reefs, but there are plenty of caves, sunken English warships, Greek ruins and the very James Bond-like underwater submarine factory. **Akvamarin** (*Nazukina 5;* ☎ *0692 637 252;* e *aquamarine3694@mail.ru; www.voliga.ru*) is the most experienced dive shop, offering about 60 different dive sites of varying difficulty, as well as a range of certification courses. Their extensive English website has all the current prices, although most two-tank dives cost around US$55. Winter diving has much better visibility than in the summer, but requires the use of a dry suit, which they rent out.

CAPE AIYA МЫС АЙЯ

This small national park marks the beginning of Crimea's southern coast with a striking change in vegetation and physical terrain. Here is one spot where natural Crimean flora and fauna have remained undisturbed. The many millennium junipers and Crimean strawberry trees scent the air, as do the rare orchid species. Some of Crimea's endangered animals are also prominent here, including eagles and falcons. Level walking trails cut through to the very beautiful coastline from the village of Goncharnoye, which can be reached by bus or taxi from the Sevastopol–Foros road.

THE SOUTH COAST ЮЖНЫЙ БЕРЕГ

The narrow strip of sea coast between the Black Sea and the jagged ridge of the Crimean mountain chain has the warmest weather in all of Ukraine and is consequently mobbed by tourists from May to September. The natural attractions and gorgeous climate are worthy of such attentions, with their stunning mountain landscapes that drop into the hundreds of tiny coves and tempting beaches that dot the shoreline of this 'Russian Riviera'. By definition, this sliver of Ukraine actually does exhibit a Mediterranean climate complete with aromatic evergreen shrubs, turquoise waves, sunshine and dry air, yet any such comparisons fall short of describing the very unique world of Crimea's beautiful southern shore. Here vacationers gather, play and relax, soaking in the exotic surroundings that somehow occur so close to the less inviting landscapes of home. This is the region that most people associate with Crimea, and only seeing is believing when it comes to the sheer popularity of the coast.

The joint metropolis of Yalta and Alushta forms the most active centre for accommodation and transport, and is the most central starting point for mountain treks. It's hard not to be disappointed by the pseudo-tropical resort culture that seems to permeate the area. The Russian/Ukrainian nations have been vacationing in this spot for over two hundred years and certain coastal areas are a tad overdeveloped. Bolshaya Yalta (Greater Yalta) is expanding into a continuous holiday zone stretching from Foros and Gurzuf, but this has not erased the distinct character of the smaller seaside towns within. These little hovels were the Mecca of the Soviet bohemian movement and there are still tiny patches where travellers sleep on the beach and live off the fish they catch. People seeking a quiet rest by the sea (or mountains) have usually discovered their own secret spot to which they return year after year.

YALTA ЯЛТА

Yalta is Russia's most popular tourist trap and should be enjoyed as such, for this fabulous little city holds much more appeal than its stony urban beaches and imported palms might first suggest. In the shadows of the concrete high-rises and glossy souvenir arcades lies a historic town of turn-of-the-century beach houses now overgrown with vines and flowers and swept by the romantic glow of the Yalta lighthouse. There was a time when Soviet citizens went crazy for the delights of Yalta, but only because they were not allowed to go anywhere else, in which case the sweeping mountain view against the open sea *would* be truly spectacular. But now that people have the freedom and money to travel elsewhere, over two million 'locals' still flood this resort town – in spite of the slightly ridiculous expense and the frenetic display of holiday atmosphere. Yes – even with the tourist minions marching in lockstep, the sprawl of Yalta has preserved a few lines of the poetry that has made it so popular. A national park completely surrounds the city and many smaller trails branch off from the outskirts and into the wilds of Crimea. Old palaces and hidden memorials offer up nostalgia for this mystical coastline, felt even by first-time visitors, and thousands of children from landlocked interiors greet the ocean for the first time, an excitement that lingers every day. Finally, given its reputation and location, it is nigh-on impossible to avoid Yalta. Every road and tourist attraction seems to lead this way, including Ai-Petri, the Grand Canyon and 'Bear Mountain', Aiyu-Dag.

As told by tour guides to starry-eyed holiday-makers, once upon a time, an ancient Greek ship was lost in a Black Sea storm so vicious the sailors believed they would die drifting endlessly. When they caught a glimpse of Aiyu-Dag's purple outline, they began shouting 'Yalos! Yalos!' meaning 'Shore!' The beachside community of castaways grew into the town pronounced *Yalta*, which had a short-lived Genoese and Turkish existence before the Russians built the first stone buildings and the port in the 1830s. Besides the fishing (which still goes on today), Yalta was the place to go for cures from all the nasty diseases so common in St Petersburg. In keeping with the late 19th-century fashion for being Russian and patriotic, the gentry began choosing Yalta over the European seaside spas. The last tsar, Nikolai II, built his summer palace here – it was later used by the Allied leaders in 1945 to finalise post-war plans for Europe. Yalta continued to be the favoured retreat of Soviet leaders but swiftly assumed a capitalist role at independence. (Lenin's statue now faces a beachside McDonald's.) A dedicated mafia has really spruced things up and as a result, Yalta is now one of the most expensive cities in Ukraine.

GETTING THERE AND AWAY A beaten path leads to Yalta from Simferopol via Alushta. Most people fly or take the train to Simferopol and then choose between the numerous buses, *marshrutka* and private taxis – even the trolley – which all leave from Simferopol's train station and end up at Yalta's *avtovokzal* (the trip takes from 1½ to 2 hours). The trolley takes the longest and is the cheapest, but after 15 minutes the novelty of going 20 miles per hour wears off and you'll wish you were on a fast minibus or in your own taxi. Taxis from Simferopol airport will stake very high prices, but with strong competition it should cost only around US$70 to get to any hotel that's situated on the south coast.

Another alternative is to consider reaching Yalta via Sevastopol. The road is narrower and more pot-holed, but the views are stunning, particularly in spring. Regular *marshrutka* and buses run to and from Sevastopol (2 hours) and with the recent opening of the airport in Sevastopol, this has become a more interesting itinerary than negotiating the crowds of Simferopol.

Several long-haul, upscale bus services also travel directly to Yalta from Kiev, Odessa, Dnepropetrovsk, and the like, but always through Simferopol. Check out Autoluks (*Yalta bus station; Moskovskaya 8;* ⟍ *0654 233 974*).

Getting around the south coast is very easy. There is an open platform at the Yalta bus station from which various forms of wheeled transport leave all day long to the coastal towns, usually in a circle via Sevastopol or to Alushta. Buses to more distant destinations like Feodosiya and Kerch run twice daily, leaving early in the morning or late in the afternoon. Smaller *marshrutka* run down to Alupka and Foros or up to Nikita and Gruzuf, stopping anywhere you want along the way. Besides the *avtovokzal*, the main *marshrutka* junction is at the square of Pushkina by the movie theatre 'Spartak'.

Yalta is also a popular cruise-ship destination, but these days Black Sea cruises originate only in Turkey or the Mediterranean. There is still one passenger ship that leaves every Tuesday from Yalta to Istanbul and that returns the following Monday. The journey costs US$100 single/US$200 return. Tickets can be purchased at the *Morskoy Vokzal* (sea station) at Roosevelt 5 (⟍ *0654 323 064*).

WHERE TO STAY Yalta seems to be made out of hotels but still provides a relatively small supply when considering the inflated demand. The result is complete overpricing and a lot of difficulty in getting a room during the highest season: most resorts have a complex pricing structure with three to four different prices depending on when you come. July and August are often twice as expensive as January to April, whereas New Year, May to June, and September are in between the two. For extended stays, or if you are trying to save money, then renting an apartment can be a very good option (whether or not you are looking, you will be approached upon arrival). Here are just a few of the hotels in the area (all middle-range and luxury hotels accept credit cards):

Luxury

🏠 **Oreanda** Lenina 35/2; ✆ 0654 390 608; f 0654 328 336; e info@hotel-oreanda.com;www.hotel-oreanda.com. As Yalta develops into a more showy resort, a few choice hotels outdo all others in pretence and self-promotion. The Oreanda stands near the top of the pile, with the kind of limitless grandeur beloved by Victorians and the local mafia. Considered to be the best in Yalta proper, this century-old hotel is right on the waterfront and furnished to the highest standard. Everything looks brand new, the rooms are remarkably spacious and nicely decorated, and most of the staff speak English. An in-house Japanese/Chinese restaurant evokes luxury with ritzy entrées, while the extravagant nightclub is slightly more hilarious. Use of the private beach and the elaborate pool complex is inc in the room price, and several local tours can be arranged in-house. Superior rooms face the sea, standard ones face the mountains, with a 40% price difference between the two. *Sgls US$220/280, dbls US$280/350, suites US$400/500 low/high season; colossal apartments US$1,000.*

🏠 **Palmira Palace** Alupkinshoe Shosse 12, No 3; ✆ 0654 275 353; f 0654 247 000; e marketing@palmira-palace.com; www.palmira-palace.com. A recent and welcome arrival to the Crimean coast, the Palmira Palace offers a classic Crimean resort vacation, but with a modern approach and world-class criteria. Sun-filled rooms overlook an undisturbed view of the Black Sea, and the clean, private beach is arguably Yalta's best. The white-pillared 'palace' was once the luxury residence of Duke Dmitri Romanov, the mischievous nephew of Tsar Nikolai II. Located in the sleepy town of Alupka, guests are within walking distance of the famous 'Swallow's Nest' castle, yet far enough away from Yalta to avoid the ongoing hubbub. Peace and quiet are part of this resort's appeal, along with its extensive professional spa that offers a series of seawater swimming pools, an array of massage and spa treatments, and an indoor complex featuring Turkish, Finnish, Russian and Japanese baths. Not only is the Palmira arguably the best hotel in Crimea, it's also one of the most progressive in Ukraine, with bona fide non-smoking rooms, wide wheelchair access and rooms adapted for disabled guests, and a family-friendly policy that offers great perks for children. Rooms come in 3 categories, based on size, amenities and view, all of which feature king- or queen-size beds. Every category offers a lot of space and comfort, with impressively sound and modern plumbing. B/fast is inc, with options for HB and FB. The hotel is about an US$8 taxi ride from central Yalta, but they can arrange a pickup at either Sevastopol or Simferopol airports. *Category C rooms are good value for money at US$120–180 for 2; category B rooms US$150–230; category A US$300–400.*

🏠 **Primorsky Park Hotel**, Primorsky Park; ✆ 0654 320 032; f 0654 321 011; e reservation@ppark.ru; www.ppark.ru. A new and flashy resort right in the middle of Yalta's secluded, tree-filled 'seaside park'. Every room is classified as a luxury suite, with modern furnishings and balconies that offer superb Black Sea views. Private beach, pool, sauna, and a modish in-house restaurant attract a ritzy Russian clientele. *US$150–200 in the off season, and US$300–450 during Jul and Aug.*

🏠 **Paradise** Sosnovy Bor 37; ✆ 0654 326 051; f 0654 336 649. Near Massandra, this is a small but fully refurbished resort with only 7 suites. Its individual attention to guests and quiet location are its greatest attributes. *High-season US$80–120.*

Middle range

🏠 **Bristol** Roosevelt 10; ✆ 0654 271 603; f 0654 271 609; e office@hotel-bristol.com; www.hotel-bristol.com.ua. Yalta's most historic hotel has been welcoming visitors for the past 150 years, and a recent renovation has helped to preserve a long tradition of hospitality. Rooms are modern, comfortable and clean, with great beds and trouble-free bathrooms. This 'English'-style hotel is also well-managed, which sets it apart from many others in the city. Located right next to the port, the Bristol is central to the city's oldest promenade, which puts most of Yalta's attractions within walking distance. A fantastic in-house tourist service can arrange car rentals, drivers, boat trips and local excursions, and the restaurant offers a creative blend of local Crimean cuisine with Ukrainian and Mediterranean classics, as well as a fine b/fast, inc in the price. (Americans may also want to ask to see the 'Roosevelt Room', a memorial meeting space for the local Rotary Club.) *Standard rooms US$70–120,*

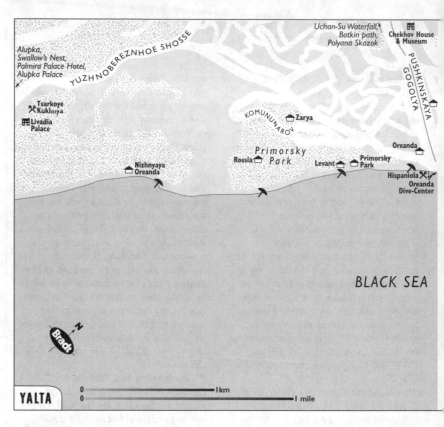

YALTA

0   1km
0   1 mile

*business-class rooms (with internet) US$90–140,
and suites US$120–280.*

🏠 **Yalta** Drazhinskovo 50; ☎ 0654 270 260;
f 0654 353 093; e info@hotel-yalta.com;
www.hotel-yalta.com. This 16-storey hotel represents
Inturist's grandest moment: an Olympic-size saltwater
pool, 3 gigantic restaurants, a behemoth cinema
complex, and live dolphins that swim beneath a
towering stadium. Indeed, the Hotel Yalta is Ukraine's
largest hotel — a staggering feat or benign
misfortune depending on your point of view. With
over 1,000 rooms of varying categories, the Yalta
accommodates nearly every standard and budget. The
very smallest are of the classic Soviet variety, but
renovated and furnished IKEA-style. The grandest are
the illustrious suites on the top floor that offer quite
a view of the entire southern coast. The complex is
located about one mile past the port near Massandra,
about a US$3 taxi ride from Yalta's centre, and is
extremely popular with groups. *Dbl occupancy rooms
US$30 off season (US$75 in summer), suites US$150
(US$300 in summer), although the great majority fall
into the US$40–90 range.*

Palace Chekhova 8; ☎ 0654 324 380; f 0654 230
492. This is one of Yalta's originals, still functioning
in a Victorian pension style, with a choice of the
number of meals you take at the hotel. All rooms
have AC. *Sgl US$50, dbls US$60–80. The US$85
suites have queen-size beds.*

🏠 **Levant** Primorsky Park; ☎ 0654 231 133;
f 0654 231 134; e bron@krasotel.ru;
www.krasotel.ru. Small and modern, this cement and
glass hotel is right on the edge of Yalta's busy stone
beach and therefore close to the city's attractions
and the very green Primorsky Park. Rooms are
pretty average on the whole. The sun deck is
carpeted with astro-turf and things can be a little
noisy at night. B/fast inc. *Rooms US$60–140
(standard), US$80–200 (classic) and US$150–300
(luxury).*

🏠 **Massandra** Drazhinskovo 48; ☎ 0654 272 427;
hotel-massandra@optima.com.ua. Built in lovely
Massandra Park, this is one of the few hotels whose
quality of service is higher than its very reasonable
prices. Rooms are basic but clean and amenable, while
the stately Neoclassical exterior offers a more honest

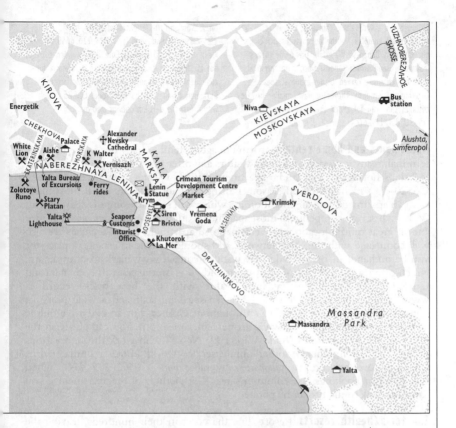

portrayal of the classic Crimean holiday. Also, in summer, rooms with AC cost extra. *Dbl US$40, suites US$80 (off season) and in summer US$80–120.*

🏠 **Vremena Goda** Rudanskovo 23; ☎ 0654 326 012; f 0654 328 771; e pms@crimea.com; www.vremenagoda.com. A very personal, remodelled hotel right in the city centre with indoor pool, sauna, private beach access and a fine restaurant. The rooms are pleasant and comfy, not to mention very affordable for what you get. *Sgls US$40*

Budget *(cash only)*
🏠 **Krym** Moskovskaya 1/6; ☎ 0654 275 300. This slightly dingy Stalinist building overlooks the central square right near the port, and features the cheapest beds in all of Yalta. A nice old lady usually sits at the front and will try to talk you out of staying here, but persistence gets good results. Hot water is sporadic, and prices double during the high season. Plus there's a lovely little restaurant on the second floor serving homey Ukrainian food. *A dbl with bath is only US$20, a sgl US$15. Rooms with just a sink are US$10 and suites are US$30.*

(US$60 in season), dbls US$50 (US$75), large suites from US$90 (US$120).

🏠 **Krimsky** Basseinaya 20; ☎ 0654 231 209; f 0654 231 215; e krimsky@yalta.crimea.ua; www.krimsky-otel.com.ua. A clean and bright exterior invites holiday-makers into rather common rooms with newly refurbished Soviet-style bathrooms. The outdoor swimming pool is a plus, although it's a fair walk to the beach itself. *In the off season, rooms US$30–60, in Jul/Aug US$50–90.*

🏠 **Energetik** Pushkinskaya 23; ☎ 0654 329 305. Technically, this is a seaside resort complete with Soviet-era healing methods; however, for the sake of price, the complex counts as rather central budget accommodation with better deals for longer stays (near Primorsky Park). A rather fun place if you can get into the experience. *Around US$20.*

🏠 **Niva** Kievskaya 44; ☎ 0654 324 392. Fairly cheap rooms of the very bare Soviet variety. Shared bathrooms in most cases. *Around US$4 pp.*

🏠 **Polyana Skazok** Kirova 167; ☎ 0654 395 219.

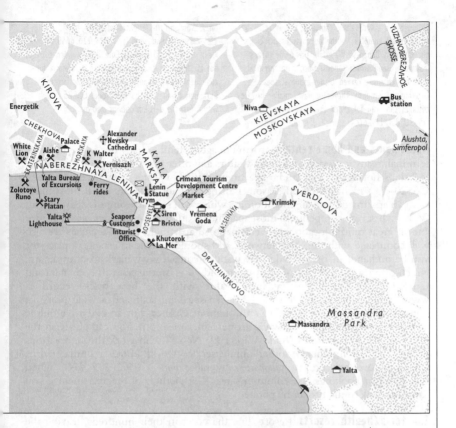

Although it's called Yalta's 'camping', this is really a grand motel complex on the outskirts of the city, not far from Uchan-Su Waterfall. The name means 'Fairytale Glade' which sounds much more mystical than the chainsaw-carved Disney-esque statues covering the grounds. They also have smaller private cottages that run for much the same price. *Sgls US$30, dbls US$60, but prices fluctuate depending* on season and the length of stay.

🏠 **Zarya** Kommunarov 7; ☎ 044 220 6650 (in Kiev); e kurort@i.kiev.ua. Cute little wooden cottages not far from the beach with a central cafeteria for communal meals. Popular with young Russian and Ukrainian families on holiday. *About US$25 a night with b/fast; full pension options also available.*

Apartments and home rentals

Apartment agents tend to hang out at the Yalta bus terminal, ready to swoop on foreign visitors and offer them an array of alternatives to Yalta's hotels. A clean studio apartment with hot water should cost between US$20–30 a night in the off season. During July and August, you'll most likely want an apartment with air conditioning, which will start at around US$100/night. With such severe competition, most apartments offered to foreigners are very nice and in great central locations. Several national apartment rental agencies are also well connected with the Yalta network, and should be able to arrange a place for you beforehand. In Britain, you may want to contact www.blacksea-crimea.com, which offers a great choice of apartments and villas on the coast in both Yalta and Gurzuf. The online agency in Ukraine with the best track record is www.travel2crimea.com, with local English-speaking staff and a wide range of options, including rural homestays throughout Crimea. For an extensive online source of apartments, visit: www.apartmentsincrimea.com. You can also visit the office of Yalta Apartments (*Karla Marksa 11; No 28*) who work through various brokers on the internet. Another online service works under a similar name: www.yaltapartment.com (e *yaltapartments@yahoo.com;* ☎ *0662 205 464*). When making prior bookings, use common sense. Get pictures of the apartment if you can and speak to the broker by phone.

Sanatoria/health resorts

Resorts line the coast in their hundreds, leaving the discriminating traveller with a lot of choice as to where one might rest and recover from the toils of Ukraine proper. Although Palmira Palace and Yalta are listed as hotels, they do function as modern resorts. Here are a couple of the more traditional 'sanitoria' establishments that are increasing their experience with foreigners. Visitors are promised a very Slavic holiday experience, complete with doctor's examination and prescribed spa treatments. One might consider using a hotel-booking agency (like *www.travel2crimea.com*) to work out any nuances that come with stays of greater than three days.

🏠 **Sosnova Roscha (Gaspra)** Alushtinksoye Shosse; ☎ 0654 242 247; f 0654 242 301. Right at the base of Ai-Petri. New rooms and new equipment make this quite a plush resort and the health clinic is very modern. *About US$115 for 2 people in season, which includes all meals and 'diagnostika'.*

🏠 **Nizhnyaya Oreanda** In the Yalta suburb of Oreanda; Lower Oreanda gardens; ☎ 0654 312 548, 322 212. This rather functional-looking resort is now the favourite of Ukrainian parliamentarians and was only recently opened up to the foreign proletariat who can pay. The secluded beachfront and fancy rooms come with lots of Slavic elitism. *Prices fluctuate, but hover around US$120.*

🏠 **Dnepr** Alupkinskye Shosse 13; ☎ 0654 247 365; f 0654 247 197; e dnepr@mail.ylt.crimea.com; www.haraksdnepr.com.ua. In peaceful Gaspra, the Dnepr is a classic sanatorium that has changed little in the century or so that it's been treating weary Ukrainians. Hidden among a forest of cypress trees, the gingerbread-style mansions are charming, and offer spa packages lasting 3–24 days. Dnepr also offers one of the best deals for foreign guests. *US$40–60 with treatments.*

🏠 **Rossia** Kommunarov 12; ☎ 0654 310 471; f 0654 321 837; e rossia@yalta.crimea.ua; www.rossia.yalta.crimea.ua. An old-style USSR holiday and health sanatorium that's evolved into a middle-class hideaway inside of Yalta. The resort services (including medical treatments) are curious but nice, and the rooms are calm, if slightly bare. US$50–100.

✕ WHERE TO EAT
Yalta may not rank among the world's gourmet greats, but there is more on offer than the expected fish 'n' chips and soft-serve ice cream. Indeed, a multitude of restaurants lines the south coast and caters to every holiday taste and budget. There are also plenty of all-night food shops and delicatessens open in the cities and along roadsides.

Fine/themed dining

✕ **K Walter** Naberezhnaya/Morskaya 1; ☎ 0676 524 060. Right on Yalta's main promenade, this fine establishment occupies the façade of Yalta's historic Marino Hotel, with a panoramic view of the waterfront through its elegant 2-storey windows. The food is mostly Asian fusion (Japanese/Vietnamese) but there are some original European dishes too (eg: 'the noblewoman', a veal fillet with cream, and 'the pauper's bag', a heavy pile of meat and potatoes). One of the better meals you will eat in Yalta. Credit cards accepted. *Mains from US$10; open 10.00–midnight.*

✕ **Oreanda** Lenina 35/2 (on the ground floor of the hotel; see page 333 for contact details) serves exquisite Ukrainian food and hosts an original Turkish buffet in the evening. Credit cards accepted. *Main dishes US$10–15. Open 08.00–23.00.*

✕ **Hispaniola** Right across from Oreanda. This pirate ship outside Oreanda (an abandoned film set) is not nearly as tacky as it might seem – the food is accurately Greek with lots of seafood; the atmosphere is dressy but relaxed. Credit cards accepted. *Mains from US$20; open 14.00–midnight.*

✕ **Bely Lev** Naberezhnaya Lenina 31A; ☎ 0654 327 736. Despite what you might think, the 'White Lion' is not named after the 1980s rock band, but rather the white marble lions that decorate many of Yalta's imperial palaces. Inside there's more gold moulding than at Versailles, as well as lace, crystal and polished silver galore. The menu incorporates rich Greek and Russian favourites: mutton, quail, lobster, fried oysters and roasted kebabs. Cash only. *Mains from US$10–15; open 12.00–midnight.*

✕ **Zolotoye Runo** Naberezhnaya Lenina 8; ☎ 0654 324 001. A wooden ship on iron stilts with Las-Vegas style light effects? Yet another supper club that epitomises exotic Yalta. Starry-eyed couples, fancy food displays, and kids dodging the waves far below. Behind all the kitsch is a thoughtful chef who cooks up an impressive and diverse menu. Definitely go at night if you can. Credit cards accepted. *Mains from US$10; open 10.00–midnight.*

✕ **Tsarskoye Kukhnya** Next to the Livadia Palace. A semi-sophisticated restaurant that serves very refined Russian dishes, typically banquet-style, to very large groups. Credit cards accepted. *Mains from US$8; open 11.00–midnight.*

✕ **Khutorok La Mer** Sverdlova 9; ☎ 0654 271 815. The 'boondocks' has established a well-known presence among Ukraine's largest cities, but this version of the popular restaurant franchise is literally 'by the sea', and therefore a little more jolly than usual. The jazzy atmosphere, sound Ukrainian menu and a huge collection of wine make it a popular night-time hangout. Try to get a table by a window for an incredible sea view. Ukrainian staples, plus seafood. Credit cards accepted. *Mains from US$15; open 11.00–02.00.*

✕ **Stary Platan** Yekaterinskaya 1 (basement); no phone. This old wine cellar doubles as a restaurant for wine connoisseurs who want some fine nibbles to go with their Crimean wines. Owned and managed by the Massandra vineyard, each featured dish is specifically designed as an accompaniment for a particular Massandra wine (there is a separate wine shop at the entrance). Credit cards accepted. *Mains from US$10; open 11.00–23.00.*

Yalta classics An abundance of less dressy establishments (and pizza places) line the *naberezhnaya*, and every summer there are a few dozen new outdoor grills that set up shop along the promenade. Yalta's outdoor market borders Moskovskaya, with plenty of food shops and smaller eating establishments. Rudanskovo also sports a few late night bakeries. Here are a few worth mentioning:

✕ **Aishe** Lenina 9; ☎ 050 696 3825. Crimean Tatar café and teahouse that serves the most authentic cuisine in Yalta. The *plov* is unbeatable, and everything is rather affordable and delicious. Highly recommended. Cash only. US$5 entrées; open 10.00–midnight.

✗ **Vernisazh** Corner of Naberezhnaya and Kirova; no phone. An extensive outdoor café run by a kind Armenian family. Salads, seafood and shish kebabs are the main fare, as well as traditional Armenian food. Everything on the menu is under US$5 and it's written in English. Cash only. Open 11.00–23.00.

✗ **Siren** Roosevelt 6; ☎ 0654 271 899. A homey cafeteria near Hotel Bristol that serves old-fashioned Soviet fare for less than a dollar. Affectionately named 'the mermaid', the food is hygienic, while the lunchtime crowds are fascinating. Open 10.00–19.00. Cash only.

LOCAL TOUR OPERATORS AND TOURIST INFORMATION
In stark contrast to the rest of the country, Yalta suffers from too much tourist information.

Inturist Central office: Roosevelt 5; ☎ 0654 327 604; e intour@yalta.crimea.ua. As the most experienced Inturist veterans are still employed, this office has the authority and connections to get most things done for travellers, including arranging local excursions, transport and accommodation. They offer plenty of tours in any language imaginable and can also arrange Russian lessons for visitors. Please note that despite their location on the cruise dock and their highly knowledgeable staff, this is a private travel agency and not a public tourist information centre. In summer, the lines of cruise-ship tourists stretch out the door, and they start charging you US$1 for questions like 'Where is the beach?' and 'Which bus do I take to get to …'

Crimean Tourism Development Centre 1/6 Moskovskaya; ☎ 0654 3242 43; f 0654 271 708; e resort@yalta.crimea.ua. Another private tourist agency that looks, feels, and smells like a tourist information booth. They do best with group tours, but can meet individual demands for practically anything. Just walk up to their office on the second floor of Hotel Krym (off of the main square).

Yalta Inform Servis Moskovskaya 8; ☎ 0654 325 777; e yalta-inform@ukr.net. In the lower level of the avtovokzal you'll find Yalta Inform who can organise small tours and accommodation upon arrival.

Bureau of Excursions Ekaterinskaya 3 This company has been around since 1847 and is still a good place to get a guided tour and find out about local attractions.

Oreanda Dive Center ☎ 0654 390 920; e oreanda-divers@ukr.net. If you are keen to dive, this is next to the wooden ship Hispaniola and offers 2-tank dives including equipment for US$80. (It looks murky but if you go out on the right day, the big fish and odd wrecks can be rewarding.) They can also make arrangements for mountain-bike rentals.

The booths on the *naberezhnaya* sell tickets to local sites for group bus tours. You don't have to speak Russian to see the palaces and gardens so it can be a good deal if you don't want the hassle of organising your own transport. US$7 to US$10 is the normal price to pay for any tour.

While dozens of foreign Black Sea cruises stop in Yalta, there are no cruises to and from Yalta starting in Ukraine itself. Short **ferry rides** and 'sea excursions' leave from the port (*right across from the post office, which is to the left of the main square when facing Lenin;* ☎ *0654 324 274*). The most popular option is a two-hour cruise that takes visitors to the Swallow's Nest and back, for around US$10.

WHAT TO SEE AND DO Walking up and down the *naberezhnaya* comes naturally in Yalta, as does beachcombing, sunbathing, swimming, and shopping for cheesy souvenirs. Yet there are some real attractions in Yalta besides the electronic mayhem on the boardwalk and the standing-room-only beaches. **Primorsky Park** is a calm green spot by the sea with cypress woods, several monuments and some of the older sanatoria, making it a good place for a stroll. **Alexander Nevsky Cathedral** on Sadovaya was built by Alexander III in remembrance of his father, Alexander II. The church has brand-new gold domes and displays original mosaics inside and out. The **Chekhov House and Museum** (*Kirova 112; open 10.00–17.00, closed Mon and Tue*) was the private 'white *dacha*' of author and playwright Anton Chekhov who came often to Yalta to work and rest between 1898 and 1904. He wrote a great many of his short stories here, as well as the plays *The Cherry Orchard* and *Three Sisters*.

CRIMEAN HOLIDAY EATS

Tasty favourites of Crimea's southern coast. When in Rome ...

- **Massandra wine** Typically, a sweet white Madeira or other dessert wine. Grown and bottled nearby and served in all the local restaurants.
- **Russian *blyny* (pancakes)** Lots of pancake stands in and around Yalta and Alushta. Filled and served like crêpes, sweet and savoury.
- **Crimean *baklava*** Sold on the beach, but not the filo pastry, rosewater dainties you might already know. Big, hand-sized diamonds of sweet, crispy pastry. Sold on the beach.
- ***Shashlyky/kebabs*** Normally pork or beef, sometimes lamb, seasoned and roasted on roadside grills or on the beach.
- **Saltfish** Dried chewy pieces of fish, served as snacks with beer.
- **Nuts** Those purple or red concoctions that look like candles. These are usually almonds or walnuts tied to a string, then dipped in a solution of grape juice and corn starch, forming a rubbery confection. A rather bizarre treat.
- **Plombir** Hard frozen vanilla ice cream that you can chew from the cone.
- **Honey** Sold at roadside stands; check to make sure it's local.
- **'Health' juice** Fresh fruit juice (apple, cherry, pear, etc) served out of communal glasses inside food stores for a few kopecks.

Chekhov was also responsible for making Crimea so popular among the Russian intelligentsia (Rachmaninoff often visited and entertained the writer on the piano in his study). While the museum at the entrance is tediously Soviet, the guided tour of the house and the gardens is reflective of the period and offers a great perspective on Yalta's place in Russia's cultural history.

In Yalta's southern suburbs stands the gleamingly white **Livadia Palace** (*open 10.00–17.00 every day except Wed; entrance US$4*), built by Tsar Nikolai II as his family's summer residence. The white renaissance mansion was completed in 1911 and is surrounded by a simple but vast garden overlooking the sea (livadia means 'meadows' in Greek). The white marble from which the palace is built was quarried in Inkerman (near Sevastopol), and the modern design is far less ostentatious than in those palaces built by other St Petersburg aristocrats. The Romanovs spent only four summers here before their arrest and eventual execution in Yekaterinburg – the small chapel in the back of the palace is an active shrine to their memory and Orthodox sainthood. A guided tour creates a wistful mood, showing original artefacts and photographs of Russia's last royal family and taking visitors through the sunlit chambers, bedrooms and historic dining hall where the momentous Yalta Conference took place. Here, in February 1945, Stalin, Churchill and Roosevelt discussed the fate of Germany after World War II, and adopted the 'Declaration on Liberated Europe'. Among the dozens of historic decisions taken, Stalin conceded to the Soviet Union's membership in the United Nations, finalising the preparations of the Dumbarton Oaks Conference and, as some claim, making Ukraine the birthplace of the UN. During the nine-day conference, the American delegation was housed in the Livadia Palace, while the British delegation stayed at the nearby Alupka Palace and the Russians at Yusupovsky in Koreiz.

It was rumoured that Stalin disliked Livadia Palace, allowing it to remain empty and unused for much of the 1950s. It was later opened as a basic holiday resort until the 1970s, when US President Nixon came to the USSR and attended a meeting there. Prior to the summit, Soviet leaders scrambled to assemble enough 'period' furniture to give the appearance that the palace had been a commemorative museum since the days of the Yalta Conference. In fact, the 'museum' began functioning as a public museum only in 1994. Taxis can get you from central Yalta to Livadia in five to ten minutes. The No 5 *marshrutka* connects the bus station and central market to Livadia.

Short walks from Yalta Yalta's great natural attraction also happens to be Europe's highest waterfall. **Uchan-Su** means 'flying water' in Tatar, and the water really does fly from a height of 98m. From the Yalta bus station take the 'taxi-bus' with the sign Водапад (*Vodapad*, 'Waterfall') which stops at the restaurant where the trail begins. Also, the **Botkin Path** leads to the falls from Polyana Skazok. Gently ascending into the Crimean Game Preserve, this trail is named after Sergei Botkin, the private doctor of Tsar Nikolai II. He made the startling discovery that walking in the outdoors was good for one's health and recommended the tsar's family take daily strolls 'in nature'. The 8km path is tame with a few rocky inclines, but the tall pines and skittish birdlife do make you feel healthy, and it's a good introduction to the Crimean Mountains. The **Tsar's Path** was the trail actually used by the tsar and his family in their daily 'constitutional' to cure their tuberculosis. It begins behind Livadia Palace and winds through 6km of mountainside to Gaspra. To take away the bourgeois stigma of the place, it was called the 'Sunny Path' during Soviet days and this is the name still carved on the stone markers. The trail *is* rather sunny and stays level at about 100m above sea level. Besides an occasional stumble across construction sites, the path is lined with forests of twisted trees and the air smells heavily of cypress. There are several lookout points along the way from which there are tremendous views of the sea and Ayu-Dag. Beware of uncovered manholes! Just past the 5km mark there is a turn-off that descends through pine scrub, then hillside vegetable gardens to the **Swallow's Nest** (see page 341).

Further walks Ai-Petri (Ай-Петри) is the craggy mountain with a row of rock teeth standing high above Alupka. This may be the heart of the Yaltinsky Mountain Forest Reserve but it is also the most visited natural spot in Crimea due to the road and cable car that go right to the summit. The Taraktash trail from Uchan-Su is slightly uneventful since it follows the winding road most of the way (though it's great for mountain bikes). For extended walks it is better to cross the 'Yaila' from above the Yalta road and swing back around. There are also two trails through the woods from Alupka, so a long trek may lead from the sea back towards Bakhchisarai via Ai-Petri. The summit is 1,234m high and the landscape behind the peak is characterised by its strange moon-like rock formations. Deep snow covers the summit from December until late April. The view of the Crimean coast from the top of Ai-Petri is spectacular – if you can work it into your travels then do. At the same time, it should be noted that the cable car from Alupka up to the top of Ai-Petri is so popular that the wait in summer can be up to three hours. Furthermore, it's old and fatigued and probably dangerous (I wouldn't get on it). The lazy traveller can negotiate a taxi or join an organised tour – ask at your hotel.

Crimea's **Grand Canyon** is unique in that it was created by tectonic activity rather than simple erosion and therefore looks like a deep crack running through rolling green hillsides. The gorge is between Yalta and Bakhchisarai, about 4km from the village of Sokolinoe and accessed from either end. One trail passes above the north side, another descends into the canyon. It is grand in terms of its wonderful trekking and striking scenery but not in size: the deepest cleft is 320m and the length is a little over 3km. Still, it's a truly beautiful walk – the Auzun-Uzen River trickles or tumbles through these tight walls depending on the season and the small clear pools and waterfalls make inviting swimming spots.

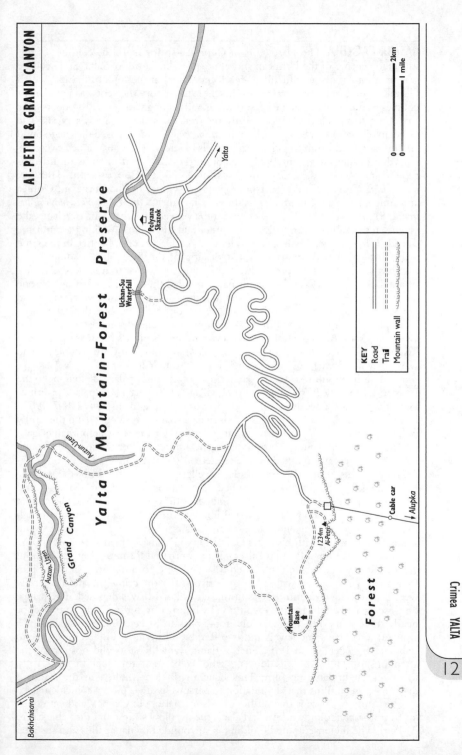

Al-Petri & Grand Canyon

Yalta Mountain-Forest Preserve

Bakhchisarai

Grand Canyon

Auzun-Uzen

Auzun-Uzen

Uchan-Su
Waterfall

Polyana
Skazok

Yalta

Mountain
Base

1234m
Al-Petri

Forest

Cable car

Alupka

KEY
Road
Trail
Mountain wall

0   2km
0   1 mile

GASPRA ГАСПРА The sharp cliffs of **Cape Ai-Todor** mark the confines of this intriguing corner of the Crimean shoreline, just 7km south of Yalta. St Theodore was the founder of the difficult-to-reach monastery at the top of the cape, which fell into ruin during medieval times. In the 19th century the spot was popular for couples wanting a view up the coast towards Yalta, along with a small wooden *dacha* that hung to the cliff-side, commonly referred to as the 'Swallow's Nest'. The German oil baron Von Shteingel bought the *dacha* in 1912 and used the site to build an imitation Gothic mini-castle as a gift to his mistress. It was abandoned two years later due to the war and in 1927 a major earthquake left it in ruins until it was rebuilt in the 1970s. Today the **Swallow's Nest** (**Ласточкино Гнездо**; *Lastochkino Gnyezdo*) is the over-photographed symbol of good times in Crimea and functions as an 'élite' Italian seafood restaurant (❱ *0654 247 571; main dishes from US$15; open 10.00–22.00*). Perched at the very edge of the stone overhang, the view is remarkable – especially if you are afraid of heights. Walking around the outside is free; if you step inside, you'll be served US$4 cups of coffee in the same spirit that you'll find in snack bars at the top of the Eiffel Tower. Indeed, the Swallow's Nest bears the proud title of Ukraine's very first tourist trap. A cluster of outdoor cafés and souvenir stands have crowded the winding stairway that one takes to get there from the road (several hundred steep stone steps that go up and down). The squadrons of tour buses never stop arriving, but the celebratory atmosphere is actually quite fun. Also, the tiny cove beneath the castle is a popular swimming spot. Any hotel can arrange a visit to the Swallow's Nest, as can any taxi driver. For public transport, just jump on *marshrutka* No 27 towards Alupka. If you want to avoid crowds, consider taking the ferry from Yalta.

Most of the health resorts you see in Gaspra were once palaces belonging to the Russian aristocracy. In the neighbouring village of **Koreiz** is the palace of Prince Felix Yusopov – the wealthiest man in the world during his lifetime (1887–1967). His home at Ai-Todor was just one of his five permanent residences and the family (who were actually Tatar) owned so much land in Crimea that Felix's father gave his mother a mountain as a birthday present. Quite a colourful character, young Felix gained an early reputation in St Petersburg due to his penchant for cross-dressing in his mother's frocks and jewellery and flirting with the visiting European gentry. His theatre even gained the attentions of England's King Edward VII, who sought after the 'mysterious and beautiful young woman' he had seen at the Paris Opera. Yusopov later married into the ruling Romanov family through the tsar's niece, putting him close to the affairs of state, namely the Rasputin scandal. Conspiring with his lover Grand Duke Dmitri Romanov (whose nearby palace is now the hotel Palmira Palace), Felix murdered Rasputin, but not without great difficulty (feeding him poisoned cake and wine, beating him, shooting him four times, and then drowning him in a river). For the crime, he and his family were exiled to their country estate until Tsar Nikolai II was deposed. The prince only escaped arrest during the revolution by hiding out in this Crimean palace for nearly three years. He did make one foray back to St Petersburg (disguised as a woman) to collect some jewels and two Rembrandts, which funded his escape to Italy and his later life in Paris. Such a flamboyant life story did not escape the attentions of Hollywood producers, who Felix sued for libel in the 1930s, following an unflattering film. This benchmark case resulted in the standard disclaimer on all films that any relation to persons living is purely coincidental.

The Yusopov palace is one of the less-visited palaces in Crimea, and yet not so far from the better known Livadia Palace, the Swallow's Nest and the cable car to Ai-Petri. The melon-coloured building is surrounded by date palms and sits atop

TREKKING IN CRIMEA

Experienced hikers and mountain climbers may be amused by the over-cautious attitude that permeates local minds in regards to exploring Crimea's rocky terrain. Much of this stems from Soviet days when everything was hyper-regulated and 'adventuring' non-existent. These are not difficult mountains. Crimea's tallest peak is Roman Kosh, which at 1,545m is a hill by world standards. That said, these mountains are known to be particularly dangerous for two reasons: firstly, very sporadic weather can turn a sunny sky into thick fog in minutes, and secondly, the unique terrain has one side gradually sloping upwards and then the other side dropping 800m to the sea. Several people die each year in these mountains – most of them inexperienced climbers who fall from unexpected drop-offs. Others get caught out by cold or wet weather and freeze, even in summer. When planning any hike, be wise and be prepared.

Gorna Spasatelnaya Sluzhba is the local Mountain Rescue Service based in Yalta (*Prigorovskaya 10;* ✆ *0652 328 715; www.kss.crimea.ua*). If you are going out on your own you must (technically) contact them and register yourself. They offer good information and if you *are* stopped along the way, this will be the one case where it was better to have asked permission than to seek forgiveness. The Service also has branch offices in several other Crimean cities, including a post right near the Simferopol train station. Check their website for further information. Caution is also needed when taking trails that pass through government-regulated reserves. Foreigners caught without a guide or a licence will have problems, although in recent years, a US$5 bill seems to solve such problems. All trails mentioned in this book are free and open, but I still recommend hiring a guide for longer treks.

Working with a private guide or company allows you to circumvent all the hassle. One of the best in the business is Sergei Sorokhin, a Crimean native who has an excellent reputation for tailor-made individual walking (or biking) tours throughout the peninsula. In addition to Russian and Ukrainian, he speaks fluent English and French, and knows the mountains extremely well (**e** *sergey@velocrimea.com; www.mt.crimea.com; a 2-day all-inclusive package – 3 meals a day, gear provided – costs around US$180 for a couple*). He can also design extensive walking tours that last up to several weeks for up to three or four people. His highly informative website is useful for planning trips.

Another good company is Outdoor Ukraine (*www.outdoorukraine.com*) which works in both Crimea and the Carpathians. Try Ukraine (*www.tryukraine.com/crimea/treks.shtmlNo 6*) also advertises a whole summer season of organised and privately guided hikes throughout Crimea. Travellers can book guides and tours online, and find a wealth of information on local hiking, including weather and hiking forecasts.

a pyramid-shaped mountain with a fantastic view of the Crimean range and the seashore. To get there from Yalta, take *marshrutka* No 32 or No 27 (direction Miskhor). If you walk from the main road, turn left at the Lenin statue and walk about 300m (*open 10.00–18.00, closed Sun; entrance US$3*).

ALUPKA АЛУПКА Tiny Alupka lies beneath the Ai-Petri mountain chain, and has recently transitioned from being a sleepy little seaside town to being a major tourist attraction in Greater Yalta. The town's name derives from the ancient Greek for 'fox', and in ancient Greek times, there were most likely foxes here. In spite of the abundant Soviet-era sanitoria in the area, the cypress forests and rocky coves are spectacular.

12

Once upon a time, such a dramatic backdrop caught the attention of one Count Vorontsov, and this is where he later chose to build his very ostentatious palace. Blending English Tudor elements with an exotic oriental style, the Alupka or Vorontsov Palace was completed in 1848 as a private residence for the count and his family. Several Vorontsovs colour the history of the area, but this one is Mikhayil Semyonovich – the one who was Governor General of New Russia and who encouraged the settling of Crimea; the one who was Catherine the Great's godson, and whose wife had an affair with Pushkin (see page 286). Vorontsov spent over twenty years and nine million pieces of silver building this elaborate palace but never actually lived in it due to the pressures of his post in far-off Odessa.

The fanciful building complex and the vast gardens make up the ever-popular **Alupka Palace Museum** (*open daily 09.00–17.00; entrance US$2*). The interior could easily be the most well-furnished exhibit in Crimea today – it's quite beautiful and well preserved. Walking on the polished floors of the palace brings you into the whimsical 'blue room' (made to look like Wedgwood), the glass conservatory filled with exotic plants and statues, and the imitation 16th-century English dining hall. Having been raised and educated in England, Vorontsov was a dedicated Anglophile and his home reflects his adoration for English style and art. During the Yalta Conference, Winston Churchill and the British delegation stayed at the palace, and today, the halls are still used to host important state dinners. Legend has it that Churchill found a physical likeness in one of the marble lions that adorns the outer steps, beneath the oft-photographed 'Moorish Arch' that creates a panoramic view of the sea. The eye-catching palace and the park make for pleasant walking among the palm trees and flowers. In contrast to the orderly gardens on top, the lower park was designed to blend with the surrounding environment; 'Chaos' is a wild arrangement of rock piles that will tempt amateur climbers. The lower trail leads to a popular but relatively clean beach below.

As 'Greater Yalta' grows into a necklace of seaside towns, Alupka has been relegated to the southeastern thoroughfare of Alupkinskoye Shosse which leads from Yalta and Gaspra. Unfortunately, most of the original town has been taken over by complexes like the Palmira Palace resort. To get to Alupka from the Yalta bus station, take *marshrutka* No 32 or No 26. You can also take the ferry to the Swallow's Nest, climb the stairs to the cluster of cafés at the top, and then catch a taxi onwards.

FOROS ФОРОС At the southernmost tip of Crimea is the small town of Foros, on a very peaceful bit of coastline surrounded by thick forest and broken rock walls that are easily accessible for trekking and climbing. Far from the fray of Yalta, Foros is an attractive vacation spot if you're looking to get off the beaten path. Above the pass at Baidarskiye Gate one trail leads to the small peak Eagle's Nest. The eastern trail follows the top of the wall for 15km to **Hell's Staircase** (**Чёртовая Лестница**). There are various degrees of climbing difficulty on offer here: the least difficult path is fine for simple trekking and goes to the plateau from which the old Genoese road once led to Sevastopol. The Foros wall, meanwhile, is about 600m high, and is a challenging climb to be attempted by experienced climbers only.

Foros is usually portrayed by the miniature cake-like church that clings to the edge of a 400m-high precipice. A nobleman by the name of Kuznetsov built the Byzantine-style **Resurrection Church** in 1892 after his daughter was nearly killed – her runaway horse stopped just at the edge of the cliff (its common name is the Traveller's Church). Others claim the church was built in honour of Tsar Alexander III who miraculously survived a train wreck. Whatever the case, it's a church dedicated to near misses when travelling, which is a rather compelling reason to visit it. The high, undisturbed view from Ukraine's southernmost point is also worthy of mention.

Foros was also the beloved holiday destination of Raissa Gorbachev, who talked her husband into building their own modernist *dacha* in the village. Here, in August 1991, Mikhail Gorbachev was placed under house arrest in a failed attempt to overthrow his reform government back in Moscow. From the main road, you can spot the **Gorbachev *dacha***, with its bright orange diagonal roof.

Foros marks the midway point on the 1½-hour Sevastopol to Yalta route and minibuses run by about once an hour in either direction. That means that it's far easier and more direct to get to Foros from Sevastopol (only 40km away), from where there's air and train transport to the rest of the country.

Where to stay and eat Foros embodies a much less commercialised part of Crimea and so options are pleasantly kept to a minimum. The lack of upscale accommodation is made up for by the fact that you might have the peace and quiet that Yalta lacks. The main resort is **Foros** (\ *0654 792 244;* e *sforos@mail.ylt.crimea.com; www.foros.com.ua*) consisting of an average Soviet-style high-rise sanatorium and cafeteria. Rooms cost US$50–100 a night.

YALTA TO ALUSHTA

MASSANDRA МАССАНДРА Yalta has swallowed up its sprawling eastern suburb but Massandra still exhibits a very separate sense of place in its palaces, gardens, and small hotels (listed under *Yalta*). For the past two hundred years, the town's name has been connected to the wine produced on these hillsides and prevalent 'sampling stations' lure tourists from the roadside. The French chateau-style **Massandra Palace** was originally commissioned by one of the Vorontsovs (the family of the Russian general ruling over Crimea) but the project was abandoned and only taken up by Alexander III a decade later in 1889, and it was completed in 1902. A visit inside shows the obsession of the Russian royalty with imitating English and French Baroque styles from centuries past. Interestingly, sun-shy Stalin chose the palace as his summer residence over the elegant white Livadia, preferring to spend his time indoors in seclusion. The consolidation of Ukrainian wine-making at Massandra can be attributed to Stalin, after he gathered the entire wine reserve of the Soviet Union and locked it up in the vicinity of the palace. The estate gardens now make up the beautiful and extensive **Massandra Park** and the complex is open to visitors all week long (*10.00–18.00*).

If you are keen to taste some Crimean wine *en place*, there are plenty of opportunities. **Massandra Wineries** (*www.massandra.ru*) is actually based at the palace, with wine tours and wine-tasting available to visitors. Group tours to the Crimea region will almost always incorporate an afternoon of wine-tasting, usually in conjunction with one of the palace tours and a visit to any of the caves that line the southern coast, the most noted of which is near the Alupka Palace. A typical visit will include a tour through the cool underground caverns past giant oak barrels and rows upon rows of dusty bottles of wine. Then, a formal *degustation* will take place, in which eight to ten different wines will be tasted and discussed at length. The grapes in Crimea perform best in sweet dessert wines, and the repertoire of wines offered to tourists reflects this, with muscat, madeira and port predominating. Massandra wineries are most proud of a bottle of their 200-year-old sherry that sold for US$50,000 at a Sotheby's auction.

Almost any tour agency can arrange a wine-tasting (eg: Inturist); or, if you are in Yalta, contact the Magarach Wine Institute (*Yantarnaya 7;* \ *0654 336 529;* f *0654 654 336 998;* e *magarach@yalta.org; www.magarach.com*). Of the many alluring properties offered in their wine, the 'reduced effect of radio-nuclides' is hard to beat.

NIKITA НИКИТА Further up the coast lies the very small **Cape Martyan Reserve**, one of the few remaining spots of natural Crimean plant growth, which includes the elusive juniper mistletoe. This is also a prized spot for birdwatching year-round. Several Crimean reptiles also survive on the tiny cape, while the area off the coast is noted for its biodiversity of fish species. The miniscule reserve is open for visitors to walk through, but expresses the severe plight of Crimean conservation, in that only tiny pockets have been sealed off, while the rest of the coast is developed. The **Nikitsky Botanical Gardens** is behind the reserve and contains a mind-blowing collection of 28,000 plant species, all growing in the park. A Russian botanist founded the gardens in 1812 under imperial orders to establish a place where all plants of the world could be collected, acclimatised and distributed throughout 'Russia'. The park has shifted from its original agricultural goals to new aesthetic heights, with stunning floral displays and incredible tree exhibits of sequoia and cedars of Lebanon. An on-site café serves exotic fruits and nuts that are grown in the gardens. Just say 'Nikita' to a taxi driver, and he will bring you to the entrance, or take *marshrutka* No 34, which goes to the Nikitsky Gardens from Yalta.

GURZUF ГУРЗУФ At one time, all of Crimea used to look like Gurzuf, with its little wooden houses, stone *dachas* and fishing boats. The Genoese left a few ruins here but the Russians like to remember the town as the spot where Pushkin came to holiday. The town still caters to a resort crowd but is less brash than Yalta proper. These are Crimea's best pebble beaches and a few seaside caves make it an interesting place for swimming. Gurzuf is 15km from Yalta and can be reached by most forms of transport, including regular *marshrutka* services. In the summer, a taxi from Yalta will cost around US$8.

Where to stay In the summer months, staying in semi-quiet Gurzuf can be a much better option than dealing with hectic nearby Yalta.

Thyssen House Leningradskaya 96; ☎ 0504 730 996; e thyssen-house@mail.ru; www.thyssen-house.crimea.ua. Gurzuf's newest and classiest hotel. The mysterious 'miracle castle' is not far from Artek, with individually decorated suites, a first-rate restaurant and great customer service. B/fast inc, credit cards accepted. *Rooms US$100–150 in low season, to US$150–300 in high season.*

Ai-Danil Gurzuf 3; ☎ 0654 335 360; f 0654 335 340. The high-rise sanatorium at the far end of the shore closest to Yalta, offering fairly comfortable rooms and a few of the 'lux' variety. It also has a very nice sandy beach, a rare luxury in these parts.

Packages with meals included are available. *US$50–90 in season for the regular rooms, a bit higher for the suites.*

Hotel Marina Leningradskaya 68A; ☎ 0652 524 738; f 0652 524 908; e administrator@hotel-marina.crimea.ua; www.hotel-marina.crimea.ua. A newer, recently refurbished option, the hotel is smaller and a little more personable. *From US$40.*

Pushkino Naberezhnaya 3; ☎ 0654 363 390; e pushkino@mail.ylt.crimea.com. The humblest of them all, it is closer to the city and right on the beach. All rooms have their bathrooms. *Around US$30 pp.*

AIYU-DAG АЮ-ДАГ 'Bear Mountain' is the landmark stone hill that can be seen from most of the south coast. Its sides are mainly cliffs and rocky overhangs while its back and summit are covered with thick pine scrub. Many believe the Tatar name *Aiyu* (Bear) is just a mispronunciation of the Greek word '*Ai*' ('Holy'). I think a good look at the mountain settles the argument. The oft-told legend is that a shipwrecked girl was rescued by a family of wild bears who were enchanted with her singing. The captain of a passing ship found her and took her away while the bears were hunting. The bears saw the departing ship on the horizon and quickly knelt at the shore to drink up the Black Sea and bring the girl back. In return, the girl began singing to stop them draining the sea. All the bears stopped, except for the oldest who was deaf and continued to drink the sea. There is a likeness when viewed from Yalta. The trail to Aiyu-Dag's summit begins in the town of **Partenit** (Партенит), backtracks along the cape, and then rises directly north to the top.

ALUSHTA АЛУШТА

Alushta is Yalta's biggest competitor, offering the same seaside amusements with less bawdiness, lower prices and a bit more greenery. The Alushta beaches are long and not nearly as crowded, running for miles up Crimea's eastern coast. The Demerdzhi Mountains and Chatyr-Dag loom in the background and Alushta is a good base from which to hike these mountains, as well as Babugan Yaila and Roman Kosh (see page 349). Three national parks are all close by; the largest is the Crimean Nature Preserve with the best animal life in the peninsula, but as it's also the Ukrainian president's private hunting grounds, it can be visited only with a special permit.

As a town, Alushta seems to have always been on the fringe of Crimea's history. Aluston was the Greek/Byzantine fortress built here in the 6th century which later extended to a chain of forts in the nearby mountains. For a while, the town was the last outpost of the Feodor principality and was named Lustia by the Genoese in nearby Sudak. The Russians put Alushta back on the map when it became the junction of their coastal road from Simferopol, but it was only during Soviet times that the site was considered a possible resort and a few sanatoria were built along the shoreline. Now the waterfront is a huge piece of pavement, filled with outdoor cafés in the summer and rather empty in the winter.

GETTING THERE AND AWAY Alushta is the halfway point between Simferopol and Yalta, so hourly buses pass through, including the nicer private line running between Simferopol and Sevastopol. The bus station is at the north end of the town at Simferopolskaya 1, and the long-distance trolleybus station is at Gorkovo 4. A private taxi from Simferopol or Yalta will cost US$15. Presently, there are no passenger ships sailing to Alushta.

WHERE TO STAY Health resorts are the mainstay of Alushta's economy and so in summer it is not the easiest place to find short-term accommodation (ie: less than a week). During the tourist rush, either book a spa package well in advance, or consider renting a private apartment.

Spa resorts

More (the Sea) Naberezhnaya 25; 📞 0656 025 949; f 0656 025939; e sale@more-ua.com; www.more-ua.com. A brand-new, and very quiet and secluded resort in the heart of Alushta. Out of all the local sanitaria and spas, the More feels the most similar to a Western-style spa, with recommended 3- and 6-day revitalisation programmes at very good prices (around US$200 for a week of treatments). The hotel is modern, efficient and customer friendly – room quality varies from basic to grand. B/fast inc and credit cards accepted. Sgl/dbl economy class US$70/90; comfort class US$90/130. A family-size 'duplex' or private villa is US$300.

Mindalnaya Rosha Naberezhnaya 4A; 📞 0656 025 971; f 0656 025 980; e infor@mindal.com.ua. Another new-and-improved Alushta beachfront property, the 'Almond Grove' caters to families with children. The complex includes a fine restaurant and the entertaining waterpark, complete with wave pool, waterslides, etc. There are 3 separate buildings. B/fast inc and credit cards accepted. All rooms are of superior quality, but size and view affect the price, ranging from US$85 to US$175, with slightly higher prices in Jul and Aug.

A CRIMEAN NEVERLAND Of the many nostalgic complaints heard in Ukraine today (besides the price of sausage), the one heard most from parents is the end of free, month-long holidays in Crimea for children. Back in the good old days of the USSR, a youthful chorus echoed from the rocky beaches that stretch between the town of Gurzuf and Bear Mountain (Aiyu-Dag). Here, almost every year, nearly 30,000 well-behaved Soviet children were rewarded with trips to the town-sized holiday complex of Artek, where they spent the summer playing, swimming, hiking, sunbathing, and learning to be model Soviet citizens. Founded in 1925 – just after the inception of the Soviet Union – Artek served an important social function through its cheerful indoctrination and paramilitary-like holiday regimens. Soviet celebrities like cosmonaut Yuri Gagarin would come and give inspirational talks to the youth and present medals and certificates. As the international communist movement spread in the 1960s and 1970s, Artek welcomed delegations of children from all over the world, including Cuba, Asia, western Europe, and even Britain. Thus, the Soviet government delivered the annual perks of a sun and beach holiday to those who lived in the more dreary parts of the empire. Although there were dozens of such children's 'bases' throughout the communist bloc, Artek was by far the largest, with over 150 buildings covering 4km².

Today, Artek still functions under the mandate of an International Children's Centre, although 'child' is more loosely defined. The uniforms are strikingly similar to those of the young pioneers, only now with Ukrainian light blue ties instead of Communist red. The majority of guests are children sent at the behest of the Ukrainian or Russian governments, most of whom are still hosted free of charge or with significant subsidies. If you are keen to send a child off, or to volunteer your help, contact **Artek** (❁ *0654 363 080;* f *0654 363 217;* e *artek@artek.org;* *www.artek.org*).

Hotels

🏠 **Hotel Korona** Utess village; ❁ 0656 021 993; e hotelkorona@rambler.ru; www.hotelkorona.ru. 2-storey luxury apartments in a small village outside of Alushta. Located inside a Gothic castle with an outdoor swimming pool and a dive centre. *US$30–150 in the off season, US$55–250 in the high season.*

🏠 **Krymskiye Zori** Oktybrskaya 5; ❁ 0656 025 500; f 0656 025 501; e zori@alushta.sf.ukrtel.net; www.crimeanzori.com. Big and sunny hotel/resort in the centre of Alushta, on the waterfront. Every room has a big, open balcony. Indoor pool and beach access. *US$30–45 in low season, US$80 during late summer.*

🏠 **Alushta** Oktyabrskaya 50; ❁ 0656 055 062; f 0656 055 278; e hotel_alushta@mail.ru. Small, convenient hotel with remodelled rooms and private clean bathrooms. The location up in the hills is more conducive to hiking rather than beachgoing. Cash only. *US$30–50.*

🏠 **Spartak** Perekopskaya 9; ❁/f 06560 3 44 33. Small and comfy with quite basic, Soviet amenities but a worthy cultural experience all the same. Cash only. *Rooms US$30–40.*

✖ **WHERE TO EAT** Beach foodstands and cafés are in abundance all along the waterfront, and there's more culinary diversity here than first meets the eye. In addition, nearly every hotel and spa has its own restaurant, some of which are included in the price of accommodation. **Vodolei** (Aquarius) is not far from the seaport on the waterfront and serves more refined food as well as the traditional Crimean *shashlyk*. On your way out of Alushta, you might try **Lesnoi** (❁ *0656 034 360*), a stone cottage in the mountains 5km away from the city on the Alushta–Yalta road, with large terraces for outdoor dining. Besides the restaurant they have a few deluxe suites for overnight guests as well as a sauna.

WHAT TO SEE AND DO Besides the sunshine and water there are some very unique landscapes to explore in the area. The **Crimean Nature Preserve** is a guarded 70,000-acre mountain space filled with what remains of Crimean wildlife: mouflon, mountain goats, gazelles, foxes and incredible bird species. It is a very difficult place to visit and the private companies that can arrange a permit usually sell the tour as a hunting trip. Crimea's tallest mountain, **Roman Kosh** (1,545m) is inside the preserve and therefore, officially off-limits. Non-rebellious mountain climbers will either have to go through a private company or with a private guide. If you go it alone, be prepared to get stopped and pay small trespassing fees of around US$5. A lot of interested tourists have created a positive demand to open these areas up, so if you venture this way, speak up. There are rumours of a public national park being created. There are many other hiking spots near Alushta: on the Alushta–Simferopol road is Angarskii Pass which is the trekking centre to both **Chatyr-Dag** and **Demerdzhi**. All buses as well as the trolley will stop at Angarskii Pass, and a taxi from Alushta costs US$7.

DEMERDZHI ДЕМЕРДЖИ

The Demerdzhi massif is directly north of Alushta and is much more removed from civilisation than other popular hiking spots in Crimea (see map on page 350). The strange rock forms and tall stone fingers make up an alien landscape, with interludes of open mountain plains covered with tall grasses and wildflowers. This is one of the highest plateaux in Crimea so the view of the peninsula is striking. Wind erosion has formed the layered cylindrical shapes and Soviet-era guides have attached names and legends to almost every single rock formation. The Tatars also had their names and *Demerdzhi* means 'Smith' after the legend of an evil blacksmith that once lived here. Some truly beautiful sites include the powerful waterfall **Dzhur-Dzhur** and the staggering **Valley of Ghosts**. Most Crimean tour companies offer treks in Demerdzhi, but this is also the best place on the peninsula for independent hikers. There are plenty of trails so that hikes can be shortened or lengthened to fit your whim. The following is a suggested walk:

DAY 1 Angarskii Pass to Polyana Man passing by Pakhkal-Kaya Mountain (1,137m). Man's Glade is a good outlook point with established campsites.

DAY 2 Continue through the forest passing North Demerdzhi Mountain (1,356m) and then turning east beneath the Yurkiny Cliffs. Camp above Dzhurla Waterfall.

DAY 3 Climb from the waterfall to the summit of South Demerdzhi (1,239m), then descend into the Valley of Ghosts. Either finish by hiking into the village of Luchistoye or continue towards Dzhur-Dzhur.

DAY 4 Visit the Dzhur-Dzhur Waterfall (which boasts the largest volume of flowing water in Crimea). From here follow the Ulu-Uzen River 10km to the beach at Solnechnogorskoye.

A longer trek could continue on to **Karabi-Yaila** which is a much wider plateau to the northeast. The hills are riddled with caves and similar rock formations to Demerdzhi but the trails are much longer and much further from any village.

FEODOSIYA ФЕОДОСИЯ

As the unofficial capital of Crimea's eastern shore, Feodosiya is nobly different from the built-up southern coast. There is no gaudy post-Soviet investment to

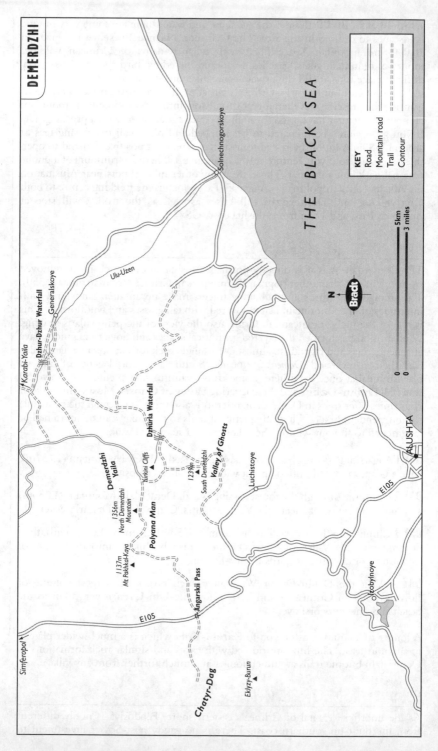

DEMERDZHI

THE BLACK SEA

KEY
Road
Mountain road
Trail
Contour

Solnechnogorskoye

Ulu-Uzen

Generalskoye

Dzhur-Dzhur Waterfall

Karabi-Yaila

Dzhürla Waterfall

Demerdzhi
Yaila

Türkini Cliffs

1356m
North Demerdzhi
Mountain

1239m

Valley of Ghosts

South Demerdzhi

Polyana Man

Luchistoye

1137m
Mt Pakhka-Kaya

ALUSHTA

E105

Simferopol

E105

Angarskii Pass

Izobylnoye

Chatyr-Dag

Eklyzy-Burun

5km
3 miles

N
Bradt

detract from the bite-sized national parks or the stunning landscapes that surround the city, and thus local attitudes remain pleasantly uncomplicated. The city stretches flat across a long seaside plain with ultra-wide streets and brightly painted Russian classical buildings that keep things light and cheerful. Children playing on the beach and resorts advertising mudbaths are unfazed by the coming and going of giant cargo ships or the never-ending action at the seaside railway station. Prospekt Lenina (as the main promenade will always be known) is lined with tall silver birch trees for its entire length and old-fashioned lanterns light the city at night for evening strolls. In short, Feodosiya is a quaint town with a redeeming character and unadulterated coastline.

The Greeks claimed Theodossia ('Given by God') in the 6th century BC and quickly transformed it into a major centre for grain exports. The Huns destroyed the city in the 4th century AD and Feodosiya was then ruled by the Khazar khaganate. The Genoese arrived in the 13th century and made Kaffa their capital and it was soon the centre of trade for the Black Sea. The towers of their fortress are still standing in random spots throughout the city. With so many ships, and rats, Kaffa soon went down in history as the official entry point of the bubonic plague into Europe following a Mongol raid in 1347 (the Black Death ensued). In 1475 the Crimean Tatars finally conquered the city for the Turks who nicknamed it Little Istanbul. Like Yevpatoria in the west, Feodosiya was vital to the Turkish slave trade and during the 1600s the Zaporizhzhyan Cossacks made repeated attacks on the city to free Ukrainian captives. After occupation (or liberation) in the 18th century, the Russians declared Feodosiya a free trade zone which helped to make it a very cosmopolitan town of merchants. The famous Armenian artist Aivazovsky was born here and returned to live here even when he became famous and wealthy. His own investment made the town what it is today, and he is honoured in several museums and numerous statues and plaques.

GETTING THERE AND AWAY Even though there are direct trains from Feodosiya to mainland Ukraine via Dzhankoi, the train schedule can be quirky. There is a train to and from Moscow every other day via Kharkiv and regular trains to Simferopol and Kerch. If there are no direct trains to Ukraine/Russia on the day you want to leave, motoring to Simferopol is better than taking the very slow train to Dzhankoi and then switching to a train that originated in Simferopol anyway. If you plan things in advance and have a return ticket, then you should avoid any hitches. Buses are quicker and provide the only way to get to the smaller towns further down the coast, namely Sudak (1 hour) and Koktebel (20 minutes). Kerch is two hours away and there is a 19-hour night bus to Kiev.

From the bus station in Yalta, there are plenty of *marshrutka* listing Feodosiya as their destination. Almost all of these buses pass through Simferopol (2 hours), from which it's another 2½ hours to Feodosiya. Tickets cost under US$10. In Feodosiya, the bus station is at the north end of town (*Engelskaya 28*) across from St Catherine's Church. If you'd like to see the very beautiful and practically virgin coastline between Alushta and Feodosiya, you may be lucky enough to catch one of the rare *marshrutka* that take the coastal road (in summer only). It's a hairy ride, with lots of hairpins and a promise of motion sickness, but then, isn't it all about the view?

12

WHERE TO STAY

Lydia Libknekhta 13; \ 0656 230 901; f 0656 221 112; e recpt@lidiya-hotel.com; www.lidiya-hotel.com. The poshest place in Feodosiya and very central, if a little expensive. Most of the staff speak English, rooms are spotlessly clean and rather comfortable, and overall this is a well-managed establishment. Aside from the indoor pool, its restaurant has a talented chef who specialises in 'health food', as well as some of the fresher Russian classics. A full meal should cost under US$25. *Basic sgls/dbls US$35/$45 in low season and US$55/$70 in high season, and double that (around US$150–200) for the spruced-up larger rooms, and US$300–600 for the apts.*

🏠 **Sunflower Guesthouse** Fedko 59; ✆ 0507 693 421. Clean and new B&B style accommodation with all en-suite rooms, just steps away from the beach. Credit cards accepted. *US$2030 in low season, US$50–60 in high season.*

🏠 **Robinson's Hut** (Khizhina Robinsona) Kerchenskoye Shosse 72B; ✆ 0656 247 264; f 0656 247 581. A slightly more upscale, family-friendly beachside hotel/motel resort with a fun restaurant. All-new remodelling and furnishing and a nice sauna.

Credit cards accepted. *In low season US$50–80, in summer US$100–200, with smaller private beachside cottages from US$250/night.*

🏠 **U Sestry** Russkaya 2; ✆ 0656 230 235 or 0656 235 362. A new little B&B smack dab in the centre of old Feodosiya; petite and affordable, and right next to the Yatsek Café. Very clean. Cash only. *Prices range (by season) from US$15 pp for a shared dbl to US$70 for a balconied suite in season.*

🏠 **Astoria** Lenina 9; ✆ 0656 524 435. The deteriorated Soviet hotel across from the train station. Hot water is sporadic in winter and regulated in summer. A restaurant next door serves the usual Ukrainian meal of borsch and meat. Cash only. *Suites US$25, rooms with a shower and toilet US$15–20, just a bed is US$7.*

✕ **WHERE TO EAT** Every hotel in Feodosiya also has a good restaurant, especially the Lydia. There are also a lot of foodstands and small cafés by the beach. The following are recommended.

✕ **Dacha Stambul** Lenina 47; ✆ 0656 230 082. An old Soviet diner that occupies the ground level of an incredible mansion once owned by the Tatar magnate of Kaffa. Despite the name, there is nothing Tatar on the rather unoriginal, low-priced menu (pork, fish, pelmenny, etc) but it might be worth eating there just to see the inside of one of Feodosiya's most beautiful buildings. *Mains from US$6; open 11.00–01.00.*

✕ **Yatsek Café** Russkaya 2; ✆ 0656 230 235; f 0656 235 362. Classy little European café with outdoor seating, serving coffee, tea and desserts, as

well as delicious and filling meals. *Mains from US$5; open 08.00–midnight. Cash only.*

✕ **Bulvarnaya Gorka** Kavaleryskovo Korpus 5A; ✆ 0676 508 191; f 0679 466 367; bulvarnaya_gorka@mail.ru; www.bulvarnaya-gorka.ru. New themed restaurant on the outskirts of Feodosiya that passes as the local gourmet eatery, featuring Ukraine's recent fascination with fusion cuisine, as well as an all-out celebration of the former bourgeois taboo, with international dishes and grandiose table settings. *Mains from US$12; open 09.00–midnight.*

WHAT TO SEE AND DO People come to Feodosiya to relax and enjoy the beach and good weather of Crimea. **Dvuyakornaya Bay,** south of the city, has some clean shoreline and is a beautiful place to walk. North of the city is the ever popular (and clean!) **Golden Beach,** as well as the remains of the **Genoese Fortress** of Kaffa. Built in 1623, the **Mufti-Djamy Mosque** is worth visiting, as is **St Georgy's Armenian Church**, from the 11th century. For help with local excursions see the **Krymtur** office at Voikova 46 (✆ 0656 232 031). The main attraction in Feodosiya is the **Aivazovsky Museum** (*each ticket costs 5UAH; open 09.00–20.00, closed Wed*) or, more correctly, museums. His picture gallery and house are combined as one building but have two separate entrances and require two separate tickets; both are filled with his paintings. Aivazovsky's genius lay in his ability to paint water and his seascapes have become a standard of technique and emotion in mastering the most difficult natural element. The Feodosiya collection is the largest in the world, a fraction of which is on display. The museum and house are on Galereinaya 2 at the corner of Prospekt Lenina.

OUTSIDE FEODOSIYA
Koktebel КОКТЕБЕЛЬ Koktebel was Crimea's special little secret until just a few years ago. This beautiful seaside village lies 10km south of Feodosiya inside

a calm and pristine bay surrounded by small hills and lined with spotless beaches. Somehow the place avoided the fate of Soviet development, yet is now dealing with its increased popularity among those yearning for the peaceful holidays on offer.

The name Koktebel is Crimean Tatar for 'land of the blue hills' – an appropriate toponym for the magnificent vistas that surround the area. The village went largely unnoticed until 1899, when the Russian symbolist poet M A Voloshin settled in Koktebel and started a commune based on his own philosophies of freedom, which included naturism. Soon Koktebel became the secret summer hangout for St Petersburg bohemians and Soviet discontents. The secret is very much out but this is still a very open and relaxed place with most visitors pitching tents on the shore (the nudist beach occupies a kilometre of soft sand to the east of the bay). Whole families are known to camp here for much of the summer, so things can get a little busy come July and August.

Koktebel also has a significant Crimean Tatar population who fortunately run many of the local restaurants and food stands – this is the right place to sample yummy *lagman* noodle soup and *köbete* meatballs. There are some fantastic trails from the beach going up and down the coast, into the hills, and on to Kara-Dag. The only factor saving this gem of a town from total overcrowding is that it's not a particularly easy place to get to, especially from Russia, which is where most of the summer guests hail from. In summer, there is a direct *marshrutka* from the Simferopol train station – just look for the signs. For those with the foresight to make it to Feodosiya, it's an easy 10km taxi, *marshrutka* or bus ride to the village.

Where to stay and eat The tiny village has become significantly 'developed' in recent years, with a few more options for guests who don't want to sleep in the clothing-optional tent city.

Hotel Galeon Desyatnikov 7B; \ 0656 224 901; e galleon@feo.net.ua; www.galeon.com.ua. Sleek and modern, with sizeable, fresh rooms and a tempting outdoor swimming pool. Credit cards accepted. *Rooms US$50–150, with some nice 'apartments' for* considerably more.

Medved (The Bear; Shkolny) 1G; \ 0503 640 033 Has a mafia feel too it, but it too has a nice pool. *Rooms US$40–100.*

Koktebel is also becoming a popular place to rent a beach house or villa. Ask at any of the online agencies listed for Yalta (see page 336). In addition to both of the hotels, there are dozens of small beachside cafés lining the Naberezhnaya

Kara-Dag КАРА-ДАГ The **Kara-Dag Nature Reserve** was established in 1979 in an attempt to preserve some of Crimea's endangered animal species living in this untouched wilderness. The sharp cliffs that rise up from the sea are the broken remnants of an ancient underwater volcano that erupted over 100 million years ago. The translation of the Tatar name, 'Black Mountain', refers to its volcanic past. The park surrounds one mountain on the bay of Koktebel, and there is an easy walking trail from the town and around the hillside. Foxes, weasels, badgers, jerboas and rock martens live in the park and common bird species include the kingfisher, Eurasian hoopoe, European roller, common crossbill, little bittern and European bee-eater.

Sudak СУДАК The Genoese came to 'Surozh' in 1365 and built the monumental square fortress to protect their trade centre at this, the official end of the Silk Road to China. The ramparts and some ruins remain draped across the coastal hills and the lower wall is over 2km long. This is Sudak's only real 'site', but it is easy to

Ivan (Hovhannes) Konstantinovich Aivazovsky was the son of an Armenian merchant and his wife who had come to Feodosiya from Galicia. As a boy, his charcoal graffiti on the town walls was brought to the attention of the Feodosiya governor, who arranged for his education in Simferopol and later at the St Petersburg Academy. In the capital his talent was praised and he was granted sponsorship to travel and paint. In 1845 Aivazovsky was appointed the official artist of the navy, which suited his favourite subjects: shipwrecks, ferocious storms and sea battles. As his style developed, the human elements slowly disappeared and the sea became the prominent focus rather than the background of the painting. His uncanny ability to deal with water, light and air brought him great fame and his ability to produce paintings quickly made him rich. He built his home and studio in Feodosiya and designed a special gallery to enable the townspeople to come and see his work. This kind of generosity sounds big-headed, but there was really no other place to display his work in the small town, and the hall became the cultural centre for eastern Crimea. Aivazovsky left the room in his will 'to the citizens of Feodosiya' and famous pianists are still invited to play here. The Feodosiya Museum displays many of his true masterpieces including *Chtlb Djky* ('Among the Waves'), a vast picture of nothing but water and wind, which he painted at the age of 82. His Crimean paintings are rightfully displayed with local scenes in Feodosiya, Yalta and Koktebel, and the exhibit also shows works from Aivazovsky's religious phase, when he attempted to paint scenes from the Bible. His human figures always appeared crude, so he leaned towards stories that involved water: Moses crossing the Red Sea, Christ walking on water, and the Flood. He was also a true philanthropist, supplying Feodosiya with water, funding the town's museum, starting an art school and lobbying for the modern commercial port and railroad. He is buried in the Armenian church in Feodosiya (on Ulitsa Timiryazeva) with the epitaph 'A man who was born to die left an undying memory'.

spend a full day exploring the walls and 14 towers on top of the conical mountain. The city beach is long and sandy and once upon a time the Soviet rose-oil processing plant gave a sweet smell to the air. Another attraction is the shallow turquoise bay at **Novy Svyet** ('New Light') which is a 7km jaunt down the coast from the fort in Sudak. This very secluded spot is distinctive for its ancient junipers and is supposedly the first place to see spring in Crimea. The rocky coastline between Cape Koba-Kaya and Cape Chi-khen is simply magnificent. If you've spent the whole time wandering around Crimea looking for a spot without any other people, this is it.

Where to stay and eat

The Grand Fireinaya Hill; ☎ 0656 631 162; e sudak-grand@yandex.ru. By far the grandest (and the newest) hotel, advertised as a tourist complex complete with swimming pool, games, private beach access and a number of quality restaurants. *The spacious and fashionable rooms cost US$85–120.*

Hotel Gorizont Turisticheskoye Shosse 8; ☎ 0656 622 179; e tokgorizont@mail.ru. An average high-rise beachside hotel, and not expensive. *US$20–40.*

Parus Naberezhnaya 29; ☎ 0656 622 377; f 0656 632 272; e hotel-parus@mail.ru. Recently remodelled hotel located near the beach and has a very good restaurant. *Rooms US$40–80.*

LOCAL TOUR OPERATORS AND TOURIST INFORMATION Azart Travel Company (☎ 0656 631 312) are good fixers for this less-travelled bit of Crimea, and can organise anything, from hotels to guides and tours. If you are a diver, try the Shelf

Diving Centre (*Alushtinskaya 7/4;* \ *0656 632 688;* e *shelf-opsha@ukr.net*). They do trips out to the capes and around Kara-Dag. The visibility tends to be better in these areas, with a lot more fish than the areas closer to Yalta.

KERCH КЕРЧЬ

This very functional port lies at the easternmost tip of Crimea and represents the very end of the line, or the very beginning, depending on your route. Russia looms on the other side of the water and the city has become an important gateway into Asia for round-the-world travellers, since crossing the strait by boat feels more deliberate than driving across the unmarked plains of central Russia. A decade ago special ferries carried trains from one side to the other; there are now plans to build a bridge, though Ukrainians aren't very keen on that idea. Kerch really took a beating in World War II, so much of its old Greek charm has been replaced by the elegance of Soviet industry and shipping. Still, the 175,000 inhabitants like to flaunt their unique ancient sights and the coastal area south of the city is really quite pleasant.

The original Greek colony of Panticapaeum was founded in the 6th century BC and within a century had developed into the independent Bosporos kingdom called Karsha. Several ports were built on both sides of the Kerch Strait and inhabited mainly by Cimmerian descendants. Ruins of some of these are now underwater and make for curious diving today. Legends claim the Apostle Andrew first set foot on Slavic soil near Kerch during the 1st century AD (although there are competing claims elsewhere in Crimea). At around the same time a significant influx of Jews arrived from the Middle East – the area was brought into Kievan Rus as a tributary but was later lost to the Golden Horde. During the Genoese era, 'Cerccio' was used as a trade warehouse, while the Turks realised the strategic importance of the Kerch Strait, connecting the Sea of Azov to the Black Sea, and built Eni-Kale to control the waterway. Russia took Kerch from the Turks more than a decade before the rest of Crimea, but it quickly fell by the wayside and stood almost as a ghost town for one hundred years. Only in the Soviet industrial revolution of the 1920s did the population begin to grow again. Kerch is remembered for its heroic stand against Nazi Germany in World War II: for six months of 1942 a resistant force in the Aszhimushkaisky stone quarries kept the city free.

After the Russia–Ukraine split at independence and the resulting tension over Crimea, the future seemed rather uncertain for Kerch. But thanks to its importance as a strategic port and an international border, there seems to be a lot more industrial investment and a lot more bustle here now. Trade and transport remain the major occupations for locals, and most travellers are here on their way to and from Russia, or to have a look at the plethora of Greek ruins.

GETTING THERE AND AWAY Kerch is a little farther than most people first expect. There is an overnight train from Simferopol, but despite the fact that it's only 200km away, it's painfully slow. There is a daily train to and from Kiev (almost 24 hours), Moscow (via Kharkov) and Kherson. A local train travels to and from the connecting station at Dzhankoi and transport to the city centre from the *vokzal* is frequent. The bus station is located at Yeryomenko 30, right next to a huge and exciting market. Buses to Simferopol take five hours and pass through Feodosiya (two hours away). Also, many of the international bus routes to and from southern Russia stop here before heading to the Ukrainian mainland. Kerch has a ferry to Russia that leaves from Port Krym at the easternmost end of the peninsula (take bus No 1 from the bus station). The journey takes 30 minutes and costs US$5.

Crossing to Russia requires advance preparation since there is no chance of getting a Russian visa on the spot.

WHERE TO STAY Although Kerch is part of Crimea it has a very eastern Ukrainian feel to it, with the kind of salty hospitality to match.

Zaliv Kurortnaya 6A; ☎ 0656 134 508. The higher-standard hotel usually recommended to foreigners, *Average rooms US$40–70.*
Kerch Kirova 11; ☎ 0656 121 155. In a better location, right across from the sea station in the city centre; it also has an office to help with short-term

apt rentals for longer stays. *Rooms from US$25.*
Meridian Sverdlova 83; ☎ 0656 120 556 Rooms come with showers and toilets, and there is a nice restaurant. *US$20/40*
Moryak Gagarina 3; ☎ 0656 157 257. Cheaper, more basic rooms.

WHERE TO EAT You'll have your best luck on Lenina, where lots of new cafés have popped up in recent years.

Grifon Teatralnaya 35; ☎ 0656 122 078. Russian, café-style food in the city centre. Cash only. *Mains from US$5; open 09.00–022.00.*
Captain Nemo Gagarina 1; ☎ 0656 156 257. Slightly hilarious themed dining by the sea. Seafood, 'European' and Russian meals. Credit cards accepted. *Mains from U$7; open 11.00–23.00.*

Na Dvoryanksy Teatralnaya 37; ☎ 0656 128 274. An illusion of aristocratic, fine-dining. Cash only. *Mains from US$10; open 10.00–22.00*
Stary Dvor (The Old Courtyard) Lenina 19; ☎ 0656 120 259. Good classic Russian food (meat and potatoes), with outdoor seating in summer. *Mains from US$4; open 11.00–midnight.*

WHERE TO DRINK Kerch is a town of sailors and travellers, so nightlife tends to be raucous and rowdy with plenty to drink.

Chai Dom (House of Tea) Teatralnaya 34; ☎ 0656 121 667. A feelgood oriental café with international teas, potent coffee and hookah pipes! Highly recommended. Cash only. *Open 09.00–23.00.*
Metro Bar Lenina 3; ☎ 0656 122 053. Crimea discovers the wonderful combination of (authentic)

pizza and beer. *From US$4; open 11.00–23.00.*
Mithridates Bar Sovetskaya 25; ☎ 0656 123 097. The city's old namesake and a fun place for late-night drinking. Also serves decent food. Cash only. *Open late.*

LOCAL TOUR OPERATORS AND TOURIST INFORMATION

Chernomorochka Marata 2; ☎ 0656 128 280; e travel@kerch.net. Offers an array of day tours in Kerch and Crimea. Good with small groups and individuals.
Bosporos Tours Naberezhnaya 2, No 204; ☎ 0656 128 255. Located right on the waterfront, with English-speaking guides.

Prestige Tour Near Kerch central bus station; ☎ 0656 121 474 or 123 879. Local bus tours and longer excursions throughout Crimea.
Kerch State History and Culture Preserve Sverdlova 7; ☎ 0656 120 475. Official office for all the local Greek ruins. Good for the serious antiquities buff.

WHAT TO SEE AND DO The sights of Kerch are not to be underestimated. From the centre are the long Mitridatskaya steps (432 of them) rising up to the top of Mitridat Hill and crowned with a pair of foreboding griffins. This is the largest concentration of ancient sites in Kerch and was once the acropolis of Panticapaeum that included a temple to Apollo. A few pillars are still standing, while the other ruins are pieces of the successive kingdoms. At the bottom of the steps in the park is the St John the Baptist Church, built in the 8th century; its original frescoes are still intact today (during the Soviet era it was used as a gem museum). The Melek-Chesmensky Tomb was the mausoleum of the Bosporan kings and is conveniently located right behind the central bus station (*closed Mon*). The Adzhimushkai stone quarries are to the northeast of the city and there is a museum commemorating the heroic resistance on Ulitsa Skifskaya (*open 09.00–17.00; closed Mon*). Further down the same road is Tsarsky Kurgan, a 4th-century tomb also used by the Bosporan kings, with a temple-like burial chamber at the end of a long corridor entrance beneath a manmade hill. At the very end of the peninsula near the ferry dock is the Turkish castle of Eni-Kale. The fortress was designed by the French in 1703 to give the Turks an edge over the Russians. It is quite large and provides a good view of the busy channel. Further down the coast are the Greek ruins of Nimfei and Eltigen, as well as plentiful beaches. The beaches of Kerch vary widely – much of the Black Sea coast is quite rocky, with the nicer beaches further out. Going up to the north coast and trying out the Sea of Azov will bring you to some fabulous clear and sandy stretches.

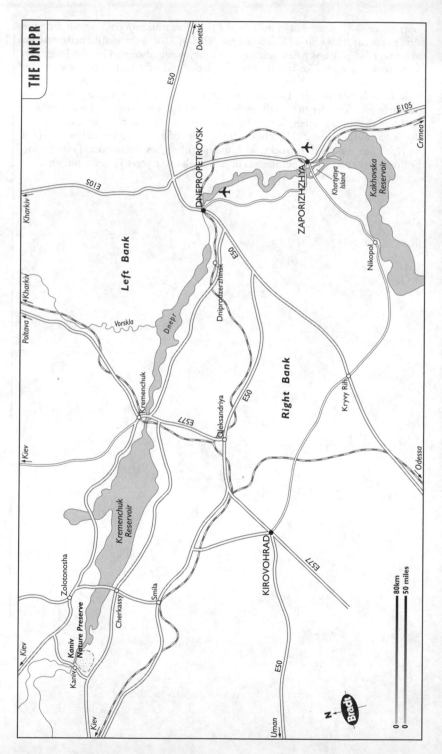

THE DNEPR

The Dnepr
Днепр

At 2,286km (1,420 miles), the Dnepr is Europe's third-longest river (after the Volga and Danube) and Ukraine's defining waterway. Early Ukrainian civilisation was born from the Kievan Rus trade routes along the Dnepr and the Zaporizhzhyan Cossacks founded their earliest independent government on the river's largest island (see page 375). The region's heavy industry and history does have an appeal, while the obvious natural beauty of the Dnepr's wide banks make up some of Ukraine's more glorious scenery. For tourists, cruising down the river has long been the 'thing to do' when visiting Ukraine, but those who are not travelling by ship may still find they keep crossing the Dnepr on their journey as the river has always marked the cultural and political boundary between east and west. The river's environs (and indeed the entire country) are usually described in terms of right bank/left bank, based on a person facing south from Kiev, and travellers will notice the mingling of Russian and Ukrainian language and culture along this historical border.

The Dnepr (*Dnipro* in Ukrainian) begins as a set of streams in the woodlands of western Russia before winding through the forests and swamps of southern Belarus and flowing down the centre of Ukraine. To fulfil Soviet demands for electrical power and industrial prestige, the river was dammed in half a dozen places, forming a series of vast reservoirs that, though no longer providing power, still offer calm seas for local recreation. In summer, boating and swimming are very popular and in winter the river freezes solid and is busy with ice fishermen.

Despite what you may see or hear from locals, the Dnepr is an extremely polluted river, albeit a very scenic one. A glimpse of industrial cities like Dnepropetrovsk and Zaporizhzhya should assist your imagination in guessing what has gone into the water since the time when the ancient Greek historian Herodotus claimed the Dnepr's water was the cleanest he ever drank. Focus on what's above the surface and appreciate the view.

GETTING AROUND

The most obvious form of transport on the river would be a boat, and a limited public river transport service once connected certain cities (eg: Kiev–Cherkassy); however, these have dwindled in favour of private river cruises. Each river city features a 'river station' (речной вокзал; *rechnoi vokzal*) that can give you the latest information on available routes (in summer only). The main rail line does not follow the river, but crosses to the right bank from Dnepropetrovsk to Kiev, or else sweeps north then west through left-bank Ukraine. If you want to travel by land along the river, motor transport is the best option; the right bank road from Cherkasy to Zaporizhzhya offers a rather picturesque stretch, but makes for a bumpy ride.

From Cherkassy you can't always see to the river's other side, as it's built along the widest point of the Dnepr. Several waterfront parks and a youthful atmosphere make it a pleasant place to come in summer, but few cruises will stop long in Cherkassy, and if they do, it will probably be for functional reasons. The most famous site is the nearby **Korsun Hill of Eternal Glory**, where a giant iron woman holds a flaming torch in honour of the war dead.

The city was officially founded in the 14th century as a Dnepr River outpost from Kiev. Later, Cherkassy belonged to the string of forts demarcating the end of civilisation and the beginning of the 'wild field'. For a few centuries, the river port was a Cossack stronghold embroiled in constant battles with the Tatars from the south. This was followed by two centuries of Polish rule, with the exception of Khmelnytsky's liberation war and the peasant uprisings from 1648 to 1654. Russia finally annexed Cherkassy in 1793. Few signs of the old city are left, since both the civil war and World War II were especially destructive. Hitler is said to have flattened the city completely. Today, Cherkassy seems to be the favoured town of foreign students who come here to study Russian. Other visitors come by boat, sailing down from Kiev for the day.

More interesting than the city is the actual region of Cherkassy where there is still the sense of a 'wild field'. Ukraine's greatest heroes – Taras Shevchenko and Bohdan Khmelnytsky – were born in the modest villages that still spread across a rather empty plain. Most visitors coming to the region visit the Shevchenko Museum upriver at **Kaniv**, or the gardens and town of **Uman** in the west (covered in *Chapter 7*; see page 177).

GETTING THERE AND AWAY People can fly to Cherkassy but considering Kiev Borispol is about a two-hour drive, it would seem silly. It's generally possible to fly here only from Kiev, Moscow and Crimea. The airport is at Smilyanska 168 and air tickets can be purchased at the office at Ostafia Dashkovicha 30 (↘ 0472 453 286). The train station is at Krupskoyi 1. However, the main lines do not run through here, and the trains that do come through tend to be going north and south. Connections to Kiev are longer than they need to be (over 3 hours). Longer routes service Moscow, Lviv and Poltava, but journeys to these cities from Cherkassy are always slow. You might consider going to Kiev and enjoying your pick of faster trains. From either Kiev or Cherkassy to the other it is wisest to take the bus. The central bus station in Cherkassy is next to the airport (*Smilyankska 162*). Nearly all Kiev buses travelling to any Dnepr River cities will stop in Cherkassy, so that every day there are connections with Kaniv, Kremenchuk, and Dnepropetrovsk, as well as Poltava, Kirovohrad and Uman. Cherkassy is the one city where there is regular river transport to and from Kiev, although the trip can take a leisurely five hours or more. The river station is at the end (or beginning) of Geroyiv Stalingrada (↘ 0472 452 727).

⌂ WHERE TO STAY

⌂ **Hotel Dnepr** Frunze 1; ↘ 0472 472 360. Located right next to the riverfront, the Dnepr is considered the city's very best hotel following an all-over renovation in 2001. Inside, the hotel is refreshingly clean and well managed. Credit cards accepted and b/fast inc. *Basic sgl rooms US$65, nicer rooms US$80–100, suites US$120.*

⌂ **Tsentralny** Lenina 30; ↘ 0472 452 170. As the name implies, this solid, standard hotel is right in the city centre, with small but clean rooms. Credit cards accepted. *Sgls US$30–40 depending on size and amount of furniture. Dbls US$45–65, suites from US$75.*

⌂ **Rosova** Frunze 28; ↘ 0472 450 321. Also on the waterfront, but of a lesser standard and with slightly lower prices. Credit cards accepted. *US$40–80.*

Hotel Cherkassy Lazareva 6; ☎ 0472 476 584. One of the less expensive options in town, but rather shabby. Popular with the backpacker crowd. Cash only. *Some rooms for less than US$25.*

Hotel Ukrayina Lisova 1; ☎ 0472 321 053. Not-so-central, very basic Soviet-era hotel. Cash only. *Sgl US$30, dbl US$50, suite US$85.*

✖ **WHERE TO EAT** Each hotel features its own restaurant, the best of which is at Hotel Dnepr. Otherwise, with such a large student population, there is no lack of inexpensive eateries in town, as well as a few new posh dining spots.

✖ **Stare Misto** Khreschatyk 200; ☎ 0472 540 515. Fancy, old-style Ukrainian restaurant with rich Slavic dishes. *Mains from US$8; open 11.00–midnight.*

✖ **Peking** Gogolya 413; ☎ 0472 470 041. Never-fail Chinese food. *Mains from US$3; open 10.00–22.00.*

✖ **Magnolia** Shevchenka 209; ☎ 0472 472 265. Upscale café and bar near the centre. Good business lunches and lots of beer on tap. *Mains from US$5; open 10.00–midnight.*

✖ **Café Sladkarnitsa** Shevchenka 195; no phone.

Cherkassy's French cuisine specialist. A cheery café with some outdoor seating. *Mains from US$5; open 08.00–22.00.*

✖ **Café Yaroslavna** Vyshnevetskovo 24; ☎ 0472 455 125. Popular city café, with good salads, lunches and great desserts. *Mains from US$4; open 09.00–22.00.*

✖ **Kreschatyk** Khreschatyk 180; ☎ 0472 544 162. A more refined local restaurant, serving meat and potatoes and Ukrainian specialities. *Mains from US$8; open 10.00–23.00.*

KANIV КАНІВ

The poet Taras Shevchenko – Ukraine's ultimate hero – requested that he be buried near this tiny village on a bluff overlooking the Dnepr River. His desire was fulfilled after his death and now visitors stream in from all over the world to see his grave at this very serene location. Kaniv itself was founded as one of the original fortresses marking the line between civilisation and the open 'wild field' and later became an important Cossack stronghold. Before the Russian Revolution and throughout Khruschev's rule, Shevchenko's grave was a popular site for clandestine meetings of nationalists and intellectuals. The **Taras Shevchenko Literary Museum** is on top of the main hill near his grandiose grave (☎ 0473 622 365; open 09.00–18.00; entrance 5UAH). The poet lived for a while in the smaller restored cottage in the woods behind. Just three miles south of the village is the **Kaniv Nature Preserve**, founded in 1926 to protect natural Ukrainian plant species. The park is open for walking and enjoying some very lovely views of the river (there's also a chance to see the rare white stork, which lives here periodically). The main office of the preserve is located in the village (☎ 0473 624 531; e reserve@aquila.freenet.kiev.ua). There is a hotel within the reserve, which can accommodate visitors for about US$20 per night, but you must check with the park service first. Kaniv can be reached by car or bus from Kiev (2+ hours) or Cherkassy (1 hour), and some Ukrainian tour agencies offer boat excursions to Kaniv as a day trip from Kiev. There are also a number of small *elektrichki* trains which go to Kaniv from Kiev, typically through Pereyaslav Khmelnytsky.

KREMENCHUK КРЕМЕНЧУК

Kremenchuk's dam is the cause of the immense Kremenchutsky Reservoir (the big blue spot on the map of Ukraine) and the hydro-electric plant used to provide energy locally and run the giant chemical carbon plant in Soviet days. An atmosphere of heavy industry does not prevent most cruises from stopping here to enjoy the parks and sandy river beaches, and this odd junction of east and west Ukraine. The scant tourist amenities are discouraging, and many opt to go and stay in Dnepropetrovsk instead. If you must remain in town, there are two choices:

Hotel Ontario (*Butyrina 15*) costs US$120–200 and is not even close to being worth it. **Dneprovskye** (*Khalamenyuka 8;* ✆ *0536 622 537*) has rooms for under US$30 but the experience resembles camping indoors. If you feel lost and confused, ask for direction at the **Kremenchuk Bureau of Excursions** (*Pervomaiskaya 1;* ✆ *0536 630 177*).

GETTING THERE AND AWAY A frequent overnight train runs between Kiev and Kremenchuk (8 hours) but only during the tourist season (June–September and New Year). Another train connects to Kirovograd (3 hours) and Poltava (3 hours), but buses are quicker and more frequent. Private buses (Avtoluks and Gunsel) also travel to and from Kiev (4 hours) and Dnepropetrovsk (2 hours). The bus station is at Vorovskovo 32/6 (✆ *0536 620 504*). River transport schedules change frequently; ask at the river station on Pervomaiskaya.

KIROVOHRAD КІРОВОГРАД

West of Dnepropetrovsk and smack bang in the middle of the country, Kirovohrad appears to be one of the less glamorous corners of the country, although it's a completely honest destination. Simultaneously industrial and extremely rural, the city seems to exist in an odd state of limbo, trying to figure out its place in the new Ukraine.

The city was first drawn up from plans entitled 'New Serbia', a ploy to bring repressed Orthodox Serbian farmers into the area as a buffer against the Turks. Alas, the Serbian settlement was short-lived, as the constant raids from the Tatars led to the construction of St Elizabeth's fortress in 1752, from which grew the city Yelizavetgrad. Throughout the Russian Empire this was nothing more than a lacklustre military outpost – until the revolution. The oft-recounted anecdote from the Russian civil war – that the city kept three or four different flags on hand, never knowing which army would be in power by morning – is actually attributed to Kirovohrad. The legend makes sense in this town, in the very middle of Ukraine and without any natural protections. In the post-revolution years, the city was renamed Zinovyevsk, for famous Bolshevik revolutionary Grigor Zinoviev, who was born and raised here. In 1934, either Stalin's guilt or paranoia led to the creation of a cult around communist favourite Sergei Kirov, who had recently been assassinated (most likely under Stalin's orders). Hence Kirovohrad, the Kirov ballet, and dozens of factories, train stations and cities across the former Soviet Union.

There is very little in the way of tourist attractions in the area, but the brave and adventurous still make their way to Kirovohrad to share the town with the 250,000 people who live here. It boasts an interesting blend of architecture – undisturbed Soviet industrial alongside pre-revolutionary Russian Neoclassical. Many guests will be taken on a tour, which focuses on the natural history museum, but that's about all.

GETTING THERE AND AWAY One overnight train comes and goes from Kiev (5 hours), but most people travel here through Dnipropetrovsk, which is only two hours by train or bus. An army of *marshrutka* buzz back and forth between the two cities. Further transport takes you south to Kherson and Mikolayiv or Odessa. There is an airport in Kirovohrad, with sporadic connections to Kiev and Crimea (*Ostrovskovo 2;* ✆f *0522 222 471;* e *kirovogr.travel@kiyavia.com*).

🏠 WHERE TO STAY

🏠 **Catalonia** Karla Marksa 21; ✆ 0522 224 536. Upscale modern hotel, housed in a posh and very historical Neoclassical brick building. Rooms are spacious, well decorated and tidy, while service is impeccable. Internet access, personal service, and everything the business traveller would expect to

Leisurely river cruises up and down the Dnepr were one of the first package deals to be touted to foreigners and are now among the most organised trips in the country. The river does not take that long to travel down, but passes lots of interesting places, so itineraries usually hit half the sites on the way down, and the others on the way back. A typical journey will begin in Kiev, make a midway stop in Odessa, Sevastopol or both, and then return to Kiev, in around two weeks. The most popular ports of call tend to be Kaniv, Kremnechuk, Dnepropetrovsk, Zaporizhzhya and Kherson. Although some may find the concept of a cruise a little banal, travelling the Dnepr in this way offers a rather comprehensive introduction to the country and a back door view of all that takes place here in the summer months.

The best time to travel down the Dnepr is in May and June, when the willow trees are just turning green, the flowers are still blossoming and the river is not too busy. At the same time, the autumn is remarkably rich in colour and warm. Every single Ukrainian tour agency will advertise their 'unique' Dnepr cruise when really they are just ticket dealers, but for now it is the only way to secure a spot. Passage is almost always on the MS *Marshal Koshevoy*, a 'vintage' East German riverboat circa 1989. When checking prices, make sure you know what is and is not included in the fee, since land excursions are sometimes extra. An all-inclusive 15-day cruise with a 'boat deck' cabin (at the top of the ship) costs around US$2,000 per person, or US$1,100 if sharing a suite. A 10–12-day cruise on the main or lower decks will cost around US$900 per person. Groups of 20 or more can negotiate significant discounts. Many Western travel agencies advertise Dnepr and Black Sea combinations, as do quite a few Russian-based tour operators. All the tour companies listed in *Chapter 4* offer some form of Dnepr River cruise. The following companies specialise in Dnepr cruises:

Imperial Travel 43 Highwood Rd, East Norwich, NY 11732, USA; ☎ +1 516 922 4640; f +1 516 922 4995; e info@imperialtravel.net; www.imperialtravel.net. A respected cruise agency with two different itineraries, both embarking from Kiev.

Noble Caledonia 2 Chester Close, Belgravia, London SW1X 7BE, UK; ☎ 020 7752 0000; f 020 7245 0388; e info@noble-caledonia.co.uk; www.noble-caledonia.co.uk. Offering diverse combinations of Dnepr and Black Sea cruises.

Viking River Cruises 5700 Canoga Av, Suite 200 Woodland Hills, CA 91367, USA; ☎ +1.818.227.1234; UK ☎ 0870 850 1690; www.vikingrivers.com. One of the most prominent companies in the business.

have. *Dbls US$95, suites US$120.*

🏠 **Europe** Karla Marksa 13/16; ☎ 0522 246 809; e europe@kw.ukrtel.net; www.europe.kw.ukrtel.net. The city's 'main' hotel, with comfortable, renovated rooms, albeit in an old concrete shell of a building. Much of the interior has that old Soviet chic feel, but the staff are friendly and there's hot water. *A range for every budget: the nicer, remodelled rooms US$30–40 for a sgl, US$55–90 for a dbl.*

🏠 **Turist** Ushakova ☎ 0522 244 680; f 0522 293 332. A die-hard Soviet hotel with all the extras, including nightclub, gym, business centre and restaurant. *Dbls US$45; suites US$80.*

🏠 **Ukrayina** Dzerzhinskovo 82/40; ☎ 0522 226 641; f 0522 222 545. Dormitory-style accommodation for less than US$15 pp. A few rooms have private bathrooms with hot water.

✖ **WHERE TO EAT** Kirovohrad is just catching on to the dining-out craze. In addition to the hotel restaurants, there are a few nice independent eateries. Otherwise, there are plenty of food shops and markets around town. Alas, cash is more widely accepted than plastic.

TARAS SHEVCHENKO (1814–61)

No matter where you travel in Ukraine, you are bound to see the portrait of a gentle old man with contemplative brow and drooping moustache – Taras Hryhorovich Shevchenko. In his life, Shevchenko was a poet, a philosopher, a painter and a prisoner; nowadays, he represents the liberation of the Ukrainian nation.

Shevchenko was born a serf in Moryntsy, a village on the right bank of the Cherkassy region. Both of his parents died before he was 12, and as an orphan he worked as a shepherd and was trained as a servant. Eventually his master brought the boy to Vilnius and then St Petersburg where he was allowed limited study with a painter. Other artists noticed the boy's sketching and held a lottery to raise enough money (2,500 roubles) to purchase his freedom. Shevchenko was then accepted into the St Petersburg art academy where he won many prizes for his paintings, and also began a compilation of poems that was published in 1840 under the title *Kobzar*. Named after the wandering bards of Ukraine, the book uses artful verse to express both the beauty and hardship of Ukrainian life. The book was a success and is now the most sacred text in Ukraine aside from the Bible.

The poet's fame and nationalistic philosophy eventually brought him under the scrutiny of Tsar Nikolai I who ordered his arrest for being involved with a clandestine Ukrainian group, the brotherhood of St Cyril and Methodius. He was first imprisoned in Siberia and later assigned a place in the army in central Asia. During this decade of exile, the tsar commanded that Shevchenko be prohibited from drawing or writing, but the poet continued both in secret, and many of these works are on display in the art museums of Kiev and Kharkiv today. After gaining his freedom, the exhausted Shevchenko lived for only four more years. His death came just seven days before the universal emancipation of the serfs, and his life of captivity became the symbol of oppressed Ukrainians in the Russian Empire. Shevchenko's poems also illustrated the national cause and built a bond between various movements and societies in Ukraine, as well as other parts of the empire and throughout the Ukrainian diaspora.

By the time Ukraine had its first brief taste of independence in 1918, Shevchenko was revered as the country's greatest hero. Ukrainians still quote Shevchenko's reference to Ukraine when he spoke of 'this land of ours that is not ours'. During the Soviet regime, Shevchenko's anti-Russian voice was toned down and the poet was represented as the universal voice of the repressed peasantry; however, since 1991, most nationalists have used his image as a convenient substitute for the former cult worship of Lenin. Every city has at least one statue of the poet and a street named after him, and schoolchildren must memorise long tracts of his poetry. Socialist or nationalist, Shevchenko was a man who truly loved his country. Shevchenko was buried in St Petersburg, but his body was later moved to Kaniv in order to fulfil the desires of his poem 'Testament', in which he had envisioned his final resting place: a high mound overlooking the surging Dnepr and the endless fields of Ukraine.

✗ **Maksim** Preobrazhenskaya 17; ➘ 0522 244 831. European-style café with set menu lunches, wonderful desserts and a wide range of light meals or heavier Ukrainian dishes. *Mains from US$7; open 11.00–23.00.*

✗ **Cossack Zastava** Moskovskaya 202; ➘ 0522 212 241. Fun, Ukrainian Cossack themed restaurant, with delicious Ukrainian staples (*varenniki, holubtsi, deruny,* etc.). *Mains from US$6; open 11.00–midnight.*

✗ **Vesna** Lenina 13; ➘ 0522 223 479. 'Spring': a classical, posh dining venue for the local élite. A nice range of salads, fish and meat dishes. *Mains from US$8; open 10.00–midnight.*

✗ **Grand Pizza** Karla Marksa 21; ➘ 0522 243 603. Big, Italian-style pizzas right next to Hotel Catalonia. *Mains from US$8; open 11.00–23.00.*

DNEPROPETROVSK ДНЕПРОПЕТРОВСЬК

Pronounced almost the way that it's spelled, Dnepropetrovsk is Ukraine's third-largest city and represents the country's mighty industrial fist. Nestled upon a sharp bend in the Dnepr River, the city is often cast in a deep fog that hides the flagging steel factories and decaying city blocks while highlighting the city's sleek new dynamic, including Ukraine's first bona fide skyscrapers – the not-yet-famous twin towers of Dnepr. The paradox of the city's gritty nature versus the lavish business climate is worthy of Dickens, and the bawdy culture of local *byznesmeny* adds a touch of Las Vegas to the streets. Over one million people make up this metropolitan hotchpotch, and the lively wheeling and dealing that goes on in the markets and flashy shops reminds visitors that this is not a city of sights, but rather a place to see and be seen in the new business-minded Ukraine.

The river occupies a central focus in everyday life and there's a lot less pomp and a lot more party than in Kiev. At the largest port on the lower Dnepr and the biggest city in the centre of the country, all river cruises make at least a one-day stop. If you are travelling by rail or car, Dnepr also makes a convenient alternative to Kiev for an east–west gateway.

HISTORY Orthodox monks founded the first permanent settlement here in the 9th century on what is today called Monastyrsky (Monastery) Island, right where the Dnepr flows directly east before turning sharply to the south at the confluence of the Samara River. The monks were left in peace for several centuries, until the Poles arrived: in an attempt to counter the independent island fortress of the Zaporizhzhyan Sich downriver, the Poles built their own fortress near this same spot named *Kodak*. However the Zaporizhzhyan Cossacks soon took it over. By 1776, the Russian Empire had finally secured the Zaporizhzhyan lands and Catherine the Great looked to build a centrally located southern capital that would rule supreme in 'New Russia'. The chosen sight was conveniently close to the two former Cossack bases, though spring floods and swampy fields hampered the building of palaces (still a problem today). Eventually, General Potemkin was able to carry out his lover's orders and the city of Yekaterinaslav rose up from the high banks of the Dnepr. Unfortunately, the original plans were never finished and the city named after Catherine herself was a fraction of its intended size.

In 1883, a new metal bridge was built across the Dnepr River and through Yekaterinaslav, completing a rail connection that could carry coal from Donetsk to the steel mills in Kryvy Rih. Soon a gigantic steelworks had been built on site and the city joined in Ukraine's rapid, but very localised, industrial revolution. A very few but very remarkable turn-of-the-century buildings remain from this boomtown period, while the largely imported Russian working-class population made the town a hotbed of revolutionary activity. After the tumultuous civil war, the city was renamed Dnepropetrovsk in an attempt to cast off Tsarist allusions and to honour the first general secretary of the Ukrainian Communist Party, Petrovsky. His noble statue stands just outside the city's train station, with his left hand pointing to the east, all of which is symbolic.

'Dnepr' rose up to be the primary city in the Soviet Union for metalworks and engineering, and as a leader in the Soviet space programme. For several decades, metal pipes of all shapes and sizes were the local speciality and the city still carries the tributes to its industrial workforce (i.e: Glory to the Metallurgists!). Dnepr has made a smooth transition (more or less) from the Soviet steel industry to the world of international business and finance, although that success can be attributed to the city's notoriously shady oligarchs. Ukraine's former president Leonid Kuchma was

13

raised, educated and made his political career in Dnepr. Luckily, the city's current élite has chosen to invest its tremendous wealth and power back into the city.

GETTING THERE AND AWAY

By air Dnepropetrovsk International Airport is probably the busiest airport in the country outside of Kiev, situated 13km (8 miles) southeast of the city centre (✆ *0562 650 496*). **Austrian Airlines** has one flight daily to and from Vienna, although due to the schedule, some transatlantic connections may require a stopover in Vienna. The Austrian Airlines office is located at Dnepropetrovsk Airport (✆ *0562 771 209*). **Dniproavia** (*Naberezhna 37;* ✆ *0562 441 757*) is the locally based airline, with daily flights to Kiev, connections to Volgograd, Yerevan, Istanbul and Tblisi, and a three-times-a-week service to Frankfurt, Germany. **Aerosvit** (*airport;* ✆ *0567 771 986;* e *aerosvit@email.dp.ua; www.aerosvit.com.ua*) has the most convenient daily flights to Kiev; and **Aeroflot** still flies once a day to and from Moscow's Sheremetevo I Airport.

By rail Dnepr serves as the primary rail junction between the industrial east, Kiev, the west, and many of the southern lines to Crimea. Even if you never plan on staying here, it is likely that you may have spent a small moment parked in this city while you slept during a long train journey. The once daily *Dnipro* overnight train goes to and from Kiev (9 hours), but there are at least ten daily trains that make the same journey, sometimes in less time (6–7 hours). Trains from Dnepr to Donetsk (4 hours) are frequent and practically all trains between Russia and Crimea make a stop here as well. Other daily trains connect with Kharkiv (4 hours), Odessa (11 hours) and Lviv (20 hours). The Dnepropetrovsk central train station is located on Ploscha Petrovskovo at the end of Karla Marksa. Buy tickets in the *kassa* located through a separate entrance on the left wing of the station (when facing the station from the street), although most local hotels can do it for you.

By bus The central bus station (*Kurchatova 6;* ✆ *0567 784 090*) is within walking distance of the train station. Ukraine's two major private companies both have offices in the main station. **Avtolux** (✆ *0567 783 979*) has four daily connections to Kiev (7 hours), as well as two daily buses to Zaporizhzhya (1 hour) and Yalta (9 hours). **Gunsel** (✆ *0562 318 460*) also has a quick bus three times a week to Kiev (7½ hours) via Kremenchuk and Borispol Airport, as well as one daily bus to Donetsk (4 hours). All other public buses are yours for the picking, and they do go everywhere. The most obvious regional connections are to Zaporizhzhya (2 hours), Kryvy Rih (4 hours), Poltava (3½ hours) and Donetsk (4 hours), while farther destinations include Simferopol, Yalta, Lviv and Kharkiv. Of note is the reliable *marshrutka* service which runs every 25 minutes to and from Zaporizhzhya in a little less than two hours.

By boat As in Kiev, there is plenty of boat traffic during the warmer seasons, although most of it is organised cruises that seldom originate in Dnepropetrovsk. From Dnepr, there are regular pleasure cruises in summer, which leave from the main dock on Naberezhnaya and sail downriver and back in a little less than an hour. Find out more at the river station (*Gorkovo 1;* ✆ *0562 498 267*).

GETTING AROUND Dnepropetrovsk opened its single-line metro in 1996 and then closed it a week later due to heavy leaking. The soggy ground of the riverbank was not ideal for tunnelling. However, these days the subway is back up and running and for 60 kopecks you can travel from the train station out to any of Dnepr's great residential neighbourhoods, all located very far away from the city centre. Inside the city itself, there is a main tram line which originates from the train station and runs the length of Karla Marksa, which is more convenient than it may look. *Marshrutka* dart about the city as well, with main pick-up/drop-off points located at the train station, bus station, and the circus (Kotsyubinsky).

Flagging down a taxi is not so easy in this town. Either locate the taxi queues outside hotels and the stations, or call Radio Taxi (↘ *053, locally*), Dnepr Taxi (↘ *0562 333 333*), Economy Taxi (↘ *0567 449 999*) or City Taxi (↘ *0562 349 349*).

COMMUNICATIONS At the central post office (*Karla Marksa 62;* ↘ *0562 454 023*) you can make international calls and use the internet. The city's most reliable internet café is called **Internet Café** (*Karla Marksa 20, underground; open 24 hours*) and is clean and smoke-free.

WHERE TO STAY There is big money in Dnepr and those that have it want it to be known. Those who do not still aspire to such grandeur and charge the same prices. Such a race to the top affects accommodation, so that this city boasts many 'luxury' hotels with varied degrees of 'luxury'. Finding good value for money is difficult, as is finding low-priced rooms. If you are planning on spending US$100 or more a night, stay at the Grand, where that money buys the most comfortable stay at an unbeatable location. If you really want to conserve your cash, it's best to rent an apartment. The general shortage of hotels in such a big city often leads to the city getting booked out completely – this is one place where it pays to book ahead.

Luxury The following all accept credit cards and staff are English-speaking.

Grand Hotel Korolenka 2; ↘ 0562 341 010; f 0562 340 200; e admin@grand-hotel-ukraine.dp.ua; www.grand-hotel-ukraine.dp.ua. Dnepr's most luxurious hotel has developed into very elegant, boutique-style accommodation. The rooms are impeccable and the location right in the centre of Karla Marksa is unbeatable. The building was the home of a successful merchant back during the last years of the empire but today the businessmen are back en masse and the atmosphere is decidedly corporate. The small swimming pool and extensive fitness club are the city's very best, and keeping in line with the extravagance, the restaurant serves a blend of Chinese and Ukrainian dishes. *Sgls US$100–175, dbls US$200, the decked-out presidential suite US$625.*

Academy Karla Marksa 20; ↘ 0563 700 505; f 056 370 2931; e info@academia.dp.ua; www.academia.dp.ua. A slightly smaller but very refined option, the Academy has only 20 rooms, all of them immaculate. Amenities include a decent fitness room, sauna and bar, and the restaurant specialises in Ukrainian and Jewish cuisine. Personal care and a comfortable use of English sets it apart from most. *US$120 for large sgl, US$190 for dbl, US$300 for suite.*

Astoria Luxe Karla Marksa 66A; ↘ 0563 704 270; e Astoria-lux@a-teleport.com. This swish hotel stands at the head of Dnepr's main drag (near the opera house) and stole its name from the Astoria Hotel next door (which was the original). It caters to a clientele with expensive tastes. Visitors will find the big beds to be bouncy and the bathrooms spacious. The popular cocktail lounge, swimming pool and sauna are definite highlights. *A 'semi-suite' costs US$120 and the super-plush suites US$190.*

Astoria Karla Marksa 66; ↘ 0562 384 803; f 0563 704 352; e hotel@astoria.dp.ua; www.astoria.com.ua. The original Astoria occupies one of the remaining historic buildings on Karla Marksa, built in old Yekaterinaslav in 1913. In the heat of the Russian Civil War, famed anarchist Nestor Makhno stayed at this hotel and made a fiery speech from its balcony. Today the hotel's long hallways and tall ceilings benefit from recent remodelling. In fierce competition with the Astoria next door, this one has a pool, sauna and a hair-styling salon. *Rooms US$110–145.*

Park Hotel Voroshylova 21D; ↘ 0567 266 001; f 0567 266 002. A classy new art-deco boutique hotel with chic design and attention to detail. *US$100 for a very nice sgl room, US$150 and upwards for dbls and suites.*

Middle range *(all of the following accept credit cards)*

🏠 **Nadezhda** Naberezhnaya Lenina 16A; ☎ 0567 782 115; f 0567 417 077; e hotel@ nadegda.dp.ua; www.nadegda.dp.ua. A calm hotel right next to the river with friendly service and newly refurbished rooms. Prices are per room as opposed to pp. *A room with a queen-size bed costs US$85, whereas a larger 2-room suite costs US$100, which can sleep up to 3.*

🏠 **Zhovtneva** Ploschad Shevchenko 4A; ☎ 0562 448 803; f 0562 722 065. Built in the vaguely historical district of the city next to Park Shevchenko, the 'October' was built as a rather functional hotel in Soviet times but underwent major reconstruction in 2006, bringing it up to international standards of comfort and cleanliness. Monastyrsky Island is within walking distance, the neighbourhood is generally quieter and there are several nice restaurants close by. *US$90–100 per room.*

🏠 **Dnipropetrovsk** Naberezhnaya Lenina 33; ☎ 0562 455 327; f 0567 444 156; e booking@ hotel.dp.ua; www.hotel.dp.ua. Right on the river and just two blocks down from the main bridge, this 11-storey former Inturist hotel has a great view of the city from either side, and is usually offered to package tourists as the cheaper alternative to the Grand. On average, rooms are smallish but modern and comfy; each is equipped with shower or bath and for US$10–15/day there is the option of FB. The 2-room suites (for US$65–75) are also not a bad deal. The ancient Egyptian bowling club on the first floor is also worth a visit. *Rooms around US$50 for a sgl and US$55 for a large dbl.*

🏠 **Tsentralnaya** Karla Marksa 50; ☎ 0562 450 347. As the name implies, this hotel is centrally located on the main street of the city and occupies a remodelled Soviet high-rise. The prices are quite reasonable given the central location and standards of comfort have improved to make this a very popular option among younger couples and families. *Sgl US$60; dbl 'suites' US$80.*

Budget *(accept cash only)*

🏠 **Sport** Schorsa 4; ☎ 0562 361 706. Right in front of the city's football stadium, this is where Soviet athletes were housed way back when. Much of the interior has been remodelled to a degree and the service is sound, but the old Soviet protocol pervades in the rooms (small bathrooms, all sgl beds). Because of its low prices this place fills up with groups fast. *Rooms US$35 sgl, US$70 twin.*

🏠 **Sverdlovsk** Sverdlova 6; ☎ 0562 428 825. This dilapidated Soviet-style hotel is still in business although there are no signs, making it almost impossible to find. It's the teal and tan tiled building at the very start of Sverdlova, but the entrance is at the back (walk around the left side) and the hotel now starts on the 4th floor. The location is also not too hot (it's about 4 uphill blocks south of Karla Marksa) and the management is notoriously rude and unfriendly. *Still, a sgl room with en-suite bathroom goes for a mere US$25. For slightly less you can share a room with Dnepr's students and transients.*

🏠 **Avtovokzal** Kurchatova 10; ☎ 056 778 3965; e dopas@dopas.dp.ua. Proudly displaying its one single star, this bus station hotel caters to travellers coming and going, but it is conveniently located near the train station and therefore the rest of the city's transport routes. Follow the bed signs up to the 5th floor. *For US$20 you can get a very bare room (with bathroom) to yourself or pay US$6 for a bed in a dormitory room of 3–5 people.*

Renting apartments Sometimes renting a whole private apartment is a cheaper option for longer stays, and even for just one night. '**Apartments**' is recommended by the city and has a few luxurious options in the very centre (*Komsomolskaya 35/1;* ☎ *0562 321 808; www.apartments.dp.ua*).

✖ **WHERE TO EAT** The meeting of local mobster dollars with an inherent longing for exotic tastes and sophistication has given birth to some wild and wacky dining establishments in Dnepropetrovsk. Keep in mind that laughing at the menu, themes or décor is not taken well. Keep a straight face, enjoy the meal and remember, this is Dnepr.

Ukrainian and Russian

✖ **Kozatska Fortetsya** Artyoma 3; ☎ 0562 321 783. The 'Cossack Fortress' is one of the city's better

Ukrainian-themed restaurants with cheerful service and charming décor. Fresh vegetables, good salads,

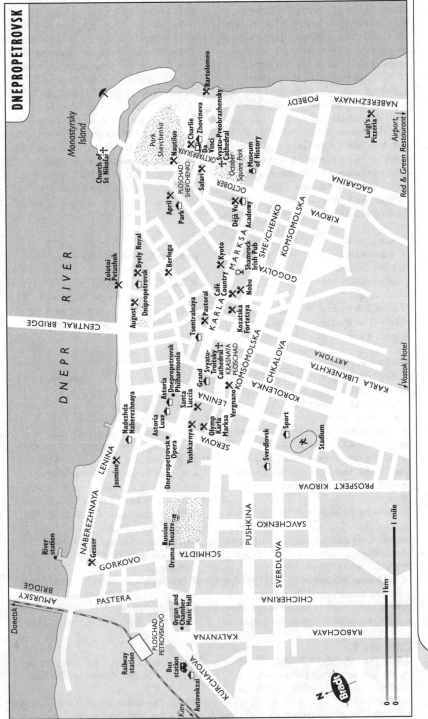

DNEPROPETROVSK

DNEPR RIVER

DNEPR RIVER

Monastyrsky Island

Church of St Nikolai

AMURSKY BRIDGE

CENTRAL BRIDGE

Donetsk

Kiev

Railway station

Bus station

Autovokzal

PLOSCHAD PETROVSKVO

Organ and Chamber Music Hall

River station

Gesser

GORKOVO

Russian Drama Theatre

Jasmine

Dnepropetrovsk Opera

Astoria Luxe

Astoria

Santa Luccia

Nadezhda Naberezhnaya

Yushkarnya

Olymp

August

Dnipropetrovsk

Byely Royal

Zolotoi Petushok

Berloga

April

PLOSCHAD SHEVCHENKO Park

Safari

Park Shevchenko

Nautilus

Charlie

Da Vinci

Zhovtneva

Bartolomeo

Svyatu-Preobrazhensky Cathedral

October

Museum of History

Svyatu-Troitsky Cathedral

Grand

Vergnano

Dnepropetrovsk Philharmonia

Tsentralnaya

Pastoral

Café Country

Kozatska Fortetsya

Nobu

Kyoto

Déjà Vu

Shamrock Irish Pub

Academy

Square Park

KRASNAYA PLOSCHAD

Sverdlovsk

Sport

Stadium

Luigi's Pizzeria

NABEREZHNAYA

Airport, Red & Green Restaurant

Vostok Hotel

NABEREZHNAYA

LENINA

NABEREZHNAYA

PASTERA

SCHMIDTA

KURCHATOVA

KALYNYNA

PUSHKINA

SAVCHENKO

SVERDLOVA

CHICHERINA

RABOCHAYA

PROSPEKT KIROVA

SEROVA

LENINA

KARLA MARKSA

SVYATU-TROITSKY

KOMSOMOLSKA

KOROLENKA

CHKALOVA

KARLA LIBKNEKHTA

ARTOMA

KARLA MARKSA

GOGOLYA

SHEVCHENKO

KOMSOMOLSKA

KIROVA

GAGARINA

POBEDY

NABEREZHNAYA

OKTYABRSKAYA

OCTOBER

The Dnepr DNEPROPETROVSK

13

0   1km

0   1 mile

Bradt

369

delicious hand rolled *varennyky* and homemade vodka make it popular for parties. There is live Ukrainian folk music every night and this is one of the few places in Dnepr where you'll hear Ukrainian spoken. *Entrées US$5–10; open 24 hours.*

✗ **Yushkarnya** Karla Marksa 83; no phone. A popular café in the heart of the city that's always packed. Genuine *borsch* and a genuine clientele. *A whole meal costs US$5; open 11.00–22.00.*

✗ **Berloga** Demyana Bednovo 11; ☎ 0562 374 211. Built to resemble a crude hunting lodge where people can enjoy the simple recipes of old Ukraine and the Carpathians. The atmosphere is quite calm and the food is especially tasty, although beware of the items on offer for shock value (eg: bear meat). *Entrées from US$15.*

Asian

✗ **Nobu** Karla Marksa 49; ☎ 0567 446 055; www.nobu.com.ua. Upscale sushi bar with traditional Japanese cuisine. *US$10 minimum; open 11.00–midnight*

✗ **Kyoto** Karla Marksa 34b; ☎ 0563 702 885. One of many Japanese restaurants in Dnepr, but worthy of special mention for its authenticity and good

Themed dining

✗ **April** Vorshilova 21D; ☎ 0562 726 000. French, Italian and southeast Asian fusion food prepared right at your table with much flair. *Entrées from US$20; open 11.00–midnight.*

✗ **Safari** Fuchika 12b; ☎ 0562 389 859. Suave and sophisticated, this urban grill and bar is rather laidback. The menu caters to those who appreciate simple gourmet food. Grilled meat and thoughtful side dishes. *Open 11.00–midnight; US$20–30 entrées.*

✗ **Charlie** Per Oktyabrsky 6; ☎ 0562 465 219. In honour of Charlie Chaplin, this combination restaurant/casino dishes out a tasty array of French *haute cuisine*, sushi and Italian antipasti. *Entrées from US$15; open 11.00–midnight.*

✗ **Red & Green** Dobrovoltseva 3; ☎ 0562 361 728. Combination bar/restaurant designed around the theme of sailing around the world. Live jazz, hearty appetisers, and cuisine representing the 4 corners of

Cafés and bars

🖵 **Da Vinci** Oktyabrsky 6; ☎ 0563 737 008. By day, this is an artsy French patisserie with metallurgic sculpture based on Da Vinci's designs, serving intense coffee, rich chocolate desserts and light meals. When the sun goes down, out come the

✗ **Zolotoi Petushok** Naberezhnaya Lenina 37; ☎ 0562 343 559. Housed in log cabin built atop a river barge on the Dnepr River, the 'Golden Rooster' exhibits the very best of Dnepr extravagance with a menu of Russian cuisine that includes whole suckling pig, quails on skewers and deer-tongue kebabs. *Entrées US$15–25; open 12.00–midnight*

✗ **Gesser** Gorkovo 22; ☎ 0567 782 756. Specialising in beer and all the food that goes with it, including a lot of wild game and hearty Russian meals. Accepts credit cards. *US$10 for most dishes.*

✗ **August** Naberezhnaya Lenina 33; ☎ 0562 450 150. Outdoor terrace right on the Dnepr, along with a riverboat. Tasty grilled food and live music (that's not annoying) make for pleasant evenings in summertime. *Mains from US$7; open 12.00–midnight.*

service. The US$10 business lunches are popular. *Open 11.00–23.00.*

✗ **Jasmine** Naberezhnaya Lenina 15A; ☎ 0562 342 238. A hole-in-the wall underground Chinese restaurant like you'd find in most cities in the world. With karaoke and billards. *Mains from US$4; open 11.00–22.00.*

the globe. It also boasts the largest wine selection in the city. *Entrées from US$10; open 11.00–midnight.*

✗ **Olymp** Karla Marska 83; ☎ 0562 455 237. Tasteful Mediterranean–Japanese (?) restaurant with an uncommonly serene and respectable atmosphere. Live violin and piano music keeps the mood pleasant, and the cuisine is delicate, if slightly unusual (eg: veal in strawberry sauce). *Entrées US$7–20; open 11.00–midnight.*

✗ **Déjà Vu** Karla Marksa 20; ☎ 0563 702 930. Celebrating jazzy 1950s Americana with bright lights and boisterous parties. Food is everything from sandwiches to steaks. *Entrées from US$8; open 10.00–midnight.*

✗ **Café Country** Karla Marksa 53A; ☎ 0563 704 265. Ukrainian cowgirl waitresses serve American–Ukrainian fusion cuisine in the heart of the city. *Entrées from US$5; open 08.30–23.00.*

hookah pipes and the absinthe, served from the enclosed bar, 'Absinthe'. *Mains from US$7; open 10.00–23.00.*

✗ **Luigi's Pizzeria** Naberezhnaya Pobedy 44; ☎ 0562 319 329. Does Italian pizza as simple or as complicated as you want it; with a popular bar. *Meals for under US$12; open 10.00–22.00.*

✗ **Pastoral** Karla Marksa 46; ☏ 0562 362 866. Refined techno-urban café serving delicious coffee, delectable pastries, soup and sandwiches at lunchtime, and a believably Victorian 'English' tea at 4. *Mains from US$4; open 10.00–midnight.*

☕ **Santa Luccia** Karla Marksa 83; ☏ 0562 455 237. Hip Italian-style coffee joint with stylish, ill-balanced tables and plush red couches. *Open 11.00–23.00.*

🍺 **Shamrock Irish Pub** Karla Marska 41; ☏ 0562 362 335; web: www.shamrock.dp.ua. Probably the city's friendliest bar (it's Irish) with a renowned happy hour. They have 8 beers on tap with plates of hearty food that go well with beer. The only place in Dnepr to drink Newcastle Brown Ale. *Open 12.00–midnight.*

✗ **Vergnano** Korolenko 10; ☏ 0562 341 598. Another Italian-themed café, but with authentic Italian food and an unpretentious atmosphere; it serves Vergnano-brand coffee. *Open 10.00–22.00.*

ENTERTAINMENT AND NIGHTLIFE For theatre, try the Gorky Russian Drama Theatre (*Karla Marksa 97;* ☏ *0567 784 857*). The circa 1970 **Dnepropetrovsk Opera** is not the most famous in the country, but what's on offer is usually very entertaining, be it opera or Russian rock (*Karla Marksa 72A;* ☏ *0567 784 469*). For traditional classical music, there is always something interesting on at the **Dnepropetrovsk Philharmonia** (*Lenina 6;* ☏ *0563 729 640*) and the **Organ and Chamber Music Hall** (*Kalinina 6;* ☏ *0562 523 005*).

The Dnepr night scene changes rapidly – it's good to get advice from locals or ask at your hotel. The bi-weekly magazine *Afisha* gives a rundown of what's on and is available for free in most hotels or at news stands. Dnepr boasts more casinos and strip bars than anywhere else in Ukraine, which is quite an accomplishment. Bartolomeo (*Naberezhnaya Pobedy 9/6;* ☏ *0563 701 500*) takes the cake when it comes to post-Soviet splendour gone completely mad. Dedicated to the concept of the first explorers, the life-size 15th-century Portuguese ship and surrounding complex is 'not a restaurant, not a club, not a hotel, but a whole world'. Besides the various restaurants, there is a yacht club, Russian bathhouse, tennis courts, children's zoo, casino and a very rowdy nightclub. Balaton (*Leningradskaya 68;* ☏ *0567 793 001*) is a more traditional nightclub with cabaret shows and dance music.

Dnepr's discos range from the rather innocent to the very hardcore. SFERA plays house and techno music with regular visiting DJs (*Naberezhnaya Pobedy 82;* ☏ *0562 360 011*). Ministerstvo (*The Ministry; Karla Marksa 81;* ☏ *0567 780 610*) is youthful and heavy on rhythm, while Reporter is a more laidback place, with cocktails and lounge music (*on the corner of Karla Marksa and Barrikadny;* ☏ *0562 375 375*).

WHAT TO SEE AND DO Strolling along the riverbank and watching the boats go by is the number one pastime in Dnepr; the second is to go shopping and the third is to go out at night. Visitors should try all three. In the summer, most activity takes place on Naberezhnaya Lenina or the riverside walkway. Dnepr's prominent high street is the very long Prospekt Karla Marksa, a classic example of socialist city planning and the most civilised stretch of the city. If you can't find it here (shops, post office, food stands, souvenirs), then you won't find it anywhere. One or two blocks from the main drag takes you into the squalor of Dnepr's no man's land: abandoned buildings, ongoing construction projects and giant rubbish heaps. Walking up and down Karla Marksa takes you to some of the city's more traditional sites, including the city's Museum of History (*Karla Marksa 18;* ☏ *0562 463 426; open 10.00–16.00, closed Mon*). The museum itself is as much of an architectural monument as the impressive lifesize diorama inside portraying the World War II defence of the Dnepr River. Dnepr's very own Krasnaya Ploschad (Red Square) is the ironic address of the yellow and gold Russian Orthodox Svyato-Troitsky Cathedral, one of the most unique buildings left from the original Yekaterinaslav.

Dnepr's other famous church is the single-domed Svyato-Preobrazhenskaya Cathedral on Oktyabrskaya Square, at the top of the hill overlooking Park Shevchenko. Here locals congregate for summer walks, dominos and conversation, and this is also a path leading to the bridge that goes to Monastyrsky Island. The island is bigger than it looks and is popular for long walks. The site of the original monastery on which Dnepropetrovsk was founded is marked with a cross on the northern tip of the island, close to the recently constructed **Church of St Nikolai**. A sandy beach, freshwater aquarium and various outdoor cafés attract good-sized crowds when the weather is nice.

LOCAL TOUR OPERATORS If you find you need help with anything in Dnepr – be it sightseeing, planning excursions, interpretation, a guide, or booking hotels and transport – contact **Voyage Service** (*31 Г Blagoyev;* ✆ *0562 388 878;* e *info@voyages.com.ua*). They speak English and are very helpful.

ZAPORIZHZHYA ЗАПОРІЖЖЯ

Essentially, Zaporizhzhya offers a happy medium between the core identity of Ukrainian tradition and the legacy of Soviet engineering. Tourists like to think of Cossacks when they come to Zaporizhzhya but usually find the city's surface is a blackened shrine to Ukraine's heaviest industry.

These two extremes don't seem to bother present-day Zaporizhians, who are just as proud of the hydro-electric dam as they are of the archaeological remnants of the Scythians and the most famous of Cossack bands. The name Zaporizhzhya comes from the Ukrainian *za porihy*, meaning 'beyond the rapids'. After passing through the most dangerous part of the journey, early traders sailing from Kiev used to stop on the island of Khortytsya to catch their breath or offer a sacrifice of thanks. Surrounded by rushing water, the large island offered both security and space and new prehistoric sites are still being discovered here. The Cossacks came to the island in the 16th century and founded a fortress town and the first universal movement for Ukrainian independence. As an island in the middle of the Dnepr, the Zaporizhian Sich was a neutral milieu left undefined by cultural concepts of the Russian left bank or Polish right bank and today, Zaporizhians use Russian and Ukrainian interchangeably.

In an attempt to wipe the Cossacks off the map, Catherine the Great destroyed the Sich in 1775 and renamed the city Aleksandrovsk and it was known as this until 1921, when the Soviets reinstated its original name. Due to its prime location on the river and within the emerging industrial basin, Zaporizhzhya was allotted the fate of 'metal town' during Stalin's five-year plans. The Dneproges Dam was started in 1932 in order to provide hydro-electric power to Zaporizhzhya's many factories. It was the first in Ukraine, took decades to finish, was partially destroyed in World War II and was then rebuilt. Today it's an impressive sight to see, especially from the top. During Soviet times, the name Zaporizhzhya also equated with the smallest and cutest of the Soviet-made cars, the Zaporozhets, which were manufactured in the city's largest factory. The complex has since been taken over by Korea's Daewoo firm and renamed Avtozaz; you can't miss it coming in from the train station.

Block after city block of square buildings, the steelworks, and hundreds of billowing smokestacks make Zaporizhzhya the prototype of the perfect Soviet city, complete with Prospekt Lenina as the city's singular axis. Frankly, the decades of smoke and residue make this one of Ukraine's dirtiest towns and it was not too long ago that breathing around here was hard on the lungs. The decline in heavy industry has cleared the air to some degree but when the wind is right, you can smell Zaporizhzhya before you see it. All Dnepr cruises will stop in Zaprorizhzhya to see Khortytsya and the Cossack Museum, but you should also make an effort to take in the city's behemoth industrial elements as historical monuments in their own right.

GETTING THERE AND AWAY

By air Zaporizhzhya does have its own airport with daily flights to Kiev (either Borispol or Zhulyany) and three flights a week to Moscow on the local airline Matursich (✆ 0612 642 565). There are occasional flights to Simferopol as well in summer. Contact the Inturist air ticket agency at Lenina 135 (✆ 0612 230 562; f 0612 246 609; e hamalia@mail.zp.ua; www.travel.zp.ua). The much larger Dnepropetrovsk Airport is only 45 minutes away by car and is the better option, with direct flights to Europe and the rest of Ukraine.

By rail Zaporizhzhya's train station is at the very end (or very beginning) of Prospect Lenina and has only just been remodelled. It now sports a stunning interior complete with a full-size copy of Repin's *Zaporizhian Cossacks* painted on the ceiling (see page 413). At one end is a comfy climatised waiting room that costs 5UAH to enter. From Kiev there are three rail connections per day, taking from ten to 12 hours. The main 'Zap' train leaves at around 20.00 and gets to Kiev at 07.30. Locally, practically all Zaporizhian trains come through Dnepropetrovsk (1 to 2 hours) as well as all trains between Russia and Crimea, meaning there are daily connections to Kharkiv (7 hours) and Simferopol (7 hours). In summer, the number of trains doubles, yet space becomes more limited. Local east–west trains join Krivy Rih (2 hours) and Donetsk (4 hours) daily, as well as Odessa (10 hours) and Lviv (24 hours). Book train tickets at the station or at any of the hotel offices.

By bus The central bus station is at Lenina 22 (✆ 0612 244 046). Local buses and *marshrutka* run back and forth from Dnepropetrovsk (1 to 2 hours), as well as the airports and Donetsk (3 hours). **Avtoluks** buses go from Kiev (9 hours) to Yalta (8 hours) and back via Zaporizhzhya twice a day (17 hours total).

By boat A lot of cruises come in at Port Lenina at Leonova 1A, but the central river station is at Gliserna 1 (✆ 0612 641 530). As with all boats on the Dnepr, schedules are highly sporadic so it's best to check with the Inturist Hotel (see *Where to Stay*) or else investigate your options on arrival. A typical local boat tour will circumnavigate Khortytsya Island in about an hour and a half.

GETTING AROUND Prospekt Lenina runs northwest to southeast and is the city's heart, with everything of note on it or less than a block away. The No 12 tram goes all the way to the train station, but this can be a rather slow way to travel. *Marshrutka* run up and down the entire length of Lenina – check to make sure the sign says *po proskpektu* (по проспекту) to avoid taking the scenic route all the way to Zaporizhzhya's less scenic neighbourhoods. Zaporizhzhiyan Taxis are also fairly cheap; dial locally ✆ 008, 056 or ✆ 0612 490 490.

WHERE TO STAY

Inturist Zaporizhzhya Lenina 135; ✆ 0612 230 500; f 0612 230 575; e hotel@intourist.com.ua; www.intourist.com.ua. Good things have happened to Inturist in recent years, so this is really the best option for a night's sleep in the city, thanks to its great location on the square and at the centre of all things connected to the local tourist industry. Rooms are divided into 3 classes: economy, standard and business, with the business-class rooms occupying the top 2 floors of the hotel. B/fast is inc, credit cards are accepted and the staff speak English. In addition, Inturist houses 2 quality restaurants, the city's main travel agency, a sauna, night club and secure parking. These are clean, tastefully renovated rooms of international standard, complete with queen-size beds and in-room high-speed internet. *Sgls US$80, dbls US$90, jacuzzi suites US$130, 2-room apts US$150.* 'Standard' class also includes new furniture: sgls US$60; dbls US$75. 'Economy' class still feels like economy but is inexpensive: US$30–40.

🏠 **Hotel Ukrayina** Lenina 162A; ☎ 0612 346 673; f 0612 890 505; e gukr@reis.zp.ua; www.ukraine.zp.ua. Once the haunt of Soviet industry bosses, the Ukrayina still affects a slightly Soviet air, but maintains a clean and professional operation with spotless bathrooms, friendly service and a quiet atmosphere. The hotel is right across the street from the Inturist and about half of the rooms have been renovated with new beds and furniture, including queen-size beds in the suites (the hotel is most proud of its suite with mirrored ceilings; US$100/night). There's also a classy Finnish sauna and a traditional Ukrainian b/fast is inc; credit cards

accepted. *New rooms US$65 for sgls and US$70 for dbls, and slightly lesser quality rooms cost US$40–60.*

🏠 **Hotel Praga** Shevchenko 28; ☎ 0612 240 711; e praga@mail.zp.ua. One of Zaporizhzhya's latest arrivals – a small boutique motel with 'luxury' accommodation, meaning dbl beds, en-suite bathrooms and an intimate setting. B/fast inc, credit cards accepted. *Rooms US$80–100.*

🏠 **Teatralnaya** Chekistov 23; ☎ 0612 642 438. Those on small budgets will find refuge at the slightly dilapidated Stalinist hotel right next to Zaporizhzhya's dramatic theatre (one block off Lenina). Cheery Ukrainian murals and Soviet-era stained glass brighten the place up and despite appearances, there is always hot water. A few rooms have been renovated to a degree: a dbl luxury suite (with heating and cooling) costs US$70 but you'd be better off spending that at one of the other hotels. *Sgls/dbls with bath and toilet US$30/$40. Hostel-type accommodation with a shared bathroom down the hall is US$20 sgl, US$24 dbl; cash only.*

✗ **WHERE TO EAT AND DRINK** Zaporizhzhya's high street has switched on the bright lights so that as long as you're cruising Prospekt Lenina, you're likely to find something to suite your fancy. The restaurants in the two main hotels are worthy of mention and accept credit cards.

✗ **Vremena Goda (Time of the Year)** Lenina 135, 2nd floor; ☎ 0612 230 800. The Inturist's Vremena Goda is a sunny European-style restaurant specialising in poultry, pasta and salads. *Entrées from US$6; open 12.00–midnight.*

✗ **Banzay** Lenina 135; ☎ 0612 230 900; e info@tsa-tsa.com.ua; www.tsa-tsa.com. More upscale, this is a clever little Japanese restaurant with a Japanese chef rolling fresh sushi and cutting sashimi at the bar. *Sushi from US$5, mains from US$10; open 12.00–midnight.*

✗ **Ukrayina** Offers a traditional menu from all of Ukraine's regions (borsch, meat and fish). *Mains from US$7; open 08.00–midnight;*

✗ **Pau Bau Pizzeria** Tsentralny 4; ☎ 0612 200 476. Right next to the Inturist and on the bustling central square. Their pizza is big and delicious and inexpensive. *Pizza around US$5; open 10.00–23.00.*

♀ **O'Brien's Pub** Lenina 169; ☎ 0612 325 723. A little walk north takes you to the requisite Irish watering hole serving good meals and Guinness. *Open 12.00–midnight.*

✗ **Traktir** Gorkovo 43; across from hotel Teatralnaya; ☎ 0612 646 517. For fine dining Zaporizhzhya-style, enjoy a gourmet meal here with

its turn-of-the-century setting, quiet mood and old-time recipes (eg: rabbit in mustard sauce, German strudel). They also serve refined Ukrainian cuisine and some nice vegetarian dishes, with entrées from US$8. *Open 11.00–midnight.*

✗ **Park Avenue** Lenina 87A; ☎ 0612 138 188. There are plenty of cafés all the way up and down Lenina, some better than others; for something a little more modern and upscale (with great steak) try this grill. *Entrées from US$10; open 24 hours.*

✗ **Vkusnyashka Café** Lenina 58; ☎ 0612 643 267. If you want to eat the way Zaporizhzhya natives do, this is the place. This cute neighbourhood eatery serves simple meals of fish, steak, pizza and the like, both quickly and with ambience.

☕ **Lira Coffee House** Lenina 146. For coffee and dessert, Lira Coffee House is a must. Less than a block from the Inturist, this quaint new cafe is the only smoke-free establishment in Zaporizhzhya, serving real espresso, 'American-style' coffee, cappuccino, and the best cup of hot chocolate (black or white) in all of Ukraine, all for just US$1. The pastries and ice-cream sundaes also seem to be made with love. *Open 09.00–23.00.*

LOCAL TOUR OPERATORS Inturist Zaporizhzhya still functions as the leading tour operator in the area, with a convenient walk-in office on the main floor (*Lenina 135;* ↘ *0612 336 127; www.intourist.com.ua; open 09.00–17.30, closed Sat–Sun*). This is the easiest place in the city to buy train, plane or bus tickets, arrange cruises, visits to Khortytsa and English-language city tours, and to rent a car.

WHAT TO SEE AND DO Anyone who is up to it should definitely walk across the Dneproges Dam for the view of Khortytsya and the river, and for the swell of Stalinist emotion that grips the heart in the presence of this famous Soviet landmark. Otherwise, enjoy the beauty of Khortytsya Island and the kind and peculiar people of Zaporizhzhya.

Khortytsya Island ХОРТИЦЯ Of the Dnepr's 256 islands, Khortytsya is the largest at 12km long and 2.5km wide. It is also one of the most beautiful places in the country, giving a taste of what the Ukrainian steppe looked like before it was settled. Walking around in summer reveals an incredible display of wildflowers, grassy meadows and willow trees that drag their branches in the blue Dnepr. The north end of the island is very rocky, with slanted cliffs up to 30m high, while the south end of the island sinks into river marsh with numerous rivulets and flooded basins. The diversity of the landscape over such a small space makes the island ideal for exploring on foot, while the amount of greenery makes it hard to believe that a grimy industrial city of one million people is just on the other side of the river. The Ukrainian government declared the area a national park in 1993 but much work remains to be done in order to identify and fix up the sights and to facilitate accessibility.

The island is named for the Slavic god of the sun, Khoros, although some believe it comes from the Turkish root *ort* ('the middle'), since it is in the centre of the Dnepr. In spring and summer, things are very green, with lots of dark purple flowers, steppe grass and lovely butterflies. Guides will tell you that there are over 100 archaeological sites on the island, dating from the Stone Age up to the time of the Cossacks; however, few are in plain view or clearly identified except for some vague Cossack ruins and the old burial mounds. Some well-marked trails make walking easier. If you are tempted to wade in the water, beware of *chyortov orekhy* (hell nuts), the spiny seedpod of a Dnepr water plant that grows in shallow water. Their iron hard spikes will easily pierce through anything and cause tremendous pain to tender feet.

The first Zaporizhian Sich (there were actually eight in all) was founded near Khortytsya in around 1550 by *hetman* Dmytro Baida. Today the island of Baida lies in the river's eastern channel, and on its northern end are the remnants of the first 16th-century Cossack fortress, built to ward off Tatar invaders. A wooden stockade was later built on the main island, and the ranks of Cossacks increased with the arrival of a number of runaway serfs, freemen and societal nonconformists who were all granted equal status as part of the Sich. Present-day Ukrainians view the Zaporizhian Cossacks as the predecessors to the country's independent government.

Where to stay and eat There are two hotels located on Khortytsya itself, although both are rather small.

🏠 **Hotel Khortytsya** ↘ 0612 865 385. The old Inturist-style resort that fills up quickly in summer, located just across the bridge. Standards are rather low, as are the prices. *Sgls from US$35.*

🏠 **Hotel Nayada** Nauchny Gorodok 76A; ↘ 0612 865 334. A much nicer private luxury hotel with a private beach on the river. There are only a few rooms but each is large, clean and comfortable, with

24hr hot water. *US$60 sgl; US$100 dbl.*

✗ **Cossack Podvira** Out on the island there are a few different 'Cossack' restaurants, open only in summer. The best of these is, a restaurant establishment that sells package deals that generally include transport to and from your hotel or boat, a meal and a Cossack riding show. Call ☎ 0612 332 556 for more infomation, or enquire at the Zaporizhzhya Intourist travel office.

✗ **Zaporozka Sich** ☎ 0612 522 552. Another club on the island that serves hearty Ukrainian meals but forces the Cossack theme a bit much. *Mains from US$8.*

✗ **Slobodka** Gorkovo 115; ☎ 0612 642 727. Not just a restaurant, Slobodka also features a sauna, bar and small convenience store selling handy travel food and drinks. This modern café is popular among young people and serves *square meals for under US$10.*

What to see and do The island's main attraction is the very impressive **Zaporizhian Cossack Museum** (☎ *0612 527 317; open 10.00–17.00, closed Mon; entrance 3UAH, 6UAH with a guide; www.hortica.org.ua).* The iron sculpture at the entrance of the museum shows the sun, oak tree, leaves and arrows, an array of important Cossack imagery, and the actual building is not far from the ruins of the original fortress gate of the Zaporizhian Sich. The museum covers the whole history of the city and the island, and visitors should expect to spend at least two hours here if they want to see everything in the exhibit. The guided tour is pretty informative and interesting, and is now available in English, Polish and French.

The exhibition begins with artefacts from the Stone and Bronze ages and then shows one of the country's best collections of Scythian objects, which were mostly found on the island on current archaeological digs. A variety of daggers, swords, arrowheads and slingshots show the warlike nature of the Scythians, who believed they were the descendants of Hercules (via his son Skyf). Several large burial mounds (*kurhany*) can still be seen on the island, from which the jewellery, weapons and armour have been recovered. To watch over the dead, Scythian 'stone grandmothers' were placed on the mounds, and several of these are on display in the museum and around the island. There are also objects left on the island from the days of Kievan Rus traders, including a 9th-century iron anchor, as well as archaeological finds from the Mongol and Tatar invasions. Another major portion of the museum is dedicated to the life and history of the Zaporizhian Cossacks. Weapons, clothing and a full-size Cossack ship are just a few of the items on display, along with famous portraits of rebel Cossack leaders Khmelnytsky and Ivan Mazepa, surrounded by some of their own belongings.

After the Cossacks left, Khortytsya fell prey to Catherine the Great's ethnic juggling. The empress assigned the land to a large group of Swiss Mennonites, whose lives are also represented in the exhibit. The Swiss were known to be peaceful, but they are also to blame for the lack of trees on the island today. Unable to deal with the Ukrainian winter, they burnt all the wood they could find. (One ancient oak spent 6,000 years underwater before popping up to the surface; it's now on display near the museum entrance.) The Mennonites stayed for more than a century and some of their buildings can still be seen on the lower half of the island. The museum also features several dramatic dioramas, including one that portrays the death of Kievan Prince Svyatoslav, who was unexpectedly attacked by the Pechenegs, supposedly on Khortytsya (see page 16). Another display shows the Soviet liberation of Zaporizhzhya in a World War II battle on 14 October 1943 (Hitler is rumoured to have come to Zaporizhzhya on four different occasions during the Nazi occupation).

Within walking distance of the museum are two interesting ancient sights: a Scythian **burial mound**, or *kurhan,* and the Neolithic **Stone Ring**, a sacred stone circle in the spirit of Stonehenge but slightly less impressive. Further out on the northwestern side of the island, visitors can glimpse the remnants of the 18th-

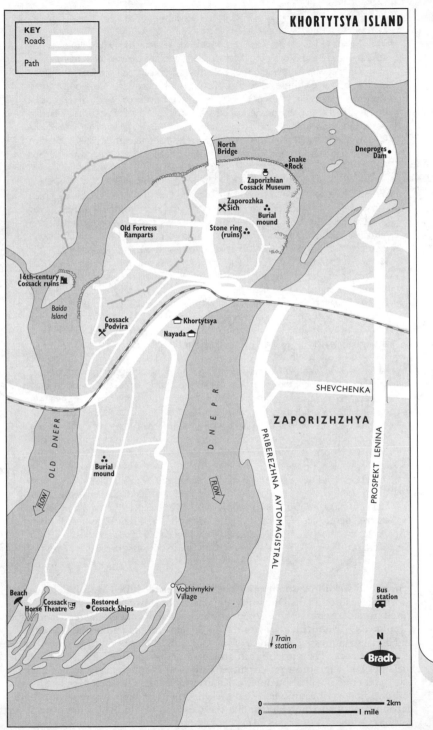

KEY
Roads
Path

North
Bridge

Snake
Rock

Dneproges
Dam

Zaporizhian
Cossack Museum

Zaporozhka
Sich

Burial
mound

Stone ring
(ruins)

Old Fortress
Ramparts

16th-century
Cossack ruins

Baida
Island

Cossack
Podvira

Khortytsya

Nayada

SHEVCHENKA

ZAPORIZHZHYA

D N E P R

PRIBEREZHNA AVTOMAGISTRAL

PROSPEKT LENINA

OLD DNEPR

FLOW

FLOW

Burial
mound

Vochivnykiv
Village

Beach

Cossack
Horse Theatre

Restored
Cossack Ships

Bus
station

Train
station

N

Bradt

0   2km
0   1 mile

The Zaporizhian Cossacks were responsible for securing the 'wild field' of south-central Ukraine and ousting the Tatar invaders, and are credited with many other daring feats of war. Despite the rough and rowdy reputation of the Cossacks, life in the Zaporizhian Sich resembled that of a warrior's monastery. No women were allowed on the island, the violation of which was punishable by death. It is probably true that Cossacks were prone to heavy drinking, but this was permitted only in peacetime. New entrants took vows, underwent a series of tests and rituals and lived by a semi-disciplined code. Legend suggests that one of these rites of passage required a Cossack to single-handedly steer a boat upriver through the Dnepr rapids.

The official mark of the Cossack was his haircut, called the chub: the head was shaved bald except for a single ponytail springing from the top of the head. A man had to live as a Cossack for seven years before he was granted the title and allowed to wear the chub. Until that time, regardless of his age, he was referred to as a *molodnyk* (youth) and a bowl was placed on his head and the hair trimmed around the edge. Cossack dress was distinctive: long baggy trousers were convenient for hiding curved swords and horseback riding. An oversized coloured sash was used as a belt or for a carrier bag slung over the shoulder. Different colours of sashes held different meanings and were supposed to be at least 3m long and wide 'like the Dnepr'. Tying the sash involved at least two people, or else it could be hung from a tree and slowly wound around the waist. The other vital Cossack accessory was a clay pipe. A Ukrainian saying often attributed to the Zaporizhian Sich is 'Lyulky ta zhinky ne pozyhai!' (A pipe or a wife can never be changed).

At its greatest, the Sich consisted of 20,000 Cossacks of 72 different nationalities. In war, the Cossacks abided by vague military hierarchies, but within the Zaporizhian Sich, the group was highly democratic and each Cossack had an equal voice around the table of the *rada,* a title used now by the Ukrainian parliament. An elected *hetman* presided and led the Cossacks into battle, but decisions about who to attack and who to join forces with were often made democratically. Land on the island was distributed among the ranks and when they were not preparing for war the Cossacks farmed their plots, hunted and fished, and kept bees for honey.

Of all the various Cossack bands, the Zaporizhian Sich was the largest, most serious, and most annoying to the Russians, Poles and Turks. Catherine the Great offered a 1,000 rouble bounty on the head of any Zaporizhian, and her forces attacked the Sich in 1775, razing it to the ground. The Cossacks scattered (some went to farm the Black Sea coast and others joined new bands), but today it is still the Zaporizhians who are remembered as Ukraine's greatest heroes.

century Cossack fortress ramparts. These walls guarded the Cossack flotilla, once a formidable force on the Dnepr River and Black Sea. Two of these ships have been raised from the bottom of the Dnepr and are currently undergoing renovation; the **Chaika** and **Brigantina** date from 1736–39, close to the end of the Cossack era, and both are impressive examples of the Cossacks' ability to fight on water as well as on horseback. The museum can arrange tours for anyone interested in seeing the ships, although most pre-arranged tours will stop here anyway. Most group tours and cruises will also come to Khortytsya for the **Cossack Horse Show,** a rousing outdoor theatre where Cossack he-men test their bravery with death-defying equestrian stunts not unlike the Cossacks of old. The show runs from April to October (↘ *0612 348 241*).

Getting out to Khortytsya is not too difficult, but getting around the island itself is tricky. Taking a taxi from anywhere on Proskpekt Lenina should cost around US$5. Otherwise the No 30 *marshrutka* runs to and from the island. The best way to walk to Khortytsya is to cross the Dneproges Dam on foot, circle around, cross the northern bridge and walk along the northern coast of the island to the museum (about 5km).

Bear in mind that the island is large and fairly sparse, except for a few scattered villages and farms. Many come over to the island for serious hiking or biking, both worthy pursuits on Khortytsya.

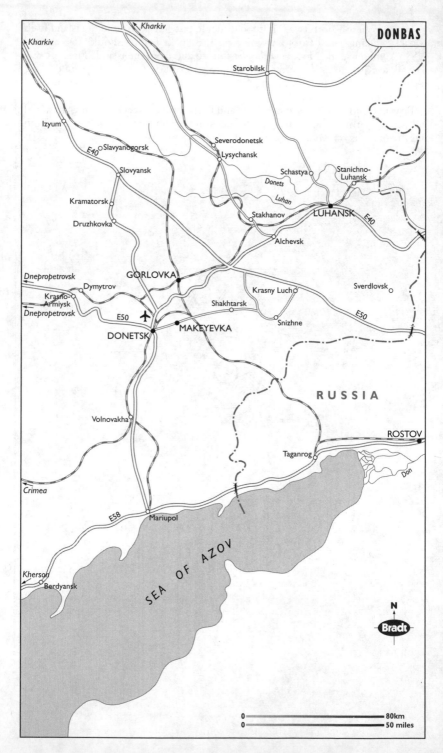

Kharkiv

Kharkiv

Starobilsk

Izyum

E40 Slavyanogorsk

Severodonetsk
Lysychansk

Slovyansk

Schastya

Stanichno-
Luhansk

Donets

Luhan

Kramatorsk

Stakhanov

LUHANSK E40

Druzhkovka

Alchevsk

Dnepropetrovsk

Dymytrov

GORLOVKA

Krasno-
Armiysk

Krasny Luch

Sverdlovsk

Dnepropetrovsk

E50

Shakhtarsk

DONETSK MAKEYEVKA

Snizhne

E50

RUSSIA

Volnovakha

ROSTOV

Taganrog

Don

Crimea

E58

Mariupol

SEA OF AZOV

Kherson
Berdyansk

N

Bradt

| 0 | 80km |
| 0 | 50 miles |

14

Donbas
Донбас

The wholly Russian population and machine-wrought landscape of the Donets River basin contrast sharply with the nostalgic Ukrainian dream of quaint survival on the open steppe. The cluster of mines, factories and cities between Donetsk and Luhansk is home to Ukraine's most obvious proletariat and represents the industrial heart of the country. Only the intrepid few who travel to Ukraine's far east can hope to understand this country's complex spectrum of experience.

Coal (*ugol*) dominates space and time in Donbas. For the past 200 years, millions of lives have been dedicated to extracting load after load of anthracite (for thermal power) and bituminous coal (for coking steel) up from the ground. An inverted earth bares open pits turned to misshapen mountains of black slag, and the strong smell of burning carbon is bound to become a fond souvenir of your visit. Things are not all smokestacks and rust piles though. Sunflowers cover the fields of Donbas in summer, and people still tend to their vegetable patches and goat herds like they do in the rest of the country. Further away from Donetsk there are some lovely green areas of hills and forest. Even more comforting to travellers should be the strong confirmation that what you see is what you get. There is no room for tourist show among the stark setting of Ukraine's dirty work, and for every Ukrainian who snubs the east as a polluted coal stove, there is another one that calls it home. Plus, it's touching to visit a place that makes you cough.

HISTORY

The Donbas was a largely unsettled area until Russia began its industrial revolution in the 19th century. The nearby metallurgical centres of Kryvy Rih and Zaporizhzhya required tremendous amounts of energy and the carboniferous deposits of the east facilitated a concentration of industry. By the time of Tsar Nikolai II, 99% of the coal used in the empire came from the Donbas. A demand for semi-skilled labour brought a continuous influx of ethnic Russians, who formed a strong political bloc in support of communism and still constitute a major force in Ukraine. Throughout the Soviet Union, the coal miners of Donbas were lauded as national heroes of labour, especially during World War II when they were forced to flood all the mines to prevent any resource benefit to Germany. In 1989, after the uncertain years of *perestroika*, the miners went on strike to demand better living conditions and higher wages, voicing national discontent with the communist government. Political leaders responded positively and without punishment, ushering in a new era of change, but what followed offered little solace. The first decade of Ukrainian independence has hit the industrial workers hardest as the demand for Soviet production has all but ceased. Strikes in and around Donetsk continued throughout the 1990s as inflation ruined miners' pensions and salaries, and the relaxed state of governance made mines even more dangerous. President Kravchuk settled with the miners by printing so much money that it nearly doubled Ukraine's GDP and exacerbated inflation everywhere else in the country. In 2002, another deadly explosion confirmed once more that Ukraine's mines were grossly outdated and decrepit, but closing the mines is not an option when so many people depend on the meagre but regular monthly income. Donbas looks longingly to the stability of its industry under the former Soviet government and the area is known for its fierce support of Victor Yanukovych, a local hero and the big loser in the Orange Revolution. Ethnic tensions with the centre and west of the country are still real. Besides Crimea, Donbas is the only region to have both Russian and Ukrainian listed as official languages, but easterners still feel at odds within their own country and wonder if they are not on the wrong side of the border with Russia. There's no avoiding Ukraine's most vivid economic and political questions when travelling in Donbas, and while the rest of the country diligently tries to get foreigners to discard all notions of the Soviet-era, around here, hanging on to some of those preconceived ideas will help make sense of what Ukraine's transition to capitalism really means.

GETTING AROUND

Donbas is a concentrated region that was blessed with lots of railways and paved roads for industrial use. Donetsk is the main transport hub to and from Kiev, Kharkiv and Dnepropetrovsk , and getting to Luhansk or Mariupol is a simple case of taking a further train. Local buses tend to be very slow and tedious, but frequent, while the private bus service is a quick and efficient way to connect to the rest of the country. *Marshrutka* also join all the smaller towns together and are quick, if a little cramped.

DONETSK ДОНЕЦЬК

The 'black pearl' of the east is the country's heavy industrial capital and the largest city in Donbas. Before it was a ever a city, the entire area was a large-scale engineering project so that today, coal belts and slag heaps dot the city skyline and most of the round lakes you see are former pit mines filled with water. Coal is such a pervasive element in the life of Donetsk, that their world famous football team is named the *Shakhtyory* ('The Miners') and the various city monuments feature burly men gripping oversized jackhammers.

Donetsk bemoaned the break-up of the Soviet Union more than anywhere else in Ukraine, yet the reality of its coal resource paired with Donetsk's infamously unrestrained oligarchs has quickly turned the city into a booming metropolis. Unlike many other million-inhabitant cities of Ukraine, Donetsk actually *feels* like a big city, with shiny modern buildings, bright lights and more flashy cars than you can count. Tree-lined streets, big square parks and a recent dedication to cleanliness also contribute to the urban buzz. With such a large base for energy, chemical and metal production, business travellers are the most likely visitors to Donetsk; however, the city is also fairly conducive to curious wandering.

HISTORY The city of Donetsk was founded in 1869 at the site of an earlier attempt at coal mining. The Welshman John Hughes – an entrepreneur from Merthyr Tydfil – was offered a contract by Tsar Alexander II to start the New Russia Company with the intention of producing smelted iron and eventually steel for railroad construction. Most of the first railway tracks in Russia and Ukraine were hammered out in Donetsk, including those used to build the Trans-Siberian railroad. The town built to house the collection of coal miners and steelworkers was called Yuzovka ('Little Hughes') after the Welshman, and the concentration of so many industrial labourers meant Yuzovka was a Bolshevik stronghold throughout the revolution. Both White and Red armies fought viciously for control over the fuel-rich city during the civil war. After Lenin's death in 1924, 'Yuzovka' was changed to 'Stalino', a name it kept until 1961. The name of the nearby River Don seemed a safe bet after the legacy of one foreign businessman and a mentally disturbed dictator, so the city has since been called Donetsk. Heavy unemployment and intensive pollution weighed on Donetsk during the early years of Ukrainian independence, yet with the richest mineral deposits in the country, the city quickly secured its wealth and stability. Thus the famous Donetsk clans progressed from small-town mafia holdings to vying for power with Kiev – a very real tension that continues today.

GETTING THERE AND AWAY

By air Donetsk Airport is on the north side of the city on Vzletnaya and now counts itself as one of Ukraine's busiest international airports and the hub of the quickly growing local airline **Donbassaero** (*Artyoma 167;* ⚊ *0622 588 482;* f *0623 456 761;* e *zakaz@donbass.aero; www.donbass.aero*). You can also buy air tickets at **Pallada-Avia** (*Universitetskaya 2A;* ⚊ *0623 456 810*) or at any of the tour agencies listed here. Direct daily flights connect Donetsk to both Kiev Zhulyany and Borispol (1½ hours), and Moscow Domodedovo (2 hours). Regular flights also service Odessa (2 hours) and Kharkiv (1 hour). Austrian Airlines also offers a daily service to and from Vienna and Lufthansa connects to Frankfurt and Munich, making Donetsk a good entry point into eastern Ukraine.

By rail Donetsk is the leading eastern destination for Ukrainian trains, so finding any direct train connection is not difficult. The daily train to and from Kiev, dubbed the 'Little Lump of Coal', leaves Kiev in the evening at around 21.00 and gets to Donetsk at 09.00 the next morning, travelling through Dnepropetrovsk (5 hours). There are daily rail connections with Luhansk (3 hours), Zaporizhzhya (4 hours), Kharkiv (8 hours), Simferopol (11 hours), Odessa (15 hours) and Lviv (28 hours). Frequent Russian trains between Moscow and the south of Russia pass through Donetsk; the first stop across the border is in Rostov-na-Donu (4 hours). Trains coming in and out of Donetsk are required to move very slowly so as not to cause any cave-ins in the mines beneath.

By bus Buses are quick and convenient around eastern Ukraine, especially for travel between Donetsk and Sloboda or the Dnepr region. The main station is at the south end of the city (*Ploschad Kommunarov;* ⚊ *0622 664 123*). Frequent public buses go to Luhansk (2½ hours) and to Mariupol (2 hours). There are also regular connections to Kharkiv (6 hours) and Dnepropetrovsk (4 hours). For overnight services to the capital, there's **Avtoluks** (*Aksakova 21;* ⚊ *0622 667 139*), and **Gunsel** (*Prospekt Kievsky 10;* ⚊ *062 385 6869*) also has a second daytime bus back and forth to Kiev (11 hours) via Poltava (7 hours) and Dnepropetrovsk (4 hours).

GETTING AROUND Thousands of coal mines tunnel beneath the city like an ant farm, which is the reason Donetsk has no metro. Getting around above ground is not terribly difficult since the city was thankfully planned by a British businessman and not a team of Soviet planners. Trams and trolleys run on the main boulevards (Artyoma, Universitetskaya, Mira and Kommunarov). For a taxi, call ⚊ 058 locally, or ⚊ 0622 530 160.

WHERE TO STAY Even though Donetsk is by no means a tourist town, a number of nice hotels have opened to accommodate foreign businessmen and local high-

ALEKSEI GRIGORYEVICH STAKHANOV (1906–77)

When Comrade Stalin let loose a series of five-year plans to industrialise the country in a speedy rush, many Soviet citizens (and party bosses) were secretly sceptical. Still, the party urged people to strive harder and produce more in order to bring the Soviet Union to its feet in record time. On 31 August 1935, a 29-year-old coal miner by the name of Aleksei Stakhanov extracted 102 tons of coal in just six hours during a work contest held by the local Komsomol ('Young Communist League') organisation.

At the time, this was ten times that of a miner working in England and 14 times that of fellow Soviet miners. The young man's feat was publicised as a grand achievement of matching self-will with social consciousness and soon the excitement of the Stakhanovite movement had taken over the USSR. Every worker was expected to take on superhuman work feats and those who didn't succeed were deemed saboteurs against the regime. The over-achievers were recognised as heroes of labour, a rare individual attention in an otherwise faceless collective society. As for Stakhanov, he was rewarded personally by Stalin, made a national hero and eventually became the Soviet Union's Minister of Mining Industry. The city of Stakhanov and Stakhanov mine (midway between Donetsk and Luhansk) still stand in his honour.

rollers, including Ukraine's most impressive hotel, the Donbass Palace. Most encouraging is the city's accepted tendency to charge per room rather than per guest. You might find Donetsk is the place to splurge a little, since you tend to get what you pay for in this town.

Luxury (all accept credit cards and include breakfast)

Donbass Palace Artyoma 80; ☎ 0623 434 333; f 0623 434 127; e info@donbasspalace.com; www.donbasspalace.com. The Donbass Palace is the country's very best hotel by international reputation and standard. Every detail has been carefully considered and every service is performed with the utmost elegance, to the point of being surreal. Aside from the chandeliers, gilded furniture, glass elevators, luxury spa and perfect rooms, there are 2 absolutely exquisite gourmet restaurants, a weekly chocolate buffet and an afternoon high tea that would put Queen Victoria to shame. The executive floor features personal butlers, whirlpool baths and a private chef. The hotel also offers wheelchair-accessible rooms and special services for disabled travellers. The hotel's concierge can and will do anything for you, including arranging personally guided, mile-underground tours to the coal mines or doorstep delivery of up-to-date newspapers from your choice of 80 different countries. *Sgl standard rooms US$320; junior suites with king-size beds US$400, larger suites US$500.*

Viktoria Mira 14A; ☎ 0623 814 700; f 0623 814 747; e info@victoria.ua; www.victoria.ua. Featuring the avant-garde design of 21st-century

Donetsk, the Victoria blends contemporary style with classic Russian hospitality, meaning rooms are fashionable and comfy, but the frequent parties downstairs can get raucous. The location in Park Komsomola is quite nice. *Dbl rooms from US$100.*

Prague Dubravnaya 101; ☎ 0623 811 166; f 0623 811 177; e prague@prague.donetsk.ua; www.prague.donetsk.ua. Intimate 'business' hotel with individually decorated rooms and optimal service for business travellers. *Rooms US$115–180.*

Legion Ovnatanyana 16A; ☎ 0623 859 565; e hotel@legion.dn.ua; www.hotel-legion.dn.ua. More a spa than a hotel, rooms are tactfully simple but elegant. All beds are at least queen size and the bathrooms are warm and spacious. A gourmet restaurant, health club and full-size swimming pool make the Legion a posh daytime hangout for prosperous locals. *Prices fall into 2 categories: 'prestige' for US$120 and the larger 'lux' for US$190.*

John Hughes Chelyuskintsev 157; ☎/f 0623 810 848; e hotel@johnhughes.dn.ua; www.johnhughes.dn.ua. In theory this hotel is built to look like 19th-century Yuzovka and advertises 'English' service, perhaps ironically. They do take care of their guests and can handle any request. There is

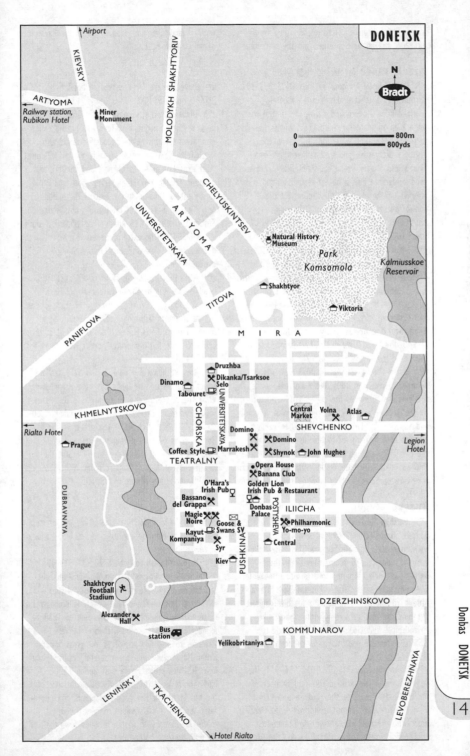

DONETSK

N

Bradt

0   800m
0   800yds

Airport

KIEVSKY

MOLODYKH SHAKHTYORIV

ARTYOMA
Railway station,
Rubikon Hotel

Miner
Monument

CHELYUSKINTSEV

UNIVERSITETSKAYA

ARTYOMA

Natural History
Museum

Park
Komsomola

Kalmiusskoe
Reservoir

TITOVA

Shakhtyor

Viktoria

PANIFLOVA

M I R A

KHMELNYTSKOVO

Druzhba
Dikanka/Tsarksoe
Selo

Dinamo
Tabouret

SCHORSKA

UNIVERSITETSKAYA

Domino

Central
Market

Volna

Atlas

SHEVCHENKO

Rialto Hotel

Prague

Coffee Style

Marrakesh

Domino

Domino
Shynok

John Hughes

Legion
Hotel

TEATRALNY

Opera House
Banana Club

O'Hara's
Irish Pub

Golden Lion
Irish Pub & Restaurant

DUBRAVNAYA

Bassano
del Grappa

Magie
Noire

Donbas
Palace

ILIICHA

POSTYSHEVA

Kayut
Kompaniya

Goose &
Swans SV

Philharmonic
Yo-mo-yo

Syr

Central

Kiev

PUSHKINA

Shakhtyor
Football
Stadium

Alexander
Hall

DZERZHINSKOVO

Bus
station

KOMMUNAROV

Velikobritaniya

LENINSKY

TKACHENKO

LEVOBEREZHNAYA

Hotel Rialto

a very limited number of rooms, but they are well furnished and all have internet, and the restaurant serves hearty Germanic food to match the Bavarian décor. *US$90–100.*

Middle range *(all accept credit cards)*

Central Hotel Artyoma 87; \/f 0623 323 332; e central@hotel-central.com.ua; www.hotel-central.com.ua Modern and flashy, the Central has set a high standard for welcoming business travellers to Donetsk. Location is central and convenient, attitudes progressive and the staff very efficient. There's also a gym, sauna, tour and ticket agency, a good conference hall, a decent restaurant and wi-fi internet on the main floor. *All rooms feature comfortable queen-size beds and shiny en-suite bathrooms; sgls US$85, corporate suites US$130, suites US$200.*

Rubikon Pryvokzalnaya 1; \ 0623 057 503; e rubicon@skif.net; www.rubikon-hotel.com. This brand-new hotel stands right next to the rail station and is convenient for anyone catching a train or just getting off. Rooms are clean and modern, beds and bathrooms are warm and comfortable. *A shared room (with a same-sex stranger) US$30 pp; sgls US$60, dbls US$70, suites US$120. Larger suites can be rented at half price for 12hr stays.*

Rialto Tkachenko 145; \ 0623 329 341. Refurnished nicely in 2001, the Rialto lies in the southwestern corner of the city and is best reached by cab. It uses a quirky classing system of regular and superior standards that are equal in comfort but not in floorspace. All bathrooms are new and the plumbing is good; most rooms come with showers, some with bath. An in-house tour agent can take care of ticket booking and the sauna and gym

are above average for this type of hotel. *Sgls US$80, dbls US$100.*

Dinamo Otechestvennaya 10; \ 0623 420 385; home.skif.net/~ticons. Ikea seems to be the major inspiration for this newly remodelled outfit, also located in the town centre. Quality of stay will meet most expectations for cleanliness and comfort, and a pleasant enough restaurant serves good food on sturdy tables. Dinamo is the best of the middle-range hotels in terms of price and guests' welfare. *Standard rooms US$45, junior suites US$60, 2-room suites US$100 (the extra room seems a bit unnecessary). Some unfinished rooms may be available for less.*

Atlas Shevchenko 20; \ 0622 939 116. This hotel is a 4-star by Ukrainian standards, which means nothing really; the advantage of staying here is that it comes with some of the benefits of a former Inturist hotel. *Rooms from US$40 up to the US$100 suite, but a good dbl can be had for US$70–90.*

Kiev Pushkina 4; \ 0622 920 525. Standard Soviet hotel where the lobby has been remodelled while the rest has gone on to preserve its former Soviet charm. As there are a limited number of dbls, the Kiev's a better choice if you are travelling alone. Hot water is only on during the day, and the rundown café is the only real amenity. Still, the location is not bad and b/fast is inc. *Sgl US$50, dbl US$90 and suites run up to US$100.*

Budget

Druzhba Universitetskaya 48; \ 0623 373 331; e drujba@mail.donbass.com; www.internet.dn.ua/hotel_drujba. This hotel follows a Soviet floorplan, so rooms may seem rather narrow, but new carpeting and furniture make for a decent night's stay. Note that the beds are a little hard and the bathrooms a bit disorganised, but how can you go wrong with a name like 'Friendship'? *Sgls US$30, dbls US$40, and the US$70 suites are good value for money if you are travelling as a pair.*

Shakhtyor Titova 15; \ 0622 556 614. The largest hotel in Donetsk in terms of number of rooms, situated next to the stadium and across from the city park. *Room standards remain very basic, and the dbls with shower and toilet cost US$25. Take away these amenities and the price*

drops all the way down to US$10 a night, or step up a level to remodelled 'lux' and pay US$40 for a suite.

Velikobritaniya Postysheva 20; \ 0623 051 951. The 'Great Britain' is crumbling and old, but has far more character than the flashy 4-stars elsewhere. This pink and blue beauty is probably the most historic building in the city, built in 1880 by founder John Hughes himself (hence the very Victorian rooms), and visited by the great Soviet writer Mayakovsky who spent several inspired nights here. It's also probably the best option for backpackers since it is within walking distance of the bus station, a few good restaurants and internet cafés, and the mine/stadium complex. *Cheapest room US$15 sgl with shared facilities down the hall; dbl with en-suite bathroom US$35.*

WHERE TO EAT

WHERE TO EAT Wow. Eating out in Donetsk competes with going to Disneyland as this has got to be the wackiest range of themed dining and costumed waiting staff in all of Ukraine. If you're the kind of traveller that insists on eating whatever the locals are having, right now the locals in Donetsk are craving anything that's strange, foreign, exotic or expensive. Sit back and enjoy the show – if you're lucky, you might still find a place that serves Russian/Ukrainian food. Nowadays, Donetsk is very comfortable with plastic, and unless otherwise noted, the following accept credit cards.

Ukrainian/Russian

Shynok Artyoma 127; ☎ 0622 920 282. The sarcastic Donetsk response to the Ukrainian folk restaurant-craze, complete with the décor and a satisfying menu of *borsch* and *varenniki*, as well as a few more adventurous dishes. *Mains from US$5; open 11.00–midnight.*

Dikanka/Tsarksoe Selo Schorsa 37. A combined Ukrainian/Russian restaurant with 2 separate menus and entrances. Both have authentic food without a lot of the frills found in most Donetsk establishments. *Varenniki* and *holubtsi* are to be had at Dikanka, while the 'Tsar's village' offers refined Russian classics (lots of meat!). *Mains from US$5–10; cash only; open 10.00–23.00.*

Goose & Swans SV Grinkevicha 11; ☎ 0623 375 156. Traditional Russian food served in a theme-park setting with a lively chef who cooks everything right in front of you. Try the very authentic fish soup (*ukha*). *Mains from US$6; open 11.00–midnight.*

Gourmet/fine dining

The Donbass Palace Artyoma 80; ☎ 0623 434 333; f 0623 434 334; e info@donbasspalace.com; www.donbasspalace.com. The mighty 'palace' features 4 different dining establishments, each a spectacle in its own right: Brasserie, L'Opera, fusion/sushi bar and Teppanyaki Grill. See below for details.

The Brasserie ☎ 0623 424 437. Evokes 1930s Paris, with a shaded sidewalk and light-to-heavy meals of pasta, salads, fish and steaks. The double-baked goat's cheese soufflé and *real* Dover sole are recommended. *Mains from US$20; open 06.30–midnight.*

L'Opera The über-grandiose dining experience, starting with Beluga caviar, moving on to duck confit or venison in elderberries, and ending with truffle-esque desserts, all on gold-rimmed plates. *Mains from US$25; open 12.00–23.00.*

A fusion/sushi bar ☎ 0623 434 452. Remains from the time when that was trendy, but serves more as a kind of happy-hour cocktail bar with fishy appetisers *Open 16.00 to 23.00.*

Teppanyaki Grill This Indonesian grill features an Indonesian chef who prepares such delicacies as the chilled cappuccino soup and a set 'Donbass' menu with (no kidding) *kobe* beef, if you are so inclined. *Open 11.00–23.00.*

Magie Noire Grinkevicha 7; ☎ 0623 042 969. French *restoratoniste* restaurant: sombre and chic, with dark mafia undertones. *Foie gras* seems to be a common ingredient. *Mains from US$25; open 12.00–midnight;*

Bassano del Grappa Grinkevicha 8; ☎ 0623 810 858; e bassano@mail.donbass.com, www.bassano.dn.ua. Quiet, upscale Italian restaurant with a strong reputation for classy food that's served with simple elegance. Fresh pasta, brick oven-baked pizzas, creative salads and delicate soups. The Italian wine list is quite distinctive, if pricey. *Mains from US$20; open 11.00–23.00.*

Exclusively Donetsk

Syr (Cheese) Universitetskaya 2A; ☎ 0623 324 888. The fluorescent yellow walls pock-marked with holes to make them look like cheese might be too disconcerting, but the food at this rather fancy restaurant is truly delicious. Dedicated to the unbeatable combination of cheese and wine, 'Cheese' serves anything with cheese in it: cheese soup, quiche, cheese puffs, blue-cheese steaks, cheesecake, mascarpone tiramisu, and 25 kinds of European cheese on their own. Their signature dish is a delicious fried camembert for US$9. *Mains US$10–15; open 11.00–23.00.*

Yo-mo-yo Illycha 15B; ☎ 0623 859 566. Fantastic Georgian restaurant in the heart of the city, meaning good food, great wine and good times. Along with the typical Georgian staples, they serve venison and pheasant, and they make their own vodka. *Mains from US$10; open 11.00–midnight.*

✗ **Banana Club** Artyoma 80A; ☏ 0623 125 858. Lively Cuban/South American café. There's a lot of cooking with alcohol, so everything on the menu comes flambéd if you want it to. The ethnic bent is largely affected, but also amusing. *Mains from US$10; open 11.00–midnight.*

✗ **Marrakesh** Artyoma 127; ☏ 0623 817 474. Exotic Moroccan and French food served amidst an outlandish North African atmosphere. Considered to be some of the finest food in Donetsk. Belly-dancing is also on the menu, of course. *Mains from US$10; open 11.00–midnight.*

✗ **Volna ('The Wave')** Shevchenko 24; ☏ 0623 858 080. 'Creative cuisine' means slightly oriental, slightly strange food, served beneath the serene glow of neon lights with live shows and more. *Mains from US$20; open 11.00–23.00.*

✗ **Domino** Artyoma 129A; ☏ 0623 343 019. Swanky, imitation French chateau serving refined, quasi-European food. *Mains from US$15 a head; open 11.00–midnight.*

✗ **Donetsk Burger** Gorkovo 146; ☏ 0623 450 027. Jazzy 1950s-style diner in downtown Donetsk. Big juicy burgers cooked to order for under US$5; *open 10.00–22.00.*

Cafés and bars

☕ **Tabouret** Khmelnytskovo 88; ☏ 0623 049 221. Very funky and progressive café with modern décor and a great menu of pancakes, sandwiches and light meals. Also, lots of cool non-alcoholic cocktails, a juice bar, and exotic tea and coffee. *Mains from US$4; cash only; open 09.00–23.00.*

☕ **Coffee Style** Universitetskaya 26; ☏ 0623 350 017; www.coffee-style.dn.ua. Cool, underground coffee house serving salads, light meals, desserts and ice cream sundaes. *Mains from US$3; cash only; open 07.00–23.00.*

☕ **Kayut Kompaniya** Grinkevicha 9 (downstairs); ☏ 0623 810 381. 'The Passenger's Lounge' is pretty much an A1 hipster hangout, complete with mood lighting, a high-maintenance menu, and attractive waiters that harbour lots of attitude. A good place for coffee, drinks or lunch. *Mains from US$7; open 09.00–23.00.*

♀ **Golden Lion Irish Pub & Restaurant** Artyoma 76A; ☏ 0623 817 676. The requisite Irish pub and restaurant with a very smoky atmosphere and stolid (read authentic) Irish cuisine, including thick mutton stew. *Mains from US$10; open 10.00–02.00.*

♀ **O'Hara's Irish Pub** Pushkina 18; ☏ 0623 810 074. The other requisite Irish drinking hole and more down to earth than the Golden Lion; a good place to watch footie and eat hot snacks. Cash only; *open 'til really late.*

Hotel restaurants Don't be afraid to check out some of Donetsk's upscale hotel restaurants, which continue to try and outdo one another. **Central** (*Artyoma 87;* ☏ *0623 323 332*) is still one of the best in the city, with elegant meals for under US$15 and a deserved reputation for good wine. **Prague**, **Victoria**, **John Hughes** and **Atlas** also manage praiseworthy restaurants.

If you're sick of restaurant fare, the **central market** is on the corner of Shevchenko and Chelyuskintsev, where anything and everything is sold hot, cold, live or packaged.

LOCAL TOUR OPERATORS AND TOURIST INFORMATION

Intours Universitetskaya 48; ☏ 0623 047 192; f 062 927 192; e Info2@intours.donetsk.ua; www.intours.donetsk.ua. Located on the first floor of the Hotel Druzhba in central Donetsk. They can arrange English- and German-language guides, tickets for transport or shows, and local excursions.

Pilot Donetsk Universitetskaya 16; ☏ 0623 452 117; e pilot@dc.dn.ua. Pilot is a national tour agency, but they do have a separate office in Donetsk with a special knowledge of the city. Contact them to arrange anything from train and plane tickets to local excursions, including visits to the mines and metallurgical factories. They also speak English and are very friendly.

WHAT TO SEE AND DO People in Donetsk dig coal, do business and party hard – an odd combination but a successful one for those who live here. Be sure to get a glance of the largest of many **miner monuments**, on the corner of Artyoma and Kievsky, which features a very sincere miner presenting a huge lump of coal, as if it's a divine gift. You might also enjoy walking around some of the city's old mining complexes. One of the largest is by the Shakhtyor football stadium – the tall hill of mineral refuse is called a *terrakon* and there are dozens like it throughout the city and the rest of the oblast. Tours into the famous **Donbas coal mines** are becoming more popular, but must be done with government permission, meaning with a licensed tour agency. Any upscale hotels listed here (and tour agencies) should be able to arrange a half-day tour. These include a shaky elevator ride about half a mile underground, and the pleasant choking feeling of blackness all around. Note that because of the increased demand to visit the mines, prices can run up to US$100 per person for a tour. The **Natural History Museum** of Donetsk (*Chelyuskintsev 189A;* ✆ *0622 553 474; open 10.00–17.00; entrance 5UAH*) tells the history of mining in the town and features a bit about regional culture, but is mostly a communist tribute to the glory of labour, a quaint monument in its own right. The **Opera House** (*Artyoma 82;* ✆ *0622 338 0969*) still brings culture to the mining masses, as does the **Philharmonic Concert Hall** (*Postisheva 117;* ✆ *0622 338 0018*), which tends to offer more contemporary entertainment of extraordinary quality.

Most activity seems to centre on Artyoma and Universitetskaya, but stepping away from the bustle takes you into the 'real Donetsk': the small wooden homes with goats in the yard, the street markets, and the quiet gardens that manage to grow in spite of the coal dust. If you're a walker, then don't be afraid to venture out and about. Donetsk follows a Soviet mentality when it comes to zoning, and is therefore somewhat illogical, meaning you can go from the barnyard to the nightlights of the main square in a matter of blocks. The oldest section of Donetsk that's still standing is down near Kommunarov, on the southern side of the city: a very interesting stroll, even if it is a slightly decrepit area. **Park Komsomola,** in the north, is a very pretty forest, and in summer it's a lively hangout for youngsters and families. Otherwise, Donetsk is a crazy city for a night out on the town, with more nightclubs and discos than perhaps even Kiev. There are opportunities for clubbing and gambling every night – check out the most recent copy of *Affiche Donetsk* for the latest listings.

OUTSIDE DONETSK If you get a chance to escape the industrial glitz of Donetsk, then definitely take it. The outer oblast is nowhere near as dreary as the urban coal mines suggest. To the north, the landscape becomes more hilly – part of Ukraine's low eastern plateau that gets little attention despite its greenery and beauty. To the south, the steppe flattens out into the low beaches and grey shores of the Sea of Azov.

Gorlovka ГОРЛОВКА Mention **Gorlovka** to a Ukrainian and you'll often get a facial response of disgust or bewilderment. Famous for its black snow in winter and incredibly high rates of lung cancer, Ukraine's most austere industrial outpost consists of one single thoroughfare surrounded by sad concrete buildings and burned-out smokestacks. And yet, Ukraine's most Stalinist of urban clusters is not all doom and gloom. Fate would have it that the country's most unappealing city is inhabited by the nicest people (really!).

Gorlovka was founded as one of a series of frontier mining camps in 1867, just as the industry of Donetsk was taking hold and expanding. The city got special attention during Stalin's five-year plans, supplying coal for the rest of the Soviet Union. After the mines closed in the mid-1990s, the population plummeted to a mere 300,000, but with the recent introduction of light industry, the town's fortunes seem to be picking up. A significant student population also keeps things hopping – this is home to the Gorlovka Institute

FC SHAKHTYOR DONETSK

Few places in the world are immune from the joys of football, not even dirty Donetsk. The game was played in the grassless fields here from the very first days that the miners moved in from Russia. An official government team was established in 1936 and named Stakhonovets Stalino – a team which was made up largely of local miners, and which played in the evolving USSR league. During the Soviet era, the 'Miners' (renamed in 1963) took four Soviet cups and gained a huge following across Ukraine and Russia. In 1992 the team went private, and FC Shakhtyor Donetsk have since won the Ukrainian championship in 2002 and 2005. Their incredible popularity has expanded beyond Ukraine and across Europe, so that it is not unusual to see the telltale bright orange shirts and Soviet-esque football crest proclaiming loyalty to the good old boys of Donbas.

As with any football team that's worth anything, acquiring tickets to a Shakhtyor game is a matter of either pure luck or strategy. In principle, tickets can be purchased by calling the ticket office (☏ 0623 434 293), visiting their website (*www.shakhtyor.donbass.com*) or going to club headquarters (*Artyoma 86A;* ☏ *0623 349 898*). Still, it helps to have an inside connection. Ask a friend, business colleague or your hotel concierge. It should also be mentioned that Shakhtyor paraphernalia (bright orange and black banners, T-shirts, pens, balls, etc.) are the souvenir of choice from Donetsk.

for Foreign Languages, one of the best linguistics schools in the world, where dozens of languages are taught. Several key figures among Ukraine's rising generation of professionals are graduates of the institute, including many of the talented and well-spoken guides that you may have encountered in your travels. If you are young or simply looking for speakers of any language, pay a visit to Rudakova 27. The very pretty pink church on the main drag is also a singular rose in an otherwise grey city.

It takes a little less than an hour to get to Gorlovka from Donetsk – there are *marshrutka* back and forth all day long, or you can usually talk a taxi down to about US$25 for the trip. Most trains in the direction of Kharkiv will also make a longish stop in Gorlovka. If you're spending the night, try **Hotel Rodina** (*Dmitrova 46;* ☏ *0624 228 282*). Rooms cost US$30 for a single, US$40 for a double and US$80 for suites. The hotel is still in a state of semi-renovation, but there's also a wonderful little café named Barnsley, in honour of Gorlovka's fellow coal-mining sister city in South Yorkshire (*Pobeda 67A;* ☏ *0624 227 061*). The food is both English and 'pub', with mains from US$6 (*open 10.00–23.00*).

Makeyevka MAKEEBKA The largest of the Donetsk suburbs started as a smelting plant that quietly grew into a huge residential camp for the mines at Dmitrievsk, one of the very oldest settlements in eastern Ukraine (founded in 1690). In Stalinist fashion, the emerging industrial city of the early 20th century took the less Orthodox-sounding name of the small country village that it swallowed up – tiny Makeyevka. The city now has a population of half a million, and many of the people who say they live in Donetsk actually live here.

Despite its coal-mining legacy, Makeyevka is rather green and pleasant. Over a hundred *marshrutka* shoot back and forth to Makeyevka daily, but a taxi should cost around US$15. For longer stays, there's the remodelled and fairly modern **Hotel Victoria** (*Terrikonnaya 3;* ☏ *062 382 9100;* f *062 382 8926;* e *hotelvicktory@skif.net*). Singles cost US$55, doubles US$65 and suites US$95. There's a nice in-house restaurant as well.

SLAVYANOGORSK СЛАВЯНОГОРСЬК

A popular destination is the historic town of **Slavyanogorsk**, located about 2½ hours north of Donetsk, midway on the road to Kharkiv. Like so many cave sites in Ukraine, the chalk cliffs of Svyatogorsk were discovered and claimed by early Christian believers and have since become renowned holy sites in Orthodoxy. After Byzantine Emperor Constantine V decreed icon veneration a heresy in the 8th century AD, stalwart believers and several schools of icon painters scattered to the far edges of Christendom, including the hills up and around the Donets River, and its very clean tributary, the Severskiv River. Here, among the hidden caves, they could worship their icons in secret and practise their art freely. Over the centuries, a community emerged from the cave churches known as **Svyatogorsk Monastery**, or the 'Holy Mountain'. **St Nikolai's Church** rests atop the highest cliff and was founded first as an underground cave chapel before the above-ground portion was constructed in the late 17th century, hence it's rather Muscovite appearance. The church is small and ornate, but history buffs can be confident in knowing that this is one of the least disturbed pieces of architecture from this era. The monastery is still very active, and there's also a wooden church (most likely from the early 19th century), which is extremely rare for this eastern half of Ukraine.

Buses and taxis can get you to Slavyanogorsk from either Kharkiv or Donetsk, but one should also consider going on an organised day trip (ask any of the agencies listed). The best time to visit is in the autumn, when the leaves are beginning to change colour in the Severskiv valley, but regardless of the time of year, this is probably the most natural (and beautiful) spot in all of Donetsk oblast.

Located just outside Slavyanogorsk, the **Svyatograd Hotel** is a complex of cottages with a series of individually decorated themed rooms (*Kuibysheva 59;* \ *0626 253 008;* f *0626 255 061*). Standard rooms go for US$75 and up (for two), family rooms for US$100 and more elaborate suites for US$150.

MARIUPOL МАРІУПОЛЬ

The largest city on the Sea of Azov, Mariupol is part steel-mill, part seaside resort, and has recently become the chosen weekend getaway for those coming from the more sullen and landlocked Donetsk. In the summer, the beaches are packed with sunbathers from all over Donbas, and a limited tradition of seaside nightlife continues year-round despite the unpleasant industrial plant that makes the air taste bad. Built at the mouth of the Kalmius River, Mariupol was so named by the large influx of Greek immigrants who arrived in the 18th century and who remain the prominent face of the city today.

One of the most upscale hotels in town is the **European** (*Primorsky 9;* \ *0629 530 373;* f *0629 530 386;* e *hotel@azovmash.com; www.european.com.ua*). The modern suites are lavish but completely overpriced at US$135 to US$200 per room, with US$400 suites that look like smoking rooms on the *Titanic*. On the other hand, the European's restaurant deserves a visit, with its very elegant food and distinguished atmosphere. For a more practical night's accommodation, try **Chaika** (*Primorsky 7;* \ *0629 372 186*) or **Spartak** (*Kharlamyevskaya 13;* \ *0629 334 214*). Both have rooms for around US$35, as well as nicer suites for US$70. Mariupol is the rail terminus for a few trains from Kiev, western Ukraine and Russia, always via Donetsk. There is a new airport, but flights to and from Kiev are sporadic. In summer, you can get the rare connection to Crimea, but it's still easier just to fly to Donetsk. Buses or *marshrutka* to Donetsk take under two hours and are very regular.

LUHANSK ЛУГАНСЬК

Ukraine's easternmost city marks the final extent of one country and the beginning of the flat Russian steppe across which blows a constant wind. When the air is still, the scent of industry wafts through this 'Wild East' where hardened miners and disenchanted factory workers still linger in a forgotten Russian outpost. But even with the present industrial paralysis, over half a million people call Luhansk home.

The city was founded by order of Catherine the Great who decided to assist her military campaign to expand the Russian Empire by building an iron foundry to make cannons and cannonballs. The empress chose Luhansk for its unending supply of coal, and its proximity to iron ore and the River Luhan, for which it was first named. Then she hired Scotsman Charles Gascoigne – an international expert in ironworks – to come and set up the city's first factories. Since the tsarina's time, the city has officially changed its name four times but spent most of the 20th century as Voroshilovgrad (Voroshilov was Stalin's darling general from World War II, a man that Khruschev often referred to as a 'big bag of shit'). Only in 1990 were the insulted citizens able to go back to calling their city Luhansk, but they're still a little touchy about all the wrongs that have been delivered to them out in this Russian/Ukrainian hinterland.

Being a drab and forlorn mid-size city on the fringe of Ukraine's industrial fringe, Luhansk was once targeted by the likes of dental tourists (people who travel abroad for cheap dental work) and creepy old men shopping for mail-order brides. The rather bored and despondent populace reacted by becoming totally addicted to the internet, and today it's one of the most wired cities in the country, with computer-savvy youth outnumbering embittered post-communists ten to one. Few Ukrainian cities preserve the Soviet aesthetic like Luhansk, and visitors will find that the giant row of rusty smokestacks from the Alchevsk metal factory are just as impressive as the many Stalin-era monuments to labour and victory. You'll have a great time in Luhansk, as long as you can appreciate history and irony.

GETTING THERE AND AWAY Flying is always the fastest way to get anywhere and seeing as Luhansk is the easternmost city in the country, it makes sense to fly if your time is limited. Daily flights from Kiev (except Sundays) cost around US$150 return; a single runs at US$80, normally flying in the early evening (2 hours). You can also fly to and from Moscow. The Luhansk 'international' airport is located at the far southern end of the city, at the end of 50 Let Oborona Luhansks (✆ 0642 544 005). It has its own regional airline, **Luhansk Airlines** (Ploschad Geroyeva 5; ✆ 0642 551 651; f 0642 501 134; e lugavia@cci.lg.ua; open 08.30–18.30). Tickets can also be purchased through **Kyi Avia** (Sovyetskaya 57, No 1; ✆ 0642 420 366; open 08.00–20.00 every day).

The Luhansk train station is on Pyatyorkina on the northeastern side of the city. Getting to Luhansk involves the longest train ride inside Ukraine and the view across the vast Eurasian steppe is rather unforgettable. Most routes must pass through Kharkiv or Donetsk first. There are three daily trains to and from Kiev (18 hours) that usually leave in the early evening and get there the next afternoon, usually via Kharkiv (8 hours) or Poltava (10 hours). A few Russian trains pass through this way, but always tend to go through Donetsk as well, which is a much more accessible rail junction.

The bus station is at Oboronnaya 28. Convenient connections service Donetsk (2½ hours) and other local Donbas towns. The private **Avtoluks** bus takes 16 hours to get to Kiev via Izyum and Kharkiv (take the train, pay less and sleep better). Their office is in the main bus station (✆ 0642 542 454).

WHERE TO STAY

🏠 **Hotel Luhansk** Sovetskaya 76; ✆ 0642 343 529; f 0642 344 707. The highest building in town, the Luhansk is an 18-storey high-rise remodelled in 1999. Only about half of its floors are used as a hotel, but rooms tend to be comfortable, clean, and convenient in terms of location, although some are rather small due to the Soviet construction. The Luhansk also features a Bulgarian restaurant and an indoor swimming pool. Cash only. Most sgls US$40, although ask to see if they have any US$20 standard rooms available; twins (rarely dbls) US$50, 2-room suites US$80–120.

🏠 **Hotel Druzhba** Soroki 16A; ✆ 0642 535 353; f 0642 344 774; e druzhba@lep.lg.ua. One of the better hotels in Luhansk – modern, clean and efficient. All rooms are heated/air-conditioned and hot water is a sure thing. Standard rooms US$45–60. The **Druzhba plus** is the upscale wing inside the hotel, with much nicer rooms – dbl suites around US$70–100. The hotel has a very nice Italian restaurant. Credit cards accepted.

🏠 **Initial Club** Oboronnaya 118A; ✆ 0642 428 564; f 0642 428 688; e init@cci.lg.ua; www.initialtour.com. A new private hotel that functions according to international norms and caters to guests' needs. They also have a great in-house tour agency. Rooms are fairly spacious, with sound plumbing and good beds. US$35–80.

Apartments and accommodation alternatives With the dearth of suitable hotels, renting an apartment for even just a few nights can be a nice alternative in Luhansk. Typically, you can get a luxurious apartment with hot water from US$25–35/night. Luhansk Rental (*www.luganskrental.com*) is a professional and dependable web service that offers good deals on clean accommodation in good locations. Note that the Luhansk apartment rental agencies are in constant flux, but it's nothing a good web search can't remedy. Another recommended service is **Elit-Comfort** (*50 let obprasovanniya SSSR;* ✆ *0642 532 052; www.inform.lg.ua/elit*), which functions as a hotel, although it's actually a series of nicely remodelled private apartments from US$20–60/night. There are also very nice rooms with private bathrooms available at the **train station hotel** for US$20–40/night (*Pyatyorkina 6;* ✆ *0642 523 555*) – just follow the signs around the corner to the high-rise (rooms are on the 6th and 8th floors).

✕ WHERE TO EAT
The restaurants at Hotel Druzhba and Luhansk both have pleasant in-house restaurants for dining, but stay in your hotel too much and you're missing out on an unexpectedly diverse range of restaurants. As in much of Donbas, a penchant for wild escapism influences the ambitions of local restaurateurs.

✕ **Red Square** Shevchenko; ✆ 0642 527 069. Nostalgic tribute to Soviet times, with pretty good Russian and Ukrainian food. Mains from US$5; open 11.00–23.00.

✕ **Versailles** Titova 13; ✆ 0642 531 502. French in name and menu, Versailles has all the delusions of grandeur that this city can muster, wrapped into a prissy, upscale dining experience. Mains from US$10–15.

☕ **Café Boulevard** Kotelnikov 13; ✆ 0642 343 320. Just off the main square; serving drinks and light meals day and night. Mains from US$4; open 08.00–22.00.

✕ **Chelsea** Sovyetskaya 58; ✆ 0642 536 371. Irish and English is all the same in Ukraine and you shouldn't travel so far from home and not have a nice little pub waiting for you. Proper English food, good service, and a truly 'non-smoking' section. Mains from US$5; open 10.00–23.00.

✕ **Texas** Frunze 1B; ✆ 0642 522 309. As a Texas native, I was quite touched by this highly decorated saloon and steakhouse. Quite popular with the people of Luhansk and a good choice if you like thick 1lb steaks and basic American cuisine. Mains from US$10; open 11.00–midnight.

✕ **Silver** Demyohkina 26; ✆ 0642 533 048. Waiters dressed as pirates, seafood dishes and lots of beer. Mains from US$5; open 11.00–midnight.

☕ **Prolissok** Sovyetskaya 65A; ✆ 0642 536 219. Cute little café with outdoor seating, specialising in light meals, heavy desserts, drinks and lethal cups of coffee. Mains from US$4; open 24hrs.

✕ **Armenia** Krasnoarmeyskaya 82; ✆ 0642 522 385. Armenian restaurant right next to the Armenian church, which interpreted means absolutely fantastic food. Everything is very authentic, including fresh-baked lavash and homemade sauces. *Mains from US$10; open 10.00–midnight.*

✕ **333** University Park; corner of Budyonny and Yakira; ☏ 0642 613 600. Traditional Chinese dim sum served inside a red-roofed pagoda. *Mains from*

US$4; open 11.00–22.00.

▭ **Coffee House** Sovyetskaya 66; ☏ 0642 538 353. Quaint little coffee house off the main square. Pastries, meals, and coffee and tea. *Open 09.00–21.00.*

LOCAL TOUR OPERATORS AND TOURIST INFORMATION You can save yourself some hassle by asking someone else to arrange your entire visit to Luhansk and the surrounding region. The most professional agency is that of Initial Tour (*Oboronnaya 118A;* ☏ *0642 427 028;* f *0642 428 564;* e *info@initialtour.com;* *www.initialtour.com*). They speak English, give good tours and have a reputation for honesty and affordability. Also check out Frigat Victory (*Sovetskaya 54; No 244;* ☏ *0642 510 445;* f *0642 478 965;* e *victorya@sonata.lg.ua*).

WHAT TO SEE AND DO To truly enjoy Luhansk, always bear in mind that this is the most well-preserved Soviet city in all of Ukraine and should be enjoyed as such. While most Ukrainian cities raced to be the first to erect a statue of their national liberationist hero, Luhansk is quite proud of the fact that it was the very last city to agree to a monument to Shevchenko, standing just off of Sovetskaya Ploschad. The rest of the city is peppered with mighty Soviet-era monuments and statues that could take an entire day to visit. Begin with the three main squares (Soviet Square, Heroes' Square and Red Square) and don't miss the horse-mounted Voroshilov monument at Kotsyubinsky 14.

Luhansk is also the home town of Vladimir Ivanovich Dahl (1801–72), the founder of the first Russian-language dictionary, a ground-breaking work based on a lifelong collection of vernacular terminology, rather than the approved academic lexicon. Dahl also collected and wrote down the fairy tales and Russian proverbs from around the region, which, like his dictionary, are still in publication today. Although he was Danish by birth, he wrote under the pseudonym 'the Cossack of Luhansk' and was inducted into the Russian Academy of Sciences for his contribution to Russian learning. The Museum of Vladimir Dahl is dedicated to his memory, located in the home he lived in and on the street named after him (*Dahla 12;* ☏ *0642 524 155; open 10.00–17.00; entrance 4UAH*).

The Natural History Museum of Luhansk is not wonderfully spectacular, frozen in its original form, circa 1965. However, like all such museums in Ukraine, there's a lot to be learned and a few real gems. The copper cannon outside was one of the first made in the Luhansk foundry in 1810, and inside you'll find everything from prehistoric remains to Russian tributes to the city's Scottish founding father (*Shevchenko 2; open 10.00–17.00, closed Mon; entrance 5 UAH*).

Also, take a good look at St Nikolas Cathedral (*Mezhdunarodnaya 111*), one of the few churches actually constructed during Stalin's lifetime, in 1950, during a period of uncharacteristic calm. The Sts Peter and Paul Cathedral was completed in the 1890s (*behind Artyoma 245*) and survived the Soviet era by becoming a movie theatre.

Definitely not to be missed is the Sea of Luhansk, an old open pit mine that has naturally filled up with highly acidic water. On the far western side of the city, the 'Sea' has become a popular summer hangout, complete with its own 'beach' and beachside restaurants. Here brave windsurfers make sport with the polluted gusts that sweep across the steppe, and people pedal small boats and swim freely midst the cooling waves. Visitors can rent cottages for the night and 'camp' for as little as US$10/day. Farther outside of Luhansk is Alchevsk, where in recent years the Alchevsk metallurgical plant has become an ironic tourist destination. Tours can be arranged through local agencies.

15

Sloboda
Слобода

The city of Kharkiv and surrounding territory is the easiest region to travel to (besides Kiev) and opens up a very different corner of Ukraine. On wheels or on foot, the boundless steppe of eastern Ukraine promises hypnotic landscape viewing, for in Sloboda the rolling plains really do 'undulate'. In winter, the snow blows into drifting waves and in summer, endless sunflower fields rise and fall with the wind. Alas, the beauty of the east is too often overlooked by tour organisers as an uninteresting expanse of open land that separates a few semi-interesting cities from the rest of the country. This false perception stems from divisive attitudes that figure left-bank Ukraine was too heavily shaped by Soviet industry and collective agriculture to be of any fascination to the outsider.

The term *sloboda* derives from the Russian word for 'freedom', and was often applied to collections of free people in the old Russian Empire, such as monasteries. The Ukrainian name for this region, *Slobozhanschina,* means quite literally, 'Land of the Free' and refers to the fields of Sumy, Kharkiv and Izyum that were simply given to early settlers without charge if they would cultivate the land. Freed Ukrainian serfs and Cossacks were attracted by the offer, as were a large group of Serbians who had fled religious persecution in their own country. Nevertheless, the land deal came with a catch: the Russian government hoped the new settlers would provide a buffer against the constant raids of the Tatars. When Catherine the Great disbanded the Cossack leadership in 1765, this area fell under Russian military protection and governorship, beginning a long legacy of Russian cultural influence. Today, Sloboda falls on the esoteric Russian border – a border that could swing 100 miles in either direction and not make much difference. People here speak both Russian and a highly literary form of Ukrainian and it is no coincidence that so many of Ukraine's greatest writers, thinkers, singers and artists were born here and inspired by the simple and beautiful surroundings.

GETTING AROUND

Sloboda features the very best train in the country, the speedy Capital Express that connects Kiev to Kharkiv, but is also convenient for getting between Kharkiv, Poltava and Mirgorod. The train to Sumy is slow, so it is best to take the bus when travelling within the region. Most of Slobozhanschina's ('land in the region of Sloboda') more interesting areas are out in the country, and so unless you are in the know about the *elektrichki* trains, it is best to find the right bus or taxi, or else go with an organised tour.

KHARKIV ХАРКІВ

Ukraine's second-largest city dominates the east and easily takes the prize for most aesthetically pleasing industrial metropolis in the country (a title which means little

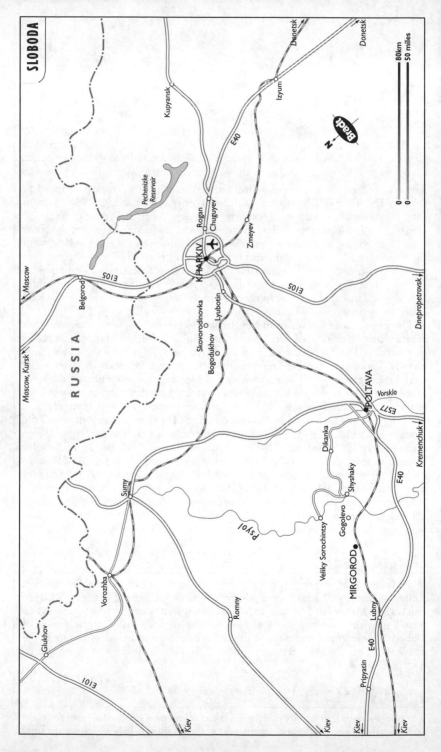

SLOBODA

Black

N

0   80km
0   50 miles

unless you've been to Donetsk or Zaporizhzhya). With a population of over two million people, Kharkiv's beauty lies in its sheer size: the constant motion of humans and its breadth of urban space. Admittedly, few come this way to sightsee, but seeing as this is a major transport hub and principally functional city, it is not surprising how many foreign visitors find themselves heading this way. Less than 20 miles from the Russian border, Kharkiv is also the easiest entry/exit point into that country. About 70% of the city is ethnic Russian and Russian is spoken first and foremost (which is why people say *Kharkóv*).

Visiting Kharkiv offers the best introduction to Ukraine's Soviet legacy and the distinct geography that comes with it: the countless war memorials, the hundreds of factories, Stalinist housing, the huge central square and the dominant public sector. The collective achievements of science, industry and art still count for a lot in this city's identity. Locals may not know the Ukrainian national anthem by heart, but they can tell you that the Soviets' nuclear programme began with a fission experiment in Kharkiv. While most of Ukraine has stripped away its emblems of the past, Kharkiv has simply reincorporated them into the present excitement. The city continues to lead the country in its industrial recovery and boasts the largest student population in Ukraine.

HISTORY Kharkiv is a young city for Ukraine, founded only in 1653 and named after a Cossack leader called Kharkach; or else the city was simply named after the River Kharkiv that flows through it. Either way, the free settlement prospered in the 17th century as a military outpost jointly defended from the Tatars by Ukrainian Cossacks and Russian army regiments. The attraction of free land and strong defence created a steady growth in population and building. Most newcomers came south from Russia and by the mid 18th century, Kharkiv had established itself as an industrial centre, with over a dozen brick factories (as in Chekhov's *Three Sisters*). In 1796 Kharkiv was officially declared the capital of the Russian Empire's Sloboda province, securing the city's primarily Russian existence.

Kharkiv University was founded in 1805 and allowed the region a stable intellectual development unseen in other areas of Ukraine. Fearing that Ukrainian language and culture were about to be swallowed up by the Russian majority, a few academics began to publish literary prose in the Ukrainian language. Known as the 'Kharkiv Romantics', this small group of writers applied the idyll of Russian romanticism to Ukrainian folklore, which later inspired the more politically minded Ukrainian intellectuals of the nationalist movement.

Still, the city was industrialised and governed as a Russian city, receiving a direct railroad link from Moscow in 1869, a whole year before Kiev even had a train station. Competition with Kiev continues to this day, and along with many other firsts, Kharkiv claims the title of Ukraine's first capital. Proximity to urban Russia and a strong industrial base meant Kharkiv lent strong support to the Bolsheviks during the Russian revolution. After Ukraine was thrown into chaos during the civil war, Lenin proclaimed Kharkiv was the rightful capital of the Soviet Republic and thus it stayed during the early years of the USSR. It suffered the wrath of the Red Army pushing forth its ideology in the city, which is why Kharkiv has very few landmark churches today. Sloboda was also one of the first regions in Ukraine to be forcefully collectivised by Stalin, and the tragic famine of 1932–33 hit Kharkiv the hardest. Thousands of starving peasants poured into the city from the countryside, and then thousands more died on the streets. The complete devastation forced the capital back to Kiev in 1934.

World War II brought another wave of destruction, and Kharkiv was battered from both sides. People know of the battles of Kursk and Stalingrad, but drawn-out Kharkiv offensives preceded each. In 1942–43, Kharkiv was captured and lost twice by the Nazis. Hitler's scorched-earth policy left the city in ruins, which is why Sumskaya and Pushkinskaya are two of the only streets with pre-war buildings.

During the latter Soviet period, Kharkiv became an industrial giant for the communist world; in 1967, the one-millionth tractor rolled out of the Kharkiv Tractor Factory, and a tank and aeroplane factory employed tens of thousands. Following independence, the machines all ground to a halt, and a city of two million was suddenly unemployed. Slowly, the many factories have been revamped to make new products and the slick-haired Russian businessman look has been adopted by local techies. (Bill Gates chose Kharkiv as his base from which to launch the Ukrainian version of Windows.) The city still leads the country in education, technology and military industry, and most of eastern (Russian-speaking) Ukraine comes to university here or to find jobs. The city's latest historical phenomenon is a sporadic influx of foreigners.

GETTING THERE AND AWAY

By air KharkIv's aviation industry has a long and glorious history, so flying is an easy and often inexpensive option, whether domestic or international. The airport is in the far south of the city off Prospekt Gagarina (❧ *0572 516 907*). A taxi into the city should cost US$3, or take the metro to Gagarina station and then the airport trolley, or the No 119 bus that leaves from the central square by Lenin's statue. Kiy Avia (*Chervonoshkilna 18;* ❧ *0572 218 441;* e *info@kiyavia.com*) flies to the most destinations from Kiev, but connections to Kharkiv are sporadic. Aerosvit (❧ *0572 195 370;* e *aerosvit@vlink.kharkov.ua; www.aerosvit.com*) is the nationally respected domestic airline which connects with Donetsk, Lviv, Kiev and Dnepropetrovsk. Aeromist (❧ *057 715 3188;* e *aeromist@interami.com*) is Kharkiv's own airline, which flies twice daily to Kiev and three times a week to Moscow. Fares change, but normally a one-way ticket to Moscow is US$100, and a one-way ticket within Ukraine is US$60. For the time being Austrian Airlines (*office near the airport; Romashkina 1;* ❧ *0572 148 953*) is the only European carrier to fly direct to Kharkiv from Vienna, four times a week. Regular charter routes serviced by Ukrainian companies include Syria, Armenia, Egypt and Turkey. In the city, most hotels have the facilities to book air tickets. The airport hotel (*Aeroflotska 16;* ❧ *0572 516 229*) is slightly unnecessary since the city is near and few will make overnight connections, but it is there.

By rail Besides Kiev, Kharkiv has the most train connections to everywhere else, so rail is usually the best option for travel. The new *Stolychny Ekspress* (Capital Express) has cut the travel time in half between Kiev and Kharkiv. The luxury train does the trip in five hours and goes back and forth twice every day. From Kharkiv, the train normally leaves at 07.00 and 16.30, and from Kiev at 06.30 and 17.30. The train makes only two stops – at Poltava (2 hours) and Mirgorod (3 hours) – and this is the fastest way to get to or from Kharkiv. First-class return tickets cost US$20, second-class tickets are about US$15. There are also several overnight trains to and from Kiev; the best is No 63/64 that takes about nine hours and leaves at around 21.00 or 22.00. Other local trains link Kharkiv with Poltava (3 hours), Sumy (4 hours), Dnepropetrovsk (5 hours), Kremenchuk (6 hours) and Donetsk (7 hours). Longer overnight routes service Luhansk (13 hours), Odessa (15 hours), Kherson (16 hours) and Lviv (20 hours).

Kharkiv is also the major hub for Russian trains, and most trains from Moscow to Crimea, Donbas and southern Russia will pass through here. It is not hard to catch a train to Moscow (14 hours), and there are daily trains to Sverdlovsk and

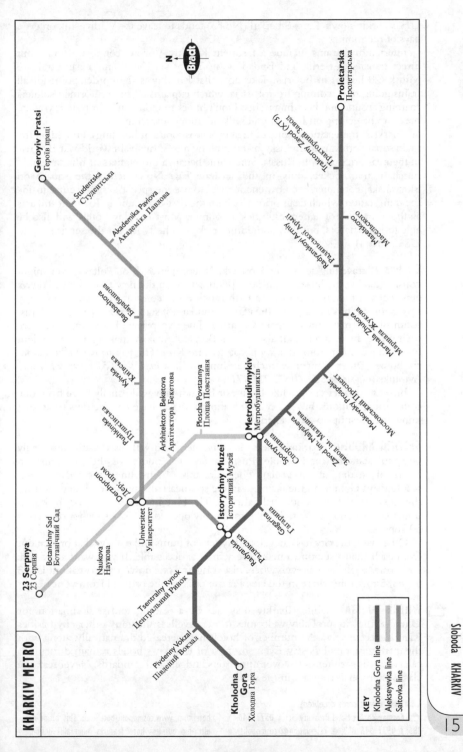

KHARKIV METRO

Geroyiv Pratsi
Героїв праці

Studentska
Студентська

Akademika Pavlova
Академіка Павлова

Botanichny Sad
Ботанічний Сад

23 Serpnya
23 Серпня

Naukova
Наукова

Barabashova
Барабашова

Kyivska
Київська

Pushkinska
Пушкінська

Arkhitektora Beketova
Архітектора Бекетова

Ploscha Povstannya
Площа Повстання

Derzhprom
Держпром

Universitet
Університет

Istorychny Muzei
Історичний Музей

Radianska
Радянська

Metrobudivnykiv
Метробудівників

Sportyvna
Спортивна

Zavod im. Malysheva
Завод ім. Малишева

Moskovsky Prospekt
Московський Проспект

Marshala Zhukova
Маршала Жукова

Maselskovo
Маселського

Radyanskoy Army
Радянської Армії

Traktorny Zavod (XTЗ)
Тракторний Завод (ХТЗ)

Proletarska
Пролетарська

Gagarina
Гагаріна

Tsentralny Rynok
Центральний Ринок

Pivdenny Vokzal
Південний Вокзал

Kholodna Gora
Холодна Гора

KEY
Kholodna Gora line
Alekseyevka line
Saltovka line

Sloboda KHARKIV

15

Ufa. Kharkiv's own Trans-Siberian (No 53) tends to leave for Vladivostok on even days of the month.

International trains include a frequent Kharkiv–Warsaw connection, rare but direct transits to Berlin and Budapest (normally via Kiev), and a daily train to Minsk (20 hours) in Belarus. Take note that Kharkiv is the border point for all trains going to or coming from Russia, which explains all the uniformed soldiers roaming around and boarding trains. Don't linger too long on your train if you are meant to be getting off here or you will fall under suspicion.

Kharkiv's train station is one of the city's most opulent buildings, located on the main square off Krasnoarmeiskaya and built by the Germans in World War II to use in their eastern push into Russia. Since time began, all foreigners in Kharkiv could purchase train tickets only in the separate *kasa* No 1 across the square on Slovyanska. Foreigners are now encouraged to use the special service centre inside the train station, which deals primarily with the first-class train to Kiev but still acts as the 'separate' foreigners-only ticket counter. Most Kharkiv hotels will also be able to issue tickets, but they sometimes tack on a hefty fee for the service (up to US$20 extra).

By bus If travelling to Sumy, Donetsk, Dnepropetrovsk or Poltava, you might consider taking the bus as a quicker option, although the new fast train to Poltava gets there in the same short time with much more comfort. There are currently seven bus stations in Kharkiv; the central and largest station is at Gagarina 22, just south of metro station Prospekt Gagarina. The two private bus companies have their offices here, and both make stops at Borispol Airport, making it a convenient way to travel to or from Kharkiv if you fly into Kiev. The trip to Kiev takes about six hours. Other companies include Gunsel (*Gagarina 7;* ⟍ *0572 199 719*) and Avtoluks (*Gagarina 22;* ⟍ *0572 215 471*).

Buses to smaller villages like Izyum or Bohodukhiv will usually leave from one of the outer stations, but the central station will also have connections or at least know the most up-to-date schedule.

GETTING AROUND Kharkiv's metro is convenient and well used with some truly beautiful stations (for example, Pushkinskaya has quotes of the poet Pushkin inscribed on the subway walls). There are three metro lines: the red connects Kholodnaya Gora to all the factories in the southeast and the green line goes from the city centre out to residential Saltovka. The blue line to Alekseyevka had been under construction since the 1980s and finally opened in 1996. One journey costs 50 kopecks.

Otherwise, the city has a developed system of trams and trolleys that branch out from each metro station to make every quarter accessible. If you want a taxi, the same rules apply here as everywhere else. Flagging one down will cost about US$3 to US$5 to go anywhere in the city. Private taxis can be ordered from your hotel.

WHERE TO STAY While Kharkiv may not be a leading tourist destination for Ukraine, the city probably welcomes more travellers than any other city besides Kiev. In recent years the number of hotels has increased dramatically, along with the quality of a night's stay. Even so, most of Kharkiv's hotels remain difficult to categorise, as each tends to cover numerous budgets and standards. Never fear, the class system shall conquer in the end.

Luxury (*credit cards accepted*)

⌂ **Cosmopolit Art Hotel** Proskury 1; ⟍ 0577 546 886; f 0577 546 880; e reservation@cosmopolit- hotel.com; www.cosmopolit-hotel.com. This brand-new, ultra-hip business hotel features minimalist design, mood lighting and lots of gadgets to please even the most demanding technophile. In addition to the high-speed internet hook-ups in every room, there's wi-fi in every corner of the hotel. There's really no other hotel like it in all of Ukraine: big modern rooms with sleek lines, avant-garde bathrooms, and lots of mirrors and glass, not to mention all the furniture, which is all made by Ukrainian artists and craftsmen. *Conference rates for standard rooms US$120, otherwise superior suites US$220, king*

Middle range *(all take credit cards unless noted)*

⌂ **Hotel Kharkiv** Ploschad Svobody 7 (metro station Universitet); ✆ 0572 456 325; f 0572 476 176; e hotel@ukrsat.kharkov.ua; www.hotel.kharkov.com. Every city has that one hotel that may not be the best, or the fanciest, but it's just 'the hotel' to stay in. That's the Kharkiv — a huge place right on the Square of Freedom with superb views of Lenin and the entire communist panorama that makes Kharkiv so grandiose. Aiming at attracting more foreign visitors, the hotel has done up a separate wing with recently remodelled and clean 'European' rooms. The separate entrance is around the corner from the main hotel and the receptionist speaks English. This is considered one of the nicer choices in Kharkiv for the time being, although that says more about Kharkiv than the hotel. To its credit, the rooms are large, the service is good and the furniture is soundly IKEA. B/fast is served in the 8th-floor café for an extra 15UAH and the business centre in the lobby has a fast internet connection and small conference room. *Sgl room with shower US$45; dbl with real dbl bed and bath US$80; 2-room suites US$70 sgl/US$120 dbl; lavish private apts US$200.*

⌂ **Hotel Kharkiv** (contact details as above) If you are looking for something slightly cheaper, you can try to get a room in the larger main part of the hotel for much less and enjoy an impressive view out over the square and park. This is a massive shell of a building — a bit dingy, and many rooms are rented for start-up businesses or private parties. Some of the rooms have been remodelled, but not all. *Dbl with toilet and shower US$30, and if you use the bathroom down the hall, your room costs only US$20. Bare sgls US$15.*

⌂ **Hotel National** Lenina 21 (metro station Naukova); ✆ 0577 021 624; f 0577 021 628. Kharkiv's former Inturist hotel kept the city's hospitality industry alive through the lean years and now offers a reliable base for travellers who come to experience the city's regeneration. Rooms tend to

suites (with king-size beds) US$280, and twin rooms (for 2 people) US$320.

⌂ **Rosinka** Hotel Balakireva 52; ✆ 0573 432 157; e rosinka@vlink.kharkov.ua. Modish, boutique hotel with only 8 rooms, but very classy and serene. Each is light and spacious with wide, luxurious beds, and impeccably modern bathrooms. The welcomed guest gets lots of personal attention. The in-house Japanese restaurant adds to the mystique. *Demi-suites are a cool US$95, full suites US$120–150.*

be cosy and have big bathtubs with 24hr hot water. When going to your room, take note of the fantastic Soviet-era stained-glass stairwell with depictions of great socialist landmarks in Eurasia. The National also boasts a tourist agency and translation service that can do city tours and arrange transport (air, train and bus). The hotel restaurant is typical of most Russian/Ukrainian enterprises and serves the staples; b/fast costs an additional US$6. *Fair sgl room with facilities US$45, a dbl US$75; the largest suites (with big beds and 2 rooms) are US$90–120.*

⌂ **Hotel Mir** Lenina 27A; ✆ 0572 322 330; f 0572 322 217. This giant high-rise does not boast the best location, but does offer the best deals in terms of quality versus price, as well as some decent budget rooms. The first 2 floors make up a commercial centre with a car showroom, the Gold Lion Casino, and a beauty salon, but the other 11 floors offer plenty of 'regular' or 'European' rooms. This tends to be the preferred hotel for foreign visitors and group tours. Hotel Mir also features one of the more professional tourist agencies in the city, and they are particularly effective in booking last-minute plane and train tickets throughout Ukraine (main floor; ✆ 0572 305 574). To get to Mir, take the metro to Naukova and then take any bus, trolley or cab north until you see it. *Regular rooms are of the Soviet fashion and cost US$40–55. European rooms are nicely remodelled and cost twice as much. The dbl with b/fast for US$60 is the best deal, but they also have some 'lux' rooms with genuine king-size beds for US$90.*

⌂ **Kievksaya** Kultura 4; ✆ 0577 143 100; f 0577 143 101; e hotelk@interswiaz.kharkov.ua; www.hotelk.kharkov.ua. Towering above Kharkiv's most historic district, the Kievskaya offers a superb location for those who like to stroll around the city and the square. The high-rise concrete hotel comes with all the accoutrements of local 'beezness' taste,

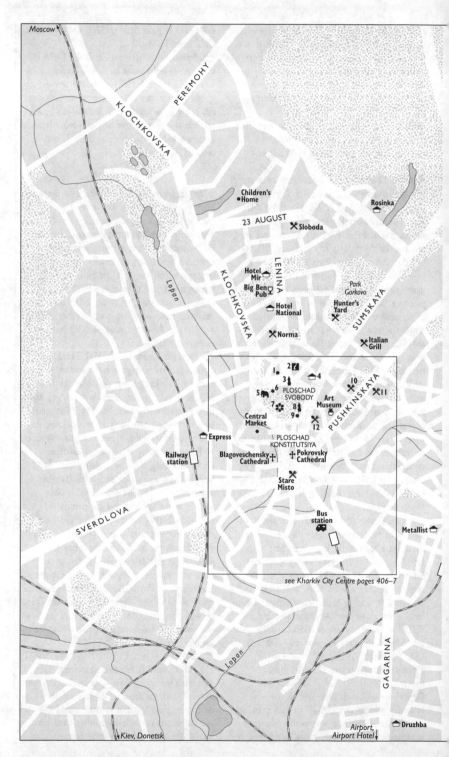

Moscow

KLOCHKOVSKA

PEREMOHY

Children's
Home

Rosinka

23 AUGUST

Sloboda

LENINA

Hotel
Mir

Big Ben
Pub

Hotel
National

KLOCHKOVSKA

Park
Gorkovo

Hunter's
Yard

SUMSKAYA

Norma

Italian
Grill

Lopan

1

2

3

4

10

5

PLOSCHAD
SVOBODY

Art
Museum

11

7

8

9

12

PUSHKINSKAYA

Central
Market

Express

PLOSCHAD
KONSTITUTSIYA

Railway
station

Blagoveschensky
Cathedral

Pokrovsky
Cathedral

Stare
Misto

SVERDLOVA

Bus
station

Metallist

GAGARINA

see Kharkiv City Centre pages 406–7

Kiev, Donetsk

Airport,
Airport Hotel

Druzhba

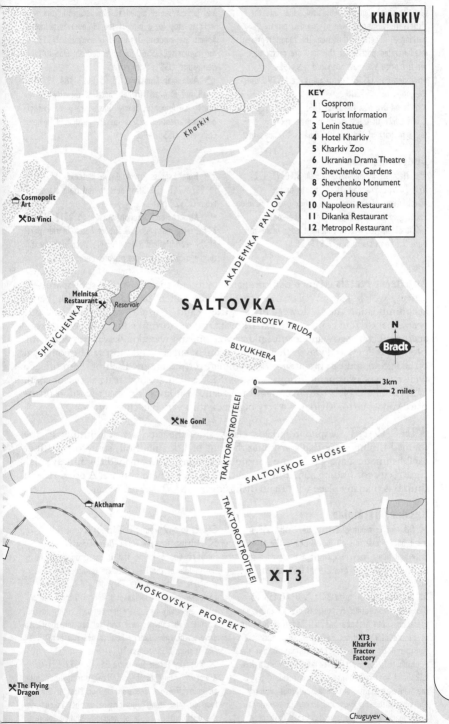

KEY
1 Gosprom
2 Tourist Information
3 Lenin Statue
4 Hotel Kharkiv
5 Kharkiv Zoo
6 Ukranian Drama Theatre
7 Shevchenko Gardens
8 Shevchenko Monument
9 Opera House
10 Napoleon Restaurant
11 Dikanka Restaurant
12 Metropol Restaurant

Cosmopolit Art

Da Vinci

Melnitsa Restaurant

Reservoir

Kharkiv

SALTOVKA

AKADEMIKA PAVLOVA

GEROYEV TRUDA

BLYUKHERA

N

Bradt

0 — 3km
0 — 2 miles

Ne Goni!

SHEVCHENKA

TRAKTOROSTROITELEI

SALTOVSKOE SHOSSE

Akthamar

TRAKTOROSTROITELEI

XT3

MOSKOVSKY PROSPEKT

XT3 Kharkiv Tractor Factory

The Flying Dragon

Chuguyev

like the sauna, tanning beds, pool tables and the glittery restaurant, as well as guarded private parking — a perk in this area. The rooms represent unadulterated post-Soviet chic and are pretty nice for the price you pay. *Standard sgls US$45, upgraded dbls US$60, demi-suites are US$90; over-the-top suites US$200.*

🏠 **Hotel Druzhba** Gagarina 185; ✆ 0572 522 091; f 0572 521 064. Just north of the airport in the southern part of the city, Druzhba is Ukraine's first

and largest 'motel' aimed at travellers with cars who want to stop for a bite at the in-house restaurant. Rooms are modern, clean and comfortable. *US$30 for regular sgl, US$60 for upgraded dbl, US$80 for demi-suite, US$120 for suite.*

🏠 **Akhtamar** Krupskaya 38; ✆ 0577 384 193. Small, but nice and friendly hotel in the city centre, run by an Armenian family. Guests are given lots of personal attention and rooms are plush and homey. *Cash only. US$50–90.*

Budget *(cash only)*

🏠 **Metallist** Plekhanovskaya 92A; ✆ 0577 372 099; f 0577 373 552. As in 'tribute to the metalworkers of Kharkov', not a rock band. This old Soviet gem is still going strong in Kharkov's industrial district, on the southeast edge of town. *Bare but bearable rooms US$15–35.*

🏠 **Hotel Express** Privokzalnaya Ploschad 1; ✆ 0572 242 414. Right next to the train station. *From US$20 pp.*

🏠 **Airport Hotel** Aeroflotskaya 16; ✆ 0577 755 347. Pretty much like all airport hotels in this part of the world: offers a good night's sleep right next to the airport. *Basic but private rooms US$20.*

Apartment rentals Many rental companies offer advance or on-the-spot apartment rentals, which like anywhere else in Ukraine, often provides you with better accommodation at a lower price. Tried and trusted companies include www.kharkovrent.com, www.kharkovapartmentsforrent.com, www.kharkov-apartment.com, www.apartments.inkharkov.com, and www.kharkovapartments.com. None of them is as dodgy as their websites might suggest and most can be contacted on Skype so you can pre-arrange everything over the phone. Each of them offers a wide range of apartments, from as low as US$30 a night to some real palaces for about US$150/night. Negotiate freely, and make sure you know the exact location of the place you agree to; Kharkiv is a very big city, with a very big 'city centre'.

✗ **WHERE TO EAT** Despite Kharkiv's classy side, the city is not immune to the themed-dining craze that's gripping the rest of Ukraine. Still, some of the finer establishments have settled into a more regular and distinguished rhythm. It's also a great city for finding something to eat, no matter where you are. A good rule of thumb is that any place with main dishes over US$5 takes credit cards.

Russian/Ukrainian

✗ **Dikanka** Lermontovska 7; ✆ 0572 587 558. A small, homey café just off Pushkinskaya. The food is tasty and filling, very inexpensive and served with lots of motherly love. *Mains from US$3; open 10.00–22.00.*

✗ **Sloboda** 23rd Avgusta 34A; ✆ 0577 155 056. Ukrainian 'restoration' restaurants are all the rage these days, but Sloboda has matched the cliché to fit the country's distinct Eastern flavour. This is considered to be Kharkiv's best restaurant, but the atmosphere is pretty laidback and fun with a live folk band in the evenings. Smoked suckling pig is the house speciality, but be adventurous and try the very authentic *kvas* and *uzvar* (a traditional drink made with dried, smoked fruit). *Cash only.*

Expect to pay around US$15 for your meal.

✗ **Melnitsa** Geroyev Truda, Zhuravlivka Park; ✆ 0572 686 671. The 'Mill' is based on an island in the middle of the River Kharkiv towards the outskirts of the old city. They do a delicious combination of Ukrainian and Georgian food and it is an especially nice place for outdoor eating in the summer. You can get here only by car, but most taxi drivers will know exactly how to get you here. *Mains from US$5; open 10.00–midnight.*

✗ **Knyazhy Terem** Sumskaya 35; ✆ 0577 511 089. A worthy tribute to the old Slavic principalities, with an impressive oak and iron interior. Most of the food on offer stems from original recipes taken from the distinguished house of Romanov: stuffed spiced oranges, milk-fed suckling pig, and delicious fish soup (*ukha*). *Mains from US$7; open 12.00–midnight.*

✕ **Podvore (The Doorway)** Chernishevskovo 12; ✆ 0577 063 137. Spacious dining hall where the kindly chef focuses on 'western Ukrainian specialties' – exotic cuisine for these parts. They also have a

Fine dining/gourmet

✕ **Chateau** Rymarskaya 30; ✆ 0577 050 806. Très sophisticated French restaurant right across from the opera house, with several different dining halls of varying themes. The food is very nice (try the soups), as is the wine. *Mains from US$15; open 10.00–23.00.*

✕ **Viensky Dom (Viennese House)** Lermontovskaya 8; ✆ 0577 043 773. Hapsburg-era precision and daintiness, with exquisite meat dishes in sauce, or fine cakes and pastries. *Mains from US$20; open 12.00–midnight.*

✕ **Metropol** Mironosytskaya 50; ✆ 0577 194 040. Swanky and expensive, the Metropol is Kharkiv's prized gourmet restaurant in terms of both food and service. The city's high-flyers come here to dine, but the menu is slightly overrated. *Mains from US$25; open 24 hours.*

✕ **Da Vinci** Proskury 1; ✆ 0577 588 888. If you've travelled elsewhere in Ukraine, you know quite well that this is kind of a chain, with similar cousins in

Asian

✕ **Yaské** Konstitutsii 18/2; ✆ 0577 312 747. Theme-decorated, underground Japanese sushi bar that advertises the best sushi in the country (they've got a lot of competition). *About US$12 pp; open 11.00–midnight.*

✕ **Bukhara** Pushkinskaya 32; ✆ 0577 162 045. Robust Uzbekistani cuisine served to you whilst you nestle among pillows and couches. Tandoor-

Special to Kharkiv

✕ **Zhyli Byli (Once upon a time ...)** Sumskaya 37; ✆ 0577 172 003. A nostalgic and humorous underground tribute to Soviet childhood, decorated with lots of forgotten knick-knacks and ties hanging from the ceiling. The food is unique and yummy. *Mains from US$2; open 09.00–22.00.*

✕ **Continent** Svobody 7; ✆ 0577 580 001. The Hotel Kharkiv's Baroque masterpiece that sadly replaced a most beloved Georgian restaurant, where guests eat languorous b/fasts and non-guests come and partake of majestic meals, inspired by the cuisines of Thailand, France and Italy. *Mains from*

nice choice of inexpensive set menus for lunches. *Mains from US$3; open 10.00–midnight.*

✕ **Stare Misto** Kvitky Osnovyanenko 12; ✆ 0572 128 095. In the heart of the old city, this small restaurant has a pub-like atmosphere with hearty food and Ukrainian beer on tap. *Mains from US$6; open 10.00–23.00.*

Kiev and Dnepropetrovsk. Here, Kharkivites consider Leonardo's contributions to art and science, whilst eating fresh pizza or seafood. It's all part of the lush cosmopolitan 'art' experience. *Mains from US$20; open 11.00–midnight.*

✕ **Napoleon** Petrovskovo 37/39; ✆ 0572 477 570. Not quite French, not quite Russian, this centrally located restaurant offers professional service and 'European' cuisine. It is correctly considered to be one of Kharkiv's nicer places to dine out. *Mains from US$15; open 11.00–midnight.*

✕ **Norma** Lenina 11; ✆ 0572 175 693. This classy café is made entirely of windows that look out on Kharkiv's busiest sidewalk, yet inside the atmosphere remains cosy and sophisticated. The food is 'high-European' and the overall menu is quite original. Basic Ukrainian dishes like *borsch* or crêpes with red caviar are also served with a flair, and this must be the first restaurant in Ukraine to have smoking and non-smoking sections. *Main dishes US$10.*

grilled meats, vegetarian food, and very authentic *plov*, *manti*, etc. *Mains from US$6; open 11.00–23.00.*

✕ **The Flying Dragon** Geroyev Stalingrada 45; ✆ 0577 148 162. One of Kharkov's long-time favourites, serving Vietnamese, Chinese and Japanese dishes inside a giant pagoda. *Mains from US$6; open 14.00–01.00.*

US$7; open 07.00–midnight.

✕ **Duby Kolduny (The Witches' Oak)** Klochkovskaya 3; ✆ 0577 511 975. Disney-esque recreation of Russian fairy-tale settings for children and adults, like 'Masha and the Bear' and 'Peter and the Wolf'. The food is quite fresh and very Russian. *Mains from US$10; open 10.00–midnight.*

✕ **Ne Goni!** 50 let VLKSM 49/8; ✆ 0577 581 258. This Saltovka establishment is downright crazy – a club and restaurant with a name that translates as 'lay off me', specialising in nothing and everything all at once. South American, Ukrainian, Italian and

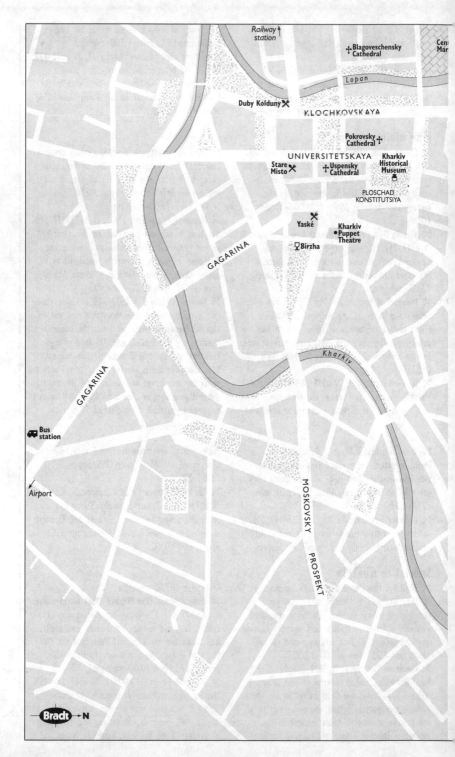

Railway
station

✝ Blagoveschensky
   Cathedral

Cen
Mar

Lopan

Duby Kolduny ✕

KLOCHKOVSKAYA

Pokrovsky ✝
Cathedral

UNIVERSITETSKAYA

Stare ✕
Misto

✝ Uspensky
   Cathedral

Kharkiv
Historical
Museum

PLOSCHAD
KONSTITUTSIYA

✕ Yaské

Kharkiv
● Puppet
Theatre

� Birzha

GAGARINA

Kharkiv

GAGARINA

🚌 Bus
   station

↙ Airport

MOSKOVSKY

PROSPEKT

Bradt ➤ N

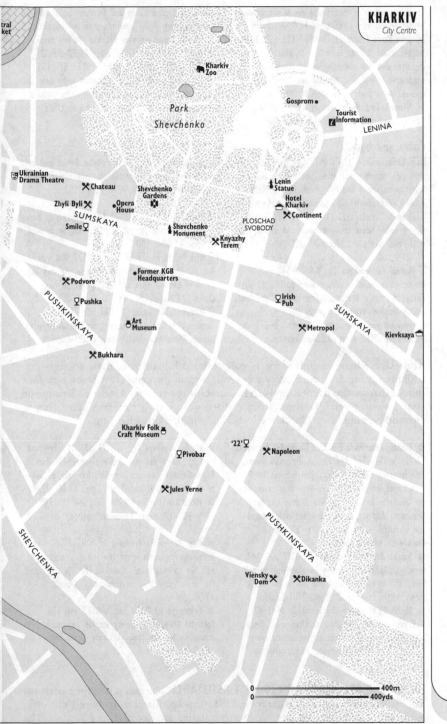

Central
Market

Kharkiv
Zoo

Park
Shevchenko

Gosprom

Tourist
Information

LENINA

Ukrainian
Drama Theatre

Chateau

Shevchenko
Gardens

Lenin
Statue

Zhyli Byli

Opera
House

Hotel
Kharkiv

Continent

Smile

SUMSKAYA

Shevchenko
Monument

PLOSCHAD
SVOBODY

Knyazhy
Terem

Former KGB
Headquarters

Podvore

Irish
Pub

Pushka

PUSHKINSKAYA

Art
Museum

SUMSKAYA

Metropol

Kievksaya

Bukhara

Kharkiv Folk
Craft Museum

'22'

Napoleon

Pivobar

Jules Verne

PUSHKINSKAYA

SHEVCHENKA

Viensky
Dom

Dikanka

0   400m
0   400yds

Czech 'fusion' cuisine continue to amaze the incoming hordes. *Mains from US$5; open 12.00–midnight.*

✘ **Jules Verne** Frunze 11; ☎ 0577 196 850. 20,000 leagues under the sea right here in Kharkiv, complete with fish swimming by your submarine window while you dine. Seafood and French-inspired cuisine. *Mains from US$6; open 10.00–23.00.*

✘ **Hunter's Yard** Novgorodskaya 85A; ☎ 0577 591 985. Channelling William Tell, this cutesy Swiss

cottage is decked out in oak furniture in an earnest effort to bring alpine atmosphere to the Ukrainian steppe. An impressive wine list, but the live music is annoying. *Mains from US$8; open 11.00–23.00.*

✘ **Italian Grill** Sumskaya 128; ☎ 0577 575 140. Pleasant and simple Italian restaurant right near the heart of the city. Refined salads, fresh pasta, and a series of grilled meat dishes. *Mains from US$6; open 11.00–midnight.*

Cafés and bars

🖵 **22** Petrovskovo 22; ☎ 0577 544 048. European-style café, complete with street-side seating, and bistro menu. Coffee and light meals (and wonderful b/fasts). *Mains from US$5; open 09.00–midnight.*

🖵 **Smile** Sumskaya 23/24; ☎ 0577 003 230. Cheery coffee house for light meals and snacks, beer, coffee and cocktails. *Coffee from US$1; open 10.00–23.00.*

🍺 **Pushka** Pushkinskaya 31; ☎ 0577 546 728. Downtown bar and restaurant done up like an old European cottage. The atmosphere is lively, the food mainly Russian/Ukrainian. A pretty child-friendly environment with a separate kids' menu in English. *Mains from US$5; open 10.00–midnight.*

🍺 **Big Ben Pub** Lenina 48; no phone. British pub in the north-central part of the city (the dining menu is fairly unremarkable). *Mains from US$3; open 11.00–23.00.*

🍺 **Pivobar** Frunze 3; ☎ 0577 192 101. Lots of beer on tap, big-screen football and the food to go with it; *open 11.00–23.00.*

🍺 **Irish Pub** Mironositskaya 46; ☎ 0577 004 940. Just like the name implies, but one of the very first in all of Ukraine. Irish and Dutch beer on tap. *Open 12.00–midnight.*

🍺 **Birzha** Moskovsky 5; ☎ 0577 581 265. Large German beer hall complete with traditional Bavarian cuisine. *Mains from US$7; open 11.00–midnight.*

NIGHTLIFE Kharkiv's club scene is concentrated but intense; there's something really big going on almost every weekend. If giant jumping crowds are not your thing, Kharkiv also happens to be A1 central for the country's independent music scene, with several famous groups that cover any genre (rap, jazz, blues, electronica, punk, etc). Check the local *Affiche* to find out what's on.

☆ **Ostannya Barrikada (The Last Barricade)** Sumksaya 73/75; ☎ 0577 548 996. Hip, all-Ukrainian literary club featuring poetry readings, jam sessions, local rock bands and any other art form that promotes the Ukrainian language (eg: The Beatles hits sung in Ukrainian). And yet, things are remarkably relaxed and apolitical – the new wave of 'Kharkiv Romantics'? *Usually open.*

☆ **Agatha Art Club** Revolyutsii; ☎ 0577 073 347; www.agata.kharkov.ua. Groovy hangout with tasty, filling and inexpensive food and lots of live music shows. *Mains from US$2; open 10.00–23.00.*

☆ **Churchill's Music Pub** Darvina 9; ☎ 0662 676 963. Probably the best place in Kharkiv for live, local music with new bands playing almost every night. *Open 14.00–23.00; most bands come on around 19.00.*

☆ **Fidele** Sumskaya 19; ☎ 0577 581 261. Feelgood evening lounge and jazz club evoking 1960s Paris. Regular film nights and incredible live jazz, as well as a very sound in-house café. *Open 11.00–02.00.*

☆ **Misto** Klochkovskaya 190A; ☎ 0577 581 702. 1970–80s club music, house and techno. *Open 24hrs.*

☆ **Dom** Akademika Proskury 3; ☎ 0577 585 749. Brand-new nightclub where the young, beautiful, or rich like to congregate in droves. The DJs are crazy; the music 'progressive electronic pop'. *Open 17.00–dawn.*

☆ **Bolero** 50 let VLKSM 56; ☎ 0577 140 738. Colourful disco where cheesy Russian pop music dominates and the show gets racy. *Open from 18.00–dawn.*

LOCAL TOUR OPERATORS AND TOURIST ASSISTANCE The going rate for a personal English-speaking guide in Kharkiv is US$10 an hour, and most hotels can offer or arrange a comprehensive two-hour walking tour of the city centre. The reception at the newer section of Hotel Kharkiv can answer your tour inquiries and the Mir Service Travel Company (see Hotel Mir) can take care of almost any travel arrangements. Along with the National, these hotels can book travel and theatre tickets.

Otherwise, your best option is the city's own tourist agency at Gosprom (*Ploschad Svobody 5, 6th Podyezd, Office No 520;* ❧ *0572 408 238;* f *0572 452 115*). The staff are friendly and helpful, and besides offering a wealth of local information, they specialise in organising very unique excursions to the surrounding areas. Finding the office is a Soviet experience: go to the big Derzhprom complex. Open the left-hand door under the right-hand concrete bridge (No 6). Don't take the elevator; just push through doors until you see the sign. If you want to get out and explore Kharkiv's beautiful outdoors, contact Stelima Tours (*Poltavsky Shlyakh 140A;* ❧ *0577 581 650;* f *0577 195 212;* e *stelima@ ukr.net; www.stelima.com.ua*). They organise lots of interesting local tours and also rent mountain bikes.

The website www.inform.kharkov.ua can also tell you what is going on, where and when.

WHAT TO SEE Trying to sightsee in Kharkiv is missing the point of the city – a city that has always played a very functional but vibrant role in Soviet and Ukrainian society. Venturing out and about is the way to go, and simply walking around the city centre or enjoying its parks is the best way to 'do' the city. Sumskaya is the oldest and most central street in the city, so named since the road leads to Sumy. Despite the destruction of the war, a few examples of Kharkiv's unique 19th-century architecture remain and today the street is where most of the action is: booksellers, theatres, cafés and clubs.

About midway up the street from the metro station Radyanska is Kharkiv's impressive **Opera House**, a modern and artistic concrete building with excellent shows practically every night. In the park across the street stands the arched 'mirrored fountain' built as a memorial to World War II. The nearby building on the corner of Sumskaya and Teatralnaya is the former KGB headquarters for Kharkiv and looks like it too.

Further up the street is the main green space for the city, the Shevchenko Gardens, centred around Kharkiv's monument to Taras Shevchenko. Although every Ukrainian town has a statue dedicated to the poet, the one in Kharkiv is remarkably moving, with its 16 human-sized bronze sculptures that spiral around his larger-than-life figure. The memorial is a three-dimensional portrait of the history and struggle of the Ukrainian people, beginning with a peasant baby, followed by the captivity of the Cossacks, and moving on to Ukrainian soldiers from both world wars. Crafted in 1935, in the Socialist Realist style, it ends with the Soviet Ukrainian triumph of a female academician and male industrialist gazing off into the enlightened future. Walking through the park (or continuing on Sumskaya) takes you to Ploschad Svobody (Freedom Square), the largest public square in Europe and the second-largest in the world (only Beijing's Tiananmen Square is larger). The open cobblestone space is still the favoured milieu for rallies, parades and mass demonstrations, directed by the imposing statue of Lenin with his arm outstretched.

The curved complex of blocks and bridges at the head of the square houses the city government and reveals the Soviet Union's early experimentation with reinforced concrete. **Gosprom** (Derzhprom in Ukrainian) is a recognised architectural feat for the country and is often used as the textbook example of Soviet post-war construction. The triple-tiered brick building on the left is the central building of Kharkiv University, founded in 1805, and named after the local noble Karazin who raised the funds to start the empire's first academy in Ukraine.

First-time visitors to Ukraine often criticise the soulless rows of concrete apartment blocks that make up so many modern Ukrainian cities. But few actually venture into these spaces. Housing in the USSR was all about giving everyone (almost) equal space, and after the utter destruction of World War II, there was some urgency in the task. An easy and quick design was standardised, and today hundreds of millions of people share identical floor plans.

As Kharkiv grew into the major manufacturing centre for the Soviet Union, the fields to the northeast were set aside to house the influx of workers and their families. In the 1970s a new metro line was extended and a grid of boulevards laid out in 15 oversized city blocks to be filled with row upon row of large-scale housing. The classic Soviet *dým* is constructed of prefabricated concrete slabs and comes in small (five floors), medium (nine floors) or large (16 floors). Nearly one thousand of these white buildings make up Saltovka, often called 'Kharkiv's bedroom'. The neighbourhood's design reinforced positive socialist ideals, with majestic street names like Geroyiv Truda ('The Heroes of Labour') and Traktorostroitelei ('The Street of Tractor Builders'), which marked the daily tram commute from Saltovka to the tractor factory.

Today, Saltovka is home to over 600,000 inhabitants, and if you ask any Russian-speaker in the world, they are bound to have a relative living here. Following the throws of marketisation, privatisation and inflation, an individual's apartment became their greatest (and usually only) stable asset. Today in Saltovka there is a great deal of buying, selling and renting going on but for the most part, people have stayed put and decided this is not a bad place to live. Things are quiet, public transport is good, and there are lots of markets and parks.

Travelling out to Saltovka is beyond the tour guide's remit, but this quintessentially Soviet suburb definitely counts as the real Ukraine. In the evening, looking closely into the hundreds of glowing kitchen windows sitting one atop the other makes it all seem a lot less soulless. To get there, take the subway to metro stations Studentska or Geroyiv Pratsi and ride the trams or trolleys into the heart of the district. Things to see include the bustling markets near Geroyev Truda and on Traktorostroitelei, the bread factory on Saltovksoe Shosse (look for the tallest smokestack), and Kharkiv's tallest building, a dizzying 23-storey concrete *dým* on Prospekt 50 let BLKCM (50 years' anniversary of the young communists' league).

Kharkiv's churches are few and far between, thanks to Stalin's wrath. The one most often shown to tourists is the gold-domed **Uspensky (or Assumption) Cathedral** (*Universitetskaya 21*) built in the late 18th century and turned into an organ recital hall during the Soviet era – if you can, it's definitely worth fitting in a concert here during your stay. The oldest surviving building in Kharkiv is two blocks north: the **Pokrovsky Cathedral** (*Universitetskaya 8*) was built in 1689 and is still undergoing restoration to preserve its unique old-Russian style. By far the most unique building in Kharkiv is the candy-striped **Blagoveschensky Cathedral** built in 1901. The fanciful brick exterior mimics the Byzantine style and the interior is one of the examples of Kharkiv's light, turn-of-the-century design. This was Kharkiv's only church to remain open during the Soviet era.

Nearby is the city's **Tsentralny Rynok (Central Market)** that ranks as a bona fide bazaar, complete with chaos and the distinct aroma of wet cardboard, flesh and fruit. Shoppers and spectators are welcome, but keep a hand on your purse/wallet and go with the flow. Walking from Ploscha Konstitutsii down **Pushkinskaya** offers another candid expression of Kharkiv's mood. Along with the shops and student complexes, you'll pass by the synagogue, art museum and the 'park of youth'.

An impressive but oft-neglected sight is **XT3** (*Khe-te-zey*) – the Kharkiv Tractor Factory. This gargantuan industrial complex supplied the communist world with farm equipment and made Kharkiv's name in the USSR. To get out to the factory, take the metro to Traktorny Zavod (XT3) station and exit on Moskovsky Prospekt. A few examples of Soviet-age tractors are on display outside and signs with human-size letters still offer words of encouragement to the proletariat.

WHAT TO DO With so many workers and students, there is plenty in Kharkiv to keep most people entertained. Number one on the list should be the **Kharkiv Museum of Art** (*Sovnarkomskaya 9/11;* ✎ *0572 477 575; open 10.00–17.00, closed Tue; entrance 4UAH*). To get there, either walk from the centre or take the metro to Arkhitektora Beketova station. Few collections in Ukraine represent so fully the country's artistic legacy, beginning with a quality display of icons and religious art. Most of the paintings are 19th-century Russian impressionist works done by local artists and using local themes such as peasants and the Ukrainian steppe. Some highlights include Semiradsky's *Pirates*, Orlovsky's *Prisoner*, Losenko's *Abel*, and Venig's *Ivan the Terrible and his mother*. The most famous painting in the museum is Ilya Repin's legendary *Zaporizhzhyan Cossacks writing a letter to the Turkish sultan*. Other works in the exhibit by Repin include his *Cossack on the steppe* and *St Nicholas saves three innocents from death*. The **Kharkiv Historical Museum** (*Universitetska 10;* ✎ *0572 228 123; open 10.00–17.00, closed Mon; entrance 5UAH*) resembles most Ukrainian history museums, with lots of old documents and some traditional clothing and craft from Sloboda. Although exhibits frequently change, the best place to buy souvenirs is at the **Kharkiv Folk Craft Museum** (*Pushkinskaya 62; open 10.00–18.00; entrance 5UAH*).

Kharkiv's very strong theatre culture rivals that of the capital and good shows can be expected year-round. The **Opera and Ballet** (*Sumskaya 25;* ✎ *0577 077 043*) usually features a new show every week of outstanding quality. The **Shevchenko Ukrainian Drama Theatre** (*Sumskaya 9;* ✎ *0577 051 366*) is housed in one of the city's oldest theatres and performs traditional comedies in Ukrainian. Kharkiv's **Theatre of Musical Comedy** (*Karla Marksa 32;* ✎ *0577 124 050*) features song and dance, with some shows geared towards children. Tickets for either can be purchased on site or from most hotels. Those who prefer the avant-garde should try the highly creative **Novaya Scena** (*Sumskaya 59, No 36;* ✎ *0577 005 964*).

Famous among children and adults in Ukraine, the **Kharkiv Puppet Theatre** (*Ploschad Konstitutsiya 24;* ✎ *0577 127 395*) puts on amusing performances during the day and in the early evening. The diverse repertoire includes the *Divine Comedy* and the uproarious *12 Chairs*.

For Soviet-style fun and games, head out to **Park Gorkovo**, Kharkiv's outdoor amusement park at the very end of Sumskaya. Trees, war memorials and carnival rides run year-round, as does a child's railroad. Another amusement is the **Kharkiv Zoo** inside the main park (*open 8.00 to 20.00; entrance 3UAH*). The menagerie is limited, but local animals are well represented: foxes, wolves, wild cats and lots of birds.

OUTSIDE KHARKIV Ukraine's most beloved painter was born and raised just outside of Kharkiv in the small village of **Chuguyev** (**Чугуев**). Ilya Repin (1844–1930) is best known for his very humanistic version of impressionism, and although he spent much of his life studying and painting in Russia, his work is most often used to illustrate Ukrainian national consciousness. His *Zaporizhzhyan*

CHILDREN'S HOME NO I When I first lived in Kharkiv, I used to visit this orphanage twice a week and help with any odd jobs or simply play with the kids. Today, Kharkiv's Children's Home No 1 houses and cares for 120 abandoned or orphaned children, ranging from the ages of two months to four years. Although suitably funded by the city government, the facility can always use outside help. If you are in the city and interested, the administration welcomes visitors offering in-kind donations or a helpful hand. Because of government regulations regarding safety standards and sterilisation, please do not show up with food, medicine or diapers. Instead, things like shoes, clothing, toys, or any fun 'extras' are the best things to bring. Any cash donations are issued with a receipt and usually put towards the constant and expensive process of baby-milk sterilisation. If you come bearing gifts, the best time to arrive is during the day between 10.00 and 13.00. If you're thinking of any large-scale projects, these can be discussed with the Head Doctor, Elena Yurievna Chistilina (*Gorodskoi Dom Rebyonka Nomer 1; Kuznetskaya 1;* ✆ *0572 321 134*).

LIFE 2 ORPHANS Kharkiv's Children's Home No 1 is just one of dozens of orphanages that benefit from the work of Life 2 Orphans, a US-based organisation which manages contributions to over 6,000 children in Ukraine. As a non-profit organisation, they rely solely on the goodwill and charity of others to continue their good work of sending money, food, clothes and medical care to Ukraine. Their proven success lies in the special attention they pay to the accountability of the institutions with which they work. Money donations and in-kind contributions go directly to the children, and often photos of the results of your gift are sent back to you. Contact them online (e *kellys@life2orphans.org; www.life2orphans.org*).

Cossacks write a letter to the Turkish sultan depicts the legendary warriors crowded round a table and composing a scathing rebuff to the sultan's offer to join forces. A little-known fact is that Repin was painting the picture when a Russian noble saw the unfinished product and wanted it for himself. As the original work had already been commissioned, Repin hurriedly made a copy and sold it to the nobleman without him knowing it was a copy. Repin was a leading member of the group of Russian artists known as 'the wanderers' and today the majority of his work is on display at the Russian Museum in St Petersburg. Some of his other well-known pieces include the *Volga Boatmen* and *Ivan the Terrible and his Son*.

The painter's first home is now a museum of his life, on Nikitinskaya Street in the centre of Chuguyev. The village is about 40km from Kharkiv, and a visit to the birthplace and museum is usually offered as a day trip (6 hours) by most hotels or Kharkiv's city tour agency.

Travelling in the opposite direction towards the town of **Bogodukhov** (**Богодухов,** 'God of the Spirits') there is a turn at **Maksimovka** (**Максимовка**) that leads to the minuscule village of **Skovorodinovka** (**Сковородиновка**), the final resting place of **Grigory Savvich Skovoroda** (1722–94), Ukrainian philosopher, poet and traveller. Skovoroda was born in Sloboda, studied in Kharkiv, Kiev and Hungary, taught in Pereyaslav and was known as an avid wanderer who criss-crossed Ukraine and much of eastern Europe on foot, telling stories, singing songs and writing poems. He never published a single book in his lifetime but is now revered as a founding father of Ukrainian intellectualism. The epitaph on his grave reads: 'The world chased me but could not catch me.' The Skovoroda memorial and museum is built in the home where the philosopher died and reveals Soviet tastes in the portrayal of his life. However, the village offers a good taste of rural Sloboda. A recent focus highlights the philosopher's love of the Ukrainian landscape, and outside the museum is a giant oak tree that supposedly shaded the philosopher in his thought, as well as two ponds where he used to swim. Kharkiv's city agency offers day trips out to Skovorodinovka, but most hotels can arrange the transport, as you can get out there only by taxi or *marshrutka*.

POLTAVA ПОЛТАВА

This quaint and orderly town represents the country's cultural heartland and is the most visited spot in left-bank Ukraine. Poltava's travel appeal is based on the area's long-standing provincial lifestyle and its convenient access from Kiev or Kharkiv – Ukraine's newest train allows visitors from either city to travel quickly and enjoy a more picturesque version of the country.

The city is best remembered for the fateful Battle of Poltava fought in 1709 during the Great Northern War, when Sweden and Russia were vying for control over the Baltic. Swedish King Charles XII planned to march on Moscow through Ukraine and made a first attack at Poltava where a Russian regiment was based near the Vorskla River. The forces of Peter the Great outnumbered the Swedes two to one and the quick defeat was inevitable. Peter left a strong military legacy in Poltava and redesigned the city to resemble a miniature St Petersburg, spreading out from a central granite obelisk in honour of the victory. The battlefield is now a park in the north of the city.

For Ukrainians, the Battle of Poltava is a tough piece of history to swallow. The Cossack *hetman* Ivan Mazepa had long been a close ally of Peter, but chose Swedish protection after the tsar grew less conscious of Ukrainian autonomy. A strong retaliation by the tsar divided the Cossack leadership and quashed all hopes for Ukraine's sovereignty. The Russian Empire was now the major power of northern Europe and would dominate this area for the next 300 years. And yet today Poltava and its environs are known throughout Ukraine as the nostalgic interior, the place where the purest form of Ukrainian language is still spoken freely, unadulterated by foreign (Russian) influence. Hearing the melodious dialect of Poltava is a delight.

All kinds of disputed metaphors are used to compare the function of Ukrainian cities to parts of the body (ie: Kiev is the head), but Poltava has always been linked to Ukraine's soul. Literature fans come this way to see the native land of writers like Gogol, Mirny, Korolenko and Kotlyarevsky – a land of cultural festivals, strong tradition and frequent country markets. Poltavschina has remained Ukraine's great agricultural prize and is known as one of the cleaner spots this side of the Dnepr.

GETTING THERE AND AWAY Riding into Poltava on the train gives the best view of the town with its perched convent and cupolas and rows of tin-roof cottages. If you are arriving from the east, enjoy the curves; this bit of track holds the record for the sharpest turn of any railroad in the world.

Poltava is the main rail stop between Kharkiv and Kiev, meaning train travel to or from anywhere else in the country should be planned through those cities. There are two train stations in Poltava: Pivdenna (*Ploscha Slavy 1*) and Kyivska (*Stepana Kondratenka 12*), on the western side of the city. Most inter-regional trains stop at Pivdenna, where foreigners must buy their tickets at the separate *Servisna Kasa* (✆ 0532 132 001). The Capital Express goes to Kyivska station, passing through Poltava twice daily in both directions to Kharkiv (2 hours) and Kiev (3½ hours). Tickets in either direction cost US$10–15 depending on class of seat.

There are also plenty of slow trains, including the main Kharkiv–Kiev connection that gets to Poltava after midnight, and a direct overnight train to and

If you visit Ukraine in winter, you may be shocked to see people running barefoot through the snow or jumping naked through holes in the ice. They splash around in the water happily and then walk back across the ice with frozen hair and smiles on their faces. These are Ukraine's *morzhei* (the Russian for 'walruses') and they are not madmen, but followers of an old form of Slavic yoga. True walruses bathe outdoors every day of the year, in rivers, lakes or the sea. The ability to withstand 0°C water takes at least six months of daily training, and an average winter swim will only last slightly longer than one minute, the time it takes to get the full 'effect'. (I've seen some old men stay in the water for more than two minutes!) Walruses claim the practice of bathing outdoors in winter strengthens their immune system to the point that they never catch cold in winter. A bather prepares for each frigid dip by doing intense physical exercise beforehand, slowly peeling off layers of clothing, widening a hole in the ice and then jumping in. Walruses normally swim in the early morning, and the best place to see them in Ukraine is on the Vorskla River in Poltava, the Kharkiv River in Kharkiv, all along the Dnepr and in Crimea.

from Kiev that conveniently arrives in the morning. To and from Kharkiv via Poltava, direct trains service Simferopol (14 hours), Luhansk (12 hours), Odessa (13 hours) and Ivano-Frankivsk (20 hours). The train to Kremenchuk (3 hours) is a popular option, but by bus the journey takes half the time.

Because train options are somewhat limited, taking the bus from Poltava can sometimes be a good idea. The private bus company Gunsel has a twice-daily service to Poltava between Kiev (5 hours) and Donetsk (6 hours). Their office is at the main bus station, best reached by taxi or the No 7 bus (*Velikotyrnovskaya 7;* ↘ *0532 663 786*). Avtoluks also has a daily service to Kiev, with an office at the main station (↘ *0532 585 019*). There are also regular buses to Kremenchuk (1½ hours), Dnepropetrovsk (4 hours) and Cherkassy (5 hours). Poltava's other bus station is better for local destinations and is located near the city centre (*Shevchenka 65a;* ↘ *0532 396 79*).

LOCAL TOUR OPERATORS If you need some extra help seeing things or getting something done, try **Eurotur** (*Gogolya 25A;* ↘ *0532 501 374;* e *evrotour@ sedtor.net.ua*). The agency has an ecological bent and does a variety of interesting local tours in and around Poltava. The Eurotur offices can be found at Chapayeva 9A; ↘ 0532 222 986; f 0532 509 626; e vegatyr-poltava@mail.ru .

WHERE TO STAY Despite its small size, Poltava is not entirely new to tourism but still lacks a strong hotel base.

Gallery Frunze 7; ↘ 0532 561 697; f 0532 563 121; e slbipol@kot.poltava.ua; www.hotel.poltava.ua. For now, the most luxurious accommodation can be found here. Small and refined, this private hotel is connected to a modern art gallery next to the new pedestrian shopping zone of the city centre. Big beds, good plumbing (24hr hot water), internet access, guarded parking and a new sauna put it a step ahead of the rest of the city. *Rooms are charged pp: dbl with shower US$95 for 1/US$120 for 2. The spacious junior*

suites with bath and shower cost US$180. According to the brochure, the luxury suites allow 'your dreams to be embodied in a reality' but this will cost you US$370/night.

Palazzo Gogolya 33; ↘ 0532 611 203. Another very sophisticated option, this brand new boutique hotel features a wide range of big and comfortable rooms, lots of personal attention, and everything necessary for business travellers (internet access, business centre, etc), and a hearty b/fast is inc. Credit cards accepted. The in-house Italian restaurant is very good and credit cards are accepted here too. *Standard rooms from US$80 sgl/US$100 dbl, with bigger 'junior' suites US$125/US$140.*

⌂ **Riviera** Rybalsky 16; ☎ 0532 572 344; e pergat@pi.net.ua; www.riviera.poltava.ua. A new, strictly 'business' hotel. *Business-class rooms US$80–120.*

⌂ **Hotel Kiev** Simnaya 2/49; ☎ 0532 224 286. A rather shoddy option, but offers a good location for independent travellers between the city centre and Kievsky train station. They do have a few decent suites with baths that cost around US$45 a night. Otherwise, the Kiev falls in the budget category in terms of price and quality. *Normal dbl with bath*

US$12, and for a bed you pay US$4.

⌂ **Hotel Turist** Mira 12; ☎ 0532 220 921. Slightly better; is near the river. Overall the complex makes a dismal impression, but they do have some remodelled rooms with clean bathrooms. *Sgl US$15, a good dbl US$20; the best-quality option is the US$60 suite.*

⌂ **Motel Poltava** Hrushevskovo 1; ☎ 0532 230 024. The former Inturist is the on the far southern edge of town. The location is terrible but the remodelled rooms are the nicest of the former Soviet variety. *Sgls US$40, new dbl with shower (24hr hot water) US$55, the slightly larger half-lux is US$75.*

The Kiev, Turist and Poltava accept cash payment only.

✖ **WHERE TO EAT** Restaurants in Poltava are on the up, with a few distinctly solid choices and lots of new cafés popping up.

✖ **Ivanova Gora** Soborna Ploshcha 2; ☎ 0532 560 003; f 0532 563 221; e iv-hora@poltava.ua; www.iv-hora.poltava.ua. Most tour groups will visit this ultra-refined restaurant. Built near the historic site of Belaya Besedka (the owners claim that a strong 'bio-energy' envelops the restaurant – see page 416). The 'luxury' restaurant serves rather unadventurous national cuisine with the exception of *Poltavsky Holushki*, a local dumpling soup. But overall the food is tasty and not expensive. A banqueting room is now the coveted venue for up-and-coming Ukrainian pop stars. *Mains from US$10; open 10.00–02.00*

✖ **Poltavska Bytva** (Battle of Poltava) R Luxembourga 72; ☎ 0532 193 391. Commemorating the famed event of the same name in food. Dishes are diverse, yet each honours Poltava's history, including a 'Swedish b/fast' and a delicious Poltava salad. *Mains from US$5; open 11.00–23.00.*

✖ **Obolon** (as in the Ukrainian beer) Oktyabrskaya 51; ☎ 0532 220 988. For something more down to earth, try Obolon near the central circle. The menu offers classic Ukrainian cuisine and nothing on it costs more than US$3; *open 10.00–midnight.*

✖ **Café Mimino** Biryuzova 15. Authentic Georgian food (soups, savoury pastries, kebabs) on offer. *Mains from US$5; open 12.00–23.00.*

✖ **Pit Stop** Kharkivske Shosse 8A; ☎ 0532 510 629. Local pizzeria that serves pizza in addition to lots of pastries and desserts. *Pizza from US$4; open 07.00–midnight.*

✖ **Café Venetsia** (**Venice**) 46 Oktyabrskaya; ☎ 0532 274 496. For sit-down coffee and pastries at teatime, b/fast time or night time, Venetsia comes highly recommended by other travellers. The very clean, very calm and very sophisticated café sells a huge range of fresh cakes, savoury rolls, and pastries baked fresh in-house every day. Handmade chocolate truffles and rich coffee make it hard to leave.

In addition, each hotel also features its own restaurant. The **Palazzo** hotel has a fantastic in-house Italian restaurant with authentic northern Italian dishes (*mains from US$10; open 10.00–23.00*). The **Riviera** hotel restaurant sticks to Russian gourmet classics like caviar, sturgeon, other fish and poultry (*mains from US$10; open 10.00–midnight*). **Gallery**'s is small but with good food; the **Hotel Kiev**'s 'Shanghai' serves convincing Chinese food with surprisingly good service; a full meal will cost under US$10.

WHAT TO SEE AND DO Much of Poltava's centre is pedestrian-only and there are parks at nearly every other block, so enjoy the walk if you can. The city spreads out from a grand roundabout centred on the tall pinnacle monument commemorating the Battle of Poltava. The circle and surrounding white Neoclassical government buildings were built as a direct replica of the Palace Square in St Petersburg. Eight boulevards lead from the circle into various city districts. Most of the action and best shops are on Oktyabrskaya and Lenina.

Poltava has preserved a few examples of whimsical, modern Ukrainian folk architecture. Two very rare structures include the very beautiful red-brick **Old Russian Village Bank** (*Oktyabrskaya 39*), and the mosaic-clad **Poltava Natural History Museum** (*Lenina 2; open 10.00–17.00, closed Wed; entrance 3UAH*). It is worth visiting the museum just to see its decorative exterior and the very traditional interior with its flower and vine design and wall painting. The full-time exhibit is like most of its kind, telling the story of Poltava through presentations on local nature, industry and agriculture. Religious art, traditional costumes and *pysanky* (coloured eggs) are also on display, along with a room dedicated solely to Chernobyl, and another to old farm equipment.

At the end of Oktyabrskaya is the **Soborny Maidan**, a park and adjoining square with a cluster of historical monuments. The most ancient remnants of Poltava are at **Belaya Besedka**, the high outcrop facing out over the southwest valley. The white-pillared, Greek-style Friendship Rotunda was built in 1953 to celebrate the 300th anniversary of the Pereyaslav union between Ukraine and Russia. On the other side of the street is a monument dedicated to the birth of Poltava, claiming the city is 800 years old (some say 1,100), although a nearby and much older Scythian ruin is marked by the single remaining tower of the **Church of the Assumption** (the rest of the church is now being rebuilt). The cute thatched-roof cottage (*Soborny Maidan No 3; ☏ 0532 272 073; open 10.00–18.00, closed Mon; entrance 5UAH*) is the restored home of writer **Ivan Kotlyarevsky** (1769–1838) who wrote *Eneida*, a Cossack parody of the *Aeneid* and the very first publication of Ukrainian prose. The exhibit is very hands-on and a simple walk around the old house and garden is interesting, even if you don't read Ukrainian.

For war buffs, military historians, interested folk and Swedes, the **Battle of Poltava History Museum** is on Shvedskaya Mogila 32 (*a street named 'Swedish Grave'; open 10.00–17.00, entrance 5UAH*). Period objects and artefacts, some owned by Peter the Great, are on display. A monument to Peter I stands next to the museum; across the street is the remarkable 19th-century Sampson's Church (the Russians defeated the Swedes on St Sampson's Day) with the Grave of Russian Brotherhood nearby. If you walk around the battlefield you can see the countless other memorials marking the front line of the Russian regiment, and showing where Peter the Great stood during the battle. To the far north is a monument to Swedish losses during the battle.

Poltava's most revered church is the **Khrestovozdvyzhensky Convent**, a mystical white edifice perched on top of the highest hill in the city. Built in 1699, this is the only Baroque cathedral in Ukraine to have kept all seven of its original cupolas. The complex consists of four buildings: a summer chapel, a smaller winter chapel, the dormitory and a choir school (ringing the small bell is said to bring blessings). A visit allows close encounters with the lives of Orthodox nuns and the singing is divine. Bus No 18 goes to the convent from the central bus station on Shevchenko. Otherwise, a taxi costs US$2.

MIRGOROD МИРГОРОД

Literally the 'City of Peace', Mirgorod was made famous first by the writer Gogol and then became renowned for its therapeutic mineral water, now sold all over Ukraine and apparently good for your intestines. The water itself tastes rather salty, but they say that's good for you. If you look closely at the label on the

Mirgorodskaya water bottles you will see the Church of the Holy Assumption with its silver turrets. The church now stands in the middle of the *kurort,* or resort complex, where countless spas heal everything from stomach aches to radiation sickness. Day visitors can drink of the water freely from the *buvyet* and sit on the lakeside beach, but don't expect much in terms of tourist amenities. Even with Mirgorod's huge resort base, access to overnight stays is often limited to Ukrainians with doctors' prescriptions. Still, money gets priority and foreigners seeking treatment should contact the *kurort* (*Gogolya 112;* ℩ *0535 552 604; www.mirgorodkurort.com*). Keep in mind that Mirgorod is still very much off the beaten path. The sanatorium with the most experience in hosting foreigners is the **Gogol** (*formerly known as Yuzhny; Mirgorodskykh Divizii 22;* ℩ *0535 546 508*). The sanatorium continues to function Soviet-style, which means lots of free health care and low prices; minimum stay 12 days, maximum 24, for around US$20–30 per night. Otherwise, the only functioning hotel is the **Mirgorod** (*Gogolya 102;* ℩ *0535 552 737*). All rooms cost under US$20, there is rarely hot water and the staff will try to keep you from staying. The only restaurant (besides the café in the town store) is **Grand Pizza** (*Gogolya 16;* ℩ *0535 553 382*). Besides pizza (US$2) and real Italian ice cream, this is the only place in Mirgorod where you can use your credit card and which has a clean bathroom.

GETTING THERE AND AWAY The Mirgorod train station (*Zheleznodorozhna 2;* ℩ *0535 552 473*) is on the main line of the Capital Express speed train linking Kiev (3½ hours) and Kharkiv (2½ hours). The bus station is directly across from the health resort complex (℩ *0535 552 204*). Buses link to the smaller villages of Poltavschina, including the famous market town of Veliky Sorochintsy.

SUMY СУМИ

Historically a large and important city of the northeast, Sumy does not warrant any particular highlighting today except that it is a pleasantly average town of the Sloboda. Founded in 1655 on the River Psyol, this was the largest of the Cossack fortresses in Sloboda. The town's name comes from the old Slavic word for bags (*suma*) after the first inhabitants found three leather bags of gold stashed in an oak tree – or so peasant legend claims. Originally, Sumy competed with Kharkiv in size and industry and during Ukraine's 19th-century sugar rush, Sumy province was growing most of the sugar beets. Civil war, the great famine and several five-year plans left an especially destructive impression on Sumy. Walking through Sumy today bears witness to the stylistic blend of Russian and Ukrainian influences in Sloboda. In recent years, the city has seen an increase in travellers who come for the summer fairs and international organ festivals.

GETTING THERE AND AWAY Sumy is slightly off the beaten path, so the trains are not always convenient. It is best to travel on one of the six daily trains to and from Kharkiv (4 hours). Coming from Kiev (twice daily) involves a very tedious seven-hour journey. Other routes from Sumy service Chernihiv (7 hours), Simpferopol (13 hours), Minsk (14 hours) and Moscow (16 hours). The train station is at the end of Prospekt Shevchenka (℩ *0542 284 537*). *Marshrutka* constantly run into the city and usually drop off by the central market. A taxi to any of Sumy's hotels will cost US$1 or less.

Sumy is only two-and-a-half hours from Kharkiv by car or taxi; the going rate is around US$40. The bus station is on the west side of town at Baumana 40 and buses go everywhere. It is probably only worthwhile taking a bus to Kharkiv (3 hours), or to the outlying areas, like Glukhiv (2½ hours).

One of the fathers of Russian literature's golden age was Nikolai Gogol (1809–52), born in Sorochintsy (Gogolevo) and schooled in Poltava. Ukrainians like to claim Gogol as their own since he was Ukrainian, took much of his material from Ukrainian folklore, and set his tales in the Poltava countryside. Russians also have a claim on Gogol since he wrote in Russian, lived in St Petersburg, and was a member of the Russian civil service. Either way, the seemingly uneventful hinterland of Poltavschina was the rural home he brought to life in his first series, *Evenings on a Farm Near Dikanka*. The fantastical stories are narrated by the tittering yokel and village beekeeper Rudy Panko who, like Gogol, is a devout Christian and a firm believer in witches, devils, magic and spells. Besides painting a rich picture of Ukrainian farm life, Panko recounts the strange things he's seen and heard.

Travellers can get to **Dikanka (Диканка)** on their own by taking one of five daily buses from Poltava's central station (1 hour). These days Dikanka is a bit of a lonely and deadbeat place, which will make it all the more endearing to true Gogol fans. Villagers are both friendly and suspicious towards outsiders but they keep Gogol's statue surrounded by fresh flowers. Due to collectivisation in the 1930s the fields seem rather vast and dramatic, but the village appears unchanged, with lots of squawking geese and children playing outside. The small town museum and single café mark the village centre, and the Troitska Church is that same church from the story *Christmas Eve*.

The most renowned of the Dikanka stories tells about the annual country fair at **Veliky Sorochintsy (Великий Сорочиний),** where a young man makes a secret pact with a Gypsy in order to win a maiden's hand. The country fair still continues each year in the late summer with lots of costumed dancers, re-enactments of Gogol's stories and Ukrainian folk singing. Gogol was also christened here in the 18th-century Transfiguration Church. To get to Veliky Sorochintsy take the bus from Mirgorod (1 hour; 5 daily).

Even after his success with the Dikanka stories, Gogol sought recognition as a professor of world history in St Petersburg. His students claimed he knew nothing about history and was therefore a failure, but that his storytelling skills were valued by all. His next published book was titled *Mirgorod* and included the swashbuckling Cossack legend Taras Bulba. A bright bronze statue of the writer sits outside the Mirgorod train station, but there is little modern reference in the town today. About 25km east of Mirgorod is Gogol's birthplace, now named Gogolevo (**Гоголево**) in his honour. Getting there by train is tricky, since only the rare *elektrichki* go there, but the village is only 25km away and taxis and buses do make the trip. The Gogol family estate and museum honours the writer.

If you have not read any Gogol, travelling in his country will make you want to – his opening lines describe the area so well, demanding from the reader in one line: 'Do you know the Ukrainian night?' *Evenings on a Farm Near Dikanka* gives a proper introduction to the superstitious culture of rural Ukraine, but his most famous book is *Dead Souls*. His dramas include *The Government Inspector* which is often performed at the Gogol Drama Theatre in Poltava (*Oktyabrskaya 23*).

WHERE TO STAY

Sumy Maidan Nezalezhnosti 1; 0542 183 068. This towering concrete high-rise rises high above the central square and was recently remodelled into a very welcoming and comfortable hotel. Everything is modern and clean, the plumbing and hot water are reliable and the staff are young and efficient. Credit cards accepted. *Sgl US$45, dbl US$60, nicer suites US$80–100.*

Hotel Khimik Pselskaya 14; 0542 224 500; f 0542 220 093. Slightly less inviting; heating, AC and a private hot-water source mean comfort, and the rooms are spacious and well furnished, but it's not as nice as the Sumy. B/fast is inc and credit cards are accepted. Khimik's restaurant is a typical Ukrainian/Russian-style endeavour serving inexpensive borsch, varenniki and lots of homemade pork sausage. Most rooms US$60, but there are few at US$25–40.

🏠 **Hotel Ukrayina** Frunze 1; ☎ 0542 222 220. The oldest accommodation in the city. Standards are low but not abysmal. There is 24hr hot water and the sauna can be rented out in 2hr segments for US$15. Sgl with shower and toilet US$20, dbl suites US$35.

🍴 **WHERE TO EAT** Quite a few new restaurants and cafés have opened up in Sumy so that the hungry traveller should have no problems finding lots of filling meals outwith the hotel restaurants listed.

🍴 **Stary Mlyn** Pereulok Dachny 9; ☎ 0542 223 604. Real home-style Ukrainian cooking is rare for a restaurant, but Stary Mlyn pulls it off very well. Housed in a restored mill converted to look like a Sloboda farmhouse, the owner and antique collector pursues a philosophy of advertising Sumy's identity through good food and a cosy atmosphere. The bar is built into the old woodstove and visitors can choose to eat up inside the mill or out on the terrace near Sumy's 'beach'. For a slight change of atmosphere and menu the management also runs the **Carpathian Kolyba** next door. Mains from US$5;

open 10.00–23.00.
🍴 **Gurman** Petropavolovskaya 65. This Armenian restaurant is a new local favourite serving authentic and spicy cuisine in a very warm setting. Mains from US$5; open 10.00–23.00.
🍴 **Chaikoff** Voskresenska 10. For fancy pastries with very fancy coffee. Pastries from US$2; open 09.00–22.00.
🍴 **Pancake Café (Blyny)** Soborna 36. Serves sweet and savoury crêpes to your taste. Pancakes from US$1; open 10.00–21.00.

WHAT TO SEE AND DO Most Sumy citizens will point the way to their former courthouse, now the **Regional Museum** (Kirova 2; ☎ 0542 221 441; open 09.00–17.00, closed Mon; entrance 1UAH). What sets the display apart from others is the wide collection of World War II memorabilia, much of it German: propaganda, helmets, guns and uniforms. (Perhaps this is retribution for the heavy looting of city treasures from this museum by the Nazis.) A permanent photography exhibit is also quite outstanding. Folk crafts, an old Sloboda farmhouse and a mini-shrine to Shevchenko complete the museum.

Sumy's three main churches deserve mention. The light blue **Spaso-Preobrazhensky Cathedral** (Soborna 31) was built in the 18th century and is very open and light on the inside, with two brassy gold domes. The mint-green **Svyato-Voskresenska Church** (Maidan Nezalezhnosti) was built in 1702 and stands as a rare monument to early Sloboda architecture, with its compact Greek-cross floor plan and triple turrets (it was also used as a fort). The stately high-domed **Troitsky Cathedral** on top of the 'old hill' is the youngest of the three, built in 1901 in imitation classic and Baroque styles. The building has only just been re-consecrated as a church after decades as a Soviet 'organ hall'. The handmade Czech organ is world famous and frequent organ festivals are played in this spacious chapel.

A number of very small but very ancient villages are spread throughout the region, all of which can be reached by bus or taxi, but which are rarely included in group tours. About two-and-a-half hours north of Sumy is the historic town of **Glukhiv** which originally belonged to 11th-century Kievan Rus and was later the hetman capital of left-bank Ukraine. It was here that Peter the Great tried and hanged an effigy of Ivan Mazepa after his 'betrayal' at Poltava (see page 413). The event took place in front of the Church of St Nicholas, built in 1686.

Appendix I

LANGUAGE

The official language of Ukraine is Ukrainian, although most Ukrainians speak both Ukrainian and Russian. In the EU and many post-colonial nations of the world, people speak a lingua franca like English or French. For a very long time, Russian was the 'international language' for many Ukrainians, not to mention the official language of the Soviet Union, promoted by the 'Friendship of Peoples' campaign. Anyone you meet over the age of 30 most likely grew up speaking Russian at school and at work. Today, the younger generation is opting towards learning English or French as their chosen second language, but many of them still know and use Russian. Obviously, you should never expect people to speak or understand English. Travellers are often surprised and complain to me that in Ukraine 'nobody speaks English'. That's because it's Ukraine.

The Cyrillic alphabet scares most people off as you are essentially learning to read all over again. Learn it. Simply knowing the letters will enliven your trip, and speaking the very basics of Russian and Ukrainian (*please, thank you, excuse me*) allows you a better connection with the land and people.

LANGUAGE POLITICS A long time ago, Russian and Ukrainian were the same language, similar to Old Church Slavonic. History and geography separated the two groups and allowed enough improvisation and evolution to turn them into two separate languages in around the 12th century. Foreign governance, namely by the Russian and Polish élite, meant for a time that the Ukrainian language survived among the lower, uneducated classes only. Strict suppression of the Ukrainian language in the 17th through to the 19th century, and all throughout the Soviet era, became synonymous with Ukraine's lack of independence and self-determination. Today, speaking Ukrainian has come to represent an important political symbol of freedom and self-determination. Although some of the protestors on the Maidan preferred speaking Russian, the slogans of the Orange Revolution were in Ukrainian. The Orange Revolution helped make Ukrainian even more 'cool', so that today you will hear Ukrainian hip hop music, and ethnic Russian politicians will only sound off on TV in Ukrainian. Like all national movements, things can swing too far in the other direction, and Ukraine's many native Russian-speakers took to making their own linguistic stance, felt most strongly in the parliamentary elections of 2006. Nowadays though, the tension over language seems to have lessened as the back and forth has created some linguistic flexibility and left the capital completely bilingual. In Kiev, it is quite common to hear Russian-speaking parents address their children in Ukrainian in the hope that their children will learn both languages. It is also very common to hear a conversation where different parties speak different languages back and forth to one another with full comprehension.

WHERE TO SPEAK WHICH You'll find that certain areas of the country speak only Ukrainian, others speak Russian, and others jump in and out of both interchangeably. Many Ukrainian cities – like Kiev – are totally bilingual. The regional chapters above imply which language is prominent in the respective areas, but the sensitive traveller will be aware and prepared for both. Throughout the country, all signs and announcements are in Ukrainian, with the exception of Crimea and a few cases in the east. The question people ask is 'How different are they?' Everyone has a different answer (they're often compared to Spanish and Portuguese) but what's most important is that they are different enough to have existed separately for nearly 1,000 years.

In western Ukraine you should make a concerted effort to speak Ukrainian (Galicia, Volhynia, the Carpathians, Podillya and Polissya). These are areas where Ukrainian was permitted to an extent and people actually use it in their homes. In Crimea, Donbas, the Dnepr and parts of Sloboda, plan on hearing and speaking Russian. In Kiev, you can speak either Russian or Ukrainian; the same goes for the western part of Sloboda (Poltava) and areas of central Ukraine (the Poltava dialect is considered the purist and most melodious form of Ukrainian). Also, keep in mind that urban areas may be Russian-speaking, but the countryside will speak Ukrainian. You will meet some people who are very fussy one way or another, and others who are happy to communicate however they can. Be sensitive and try to use a few words in whichever language they do. This is by no means intended as a language guide, but it may help to provide you with a fairly simple start.

THE CYRILLIC ALPHABET The Ukrainian alphabet is not as daunting as it may look. Many letters are the same as or use the Greek equivalent. If you think that learning a whole new language is not for you, so be it, but getting the alphabet down is the key to finding your way around and enjoying your stay. A self-proclaimed non-linguist traveller recommends finding a video shop in Ukraine and spending an hour or so reading all the Cyrillic covers of movies you know. Once you've broken the barrier of Cyrillic, you'll realise that much of Ukrainian and Russian is cognitive (like Stop/Стоп and Sport/Спорт and Surprise/Сюрприз).

Letters		Ukrainian pronunciation
А	а	'ah' as in almond
Б	б	'b' as in boat
В	в	'v' as in vivacious
Г	г	'h' as in halo
Д	д	'd' as in doctor
Е	е	'eh' as in set
Є	є	'yeh'
Ж	ж	'zh' as in mirage
З	з	'z' as in zebra
И	и	'y' (short 'i') as in myth
Й	й	closes an 'ee' sound or 'И'
І	і	long 'ee'
Ї	ї	'yee' as in old English 'ye'
К	к	'k' as in kitten
Л	л	'l' as in lemon
М	м	'm' as in man
Н	н	'n' as in nice
О	о	'o' as in Oh!
П	п	'p' as in pole
Р	р	'r'; short and rolled
С	с	's' as in sesame
Т	т	't' as in tight
У	у	'oo' as in moon
Ф	ф	'f' as in fruit
Х	х	'kh' (gutteral) as in 'Bach'
Ц	ц	'ts' as in bits

Ч	ч	'ch' as in cheddar
Ш	ш	'sh' as in shop
Щ	щ	'shch' as in fresh cheese
Ю	ю	'yoo' as in you
Я	я	'ya' as in yacht
Ь	ь	soft sign, often transliterated as an apostrophe and used after 'hard' consonants д, э, л, н, с, т, ц. 'Soften' a letter by barely making a 'y' sound (as in yes) right as you stop saying the consonant.

Russian letters

Г	г	G as in go
Е	е	*yeh* as in yes
Ё	ё	*yo* as in yo-yo
Э	э	eh, as in Ukrainian 'E'
И	и	long *ee* sound
Й	й	closes an *'ee'* sound or 's'
Ы	ы	y, like Ukrainian 'и'
Ъ	ъ	hard sign; causes an audible break in the word

Vowels are the main difference between Russian and Ukrainian sounds. Ukrainian vowels (and consonants) are always pronounced as written and tend to sound softer. Russian vowels change from long to short depending on where they fall in a word. Remember the key difference is to say *'yeh'* found in so many Russian words, and saying the same letter 'E' as *'eh'* in Ukrainian. Always remember that Г is 'H' in Ukrainian and 'G' in Russian.

Both languages are much more phonetic than English, so just sound the words out. Stresses are underlined. Test your knowledge of Cyrillic by covering the transliterations and reading down the column. (NB: To complicate matters further, the Cyrillic letter Д is handwritten as *'D'* when capitalised; *'g'* when lower case. The Cyrillic letter Т is handwritten as *three slanted lines joined with a crossbar* when capitalised; *'m'* when lower case.)

Verbs Most Ukrainian verbs are completely different from Russian. Luckily, they conjugate very similarly to one another.

Infinitives

to think	думати	*dumaty*	думать	*dumat*
to live	жити	*zhyty*	жить	*zhyt*
to wait	чекати	*chekahty*	ждать	*zhdat*
to work	працювати	*pratsyuvahty*	аботать	*rabotat*
I think	думаю	*dumayu*	думаю	*dumayu*
You (sing.) think	думаєш	*dumayesh*	думаешь	*dumayesh*
He/she thinks	думає	*dumaye*	думает	*dumayet*
We think	думаємо	*dumayemo*	думаем	*dumayem*
You (plural) think	думаєте	*dumayeteh*	думаете	*dumayete*
They think	думають	*dumayut*	думають	*dumayut*
I live	живу	*zhyvoo*	живу	*zhivoo*
You (sing) live	живеш	*zhyvesh*	живёшь	*zhivyosh*
he/she lives	живе	*zhyveh*	живёт	*zhivyot*
we live	живемо	*zhyvemo*	живём	*zhivyom*
you (plural) live	живете	*zhyvehteh*	живёте	*zhivyotyeh*
they live	живуть	*zhyvut*	живут	*zhivut*

BASICS

	Ukrainian		Russian	
Good morning	Добрий ранок	*dobry ranok*	Доброе утро	*dobre oodra*
Hello (formal)	Добрий день	*dobry dehn*	Здравствуйте	*zdrastvwytye*
Hi (casual)	Привіт	*pryveet*	Привет	*privyet*
Good evening	Добрий вечір	*dobry vecheer*	Добрый вечер	*dobry vyecher*
Good night (farewell)	Надобраніч	*nadobraneech*	Спокойной ночи	*spokoiny nochee*
Goodbye	До повачення	*do pobachennya*	До свидания	*dasvidanya*
Yes	Так	*tak*	Да	*da*
No	Ні	*nee*	Нет	*nyet*
Please	Будь ласка	*bood laska*	Пожалуйста	*pazhawsta*
But	але	*ale*	но	*no*
Thank you	Дякую	*dyakooyoo*	Спасибо	*spaseeba*
Thank you so much	дуже дякую	*duzhe dyakooyoo*	большое спасибо	*bolshoye spaseeba*
You're welcome	Нема за що	*nehma za scho*	Не за что	*nyeh za shto*
Excuse me	Пробачте	*probachteh*	Извините	*eezvineetye*
What's your name?	Як вас звати?	*yak vas zvaty?*	Как вас зовут?	*kak vas zavoot?*
My name is …	Мене звати …	*mehneh zvaty*	Меня зовут	*menya zavoot*
Nice to meet you	Дуже приємно	*duzhe pry'yemno*	Очень приятно	*ochen preeyatna*
How are you?	Як справи?	*yak spravy?*	Как дела?	*kak dyela?*
Fine, good	Довре	*dobreh*	Хорошо	*kharasho*
Bad	Погано	*pohano*	Плохо	*plokha*
Very	Дуже ·	*duzhe*	Очень	*ochen*
Attention	Увага	*uvaha*	Внимание	*vnimaniye*
Watch out	Обережно	*oberezhno*	Осторожно	*ostorozhna*
Help!	Допоможіть	*dopomozheet*	Помогите	*pamageetyeh*
I (don't) like …	мені (не) подобається (ukr)		*mehnee (neh) podobayetsya*	
	Мне (не) нравиться (rus)		*mnyeh (nyeh) nryaveetsya*	

Questions

Do you speak …?	Ви говорите?	*vy hovoryteh?*	Вы говорите?	*vy gavarityeh?*
English	по-англійськи	*pa anhleesky*	по-английский	*pa angleeskee*
Ukrainian	по-українськи	*pa ukrayeensky*	по-украинский	*pa ukrainskee*
Russian	по-россіськи	*pa rosseesky*	по-русский	*pa rooskee*
German	по-німецьки	*pa neemetsky*	по-немецкий	*pa nyemetskee*
French	по- французьки	*pa frantsoozky*	по- французкий	*pa frantsoozkee*
Do you understand?	Ви розумієте?	*vy razoomee'yeteh?*	Вы понимаете?	*vy paneemahyetyeh?*
I do not understand	Я не розумію	*ya ne razoomee'yoo*	Я не понимаю	*ya nye paneemayoo*
Repeat,	Повторите	*povtoryteh*	Повторите	*pahvtareetyeh*
(please)	Будь ласка	*bood laska*	пожалуйста	*pazhawsta*
What?	Що?	*scho?*	Что?	*shto?*
Who?	Хто?	*khto?*	Кто?	*kto?*
Why?	Чому?	*chomoo?*	Почему?	*pochyemoo?*
How?	Як?	*yak?*	Как?	*kak?*
Where?	Де?	*deh?*	Где?	*gdyeh?*

	Ukrainian		**Russian**	
on the left	на ліво	*na leevo*	на лева	*na lyeva*
on the right	на права	*na prava*	на права	*na prava*
straight ahead	прямо	*pryamo*	прямо	*pryama*
here	тут	*toot*	здесь	*zdyes*
there	там	*tam*	там	*tam*
far	далеко	*dalehko*	далёко	*dalycko*
near	блізько	*bleezko*	близко	*bleezka*

Shopping

Do you have …?	Чи ви маєте?	*chy vy mah-yehteh*	У вас есть?	*oo vas yest?*
Closed	зачинено	*zachyneno*	закрыто	*zakryto*
Open	відкрито	*vidkryto*	открыто	*otkryto*
How much?	Скільки?	*skeelky?*	Сколько?	*skoylka?*
What is it?	Що це?	*scho tseh?*	Что это?	*shto ehta?*
a lot	багато	*bohata*	много	*mnoga*
a little bit	трохи	*troshka*	чуть-чуть	*trokhy*
(too) little	мало	*malo*	мало	*mala*
How much does this cost?	Скільки це коштує? (ukr)			*skeelky tseh koshtooyeh?*
	Сколько это стоит? (rus)			*skolka ehta stoyeet?*

Needs

I want …	Я хочу	*ya khochoo*	Я хочу	*ya khachoo*
I need …	мені потрібно	*mehnee potreebno*	мне нужно	*mnyeh noozhna*
I am looking for …	Я шукаю	*ya shukayu*	Я ищу	*ya eeschoo*
May I …?	можна?	*mozhna?*	можно?	*mozhna?*
to sleep	спати	*spahty*	спать	*spaht*
to buy	купити	*koopyty*	купить	*koopeet*
to eat	їсти	*yeesty*	есть	*yehst*
to drink	пити	*pyty*	пить	*peet*

Food and drink

bread	хліб	*khleeb*	хлеб	*khlyeb*
cheese	сир	*syr*	сыр	*syr*
butter	масло	*mahslo*	масло	*mahsla*
sausage	ковбаса	*kovbassa*	колбаса	*kolbassa*
meat	мясо	*myaso*	мясо	*myasa*
fish	риба	*ryba*	рыба	*ryba*
sweets	цукерки	*tsookerky*	конфеты	*konfyety*
fruit	фрукти	*frookty*	фрукты	*frookty*
vegetables	овочі	*ovochee*	овощи	*ovoschee*
apple	яблуко	*yabluko*	яблоко	*yablako*
cherry	вишні	*vyshnee*	вишня	*veeshnya*
mushrooms	гриби	*hryby*	грибы	*greeby*
potatoes	картопля	*kartoplya*	картошки	*kartoshkee*
water	вода	*voda*	вода	*vada*
milk	молоко	*moloko*	молоко	*malako*
juice	сік	*seek*	сок	*sok*
sugar	цукор	*tsookor*	сахар	*sakhar*
tea	чай	*chai*	чай	*chai*

	Ukrainian		**Russian**	
coffee	кава	_kava_	кофе	_kofye_
beer	пиво	_pyvo_	пиво	peevo
vodka	горілка	ho_reel_ka	водка	_vodka_
ice cream	морозіво	mo_ro_zeevo	мороженое	mo_rozh_enoye
tasty	смачно	_smachno_	вкусно	_fkusno_
breakfast	сніданок	snee_danok_	завтрак	_zavtrak_
lunch	обід	o_beed_	обед	ob_yed_
dinner	вечеря	ve_cher_ya	ужин	_oozhyn_

Useful words

book	книга	_knyha_	книга	_kneega_
map	мапа	_mappa_	карта	_karta_
money	гроші	hroshee	денги	_dyengui_
ticket	квіток	_kveetok_	билет	beelyet
train	поїзд	po_yeezd_	поезд	po_yezd_
bus	автобус	av_toboos_	автобус	av_toboos_
stamps	марки	_marky_	марки	_markee_
blanket	ковдри	_kovdry_	одеяло	odeyalo
room	кімната	_keemnata_	комната	_komnata_
house	дім	_deem_	дом	dom
village	село	seh_lo_	село	sye_lo_
city	місто	_meesto_	город	_gorod_
square	площа	ploscha	площадь	ploschad
street	вулиця	_voolytsya_	улица	u_leetsa_
tree	дерево	dehrehvo	дерево	dyerevo
mountain	гора	_hora_	гора	_gora_
flower	квіти	_kveety_	цветы	tsvy_ety_
wheat	пшениця	pshe_hnytsya_	пшеница	pshe_neetsya_
sunflower	соняшник	_sonyashneek_	подсолнечник	pahd_solnyechneek_
rainbow	веселка	veh_sehlka_	радуга	ra_duga_

Descriptions

small	малий	_maly_	маленький	_malyenky_
big	великий	veh_lyky_	большой	bol_shoi_
new	новий	_novy_	новый	_novy_
old	старий	_stary_	старый	_stary_
beautiful	красний	_krasny_	красивый	kra_seevy_
important	важливо	vazh_lyvo_	важно	_vazhno_
cold	холодно	_kholodno_	холодно	_kholodna_
hot	горячий	hor_yachy_	горячий	gahr_yachee_
delicious	смачно	_smachno_	вкусно	_fgoosna_

Numbers Ukrainian and Russian numbers are fairly cognitive. If you know one to ten and the constructions, you can say any number in either language:

0	нуль	_nool_	нуль	_nool_
1	один	_odyn_	один	ah_deen_
2	два	_dva_	два	dva
3	три	_trih_	три	tree
4	чотири	cho_tyry_	четыре	chye_tyreh_
5	пять	_pyat_	пять	_pyat_

	Ukrainian		Russian	
6	шість	*sheest*	шесть	*shehst*
7	сімь	*seem*	семь	*syem*
8	вісім	*veeseem*	восемь	*vosyem*
9	девять	*dehvyat*	девять	*dyevyat*
10	десять	*dehsyat*	десять	*dyesyat*

Eleven through nineteen are formed by adding the suffix 'надцять' (shown in Ukrainian but Russian uses the same format):

11	одинадцять	*odynatsyat*
12	дванадцять	*dvanatsyat*

Twenty through to forty are slightly irregular:

20	двадцять		*dvatsat*
21	двадцять один		*dvatsat odyn*
30	тридцять		*trihtsyat*
40	сорок		*sorok*
50	пятдесять		*peedehsyat*
60	шістдесять		*sheesdehsyat*
70	сімдесять		*seemdehsyat*
80	вісімдесять		*veeseemdehsyat*
90	девятносто		*devyahnosto*
100	сто		*sto*
124	сто двадцять чотири		*sto dvatsat chotyry*
200	двісті		*dveestee*
300	триста		*trihsta*
400	чотириста		*chotyrystah*
500	пятсот		*pyatsot*
1000	тисяча		*tysyacha*

Days and time

today	сьогодні	*s'yohodni*	сегодня	*syevodnya*
tomorrow	завтра	*zavtra*	завтра	*zavtra*
the day after tomorrow	післязавтра	*peeslyazavtra*	послезавтра	*poslyezavtra*
yesterday	вчора	*fchora*	вчера	*fchyera*
Monday	понеділок	*ponehdeelok*	понедельник	*ponyedyelneek*
Tuesday	вівторок	*veevtorok*	вторник	*vtorneek*
Wednesday	середа	*sehrehdah*	среда	*sryedah*
Thursday	четвер	*chetver*	четверг	*chetvyerg*
Friday	пятниця	*pyatnytsya*	пятница	*pyatneetsa*
Saturday	субота	*soobohta*	суббота	*soobohta*
Sunday	неділя	*nehdeelya*	воскресенье	*voskresenye*
What time is it?	Котра година?	*kotra hodyna?*	Который час?	*katory chas?*
now	тепер	*tehpehr*	сейчас	*seychas*
hour	година	*hodyna*	час	*chas*
minute	хвилин	*khvylyn*	минута	*meenoota*

Months See *Chapter 3*, page 37, for months.

Appendix 2

FURTHER READING
History

Acherson, Neil *Black Sea* Hill & Wang, 1996. Colourful narrative.

Hamm, Michael F *Kiev: A Portrait* Princeton University Press, 1993. A poignant history. Using statistics from the state archives, the historian has pieced together a colourful tale of the capital just prior to the Russian Revolution.

Kuzio, Taras *Ukraine: From Perestroika to Independence* Palgrave Macmillan, 2000. A well-respected Ukraine scholar with several important publications on Ukrainian politics and economics. This is probably his most well-known book.

Reid, Anna, *Borderland* Westview, 2000. For travellers with a little less time, this comes highly recommended. As a correspondent for *The Economist* during the early years of Ukraine's transition, the author artfully connects Ukraine's past with its present regions and people in a very entertaining read.

Royle, Trevor *Crimea: The Great Crimean War, 1854–1856* Palgrave Macmillan, 2004.

Subtelny, Orest *Ukraine: A History* University of Toronto Press, 1988. A comparatively small amount has been written about Ukraine in English. The real bible of Ukrainian history is still this 700-page book.

Wilson, Andrew *The Ukrainians: Unexpected Nation* Yale University Press, 2002; 2nd edition. As the world's leading scholar on all that goes on in Ukraine today, Andrew Wilson has written a rich and accurate portrait.

Literature Sadly, too little Ukrainian literature exists in translation. To my knowledge, there have been no worthy attempts to translate Shevchenko into English.

Collected Stories of Sholom Aleichem Sholom Aleichem Family Publications, 1999; for more information, go to www.sholom-aleichem.org. Several different small publications exist; this is most common.

The Jews of Odessa: A Cultural History, 1794–1881 Stanford University Press, 1986. A more academic read, but filled with important biographies and facts. Much of Sholom Aleichem's work (translated from Yiddish) takes place in Ukraine and offers poignant insights into the relationships between the Ukrainians and Ukraine's former Jewish community.

Written in the Book of Life: Works by 19–20th Century Ukrainian Writers Progress Publishers,1982. A very hard-to-find book (but well worth the search), including stories and essays by such famed Ukrainian writers as Ivano Franko and Kotsyubinsky.

Babel, Isaac *The Complete Works of Isaac Babel* W W Norton & Company, 2002. Anyone travelling to Odessa, wanting to travel to Odessa, or simply a lover of good short stories should get their hands on a copy of this book. Edited by the author's daughter, the tome includes all of the *Odessa Stories*, as well as stark tales of Ukraine in the civil war. From a geographic standpoint, I know of no other book in English that covers so much of Ukraine.

Bulgakov, Mikhail *The Master and Margerita*. Ukrainians have mixed feelings about Bulgakov but foreigners tend to be very big fans. This is his masterpiece and is widely available in several editions. Less known in English, but quite pertinent to Ukraine is *The White Guard* (Academy Chicago Publishers, 1995), detailing the life of a family in Kiev through the Russian civil war.

Gogol, Nikolai *Evenings on a Farm Near Dikanka* I would suggest this first and foremost. These dark but comic tales portray Ukrainian folklore like nothing else. Leonard Kent has edited a *Complete Tales of Nikolai Gogol* (University of Chicago Press, 1985) with *Evenings* as well as *Mirgorod*, which includes the famous story of the Cossack hero Taras Bulba.

Safran Foer, Jonathon *Everything is Illuminated* Houghton Mifflin, 2002. Another great read is this highly acclaimed part novel, part travel tale, part Jewish memoir. The book was made into a film in 2006 and shows parts of Odessa, Lviv, and the great forests and countryside of Volhynia. The story of the *shtetl* life and the Holocaust in Ukraine is probably more accurate than even the author intended.

Language guides

Colloquial Ukrainian Routledge, 2004. Comes highly recommended.

Culture Smart! Ukraine: A Guide to Customs & Etiquette Graphic Arts Center Publishing Company, 2005. Relays cultural information and the dos and don'ts of modern Ukraine.

Ukrainian Phrasebook Lonely Planet, 2002. For additional Ukrainian language, this is a convenient pocket-size guide that can be very useful for travellers.

Hodges, Linda and Chumak, George *A Language Guide to Ukraine* Hippocrene Books, 2004; 4th edition. A hefty and very helpful companion, the book encourages travellers to use Ukrainian in their travels and many have found it to be a good companion.

Politics As should be expected, quite a lot has been written on the Orange Revolution and what it means for Ukraine.

Aslund, Anders and McFaul, Michael (eds) *Revolution in Orange: The Origins of Ukraine's Democratic Breakthrough* Carnegie Endowment for International Peace, 2006. For something more analytical.

Wilson, Andrew *Ukraine's Orange Revolution* Yale University Press, 2006. For a fascinating step-by-step account of how and what happened.

WEBSITES Ukrainians are among the most wired people on earth. The following are mostly English-language websites about Ukraine, and Ukraine-related topics.

General information

www.brama.com The ultimate site on all things Ukrainian. They have a very helpful travel post to answer any question you have.

www.encyclopediaofukraine.com Largest online information resource on Ukraine and Ukrainian history

www.artukraine.com Huge information resource on Ukrainian art, culture, and travel.

www.ukraine.org Promotional website on Ukraine

www.ukraine.com An overall online destination guide

www.infoukes.com The Ukrainian diaspora information resource

www.ukrainianweb.com Information on Ukraine-related interests

www.ukrainianstudies.uottawa.ca/orange.html Ukraine List – Ukrainian studies journal

www.RISU.org.ua Religion Information Service for Ukraine

News

www.wumag.kiev.ua Welcome to Ukraine Magazine

www.ukrainenews.com Like the title says

www.interfax.kiev.ua/eng Daily Ukraine news service in English
www.news.bbc.co.uk/2/hi/europe/country_profiles/1102303.stm BBC Ukraine profile
www.action-ukraine-report.blogspot.com Action Ukraine Report – daily news service
www.kyivpost.com Kiev's English-language newspaper online
www.nrcu.gov.ua Ukraine's National Radio Company
www.ukraineweekly.com The Ukraine Weekly News
www.ukranews.com Ukrainian News Agency
www.ukrainianjournal.com The Ukrainian Journal
www.ukrainiantime.com Ukrainian News by radio
www.internews.ua Internews Ukrainian News Service

Official resources
www.mfa.org.ua Ukraine's Ministry of Foreign Affairs – a friendly bunch
www.rada.gov.ua Ukraine's Parliament
www.president.gov.ua Ukraine's head of state online
www.un.int/ukraine Ukraine's mission to the United Nations
www.un.kiev.ua United Nations in Ukraine
www.ukrposhta.com Ukraine's postal service
www.worldbank.org/ua World Bank waxes forth on Ukraine
www.ukremb.org.uk Embassy of Ukraine to the United Kingdom
www.britishcouncil.org/ukraine.htm British Council in Ukraine
www.ukraineinfo.us Embassy of Ukraine to the United States background information
www.ukma.kiev.ua Ukraine's Kiev Mohyla Academy
www.univ.kiev.ua Ukraine's National University
www.lavra.kiev.ua Official site of the Caves Monastery
www.ic-chernobyl.kiev.ua Ukraine's Ministry of Chernobyl

Ukraine travel
www.aerosvit.com Ukraine's national airlines
www.tryukraine.com Ukraine travel website
www.travelinukraine.com Slightly chaotic but nevertheless helpful travel posting board
www.seat61.com/Ukraine2.htm Train travel information page for Ukraine
www.biztravel.kiev.ua Business travel information for Kiev
www.uazone.net Online fact book about Ukraine with travel information
www.inyourpocket.com/ukraine Online guide to Kiev
www.travel-2-ukraine.com Online travel resource and agency for Ukraine
www.outdoorukraine.com Outdoor activities in Crimea and the Carpathians
www.uatour.com Package tours in Ukraine

Organisations
www.usukraine.org The US–Ukraine Foundation
www.ucc.ca Ukraine–Canadian Congress
www.cym.org Ukrainian Youth Association
www.ukrainianmuseum.org The Ukrainian Museum
www.ugcc.org.ua Ukrainian Greek Catholic Church
www.cerkva.info Ukrainian Orthodox Church, Kiev Patriarchate
www.orthodox.org.ua Ukrainian Orthodox Church, Moscow Patriarchate
www.uaoc.org Ukrainian Autocephalous Orthodox Church
www.jewish.kiev.ua All Ukrainian Jewish Congress
www.iccrimea.org International Committee for Crimea
www.frua.org Families for Russian & Ukrainian Adoptions
www.ukrainianinstitute.org The Ukrainian Institute of America
www.huri.harvard.edu The Ukrainian Research Institute of Harvard University

www.bandura.org The Ukrainian Bandura Chorus
www.cam.ac.uk/societies/ukr Cambridge University Ukrainian Society
www.ucca.org Ukrainian Congress Committee of America
www.cossacks.kiev.ua Ukrainian Cossacks – looks like the real thing
www.ucci.org.ua The Ukrainian Chamber of Commerce & Industry
www.ffu.org.ua Ukraine's Football Federation
www.ugagb.org The Ukrainian Golf Association of Great Britain
www.naftogaz.com Ukraine's National Gas Company

Search engines

www.meta.ua English language search engine in Ukraine
www.online.com.ua Ukrainian language search engine
www.google.com/intl/uk Pronounced 'hoohle' in Ukrainian

Geneaology research

www.routestoroots.com Jewish archival research in Ukraine
www.shtetlinks.jewishgen.org/Ukraine.html In-depth Jewish history and alternative names for *shtetls* in Ukraine
www.rootsweb.com/~ukrgs/index.htm Ukrainian Genealogical Society
www.genforum.genealogy.com/ukraine Online discussion board on Ukrainian ancestry
www.torugg.org Toronto Ukrainian Genealogy Group Site
www.ukr-gensearch.netfirms.com Ukrainian Genealogy Search Mail List

Other information

www.ethnologue.com/show_country.asp?name=Ukraine Language and ethnicity in Ukraine
www.learnpysanky.com Make your own Ukrainian dyed Easter eggs
www.unicorne.org/ORTHODOXY/articles/saints_icons/main.htm Search engine for Ukrainian Orthodox saints and feast days
www.ukrainiansoccer.com Up-to-date info on Ukraine's many football teams and intrigues
www.ruslana.com.ua Official website of Ukrainian pop singer Ruslana
www.umka.com.ua Online Ukrainian music store
www.borshch.com The impossible and incomparable Ukrainian folk-punk band Borsch

WIN £100 CASH!

READER QUESTIONNAIRE

Send in your completed questionnaire for the chance to win £100 cash in our regular draw

All respondents may order a Bradt guide at half the UK retail price – please complete the order form overleaf.

(Entries may be posted or faxed to us, or scanned and emailed.)

We are interested in getting feedback from our readers to help us plan future Bradt guides. Please answer ALL the questions below and return the form to us in order to qualify for an entry in our regular draw.

Have you used any other Bradt guides? If so, which titles? . . . .
. . . .

What other publishers' travel guides do you use regularly? . . . .
. . . .

Where did you buy this guidebook? . . . .

What was the main purpose of your trip to Ukraine (or for what other reason did you read our guide)? eg: holiday/business/charity etc.. . . . .
. . . .

What other destinations would you like to see covered by a Bradt guide?
. . . .

Would you like to receive our catalogue/newsletters?

YES / NO (If yes, please complete details on reverse)

If yes – by post or email? . . . .

Age (circle relevant category) 16–25   26–45   46–60   60+

Male/Female (delete as appropriate)

Home country . . . .

Please send us any comments about our guide to Ukraine or other Bradt Travel Guides. . . . .
. . . .
. . . .
. . . .

Bradt Travel Guides
23 High Street, Chalfont St Peter, Bucks SL9 9QE, UK
☎ +44 (0)1753 893444 f +44 (0)1753 892333
e info@bradtguides.com
www.bradtguides.com

CLAIM YOUR HALF-PRICE BRADT GUIDE!

Order Form

To order your half-price copy of a Bradt guide, and to enter our prize draw to win £100 (see overleaf), please fill in the order form below, complete the questionnaire overleaf, and send it to Bradt Travel Guides by post, fax or email.

Please send me one copy of the following guide at half the UK retail price

Title		Retail price	Half price
...	....	....	....

Please send the following additional guides at full UK retail price

No	Title		Retail price	Total
...	....		....	....
...	....		....	....
...	....		....	....

Sub total	....
Post & packing	....

(£1 per book UK; £2 per book Europe; £3 per book rest of world)

Total	....

Name . . . .

Address. . . . .

Tel . . . .   Email . . . .

☐ I enclose a cheque for £. . . . . . . made payable to Bradt Travel Guides Ltd

☐ I would like to pay by credit card. Number: . . . .

Expiry date: . . . / . . .   3-digit security code (on reverse of card) . . . . .

☐ Please add my name to your catalogue mailing list.

☐ I would be happy for you to use my name and comments in Bradt marketing material.

Send your order on this form, with the completed questionnaire, to:

Bradt Travel Guides UKR/2
23 High Street, Chalfont St Peter, Bucks SL9 9QE
✆ +44 (0)1753 893444   f +44 (0)1753 892333
e info@bradtguides.com   www.bradtguides.com

Bradt Travel Guides

www.bradtguides.com

Africa

Africa Overland	£15.99
Benin	£14.99
Botswana: Okavango, Chobe, Northern Kalahari	£15.99
Burkina Faso	£14.99
Cape Verde Islands	£13.99
Canary Islands	£13.95
Cameroon	£13.95
Eritrea	£12.95
Ethiopia	£15.99
Gabon, São Tomé, Príncipe	£13.95
Gambia, The	£13.99
Ghana	£13.95
Johannesburg	£6.99
Kenya	£14.95
Madagascar	£14.95
Malawi	£13.99
Mali	£13.95
Mauritius, Rodrigues & Réunion	£13.99
Mozambique	£13.99
Namibia	£14.95
Niger	£14.99
Nigeria	£15.99
Rwanda	£14.99
Seychelles	£14.99
Sudan	£13.95
Tanzania, Northern	£13.99
Tanzania	£16.99
Uganda	£15.99
Zambia	£15.95
Zanzibar	£12.99

Britain and Europe

Albania	£13.99
Armenia, Nagorno Karabagh	£14.99
Azores	£12.99
Baltic Capitals: Tallinn, Riga, Vilnius, Kaliningrad	£12.99
Belgrade	£6.99
Bosnia & Herzegovina	£13.99
Bratislava	£6.99
Budapest	£7.95
Cork	£6.95
Croatia	£12.95
Cyprus see North Cyprus	
Czech Republic	£13.99
Dubrovnik	£6.95
Eccentric Britain	£13.99
Eccentric Cambridge	£6.99
Eccentric Edinburgh	£5.95
Eccentric France	£12.95
Eccentric London	£12.95
Eccentric Oxford	£5.95
Estonia	£13.99
Faroe Islands	£13.95
Helsinki	£7.99
Hungary	£14.99
Kiev	£7.95
Latvia	£13.99
Lille	£6.99
Lithuania	£13.99
Ljubljana	£6.99
Macedonia	£13.95
Montenegro	£13.99
North Cyprus	£12.99
Paris, Lille & Brussels	£11.95
Riga	£6.95
River Thames, In the Footsteps of the Famous	£10.95
Serbia	£13.99
Slovenia	£12.99
Spitsbergen	£14.99
Switzerland: Rail, Road, Lake	£13.99
Tallinn	£6.99
Ukraine	£14.99
Vilnius	£6.99

Middle East, Asia and Australasia

China: Yunnan Province	£13.99
Georgia	£13.95
Great Wall of China	£13.99
Iran	£14.99
Iraq	£14.95
Kabul	£9.95
Maldives	£13.99
Mongolia	£14.95
North Korea	£13.95
Oman	£13.99
Palestine, Jerusalem	£12.95
Sri Lanka	£13.99
Syria	£14.99
Tasmania	£12.95
Tibet	£13.99
Turkmenistan	£14.99

The Americas and the Caribbean

Amazon, The	£14.95
Argentina	£15.99
Bolivia	£14.99
Cayman Islands	£12.95
Costa Rica	£13.99
Chile	£16.95
Chile & Argentina: Trekking	£12.95
Eccentric America	£13.95
Eccentric California	£13.99
Falkland Islands	£13.95
Panama	£13.95
Peru & Bolivia: Backpacking and Trekking	£12.95
St Helena, Ascension, Tristan da Cunha	£14.95
USA by Rail	£13.99

Wildlife

Antarctica: Guide to the Wildlife	£14.95
Arctic: Guide to the Wildlife	£15.99
British Isles: Wildlife of Coastal Waters	£14.95
Galápagos Wildlife	£15.99
Madagascar Wildlife	£14.95
Peruvian Wildlife	£15.99
Southern African Wildlife	£18.95
SriLankan Wildlife	£15.99

Health

Your Child Abroad: A Travel Health Guide	£10.95

Index

DISCARDED